Eighth Edition

POLICING AMERICA
CHALLENGES AND BEST PRACTICES

Kenneth J. Peak
University of Nevada, Reno

PEARSON

Boston Columbus Indianapolis New York San Francisco Upper Saddle River
Amsterdam Cape Town Dubai London Madrid Milan Munich Paris Montréal Toronto
Delhi Mexico City São Paulo Sydney Hong Kong Seoul Singapore Taipei Tokyo

Editorial Director: Vernon Anthony
Acquisitions Editor: Gary Bauer
Program Manager: Alicia Ritchey
Editorial Assistant: Lynda Cramer
Director of Marketing: David Gesell
Senior Marketing Manager: Mary Salzman
Senior Marketing Coordinator: Alicia Wozniak
Project Management Team Lead: JoEllen Gohr
Production Project Manager: Jessica H. Sykes
Operations Specialist: Deidra Skahill

Senior Art Director: Diane Ernsberger
Text and Cover Designer: PreMediaGlobal
Cover Art: Jose AS Reyes/Shutterstock.com
Lead Media Project Manager: Leslie Brado
Full-Service Project Management: Saraswathi Muralidhar/
    PreMediaGlobal
Composition: PreMediaGlobal
Printer/Binder: Courier/Kendallville
Cover Printer: Lehigh-Phoenix Color/Hagerstown
Text Font: Minion Pro Regular 10/12

Library of Congress Cataloging-in-Publication Data

Peak, Kenneth J.
    Policing America: challenges and best practices / Kenneth J. Peak, University of Nevada, Reno.—Eighth edition.
        pages cm
    Includes bibliographical references and index.
    ISBN-13: 978-0-13-349565-2
    ISBN-10: 0-13-349565-5
    1. Police—United States.   2. Law enforcement—United States.   I. Title.
    HV8141.P33 2014
    363.20973--dc23

                                                                                    2013046404

10 9 8 7 6 5 4 3 2 1
V011

ISBN 10: 0-13-349565-5
ISBN 13: 978-0-13-349565-2

[There are] two points in the adventure of the diver—one, when a beggar, he prepares to plunge. One, when a prince, he rises with his pearl…

—Robert Browning, *Paracelsus*, Part I (1835)

This book is dedicated to those who have made or will soon make the "plunge" into one of our most challenging (and, when done right, gratifying) occupations.

It is also dedicated to our newest family member, Ava. May you live long and be happy—and remember the Italian proverb: *If nothing is going well, call your grandparents.*

—K. J. P.

BRIEF CONTENTS

CONTENTS

PREFACE

▶ Purposes and Approaches

Famed educator John Dewey advocated the "learning by doing" approach to education or problem-based learning. The eighth edition of this book is written, from start to finish, with that philosophy in mind and is reflected in the book's subtitle, *Challenges and Best Practices*. And, as with its seven predecessors, this book benefits from the author's many (more than thirty-five) years of combined practical and academic experience, which includes holding two positions as a police chief executive officer. Its chapters, therefore, contain a real-world flavor not found in most policing textbooks and reflect the changing times in which we live and the tremendous challenges facing federal, state, and local agents and officers every day. And again, like its seven preceding editions, this edition continues to represent my best attempt to allow the reader, to the fullest extent possible, to vicariously experience the wearing of a police uniform by providing a highly practical, comprehensive view of the world of policing. As shown above in the above "New Topics" section, included are several beneficial additions in topics as well as changes in its organization and content.

▶ Special Features and Attributes

The first aspect of the book that will be noted are its several pedagogical attributes. First, to help make this textbook more reader-friendly, each chapter begins with learning objectives and an introduction. A summary, list of key terms, review questions, "Learn by Doing," and endnotes are found at the end of each chapter. Other instructional aids found in the chapters include the Career Profiles, Comparative Closeups (looking at some aspect of policing in foreign venues), Court Closeups, tables and figures, and exhibits describing police methods and news items. Finally, a detailed index at the end of the book makes it easy for you to find information on specific topics quickly.

A few additional comments are in order concerning the "Learn by Doing" and "Career Profiles" sections of this edition, which are to further enhance its applied nature. Beginning in the early 1900s, famed educator John Dewey promulgated the "learning by doing" approach to education, or problem-based learning. This approach also comports with the popular learning method espoused by Benjamin Bloom in 1956, known as "Bloom's Taxonomy," in which he called for "higher-order thinking skills"—critical and creative thinking that involves analysis, synthesis, and evaluation. These chapter scenarios and activities place you in hypothetical situations, shifting attention away from the textbook-centered instruction and moving the emphasis to student-centered projects. These activities also allow you to practice skills in communication and self-management, act as a problem-solver, and learn about/address current community issues. Hopefully, you will be inspired to become engaged in some or all of these scenarios and activities.

The "Career Profiles," appearing in several chapters contain information provided by current police practitioners and provide the reader with their insights concerning the nature of their duties, a "typical day," and some career advice.

▶ New Topics in the Eighth Edition

Newly added topics include:

Chapter 1:	Slave patrols
Chapter 2:	New recruitment tools and methods (including social media); advantages to having women and minority police officers
Chapter 3:	Benefits of graveyard shift; fatal ambushes of officers and an analysis of officers killed; three "new generation" patrol vehicles being developed for police service; patrolling on paddleboards
Chapter 4:	Examples of crime prevention through environmental design (CPTED); police use of social networking for community policing and during disasters; Smart Policing—origins and applications; intelligence-led and predictive policing sections were moved here from Chapter 13
Chapter 5:	Advanced and familial DNA; medical examiners' duties; use of private DNA labs; Locard's exchange principle; whether there exists a "CSI effect"; use of dogs; expanded use of polygraph and social networking sites; use of three investigative tools: confidential informants, interviews, and informants
Chapter 6:	Delivering death messages under stress; private security legislation and attempts to align them more closely with public police; ASIS International
Chapter 7:	"Stand your ground" laws: warrantless searches under exigent circumstances cases; qualified immunity; decision concerning warrantless use of GPS; "consent once removed"
Chapter 8:	New police shooting cases; problems and policies concerning officers' personal use of social networking sites
Chapter 9:	New Section 1983 cases; sample high-speed pursuit policy; greater controls over use of electronic control devices
Chapter 10:	Federal agencies employing sworn personnel; new information concerning federal agencies' duties and organization; state agencies' organizations, duties, and specialization, and names
Chapter 11:	Board of Police Commissioners concept; rural/small-town policing; types/levels of police consolidation; benefits of police accreditation
Chapter 12:	New examples of attempted domestic terrorist attacks; new materials on cyberterrorism and gangs (extent, crimes, police responses); responding to active shooters/mass killings; Electronic Communications Protection Act of 1986; new strategies for methamphetamine; use of focused deterrence; bath salts and synthetic cannabinoids
Chapter 13:	New and updated immigration and homeless materials; a new section on coping with the mentally ill; police responses; Arizona immigration law; Basic Immigration Enforcement Training (BIET) program; youth arrest data; expanding hate groups; estimating extent of hate crimes
Chapter 14:	New technologies, generally; good/bad aspects of smartphones, social media, and unmanned aerial vehicles, and legislation relating to same; Kentucky phone app for terrorism; the Peacemaker vehicle; two national resources to address cybercrooks; Kelsey's Law; developments with robots; Stored Communication Act of 1986.

▶ Chapter Organization and Contents

The book's fourteen chapters are divided into five parts; some of the parts as well as chapters have been reconfigured and relocated from the previous edition so as to better organize and present their overall flow and content. Following is a description of the organization and contents of those parts and chapters that compose this eighth edition, as well as its supplemental attributes.

In Part I, the foci are on the foundations—that is, evolution and development—of policing. Chapter 1 traces policing in history, from its English origins through its migration to the United States; included are discussions of its striving for acceptance both here and abroad as well as its struggles (e.g., political influence, reform, and the civil rights movement in the United States) and transformations during this historical period. Chapter 2 charts the "making" of a police officer and begins by examining how common citizens are prepared for doing the work of policing: recruitment (to include the testing process used to discern whether one possesses the physical and psychological attributes that are sought), training (both during and after the recruit academy), and the different styles and roles of policing. Next, having hired and formed citizens into police officers, Chapter 3 takes the officers to the street, looking at the very fundamental (and at times hazardous) function of patrolling and its purposes and nature; the variations in patrol work by shift, beat, and assignment; officers' use of discretion; and the traditional traffic function.

Part II considers contemporary policing practices and challenges and begins with a discussion of community policing, community-oriented policing, and problem solving (Chapter 4), and includes this strategy's principles, strategies, and various applications, as well as Smart Policing, intelligence-led policing, and predictive policing. Next, Chapter 5 focuses on criminal investigation, including some discussion of how this field evolved, the roles of detectives, working undercover, DNA and other forms of analysis and technologies, uses of behavioral science, and recent developments in the field. This part's concluding chapter, Chapter 6, examines selected personnel issues: stress, labor relations, higher education, and the private police.

Next, in the three chapters composing Part III, we lump together several means by which police authority is constrained. More specifically, Chapter 7 looks at the rule of law: court decisions and constitutional enactments that direct and constrain police actions; the focus here is on the Bill of Rights in the Constitution, particularly the Fourth, Fifth, and Sixth Amendments. Chapter 8 considers police accountability from several perspectives, including the issue of police ethics, use of force, corruption, and discipline. Potential civil liability of the police is the focus of Chapter 9, to include various areas in which officers may be liable, and the means by which citizens may seek legal redress when they believe their civil rights have been violated.

Part IV has as its underlying theme the fact that federal and state law enforcement as well as local (municipal and county) policing in the United States doesn't just "happen" or occur in random, unplanned fashion. Such organizations are in fact organized and administered by virtue of their sovereignty, jurisdiction, and type of assignment so as to be more effective and efficient. Chapter 10 examines the organization and administration of U.S. federal and state law enforcement agencies, and Chapter 11 continues this discussion, examining the organization and administration of local (i.e., municipal police and county sheriff) agencies; included are profiles of both and comparisons with each other. Also discussed are definitions of organizations; organizational communication; functions of police executive officers, middle managers, and supervisors; influence of politics; media relations; contract and consolidated policing; and agency accreditation.

Part V, like the three previous ones, is intended to have a grouping effect in terms of common attributes, with the emphasis here being on the problems caused by special populations of criminals, the challenges they pose for the police, and some of the methods and tools being used to deal with those problems. Chapter 12 examines several criminal *syndicates* that plague our society, including terrorists, the mob (also known as La Cosa Nostra or the mafia), gangs, and drug traffickers. Methods, relevant legislation, and other tools for coping with these crime collectives is included. Chapter 13 largely moves away from this "collective" grouping of offenders as discussed in Chapter 12 and looks instead at selected *individual* offenders as well as other "people problems." Included in this chapter are crimes involving illegal immigrants (and the protection of our nation's borders), youth crimes, hate crimes, and dealing with the mentally ill and homeless populations; emphases here, as in the previous chapter, are on the best practices, relevant legislation, and other tools that are available to the police for coping with these crimes. Finally, Chapter 14 examines a wide array of exciting police technologies that exist today or are on the horizon for detecting crime, analyzing evidence, and doing everyday work.

From its beginning through the final chapter, this book provides a penetrating view of policing in America, demonstrating that this occupation inherently continues to be one of the most challenging and difficult occupations our society has ever witnessed.

▶ Instructor Supplements

MyTest and *TestBank* represent new standards in testing material. Whether you use a basic test bank document or generate questions electronically through MyTest, every question is linked to the text's learning objective, page number, and level of difficulty. This allows for quick reference in the text and an easy way to check the difficulty level and variety of your questions. MyTest can be accessed at www.PearsonMyTest.com.

PowerPoint Presentations Our presentations offer clear, straightforward outlines and notes to use for class lectures or study materials. Photos, illustrations, charts, and tables from the book are included in the presentations when applicable.

Other supplements are:

- Instructor's Manual with Test Bank
- Test Item File for ingestion into an LMS, including Blackboard and WebCT.

To access supplementary materials online, instructors need to request an instructor access code. Go to **www.pearsonhighered.com/irc**, where you can register for an instructor access code. Within 48 hours after registering, you will receive a confirming email, including an instructor access code. Once you have received your code, go to the site and log on for full instructions on downloading the materials you wish to use.

Pearson Online Course Solutions

Policing America is supported by online course solutions that include interactive learning modules, a variety of assessment tools, videos, simulations, and current event features. Go to www.pearsonhighered.com or contact your local representative for the latest information.

Alternate Versions

eBooks This text is also available in multiple eBook formats including Adobe Reader and CourseSmart. CourseSmart is an exciting new choice for students looking to save money. As an alternative to purchasing the printed textbook, students can purchase an electronic version of the same content. With a *CourseSmart* eTextbook, students can search the text, make notes online, print out reading assignments that incorporate lecture notes, and bookmark important passages for later review. For more information, or to purchase access to the *CourseSmart* eTextbook, visit **www.coursesmart.com**.

ACKNOWLEDGMENTS

I would like to extend my heartfelt gratitude to those reviewers named below who are responsible for the improvements and overall product found within this book's covers. Textbook authors—not unlike artists at their easels—constantly strive to upgrade the quality of our "pallet," so as to deliver a better product to our "gallery." Anonymous reviewers are the unheralded heroes in this regard, toiling long and hard over each chapter so as to provide the author with comprehensive, thoughtful, and cogent reviews. Their incisive and insightful work with each chapter far exceeds what I could accomplish, and in my experience my final product is immeasurably improved because of the reviewers' efforts . Again, many thanks to the following: Janice Ahmad, University of Houston–Downtown; Amber Ciccanti, Burlington County College; Paige Godier, Lake Superior State University; Steve Martin, Des Moines Area Community College; Matthew Morgan, Indiana State University; Barry Parker, Palo Alto College; and Aaron Westrick, Lake Superior State University and North Central Michigan College.

Finally, this edition, like its seven predecessors, is the result of the professional assistance and forbearance of several people at Pearson Education, several of whom have stayed the course with me over several editions of this and other textbooks. Specifically, I wish to acknowledge the yeoman's efforts of Gary Bauer, Executive Editor; Sara Eilert, Senior Acquisitions Editor; Alicia Ritchey, Program Manager; Jessica Sykes, Project Manager; and Elisa Rogers, freelance developmental editor. Their work with this edition resulted in many beneficial changes as well as a final product of which I am quite proud.

ABOUT THE AUTHOR

Ken Peak's career as a practitioner and educator in law enforcement and criminal justice spans more than three decades, including nearly eight years as a police chief executive and beat officer. He is currently a full professor and former chairman of the Department of Criminal Justice, University of Nevada, Reno, where he was named teacher of the year by the university's honor society. He entered municipal policing in Kansas in 1970 and subsequently held positions as a nine-county criminal justice planner in Kansas; director of a four-state Technical Assistance Institute for the Law Enforcement Assistance Administration; director of university police at Pittsburg State University in Kansas; acting director of public safety at the University of Nevada, Reno; and assistant professor of criminal justice at Wichita State University. His other authored or coauthored textbooks include *Justice Administration: Police, Courts, and Corrections Management* (7th ed.); *Community Policing and Problem Solving: Strategies and Practices* (6th ed., with Ronald W. Glensor); *Police Supervision and Management: In an Era of Community Policing* (3rd ed., with R.W. Glensor and L. K. Gaines); *Women in Law Enforcement Careers: A Guide for Preparing and Succeeding* (with V. Lord); and *Policing Communities: Understanding Crime and Solving Problems* (an anthology). He served as General Editor for the *Encyclopedia of Community Policing and Problem Solving*, has published two historical books—*Kansas Temperance: Much Ado about Booze, 1870–1920* (with P. Peak) and *Kansas Bootleggers* (with Patrick G. O'Brien)—and is author or coauthor of more than sixty journal articles and invited book chapters. He has served as chairman of the Police Section of the Academy of Criminal Justice Sciences, Vice Chair of the ACJS Academic Review Committee, and president of the Western and Pacific Association of Criminal Justice Educators. His teaching interests include policing, administration, victimology, comparative criminal justice systems, and planned change in criminal justice. He received two gubernatorial appointments to statewide criminal justice committees while residing in Kansas and holds a doctorate from the University of Kansas.

Foundations: Development of American Policing and Police Officers

In Part 1, the foci are on the foundations—that is, evolution and development—of policing. Chapter 1 traces policing in history, from its English origins through its migration to the United States; included are discussions of its striving for acceptance both here and abroad as well as its struggles (e.g., political influence, reform, and the civil rights movement in the United States) and transformations during this historical period. Chapter 2 charts the "making" of a police officer and begins by examining how common citizens are prepared for doing the work of policing: recruitment (to include the testing process used to discern whether one possesses the physical and psychological attributes that are sought), training (both during and after the recruit academy), and the different styles and roles of policing. Next, having hired and formed citizens into police officers, Chapter 3 takes the officers to the street, looking at the very fundamental (and at times, hazardous) function of patrolling and its purposes and nature; the variations in patrol work by shift, beat, and assignment; officers' use of discretion; and the traditional traffic function.

(Courtesy Stocksnapper/Shutterstock.)

1 History
From English Origins to the United States

LEARNING OBJECTIVES

As a result of reading this chapter, the student will be able to:

1. *Explain the four major police-related offices and their functions during the early English and colonial periods*

2. *Describe the major contributions of selected individuals to the development of policing (e.g., Peel's "principles," Vollmer's professionalization)*

3. *Explain the legacies of colonial policing that remained intact after the American Revolution*

4. *Delineate where professional policing began in the United States, and the role played by Southern slave patrols in that historical perspective*

⑤ Explain the three primary eras of policing in the United States, and the main characteristics of each

⑥ List the three early issues of American policing and to describe their present status

⑦ Describe the unique characteristics of law enforcement as it existed in the Wild West

⑧ Explain the definitions and advantages of the political and professional eras of policing

⑨ Describe the fundamental nature of the civil rights movement, and how the police and minorities were often pitted against one another

⑩ Describe what led to the development of the community-oriented policing and problem-solving (COPPS) era and some of its main features

⑪ Explain how today policing has come full circle, returning to its origins

⑫ Describe the three generations of community-oriented policing and problem solving

. . . .

Introduction

The #'s on colea is presic #

To understand contemporary policing in America, it is necessary to understand its antecedents; we will gain a better understanding of this history by looking at its three eras. The police, it has been said, are "to a great extent, the prisoners of the past. Day-to-day practices are influenced by deeply ingrained traditions."[1] Another reason for analyzing historical developments and trends is that several discrete legacies have been transmitted to modern police agencies. In view of the significant historical impact on modern policing, it is necessary to turn back the clock to about A.D. 900.

①

Therefore, we begin with a brief history of the evolution of four primary criminal justice officers— sheriff, constable, coroner, and justice of the peace—from early England to the twentieth century in America. We then examine policing from its early beginnings in England to the American colonial period, when volunteers watched over their "human flock." The concepts of patrol, crime prevention, authority, professionalism, and discretion can be traced to the colonial period. We move on to the adoption of full-time policing in American cities (beginning with the Southern **slave patrols** and then what is termed the *political era*, with its predominant issues, political influences, and other problems) and on the Western frontier. Then we consider the reform (or professional) era, the movement to professionalize the police by removing them from politics (and, at the same time, the citizenry) and casting them as crime fighters; included here is a look at the tumultuous 1960s and 1970s, which often saw the police pitted against minority groups who were seeking equal rights. Next, we discuss the movement away from the professional model into the community era, centering on the influence of the President's Crime Commission; this portion of the chapter also briefly considers community-oriented policing and problem solving (COPPS, discussed thoroughly in Chapter 4), including its three eras. Included at the chapter's end are a summary, key terms, review questions, and several scenarios and activities that provide opportunities for you to learn by doing.

. . . .

▶ English and Colonial Officers of the Law

All four of the primary criminal justice officials of early England—the sheriff, constable, coroner, and justice of the peace—either still exist or existed until recently in the United States. Accordingly, it is important to have a basic understanding of these offices, including their early functions in England and, later, in America. Following is a brief discussion of each.

Sheriff

The word sheriff is derived from the term *shire reeve*—*shire* meaning "county" and *reeve* meaning "agent of the king." The shire reeve appeared in England before the Norman conquest of 1066. His job was to maintain law and order in the tithings. (Tithings will be discussed further in the next section.) The office survived in England, although the sheriff was never a popular officer in England, and since the nineteenth century the sheriff has had no police powers. When the office began, the sheriff assisted the king in fiscal, military, and judicial affairs and was referred to as the "king's steward." As men could buy their appointment from the Crown, the office was often held by nonresidents of the county who seemed intent only upon fattening their purses and abusing the public. In addition, English sheriffs were often charged with being lazy in the pursuit of criminals. Indeed, by the late thirteenth century, sheriffs were forbidden to act as justices. The position of coroner was created to act as a monitor over the sheriff. Thereafter, the status and responsibility of the position began to diminish. In response, just before his death, King Edward I granted to the counties the right to select their sheriffs. With the subsequent appearance of the justice of the peace, the sheriff's office declined in power even further. At the present time in England, a sheriff's only duties are to act as officer of the court, summon juries, and enforce civil judgments.[2]

The first sheriffs in America appeared in the early colonial period, where control over sheriffs has rested with the county electorate since 1886. Today, the American sheriff remains the basic source of rural crime control. When the office appeared in the American colonies, it was little changed from the English model. However, the power of appointment was originally vested in the governor, and the sheriff's duties included apprehending criminals, caring for prisoners, executing civil process, conducting elections, and collecting taxes.[3]

In the late nineteenth century, the sheriff became a popular figure in the legendary Wild West (discussed later in this chapter). The frontier sheriffs often used the concept of *posse comitatus*, an important part of the criminal justice machine that allowed the sheriff to deputize common citizens to assist in the capture of outlaws, among other tasks. Overall, by the turn of the twentieth century the powers and duties of the sheriff in America had changed very little in status or function. In fact, the office has not changed much today.

Constable

Like the sheriff, the constable can be traced back to Anglo-Saxon times. The office began during the reign of Edward I, when every parish or township had a constable. As the county militia turned more and more to matters of defense, the constable alone pursued felons—hence the ancient custom of citizens raising a loud "hue and cry" and joining in pursuit of criminals lapsed into disuse. During the Middle Ages, there was as yet no high degree of specialization. The constable had a variety of duties, including collecting taxes, supervising highways, and serving as magistrate. The office soon became subject to election and was conferred upon local men of prominence. However, the creation of the office of justice of the peace around 1200 quickly changed this trend forever; soon the constable was limited to making arrests only with warrants issued by a justice of the peace. As a result, the office, deprived of social and civic prestige, was no longer attractive. It carried no salary, and the duties were often dangerous. In addition, there was heavy attrition in the office, so the constable's term was limited to one year in an attempt to attract officeholders; in 1856 Parliament completely discarded the office.[4]

The office of constable experienced a similar process of disintegration in the colonies. However, the American constables, usually two in each town, were given control over the night watch. By the 1930s, constitutions in twenty-one states provided for the office of constable, but constables still received no pay, and like their British colleagues they enjoyed little prestige or popularity after the early 1900s. The position fell into disfavor largely because most constables were untrained and were believed to be wholly inadequate as officials of the law.[5]

Coroner

The office of coroner is more difficult to describe. It has been used to fulfill many different roles throughout its history and has steadily changed over the centuries. There is no agreement concerning the date when the coroner first appeared in England, but there is general consensus that the office was functioning by the end of the twelfth century.

From the beginning, the coroner was elected; his duties included oversight of the interests of the Crown, not only in criminal matters but in fiscal matters as well. In felony cases, the coroner could conduct a preliminary hearing, and the sheriff often came to the coroner's court to preside over the coroner's jury. The coroner's inquest provided another means of power and prestige, determining the cause of death and the party responsible for it. Initially, coroners were elected for life. Soon becoming unhappy with the absence of compensation, however, eventually they were given the right to charge fees for their work.[6]

As was true of sheriffs and constables, at first the office of the coroner in America was only slightly different than what it had been in England. The office was slow in gaining recognition in America, as many of the coroners' duties were already being performed by the sheriffs and justices of the peace. By 1933, the coroner was recognized as a separate office in two-thirds of the states. Tenure was generally limited to two years. By then, however, the office had been stripped of many of its original functions, especially its fiscal roles. In many states, the coroner legally served as sheriff when the elected sheriff was disabled or disqualified. However, since the early part of the twentieth century, the coroner in the 2,000 coroners' offices in the U.S. has basically performed a single function: determining the causes of all deaths by violence or under suspicious circumstances. The coroner or his or her assistant is expected to determine the causes and effects of wounds, lesions, contusions, fractures, poisons, and more. The coroner's inquest resembles a grand jury at which the coroner serves as a kind of presiding magistrate. If the inquest determines that the deceased came to his or her death through criminal means, the coroner may issue a warrant for the arrest of the accused party.[7]

The primary debate regarding the office of coroner has centered on the qualifications needed to hold the office. Many states have traditionally allowed laypeople, as opposed to physicians, to be coroners. Thus people of all backgrounds—ranging from butchers to musicians—have occupied this powerful office.[8]

Justice of the Peace

The justice of the peace (JP) can be traced back as far as 1195 in England. By 1264 the *custos pacis*, or conservator of the peace, nominated by the king for each county, presided over criminal trials. Early JPs were wealthy landholders. They allowed constables to make arrests by issuing them warrants. Over time, this practice removed power from constables and sheriffs. By the sixteenth century, the office came under criticism because of the caliber

▲ Justice of the Peace Roy Bean, Langtry, Texas, about 1900. *(Courtesy U.S. National Archives "Judge Roy Bean, the 'Law West of the Pecos,' holding court at the old town of Langtry, Texas in 1900, trying a horse thief. This building was courthouse and saloon. No other peace officers in the locality at that time." 111-SC-93343.)*

of the people holding it. Officeholders were often referred to as "boobies" and "scum of the earth."[9] The only qualification necessary was being a wealthy landowner who was able to buy his way into office.

By the early twentieth century, England had abolished the property-holding requirement, and many of the medieval functions of the JP's office were removed. Thereafter, the office possessed extensive but strictly criminal jurisdiction, with no jurisdiction whatsoever in civil cases. This contrasts with the American system, which gives JPs limited jurisdiction in both criminal and civil cases.

The JP's office in the colonies was a distinct change from the position as it existed in England. JPs were elected to office and given jurisdiction in both civil and criminal cases. By 1930, the office had constitutional status in all of the states. JPs have long been allowed to collect fees for their services. As in England, it is typically not necessary to hold a law degree or to have pursued legal studies in order to be a JP in the United States.[10]

Perhaps the most colorful JP was Roy Bean, popularized in film as the sole peace officer in a 35,000-square-mile area west of the Pecos River, near Langtry, Texas. Bean was known to hold court in his shack, where signs hung on the front porch proclaimed, "Justice Roy Bean, Notary Public," "Law West of the Pecos," and "Beer Saloon." Cold beer and the law undoubtedly shared many quarters on the Western Frontier.

JPs are today what they perhaps were intended to be—lay and inexpert upholders of the law. On the whole, the office has declined from dignity to obscurity and ridicule. As one observer noted, this loss of prestige can never be recovered.[11]

▶ The Old English System of Policing

Like much of the American criminal justice system, modern American policing can be traced directly to its English heritage. Ideas concerning community policing, crime prevention, the posse, constables, and sheriffs developed from English policing. Beginning about A.D. 900, the role of law enforcement was placed in the hands of common citizens. Each citizen was responsible for aiding neighbors who might be victimized by outlaws.[12] No formal mechanism existed with which to police the villages, and the informal voluntary model that developed was referred to as "kin police."[13] Slowly this model developed into a more formalized community-based system.

After the Norman conquest of 1066, a community-based system called "frankpledge" was established. This system required that every male above the age of twelve form a group with nine of his neighbors. This group, called a tithing, was sworn to help protect fellow citizens and to apprehend and deliver to justice any of its members who committed a crime. Tithingmen were not paid salaries for their work, and they were required to perform certain duties under penalty of law.[14] Ten tithings were grouped into a hundred, directed by a constable who was appointed by a nobleman. The constable was the first police official with law enforcement responsibility greater than simply protecting his neighbors. As the tithings were grouped into hundreds, the hundreds were grouped into shires, which are similar to today's counties.

By the late sixteenth century, however, wealthier merchants and farmers became reluctant to take their turn in the rotating job of constable. The office was still unpaid, and the duties were numerous. Wealthier men paid the less fortunate to serve in their place until there came a point at which no one but the otherwise unemployable would serve as constable. Thus from about 1689 on, the demise of the once-powerful office was swift. All who could afford to pay their way out of service as constable to King George I did so.[15]

Meanwhile, the JP was rewarded in proportion to the number of people he convicted, so extortion was rampant. Ingenious criminals were able to exploit this state of affairs to great advantage. One such criminal was Jonathan Wild, who, in the early 1700s obtained single-handed control over most of London's criminals. Wild's system was simple: After ordering his men to commit a burglary, he would meet the victim and courteously offer to return the stolen goods for a commission. That he could have operated such a business for so long is a testimony to the corrupt nature of the magistrates of the "trading justice" period.[16]

This early English system, in large measure voluntary and informal, continued with some success well into the eighteenth century. By 1800, however, the collapse of its two primary offices and the growth of large cities, crime, and civil disobedience required that the system be changed. The British Parliament was soon forced to consider and adopt a more dependable system.

Policing in Colonial America

The first colonists transplanted the English policing system, with all of its virtues and faults, to seventeenth- and eighteenth-century America. Most of the time, the colonies were free of crime as the settlers busied themselves carving out a farm and a living. Occasionally colonists ran afoul of the law by violating or neglecting some moral obligation. They then found themselves in court for working on the Sabbath, cursing in public, failing to pen animals properly, or begetting children out of wedlock. Only two "crime waves" of note occurred during the seventeenth century, both in Massachusetts. In one case, between 1656 and 1665, Quakers who dared challenge the religion of the Puritan colony were whipped, banished, and, in three instances, hanged. The second "crime wave" involved witchcraft. Several alleged witches were hanged in 1692 in Salem; dozens more languished in prison before the hysteria abated.[17]

Once colonists settled into villages, including Boston (1630), Charleston (1680), and Philadelphia (1682), local ordinances provided for the appointment of constables, whose duties were much like those of their English predecessors. County governments, again drawing on English precedent, appointed sheriffs as well. The county sheriff, appointed by a governor, became the most important law enforcement official, particularly when the colonies were small and rural. The sheriff apprehended criminals, served subpoenas, appeared in court, and collected taxes. The sheriff was also paid a fixed amount for each task performed; the more taxes he collected, for example, the higher his pay.[18] 5

Criminal acts were so infrequent as to be largely ignored. Service as a constable or watchman was obligatory, and for a few years citizens did not seem to mind this duty. But as towns grew and the task of enforcing the laws became more difficult and time consuming, the colonists, like their English counterparts, began to evade the duty when possible. The "watch-and-ward" responsibility of citizens became more of a comical "snooze-and-snore" system. New Amsterdam's Dutch officials introduced a paid watch in 1658, and Boston tried the concept in 1663, but the expense quickly forced both cities to discontinue the practice.[19]

Unfortunately for these eighteenth-century colonists, their refusal to provide a dependable voluntary policing system came at a time when economic, population, and crime growth required a reliable police force. The citizen-participation model of policing was breaking down, and something had to be done, especially in the larger colonies. Philadelphia devised a plan, enacted into law, restructuring the way the watch was performed. The law empowered officials, called wardens, to hire as many watchmen as needed; the powers of the watch were increased; and the legislature levied a tax to pay for it. Instead of requiring all males to participate, only male citizens interested in making money needed to join the watch. Philadelphia's plan was moderately successful, and other cities were soon inspired to follow its example and offer tax-supported wages for watches.[20]

From the middle to the late eighteenth century, massive social and political unrest caused police problems to increase even more. From 1754 to 1763, the French and Indian War disrupted colonial society. In 1783, after the American Revolution had ended, property and street crime continued to flourish, and the constabulary and the watches were unable to cope with it. Soon it became evident that, like the English, the American people needed a more dependable, formal system of policing.

Legacies of the Colonial Period

As uncomplicated and sedate as colonial law enforcement seems, especially when compared to contemporary police problems, the colonial period is very important to the history of policing because many of the basic ideas that influence modern policing were developed during that era. Specifically, the colonial period transmitted three legacies to contemporary policing.[21]

First, as just discussed, the colonists committed themselves to local (as opposed to centralized) policing. Second, the colonists reinforced that commitment by creating a theory of government called republicanism. Republicanism asserted that power can be divided, and it relied on local interests to promote the general welfare. Police chiefs and sheriffs might believe that they alone know how to address crime and disorder, but under republicanism, neighborhood groups and local interest blocs have input with respect to crime-control policy. Republicanism thus established the controversial political framework within which the police would develop during the next two hundred years.[22]

Finally, the colonial period witnessed the onset of the theory of crime prevention. This legacy would alter the shape of policing after 1800 and would eventually lead to the emergence of modern police agencies.

The population of England had doubled between 1700 and 1800. Parliament, however, had done nothing to solve the problems that arose from social change. Each municipality or county, therefore, was left to solve its problems in piecemeal fashion. After 1750, practically every English city increased the number of watchmen and constables, hoping to address the problem of crime and disorder but not giving any thought to whether this ancient system of policing still worked. However, the cities did adopt paid, rather than voluntary, watches.[23]

London probably suffered the most from this general inattention to social problems; awash in crime, whole districts had become criminal haunts that no watchmen visited and no honest citizens frequented. Thieves became very bold, robbing their victims in broad daylight on busy streets. In the face of this situation, English officials still continued to

▲ Henry Fielding. *(Courtesy Library of Congress, Prints & Photographs Division, [LC-USZ62-103879].)*

prefer the existing policing arrangements over any new ideas. However, three men—Henry Fielding, his half brother John Fielding, and Patrick Colquhoun—began to experiment with possible solutions and laid the foundation on which later reformers would build new ideas.

Henry Fielding's acute interest in, and knowledge of, policing led to his 1748 appointment as chief magistrate of Bow Street in London. He soon became one of England's most acclaimed theorists in the area of crime and punishment. Fielding's primary argument was that the severity of the English penal code, which provided for the death penalty for a large number of offenses, including the theft of a handkerchief, did not work in controlling criminals. He believed the country should reform the criminal code to deal more with the origins of crime. In 1750, Fielding made the pursuit of criminals more systematic by creating a small group of "thief takers." Victims of crime paid handsome rewards for the capture of their assailants, so these volunteers stood to profit nicely by pursuing criminals.[24]

When Henry Fielding died in 1754, John Fielding succeeded him as Bow Street magistrate. By 1785, his thief takers had evolved into the Bow Street Runners—some of the most famous policemen in English history. While the Fieldings were considering how to create a police force that could deal with changing English society, horrible punishments and incompetent policing continued throughout England.

Patrick Colquhoun was a wealthy man who was sincerely interested in improving social conditions in England. In 1792, Colquhoun was appointed London magistrate, and for the next quarter of a century he focused on police reform. Like the Fieldings, he wrote lengthy treatises on the police, and he soon established himself as an authority on police reform. Colquhoun believed that government could, and should, regulate people's behavior. This notion contradicted tradition and even constitutional ideals, undermining the old principle that the residents of local communities, through voluntary watchmen and constables, should police the conduct of their neighbors. Colquhoun also endorsed three ideas originally set forth by the Fieldings: (1) the police should have an intelligence service for gathering information about offenders; (2) a register of known criminals and unlawful groups should be maintained; and (3) a police gazette should be published to assist in the apprehension of criminals and to promote the moral education of the public by publicizing punishments such as whipping, the pillory, and public execution. To justify these reforms, Colquhoun estimated that London in 1800 had 10,000 thieves, prostitutes, and other criminals who stole goods valued at more than a half million pounds from the riverside docks alone.[25]

Colquhoun also believed that policing should maintain the public order, prevent and detect crime, and correct bad manners and morals. He did not agree with the centuries-old notion that watchmen—who, after all, were amateurs—could adequately police the communities. Thus Colquhoun favored a system of paid professional police officers who would be recruited and maintained by a centralized governmental authority. Colquhoun believed that potential criminals could be identified before they did their unlawful deeds.[26] Thus began the notion of proactive policing—that is, preventing the crime before it occurs. Colquhoun died before his proposals were adopted, and as the eighteenth century ended, the structure of policing in England and America was largely unchanged. However, both nations had experienced the inadequacies of the older form of policing. Although new ideas had emerged, loyalties to the old system of policing would remain for some time.

▶ Police Reform in England

Two powerful trends in England (and, later in the United States) brought about changes in policing in the early and mid-nineteenth century. The first was urbanization, and the second was industrialization. These developments generally increased the standard of living for western Europeans. Suddenly, factories needed sober, dependable people who could be trusted with machines. To create a reliable workforce, factory owners began advocating temperance. Clearly a new age, a new way of thinking, had begun. Crime also increased during this period. Thus social change, crime, and unrest made the old system of policing obsolete. A new policing system was needed, one that could deal effectively with criminals, maintain order, and prevent crime.[27]

England began witnessing food riots (due to food scarcity and high prices) and increases in crime. The British army, traditionally used to disperse rioters, was becoming less effective as people began resisting its commands. In 1822, England's ruling party, the Tories, moved to consider new alternatives. The prime minister appointed Sir Robert Peel to establish a police force to combat the problems. Peel, a wealthy member of Parliament who was familiar with the reforms suggested by the Fieldings and Colquhoun, found that many English people objected to the idea of a professional police force, thinking it a possible restraint on their liberty. They also feared a stronger police organization because the criminal law was already quite harsh, as it had been for many years. By the early nineteenth century, there were 223 crimes in England for which a person could be hanged. Because of these two obstacles, Peel's efforts to gain support for full-time, paid police officers failed for seven years.[28]

Peel finally succeeded in 1829. He had established a base of support in Parliament and had focused on reforming only the metropolitan police of London rather than trying to create policing for the entire country. Peel submitted a bill to Parliament. This bill, which was very vague about details, was called "An Act for Improving the Police in and Near the Metropolis." Parliament passed the Metropolitan Police Act of 1829. The General Instructions of the new force stressed its preventive nature, specifying that "the principal object to be attained is 'the prevention of crime.' The security of person and property will thus

▲ Sir Robert Peel. *(Courtesy Library of Congress, Prints & Photographs Division, [LC-USZ62-96480].)*

be better effected, than by the detection and punishment of the offender after he has succeeded in committing the crime."[29] The act called on the home secretary to appoint two
police commissioners to command the new organization. These two men were to recruit "a
sufficient number of fit and able men" as constables.[30] Peel chose a former military colonel,
Charles Rowan, as one commissioner, and a barrister (attorney), Richard Mayne, as the
other. They divided London into seventeen divisions, using crime data as the primary basis
for creating the boundaries. Each division had a commander called a superintendent; each
superintendent had a force of 4 inspectors, 16 sergeants, and 165 constables. Thus London's
Metropolitan Police immediately consisted of nearly 3,000 officers. The commissioners
decided to put their constables in a uniform (a blue coat, blue pants, and a black top hat)
and to arm them with a short baton (known as a "truncheon") and a rattle for raising an
alarm. Each constable was to wear his own identifying number on his collar, where it could
be easily seen.[31]

Interestingly, the London police (nicknamed "bobbies" after Sir Robert Peel) quickly
met with tremendous public hostility. Wealthy people resented their very existence

and became particularly incensed at their attempts to control the movements of their horse-drawn coaches. Several aristocrats ordered their coachmen to whip the officers or simply drive over them. Juries and judges refused to punish those who assaulted the police. Defendants acquitted by a hostile judge would often sue the officer for false arrest. Policing London's streets in the early 1830s proved to be a very dangerous and lonely business. The two commissioners, Rowan and Mayne, fearing that public hostility might kill off the police force, moved to counter it. The bobbies were continually told to be respectful yet firm when dealing with the public. Citizens were invited to lodge complaints if their officers were truly unprofessional. This policy of creating public support gradually worked; as the police became more moderate in their conduct, public hostility also declined.[32]

Peel, too, proved to be very farsighted and keenly aware of the needs of both a professional police force and the public that would be asked to maintain it. Indeed, Peel saw that the poor quality of policing contributed to social disorder. Accordingly, he drafted several guidelines for the force, many of which focused on community relations. He wrote that the power of the police to fulfill their duties depended on public approval of their actions; that as public cooperation increased, the need for physical force by the police would decrease; that officers needed to display absolutely impartial service to law; and that force should be employed by the police only when attempts at persuasion and warning had failed, and then they should use only the minimal degree of force possible. Peel's remark that "the police are the public, and the public are the police" emphasized his belief that the police are first and foremost members of the larger society.[33]

During this initial five-year period, Peel endured the largest police turnover rate in history. Estimates vary widely, but the following is thought to be fairly accurate: 1,341 constables resigned from London's Metropolitan Police from 1829 to 1834; that's roughly half of the constables on the force. The pay of three shillings a day was meager, and probably few of the officers ever considered the position as a career.[34]

Peel proved very prescient, giving his early police practitioners a number of principles of policing that even today prove relevant to the policing community. As examples, Peel argued early on that the police should be organized along military lines and under governmental control—certainly two facets of modern policing that are prevalent. He also believed that the distribution of crime news is absolutely essential, and that police should not be deployed in willy-nilly fashion, but rather based on activities and calls for service as dictated by time and area. Peel recognized as well that police officers must be able to control their temper, present a good appearance, be properly hired and trained (and sent out on the streets only after satisfactorily completing a probationary period), and be identifiable with a badge number. He believed that the public should have easy access to police headquarters—which must be centrally located and contain excellent records. His principles also expressed the belief that crime *prevention* was as important as crime *suppression*, and that public approval of police actions is paramount. Indeed, he argued that the very authority given to the police is dependent on the public's approval of their existence, actions, and behavior. Furthermore, Peel included a principle that, again in a very foresighted manner, stands at the heart of today's community policing and problem solving era: The police must always recognize that they require the willing cooperation of the public if there is to be public observance of laws. This principle stands today as one of the hallmarks of Peel's viewpoints, underscoring his aforementioned, classical statement that "the police are the public, and the public are the police." And, in keeping with that directive, Peel noted that the need for the police to exercise force will *decrease* as public cooperation *increases*. Indeed, Peel appeared to be quite apprehensive concerning the use of force by police, arguing that such force should be employed only as a last resort—when the officer's powers of persuasion, warning, and so on failed to secure public compliance. Moreover, Peel maintained that the police should be impartial in their enforcement of the laws, without regard to one's wealth or public standing.[35]

Note that Peel's emphasis is on the *prevention* of crime. Peel felt that all efforts of the police were to be directed toward that end, and all other work of the police flowed from attempting to prevent crimes from occurring: the security of person and property, the preservation of the public tranquility, and ultimately the arrest, conviction, and punishment of those who in fact commit crimes. By the same token, Peel is implying that when many offenses are committed in a given area, police leaders and planners must recognize that their efforts are lacking in that locus and must govern their actions accordingly.

Also note that Peel's principles of 1829 relate very closely to the tenets of community policing—the current era of policing. Peel observed that the police are situated to proactively curb criminal activity and to provide order in the community, are no different from the people they are to serve, and should be visible in the community and interact with its citizens.

If Peel could speak today, however, he would likely indicate great displeasure with both the political and the reform (professional) eras of policing that came to pass in the United States (discussed below) because their motives and practices served to move the police away from his views of policing and into directions that were in opposition to his nine principles.

▶ Policing Comes to the United States

The English experiment with policing was not going unnoticed in the United States, where Peel's experiments with the bobbies were being closely watched. However, industrialization and social upheaval had not reached the proportions here that they had in England, so there was not the same urgency for full-time policing. Yet by the 1840s, when industrialization began in earnest in America, U.S. officials began to watch the police reform movement in England more closely. Eventually, of course, policing would become entrenched in America and evolve through three full eras: political, reform, and community (see Table 1-1 ■).

It will be seen below that the onset of full-time policing (defined as a paid, full-time police force with citywide jurisdiction that was charged solely with police duties)[36] in the United States is commonly said to have occurred in New York City in 1844. However, a number of prominent police historians and experts believe that the first organized, publicly funded, "modern" form of policing occurred in the South in the form of slave patrols.[37] It has been further argued that the Southern slave patrols were not only a precursor to

TABLE 1-1 The Three Eras of Policing

	Political Era (1840s to 1930s)	Reform Era (1930s to 1980s)	Community Era (1980s to Present)
Authorization	Politics and law	Law and professionalism	Community support (political), law, and professionalism
Function	Broad social services	Crime control	Broad provision of services
Organizational design	Decentralized	Centralized and classical	Decentralized using task forces and matrices
Relationship to community	Intimate	Professional and remote	Intimate
Tactics and technology	Foot patrol	Preventive patrol and rapid response to calls	Foot patrol, problem solving, and public relations
Outcome	Citizen and political satisfaction	Crime control	Quality of life and citizen satisfaction

Source: Adapted from George L. Kelling and Mark H. Moore, *The Evolving Strategies of Policing* (Washington, D.C.: U.S. Department of Justice, National Institute of Justice Perspectives on Policing, November 1988).

today's system but actually marked the first real advances in American policing.[38] Therefore, because the true origins of policing in America are somewhat debated, next we briefly discuss the Southern slave patrols.

Southern Slave Patrols

From the time Dutch slave ships began to bring slaves to the U.S. colonies as early as 1670, colonists began attempting to control slaves through informal means. For example, in many colonies and states, anyone could legally apprehend, chastise, and even kill any slave found off of his or her plantation, and runaway slaves could even be killed in some states.[39] The "slave codes" of the day defined slaves as mere property of their masters who were indentured for life; slaves were valuable property, and thus slave masters were given the right to control their "property" through discipline and punishment.

The slave patrols eventually became the legal mechanism for enforcing these codes; as a formal means of social control, particularly in rural areas of the Southern colonies, these patrols were to maintain the institution of slavery as well as capture runaway slaves and

▲ Some prominent police historians argue that the first form of modern policing occurred in the South in the form of slave patrols. *(Courtesy © North Wind Picture Archives/Alamy.)*

protect the white majority from slave uprisings and crimes. Members of such patrols in South Carolina and other states could enter the home of anyone—black or white—who was suspected of harboring slaves who were runaways or had violated the law.[40]

According to Phillip Reichel, the first such patrol was probably organized as a special enforcement arm in South Carolina in 1704.[41] Unlike the watchmen, constables, and sheriffs (discussed above) who had some nonpolice functions, these slave patrols, which continued operating through the antebellum period, functioned "solely for the enforcement of colonial and state laws."[42] Slave patrols often worked in combination with local militias and police and, although generally small in size, were well-armed and often visited plantations where they were allowed to flog slaves who were violating the codes.[43] Indeed, the right of patrols to administer such punishment existed in a number of states: patrols in Georgia, Arkansas, and South Carolina could administer twenty lashes, while North Carolina, Tennessee, and Mississippi permitted fifteen lashes.[44] Any hopes held by slaves for a better life were no doubt dashed—and the existence of slave patrols no doubt enhanced—by the infamous 1857 U.S. Supreme Court decision, *Scott v. Sanford*, in which a slave named Dred Scott was in effect told that he could not sue for his freedom: he was mere "property" and had no rights which white men needed to respect.

In sum, at the very least, when trying to understand the development of modern-day policing in America, Southern slave patrols can be said to represent a form of policing that was neither informal nor modern; in fact, they were probably more developmental or transitional in nature and created by the dominant class to preserve its control over the minority population of their day.

▶ The Political Era—1840s to 1930s

Imitating Peel

When the movement to improve policing did begin in America in the 1840s, it occurred in New York City. (Philadelphia, with a private bequest of $33,000, actually began a paid daytime police force in 1833; however, it was disbanded three years later.) The police reform movement had actually begun in New York in 1836, when the mayor advocated a new police organization that could deal with civil disorder. The city council denied the mayor's request, saying that, instead, citizens should simply aid one another in combating crime.

Efforts at police reform thus stayed dormant until 1841, when a highly publicized murder case resurrected the issue, showing again the incompetence of the officers under the old system of policing. Mary Cecilia Rogers left her New York home one day and disappeared; three days later, her body was discovered in the Hudson River. The public and newspapers clamored for the police to solve the crime. The police appeared unwilling to investigate until an adequate reward was offered.[45] Edgar Allan Poe's 1850 short story "The Mystery of Marie Roget" was based on this case. The Rogers case and the police response did more to encourage police reorganization than all of the previous cries for change. Thus began the political era of policing.

In 1844, the New York State legislature passed a law establishing a full-time preventive police force for New York City. However, this new body came into being in a very different form than in Europe. The American version, as begun in New York City, was deliberately placed under the control of the city government and city politicians. The American plan required that each ward in the city be a separate patrol district, unlike the European model, which divided the districts along the lines of criminal activity. The process for selecting officers was also different. The mayor chose the recruits from a list of names submitted by the aldermen and tax assessors of each ward; the mayor then submitted his choices to the city council for approval. This system adhered to the principles of republicanism and resulted in most of the power over the police going to the ward aldermen, who were seldom concerned about selecting the best people for the job. Instead, the system allowed and even encouraged political patronage and rewards for friends.[46]

The law also provided for the hiring of 800 officers—not nearly enough to cover the city—and for the hiring of a chief of police, who had no power to hire officers, assign them to duties, or fire them. Furthermore, the law did not require the officers to wear uniforms; instead, they were to carry a badge or other emblem for identification. Citizens would be hard-pressed to recognize an officer when they needed one. As a result of the law, New York's officers would be patrolling a beat around the clock, and pay scales were high enough to attract good applicants. At the same time, the position of constable was dissolved. Overall, these were important reforms over the old system and provided the basis for continued improvements that the public supported.[47]

It did not take long for other cities to adopt the general model of the New York City police force. New Orleans and Cincinnati adopted plans for a new police force in 1852, Boston and Philadelphia followed in 1854, Chicago in 1855, and Baltimore and Newark in 1857.[48] By 1880, virtually every major American city had a police force based on Peel's model.

Early Issues and Traditions

Three important issues confronted these early American police officers as they took to the streets between 1845 and 1869: whether the police should be in uniform, whether they should be armed, and whether they should use force.

The issue of a police uniform was important for several reasons. First, the lack of a uniform negated one of the basic principles of crime prevention—that police officers be visible. Crime victims wanted to find a police officer in a hurry. Further, uniforms would make it difficult for officers to avoid their duties since it would strip them of their anonymity. Interestingly, police officers themselves tended to prefer not to wear a uniform. They contended that the uniform would hinder their work because criminals would recognize them and flee and that the uniform was demeaning and would destroy their sense of manliness and democracy. One officer went so far as to argue that the sun reflecting off his badge would warn criminals of his approach; another officer hired an attorney and threatened to sue if he were compelled to don a uniform. To remedy the problem, New York City officials took advantage of the fact that their officers served four-year terms of office; when those terms expired in 1853, the city's police commissioners announced they would not rehire any officer who refused to wear a uniform. Thus New York became the first American city with a uniformed police force. It was followed in 1860 by Philadelphia, where there was also strong police objection to the policy. In Boston (1858) and Chicago (1861), police accepted the adoption of uniforms more easily.[49]

A more serious issue confronting politicians and the new police officers was the carrying of arms. At stake was the personal safety of the officers and the citizens they served. Nearly everyone viewed an armed police force with considerable suspicion. However, after some surprisingly calm objections by members of the public, who noted that the London police had no need to bear arms, it was agreed that an armed police force was unavoidable. Of course, America had a long tradition that citizens had the right—sometimes even the duty—to own firearms. And armed only with nightsticks, the new police could hardly withstand attacks by armed assailants. The public allowed officers to carry arms simply because there was no alternative, which was a significant change in American policing and a major point of departure from the English model. Practically from the first day, then, the American police have been much more open to the idea of carrying weapons.[50]

Eventually the use of force, the third issue, would become necessary and commonplace for American officers. Indeed, the uncertainty about whether an offender was armed perpetuated the need for an officer to rely on physical prowess for survival on the streets. The issue of use of force will be discussed further in Chapter 8.

Attempts at Reform in Difficult Times

By 1850, American police officers still faced a difficult task. In addition to maintaining order and coping with vice and crime, they would, soon after putting on the uniform, be separated from their old associates and viewed with suspicion by most citizens.

With few exceptions, the work was steady, and layoffs were uncommon. The nature of the work and the possibility of a retirement pension tied officers closely to their jobs and their colleagues. By 1850, there was a surplus of unskilled labor, particularly in the major eastern cities. The desire for economic security was reason enough for many able-bodied men to try to enter police service. New York City, for example, paid its police officers about twice as much as unskilled laborers could earn. Police departments had about twice as many applicants as positions. The system of political patronage prevailed in most cities, even after civil service laws attempted to introduce merit systems for hiring police.[51]

In New York, the police reform board was headed by Theodore Roosevelt, who sought applications for the department from residents in upstate areas. When these officers, later called bushwhackers, were appointed, they were criticized by disgruntled Tammanyites (corrupt New York City politicians) who favored the political patronage system. The Tammanyites complained that the bushwhackers "could not find their way to a single station house."[52] Roosevelt's approach violated the American tradition of hiring local boys for local jobs.[53] Citizens saw these new uniformed anomalies as people who wanted to spoil their fun or close their saloons on Sunday.

Tradition became the most important determinant of police behavior: A major teaching tool was the endless string of war stories the recruit heard, and the emphasis in most departments was on doing things as they had always been done. Innovation was frowned upon, and the veterans impressed on the rookies the reasons why things had to remain the same.[54] The police officers of the late nineteenth century were kept busy with riots, strikes, parades, and fires. These events often made for hostile interaction between citizens and the police. Labor disputes often meant long hours of extra duty for the officers, for which no extra pay was received. This, coupled with the fact that the police did not engage in collective bargaining, resulted in the police having little empathy or identification with strikers or strikebreakers. Therefore the use of the baton to put down riots, known as the "baton charge," was not uncommon.[55]

During the late nineteenth century, large cities gradually became more orderly places. The number of riots dropped. In the post–Civil War period, however, ethnic group conflict sometimes resulted in individual and group acts of violence and disorder. Hatred of Catholics and Irish Protestants led to the killing and wounding of over one hundred people in large eastern cities. Still, American cities were more orderly in 1900 than they had been in 1850. The possibility of violence involving labor disputes remained, and race riots increased in number and intensity after 1900, but daily urban life became more predictable and controlled. And then American cities absorbed millions of newcomers after 1900.[56]

Increased Politics and Corruption

A more developed urban life also promoted order. Work groups and social clusters provided a sense of integration and belonging. Immigrants established benefit societies, churches, synagogues, and social clubs. Irish-Americans constituted a heavy proportion of

▲ Turn of the century tools. *(Courtesy © Michael Matthews—Police Images/Alamy.)*

the police departments by the 1890s; they made up more than one-fourth of the New York City police force as early as the 1850s. Huge proportions of Irish officers were also found in Boston, Chicago, Cleveland, and San Francisco.[57]

Ethnic and religious disputes were found in many police departments. In Cleveland, for example, Catholics and Masons distrusted one another, while in New York, the Irish officers controlled many hirings and promotions. And there were still strong political influences at work. Politics were played to such an extent that even nonranking patrol officers used political backers to obtain promotions, desired assignments, and transfers.

Police corruption also surfaced at this time. Corrupt officers wanted beats close to the gamblers, saloonkeepers, madams, and pimps—people who could not operate if the officers were "untouchable" or "100 percent coppers."[58] Political pull for corrupt officers could work for or against them; the officer who incurred the wrath of his superiors could be transferred to the outposts, where he would have no chance for financial advancement.

In New York, officers routinely committed perjury to protect one another against civilian complaints. An early form of "internal affairs" thus developed in the 1890s: the "shoofly," a plainclothes officer who checked on the performance of the patrol officers. When Theodore Roosevelt served as police commissioner in New York, he frequently made clandestine trips to the beats to check on his officers; any malingerers found in the saloons were summoned to headquarters in the morning.[59]

Meanwhile, on the American Frontier . . .

While large cities in the East were struggling to overcome social problems and establish preventive police forces, the western half of America was anything but passive. Many historians believe that the true character of Americans developed on the frontier. Rugged

Career Profile

Name: Francis O'Neill, Chicago
Position: Chief of Police, Chicago, Illinois, 1903

The watchman of a century ago with his lantern and staff who called out the passing hours in stentorian tones during the night is now but a tradition. He has been succeeded by a uniformed constabulary and police who carry arms and operate under semi-military discipline. The introduction of electricity as a means of communication between stations was the first notable advance in the improvement of police methods. I remember the time when the manipulation of the dial telegraph by the station keeper while sending messages excited the greatest wonder and admiration. The adoption of the Morse system of telegraphy was a long step forward and proved of great advantage. In 1876, all desk sergeants were required to take up the immediate study of the Morse system of telegraphy. Scarcely one-fourth of them became proficient before modern science, advancing in leaps and bounds, brought forth that still more modern miracle—the telephone. Less than one-quarter century ago the policeman on post had no aid from science in communicating with his station or in securing assistance in case of need. When required by duty to care for the sick and injured or to remove a dead body, an appeal to the owner of some suitable vehicle was his only resource. These were desperate times for policemen in a hostile country with unpaved streets. The patrol wagon and signal service have effected a revolution in police methods. The forward stride from the lanterned night watch, with staff, to the uniformed and disciplined police officer of the present, equipped with telegraph, telephone, signal service, and the Bertillon system of identification [discussed in Chapter 5], is indeed an interesting one to contemplate.

Source: "Career Profile" from PROCEEDINGS OF THE INTERNATIONAL CHIEFS OF POLICE, TENTH ANNUAL CONVENTION, MAY 12–14. Copyright © 1903 by International Association of Chiefs of Police. Used by permission of International Association of Chiefs of Police.

individualism, independence, and simplicity of manners and behavior lent dignity to American life.

Most Americans are fascinated by this period of police history, a time when heroic marshals engaged in gunfights in Dodge City and other wild cowboy towns. But this period is also riddled with exaggerated legends and half-truths. During the second half of the nineteenth century, the absence of government created a confusing variety of forms of policing in the West. Large parts of the West were under federal control, some had been organized into states, and still others were under Native American control, at least on paper. Law enforcement was performed largely by federal marshals and their deputies. Once a state was created within a territory, its state legislature had the power to attempt to deal with crime by appointing county sheriffs. Otherwise, there was no uniform method for attempting to control the problems of the West.

When the people left the wagon trains and their relatively law-abiding ways, they attempted to live together in communities. Many different ethnic groups—Anglo-Americans, Mexicans, Chinese, Native Americans, freed African Americans, Australians, Scandinavians, and others—competed for often scarce resources and fought one another violently, often with mob attacks. Economic conflicts were frequent between cattlemen and sheepherders, and they often led to major range wars. There was constant labor strife in the mines. The bitterness of slavery remained, and many men with firearms skills learned during the Civil War turned to outlawry after leaving the service. (Jesse James was one such person.) In spite of these difficulties, westerners did manage to establish peace by relying on a combination of four groups who assumed responsibility for law enforcement: private citizens, U.S. marshals, businessmen, and town police officers.[60]

Private citizens usually helped to enforce the law by joining a posse or making individual efforts. An example of citizen policing was the formation of vigilante committees. Between 1849 and 1902, there were 210 vigilante movements in the United States, most of them in California.[61] While throughout history many vigilante groups have practiced "informal justice" by illegally taking the law into their own hands, breaking the law with violence and force, they also performed valuable work by ridding their communities of dangerous criminals. The Career Profile that is presented is an essay written at the dawn of the twentieth century and reflects the changes in technologies and methods of that era.

Federal marshals were created by congressional legislation in 1789. As marshals began to appear on the frontier, the vigilantes tended to disappear. The marshals enforced federal laws, so they had no jurisdiction over matters not involving a federal offense. They could act only in cases involving theft of mail, crimes against railroad property, murder on federal lands (much of the West was federal property for many decades), and a few other crimes. Their primary responsibility was in civil matters arising from federal court decisions. Federal marshals obtained their office through political appointment; therefore, they did not need any prior experience and were politically indebted. Initially, they received no salary but were instead compensated with fees and rewards. Because chasing outlaws did not pay as much as serving civil process papers, the marshals tended to prefer the more lucrative, less dangerous task of serving court paperwork. Congress saw the folly in this system and, in 1896, enacted legislation providing regular salaries for marshals.[62]

When a territory became a state, the primary law enforcement functions usually fell to local sheriffs and marshals. Train robbers such as Jesse James and the Dalton Gang were among the most famous outlaws to violate federal laws. Many train robbers became legendary for having the courage to steal from the despised railroad owners. What is often overlooked in the tales of these legendary outlaws is their often total disregard for the safety and lives of their victims. To combat these criminals, federal marshals found their hideouts, and railroad companies and other businesses often offered rewards for information leading to their capture. Occasionally, as in the case of Jesse James and the Daltons, the marshals' work was done for them—outlaws were often killed by friends (usually for a reward) or by private citizens.[63]

Gunfights in the West actually occurred very rarely; few individuals on either side of the law actually welcomed stand-up gunfights. It was infinitely more sensible to find cover from which to have a shootout. Further, handguns were not the preferred weapon—a double-barreled shotgun could do far more damage than a handgun at close range.

Local law enforcement came about as people settled into communities. Town meetings were held during which a government was established and local officials were elected. Sheriffs quickly became important officials, but they spent more time collecting taxes, inspecting cattle brands, maintaining jails, and serving civil papers than they did actually dealing with outlaws. In addition, with the growing use of U.S. marshals to uphold the law (some of the more storied ones being Wyatt Earp, "Wild Bill" Hickok, and William "Bat" Masterson), most people were inclined to be law abiding.[64]

Only forty-five violent deaths from all causes can be found in western cow towns from 1870 to 1885, when they were thriving. This low figure reflects the real nature of the cow towns. Businessmen had a vested interest in preventing crime from occurring and in not hiring a trigger-happy sheriff or marshal. They tended to avoid hiring individuals like John Slaughter, sheriff of Cochise County, Arizona, who never brought a prisoner back alive for eight years. Too much violence ruined a town's reputation and harmed the local economy.[65]

The Entrenchment of Political Influence

Partly because of their closeness to politicians, police during the early twentieth century began providing a wide array of services to citizens. In some cities, they operated soup lines, helped find lost children, and found jobs and temporary lodging in station houses for newly arrived immigrants.[66] Police organizations were typically quite decentralized, with cities divided into precincts and run like small-scale departments, hiring, firing, managing, and assigning personnel as necessary. Officers were often recruited from the same ethnic stock as the dominant groups in the neighborhoods and lived in the beats they patrolled, and they were allowed considerable discretion in handling their individual beats. Detectives operated from a caseload of "persons" rather than offenses, relying on their charges to inform on other criminals.[67]

Officers were integrated into neighborhoods. This strategy proved useful; it helped contain riots, and the police helped immigrants establish themselves in communities and find jobs. There were weaknesses as well: The intimacy with the community, closeness to politicians, and decentralized organizational structure (and its inability to provide supervision of officers) also led to police corruption. The close identification of police with neighborhoods also resulted in discrimination against strangers, especially ethnic and racial minorities. Police officers often ruled their beats with the "end of their night-sticks" and practiced "curbside justice."[68] The lack of organizational control over officers also caused some inefficiencies and disorganization; thus the image of the bungling Keystone Kops was widespread.

▶ The Reform Era: 1930s to 1980s

Attempts to Thwart Political Patronage

During the early nineteenth century, reformers sought to reject political involvement by the police, and civil service systems were created to eliminate patronage and ward influences in hiring and firing police officers. In some cities, officers were not permitted to live in the same beat they patrolled in order to isolate them as completely as possible from political influences. Police departments became one of the most autonomous agencies in urban government.[69] However, policing also became a matter viewed as best left to the discretion of police executives. Police organizations became law enforcement agencies with the sole goal of controlling crime. Any noncrime activities they were required to do were considered "social work." The reform era of policing (also termed the professional era of policing) would soon be in full bloom.

The scientific theory of administration was adopted, as advocated by Frederick Taylor during the early twentieth century. Taylor first studied the work process, breaking down jobs into their basic steps and emphasizing time and motion studies, all with the goal of maximizing production. From this emphasis on production and unity of control flowed the notion that police officers were best managed by a hierarchical pyramid of control. Police leaders routinized and standardized police work; officers were to enforce laws and make arrests whenever they could. Discretion was limited as much as possible. When special problems arose, special units (e.g., vice, juvenile, drugs, tactical) were created rather than problems being assigned to patrol officers.

The Era of August Vollmer

The policing career of August Vollmer has been established as one of the most important periods in the development of police professionalism (see Exhibit 1-1 ■). In April 1905 at age twenty-nine, Vollmer became the town marshal in Berkeley, California. At that time, policing had become a major issue all across America. Big-city police departments had become notorious for their corruption, and politics rather than professional principles dominated most police departments.[70]

Vollmer commanded a force of only three deputies; his first act as town marshal was to request an increase in his force from three to twelve deputies in order to form day and

EXHIBIT 1-1

THE CRIB OF MODERN LAW ENFORCEMENT

A Chronology of August Vollmer and the Berkeley Police Department

1905   Vollmer is elected Berkeley town marshal. Town trustees appoint six police officers at a salary of $70 per month.

1906   Trustees create detective rank. Vollmer initiates a red light signal system to reach beat officers from headquarters; telephones are installed in boxes. A police records system is created.

1908   Two motorcycles are added to the department. Vollmer begins a police school.

1909   Vollmer is appointed Berkeley chief of police under a new charter form of government. Trustees approve the appointment of a Bertillon expert and the purchase of fingerprinting equipment. A modus operandi file is created, modeled on the British system.

1911   All patrol officers are using bicycles.

1914   Three privately owned autos are authorized for patrol use.

1915   A central office is established for police reports.

1916   Vollmer urges Congress to establish a national fingerprint bureau (later created by the FBI in Washington, D.C.), begins annual lectures on police procedures, and persuades biochemist Albert Schneider to install and direct a crime laboratory at headquarters.

1917   Vollmer has the first completely motorized force; officers furnish their own automobiles. Vollmer recruits college students for part-time police jobs. He begins consulting with police and reorganizing departments around the country.

1918   Entrance examinations are initiated to measure the mental, physical, and emotional fitness of recruits; a part-time police psychiatrist is employed.

1919   Vollmer begins testing delinquents and using psychology to anticipate criminal behavior. He implements a juvenile program to reduce child delinquency.

1921   Vollmer guides the development of the first lie detector and begins developing radio communications between patrol cars, handwriting analysis, and use of business machine equipment (a Hollerith tabulator).

Following his retirement from active law enforcement in 1932, Vollmer traveled around the world to study police methods. He continued serving as professor of police administration at the University of California, Berkeley, until 1938, and authored or co-authored four books on police and crime from 1935 to 1949. He died in Berkeley in 1955.

night patrols. Obtaining that, he soon won national publicity for being the first chief to order his men to patrol on bicycles. Time checks he had run demonstrated that officers on bicycles would be able to respond three times more quickly to calls than men on foot possibly could. His confidence growing, Vollmer next persuaded the Berkeley City Council to purchase a system of red lights. The lights, hung at each street intersection, served as an emergency notification system for police officers—the first such signal system in the country.[71]

In 1906, Vollmer, curious about the methods criminals used to commit their crimes, began to question the suspects he arrested. He found that nearly all criminals used their own peculiar method of operation, or modus operandi. In 1907, following an apparent suicide case that Vollmer suspected of being murder, Vollmer sought the advice of a professor of biology at the University of California. He then became convinced of the value of scientific knowledge in criminal investigation.[72]

Vollmer's most daring innovation came in 1908: the idea of a police school. The first formal training program for police officers in the country drew on the expertise of university professors as well as police officers. The school included courses on police methods and procedures, fingerprinting, first aid, criminal law, anthropometry, photography, public health, and sanitation. In 1917, the curriculum was expanded from one to three years.[73] In 1916, Vollmer persuaded a professor of pharmacology and bacteriology to become a full-time criminalist in charge of the department's criminal investigation laboratory. By 1917, Vollmer had his entire patrol force operating out of automobiles; it was the first completely mobile patrol force in the country. And in 1918, to improve the quality of police recruits in his department, he began to hire college students as part-time officers and to administer a set of intelligence, psychiatric, and neurological tests to all applicants. Out of this group of "college cops" came several outstanding and influential police leaders, including O. W. Wilson, who served as police chief in Wichita and Chicago and as the first dean of the school of criminology at the University of California. Then, in 1921, in addition to experimenting with the lie detector, two of Vollmer's officers installed a crystal set and earphones in a Model T touring car, thus creating the first radio car.

These and other innovations at Berkeley had begun to attract attention from municipal police departments across the nation, including Los Angeles, which persuaded Vollmer to serve a short term there as chief of police beginning in August 1923. Gambling, the illicit sale of liquor (prohibition was then in effect), and police corruption were major problems in Los Angeles. Vollmer hired ex-criminals to gather intelligence information on the criminal network. He also promoted honest officers, required 3,000 patrol officers to take an intelligence test, and, using those tests, reassigned personnel.[74] He was already unpopular with crooks and corrupt politicians, and these personnel actions made Vollmer very unpopular within the department as well. When he returned to Berkeley in 1924, he had made many enemies, and his attempts at reform had met with too much opposition to have any lasting effect. It would not be until the 1950s, under Chief William Parker, that the Los Angeles Police Department (LAPD) would become a leader in this reform era of policing.[75]

Vollmer, although a leading proponent of police professionalism, also advocated the idea that the police should function as social workers. He believed the police should do more than merely arrest offenders that they should also seek to prevent crime by "saving" offenders.[76] He suggested that police work closely with existing social welfare agencies, inform voters about overcrowded schools, and support the expansion of recreational facilities, community social centers, and antidelinquency agencies. Basically, he was suggesting that the police play an active part in the life of the community. These views were very prescient; today, his ideas are being implemented in the contemporary

▲ August Vollmer as town marshal, police chief, and criminalist. *(Courtesy Samuel G. Chapman)*

movement toward community policing and problem-oriented policing. Yet the major thrust of police professionalization had been to insulate the police from politics. This contradiction illustrated one of the fundamental ambiguities of the whole notion of professionalism.[77]

In the late 1920s, Vollmer was appointed the first professor of police administration in the country at the University of Chicago. Upon returning to Berkeley in 1931, he received a similar appointment at the University of California, a position he held concurrently with the office of chief of police until his retirement from the force in 1932. He continued to serve as a university professor until 1938.[78]

The Crime Fighter Image

The 1930s marked an important turning point in the history of police reform. O. W. Wilson emerged as the leading authority on police administration, the police role was redefined, and the crime fighter image gained popularity.

Wilson, who learned from J. Edgar Hoover's transformation of the Federal Bureau of Investigation (FBI) into a highly prestigious agency, became the principal architect of the police reform strategy.[79] Hoover, appointed FBI director in 1924, had raised the eligibility and training standards of recruits and had developed an incorruptible crime-fighting organization. Municipal police found Hoover's path a compelling one.

Professionalism came to mean a combination of managerial efficiency and technological sophistication and an emphasis on crime fighting. The social work aspects of the policing movement fell into almost total eclipse. In sum, under the professional model of policing, officers were to remain in their "rolling fortresses," going from one call to the next with all due haste. As Mark Moore and George Kelling observed, "In professionalizing crime fighting . . . citizens on whom so much used to depend [were] removed from the fight."[80]

The Wickersham Commission

Another important development in policing, one that was strongly influenced by August Vollmer, was the creation of the Wickersham Commission. President Calvin Coolidge had appointed the first National Crime Commission in 1925, in an admission that crime control had become a national problem. This commission was criticized for working neither through the states nor with professionals in criminal justice, psychiatry, social work, or the like. Nevertheless, coming on the heels of World War I, the crime commission took advantage of FBI Director J. Edgar Hoover's popular "war on crime" slogan to enlist public support. Political leaders and police officials also loudly proclaimed the "war on crime" concept; it continued the push for police professionalism.

Coolidge's successor, President Herbert Hoover, became concerned about the lax enforcement of Prohibition, which had taken effect in 1920. It was common knowledge that an alarming number of American police chiefs and sheriffs were accepting bribes in exchange for overlooking moonshiners; other types of police corruption were occurring as well.

Hoover replaced the National Crime Commission with the National Commission on Law Observance and Enforcement—popularly known as the Wickersham Commission after its chairman, former U.S. Attorney General George W. Wickersham. This presidential commission completed the first national study of crime and criminal justice, issued in fourteen reports. Two of those reports, the "Report on Police" and the "Report on Lawlessness in Law Enforcement," represented a call by the federal government for increased police professionalism.

The "Report on Police" was written in part by August Vollmer, and his imprint on this and other reports is evident. The "Report on Lawlessness in Law Enforcement" concerned itself with police misconduct and has received the greatest public attention, both then and now. The report indicated that the use by the police of third-degree suspect interrogation methods (including the infliction of physical or mental pain to extract confessions) was widespread in America. This report, through its recommendations, mapped out a path of professionalism in policing for the next two generations. The Wickersham Commission recommended, for example, that the corrupting influence of politics should be removed from policing. Police chief executives should be selected on merit, and patrol officers should be tested and should meet minimal physical standards. Police salaries, working conditions, and benefits should be decent, the commission stated, and there should be adequate training for both preservice and in-service officers. The commission also called for the use of policewomen (in cases involving juveniles and females), crime-prevention units, and bureaus of criminal investigation.

Many of these recommendations represented what progressive police reformers had been wanting for the previous forty years; unfortunately, President Hoover and his administration could do little more than report the Wickersham Commission's recommendations before leaving office.

Police as the "Thin Blue Line": William H. Parker

The movement to transform the police into professional crime fighters found perhaps its staunchest champion in William H. Parker, who began as a patrol officer with the LAPD in 1927. Parker used his law degree to advance his career, and by 1934 he was the LAPD's trial prosecutor and an assistant to the chief.[81]

Parker became police chief in 1950. Following an uproar over charges of police brutality in 1951, he conducted an extensive investigation that resulted in the dismissal

▼

or punishment of over forty officers. Following this incident, he launched a campaign to transform the LAPD. His greatest success, typical of the new professionalism, came in administrative reorganization. The command structure was simplified as Parker aggressively sought ways to free every possible officer for duty on the streets, including forcing the county sheriff's office to guard prisoners and adopting one-person patrol cars. Parker also made the rigorous selection and training of personnel a major characteristic of the LAPD. Higher standards of physical fitness, intelligence, and scholastic achievement weeded out many applicants, while others failed the psychiatric examinations.

Once accepted, recruits attended a thirteen-week academy that included a rigorous physical program, rigid discipline, and intensive study. Parker thus molded an image of a tough, competent, polite, and effective crime fighter by controlling recruitment. During the 1950s, this image made the LAPD the model for reform across the nation; thus the 1950s marked a turning point in the history of professionalism.[82]

Parker conceived of the police as a "thin blue line"—a force that stood between civilization and chaos and protecting society from barbarism and Communist subversion. He viewed urban society as a jungle, needing the restraining hand of the police; only the law and law enforcement saved society from the horrors of anarchy. The police had to enforce the law without fear or favor. Parker opposed any restrictions on police methods. The law, he believed, should give the police wide latitude to use wiretaps and to conduct search and seizure. For him, the Bill of Rights was not absolute but relative. Any conflict between effective police operation and individual rights should be resolved in favor of the police, he believed, and the rights of society took precedence over the rights of the individual. He thought that evidence obtained illegally should still be admitted in court and that the police could not do their jobs if the courts and other civilians were continually second-guessing them.

Basically, Parker believed that some "wicked men with evil hearts" preyed on society and that the police must protect society from attack by them. But Parker's brand of professional police performance lacked total public support. Voters often supported political machines that controlled and manipulated the police in anything but a professional manner; the public demanded a police department that was subject to political influence and manipulation and then condemned the force for its crookedness. The professional police officer was in the uncomfortable position of offering a service that society required for its very survival but that many people did not want at all.[83]

1960s and 1970s: The Struggle for Civil Rights

Certainly any review of the history of policing would be lacking if it did not discuss the civil rights movement that predominated the late 1960s and 1970s and pitted the nation's police against many of its college-age youths and minority groups (with many members of both groups viewing the police as "pigs" and representing the "establishment"). National groups (e.g., Students for a Democratic Society, Black Panthers, Student Nonviolent Coordinating Committee) represented both sides, some violent, others nonviolent. As Benjamin Disraeli once said, "No man will treat with indifference the principle of race. It is the key to history."[84]

The 1960s were a time of great tumult, civil disobedience, social turbulence, and tremendous progress in civil rights. Inner-city residents rioted in several major cities, protestors denounced military involvement in Vietnam, and assassins' bullets ended the life of President John F. Kennedy (1963) as well as those of his brother U.S. Senator Robert F. Kennedy (1968) and Dr. Martin Luther King, Jr. (1968). The country was witnessing tremendous upheaval, and incidents such as the Democratic National Convention (1968) in Chicago raised many questions about the police and their function and role; each night Americans witnessed scenes on national television of Chicago police officers gassing and clubbing protesters, news photographers and reporters, and other citizens in what was subsequently termed in the investigative Walker Report and in many other accounts as the Chicago "police riot."[85]

The reform (or professional) era of policing was in bloom, however, so the police were firmly ensconced in their patrol vehicles, being reactive to crime and quite removed from personal contact with the public while on random patrol and focusing on quantitative measures of their effectiveness: numbers of arrests, response time, calls for service, numbers of officers in patrol cars, numbers of miles officers drove per shift, and so on. Police training and university police science programs were booming, the latter making campuses rich with these "cash cow" programs taught largely by practitioners, with federal grants and GI benefits paying for officers' tuition, books, and often their living expenses. But the failure of the professional era became most apparent during the aforementioned urban riots, sit-ins, sniper attacks against police, gang violence, and other forms of unrest and upheaval of the time.

Specifically, Harlem, Watts, Newark, and Detroit all were scenes of major race riots during the 1960s. There were seventy-five civil disorders involving African Americans and the police in 1967 alone, with at least eighty-three people killed, mostly African Americans. In addition, many police officers and firefighters were killed or injured. Property damage in these riots totaled hundreds of millions of dollars. The 1970s busing programs that were introduced to integrate schools resulted in white "backlash" and more interracial conflict.

In the late 1980s police–community relations appeared to worsen, with a major riot in Miami, Florida, in 1989. Also in the 1980s, affirmative action programs led to charges of reverse discrimination and more dominant-group backlash. More recent decades have witnessed burning and looting in Miami, Florida; Los Angeles, California; Atlanta, Georgia; Las Vegas, Nevada; Washington, D.C.; St. Petersburg, Florida; and other cities. These incidents have demonstrated that the same tensions that found temporary release on the streets of African American communities in the past still remain with us.

The police, viewed by many during the professional era as the "thin blue line" per William Parker, were involved in all of the social changes described above. Although at times police were used to prevent minority group members from demonstrating on behalf of civil rights, at other times the police were required to protect those same protesting minorities from the wrath of the dominant group and others who opposed peaceful demonstrations. Over time, alienation developed from these contacts. Thus, members of both groups had an uneasy coexistence with a good deal of emotional "baggage" based on what they had seen, heard, or been told of their interactions throughout history.

History has shown that problems in police–community relations are actually part of a larger problem of racism in American society. The highly respected National Academy of Sciences concluded nearly two decades ago that "black crime and the position of blacks within the nation's system of criminal justice administration are related to past and present social opportunities and disadvantages and can be best understood through consideration of blacks' overall social status."[86] More recent mass gatherings in Washington, D.C., engendered by such groups as the Southern Christian Leadership Conference and the Rainbow Coalition, have involved protests against racial profiling (discussed later), police brutality, and other perceived prejudices toward people of color; such assemblies would indicate that the Academy's statement is still valid today. Minority group members remain frustrated because the pace of gains in our society has not kept pace with their expectations.

▶ A Retreat from the Professional Model

Coming Full Circle to Peel: President's Crime Commission

Until the period described above, the 1960s and 1970s, there had been few inquiries concerning police functions and methods for two reasons.[87] First was a tendency on the part of the police to resist outside scrutiny. Functioning in a bureaucratic environment, the police, like other bureaucrats, were sensitive to outside research. Many police administrators perceived a threat to their career and to the image of the organization, and they were also concerned about the legitimacy of the research itself. There was a natural reluctance to invite trouble. Second, few people in policing perceived a need to challenge traditional methods of operation. The "If it ain't broke, don't fix it" attitude prevailed, particularly among old-school administrators. Some ideas were etched in stone, such as the belief that more police personnel and vehicles equaled more patrolling and, therefore, less crime, a quicker response rate, and a happier citizenry. A corollary belief is that the more officers riding in the patrol car, the better. The methods and effectiveness of detectives and their investigative techniques were not even open to debate.

As Herman Goldstein stated, however, "Crises stimulate progress. The police came under enormous pressure in the late 1960s and early 1970s, confronted with concern about crime, civil rights demonstrations, racial conflicts, riots, and political protests."[88]

Concurrent with, and because of, the aforementioned turmoil, five national commissions attempted to examine police methods and practices during the 1960s and 1970s, each viewing them from different perspectives. Of particular note is a commission whose findings are still widely cited today and that provided the impetus to return the police to the community: the President's Commission on Law Enforcement and the Administration of Justice. Termed the President's Crime Commission, this body was charged by President Lyndon Johnson to find solutions to America's internal crime problems, including the root causes of crime, the workings of the justice system, and the hostile, antagonistic relations between the police and civilians. Among the commission's recommendations for the police were hiring more minority members as officers to improve police–community relations, upgrading the quality of police officers through better-educated officers, promoting to supervisory positions college-educated individuals, screening applicants more rigorously, and providing intensive preservice training for new recruits. It was proposed that a higher caliber of recruits would raise police service delivery, promote tranquility within the community, and relegate police corruption to a thing of the past.[89]

The President's Crime Commission brought policing full circle, restating several of the same principles that were laid out by Sir Robert Peel in 1829: that the police should be close to the public, that poor quality of policing contributed to social disorder, and that the police should focus on community relations. Thus, by 1970 there had been what was termed a systematic demolition of the assumptions underlying the professional era of policing.[90] Few authorities on policing today could endorse the basic approaches to police management that were propounded by O. W. Wilson or William Parker. We now know much that was still unknown by the staff of the President's Crime Commission in 1967. For example, as will be seen in Chapter 3, we have learned that adding more police or intensifying patrol coverage does not reduce crime and that neither faster response time nor additional detectives will improve clearance rates.

▶ The Community Era: 1980s to Present

In the early 1970s, it was suggested that the performance of patrol officers would improve by redesigning their job based on motivators.[91] This suggestion later evolved into a concept known as team policing, which sought to restructure police departments, improve police–community relations, enhance police officer morale, and facilitate change within the police organization. Its primary element was a decentralized neighborhood focus for the delivery of police services. Officers were to be generalists, trained to investigate crimes and basically attend to all of the problems in their area; a team of officers would be assigned to a particular neighborhood and would be responsible for all police services in that area.

In the end, however, team policing failed for several reasons. Most of the experiments were poorly planned and hastily implemented, resulting in street officers who did not understand what they were supposed to do. Many mid-management personnel felt threatened by team policing and did not support the experiment.

There were other developments for the police during the late 1970s and early 1980s. Foot patrol became more popular, and many jurisdictions (such as Newark, New Jersey; Boston, Massachusetts; and Flint, Michigan) even demanded it. In Newark, an evaluation led to the conclusions that officers on foot patrol were easily seen by residents, produced a significant increase in the level of satisfaction with police service, led to a significant reduction of perceived crime problems, and resulted in a significant increase in the perceived level of neighborhood safety.[92]

These findings shattered several long-held myths about measures of police effectiveness. In addition, research conducted during the 1970s suggested that information could help police improve their ability to deal with crime. These studies, along with studies of foot patrol and fear reduction, created new opportunities for police to work with citizens to do something about crime problems. Police discovered that when they asked citizens about their priorities, citizens appreciated their asking and often provided useful information.

Simultaneously, the problem-oriented approach to policing was being tested in Madison, Wisconsin; Baltimore County, Maryland; and Newport News, Virginia. Studies there found that police officers have the capacity to do problem solving successfully and can work well with citizens and other agencies. Also, citizens seemed to appreciate working with police. Moreover, this approach gave officers more autonomy to analyze the underlying causes of problems and to find creative solutions. Crime control remained an important function, but equal emphasis was given to prevention.

In sum, following are some of the factors that set the stage for the demise of the professional era and the emergence of the community era of policing (discussed in Chapter 4):

- Narrowing of the police mission to crime fighting
- Increased cultural diversity in our society
- Detachment of patrol officers in patrol vehicles
- Increased violence in our society
- Scientific view of management, stressing efficiency more than effectiveness, quantitative policing more than qualitative policing
- Increased dependence on high-technology equipment rather than contact with the public
- Isolation of police administration from community and officer input
- Concern about police violation of the civil rights of minorities
- Burgeoning attempts by the police to adequately reach the community through crime prevention, team policing, and police–community relations

Today, COPPS is recognized as being on the cutting edge of what is new in policing.[93]

Summary

This chapter has presented the evolution of policing through its three eras, and some of the individuals, events, and national commissions that were instrumental in taking policing through those eras. It has also shown how the history of policing may be said to have come full circle to its roots, wherein it was intended to operate with the consent and assistance of the public. Policing is now attempting to throw off the shackles of tradition and become more community oriented.

This historical overview also reveals that many of today's policing issues and problems (most or all of which are discussed in subsequent chapters) actually began surfacing many centuries ago: graft and corruption, negative community relations, police use of force, public unrest and rioting, general police accountability, the struggle to establish the proper roles and functions of the police, the police subculture, and the tendency to withdraw from the public, cling to tradition, and be inbred. All in all, however, it would seem the police learned well their lessons from history, as these problems do not pervade the nation's 17,000 agencies or their 800,000 officers. As we will see, the community era is spreading and thriving in today's police world.

Key Terms

August Vollmer
civil rights movement
community era of policing
constable
coroner
Democratic National Convention (1968)

justice of the peace (JP)
modus operandi
political era of policing
President's Crime Commission
principles of policing
professional era of policing
reform era of policing

republicanism
sheriff
slave patrols
team policing
Wickersham Commission
William H. Parker

Review Questions

1. What were the major police-related offices and their functions during the early English and colonial periods?
2. What legacies of colonial policing remained intact after the American Revolution?
3. List the three early issues of American policing, and describe their present status.
4. What unique characteristics of law enforcement existed in the Wild West? What myths concerning early western law enforcement continue today?
5. Explain the function of slave patrols, and how it might be argued that they were the first form of policing in the United States.
6. What were some of the major characteristics of the political and reform eras of policing? How did they square with the earlier principles of policing as set forth by Sir Robert Peel?
7. What led to the development of the contemporary community-oriented policing and problem-solving era, and what are some of its main features?
8. How can it be said that policing has come full circle, returning to its origins?

Learn by Doing

As indicated in the Preface, this section (here and at the ends of all the other chapters of this book) comports with the early 1900s teaching of famed educator John Dewey, who advocated the "learning by doing" approach to education, or problem-based learning. It also comports with the popular learning method espoused by Benjamin Bloom in 1956, known as Bloom's Taxonomy, in which he called for "higher-order thinking skills"—critical and creative thinking that involves analysis, synthesis, and evaluation.[94] The following scenarios and activities will shift your attention from textbook-centered instruction and move the emphasis to student-centered projects. By being placed in these hypothetical situations, you can thus learn—and apply—some of the concepts covered in this chapter, develop skills in communication and self-management, solve problems, and understand and address current community issues.

1. You have been tasked by the police chief to develop—and present—a one-hour History of Policing class as part of the curriculum at the Regional Police Academy. Prepare an outline, timeline of police history, and presentation that will satisfy this request. Be sure to include the major developments for each policing era.

2. Your criminal justice professor assigns you to examine your local police organizations and then, if they exist, to compare the duties of the four early English policing offices (e.g., sheriff, constable, justice of the peace, coroner) with their present status and function (or, if more appropriate, at the time of their demise) in your particular area.

3. Assume that, as part of an assigned research paper on the history of policing, you seek to interview a retired police officer(s) concerning the changes in police methods and philosophy over the past several decades (as well as areas in which policing has remained unchanged); hopefully you would be particularly determined to locate and interview a woman who entered the field as a sworn officer in the 1970s or 1980s, and learn the unique challenges that were faced.

Notes

1. Samuel Walker, *The Police in America: An Introduction* (New York: McGraw-Hill, 1983), p. 2.
2. Bruce Smith, *Rural Crime Control* (New York: Columbia University, 1933), p. 40.
3. Ibid., pp. 42–44.
4. Ibid.
5. Ibid.
6. Ibid., pp. 182–84.
7. Ibid., pp. 188–89.
8. Ibid., p. 192.
9. Ibid., pp. 218–22.
10. Ibid., pp. 245–46.
11. Ibid.
12. Craig Uchida, "The Development of American Police: An Historical Overview," in *Critical Issues in Policing: Contemporary Readings*, eds. Roger G. Dunham and Geoffrey P. Alpert (Prospect Heights, IL: Waveland Press, 1989), p. 14.
13. Charles Reith, *A New Study of Police History* (London: Oliver and Boyd, 1956).
14. Carl Klockars, *The Idea of Police* (Beverly Hills, CA: Sage, 1985).
15. Ibid., pp. 45–46.
16. Ibid., p. 46.
17. David R. Johnson, *American Law Enforcement History* (St. Louis: Forum Press, 1981), p. 4.
18. Ibid., p. 5.
19. Ibid.
20. Ibid., p. 6.
21. Ibid., p. 1.
22. Ibid., pp. 8–10.
23. Ibid., p. 11.
24. Ibid., p. 13.
25. David A. Jones, *History of Criminology: A Philosophical Perspective* (Westport, CT: Greenwood Press, 1986), p. 64.
26. Johnson, *American Law Enforcement History*, pp. 14–15.
27. Ibid., pp. 17–18.
28. Ibid., pp. 18–19.
29. Leon Radzinowicz, *A History of English Criminal Law and Its Administration from 1750*, vol. IV, *Grappling for Control* (London: Stevens and Son, 1968), p. 163.
30. Johnson, *American Law Enforcement History*, p. 19.
31. Ibid., pp. 19–20.
32. Ibid., pp. 20–21.

33. A. C. Germann, Frank D. Day, and Robert R. J. Gallati, *Introduction to Law Enforcement and Criminal Justice* (Springfield, IL: Charles C Thomas, 1962), p. 63.

34. Clive Emsley, *Policing and Its Context, 1750–1870* (New York: Schocken, 1983), p. 37.

35. For more information concerning Peel's principles, see Pamela D. Mayhall, *Police-Community Relations and the Administration of Justice*, 3d ed. (New York: John Wiley & Sons, 1985), p. 425; also see Charles Reith, *A Short History of the British Police* (London: Oxford University Press, 1948).

36. Selden D. Bacon, *The Early Development of American Municipal Police: A Study of the Evolution of Formal Controls in a Changing Society*, unpublished dissertation, Yale University, University Microfilms No. 6646844, 1939.

37. See, for example, Samuel Walker, *A Critical History of Police Reform: The Emergence of Professionalism* (Lexington, MA: Lexington Books, 1977); Samuel Walker, *Popular Justice* (New York: Oxford University Press, 1980); also see Phillip Reichel, "Southern Slave Patrols as a Transitional Police Type," *American Journal of Policing* 7 (2) (1988): 51–77.

38. M. P. Roth, *Crime and Punishment: A History of the Criminal Justice System* (Belmont, CA: Wadsworth, 2005).

39. Phillip Reichel, "Southern Slave Patrols as a Transitional Police Type," *American Journal of Police* 7(2) (1988), p. 57.

40. Sally Hadden, *Slave Patrols: Law and Violence in Virginia and the Carolinas* (Cambridge: Harvard University Press, 2001), pp. 185–187.

41. Phillip Reichel, "Southern Slave Patrols as a Transitional Police Type," *American Journal of Police* 7(2) (1988), p. 59.

42. Ibid., p. 68.

43. Sally Hadden, *Slave Patrols: Law and Violence in Virginia and the Carolinas*, pp. 185–187.

44. Phillip Reichel, "Southern Slave Patrols as a Transitional Police Type," *American Journal of Police* 7(2) (1988), p. 72.

45. Johnson, *American Law Enforcement History*, p. 26.

46. Ibid., pp. 26–27.

47. Ibid., p. 27.

48. Ibid.

49. Ibid., pp. 28–29.

50. Ibid., pp. 30–31.

51. James F. Richardson, *Urban Policing in the United States* (London: Kennikat Press, 1974), pp. 47–48.

52. James F. Richardson, *The New York Police: Colonial Times to 1901* (New York: Oxford Press, 1970), p. 259.

53. Richardson, *Urban Policing in the United States*, p. 48.

54. Richardson, *The New York Police*, pp. 195–201.

55. Richardson, *Urban Policing in the United States*, p. 51.

56. Ibid.

57. Ibid., pp. 53–54.

58. Ibid., pp. 55–56.

59. Ibid., pp. 59–60.

60. Johnson, *American Law Enforcement History*, p. 92.

61. Ibid.

62. Ibid., pp. 96–97.

63. Ibid., p. 98.

64. U.S. Department of Justice, United States Marshals Service, "The Marshals Service Turns 215," www.usmarshals.gov/monitor/215-0402.pdf (accessed March 5, 2013).

65. Johnson, *American Law Enforcement History*, pp. 100–101.

66. Eric H. Monkkonen, *Police in Urban America, 1860–1920* (New York: Cambridge University Press, 1981), p. 158.

67. John E. Eck, *The Investigation of Burglary and Robbery* (Washington, D.C.: Police Executive Research Forum, 1984).

68. George L. Kelling, "Juveniles and Police: The End of the Nightstick," in *From Children to Citizens*, vol. II, *The Role of the Juvenile Court*, ed. Francis X. Hartmann (New York: Springer-Verlag, 1987).

69. Herman Goldstein, *Policing a Free Society* (Cambridge, MA: Ballinger, 1977).

70. August Vollmer, "Police Progress in the Past Twenty-Five Years," *Journal of Criminal Law and Criminology* 24 (1933): 161–75.

71. Alfred E. Parker, *Crime Fighter: August Vollmer* (New York: Macmillan, 1961).

72. Nathan Douthit, "August Vollmer," in *Thinking About Police: Contemporary Readings*, ed. Carl B. Klockars (New York: McGraw-Hill, 1983), p. 102.

73. Ibid.

74. Paul Jacobs, *Prelude to Riot: A View of Urban America from the Bottom* (New York: Random House, 1966), pp. 13–60.

75. Ibid.

76. Samuel Walker, *A Critical History of Police Reform: The Emergence of Professionalism* (Lexington, MA: Lexington Books, 1977), p. 81.

77. Ibid., pp. 80–83.

78. For a chronology of Vollmer's career and a listing of his publications, see Gene E. Carte and Elaine H. Carte, *Police Reform in the United States: The Era of August Vollmer, 1905–1932* (Berkeley: University of California Press, 1975).

79. Orlando Wilson, *Police Administration* (New York: McGraw-Hill, 1950).

80. Mark H. Moore and George L. Kelling, "'To Serve and Protect': Learning from Police History," *The Public Interest* 70 (Winter 1983): 49–65.

81. Johnson, *American Law Enforcement History*, pp. 119–20.

82. Ibid., pp. 120–21.

83. Richardson, *Urban Policing in the United States*, pp. 139–43.

84. Benjamin Disraeli, *Endymion* (New York: D. Appleton & Co., 1880), pp. 249–50.

85. Daniel Walker, *Rights in Conflict: The Violent Confrontation of Demonstrators and Police in the Parks and Streets of Chicago During the Week of the Democratic National Convention of 1968—A Report Submitted to the National Commission on the Causes and Prevention of Violence* (Steubenville, OH: Braceland Brothers, 1968), p. 233; also see "Chicago Examined: Anatomy of a Police Riot," *Time*, December 6, 1968, www.time.com/time/magazine/article/0,9171,844633-5,00.html (accessed March 5, 2013).

86. National Academy of Sciences, *A Common Destiny: Blacks and American Society* (Washington, D.C.: National Academy Press, 1989), p. 453.

87. Peter K. Manning, "The Researcher: An Alien in the Police World," in *The Ambivalent Force: Perspectives on the Police*, 2nd ed. (Hinsdale, IL: Dryden Press, 1976), pp. 103–21.

88. Herman Goldstein, *Problem-Oriented Policing* (New York: McGraw-Hill, 1990), p. 9.

89. William G. Doerner, *Introduction to Law Enforcement: An Insider's View* (Englewood Cliffs, NJ: Prentice Hall, 1992), pp. 21–23.

90. Samuel Walker, "'Broken Windows' and Fractured History: The Use and Misuse of History in Recent Police Patrol Analysis," in *Classics in Policing*, eds. Steven G. Brandl and David E. Barlow (Cincinnati, OH: Anderson, 1996), pp. 97–110.

91. Thomas J. Baker, "Designing the Job to Motivate," *FBI Law Enforcement Bulletin* 45 (1976): 3–7.

92. Police Foundation, *The Newark Foot Patrol Experiment* (Washington, D.C.: Author, 1981).

93. Ibid., p. 71.

94. Benjamin S. Bloom, *Taxonomy of Educational Objectives, Handbook I: The Cognitive Domain* (New York: David McKay, 1956).

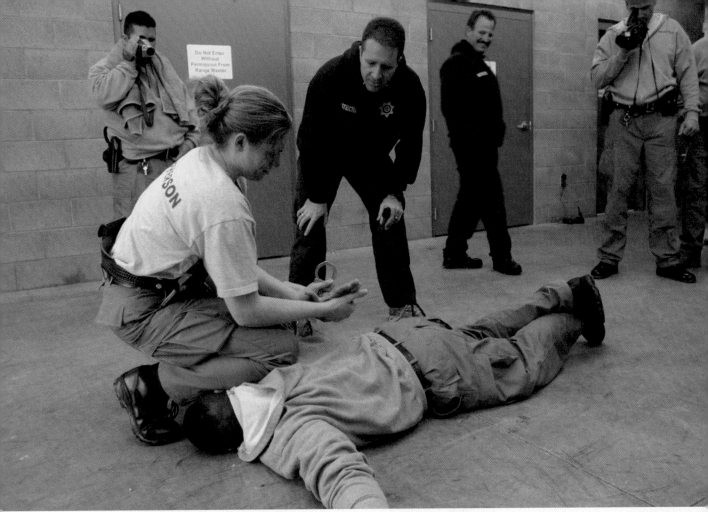

(Courtesy Washoe County Sheriff's Office.)

2 Preparing for the Street
Recruitment, Training, and Socialization

LEARNING OBJECTIVES

As a result of reading this chapter, the student will be able to:

1 *Describe some of the problems confronting today's police recruiters and some unique measures being tried to obtain a viable applicant pool*

2 *Explain the general hiring process and types of tests and examinations employed to hire and train police officers*

3 *Describe the assessment center concept and its functions for hiring and promoting the best personnel*

4 *List the kinds of skills and knowledge that are imparted to police trainees during their academy training, including the typical subjects or topics that are found in the curriculum*

⑤ Describe the methods and purposes of both the FTO and PTO programs

⑥ Describe what is meant by the term working personality *and how it is developed and functions*

⑦ Define police cynicism and how it operates

⑧ Delineate the ideal traits of police officers

⑨ Describe the primary functions and styles of policing

⑩ Explain the status and advantages of women and minorities serving in police ranks

· ·

Introduction

This chapter generally describes how an officer's career begins and, to a large extent, how his or her occupational personality is formed. Studying the subculture of the police helps us define the "cop's world" and the officer's role in it; this subculture shapes the officer's attitudes, values, and beliefs.

The idea of a police subculture was first proposed by William Westley in his 1950 study of the Gary, Indiana, Police Department, where he found, among many other things, a high degree of group cohesion, secrecy, and violence.[1] It is now widely accepted that the police develop traditions, skills, and attitudes that are unique to their occupation because of their duties and responsibilities.[2]

We begin at the threshold, looking at some of the methods, challenges, and problems connected with the recruitment of qualified individuals. Then we track the typical police applicant's progression through what has been termed the "hurdle process," or various types of tests that may be employed—written, psychological, physical, oral, character, and medical screening—and also discuss the assessment center.

Next we examine formal police training at the academy, where the initiation of the officer-to-be into the police subculture commences in earnest; included are their typical curriculum and some of the informal learning that takes place there. We then look at postacademy training—the field training officer concept—and in-service training later in one's career. Following that, we take a look at how officers adopt their working personality: formal and informal rules, customs, and beliefs of the occupation. This portion of the chapter includes an assessment of the traits that make a good officer. Then we examine the roles, functions, and styles of policing, following which we consider women and minorities in policing. A summary, review questions, and several scenarios and activities that provide opportunities to learn by doing conclude the chapter.

· ·

▶ First Things First: Recruiting Qualified Applicants

Wanted: Those Who Walk on Water

Recruiting that results in an adequate pool of applicants is an extremely important facet of the police hiring process. August Vollmer stated:

> [Law enforcement candidates should] have the wisdom of Solomon, the courage of David, the patience of Job and leadership of Moses, the kindness of the Good Samaritan, the diplomacy of Lincoln, the tolerance of the Carpenter of Nazareth, and, finally, an intimate knowledge of every branch of the natural, biological and social sciences.[3]

—POLICE ORGANIZATION AND MANAGEMENT, 3rd ed. by Vivian Anderson Leonard and Harry W More. Published by Foundation Press, MN.

Many people believe that the police officer has the most difficult job in America. Police officers are solitary workers, spending most of their time on the job unsupervised. Also, people who are hired today will become the supervisors of the future. For all these reasons, police agencies must attempt to attract the best individuals possible.

Police applicants typically come from lower-middle-class or working-class backgrounds;[4] they generally have a high school education and a history of employment. They also tend, at the application stage, to be enthusiastic, idealistic, uninformed about the reality of police work, and very different from the stereotype of the police officer as authoritarian, suspicious, and insensitive.[5]

Some studies indicate that police applicants are primarily motivated by the need for job security.[6] Other researchers have found that both males and females listed the same six factors—desire to help people, job security, crime fighting, job excitement, prestige, and a lifetime interest—as strong positive influences in their career choices.[7] Joel Lefkowitz concluded that police candidates were lower than average in their desire to do autonomous work,[8] and other studies have indicated that applicants tend to favor a more directive leadership style. Such findings are not unusual, given that most police agencies are highly structured and paramilitary in nature. Studies do not establish that police candidates fit the stereotypes of harsh, controlling people who wish to dominate others. Leadership, or the ability to take charge of situations, is a desirable attribute, however. Some researchers have found that the typical police applicant is very similar to the average college student.[9]

Bruce Carpenter and Susan Raza, using the Minnesota Multiphasic Personality Inventory (MMPI), found that police applicants differed from the general population in several important ways.[10] Police applicants, they learned, are somewhat more psychologically healthy, are generally less depressed and anxious, and are more assertive and interested in making and maintaining social contacts. Furthermore, few police aspirants have emotional difficulties, and they have a greater tendency to present a good impression of themselves than the general population does. They are a more homogeneous group.

Female police applicants tend to be more assertive and nonconforming and to have a higher energy level than male applicants; they are also less likely to identify with traditional sex roles than male applicants. Older police applicants tend to be less satisfied, have more physical complaints, and are more likely to develop physical symptoms under stress than younger applicants. Applicants to large city police forces are generally less likely to have physical complaints and have a higher energy level than applicants to small- or medium-sized agencies. (This is probably explained by the fact that applicants in large cities are significantly younger.[11]) Some departments are under a mandate to recruit special groups of people, such as women, African Americans, and Hispanics; several cities have also recruited homosexuals.

What psychological qualities should agencies seek? According to psychologist Lawrence Wrightsman,[12] it is important that police applicants be incorruptible and have high moral character. They should be well adjusted, able to carry out the hazardous and stressful tasks of policing without "cracking up," and be thick-skinned enough to operate without defensiveness. They should have a genuine interest in people and a compassionate sense of the innate dignity of others. Applicants should also be free of emotional reactions, they should not be impulsive or overly aggressive, and they should be able to exercise restraint. This is especially important given their active role in crime detection.

Finally, they need logical skills to assist in their investigative work. An interesting example of some of the logical skills needed for police work is provided by Al Seedman, former chief of detectives in the New York City Police Department (NYPD):

> In the woods just outside of town they found the skeleton of a man who'd been dead for three
> months or so. I asked whether this skeleton showed signs of any dental work. But the local

cops said no, although the skeleton had crummy teeth. No dental work at all. Now, if he'd been wealthy, he could have afforded to have his teeth fixed. If he'd been poor, welfare would have paid. If he was a union member, their medical plan would have covered it. So this fellow was probably working at a low-paying non-unionized job, but making enough to keep off public assistance. Also, since he didn't match up to any family's missing-person report, he was probably single, living alone in an apartment or hotel. His landlord never reported him missing, either, so most likely he was also behind on his rent and the landlord probably figured he had just skipped. But even if he had escaped his landlord, he would never have escaped the tax man. The rest was simple. I told these cops to wait until the year is up. Then they can go to the IRS and get a printout of all single males making less than $10,000 a year but more than the welfare ceiling who paid withholding tax in the first three quarters but not in the fourth. Chances are the name of their skeleton will be on that printout.[13]

—CHIEF! by Albert A. Seedman and Peter Hellman. Published by Point Judith Press, © 1974.

Other desirable traits of entry-level officers are discussed later in this chapter.

Recruiting Problems and Successes

Certainly the recruitment of quality police officers is a key to the values and culture of any police organization. The current "cop crunch" is exacerbated in many cities by exploding growth, a competitive job market, fiscal challenges, and struggles to retain diversity.[14] Furthermore, this crunch comes at a time when today's police need a stronger focus on problem-solving skills, ability to collaborate with the community, and a greater capacity to use technology.[15] Adding to the problems are today's higher incidence of obesity, major debt, drug use, and criminal records that are found among potential recruits.[16] Leaving no stone unturned, however, agencies are using all types of techniques to locate and attract applicants. Agencies in many cities are disseminating their latest recruiting news, updates, and hiring information on social networking sites, and urge citizens to go to their recruiting unit's Facebook page. Furthermore, some agencies are asking job candidates to waive their privacy rights and even provide their passwords, text messages, and identities in order that background investigators may access their social media sites. Perhaps another factor relating to recruitment concerns entry-level salaries. According to a federal survey, the entry-level average salary of police officers in smaller jurisdictions averages about $26,000, and $49,500 in the largest jurisdictions.[17]

Recruiting and retaining women and minorities in police service remain particularly problematic. Gender bias (reflected in the absence of women being hired and promoted to policy-making positions) and sexual harassment concerns prevent many women from applying and cause many female officers to leave—and quickly: About 60 percent of female officers who leave their agency do so during their second to fifth years on the job.[18] Police agencies now use various practices for attracting women and minorities to the applicant pool and/or to increase the likelihood of their being hired. Studies show that one of the most effective means to do so—even more important than raising starting salaries—is for agencies to enhance their recruiting budget so that targeted recruitment activities can be accomplished. Police agencies typically do not give specific advantages—such as lower fitness standards or preference in the waiting list—to women or minorities; however, targeted recruitment strategies have been shown to be beneficial for generating larger recruitment pools and hiring underrepresented groups.[19] Examples of such strategies include: conducting career fairs, travelling to other cities and states to recruit, advertising heavily on the Internet, and so on; the U.S. Border Patrol has advertised during televised professional football games and even sponsored a NASCAR race car.[20] Women and minorities in policing are discussed in detail below.

▶ Testing

Hurdle Process

Even though a person meets the minimum qualifications for being a police officer (age, education, no disqualifying criminal record), much work still remains to be done before he or she is ready to be put to work as a police officer. The new recruit must successfully complete what is known as the hurdle process. In this section, we consider some kinds of tests that are used to weed out undesirable candidates.

Tables 2-1 ■ and 2-2 ■ show the kinds of tests and background checks that are used in selecting new officer recruits. Both tables are organized by agency size, from under 2,500 to more than 1 million. A study by the federal Bureau of Justice Statistics (see Tables 2-1 and 2-2) found that nearly all local police agencies use criminal record checks, and nearly all employ background investigations (99 percent), and driving record checks (99 percent) to screen applicants. Personal interviews (99 percent), psychological evaluations (72 percent), written aptitude tests (48 percent), personality inventory (46 percent), and polygraph exams (26 percent) are also used.[21] Certainly not all types of tests shown in Figure 2-1 ■ are employed by all of the 17,000 police agencies in America, nor are these tests necessarily given in the sequence shown. Under affirmative action laws and court decisions, a burden rests with police administrators to demonstrate that the tests used are job related. This so-called hurdle process[22] shown in Figure 2-1 can require more than three months to complete, depending on the number and types of tests used and the ease of scheduling and performing them.

Written Examinations: General Knowledge and Psychological Tests

Measures of general intelligence and reading skills are the best means a police agency can use for predicting who will do well in the police academy.[21] Of course, any such test must be reliable and valid. To achieve reliability and validity, many (if not most) police agencies purchase and use "canned" test instruments—those prepared by professional individuals or companies.

TABLE 2-1 Interviews, Tests, and Examinations Used in Selection of New Officer Recruits in Local Police Departments, by Size of Population Served

	Interviews, Tests, and Examinations Used to Select New Officer Recruits					
Population Served	**Personal Interview**	**Psychological Evaluation**	**Written Aptitude Test**	**Personality Inventory**	**Polygraph Exam**	**Voice Stress Analyzer**
All sizes	99%	72%	48%	46%	26%	5%
1,000,000 or more	100	100	100	85	77	0
500,000–999,999	97	100	90	68	74	13
250,000–499,999	96	100	96	67	83	7
100,000–249,999	98	99	88	64	77	13
50,000–99,999	99	100	87	66	63	13
25,000–49,999	100	98	83	64	51	9
10,000–24,999	100	94	76	57	42	11
2,500–9,999	100	82	56	44	26	5
Under 2,500	98	48	20	38	10	2

Note: List of selection methods is not intended to be exhaustive.

Source: "Interviews, Tests, and Examinations Used in Selection of New Officer Recruits in Local Police Departments, by Size of Population Served" from LOCAL POLICE DEPARTMENTS, 2007 (WASHINGTON, DC). Published by Bureau of Justice Statistics, © 2010.

TABLE 2-2 Background Checks Used in Selection of New Officer Recruits in Local Police Departments, by Size of Population Served

Population Served	Background Checks Used to Select New Officer Recruits			
	Criminal Record Check	Background Investigation	Driving Record Check	Credit History Check
All sizes	100%	99%	99%	61%
1,000,000 or more	100	100	100	85
500,000–999,999	100	100	100	97
250,000–499,999	100	100	98	96
100,000–249,999	100	100	100	94
50,000–99,999	100	100	100	93
25,000–49,999	100	100	100	90
10,000–24,999	100	100	100	78
2,500–9,999	100	99	99	65
Under 2,500	100	99	97	41

Note: List of selection methods is not intended to be exhaustive.

Source: Background Checks Used In Selection Of New Officer Recruits In Local Police Departments, By Size Of Population Served, Local Police Departments, 2007 (Washington, DC: Author, December 2010), Bureau of Justice Statistics, 2010.

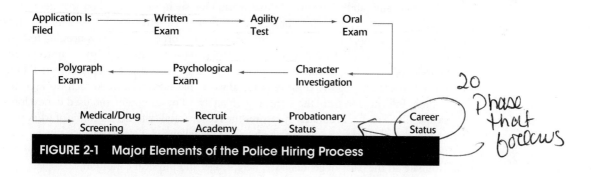

FIGURE 2-1 Major Elements of the Police Hiring Process

Larger police departments and state police agencies use four types of written tests: cognitive tests (measuring aptitudes in verbal skills and mathematics, reasoning, and related perceptual abilities), personality tests (predominantly the Minnesota Multiphasic Personality Inventory [MMPI]), interest inventories (the Strong-Campbell, the Kuder, and the Minnesota Interest tests), and biographical data inventories.[22]

Over time, research findings have been mixed concerning the implications of written examinations. For example, a 1962 study of deputy sheriffs found that candidates with written test scores above the 97th percentile were most apt to be successful in their careers.[23] However, a study of the Tucson, Arizona, Police Department determined that the IQ scores of officers who dropped out of the force were significantly higher than those of a norm group. The study concluded that one can be too bright to be a cop, unless an alternate career development program can be developed to challenge and use highly intelligent people.[24] Of course, there is much more to police work than reading skills.

General intelligence tests are often administered and scored by the civil service or the central personnel office. Most frequently, those who fail the entrance examination (that is, they do not make the minimum score, which is usually set at 70 percent) will go on to other careers, although most jurisdictions allow for a retest after a specified period of time. The names of those who pass are forwarded to the police agency for any further in-house testing and screening.[25]

Another form of written examination for police applicants is the psychological screening test. There are two major concerns in using such tests to screen out applicants: stability and suitability. Candidates must be carefully screened in order to exclude those who are emotionally unstable, overly aggressive, or suffering from some personality disorder. The two primary tests of suitability of police candidates are the MMPI and the California Personality Inventory (CPI).[26] Stability is a major legal concern. If an officer commits a serious, harmful, and inappropriate act, the question of his or her stability will be raised, and the police agency may be asked to provide documentation about why the officer was deemed stable at the time of employment. It has been found that 2 to 5 percent of the police applicant pool may be eliminated due to severe emotional or mental problems.[27]

Physical Agility

Entry-level physical examinations range from a minimally acceptable number of push-ups to timed running and jumping tests to tests of strength and agility, such as dragging weights, pushing cars, leaping over six-foot walls, walking on horizontal ladders, crawling through tunnels, and negotiating monkey bars. The problem is that very few of these activities are actually performed by police officers on the job.

The challenge for police executives, and an area of lawsuit vulnerability, is selecting a truly job-related physical agility test. Police agencies must determine the nature and extent of physical work performed by police officers and use that information to develop an instrument to measure applicants' ability to perform that work. One such test is based on the theory that police officers must perform three basic physical functions: getting to the problem (possibly needing to run, climb, vault, and so forth), resolving the problem (perhaps needing to fight or wrestle with an offender), and removing the problem (often requiring that the officer carry heavy weights). To establish the testing protocol for a given jurisdiction, the officers fill out written forms concerning the kinds of physical work that they performed each workday for one month. Information from the forms is then analyzed by computer and used to develop a physical agility test that accurately measures the recruit's ability to do the kinds of work performed by police officers in that specific locale.[28] If challenged in court, agencies using such tests can show that they test for the actual job requirements of their jurisdiction and do not discriminate on the basis of gender, race, height, age, and physical condition.

Personal Interview

As noted in Table 2-1, the personal interview is used by 99 percent of all police agencies as part of the selection process.[29] Candidates appear individually before one or more boards that are composed of members of the police agency and often the community. Candidates may also be asked to participate in a clinical interview with a psychologist; studies have indicated that the clinical interview complements the written psychological test.[30]

The purpose of the interview is to assess aspects of the candidate that cannot be measured on other tests, such as appearance, ability to communicate and reason (often using situational questions), and general poise and bearing. The interview is not normally well suited for judging character, dependability, initiative, or other such factors.

A primary advantage of the interview is that evaluators can ask applicants to explain how they would behave and use force in given situations because any number of possible scenarios exist. Following are five examples of the kinds of situations that might be posed to police applicants to see how well they think on their feet, develop appropriate responses, and prioritize their actions:

1. You are dispatched to a neighborhood park to check out a young man who is acting strangely. Upon arrival, you see the youth standing near a group of children playing on a merry-go-round. He is holding a .22-caliber rifle. What is your next action?

2. You are in the men's locker room at the end of your shift. You hear another male officer talking about a female officer's body. What do you do?

3. You are at home watching a football game on a weekend. Your neighbor comes to your door and frantically claims that his door has been kicked in and that he believes someone is inside. What do you do? What if the neighbor tells you that his daughter is upstairs in his house? How would you proceed?

4. You are in a downtown area making an arrest. A crowd gathers and you begin to hear comments about "police harassment." Soon the crowd becomes angry. How do you react?

5. You and another officer are responding to a burglary call at an office building. While searching the scene, you observe the other officer remove an expensive fountain pen from the top of a desk and put it in his pocket. What do you do?

Character Investigation

As indicated earlier, nearly all (99 percent) local police departments use background checks or character investigations—probably the most important element of the selection process. If done properly, the character investigation will also be one of the most time consuming and costly elements of the process.

Character is one of the most subjective yet most important factors an applicant brings to the job, and it cannot be measured with data and interviews. A character investigation involves talking to the candidate's past and current friends, coworkers, teachers, neighbors, and employers. The applicant should be informed that references will be checked and that in the course of reviewing them, the investigation may spread to other references and others who are known to the applicant. No expense should be spared in talking with anyone who has personal knowledge of the candidate and can provide crucial information; if the job is done properly, the investigator will not only have a complete knowledge of the person's character but will also know where any skeletons may be buried in the applicant's background.

Polygraph Examination

As shown in Table 2-1, 26 percent of the nation's police agencies—and much higher proportions of larger agencies—conduct polygraph examinations as part of their selection process.[31] These agencies are willing to devote the extra resources necessary to help them determine that their applicants are honest and to secure higher-quality employees.

A survey of the benefits of polygraph examinations for police applicants by Richard Arther, director of the National Center of Lie Detection, supported the need for the polygraph for police recruitment:[32]

- An applicant for a police position in Lower Merion, Pennsylvania, came to that agency highly recommended by a police lieutenant and his employer at a home for blind, retarded children. During the polygraph examination, however, the applicant admitted to at least fifty instances of sexually abusing the children under his care.

- An applicant with the Wichita, Kansas, Police Department admitted to the polygraphist that he had been involved in many burglaries. The detective division was able to clear eight unsolved crimes as a result of the applicant's confession.

- A police officer in one California police department applied for employment in the Salinas, California, Police Department. He appeared to be a model police officer, was in excellent physical condition, and was familiar with state codes. His previous experience made him a potentially ideal candidate. However, during the polygraph exam, he admitted to having committed over a dozen burglaries while on duty and to having used his patrol car to haul away the stolen property. He also admitted to planting stolen

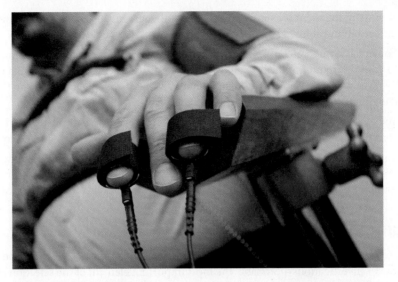

▲ The polygraph, which measures several physiological features, is used to detect lies and deception. *(Courtesy pefostudio5/Shutterstock.)*

narcotics on innocent suspects in order to make arrests and to having had sexual intercourse with girls as young as sixteen, in his patrol car.

- An applicant for the San Diego Sheriff's Department admitted to that agency's polygraphist that on weekends he would go from bar to bar pretending to be drunk. He would then seek out people to pick fights with, since he could only have an erection and orgasm while inflicting pain on others. In addition to these sadistic tendencies, he also admitted that he got rid of his frustrations by savagely beating "niggers, Chicanos, and long-haired pukes who cause all the trouble."

These are but a few examples of how the investment of time and money for polygraph examinations can spare the public and police agencies a tremendous amount of trouble and expense later. It is doubtful that few (if any) of these behaviors would have surfaced during the course of a personal interview or a background investigation. Polygraph testing will be discussed in greater detail in Chapter 5 in connection with criminal investigations.

Medical Examination and Drug Screening

Someone once said that some police medical examinations are often of the "Can you hear thunder/see lightning?" variety—meaning that they are cursory at best. It is also widely believed that policing is only for those young people who are in peak physical condition. Whether these statements are facetious or not, it is certainly true that policing is no place for the physically unfit. Such officers would be a hazard not only to themselves but also to their coworkers. The job, with its stress, shift work, many hours of inactivity during patrol time, and other factors, can be physically debilitating even for veteran officers, especially those who fail to exercise and eat properly, so police administrators certainly do not want applicants who are unfit. The Federal Bureau of Investigation (FBI), for example, will not consider applicants whose weight exceeds the norm for their height and body type. Unfit personnel are thought to have lower energy levels, to give less attention to duty, and to take more sick days. Early retirement and disability often result, as do increased operating expenses for replacing ill officers and hiring and training new permanent replacements.

More and more often, police agencies, like private-sector businesses, the military, and other sensitive government agencies, are compelling prospective employees to submit to a drug test. Substance abuse remains a very real problem in the workplace, resulting in poor productivity, lowered agency morale, and increased accidents and injuries.

Assessment Center

Recently, the use of an assessment center has become more popular with police agencies. While used by many departments for promotional testing and for hiring a chief executive, some agencies also use this method for hiring new personnel. An assessment center may include interviews; psychological tests; in-basket exercises; management tasks; group discussions; role-playing exercises, such as simulations of critical incidents or interviews with subordinates, the public, and news media; fact-finding exercises; oral presentation exercises; and written communication exercises. Behaviors and skills that are important to the successful performance of the position are identified and possibly weighted, and each candidate is evaluated on his or her ability to perform them.

Individual and group role-playing provides a hands-on atmosphere during the selection process. For example, candidates may be required to perform in simulated police–community problems (such as having candidates conduct a "meeting" to hear concerns of local minority groups), react to a major incident (such as a simulated shooting or riot situation), hold a news briefing, or participate in other such exercises. They may be given an in-basket situation, for example, assuming the role of the new chief or captain who receives an abundance of paperwork, policies, and problems to be prioritized and dealt with in a prescribed amount of time. To evaluate candidates' writing abilities, they may be given a specified amount of time (thirty minutes, for example) to develop a new use-of-force policy for a hypothetical or real police agency, allowing raters to assess candidates' written communication skills and their understanding of the technical side of police work, as well as the ways they think and build a case.

During each exercise, several assessors or raters analyze each candidate's performance and record some type of quantitative or qualitative evaluation score, which is then turned over to the hiring or promoting authority. Raters are typically selected who have held and now supervise the position for which candidates are testing. For example, if the assessment center is used to hire new officers, it would minimally be best that sergeants serve as raters (for promotion to sergeant, lieutenants should be raters, and so on).

Assessment centers are obviously more difficult logistically to conduct and are normally more labor-intensive and costly than traditional (mere interviewing) procedures, but they are well worth the extra investment. Monies invested at the early stages of a hiring or promotional process can help the agency to make the best hiring decisions and save untold problems for years to come.

▶ Formal Entry into Policing: Academy Training

Training Nature and Topics

Receiving an offer of employment in policing obviously is not immediately accompanied by a badge, uniform, and set of keys to your new cruiser. Completion of an academy and field training program will be one's final hurdles to becoming a full-fledged officer.

Each state and each jurisdiction has different training requirements. In some areas, one can attend basic law enforcement training at the local community college or other state-sponsored institution first and then apply to the agency of his or her choice. Other jurisdictions may require individuals to complete their in-house training program after successful completion of their hiring process or sponsor them to attend an academy elsewhere. Still others may accept one's external academy certificate but also require completion of an abbreviated version of their academy. Regardless, people must receive extensive training prior to working alone on patrol. The majority of their initial training will be classroom based, supplemented by practical exercises and scenarios. They will hold the rank of "cadet" or "police trainee" during this time, and if sponsored by a hiring agency, receive their first paycheck and be eligible to receive benefits.

There is no standard national academy curriculum, but the state may guide agencies in developing training programs. Each state has a Commission on Peace Officers Standards

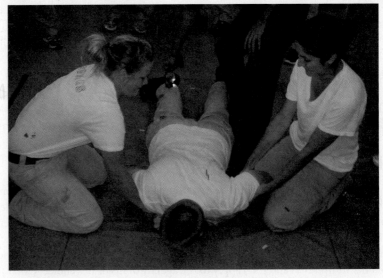

▲ In addition to classroom instruction, academy recruits receive training in such areas as felony car stops, use of less-lethal tools, physical training, and use of firearms. (*Courtesy Western Nevada State Peace Officer Academy.*)

(Courtesy Mark Ide/Pearson Education.)

(Courtesy Mark Ide/Pearson Education.)

and Training (POST) or similar entity that establishes minimum selection standards for law enforcement officers, sets minimum education and training standards, and serves as the certification or licensing authority for sworn personnel. These agencies may be helpful in obtaining an idea of the state's approach to law enforcement training.

According to the Bureau of Justice Statistics,[33] about 648 state and local law enforcement academies are operating in the United States and offering basic law enforcement training to individuals recruited or seeking to become law enforcement officers. These include local police officers, sheriff's deputies, campus police officers, state police or highway patrol officers, constables, and tribal police officers. Some academies also provide training for jail and corrections officers, probation and parole officers, fire marshals and arson investigators, private security officers, firefighters, emergency medical technicians, and animal control officers. About 40 percent of academies provided preservice training for individuals not sponsored by an employing agency and nearly 90 percent provide in-service training, especially for such units as K-9 or special weapons and tactics (SWAT) units. Some also train first-line (e.g., sergeant) or higher supervisors and field training instructors.

The average duration of basic recruit training for new municipal police and county deputy recruits is about 760 hours, with the most time being spent earning firearms skills (median instruction time of 60 hours) and self-defense skills (51 hours) . Some academies also provided training for jail officers (25 percent), corrections officers (23 percent), probation and parole officers (16 percent), fire marshals and arson investigators (16 percent), private security officers (10 percent), firefighters (8 percent), emergency medical technicians (7 percent), and animal control officers (6 percent). The median class size among all academies was 18 recruits, and overall, 86 percent of the recruits who began the academy successfully completed their studies and graduated.[34]

Table 2-3 ■ includes a summary of training topics, the percentage of academies providing each topic, and the median number of hours of instruction per topic.

New Demeanor and Uniform

As academy training begins, recruits adopt a new identity and a system of discipline in which they learn to take orders and not to question authority. They learn that loyalty to fellow officers, a professional demeanor and bearing, and respect for authority are all highly valued in this occupation. The classroom teaches the recruit how to approach situations. Outside the classroom, as recruits share war stories discussed with academy staff, they informally transmit the proper attitudes to one another. Thus, the recruits begin to form a collective understanding of policing and how they are supposed to function, and they gradually develop a common language and demeanor. Many people also believe that the police develop a swagger: a confident, authoritarian way of walking and presenting themselves. This is the beginning of the police officer's working personality.[35]

Recruits may wear a uniform for the first time during academy training, which is typically an awe-inspiring experience for them. The uniform sets recruits apart from society at large and conveys a sense of authority and responsibility to them and to the public. "Image is everything," according to a popular saying, and the choice of agency uniform can go a long way toward setting the image and tone of the department. Police uniforms come in various colors, styles, and fabrics. Some agencies even have their officers wearing blue jeans or shorts and T-shirts (e.g., for beach patrol).

The belt is one of the most important components of the patrol uniform and is certainly one of the heaviest. It often exceeds twenty pounds when laden with weapon, cuffs, baton, radio, flashlight, extra ammunition, chemical weapons, and so on. The uniform hat comes in several styles and is probably the piece of equipment that most readily identifies the officer and the department's image; each type of hat makes a certain statement to the public about the officer and his or her authority. The officer's badge also conveys a tremendous sense of authority; the most popular are customized shields, incorporating everything from the state motto and seal to symbols that convey the agency's image and philosophy. When designing its badge, a police department considers its tradition and history as well as those of the community.[36]

Suspicion: The "Sixth Sense"

Police recruits are taught to nurture a sixth sense: suspicion. A suspicious nature is as important to the street officer as a fine touch is to a surgeon. The officer should not only

▼

TABLE 2-3 Topics Included in Basic Training of State and Local Law Enforcement Training Academies

Topics	Percentage of Academies with Training	Median Number of Hours of Instruction
Operations		
Report writing	100%	20 hours
Patrol	99	40
Investigations	99	40
Basic first aid/CPR	99	24
Emergency vehicle operations	97	40
Computers/information systems	58	8
Weapons/Self-defense		
Self-defense	99%	51 hours
Firearms skills	98	60
Nonlethal weapons	98	12
Legal		
Criminal law	100%	36 hours
Constitutional law	98	12
History of law enforcement	84	4
Self-improvement		
Ethics and integrity	100%	8 hours
Health and fitness	96	46
Stress prevention/management	87	5
Basic foreign language	36	16
Community Policing		
Cultural diversity/human relations	98%	11 hours
Basic strategies	92	8
Mediation/conflict management	88	8
Special Topics		
Domestic violence	99%	14 hours
Juveniles	99	8
Domestic preparedness	88	8
Hate crimes/bias crimes	87	4

Source: Topics Included In Basic Training Of State And Local Law Enforcement Training Academies, State and Local Law Enforcement Training Academies, 2006 (February 2009), Bureau of Justice Statistics, 2012.

be able to visually recognize but also be able to physically sense when something is wrong or out of the ordinary. A Chicago Police Department bulletin stated the following:

> Actions, dress, [and] location of a person often classify him as suspicious in the mind of a police officer. Men loitering near schools, public toilets, playgrounds and swimming pools may be sex perverts. Men loitering near . . . any business at closing time may be robbery suspects. Men or youths walking along looking into cars may be car thieves or looking for something to steal. Persons showing evidence of recent injury, or whose clothing is disheveled, may be victims or participants in an assault or strong-arm robbery.[37]

> —*Excerpt from WRIGHTMAN'S PSYCHOLOGY AND THE LEGAL SYSTEM by Edith Greene and Kirk Heilbrun. Published by Cengage Learning.*

Officers are trained to be observant, to develop an intimate knowledge of the territory and people, and to "notice the normal. . . . Only then can [they] decide what persons or cars under what circumstances warrant the appellation 'suspicious.'"[38] They must recognize when someone or something needs to be checked out. The following observations often warrant a field investigation:[39]

- People who do not "belong" where they are observed.
- Automobiles that do not "look right" (such as dirty cars with clean license plates or a vehicle with plates attached with wire or in another unusual fashion).
- Businesses that are open at odd hours or that are not operating according to routine or custom.
- People who exhibit exaggerated unconcern over contact with the officer or who are visibly "rattled" when near the officer.
- Solicitors or peddlers who are in a residential neighborhood.
- Lone males who sit in cars near a shopping center or near a school while paying unusual attention to women or children.
- Persons who are hitchhikers.
- Persons who wear a coat on a hot day.

The academy also teaches neophyte officers that their major tool is their body; like mountain climbers, acrobats, or athletes, their body is an essential tool for the performance of their trade. The gun and nightstick initially fascinate the recruits, but until they are adequately trained, officers using them would be more a menace to society than a protector. Proper handling and safety measures are drilled into the recruits—the message is unequivocal that recruits will not be trusted with these potentially lethal weapons until they become proficient in their use. The new officers must be taught to measure their capacity to do the job, to assess carefully the physical capabilities of people they confront on the street, and to determine whether someone can be subdued without assistance or the risk of injury if a physical altercation should develop.[40]

The officers are also told, however, that they cannot approach every situation with the holster unsnapped or baton raised or twirling; they must demonstrate poise and not be eager to use force. The fact that the days of the club-swinging cop are gone is constantly instilled in officers. Thus, knowing that the body is a tool, the recruits are taught how to position themselves unobtrusively, whether at a vehicle stop or while engaged in a discussion on the street, in order to gain a physical advantage should trouble arise. They are taught when to use force and when to relent, to always keep control of the situation, and to feel that they would emerge victorious should force be required. Thus, in addition to weapons training, they may be given some weaponless defense training, including some holds that can be applied to subjects to bring them into compliance.

Recruits are taught some aspects of human nature and are encouraged not to be prejudicial in their actions or speech. They learn to deal with criminal suspects, offenders, victims, and witnesses and to be suspicious of "eyewitness" accounts. (e.g., twenty-five "witnesses" claimed that they helped carry Abraham Lincoln from the Ford Theater into the little house where he died; eight different people said they held his head, and eighty-four people said they were in the room that night.[41])

Recruits often participate in hands-on training, practicing their new techniques in the field in simulated situations. Quite possibly the ultimate in hands-on training occurs at the Hogan's Alley complex at the FBI Academy in Quantico, Virginia, which opened in 1987 and covers almost thirty-five acres. This facility combines training, office, and classroom space on one site, increasing training effectiveness. Hogan's Alley (the name given many early-twentieth-century training facilities, apparently after an old comic strip about

▼

mischievous Irish kids) resembles a fully developed urban area. The set includes a business area and a residential street with townhouses and apartments. The use of movie-set techniques gives the illusion of depth and space. All furnishings—including a fleet of cars, furniture, desks, and even a pool table—were forfeited by convicted criminals. Federal agents are trained in the practical skills of crime-scene investigation and photography, surveillance techniques, arrest mechanics, and investigative skills. Trainees participate in paintball gunfights with persons role-playing criminals.

▲ The FBI's "Hogan's Alley." *(Courtesy Department of Justice, FBI.)*

Other methods of police training that are currently used include computer-based training (CBT), electronic bulletin boards, satellite training and teleconferencing, online computer forums, and correspondence courses. With computer costs declining, CBT is becoming increasingly popular and has been shown to be very effective. As CBT simulates real-life situations through the use of computer-modeled problems, it closely duplicates the way we think. One study found that police officers who learned about the exclusionary rule (discussed in Chapter 7) through CBT understood the material significantly better than the non-CBT control group.[42]

Virtual reality is another available (although very costly) form of police training. Trainees wear a head-mounted device that restricts their vision to two monitors and projects a computer-generated three-dimensional illusion that engulfs the senses of sight, sound, and touch. Virtual reality may one day be commonly used for training police officers in such areas as pursuit driving, firearms training, critical-incident management, and crime-scene processing.

Finally, graduation day arrives, and the academy experience becomes a rite of passage. Graduation also means new uniforms, associates, and responsibilities and a raise in pay and status. As Arthur Niederhoffer observed, for many officers academy graduation is a worthy substitute for a college education. But "the very next morning the graduate is rudely dumped into a strange precinct where he must prove himself."[43]

▶ Postacademy Field Training

Field Training Officer (FTO) Program

Once the recruits leave the academy, their knowledge of and acceptance into the police subculture are not yet complete. Another very important part of this acquisition process is assignment to a veteran officer for initial field instruction and observation in what is sometimes called a field training officer (FTO) program. The oldest formal FTO program began in the San Jose, California, Police Department in 1972.[44] This training program provides recruits with an opportunity to make the transition from the academy to the streets under the protective arm of a veteran officer. Recruits are on probationary status, normally ranging from six months to one year; they understand that they may be immediately terminated if their overall performance is unsatisfactory during that period.

Most FTO programs consist of four identifiable phases: an introductory phase (the recruit learns agency policies and local laws), the training and evaluation phases (the recruit is introduced to more complicated tasks that patrol officers confront), and a final phase (the FTO acts strictly as an observer and evaluator while the recruit performs all the functions of a patrol officer).[45] The National Institute of Justice (NIJ), surveying nearly six hundred police agencies, found that 64 percent had an FTO program and that such programs had reduced the number of civil liability suits filed against their officers and against standardized training programs.[46] The length of time rookies are assigned to FTOs will vary; a formal FTO program might require close supervision for a range of one to twelve weeks.

Police Training Officer (PTO) Program

Another new approach to training new officers is slowly gaining traction across the nation; as with the FTO program discussed above, it is multifaceted and is an in-depth method: the police training officer (PTO) program. A PTO program seeks to take the traditional FTO program to a higher level, one that embraces new officers and evaluates them on their understanding and application of community-oriented policing and problem solving (COPPS, discussed in Chapter 4).

With a half million dollars in federal assistance, training needs were assessed and a new PTO program was recently initiated in the Reno, Nevada, Police Department and at five other national sites. Its theoretical underpinnings include adult and problem-based learning. The PTO program covers two primary training areas: substantive topics (the most common policing activities) and core competencies (the required common skills that officers engage in and that are required in the daily performance of their duties). New officers must successfully pass fifteen core competencies, specific skills, knowledge, and abilities that have been identified as essential for good policing. A learning matrix serves as a guide for trainees and trainers during the training period and demonstrates the inter-relationships between the daily policing activities and core competencies during the eight phases of the PTO program.[47]

New Technology

New technology in the training function includes software known as ADORE (Automated Daily Observation Report and Evaluation). FTOs in several agencies now field-testing the software find that it saves them time because they do not have to write reports by hand for each recruit. ADORE, which can be accessed through either a laptop or a Palm Pilot, allows FTOs to take computerized notes while watching trainees at work; it also reduces paperwork by allowing trainers to easily compile numbers for evaluating performance in dozens of categories. The software is credited with reducing FTO burnout, which is often a part of the paper-intensive evaluation process.[48]

Another new form of technology for police training that is being tested involves pursuit simulation. The training simulator is thought to be an effective means of determining how and when a vehicle pursuit should be halted. In one scenario, trainees in a simulated pursuit swerve around computerized images of a transit bus, a produce truck, a minivan, and a child on a skateboard before the chased vehicle enters a school zone, where the officer should end the hot pursuit. These simulated pursuits also allow supervisors to see how well trainees conduct themselves in accordance with their agency's pursuit policy, which is often several pages long.[49]

▲ Officer using a driving simulator. *(Courtesy Washoe County Sheriff's Office.)*

▲ Officer in SWAT training. *(Courtesy Washoe County Sheriff's Office.)*

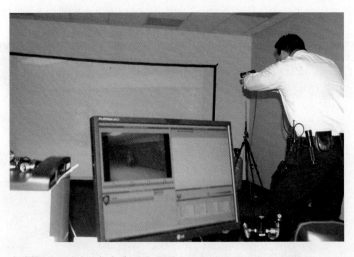

▲ Officer training in indoor range. *(Courtesy Cincinnati Police Department.)*

In-Service Training

Changes in departmental policies and procedures, court decisions, the specter of liability, and operational strategies and techniques demand that training be an ongoing process throughout a police officer's career. It is simply unreasonable to expect that the knowledge gained during basic academy training or specialized training can serve an officer for an entire career. As Roger Dunham and Geoffrey Alpert put it, "Whether an officer is overweight or out of shape, a poor shot, uses poor judgment, or is too socialized into the police subculture to provide good community policing, in-service training can be used to restore the officer's skills or to improve his attitude."[50]

In-service training is used to recertify, refresh, or provide new information to officers in the most critical areas of their job, including weapons qualification, driving, defensive tactics, first aid, and changes in the law. Most states require a minimum number of hours of in-service training for police officers, and many departments exceed the minimum requirement. News items, court decisions, and other relevant information can be covered at roll call before the beginning of each shift. Short courses ranging from a few hours to several weeks are available for in-service officers through several means, such as videos and nationally televised training programs.

▶ Working Personality: Having the "Right Stuff"

Developing a Police Personality

Since William Westley first wrote about the police subculture in 1950, the notion of a police personality has become a popular area of study. In 1966, Jerome Skolnick[51] described what he termed the *working personality* of the police. He determined that the police role contained two important variables: danger and authority. Danger is a constant feature of police work. Police officers, constantly facing potential violence, are warned at the academy to be cautious and are told many war stories of officers shot and killed at domestic disturbances or traffic stops. Consequently, they develop a "perceptual shorthand," Skolnick said, that they use to identify certain kinds of people as "symbolic assailants"—individuals whom the officer has come to recognize as potentially violent based on their gestures, language, and attire.

The police, as Skolnick stated, represent authority, but unlike doctors, ministers, and the like, they must establish their authority. The symbols of that authority—the gun, the badge, and the baton—assist them, but officers' behavior and confidence are more important in social situations. As William Westley said, an officer "expects rage from the underprivileged and the criminal but understanding from the middle classes: the professionals, the merchants and the white-collar workers. They, however, define him as a servant, not as a colleague, and the rejection is hard to take."[52] Thus, officers cannot even depend on their symbols and position of authority in dealing with the public; they are often confused when the public does not automatically observe and accept their authority.

Considerable research has compared the personality characteristics of the police with those of the general public,[53] and a number of differences have been discovered. One study found the average officer to be more intelligent, assertive, dependable, straightforward, and conscientious than civilians.[54] Other researchers who recently studied state traffic officers and deputy sheriffs using the MMPI and CPI scales reported that the officers scored high on the values of achievement, strong work ethic, ambition, leadership potential, and organizational skills.[55] Studies have also found conservatism and a high degree of cynicism among officers, although those traits are found to be present in much of the society at large. The late LAPD Chief William Parker asserted that police were "conservative, ultraconservative, and very right wing."[56]

Niederhoffer reported his classic study of police cynicism in 1967, using the NYPD as the site of a longitudinal study.[57] He found that although typical recruits begin their career without a trace of cynicism, police cynicism spikes most dramatically immediately after they leave the basic academy. This is probably because they confront the reality of the streets—the pain and criminality of society—and perhaps lose friends. Cynical veteran peers frequently reinforce the worst aspects of the job. In the period of about two to six years of service, the cynicism level continues to increase, but at a slower rate. The recruit has begun to adapt to the occupation and the people to be dealt with every day. At about mid-career (about eight to thirteen years of service), the cynicism level actually begins to decline, possibly because the officer has accepted the job and has been promoted, earns a decent salary and benefits, and realizes that he or she is about halfway to retirement. Toward the end of the career, the degree of cynicism levels off; for many officers, this is a period of coasting toward retirement.

A police officer's view of humanity may become distorted and cynical because many of the people the police deal with are offenders. They see what they feel are miscarriages of justice, such as improper or lenient court decisions, perjury on the witness stand, plea bargaining (where defendants are allowed to plead guilty to less serious offenses than charged or to fewer counts than charged, and observe fellow officers who do not live up to their code of ethics). Cynicism does have a protective feature, however: It can help to make the officer callous, allowing him or her to observe things that would sicken or horrify the average citizen without becoming mentally debilitated.

John Broderick[58] presented another view of the working personality of the police. He believed that there are actually four types of police personalities: enforcers, idealists, realists, and optimists.

Enforcers are officers who believe that the job of the police consists primarily of keeping their beats clean, making good arrests, and sometimes helping people. These officers have sympathy for vagrants, the elderly, the working poor, and others whom they see as basically good people. However, drug users, cop haters, and others frustrate the efforts of enforcers to make them "good," which makes the enforcers very unhappy. Thus, they have high job dissatisfaction and an attitude of resentment, feeling that a lot of people are hostile toward them.

Idealists, according to Broderick, are officers who put high value on individual rights and due process. They also believe that it is their duty to keep the peace, protect citizens from criminals, and generally preserve the social order. With a high percentage of college graduates, idealists' commitment to the job is the lowest of the four groups, and they are less likely to recommend the job to a son or daughter.

Realists place relatively little emphasis on either social order or individual rights, Broderick says. They seem less frustrated, having found a way to come to terms with a difficult job. For them, the reality of the job consists of manila envelopes and properly completed forms. Realists see many problems in policing, such as special privileges given to politicians. Reality is not warm bodies to be dealt with but rather the paperwork that the bodies leave behind. They work well in the ordered, predictable environment of a police records room.

Broderick's last group, the *optimists*, also places a relatively high value on individual rights. Like idealists, they see their job as people oriented instead of crime oriented. They see policing as providing opportunities to help people; they view the television version of policing as totally unrealistic and find it rewarding to spend the majority of their time in service activities. Optimists have the lowest amount of job resentment, are committed to the job, and would choose policing as a career all over again. They enjoy the mental challenge of problem solving.

What Traits Make a Good Cop?

It is not too difficult to identify a bad cop through his or her unethical or criminal behavior. It is probably more difficult for the average person to identify the traits of good officers. How can a quantitative measure assess the work of police? Is it possible to judge the quality of an officer's work? These are challenging questions for police supervisors.

A major obstacle to assessing police performance rests with the nature of police work generally and the variation in the kinds of work performed on different shifts. The police role varies according to whether the officer is assigned to the day shift, evening (swing) shift, or night (graveyard) shift (see Chapter 5 for a description of how police work varies by shift).

Dennis Nowicki[59] acknowledged that while certain characteristics form the foundation of a police officer—honesty, ethics, and moral character—no scientific formula can be used to create a highly effective officer. However, he compiled twelve qualities that he believes are imperative for entry-level police officers:

1. **Enthusiasm.** Believing in what one is doing and going about even routine duties with a certain vigor that is almost contagious.

2. **Good communication skills.** Having highly developed speaking and listening skills and interacting equally well with a wealthy person or someone lower on the socio-economic ladder.

3. **Good judgment.** Having wisdom and the ability to make good analytic decisions based on an understanding of the problem.

4. **Sense of humor.** Being able to laugh and smile in order to help oneself cope with regular exposure to human pain and suffering.

5. **Creativity.** Using creative techniques to place oneself in the mind of the criminal and accomplish legal arrests.

6. **Self-motivation.** Making things happen, proactively solving difficult cases, and creating one's own luck.

7. **Knowing the job and the system.** Understanding the role of a police officer and the intricacies of the justice system, knowing what the administration requires, and using both formal and informal channels to be effective.

8. **Ego.** Believing one is a good officer and having the self-confidence that enables one to solve difficult crimes.

9. **Courage.** Being able to meet physical and psychological challenges, thinking clearly during times of high stress, admitting when one is wrong, and standing up for what is right.

10. **Discretion.** Enforcing the spirit of the law (not the letter of the law), giving people a break, showing empathy, and not being hard-nosed, hardheaded, or hard-hearted.

11. **Tenacity.** Staying focused, seeing challenges rather than obstacles, and viewing failure not as a setback but as an experience.

12. **Thirst for knowledge.** Being aware of new laws and court decisions and always learning (from the classroom but also via informal discussions with other officers).

—"Twelve Qualities that are Imperative for Entry-level Police Officers" by Dennis Nowicki from TWELVE TRAITS OF HIGHLY EFFECTIVE POLICE OFFICERS, LAW AND ORDER. Copyright © 1999 by Hendon Publishing Company. Used by permission of Hendon Publishing Company.

▶ Roles, Functions, and Styles of Policing

Definition and Knowledge of the Police Role

Why do the police exist? What are they supposed to do? Often these questions are given oversimplified answers such as "They enforce the law" or "They 'serve and protect.'"[60]

But policing is much more complex. As Herman Goldstein put it, "Anyone attempting to construct a workable definition of the police role will typically come away with old images shattered and with a newfound appreciation for the intricacies of police work."[61] Even with all of the movies and television series depicting police in action, most Americans probably still do not have an accurate idea of what the police really do. This confusion is quite understandable because the police are called on to perform an almost countless number of tasks. Police are even used as prosecutors in some states, such as New Hampshire.

Who defines the police role? There are several groups and individuals who do:[62]

- Private citizens influence the nature of the police role through their contacts with the police, by participation in COPPS groups (discussed in Chapter 4), and through the election of public officials who set policy and appoint police administrators.

- Legislative bodies influence the role of the police by enacting statutes, both those that govern the police and those that the police use to govern others. In addition, legislative bodies determine police department budgets.

- The courts actively "police the police" by handing down decisions that regulate police conduct.

- Executives such as city managers and prosecutors help to define the police role by determining the types of cooperative agreements and evidence necessary for a prosecutable case.

- Police officers themselves define their roles by choosing to intervene in some incidents while ignoring others.

One of the greatest obstacles to understanding the American police is the crime fighter image. Many people believe that the role of the police is confined to law enforcement: the prevention and detection of crime and the apprehension of criminals. This is not an accurate view of contemporary policing.[63] It does not describe what the police do on a daily basis. First, only about 20 percent of the police officer's typical day is devoted to fighting crime per se.[64] As Jerome Skolnick and David Bayley point out, the crimes that terrify Americans the most—robbery, rape, burglary, and homicide—are rarely encountered by police on patrol: "Only 'Dirty Harry' has his lunch disturbed by a bank robbery in progress. Patrol officers individually make few important arrests. The 'good collar' is a rare event. Cops spend most of their time passively patrolling and providing emergency services."[65]

The crime fighter image persists, although it is extremely harmful to the public and individual officers.[66] The public suffers from this image because it gives rise to unrealistic expectations about the ability of the police to catch criminals. The image harms individual officers, who believe that rewards and promotions are tied only to success in capturing criminals. Also, many individuals enter policing expecting it to be exciting and rewarding, as depicted on television and in the movies. Later they learn that much of their time is spent with boring, mundane tasks that are anything but glamorous, that much of the work is trivial, and that paperwork is seldom stimulating.

Role Conflicts

Role conflicts may develop with officers and their departments. A family disturbance is a good example. Assume that Jane Smith reports to the police that her husband, John, is assaulting her. Police officers must respond to the disturbance, and the law empowers them to intervene, to enforce the law, and to maintain order. For the combatants, it is a very trying experience, not only because their family is dysfunctional but also because the police have been summoned to their home. Veteran officers might view the domestic call as trivial and inconvenient, leaving the scene as quickly as possible to go perform "real" police duties.

By the same token, the role of the police is often in the eye of the beholder. For example, the domestic argument just described might seem to fit best the category of maintaining order. However, if the responding officers are trained in crisis intervention or if they refer the couple to counseling, they are providing a social service. On the other hand, if John is found to have assaulted Jane, it is likely a criminal matter. If the police make an arrest or even just assist Jane in swearing out a warrant, the matter becomes a law enforcement issue.

The category to which this incident is assigned will vary greatly from agency to agency, officer to officer, and researcher to researcher, making it difficult to draw any solid conclusions about the police role.

Still, it is important to be as explicit as possible about the police role for several reasons. First, we can recruit and select competent police personnel only when we have a clear vision of what the police are supposed to accomplish. Second, evaluation for retention and promotion is useful only to the extent that we evaluate in terms of what the police are supposed to do. Third, budgetary decisions should be based on an accurate analysis of police roles. Fourth, efficiency and effectiveness in police organizations depend on accurate task descriptions. Fifth, public cooperation with the police depends on developing reasonable expectations of the roles of the police and the public.[67]

The police must identify those crimes on which police resources should be concentrated, focusing on the crimes that generate the most public fear and economic loss. The chief executive should have written policies to ensure that the police mission and the objectives used to achieve that mission are maintained by the police department. In other words, it is not enough for the police to "maintain order" or "provide justice." A police department may use many methods to maintain order and provide justice. In China or Saudi Arabia, those methods would be far different from those generally employed in the United States. But would "justice" result? In America, the police must maintain order without resorting to extralegal means or violating human rights.

Policing Functions and Styles

Officers may be said to perform four basic policing functions: (1) enforcing the law, (2) performing services (such as maintaining or assisting animal-control units, reporting burned-out street lights or damaged traffic signs, delivering death messages, checking the welfare of people in their homes, delivering blood), (3) preventing crime (patrolling, providing the public with information on crime prevention), and (4) protecting the innocent (by investigating crimes, police are systematically removing innocent people from consideration as crime suspects).

James Q. Wilson[68] looked at the functions of the police differently, determining that the police perform two basic functions: maintaining order (peacekeeping) and enforcing the law. Maintaining order constitutes most of the activities of the police; as noted earlier, less than 20 percent of the calls answered by police are directly related to crime control or law enforcement. Much of an officer's time is spent with such service activities as traffic control and routine patrol. Indeed, in some cases the police deliberately avoid enforcing the law in an attempt to maintain order. For example, if the police know of a busy street where many drivers speed, they may desist from setting up a speed trap during rush hours so as not to impede the flow of traffic and possibly cause accidents.

Enforcing the law means upholding the statutes, but this is not as simple and straightforward a function as it might seem. First, the police are really not very good at performing the law enforcement function; they have not traditionally been successful at preventing crime or providing long-term solutions to neighborhood disorder (although the relatively new community-policing and problem-solving concepts are addressing this shortcoming). Second, there are several types of crime—such as white-collar crime—with which the local police seldom deal. Third, the police, representing only about 2.3 officers per 1,000 population in the United States, cannot effectively control the public alone. Finally, the police are successful in solving only a fraction of the property and personal crimes that occur.[69]

Wilson also maintained that there are three distinctive policing styles:[70]

1. **Watchman style.** The watchman style involves the officer as a "neighbor." Here, officers act as if order maintenance (rather than law enforcement) is their primary function. The emphasis is on using the law as a means of maintaining order rather

than regulating conduct through arrests. Police ignore many common minor violations, such as traffic and juvenile offenses. These violations and so-called victimless crimes, such as gambling and prostitution, are tolerated and will often be handled informally. Thus, the individual officer has wide latitude concerning whether to enforce the letter or the spirit of the law; the emphasis is on using the law to give people what they "deserve." It assumes that some people, such as juveniles, are occasionally going to "act up."

2. **Legalistic style.** A legalistic style casts the officer as a "soldier." This style takes a much harsher view of law violations: Police officers issue large numbers of traffic citations, detain a high volume of juvenile offenders, and act vigorously against illicit activities, and large numbers of other kinds of arrests occur as well. Chief administrators want high arrest and ticketing rates not only because violators should be punished but also because it reduces the opportunity for their officers to engage in corrupt behavior. This style of policing assumes that the purpose of the law is to punish.

3. **Service style.** The service style views the officer as a "teacher." This style falls between the watchman and legalistic styles. The police take seriously all requests for either law enforcement or order maintenance (unlike in the watchman-style department) but are less likely to respond by making an arrest or otherwise imposing formal sanctions. Police officers see their primary responsibility as protecting public order against the minor and occasional threats posed by unruly teenagers and "outsiders" (tramps, derelicts, out-of-town visitors). The citizenry expects its service-style officers to display the same qualities as its department store salespeople: They should be courteous, neat, and deferential. The police will frequently use informal sanctions instead of making arrests.

Which Role, Function, and Style Prevail?

As we have seen, the role, function, and style of the police will differ by time and place. They will also be fluid within the agency, changing with the times, the political climate, and the problems of the day. Most police agencies do not determine which problems they address; rather, they respond to the problems that citizens believe are important, and the police agencies depend on the goals set by the community, the chief executive, and the individual officers. Sometimes roles, functions, and styles overlap, but most of the time they are distinct.

▶ Breaking Through Glass Ceilings: Women and Minorities

Some challenges and successes with recruiting women (and minorities) into policing were discussed earlier. Here, we basically consider *why* it is important to have them engaged in police work.

Women as Officers and Chief Executives

Over the last thirty years, the proportion of women police officers has grown steadily. During the 1970s, some formal barriers to hiring women were eliminated, such as height requirements; in addition, subjective physical agility tests and oral interviews were modified.[71] Some job discrimination suits further expanded women's opportunities.

Women now represent about 12 percent of the sworn personnel in local (municipal and county) police agencies,[72] State agencies as a whole have a much lower percentage of female officers than either local or federal law enforcement agencies, 6.5 percent.[73] Women account for about 15 percent of all federal sworn officers, which is a bit higher than local agencies.[74]

Although this representation of women officers is low compared to their overall proportion in the total population, it becomes even more evident in the leadership ranks, where women number only 1 percent of the police chiefs in the United States. However, inroads are being made: approximately forty women now serve as sheriffs in the United States,[75] and women serve or have served as chiefs of police in Orlando, Florida; Newark, New Jersey; Washington, D.C.; San Francisco; Boston; Detroit; and Milwaukee, as well as in a number of other cities, as "mayors are looking for sophisticated CEOs who can oversee large budgets, negotiate thorny management problems, and set sound department-wide policy."[76]

Advantages

In addition to helping the police labor force to diversify, there are certainly practical advantages to having women in uniform as well; according to a report by the National Center for Women & Policing:

1. **Female officers are proven to be as competent as their male counterparts.** The Center notes that several evaluations of the effectiveness of female officers in a number of work-related areas in several large cities (e.g., Washington D.C., St. Louis, New York City, Denver, Philadelphia) concluded that men and women were equally capable of successful performance as patrol officers.

2. **Female officers are less likely to use excessive force.** As with their competency, research both in the United States and international venues demonstrates that female officers utilize a less authoritarian style of policing that relies less on physical force—and their communications skills allow them to defuse situations.

3. **Female officers implement "community-oriented policing."** Community policing and problem solving emphasizes communication and cooperation with citizens as well as informal problem solving. The Center believes that, in addition to their communication skills, women officers demonstrate empathy toward others and interact in a way that is not designed to "prove" something.

4. **More female officers will improve law enforcement's response to violence against women.** It is critical that the police properly respond to problems of sexual and physical assaults against women; the price of failure is high, not only in terms of crimes against the victims but also the risk of litigation (particularly in domestic violence). The Center cites studies indicating that female officers have long been viewed as more effective in responding to crimes against women than their male counterparts.

5. **Increasing the presence of female officers reduces problems of sex discrimination and harassment within a law enforcement agency.** Although studies show, according to the Center, that women in law enforcement continue to face a variety of obstacles such as negative attitudes, gender discrimination, and sexual harassment, increased representation of women in policing can transform the climate within a police agency and reduce the prevalence of gender discrimination, under-utilization, and sexual harassment.[77]

Minorities as Law Enforcement Officers

Certainly as the United States becomes more diversified in its population, it is increasingly important and advantageous to have minorities as police officers serving communities in police uniforms as well. Minority citizens will naturally feel more secure in their communities when they see and know police officers of their own race, as well as (hopefully) believe that their sons and daughters can enjoy a successful career in the police service. In short, a community's

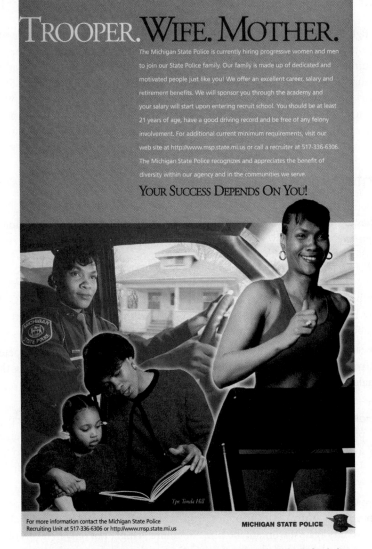

TROOPER. WIFE. MOTHER.

The Michigan State Police is currently hiring progressive women and men to join our State Police family. Our family is made up of dedicated and motivated people just like you! We offer an excellent career, salary and retirement benefits. We will sponsor you through the academy and your salary will start upon entering recruit school. You should be at least 21 years of age, have a good driving record and be free of any felony involvement. For additional current minimum requirements, visit our web site at http://www.msp.state.mi.us or call a recruiter at 517-336-6306. The Michigan State Police recognizes and appreciates the benefit of diversity within our agency and in the communities we serve.

YOUR SUCCESS DEPENDS ON YOU!

Tpr. Tonda Hill

For more information contact the Michigan State Police
Recruiting Unit at 517-336-6306 or http://www.msp.state.mi.us

MICHIGAN STATE POLICE

▲ There are many advantages to having women serve in today's law enforcement agencies, such as their being as competent as male officers and less likely to use excessive force. *(Courtesy Michigan State Police.)*

having a diversified police organization can contribute to its minorities feeling "at home" with their police, rather than believing that the police are a mere necessary evil or unwanted presence.

And, as noted above with women, the representation and recruitment of minorities also pose challenges for policing remains a difficult task, although it is absolutely essential for agencies to be well represented in this area. At present, only about 12 percent of all local police officers are African American, and 10 percent are Hispanic/Latino.[78] Probably the most difficult barrier has to do with the image that police officers have in the minority communities. Unfortunately, police officers have been seen as symbols of oppression and have been charged with using excessive brutality; they are often seen as an army of occupation.

African-American police officers face problems similar to those of women who attempt to enter and prosper in police work. Until more African-American officers are promoted and can affect police policy and serve as role models, they are likely to be treated unequally and have difficulty being promoted—a classic catch-22 situation. African Americans considering

▲ Police departments must strive to diversify their ranks, to be more representative of their communities, and to incorporate a broader set of employee cultures, cultures, and viewpoints. *(Courtesy © Jeff Greenberg/Alamy.)*

a police career may be encouraged by a survey of African-American officers, which found that most believed their jobs were satisfying and offered opportunities for advancement.[79]

An influential coalition of African Americans is the National Organization of Black Law Enforcement Executives (NOBLE), which was founded in 1976 and has fifty nine chapters in the United States. Its purposes are to unify African-American law enforcement officers at executive and command levels; to conduct research in relevant areas of law enforcement; to recommend legislation relating to the criminal justice process; to establish means and strategies for dealing with racism in the field of criminal justice; to sensitize people to the problems of the African-American community; to facilitate the exchange of information among African-American police executives; and to articulate the concerns of African-American executives in law enforcement.[80]

Summary

We began this chapter with a look at the officer's world and an explanation of how private citizens are socialized into their role as police officers and prepared for working the street; an emphasis was placed on viewing these officers as individuals rather than in the aggregate, as is often the case. The reader has seen how people are recruited, tested, and trained for their role as police officers through a series of "hurdles"; during this process they are transformed psychologically, physically, and emotionally to become competent and to function in the very challenging world of the police.

We have established that a working personality develops in police officers. Both formal training and peer relations are instructive and helpful in teaching the novice officer how to act, think, and view certain elements of the job. Unfortunately, it was shown that danger, suspicion, constantly witnessing the seedy side of humanity, and other factors also tend to inculcate in police officers another common trait: cynicism.

This chapter also examined the roles, functions, and styles of the local police in America. More than a century and a half after the adoption of the early British model of policing (discussed in Chapter 1), disagreement, conflict, and debate are still widespread concerning what we truly want our police to do, represent, and become.

The hiring process described in this chapter is certainly the ideal rather than the real. Probably few of the seventeen thousand American police agencies compel their applicants to successfully complete the entire battery of tests and screening examinations described here, nor do all departments have the inclination or resources to engage in a full-fledged FTO or PTO program that would monitor and further train new recruits. It is also doubtful that formal education requirements are being elevated for or acquired by police at the rate of the society at large. Yet, the present recruitment and training process seems to work well overall, except in those instances where a jurisdiction, sorely needing personnel, engages in rapid hiring and can easily bring substandard people into the field.

Women and minorities in policing also were discussed. The incorporation of community-oriented, problem-solving strategies of policing (which will be discussed in Chapter 6) has changed the focus of policing from a highly physical, quantitative, and hardware-oriented field to one that requires officers with communication skills, an understanding of our diverse society, and problem-solving capabilities. Women and minorities, in both philosophical and quantitative terms, have yet to be accepted in this occupation, even though studies have shown their tremendous value to the field. The argument seems compelling that until enough women and minorities are employed at all levels of a police force, policy decisions about hiring and promoting them will be ineffective or nonexistent. Strategies to encourage them to enter the field are still being developed; much more can obviously be done toward enhancing their visibility, presence, and usefulness in this occupation.

Key Terms

academy training
assessment center
computer-based training (CBT)
field training officer (FTO)
    program
hurdle process

in-service training
minority police officers
police cynicism
police training officer (PTO)
    program
policing functions

policing styles
recruiting
sixth sense
traits of good officers
women police officers
working personality

Review Questions

1. What are some of the problems confronting today's police recruiters and some of the unique measures they use to obtain a viable applicant pool?
2. What is generally the hiring process for new police officers and the kinds of tests that are commonly given to applicants?
3. Which kinds of skills and knowledge are imparted to police trainees during their academy training, and what are the typical subjects that are taught in a police academy curriculum?
4. What are the methods and purposes of the FTO and PTO programs?

5. What is meant by the term *working personality*, how was the concept developed, and what is its function?
6. What is police cynicism, and how does it operate?
7. What are the ideal traits of police officers?
8. Why is the crime fighter image possibly the greatest obstacle in accepting a realistic view of the police role?
9. What are the primary functions and styles of policing?
10. What is the status of women and minorities in policing as well as some advantages of having them represented in this occupation?

Learn by Doing

1. You are consulting with a medium-size police department that has been criticized in the media for its high levels of recruit dropouts from the basic academy as well as high percentages of recruits being failed by their field training officers (FTOs) during their probationary period. It appears at first glance that local police–community relations are such that there are not large pools of police applicants. You are to recommend better recruitment methods that will overcome these academy and FTO problems. What would you recommend?

2. Assume the same scenario as above, in #1. Now, however, the emphasis shifts to the kinds of tests that should be employed during the initial hurdle process or hiring phase. While admitting the need for improvement, the chief of police argues that there simply is not enough time, money, or other resources to employ the full range of test methods, one that would include for each recruit in a *large* agency a written examination, psychological test, physical

agility test, personal interview, character investigation, polygraph examination, medical examination, and drug screening. The chief asks you to consider each type of entry-level examination in terms of its contribution to the hiring process and the overall mission of the agency, and then—due to cost limitations—make recommendations for *six* forms of testing that should minimally be employed for hiring new officers. Which six types of tests would you recommend (defend your choices)?

3. Still assuming the same scenario as in #1 and #2, the emphasis now shifts to training. Due to a number of recent incidents involving police errors in procedure and revelations of inappropriate use of force, the department has been criticized in the media for its recruit training requirements. Looking at the nature of the curriculum and topics included in Table 2-3, which training topics do you think might be added to the curriculum? Expanded in their duration? Deleted? Defend your answers.

Notes

1. William A. Westley, *Violence and the Police* (Cambridge, MA: MIT Press, 1970).
2. Geoffrey P. Alpert and Roger G. Dunham, *Policing Urban America*, 2nd ed. (Prospect Heights, IL: Waveland Press, 1992), p. 80; for an excellent description of the evolving police role, also see Roger G. Dunham and Geoffrey P. Alpert, *Critical Issues in Policing: Contemporary Readings*, 5th ed. (Long Grove, IL: Waveland Press, 2005), pp. 1–9.
3. Quoted in V. A. Leonard and Harry W. More, *Police Organization and Management*, 3rd ed. (Mineola, NY: Foundation Press, 1971), p. 128.
4. Joel Lefkowitz, "Industrial-Organizational Psychology and the Police," *American Psychologist* 32 (5) (May 1977): 346–364.
5. R. B. Mills, "Use of Diagnostic Small Groups in Police Recruit Selection and Training," *Journal of Criminal Law, Criminology and Police Science* 60 (1969): 238–241; John Van Maanen, "Police Socialization: A Longitudinal Examination of Job Attitudes in an Urban Police Department," *Administrative Science Quarterly* 20 (1975): 207–228.
6. C. Gorer, "Modification of National Character: The Role of the Police in England," *Journal of Social Issues* 11 (1955): 24–32; Arthur Niederhoffer, *Behind the Shield: The Police in Urban Society* (New York: Anchor, 1967), p. 140.
7. M. Steven Meagher and Nancy A. Yentes, "Choosing a Career in Policing: A Comparison of Male and Female Perceptions," *Journal of Police Science and Administration* 14 (1986): 320–327.
8. Lefkowitz, "Industrial-Organizational Psychology and the Police."
9. J. D. Matarazzo, B. V. Allen, G. Saslow, and A. N. Wiens, "Characteristics of Successful Policemen and Firemen Applicants," *Journal of Applied Psychology* 48 (1964): 123–133.
10. Bruce N. Carpenter and Susan M. Raza, "Personality Characteristics of Police Applicants: Comparisons Across Subgroups and with Other Populations," *Journal of Police Science and Administration* 15 (1987): 10–17.
11. Carpenter and Raza also compared police applicants with other similar occupational groups and found that police applicants appear to be most like nuclear submariners and least like air force trainees and security guards.
12. Lawrence S. Wrightsman, *Psychology and the Legal System* (Monterey, CA: Brooks/Cole, 1987), pp. 85–86.
13. Al Seedman and P. Hellman, *Chief!* (New York: Arthur Fields, 1974), pp. 4–5.

14. Jeremy M. Wilson and Clifford A. Grammich, *Police Recruitment and Retention in the Contemporary Urban Environment: A National Discussion of Personnel Experiences and Promising Practices from the Front Lines* (Santa Monica, CA: RAND Corporation, 2009), p. 5; also available at: www.rand.org/pubs/conf_proceedings/ 2009/RAND_CF261.pdf (accessed March 5, 2013).

15. Ibid., p. 2.

16. Stephanie Slahor, "RAND Study Suggests Strategies to Address Recruiting Shortage," *Law and Order*, December 8, 2008, p. 32.

17. U.S. Department of Justice, Bureau of Justice Statistics, *Local Police Departments, 2007* (Washington, D.C.: Author, December 2010), p. 12.

18. "Plenty of Talk, Not Much Action," *Law Enforcement News*, January 15/31, 1999, p. 1.

19. William T. Jordan, Lorie Fridell, Donald Faggiani, and Bruce Kubu, "Attracting Females and Racial/Ethnic Minorities to Law Enforcement," *Journal of Criminal Justice* 37(4) (July–August 2009), pp. 333–341, http://0-www.sciencedirect.com.innopac.library .unr.edu/science/article/pii/S0047235209000658 (accessed October 24, 2013).

20. Alicia Caldwell, "Border Patrol Gets Creative to Try to Find More Recruits, Tighten Border," *Associate Press*, January 11, 2008, http://www.gadsdentimes .com/article/20080111/NEWS/801110325 (accessed October 24, 2012).

21. Hans Toch, *Psychology of Crime and Criminal Justice* (Prospect Heights, IL: Waveland Press, 1999), p. 44.

22. Philip Ash, Karen B. Slora, and Cynthia F. Britton, "Police Agency Officer Selection Practices," *Journal of Police Science and Administration* 17 (December 1990): 259–264.

23. S. H. Marsh, "Validating the Selection of Deputy Sheriffs," *Public Personnel Review* 23 (1962): 41–44.

24. William H. Thweatt, "A Vocational Counseling Approach to Police Selection" (unpublished dissertation, University of Arizona).

25. W. Clinton Terry III, *Policing Society* (New York: John Wiley & Sons, 1985), p. 194.

26. George E. Hargrave, "Using the MMPI and CPI to Screen Law Enforcement Applicants: A Study of Reliability and Validity of Clinicians' Decisions," *Journal of Police Science and Administration* 13 (1985): 221–224.

27. Dunham and Alpert, *Critical Issues in Policing: Contemporary Readings*, p. 80.

28. For a complete discussion of the Sparks Police Officers Physical Abilities Test (POPAT), see Ken Peak, Douglas Farenholtz, and George Coxey, "Physical Abilities Testing for Police Officers: A Flexible, Job Related Approach," *Police Chief* 59 (January 1992): 51–56.

29. Terry Eisenberg, D. A. Kent, and C. R. Wall, *Police Personnel Practices in State and Local Governments* (Gaithersburg, MD: International Association of Chiefs of Police, 1973), p. 15.

30. George E. Hargrave and Deirdre Hiatt, "Law Enforcement Selection with the Interview, MMPI, and CPI: A Study of Reliability and Validity," *Journal of Police Science and Administration* 15(2) (1987): 110–117.

31. U.S. Department of Justice, Bureau of Justice Statistics, *Local Police Departments, 2007*, p. 8.

32. Quoted in Charles R. Swanson, Leonard Territo, and Robert W. Taylor, *Police Administration*, 2nd ed. (New York: Macmillan, 1988), pp. 202–203.

33. U.S. Department of Justice, Bureau of Justice Statistics, "Census of State and Local Law Enforcement Agencies, 2008" (July 2011), p. 1, http://bjs.ojp.usdoj .gov/content/pub/pdf/csllea08.pdf (accessed November 5, 2013); U.S. Department of Justice, Bureau of Justice Statistics, *Local Police Departments, 2007*, p. 6, http://bjs.ojp.usdoj.gov/content/pub/ pdf/lpd07.pdf (accessed January 24, 2013); also see U.S. Department of Justice, Bureau of Justice Assistance, "Discover Policing: Training/Academy Life," discoverpolicing.org/what_does_take/?fa=training_ academy_life (accessed March 5, 2013).

34. U.S. Department of Justice, Bureau of Justice Statistics, *State and Local Law Enforcement Training Academies, 2006*, (February 2009), pp. 1–6, http:// bjs.ojp.usdoj.gov/index.cfm?ty=tp&tid=77 (accessed January 11, 2013).

35. Swanson, et al., *Police Administration*, pp. 6, 8.

36. Lois Pilant, "Enhancing the Patrol Image," *Police Chief* 59 (August 1992): 55–61.

37. Wrightsman, *Psychology and the Legal System*, p. 86.

38. Quoted in Jerome Skolnick, "A Sketch of the Policeman's Working Personality," in *The Police Community*, ed. Jack Goldsmith and Sharon S. Goldsmith (Pacific Palisades, CA: Palisades Publishers, 1974), p. 106.

39. Thomas F. Adams, "Field Interrogation," *Police*, March–April 1963, pp. 1–8.

40. Jonathan Rubenstein, "Cop's Rules," in *Police Behavior: A Sociological Perspective*, ed. Richard J. Lundman (New York: Oxford University Press, 1980), pp. 68–78.

41. Bruce Catton, "Eyewitness Reports on the Assassination of Abraham Lincoln," in *Criminal Justice: Allies and Adversaries*, ed. John R. Snortum and Ilana Hader (Pacific Palisades, CA: Palisades Publishers, 1978), pp. 155–157.

42. Tom Wilkenson and John Chattin-McNichols, "The Effectiveness of Computer-Assisted Instruction for Police Officers," *Journal of Police Science and Administration* 13 (1985): 230–235.

43. Niederhoffer, *Behind the Shield*, p. 51.
44. Dunham and Alpert, *Critical Issues in Policing*, p. 112.
45. Ibid., p. 111.
46. Ibid., pp. 112–115.
47. Kenneth J. Peak, Steven Pitts, and Ronald W. Glensor, "From 'FTO' to 'PTO': A Contemporary Approach to Post-Academy Recruit Training" (paper presented at the annual conference of the Academy of Criminal Justice Sciences, Seattle, WA, March 22, 2007).
48. "Field Trainers Have Reports Well in Hand," *Law Enforcement News*, November 15, 2000, p. 5.
49. "Pursuit Simulation Training Is No Ordinary Crash Course," *Law Enforcement News*, November 15, 2000, p. 6.
50. Alpert and Dunham, *Policing Urban America*, p. 58.
51. Skolnick, "A Sketch of the Policeman's Working Personality," p. 106.
52. Westley, *Violence and the Police*, p. 56.
53. Elizabeth Burbeck and Adrian Furnham, "Police Officer Selection: A Critical Review of the Literature," *Journal of Police Science and Administration* 13 (1985): 58–69.
54. Matarazzo et al., "Characteristics of Successful Policemen and Firemen Applicants."
55. George E. Hargrave, Deirdre Hiatt, and Tim W. Gaffney, "A Comparison of MMPI and CPI Profiles for Traffic Officers," *Journal of Police Science and Administration* 14 (1986): 250–258.
56. Quoted in Seymour M. Lipset, "Why Cops Hate Liberals—and Vice Versa," *Atlantic Monthly* 223 (March 1969): 76.
57. Niederhoffer, *Behind the Shield*, p. 140.
58. John J. Broderick, *Police in a Time of Change* (Prospect Heights, IL: Waveland Press, 1987), p. 215.
59. Adapted from Dennis Nowicki, "Twelve Traits of Highly Effective Police Officers," *Law and Order*, October 1999, pp. 45–46.
60. Samuel Walker, *The Police in America: An Introduction*, 2nd ed. (New York: McGraw-Hill, 1992), p. 61.
61. Herman Goldstein, *Policing a Free Society* (Cambridge, MA: Ballinger, 1977), p. 21.
62. Steven M. Cox, *Police: Practices, Perspectives, Problems* (Boston: Allyn & Bacon, 1996), pp. 18–19.
63. Ibid., p. 61.
64. See Albert Reiss, *The Police and the Public* (New Haven, CT: Yale University Press, 1971), p. 96.
65. Jerome H. Skolnick and David H. Bayley, *The New Blue Line: Police Innovation in Six American Cities* (New York: Free Press, 1986), p. 4.
66. Patrick V. Murphy and Thomas Plate, *Commissioner: A View from the Top of American Law Enforcement* (New York: Simon and Schuster, 1977). Also see Walker, *The Police in America*, pp. 55–56.
67. Cox, *Police*, pp. 18–19.
68. James Q. Wilson, *Varieties of Police Behavior* (Cambridge, MA: Harvard University Press, 1968), pp. 140–226.
69. Cox, *Police*, pp. 18–19.
70. Wilson, *Varieties of Police Behavior*, pp. 140–226.
71. Barbara Raffel Price, "Sexual Integration in American Law Enforcement," in *Police Ethics: Hard Choices in Law Enforcement*, ed. William C. Heffernan and Timothy Stroup (New York: John Jay Press, 1985), see also Vivian B. Lord and Kenneth J. Peak, *Women in Law Enforcement Careers: A Guide for Preparing and Succeeding* (Upper Saddle River, NJ: Prentice Hall, 2005).
72. U.S. Department of Justice, Bureau of Justice Statistics, *Local Police Departments, 2007*, p. 14.
73. Department of Justice, Bureau of Justice Statistics, *Women in Law Enforcement, 1987–2008* (Washington, D.C.: Author, June 2010), p. 3; also see U.S. Department of Justice, Bureau of Justice Assistance, *Recruiting & Retaining Women: A Self-Assessment Guide for Law Enforcement* (June 2001), https://www.ncjrs.gov/pdffiles1/bja/188157.pdf (accessed October 2, 2012).
74. Ibid., p. 2.
75. Dana Parsons, "Ready for a female sheriff?" *Los Angeles Times*, http://articles.latimes.com/2008/jun/05/local/me-parsons5 (accessed October 2, 2012).
76. Jacqueline Mroz, "Female Police Chiefs, a Novelty No More," *The New York Times* (April 6, 2008), http://www.nytimes.com/2008/04/06/nyregion/nyregionspecial2/06Rpolice.html?_r=1&pagewanted=all& (accessed October 2, 2012).
77. Kim Lonsway, Margaret Moore, Penny Harrington, Eleanor Smeal, and Katherine Spillar, *Hiring & Retaining More Women: The Advantages to Law Enforcement Agencies* (Beverly Hills, CA: National Center for Women & Policing, 2003); also see Sandra Wells and Betty Sowers Alt, *Police Women: Life with the Badge* (Westport, CT: Praeger, 2005).
78. U.S. Department of Justice, Bureau of Justice Statistics, *Local Police Departments, 2007*, p. 14.
79. Lena Williams, "Police Officers Tell of Strains of Living as a 'Black in Blue,'" *New York Times*, February 14, 1988, pp. 1, 26.
80. National Organization of Black Law Enforcement Executives, "About NOBLE," http://www.noblenational.org/aboutus.html (accessed October 24, 2012).

3   On Patrol
Methods and Menaces

LEARNING OBJECTIVES

As a result of reading this chapter, the student will be able to:

 List several of the major studies and findings of the patrol function

2 *Delineate how the patrol function is affected by the officer's shift assignment and the nature of the beat or sector to which he or she is assigned*

3 *Explain some of the hazards that are inherent in police work and patrol functions, and what circumstances tend to be present in situations involving officer fatalities*

 Describe the newly enacted legislation that allows retired officers to carry their weapons

Delineate the functions of different types of patrol vehicles, how they are used, and how the recent economic downturn affected traditional patrol functions

 Define what is meant by police discretion, its advantages and disadvantages, and the factors that can enter into the officer's decision-making process

7 Explain the nature and importance of the traffic function in patrol work

8 Describe the legal and psychological aspects of police officers' uniforms and their general appearance and the nature, purpose, and areas of potential liability with agency dress codes

9 Explain the importance—the "lifeline"—that police dispatchers provide to patrol officers

Introduction

The patrol function has long been viewed as the backbone of policing, the most important and *31* visible part of police work. It is the primary means by which the police fulfill their mission. Patrol officers are the eyes and ears of the police organization, the worker bees of community policing and problem solving, the initial responders and protectors of the crime scene, and typically the first police representative whom citizens meet. All other specialized units either directly or indirectly support the patrol function. Patrol is where the art of policing is learned, citizens go to lodge concerns and complaints, and needs of the community are met. Significantly, all police chiefs, sheriffs (unless elected without prior experience), and other high-ranking personnel began their careers as patrol officers.

Indeed, this chapter serves as a prologue to many different kinds of police activities described in later chapters, all of which branch off from the patrol function. Because patrol duties normally involve 60 to 70 percent of a police agency's workforce, this task has been a topic of considerable interest and analysis.

In addition to the patrol function, the work of policing also revolves around the discretionary use of authority: whether or not to stop and question or cite someone, to arrest, to use force, or to shoot. From the relatively innocuous traffic stop to the use of lethal force, many choices are involved, including some with serious consequences.

This chapter begins with an overview of what research has revealed concerning the patrol function. Next is a description of the culture of the beat: the purposes and nature of patrol, patrol work as a function of shift and beat assignment, and the dangers that may be confronted while on patrol. Then we consider an often overlooked yet extremely important tool for patrolling: the patrol vehicle, including automobiles, motorcycles, and other means. Following that is an examination of the discretionary use of police authority, with a view toward the various considerations that can enter into an officer's decision-making process. Then we discuss another function that is closely related to patrol—traffic; following this discussion are reviews of two important aspects of patrol that, like the patrol vehicle, are seldom examined: the legal and psychological aspects of police officers' uniforms (to include agency dress codes and litigation involving the codes), and the roles of police dispatchers—the lifeline—to patrol officers. The chapter concludes with a summary, key terms, review questions, and several scenarios and activities that provide opportunities for you to learn by doing.

Two closely related topics that are at the heart of the patrol function are discussed in later chapters: community-oriented policing and problem solving (Chapter 4) and the less-lethal and high-technology tools used by patrol officers in the performance of their duties (Chapter 14).

▶ Studies of the Patrol Function: An Overview

Because of the vast resources devoted to the patrol function and a desire to make patrolling more productive, many patrol studies have been conducted and have helped us to better understand this key police function.

The best-known study of patrol efficiency, the Kansas City Preventive Patrol Experiment, was conducted in Kansas City, Missouri, in 1973, by George Kelling and a research team at the Police Foundation. The researchers divided the city into fifteen beats, which were then categorized into five groups of three matched beats each. Each group consisted of neighborhoods that were similar in terms of population, crime characteristics, and calls for police services. Patrolling techniques used in the three beats varied: There was no preventive patrol in one beat (police only responded to calls for service), increased patrol activity in another (two or three times the usual amount of patrolling), and the usual level of service in the third. Citizens were interviewed and crime rates were measured during the year the experiment was conducted. This experiment challenged several traditional assumptions about routine police patrol. The study found that the deterrent effect of policing was not weakened by the elimination of routine patrolling. Citizens' fear of crime and their attitudes toward the police were not affected, nor was the ability of the police to respond to calls. The Kansas City Preventive Patrol Experiment (depicted in Figure 3-1 ▪) indicated that the old sacrosanct patrol methods were subject to question. As one of the study's authors stated, "[It showed] that the traditional assumptions of 'Give me more cars and more money and we'll get there faster and fight crime' is probably not a very viable argument."[1] In the mid-1970s, it was suggested that the performance of patrol officers would improve by redesigning the job based on motivators rather than by attempting to change the individual officer selected for the job (by such means as increasing education requirements).[2]

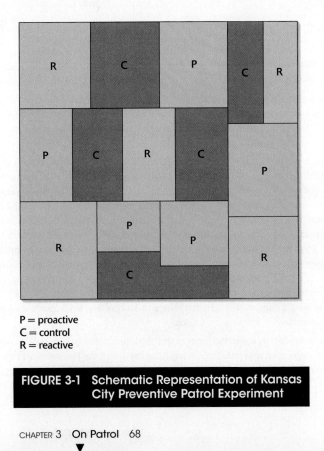

P = proactive
C = control
R = reactive

FIGURE 3-1   Schematic Representation of Kansas City Preventive Patrol Experiment

This suggestion later evolved into a concept known as "team policing," which differed from conventional patrol in several areas. Officers were divided into small teams that were assigned permanently to small geographic areas or neighborhoods. Officers were to be generalists, trained to investigate crimes and to attend to all the problems in their area. Communication and coordination between team members and the community were to be maximized; team involvement in administrative decision making was emphasized as well. This concept, later abandoned by many departments (apparently because of its strain on resources), was the beginning of the 1980s movement to return to community-oriented policing.

Two more attempts to increase patrol productivity, generally referred to as "directed patrol," occurred in 1975. The New Haven, Connecticut, Police Department used computer data of crime locations and times to set up deterrent runs (D-runs) to instruct officers on how to patrol. For example, the officer might be told to patrol around a certain block slowly, park, walk, get back in the car, and cruise down another street. A D-run took up to an hour, with each officer doing two or three of them per shift. Support for patrol officers was generally low, and the program did not reduce crime but rather displaced it. After a year, the experiment quietly died.[3] Wilmington, Delaware, instituted a split-force program, whereby three-fourths of the 250 patrol officers were assigned to a basic patrol unit to answer prioritized calls. The remaining officers were assigned to the structured unit and were deployed in high-crime areas, usually in plainclothes, to perform surveillances, stakeouts, and other tactical assignments. An evaluation of the project found that police productivity increased 20 percent and crime decreased 18 percent in the program's first year.[4]

In the late 1970s, a renewed interest in foot patrol—in keeping with Peel's view that police officers should walk the beat—compelled the Police Foundation to evaluate the effectiveness of foot patrol in selected New Jersey cities between 1977 and 1979. It was found that, for the most part, crime levels were not affected by foot patrol, but it did have a significant effect on the attitudes of area residents. Specifically, residents felt safer, thinking that the severity of crimes in their neighborhoods had diminished. Furthermore, evaluations of the Neighborhood Foot Patrol Program in Flint, Michigan, in 1985 found that foot officers had a higher level of job satisfaction[5] and felt safer on the job than motor officers.[6]

Other studies have illuminated the patrol function as well. A long-standing assumption was that as police response time increased, the ability to arrest perpetrators proportionately decreased. Thus, conventional wisdom held, more police were needed on patrol in order to get to the crime scene more quickly and catch the criminals. In 1977, a study examined police response time in Kansas City, Missouri, and found that response time was unrelated to the probability of making an arrest or locating a witness. Furthermore, neither dispatch nor travel time was strongly associated with citizen satisfaction. The time it takes to report a crime, the study found, is the major determining factor of whether an on-scene arrest takes place and whether witnesses are located.[7] It has also been found that two-person patrol cars are no more effective than one-person cars in reducing crime or catching criminals. Furthermore, injuries to police officers are not more likely to occur in one-person cars. In addition, most officers on patrol do not stumble across felony crimes in progress.[8]

While these studies should not be viewed as conclusive—different results could be obtained in different communities—they do demonstrate that old police methods should be viewed very cautiously. Many police executives have had to rethink the sacred cows of patrol functions.

▶ Patrol as Work: Culture of the Beat

Purposes and Nature of Patrol

In this chapter section, we look at the beat culture, or some of the methods and problems that are connected with the patrol function—all of which has certainly changed since Leonard Fuld observed in 1910 that "the policeman's life is a lazy life in as much as his time is spent doing nothing."[9] Today the patrol officer performs myriad duties, and danger is a constant adversary.

When not handling calls for service, today's officers frequently engage in problem-solving activities (see Chapter 4) and in random preventive patrol, hoping to deter crime with a police presence. The various forms of preventive patrol include automobile, foot, bicycle, horse, motorcycle, marine, helicopter, and even snowmobile patrols. During all of these duties, the officer is alert for activities and people who seem out of the ordinary. The method of deployment of patrol officers should take into account where and when crimes occur, attempting to distribute available personnel at the places and the times of day and days of the week when trouble and crime seem to occur with greatest frequency.

Patrol officers should also attempt to effect good relations with the citizens on their beat, realizing that they cannot apprehend criminals or even maintain a quiet sector without public assistance. In many ways, the success of the entire police agency depends on the skill and work of the patrol officers. For example, upon arriving at a crime scene, police must protect and collect evidence, treat and interview victims, locate and interview suspects and witnesses, and make important discretionary decisions such as whether to arrest someone and even perhaps whether to use their weapons. Officers must also become very knowledgeable about their beat assignment: They must be familiar with such details as where the doors and windows of buildings are, where the alleys are, where smaller businesses are located, and how the residential areas they patrol are laid out. Officers must learn what is normal on their beat and thus be able to discern people or things that are abnormal; in short, they should develop a kind of sixth sense that is grounded on suspicion—an awareness of something bad, wrong, harmful, without solid evidence. This is often termed "JDLR" (things "Just Don't Look Right").

Patrol officers may also develop certain informal rules pertaining to their beat. For example, they may adopt the belief that "after midnight, these alleys belong to me." In other words, an officer may take the position that any person who is observed in "his" or "her" alley after midnight must be checked out—especially if that person is wearing dark clothing or is acting in a furtive or surreptitious manner.

Several authors have described, often in colorful but realistic terms, the kinds of situations encountered by officers on patrol. For example, as W. Clinton Terry III put it:

> Patrol officers respond to calls about overflowing sewers, reports of attempted suicides, domestic disputes, fights between neighbors, barking dogs and quarrelsome cats, reports of people banging their heads against brick walls until they are bloody, requests to check people out who have seemingly passed out in public parks, requests for more police protection from elderly ladies afraid of entering their residence, and requests for information and general assistance of every sort.[10]

Contrary to the image that is portrayed on television, some (or even much) of the time officers devote to patrolling consists of gaps of inactivity. During those periods of time (particularly on the graveyard shift, when even late-night people and partygoers submit to fatigue and go home to sleep), patrol officers engage in a variety of activities to pass the time:

- They create "private places" for themselves—fire stations, hospitals, and other places where they can wash up, have a cup of coffee, make a phone call, or simply relax for a few moments.

- They engage in police-related activities, such as completing reports, checking license plates of vehicles that are parked at motels (to locate stolen vehicles or wanted persons), or meeting with other officers. Other more relaxing activities might include exercising in the station house workout room.

- The officer is often encouraged (beginning during recruit training) to make good use of this slack time, even while engaged in routine patrol, by engaging in "what-if" mental exercises: "What if an armed robbery occurred at (location)? How would I get there most rapidly? What would I do after arrival? Where would I find available cover?"

Of course, officers can concoct any number of scenarios and types of calls for service to keep themselves mentally honed and ready to respond in the most efficacious manner.

- An often overlooked part of policing is that patrol officers must also spend a lot of time—especially during the early part of their careers—memorizing many things: the "Ten Code," for example, and the numbering systems of streets and highways within their jurisdiction. (Indeed, new recruits can and do "wash out" during the field training phase of their careers because of their inability to read an in-car map of the city, thus preventing them from arriving at their destination promptly.)

Indeed, as Terry noted above, patrolling officers will encounter all manner of things while engaged in routine patrol—things they stumble onto as well as problems phoned in by citizens. They are assigned "attempt to locate" calls (usually involving missing persons, ranging from juveniles who have not returned home on time to elderly people who have wandered away from nursing homes); "attempt to contact" and "be on the lookout" calls (e.g., an out-of-town individual asks police to try to locate someone in order to deliver a message); and "check the welfare of" calls (involving a person who has not been seen or heard from for some time).

Finally, although the campaign begun by police in the mid-1990s encouraging the use of a nationally recognizable number—311—to alleviate the burden of nonemergency 911 calls, they remain a problem. Studies consistently show that 60 to 90 percent of them are for nonemergencies.[11] A study in New York found that 40 percent of all 911 calls were accidental (what they termed "butt calls"—calls made by people sitting on their phones).[12] Departments must continue to fight what has been called the "tyranny of 911": nonstop calls that can send officers bouncing from one nonemergency call for service to the next. Indeed, the range of "emergencies" 911 callers report boggles the mind: Some people call because they want to know when the National Football League game begins that day, some people want to know the weather report.[13] (The author witnessed one such call to a 911 dispatcher during a consulting visit in Midwest, in which the caller was reporting a goat standing on their front porch.)

▲ Today's police patrol function involves many methods of transportation other than the automobile. *(Courtesy © Jim West/Alamy.)*

Patrol Work as a Function of Shift Assignment

Although the following analysis does not apply to all jurisdictions, the nature of patrol work is very closely related to the officer's particular shift assignment. Following are general descriptions of the nature of work on each of the three daily shifts.

Officers working the *day shift* (approximately 8:00 A.M. to 4:00 P.M.) probably have the greatest contact with citizens. Officers may start their day by watching school crossings and unsnarling traffic jams. Speeding and traffic accidents are more common as people hurry to work in the morning. Officers also participate in school and civic presentations and other such programs. Most errands and nonpolice duties assigned to the police are performed by day-shift officers, such as unlocking parking lots, escorting people, delivering agendas to city council members, transporting evidence to court, and seeing that maintenance is performed on patrol vehicles. Day-shift officers are more likely to be summoned to such major crimes as armed robberies and bomb threats. This shift often has lulls, as most people are at work or in school. Usually, the officers with the most seniority work the day shift.

Officers of the *swing*, or *evening*, *shift* (4:00 P.M. to 12:00 A.M.) report to duty in time to untangle evening traffic jams and respond to a variety of complaints from the public. Youths are out of school, and shops are beginning to close; as darkness falls, officers must begin checking commercial doors and windows on their beat (new officers are amazed at the frequency with which businesspeople leave their buildings unsecured). Warm weather brings increased drinking and partying, along with noise complaints. Domestic disturbances begin to occur, and the action at bars and nightclubs is beginning to pick up—soon fights will break out. Many major events, such as athletic events and concerts, occur in the evenings, so officers often perform crowd and traffic control duties. Toward the end of the shift, fast-food restaurants and other businesses begin complaining about loitering and littering by teenagers. Arrests are much more frequent than during the day shift, and officers must attempt to take one last look at the businesses on the beat before ending their shift to ensure that none have been burglarized during the evening and night hours. That done, arrest and incident reports must be completed before officers may leave the station house for home.

The *night* (or *graveyard*) *shift* (12 A.M. to 8 A.M.) is an entirely different world. For many people, this shift has adverse effects, causing physical and psychological problems as it affects one's Circadian rhythm (also termed the "biological clock" of humans, which regulates bodily functions such as eating, sleeping, and even body temperature and hormone production) and, quite possible, one's social life as well. The night shift is usually worked by newer officers with less seniority (who also must work most weekends and holidays). While few officers probably like working this shift enough to want to devote much of their career working it, many officers actually thrive on working nights because it offers: a flurry of activity and calls for service at the outset, followed by a period of calm; less traffic is on the streets to deal with; fewer errands to run; cooler nights; and more free time to do other things such as completing offense and traffic crash reports. (Some officers would add that another benefit is having fewer departmental "brass" (administrative personnel) around.) After dark the "night people" begin to come out—those who sleep in the daytime and prowl at night, including the burglars—and thus begins the nightly cat-and-mouse game between the police and the "bad guys." Night-shift officers spend much of the night patrolling alleys and businesses, working their spotlights in search of open doors and windows in businesses and never knowing what might be lurking around the next dark corner. Such patrol work is inevitably eerie and dangerous in nature, as these officers typically work alone under the cover of darkness, often without hope of rapid backup units. Even at three or four o'clock in the morning, when boredom and fatigue begin to set in, these officers must be mentally prepared for action; when a call comes over the radio during those "wee hours," it is often a major incident or crime.

▲ Police work during hours of darkness requires extra vigilance. *(Courtesy mjay/Shutterstock.)*

Influence of an Assigned Beat

Just as the work of the patrol officer is influenced by his or her shift assignment, the nature of that work is determined by the beat assignment. Each beat has its own personality, which may be quite different from other contiguous beats in terms of its structure and demographic character, as seen in the following hypothetical examples:

- Beat A contains a university with many large crowds that attend athletic and concert events; it also contains a number of taverns and bars where students congregate, resulting in an occasional need for police presence. A large hospital is located in this sector. Residents here are predominantly middle class. A large number of shopping malls and retail businesses occupy the area. The crime rate is quite low here, as are the number of calls for service. The university commands a considerable amount of officer overtime for major events as well as general officer attention for parking problems. During university homecoming week and other major events, officers in this beat will be going from call to call while officers assigned to other beats may find themselves completely bored. One portion of the beat contains several bars that attract working-class individuals and generate several calls for service each week due to fights, traffic problems, and so forth.

- Beat B is almost totally residential in nature and is composed of the "old money" people of the community: upper- and upper-middle-class people who "encourage" routine patrols by the police. Some of the community's banks, retail businesses, and industrial complexes are also located in this area. Most people have their homes wired for security, either to a private security firm or to the local police department. The crime rate and calls for service are relatively low in this beat, but patrol covers a large amount of territory, and a major thoroughfare runs along the beat's perimeter, generating some serious traffic accidents.

- Beat C is composed primarily of blue-collar working-class residents. It generates a low to medium number of calls for service relative to the other beats, and much of its geographic area is consumed by a small airport and a large public park with a baseball diamond/golf course complex.
- Beat D is the worst in the city in terms of quality of life, residents' income levels, and police problems. Though smaller in size than the other beats, it generates a very high number of calls for service. It contains a large number of residents living on the margins of the economy, lower-income housing complexes, older mobile home parks and motels, taverns, barely surviving retail businesses, and a major railroad switching yard. Officers are constantly driving from call to call, especially during summer weekend nights. At night, officers who are engaged in calls for service—even traffic stops—are given backup by fellow officers whenever possible.

Of course, even the normal ebb and flow of beat activity is greatly altered when a critical incident occurs; for example, an act of nature (such as a tornado, an earthquake, or a fire) or a major criminal event (such as a bank robbery or a kidnapping) can wreak havoc on a beat that is normally the most placid in nature.

Three "cops' rules" are also a part of the beat culture:

1. Don't get involved in another officer's sector; "butt out" unless asked to come to a beat to assist. Each officer is accountable for his or her territory, and each officer must live with the consequences of decisions that pertain to his or her beat.

2. Don't leave work for the next duty shift; take care of such practical matters as putting gas in the patrol car and taking all necessary complaints before leaving the station house.

3. Hold up your end of the work: Don't slack off.[14]

▶ Where Danger Lurks: Occupational Hazards of Patrol

At Their Peril

Although several occupations—commercial fishing, logging, and piloting airplanes in particular—have workers dying at much higher rates than policing,[15] police officers' lives are still rife with occupational hazards. Police officers never know if the citizen they are about to confront is armed, is high on drugs or alcohol, or plans to engage in a relatively recent phenomenon known as "suicide by cop" (discussed below). Certainly an entire community, not only its police agency, is stunned when one of its officers is murdered.

Police work has always been hazardous, but a recent, alarming spike in fatal ambushes of police officers, even while violent crime is decreasing across the nation, is weighing heavily on police executives, officers, and trainers who believe a reassessment of high-risk fugitive and drug raids is in order. A U.S. Department of Justice study found that in 63 of 65 shooting deaths analyzed, nearly three-fourths of them (73 percent) were the result of ambushes or surprise attacks. In one case in Utah, one officer was killed and five others were wounded as they attempted to execute a drug-related search warrant; in Odessa,

Texas, three officers were killed as they approached a home to deal with a domestic disturbance call. Furthermore, during the first three months of 2011, five cities lost two officers each in these kinds of brutal attacks. Such a "hunter mentality" resulting in an increase of such deaths comes at a time when officers are better trained and, in most cases, wearing body armor. However, wearing body armor is no guarantee of officer safety (see Exhibit 3-1 ■); a majority of officer slayings involve shooters who ambush officers for behind and shoot at the officers' head or other unprotected areas of the body. At minimum, experts are recommending that such tactics as knocking down doors and charging inside during drug raids be replaced with either luring suspects out into the open or simply "waiting them out."[16]

Exhibit 3-1 shows the general demographic characteristics or "profile" of police officers who were feloniously killed in the line of duty in 2011. It will be seen that these officers were not of the "rookie" variety, as on average they had served for about ten years; they also tended to be slain during potentially perilous situations (e.g., making an arrest)—with a large proportion of the killers in those situations having prior arrests.

What can be learned from examining officers killed and assaulted data? Researchers determined that while no single, absolute offender profile emerged, most killers of law enforcement officers had been diagnosed as having some sort of personality disorder. Next, the victim officers were generally good-natured and more conservative than their fellow officers in the use of physical force. Finally, the killings often were facilitated by some type of procedural miscue (e.g., an improper approach to a vehicle or loss of control of a situation or individual). In sum, the study determined that these three factors combined into a "deadly mix": an easy-going officer who would use force only as a last resort, confronting an offender of aberrant behavior, and in an uncontrolled, dangerous situation.[17]

The message to officers is clear: be watchful, follow good "officer survival" procedures and training at all times, and be prepared to use some level of appropriate force if necessary. In sum, "go home safely at shift's end."

EXHIBIT 3-1

OFFICERS KILLED IN THE UNITED STATES: A PROFILE

Following is a profile of the forty-eight officers (state, local, federal, tribal, and campus) who were feloniously killed during 2012:

- The average age of the slain officers was thirty-eight years; they had worked in law enforcement for about twelve years.

- Most of the fifty-one identified assailants (33, or 65 percent) had prior arrests; they averaged thirty-two years of age, and were nearly all male.

- The officers were typically murdered with a firearm (44, or 92 percent); of these, two-thirds (32 percent) were slain with handguns.

- The majority of the forty-eight victim officers were either feloniously killed during an arrest situation (12, or 25 percent), while investigating suspicious persons (8, or 17 percent), during a traffic pursuit or stop (8, or 17 percent), or an ambush (6, or 13 percent).

- Nearly half (22, or 46 percent) of the slain officers were employed in the South.

Note that an additional forty-seven officers died in accidents during 2012; twenty-two (47 percent) of these deaths involved traffic accidents—and about 53,000 officers were assaulted while on duty.

Source: Officers Killed in the United States: A Profile, Uniform Crime Reports: Law Enforcement Officers Killed and Assaulted, Federal Bureau of Investigation, 2011.

▲ Shown is a small portion of the National Law Enforcement Officers Memorial Fund museum in Washington, D.C.; in late 2012 there were 19,660 names engraved on the memorial's walls. *(Courtesy Photo by National Law Enforcement Officers Memorial Fund.)*

A final note on danger: Although federal agents are not engaged in patrol functions, the Federal Bureau of Investigation announced in early 2013 that it would be modifying its three-decade-old firearms training regimen. Following a review of nearly 200 shootings found that about three-fourths of incidents in which agents confront suspects occur

▲ The patrol function often takes officers to places that are "brutish" and dangerous. *(Courtesy Andreas Meyer/Shutterstock.)*

at point-blank range—within three yards of agents when shots are fired—the simulated firearms training exercises that agents undergo will now have agents firing two-thirds of their rounds at targets that are from between three and seven yards away.[18] State and local agencies would be wise to examine such data and their firearms training regimens as well.

Suicide by Cop

A type of incident that certainly poses serious potential for danger to the police is suicide by cop, which is defined as "an act motivated in whole or in part by the offender's desire to commit suicide that results in a justifiable homicide by a law enforcement officer."[19]

Presently, the extent of the suicide by cop phenomenon remains unknown for two reasons:

1. Lack of both a clear definition and established reporting procedures
2. Immediate removal of suicide attempts from the criminal process and placement within the mental health arena, causing the police investigation to cease and preventing an agency from identifying a potential threat to its officers

Although it is difficult to measure, one study by a medical organization of deputy-involved shootings in the Los Angeles County, California, Sheriff's Department found that suicide by cop incidents accounted for 11 percent of all deputy-involved shootings and 13 percent of all deputy-involved justifiable homicides. The report concluded that suicide by cop constitutes an actual form of suicide.[20]

Case Study While each case of suicide by cop is different, following is an actual example of how such incidents occur:

> An officer is dispatched to an apartment building in response to a woman yelling for help. Upon arriving at the location, the officer observes a woman standing on the front steps. The officer is waved inside, and as she enters the apartment she hears a man yelling, then sees him standing in the kitchen area. When the male observes the female officer, he produces a large butcher knife and holds the blade of the knife firmly against his stomach with both hands; he appears highly intoxicated, agitated, and angry. The officer draws her service weapon and orders the man to put down the knife. The offender responds by stating, "[Expletive] you, kill me!" The officer attempts to talk with the offender, who responds by turning around and slicing himself severely on his forearm, bleeding profusely. The officer repeatedly asks him to drop the knife. The offender begins to advance toward the officer, telling her to shoot him while still ignoring her commands to drop the knife. From a distance of approximately 12 feet, he raises the knife in a threatening manner and charges the officer; she fires her weapon, striking him in the chest and hand, killing him.[21]

Arms and Armor for Duty

Jerome Skolnick and David Bayley describe how officers prepare to face the beat's dangers on their tour of duty:

> Policing in the United States is very much like going to war. Three times a day in countless locker rooms, large men and a growing number of women carefully arm and armor themselves for the day's events. They begin by strapping on [body armor]. Then they pick up a wide, heavy, black leather belt and hang around it the tools of their trade: gun, mace, handcuffs, bullets. When it is fully loaded they swing the belt around their hips with the same practiced motion of the gunfighter in Western movies, slugging it down and buckling

it in front. Inspecting themselves in a full-length mirror, officers thread their night sticks into a metal ring on the side of their belt.[22]

—Excerpt from "How Officers Prepare To Face The Beat's Dangers On Their Tour Of Duty" by Jerome H Skolnick and David H Bayley from THE NEW BLUE LINE: POLICE INNOVATION IN SIX AMERICAN CITIES. Published by The Free Press, © 1986.

As John Crank states, "This is not a picture of American youth dressing for public servitude. These are warriors going to battle, the New Centurions, as Wambaugh calls them. In their dress and demeanor lies the future of American policing."[23] As Crank also observes, police recognize many citizens for what they are: "Dangerous, unpredictable, violent, savagely cunning . . . in a world of capable and talented reptilian, mammalian . . . predators."[24]

This depiction of the people officers confront on the beat may seem overly contrived, exaggerated, or brusque. Most patrol officers with any length of service, however, can attest to the fact that certain members of our society are, as one officer put it, "irretrievable predators that just get off . . . on people's pain and on people's crying and begging and pleading. They don't have any sense of morality, [and] they don't have any sense of right and wrong."[25] During their careers, most patrol officers are verbally threatened by such individuals; they take the great majority of such threats with a grain of salt. Occasionally, however, the "irretrievable predator" who possesses no sense of morality will issue such a threat, which the officer will (and must) take quite seriously. This is a very disconcerting part of the job.

The importance of patrol officers providing backup to one another—especially during the hours of darkness—cannot be overstated, as described by Anthony Bouza:

> The sense of "us vs. them" that develops between cops and the outside world forges a bond between cops whose strength is fabled. It is widened by the dependence cops have on each other for safety and backup. The response to help is a cop's life-line. An "assist police officer" is every cop's first priority. The ultimate betrayal is for one cop to fail to back up another.[26]

—Excerpt from THE POLICE MYSTIQUE by Anthony V Bouza. Published by Da Capo Press-Plenum Publishing Corp.

In this same vein, patrol officers quickly come to know on whom they can count when everything "hits the fan"—which officers will race to assist another officer at a barroom brawl, a felony in progress, and so on—and which will not.

H.R. 218

A relatively new legislative enactment, the Law Enforcement Officers Safety Act of 2004 (H.R. 218), exempts qualified police officers from state laws prohibiting the carrying of concealed weapons and allows retired officers having at least fifteen years of service to carry a firearm.[27] The purpose of the act, its supporters state, is to afford these retired officers "protection of themselves, their families and our nation's communities." Retired officers who carry weapons under this law do not possess any police powers or immunities in other states, however, and are personally responsible for checking and understanding the laws of any jurisdictions they visit while armed.[28]

▶ The Officer's "Rolling Office"

A Sanctuary

The patrol vehicle is perhaps the most underappreciated and ignored aspect of police work—by both scholars and officers themselves. The patrol vehicle warrants greater attention because it is not only a place where officers on patrol spend a great deal of their time but also their sanctuary. It contains the myriad vital tools for accomplishing their work and, to a great extent, represents their authority.

The patrol vehicle is generally safe and comfortable, containing several essential accoutrements (a radio, spotlight, and weapons such as a shotgun or rifle) that contribute to the officer's safety. It is a mobile haven, providing comfort from inclement climates as well as against humans who would hurt the officer. The patrol car provides access to the tools of defense and is a safe place to deposit combative prisoners for transport.

Vital tools can also be stored in or mounted on the vehicle, which serves as a virtual office: the radio (for summoning assistance), warning lights and siren, defensive weapons (e.g., a shotgun or other firearm as well as a TASER electronic control device [ECD], baton, or other less lethal tool), possibly an onboard computer and video recorder, flares, cameras, and other evidence-gathering equipment. In addition, on the graveyard shift, the vehicle's spotlight can be one of the officer's greatest assets. 3 9

The police vehicle also is a rolling symbol of authority. For this reason, few people enjoy seeing a police vehicle appear in their rearview mirror; for some, it is a prelude to being issued a traffic citation or, worse, being taken to jail. Still, it can be stated that since the first police car appeared, citizens have been fascinated with the speed and imposing appearance of these vehicles.

In addition to the traditional beefed-up engines, heavy suspension, and upgraded electrical systems, some patrol cars contain additional features that mean a lot to the officers on patrol. For example, new models come with plates in the driver's seatback to protect against assault from the rear, cutouts in the driver's seat for a holster, extra-long safety belts, reinforced front steel beams and higher-rated tires for high-speed pursuits, a voice-recognition system for accessing onboard computers, a camera mounted in the overhead light bar with output to a laptop computer, an aircraft-style "blue box" accident data recorder, and crush-resistant bumpers.[29]

Exhibit 3-2 ■ describes how the demise of the Ford Crown Victoria, which remained largely unchanged since 1992, has ushered in a new generation of police vehicles—and generated a high degree of competition for police-vehicle market dominance.

EXHIBIT 3-2

THE DEMISE OF THE "CROWN VIC" VEHICLE, AND THE RISE OF A NEW GENERATION

Many police officers spend more time sitting in their patrol vehicles (or "squad car") than sitting in their home's reclining chairs; therefore, the nature of the vehicle in which they must patrol for long hours is a topic of great interest to them. Certainly the demise of the iconic Ford Crown Victoria in late-2011 caused many officers such concern in terms of what their agencies would purchase as replacements. Three top automakers are vying to dominate the market for police vehicles, and each has developed a new sedan to fill the gap.

Chevrolet created a 6.0L V8 Caprice Police Patrol Vehicle (PPV); it is advertised as having seven cubic feet more interior space than the other two competitors, and has upgrades that include larger brakes, a six-speed automatic transmission, and better stability and weigh distribution.

Dodge offers a Charger Pursuit with a 5.7L HEMI V8 engine, and includes driver's knee airbags, multistage front air bags, side-curtain airbags, rain brakes, traction control, stability control, and brake assist.

Ford has a new rear-wheel drive Police Interceptor with a 3.5L twin-turbo V6 engine and side-curtain airbags, wide-opening rear door hinges, reinforced subframe, bigger brakes, upgraded suspension, a voice-activated communications system, radar-powered cross-traffic sensors, and a blind-spot alert system.

The Los Angeles Police Department opted for Chevrolet's PPV, each of which is to be outfitted with two automatic license plate readers (that can scan eight plates at once and is connected to a criminal database), an infrared camera allowing officers to see minute details such as offenders' footprints in the dark, and a GPS attached to a computer-aided dispatch system to streamline calls of distress.

Source: "The Demise of the Crown Vic Vehicle, and the Rise of a New Generation" from SAYING GOODBYE TO THE CROWN VICTORIA POLICE CAR SAD FOR SOME, GOVERNMENT TECHNOLOGY. Published by Government Technology, © 2011.

Patrolling on Two Wheels

The escalating costs of gasoline that began in mid-2008 caused police agencies to rethink their vehicle patrol methods. Following are some of the changes that were put into effect as gas prices escalated across the United States; many of these modifications will be continued now and into the future, given the ongoing increases and unstable nature of U.S. fuel costs:

- Many officers lost the right to take their patrol cars home, or they were forced to pay for the privilege.
- Officers in some communities were told to turn off their ignition whenever they are stopped and idling for more than a minute.[30]
- Some departments switched to lower octane gasoline and installed GPS receivers in patrol cars to make dispatching more efficient.
- Some state troopers have begun sitting and monitoring traffic rather than cruising the highways, and they have increased their use of single-engine airplanes to look for speeders.[31]

Motorcycle traffic enforcement is increasingly used to assist in attempts to reduce the incidences of aggressive driving, impaired driving, speeding, and red-light running. The use of motorcycle patrol units dates to 1909, when mounted officers abandoned their horses in lieu of transportation that could keep up with the rapidly evolving motor vehicle. These specialized enforcement units are capable of diverse assignments and, due to their build, can reach a crash scene more quickly than their four-wheeled counterparts. Motorcycle patrol officers also assume a community-policing role because citizens typically tend to be more comfortable approaching an officer on a motorcycle without the perceived barrier of an enclosed vehicle. Motorcycle patrol officers are also called upon to conduct traffic safety presentations to various civic groups and organizations and are frequently used for dignitary escort and ceremonial duties.[32]

Bicycles as a means of patrol (as well as foot patrols) have declined somewhat in recent years. A recent federal Bureau of Justice Statistics survey found that only 32 percent of police agencies of all sizes used bicycles.[33] There are distinct benefits to using bicycles on patrol, however; Chris Menton determined the following:

- Bike patrols had more than double the number of contacts with people, per hour, as officers patrolling in cars

▲ An in-car computer. A GPS is mounted on the top right of the monitor. *(Courtesy Kenneth J. Peak.)*

EXHIBIT 3-3

PATROLLING ON PADDLEBOARDS

Truckee, California, with a population of about 16,000, is located in the northeastern part of the state on Interstate 80, close to Lake Tahoe and encompassing Donner Lake, which has nearly 1,000 acres of surface area. The Truckee Police Department recently unveiled a new program, the Adventure Recreation Community (ARC) team, which includes officers patrolling Donner Lake by rotating between paddleboards, mountain bikes, and a boat. Stand-up paddleboarding is performed by four cross-trained officers who are allowed to flex their schedules around community events. The sport has evolved in the area from a time when only a few people paddleboarded and few retail outlets sold the devices—many boarders having to use old windsurfing boards as a substitute— to the contemporary situation where numerous people paddleboard, several businesses sell the boards, and there are annual board races on the lake. The natural beauty of the area brings many boarders to the lake, and rather than focusing on increasing enforcement or addressing crime-related issues, the ARC program emphases include officers interacting with others on boards, engaging the outdoor community in Truckee, and emphasizing safety to people on the lake and residing in the area. Officers are trained in rescuing people who are involved in water emergencies, and view their role as providing a consistent, community-oriented philosophy.

Source: "Patrolling on Paddleboards" by Jaclyn O'Malley from PADDLEBOARDS MAKE POLICE PART OF TRUCKEE AREA'S ACTIVE LIFESTYLE. Copyright © 2012 by Reno Gazette-Journal. Used by permission of Reno Gazette-Journal.

- Bicycle officers did essentially the same level of serious and nonserious work as motor patrols.
- Incidents of public drinking, urination, and drug use were more readily discovered and dealt with by bicycle officers (the issue of stealth is important here; there is often no time for offenders to hide their drugs or open containers of alcohol).
- Bike officers have enhanced access, using alternative routes (including closed roads, sidewalks, alleyways, footpaths, and so on).[34]

Today hundreds of venues are also patrolling on their battery-powered Segways. Launched in 2001, the battery-powered Segway is, of course, much cheaper to operate than a patrol car, but it is also marketed as providing officers with more mobility than a bicycle and the ability to negotiate large crowds quickly and easily. Models come equipped with a siren, saddle bags to carry forms and other materials, and even an alarm that allows officers to park the machine while tending to business without fear of it being stolen.[35]

▶ Discretionary Use of Police Authority

Myth of Full Enforcement

The municipal police chief or county sheriff is asked during a civic club luncheon speech which laws are and are not enforced by his or her agency. The official response will inevitably be that *all* of the laws are enforced equally, all of the time. Yet the chief or sheriff knows that full enforcement of the laws is a myth—that neither the resources nor the desire to enforce them all is available, nor are all laws enforced impartially. It is neither prudent nor politically wise to list the offenses for which the police treat some offenders more harshly or more leniently or for which they look the other way (and *non*enforcement of laws is a form of discretion). There are legal concerns as well. For example, releasing some offenders (e.g., to get information about other crimes or because of a good excuse) cannot be the official policy of the agency; however, the chief or sheriff cannot broadcast that fact to the public.

Indeed, it has been stated that the "single most astonishing fact of police behavior is the extent to which police do *not* enforce the law when they have every legal right to do so."[36] As an example, police scholar George Kelling described a Newark, New Jersey, street cop with whom he spent many hours walking a beat:

> As he saw his job, he was to keep an eye on strangers, and make certain that the disreputable regulars observed some informal but widely understood rules. Drunks and addicts could sit on the stoops, but could not lie down. People could drink on side streets, but not at the main intersection. Bottles had to be in paper bags. Talking to, bothering or begging from people waiting at the bus stop was strictly forbidden. Persons who broke the informal rules, especially [the latter], were arrested for vagrancy. Noisy teenagers were told to keep quiet.[37]
>
> —Excerpt from BROKEN WINDOWS: THE POLICE AND NEIGHBORHOOD SAFETY, ATLANTIC MONTHLY by George L Kelling and James Q Wilson. Published by Tribune Media Services, © 1982.

This quote points out the inextricable link between the patrol function and discretionary use of police authority: We cannot have one without the other.

Attempts to Define Discretion

Scholarly knowledge about the way police make decisions is limited. What is known, however, is that when police observe something of a suspicious or illegal nature, two important decisions must be made: (1) whether to intervene in the situation and (2) how to intervene. The kind, number, and possible combination of interventions are virtually limitless. What kinds of decisions are available for an officer who makes a routine traffic stop? David Bayley and Egon Bittner observed long ago that officers have as many as 10 actions from which to select at the initial stop (e.g., order the driver out of the car), 7 strategies appropriate during the stop (e.g., a roadside sobriety test), and 11 exit strategies (e.g., releasing the driver with a warning), representing a total of 770 different combinations of actions that might be taken![38]

Criminal law has two sides: the formality and the reality. The formality is found in the statute books and opinions of appellate courts; the reality is found in the practices of enforcement officers. In some circumstances, the choice of action to be taken is relatively easy, such as arresting a bank robbery suspect, but in other situations, such as quelling a dispute between neighbors, the choice is more difficult. Drinking in the park is a crime according to many local ordinances, but quietly drinking at a family picnic without disturbing others is not a crime according to the reality of the law because officers uniformly refuse to enforce the ordinance in such circumstances. When the formality and the reality differ, the reality prevails.[39]

These examples demonstrate why the use of discretion is one of the major challenges facing U.S. police today. The system tends to treat people as individuals: One person who commits a robbery is not the same as another person who commits a robbery because the system takes into account why and how a person committed a crime (his or her intent, or *mens rea*). With the U.S. judicial process, when one person shoots another, a variety of possible outcomes can occur. The most important decisions take place on the streets, day or night, generally without the opportunity for the officer to consult with others or to carefully consider all the facts.

Determinants of Officer Discretion

The U.S. government is supposed to be based on laws, not on people. That axiom is simply a myth—at least in the manner in which the law is applied. Official discretion pervades all levels and most agencies of government. The discretionary power of the police is awesome. Kenneth Culp Davis, an authority on police discretion, writes, "The police are among the most important policy makers of our entire society. And they make far more discretionary determinations in individual cases than does any other class of administrators; I know of no close second."[40]

What determines whether the officer will take a stern approach (enforcing the letter of the law with an arrest) or will be lenient (issuing a verbal warning or some other outcome short of arrest)? Several variables enter into the officer's decision:

1. The *law* is indeed a factor in discretionary use of police authority. For example, many state statutes and local ordinances now mandate that the police arrest for certain suspected offenses, such as driving under the influence or committing domestic violence.

2. The *officer's attitude* can also be a factor. First, some officers are more willing to empathize with offenders who feel they deserve a break than others. Also, as Carl Klockars and Stephen Mastrofski observed, although violators frequently offer what they feel are very good reasons for the officer to overlook their offense, "every police officer knows that, if doing so will allow them to escape punishment, most people are prepared to lie through their teeth."[41] What also makes situations awkward is that the officer cannot comfortably acknowledge the real reasons for denying a citizen's appeal for discretion. Imagine a police officer saying to a traffic violator, "The city depends on traffic fines for revenue," "Sorry, I don't like people like you," "Sorry, I don't think your excuse is good enough," or "Sorry, but I don't believe you."[42] Furthermore, police officers, being human, can bring to work either a happy or an unhappy disposition. If, on the same day as reporting for duty, the officer received an IRS notice saying back taxes were owed, had a nasty spat with a significant other, and was bitten while picking up the family pet shortly before leaving for work, he or she might naturally be more inclined to enforce the letter of the law rather than dispense leniency. Personal views toward specific types of crimes also play a role; for example, perhaps the officer is fed up with juvenile crimes that have been occurring of late and thus will not give any leniency to youths he or she confronts who are involved in even minor crimes.

3. Another major consideration in the officer's choice among various options is the *citizen's attitude*. If the offender is rude and condescending, denies having done anything wrong, or uses some of the standard clichés that are almost guaranteed to rankle the officer—such as "You don't know who I am" (someone who is obviously very important in the community), "I'll have your job," "I know the chief of police," "I'm a taxpayer, and I pay your salary"—the probable outcome is obvious. On the other hand, the person who is honest with the officer, avoids attempts at intimidation and sarcasm, and does not try to "beat the rap" may fare better.

Several studies have found that not only a citizen's demeanor but also his or her social class, sex, age, and race influence the decisions made by patrol officers.[43] This possible discrimination on the part of officers points out that the police—like other citizens—are subject to stereotypes and biases that will affect their behavior.

Pros, Cons, and Politics of Discretionary Authority

Several ironies are connected with the way in which the police apply discretion. First is the inverse relationship between the officers' rank and the amount of discretion that is available. In other words, as the rank of the officer increases, the amount of discretion that he or she can employ normally decreases. The street officer makes discretionary decisions all the time, including decisions about whether to arrest, search, seize property, and so forth. But the chief of police, who does very little actual police work, may be very constrained by department, union, affirmative action, or governing board guidelines and policies. Furthermore, the chief of police knows that neither the resources nor the desire are readily available to enforce all the laws that are broken.

In addition, the issue of police discretion is shrouded in controversy. Various arguments are made both for and against discretion. Advantages include that it allows the officer to treat different situations in accordance with humanitarian and practical goals. For example, an officer pulls over a speeding motorist, only to learn that the car is en route to the hospital with a woman who is about to deliver a baby. While the agitated driver is endangering everyone in the vehicle as well as other motorists on the roadway, discretion allows the officer to be compassionate and empathetic, giving the car a safe escort to the hospital rather than issuing a citation for speeding. In short, discretionary use of authority allows the police to employ a philosophy of justice tempered with mercy.

Conversely, discretion can also carry the specter of impartiality—the ability of officers to treat different people differently for committing essentially the same offense. Critics of discretion also argue that such wide latitude in decision making may serve as a breeding ground for police corruption; for example, an officer may be offered a bribe to overlook an offense. And as Lawrence Sherman observed, another problem is that the police do not know the consequences of their discretionary decisions. He contrasted the police with artisans and navigators who receive feedback on the effects of their decisions. The police, however, have failed to create a feedback information system that tells them what happens after they leave a call or even after they make an arrest. Thus police lack knowledge about the effects of their discretionary actions on suspects, victims, witnesses, and potential criminals.[44]

Certain aspects of policing will never be completely free of discretion, however; to a large extent, the work of a police officer is unsupervised and unsupervisable. As the police strive to achieve professionalism, they will remember that discretion is a key element of a profession.

Police discretion is also part of the American political process.[45] As Kenneth Culp Davis observed, a major contributing factor to police discretion is that state legislative commands are ambiguous. Legislatures speak with three voices: (1) they enact state statutes that seemingly require full enforcement of the laws, (2) they provide only enough resources for limited enforcement of them, and (3) they consent to such limited enforcement.[46] Some observers have even questioned the legality and morality of police discretion.[47] It might also be added that the statute books are often treated as society's "trash bins." A particular behavior is viewed negatively, so a law is passed against it, and the police are stuck with the dilemma of having to enforce or ignore what may be an overly broad or unpopular law.

Other aspects of politics are found in police discretion. For example, several state and local governments restricted police use of deadly force long before the U.S. Supreme Court did away with the common law "fleeing felon" doctrine in *Tennessee* v. *Garner* (1985).[48]

▶ A Related Function: Traffic

A major figure in policing in the mid-1900s, O. W. Wilson, reportedly said that "the police traffic function overshadows every other function." That may be an overstatement today, but a strong link still exists between the patrol function and traffic control. Traffic stops account for about half (52 percent) of the contact Americans have with the police.[49] Therefore, the importance of a seemingly trivial traffic stop cannot be overstated because the manner in which the officer conducts the stop may in large measure determine the citizen's view of the police for many years to come.

Note that in this section our focus is on the police traffic function alone. In Chapter 8, which deals generally with police accountability, we extend this discussion to include accusations of racial bias that can flow from traffic stops that subsequently involve searches of citizens.

Enforcement of Traffic Laws: Triumph and Trouble

The number of U.S. traffic deaths has declined over the past six decades (largely due to airbag and safety belt use, better traffic enforcement and engineering, public education, and drunk driver legislation); still, more than 32,000 motorists, bicyclists, and pedestrians are killed each year on U.S. roadways.[50] That number is expected to increase, however, as the economy improves (and people drive more) and distracted driving continues to be a problem.

Police endeavor to reduce traffic deaths and injuries through the enforcement of traffic laws, and on its face, this is a noble undertaking. But this is a very delicate area of contact between citizens and their police. Indeed, citizens may have their one and only contact with a police officer because of some traffic-related matter; therefore, the extent to which the officer displays a professional demeanor—and the attitude and demeanor projected by the citizen—may well have long-term effects for both and carry long-term significance for both community policing (which relies heavily on community teamwork) and public relations. More than a few bond issues to hire new officers, purchase new equipment, or build a new station house have been defeated at the ballot box because of ill will created by the police traffic function.

Levels of traffic enforcement differ, too. Some departments are relatively lenient, but others have initiated ticket quotas, and some jurisdictions pressure their officers to have a "ticket blizzard" to generate revenue. Aside from often being rankled by having to pay a fine, many citizens also believe the police should be engaged in other "more important" functions ("Why aren't you out catching bank robbers?"). Therefore, traffic stops can be a major source of friction between police officers and citizens, and strict traffic enforcement policies can negatively impact police–community relations.[51] Furthermore, because of "extinction"—the process of people forgetting about the traffic citation they received and the need to obey traffic laws—the long- and even short-term deterrent effects of handing out traffic citations have been called into question.[52]

Despite citizen disgruntlement with traffic enforcement, traffic stops and citations generally remain an integral part of police work. Police administrators find such work to be easily verifiable evidence that their officers are working.[53] Traffic enforcement has even gone high tech with the advent of the traffic camera, which has been nicknamed "the photocop." Traffic cameras, either mounted on a mobile tripod or permanently fixed on a pole, emit a narrow beam of radar that triggers a flash camera when the targeted vehicle is exceeding the speed limit by a certain amount, usually ten miles per hour.

Police in Berkeley, California, have applied a new twist to the traffic function. Drivers who are "caught" driving safely and courteously are stopped and issued coupons good for movies or free nonalcoholic beverages at a local cafe. This Good Driver Recognition Program, which began with officers' donations, now receives city funding.[54]

Traffic Crash Investigation

Patrol officers have long been required to investigate traffic crashes. (*Note*: The long-used term *traffic accident* is increasingly being replaced with *traffic crash* or *collision* because *accident* implies that the crash was unintended, but with the increase in road rage incidents and other uses of motor vehicles as weapons, *collision* can include both intended and unintended crashes.) In this era of accountability and litigation, and due to the vast amount of damage done to people and property each year as a result of traffic crashes, it is essential that officers understand this process of investigation and cite the guilty party—not only from a law enforcement standpoint but also in the event that the matter is taken to civil court. Until officers receive formal training in this complex field, they are in a very precarious position.

▲ Traffic collision investigation is a major part of the police role. *(Courtesy Liga Alksne/ Shutterstock.)*

In addition to basic traffic crash investigation (TAI) training normally provided at the police academy, several agencies offer good in-service courses, and Northwestern University has a renowned crash investigation program. The process of analyzing road and damage evidence, estimating speeds, reconstructing what occurred and why, issuing citations properly, drawing a diagram of the scene, and explaining what happened in court is too important to be left to untrained officers. The public demands skilled crash investigations.

Pursuit of the "Phantom" Driver

One of the traffic-related areas in which the police enjoy wide public support is their efforts to identify, apprehend, and convict the hit-and-run (or "phantom") driver. No one thinks highly of these drivers (who are often intoxicated) who collide with another vehicle or person and leave the scene. This matter requires more of a criminal investigation than a crash investigation for the police. In some states, the killing of a human being by someone driving under the influence (DUI) is a felony. Physical evidence and witness statements must be collected in the same fashion as in a conventional criminal investigation; paint samples and automobile parts left at the scene are sent to crime laboratories for examination. The problem for the police is that unless the driver of the vehicle is identified—by physical evidence, an eyewitness, or a confession—the case can be lost. If the phantom vehicle is located, the owner can simply tell the police that his or her vehicle was stolen or is on loan. Thus, the police often must resort to psychology to get a confession by convincing the suspect that incriminating evidence exists.

Chapter 14, dealing with police technology, contains information on the use of the Global Positioning System (GPS) for investigating traffic accidents.

▶ Officers on Display: Appearance, Uniforms, and Dress Codes

The police are paramilitary in nature; as such, in addition to being hierarchical in organization, with rank and chain of command (as discussed in Chapter 11), they are typically uniformed (unless assigned to undercover work). And, as two authors stated, "The uniform stands out as one of the most important visual representations of the law enforcement profession."[55]

From the moment a neophyte officer puts on a uniform, his or her world changes; the officer is immediately and uniquely set apart from society. For some, the uniform seems to be a target for all kinds of verbal abuse and even fists or bullets; for others, it is a welcome symbol of legal authority. In any case, the uniform and the overall appearance of police officers have several psychological and legal aspects, as we will see in the following sections.

Legal Aspects

Succinctly put, police administrators have long been able to regulate the appearance of their officers. In *Kelley* v. *Johnson*[56] (1976), the U.S. Supreme Court held that police agencies have a legitimate, "rational" interest in establishing such rules and regulations. There, the Suffolk County (New York) Police Department's hair-grooming standards applicable to male members of the police force (governing the style and length of hair, sideburns, and mustaches and prohibiting goatees) were attacked as violating officers' First and Fourteenth Amendments rights of expression and liberty. The Supreme Court upheld such regulations, on the grounds they:

> may be based on a desire to make police officers readily recognizable to the members of the public, or a desire for the esprit de corps which such similarity is felt to inculcate within the police force itself. Either one is a sufficiently rational justification for regulations.[57]

Therefore, police administrators can dictate how the uniform will be worn—as well as other aspects of personal appearance (discussed below).

Psychological Aspects

Why do most agencies insist that patrol officers dress in uniforms? Certainly officers' uniforms convey power and authority; in addition, the uniform elicits stereotypes about that person's status, attitudes, and motivations. The uniform identifies a person with powers to arrest and use force and establishes order, as well as conformity within the ranks of those who wear it by suppressing individuality.[58]

Research has consistently supported suggestions about the police uniform's power and authority. In one study, individuals ranked twenty five different occupational uniforms by several categories of feelings. The test subjects consistently ranked the police uniform as the one most likely to induce feelings of safety. Studies have also shown that people consistently rate models as more competent, reliable, intelligent, and helpful when pictured in a police uniform, rather than in casual clothes.[59]

Details about a police officer's uniform, such as the style of hat or the tailoring, can also influence the level of authority emanating from the officer. For example, studies show that the traditional "bus driver" garrison cap and the "Smoky the Bear" campaign hat conveyed more authority than the baseball cap or no hat at all.[60]

An interesting experiment in deviation from the conventional police uniform occurred in 1969, in the Menlo Park, California, Police Department (MPPD). There, hoping to improve police–community relations, the police discontinued their traditional navy blue, paramilitary-style uniforms and adopted a uniform that consisted of a forest green blazer worn over black slacks, a white shirt, and a black tie. Officers displayed their badges on the blazer and concealed their weapons under the coat. Eventually, more than 400 other police departments in the United States also experimented with a blazer-style uniform.[61]

The initial results were promising: After wearing the new uniforms for eighteen months, MPPD officers displayed fewer authoritarian characteristics when compared to officers in the surrounding jurisdictions. Also, after wearing the uniforms for about a year, assaults on MPPD officers decreased by 30 percent and injuries to civilians by the police dropped 50 percent (however, other variables were deemed to be responsible for these decreases as well). The number of college-educated officers in the department increased dramatically, and the agency abolished its traditional autocratic management style during this same time period.[62]

After eight years of officers wearing blazers, however, the MPPD dropped the blazer concept, determining that it did not command respect, and returned to a traditional, paramilitary-style uniform. A final evaluation showed that, although assaults on officers had dropped during the first eighteen months of the new uniform implementation, the number of assaults steadily began to rise again until it doubled the amount of the year before the uniform change occurred. During the initial four-year period after MPPD officers returned to a traditional uniform, the number of assaults on their officers dropped steadily.[63]

Instituting (and Enforcing) a Dress Code

Many, if not most, police agencies have general orders or policies constituting a dress code—how their officers will dress and their general appearance—so as to project a professional image and have officers be properly groomed.[64] Such dress codes might address such matters as the length of hair, sideburns, beards, and goatees (whether or not they are permitted); types of sunglasses to be worn (mirrored, for example, are often banned); and tattoos (whether or not any body art is to be permitted for officers, and if they are to be covered while on duty).The wearing of uniforms and displaying of tattoos, bodily hair, and beards are only the tip of the iceberg, however. Regulations might also spell out, for example, when officers are to begin wearing their summer and winter uniforms (specified dates normally occurring in spring and fall) and the proper components of each uniform (the list can specify certain types of socks, shoes, turtleneck, patches and insignia, and prohibitions against wearing items of clothing with an identifying logo—so the jurisdiction will not be seen as endorsing a particular name brand).

Imposing the will of the police administration concerning officers' appearance and attire is not always as easy as it might appear, however; today officers show little reluctance to file lawsuits if feeling that such codes violate their rights to freedom of expression:

- A northeastern Pennsylvania man sued in late 2009, claiming his rights were violated when he was not hired with the state police because he would not have his arm tattoo removed. Applicants' tattoos are subject to review by the Tattoo and Replica Review Committee, which can insist they be removed before a job will be offered. The lawsuit seeks to determine whether "the government can require you to physically alter your body in exchange for employment," and infringes on the applicant's "freedom of choice in personal matters."[65]

- The Houston City Council voted to spend up to $150,000 to hire outside lawyers to defend the city's no-beard policy for police. Four black officers filed a federal civil rights lawsuit against the city, claiming discrimination because shaving exacerbates a skin condition that disproportionately affects black men; officers with beards are barred from wearing the Houston Police Department uniform.[66] In March 2010 a federal appeals court upheld the city's policy, saying it was not racially discriminatory.

- Des Moines, Iowa, police policy states that any tattoos, branding and intentional scarring on the face, head, neck, hands, and exposed arms and legs are prohibited. Employees who already have tattoos are exempt. The police union says the policy is unreasonable and has filed a grievance.[67]

- Other agencies have implemented or are considering policies that would require officers to either not be tattooed, or to cover the tattoos completely when on duty.[68]

As mentioned, there are certainly several legal and psychological aspects of police uniforms and dress codes. This is an area where the views of administrators toward officers' uniforms and appearance may well inherently clash with the street officers' viewpoints, as the latter tries to be more "expressive" in an era when tattoos and facial hair are more commonplace and less stigmatized.

▶ The Patrol Lifeline: Dispatchers and Communications

One group of police employees—often civilians—that a majority of police officers would no doubt say qualifies as their "unsung heroes" are police dispatchers, also called communications specialists. Neophyte police officers soon learn to highly value and rely on the knowledge, insight, and assistance of their dispatchers; they know their lives and safety may literally depend on the dispatcher's ability to determine the type, seriousness, and location of calls for service. In fact, their role is so critical that many agencies require their dispatchers to have first worked as patrol officers for a substantial amount of time in order to fully understand what the officers are facing and feeling while on patrol.

Dispatchers generally work in a centralized communications center. When handling calls, the information obtained is posted either electronically by computer or, with decreasing frequency, by hand. The dispatcher then quickly decides the priority of the incident, the kind and number of units needed, and the location of the closest and most suitable units available.

Dispatchers often are the first people the public contacts when emergency assistance is required. If certified for emergency medical services, the dispatcher may also provide medical instruction to those on the scene of the emergency and to citizens at home before the emergency personnel arrive. Particularly where communications services are combined or regional, a single dispatcher may also be responsible to take citizens' calls for, and to dispatch, fire fighters, ambulance personnel, sheriff's deputies, other outlying police department units, state troopers, and fish and game wardens.[69]

▲ Computer-aided dispatch (CAD) systems help dispatchers to provide vital information—and be a "lifeline"—to officers responding to calls for service. *(Courtesy Citrus Height Police Department.)*

Summary

This chapter has examined several issues related to the patrol function, which can be fairly stated as being the essence of policing. It discussed the purposes and nature of patrol; the influence of an officer's shift and beat; some hazards involved with patrol duties; the discretionary authority of patrol officers; the traffic function; the nature and purposes of various patrol vehicles; the legal and psychological significance of the patrol uniform; and the vital importance of the dispatch or communications function.

It was demonstrated that the patrol function is truly the backbone of policing, the primary means by which the police fulfill their mission. As noted, patrol officers do the work of community policing and problem solving, and they are the eyes and ears of the police organization. Patrol is the beginning point for all other specialized and administrative assignments, where citizens go to lodge concerns and complaints and where the needs of the community are met.

Because of the importance of patrol, researchers have tried to determine what works on patrol, and research findings on the patrol function were also presented—clearly it concerns more than just "driving around." Perhaps we have not yet reached the point of understanding how to best deploy patrol officers to their maximum effect, but research is demonstrating that some patrolling methods, which for decades were felt to be "tried and true," are myths and do not work. Ongoing research on the patrol function is needed. The fundamental—and seemingly simple—police task of seeing and being seen is indeed complicated and challenging. Knowledge of patrol utilization and effectiveness becomes more crucial because research has shown the crime-solving ability of detectives to be overrated. We have also seen that the street cop performs a variety of duties while using wide discretion in deciding how to handle problems. In essence, this chapter has attempted to put readers in the patrol officer's position by giving them a sense of what's involved in that profession.

Key Terms

beat assignment	dress code	patrol function
beat culture	Kansas City Preventive Patrol	patrol vehicle
deployment	Experiment	shift assignment
discretionary use of police authority	Law Enforcement Officers Safety Act of 2004 (H. R. 218)	suicide by cop traffic control
dispatcher	occupational hazards	uniform

Review Questions

1. What are some of the major findings of studies of the patrol function? (Include in your answer findings of the Kansas City Preventive Patrol Experiment.)
2. How is the patrol function affected by the officer's shift assignment and the nature of the beat to which he or she is assigned?
3. What are some of the occupational hazards that are inherent in beat patrol, and what does research seem to indicate should be done to prevent fatal ambushes?
4. What does H.R. 218 permit?
5. What is the "profile" of officers who are feloniously killed, and what are some related lessons that should be taught in police training and then applied by officers on the street?
6. What is meant by discretionary use of police authority, and what are some of its advantages, disadvantages, and factors that enter into the officer's decision-making process?
7. Why is the traffic function important in patrol work, and how can it bring about bad citizen–police relations?

8. What purposes and benefits are provided by patrol vehicles, and why are they so important in the safety and functions of patrol officers?
9. What are the legal and psychological aspects of police officers' uniforms and their general appearance, and the nature and purpose of an agency dress code? What types of lawsuits are officers filing in regard to dress codes?
10. How would you describe the relationship between patrol officers and police dispatchers?

Learn by Doing

1. You are a patrol sergeant, lecturing to your agency's Citizens' Police Academy about the patrol function. Someone raises her hand and asks, "Sergeant, your officers obviously can't enforce all of the laws all of the time. Which laws are always enforced, and which ones are not? What factors determine how police discretion is used?" How do you respond (without saying something like "We enforce all of the laws, all of the time," which of course would be untrue)? How would you fully explain police discretion to the citizens' group?

2. Increasing incidents involving fatal ambushes of officers has obviously become a major concern, calling for a reassessment of police training and procedural methods, especially involving drug cases. As a new lieutenant in your training academy who has studied the fatality data and reports, what new training and procedural measures would you recommend to be adopted to reduce or attempt to eliminate such fatal shootings?

3. As a police consultant, you are hired by a nearby police agency to develop a new police uniform and dress code for all sworn officers, paying attention to legal and practical aspects. Develop a dress code as well as a description of the new uniform (color, accoutrements, etc.) that you would recommend, with arguments in defense of both.

4. For a practical view of traffic problems and solutions, go to www.popcenter.org/problems/street_racing (Guide No. 26) and/or to www.popcenter.org/problems/drunk_driving (Guide No. 28). These guides are published by the federal Center for Problem-Oriented Policing. Read and describe the kinds of problems that are caused by illegal street racing and/or drunk driving. Consider the efforts described in the guides that police are using to successfully address these problems.

Notes

1. Quoted in Kevin Krajick, "Does Patrol Prevent Crime?" *Police Magazine* 1 (September 1978): 4–16.
2. T. J. Baker, "Designing the Job to Motivate," *FBI Law Enforcement Bulletin* 45 (1976): 3–7.
3. Krajick, "Does Patrol Prevent Crime?" p. 10.
4. Ibid., pp. 11–13.
5. Robert C. Trojanowicz and Dennis W. Banas, *Job Satisfaction: A Comparison of Foot Patrol Versus Motor Patrol Officers* (East Lansing: Michigan State University, 1985).
6. Ibid.
7. Ibid., p. 235.
8. Jerome H. Skolnick and David H. Bayley, *The New Blue Line: Police Innovation in Six American Cities* (New York: Free Press, 1986), p. 4.
9. Quoted in John A. Webster, "Patrol Tasks," in *Policing Society: An Occupational View*, ed. W. Clinton Terry III (New York: Wiley, 1985), pp. 263–313.
10. W. Clinton Terry III, ed., *Policing Society: An Occupational View* (New York: Wiley, 1985), pp. 259–260.
11. U.S. Department of Justice, National Institute of Justice, *Managing Calls to the Police with 911/311 Systems* (February 2005), Calling 311: Guidelines for Policymakers (February 2005), p. 4, https://www.ncjrs.gov/pdffiles1/nij/206257.pdf (accessed November 7, 2013).
12. NBC News New York, "Nearly 40 Percent of City's 911 Calls Accidental: Report," http://www.nbcnewyork.com/news/local/City-911-System-Butt-Dial-Accidental-Calls-Report-150743725.html (accessed November 8, 2013).
13. See U.S. Department of Justice, Office of Community Oriented Policing Services, *311 for Non-Emergencies* (August 2006); also see U.S. Department of Justice, National Institute of Justice, *Managing Calls to the Police with 911/311 Systems* (February 2005),

http://www.cops.usdoj.gov/Publications/managing_calls_911311.pdf (accessed November 8, 2013).

14. Elizabeth Reuss-Ianni, *Two Cultures of Policing: Street Cops and Management Cops* (New Brunswick, NJ: Transaction Books, 1983).

15. SmartPlanet, "The 10 Most Dangerous Jobs in America," January 27, 2013, http://www.smartplanet.com/blog/bulletin/the-10-most-dangerous-jobs-in-america/11396 (accessed March 5, 2013).

16. Kevin Johnson, "In light of police deaths, training is scrutinized," *USA Today* (January 11, 2012), http://usatoday30.usatoday.com/news/nation/story/2012-01-06/police-deaths-training-raids/52488196/1; Kevin Johnson, More police officers die in ambush attacks, *USA Today* (December 22, 2011), http://usatoday30.usatoday.com/news/nation/story/2011-12-21/police-officer-ambush-deaths/52147034/1 (accessed November 7, 2013).

17. Charles E. Miller III, Henry F. Hanburger, Michael Sumeracki, and Marcus Young, "The FBI's National Law Enforcement Safety Initiative," *FBI Law Enforcement Bulletin* (January 2010), http://www.fbi.gov/stats-services/publications/law-enforcement-bulletin/january-2010/the-fbi2019s-national-law-enforcement-safety-initiative (accessed November 3, 2013).

18. Kevin Johnson, "FBI focuses firearms training on close-quarters combat," *USA Today*, January 7, 2013, http://www.usatoday.com/story/news/2013/01/05/fbi-firearms-training/1811053/ (accessed January 8, 2013).

19. Anthony J. Pinizzotto, Edward F. Davis, and Charles E. Miller III, "Suicide by Cop Defining a Devastating Dilemma," *FBI Law Enforcement Bulletin* 74(2) (February 2005), www.fbi.gov/publications/leb/2005/feb2005/feb2005.htm#page8 (accessed March 5, 2013).

20. H. Range Huston and Diedre Anglin, "Suicide by Cop," *Annals of Emergency Medicine* 32(6) (December 1998): 665–669.

21. Adapted from Pinizzotto, Davis, and Miller, "Suicide by Cop Defining a Devastating Dilemma."

22. Skolnick and Bayley, *The New Blue Line*, pp. 141–142.

23. John P. Crank, *Understanding Police Culture* (Cincinnati, OH: Anderson, 1998), p. 83.

24. Ibid., p. 254.

25. Quoted in Mark Baker, *Cops: Their Lives in Their Own Words* (New York: Pocket Books, 1985), p. 298.

26. Bouza, *The Police Mystique*, p. 74.

27. See the full text of the law at www.sdsos.gov/admin-services/adminpdfs/h218enr.pdf (accessed March 5, 2013).

28. Jennifer Boyer, "Legislative Alert: President Bush Signs Concealed Carry Legislation into Law," *The Police Chief* 71(9) (September 2004), http://www.policechiefmagazine.org/magazine/index.cfm?fuseaction=display_arch&article_id=383&issue_id=92004 (accessed March 5, 2013).

29. Luke Dawson, "The Evolution of the Cop Car," *Gear* (n.d.), p. 72.

30. Ibid.

31. Shaila Dewan, "As Gas Prices Rise, Police Turn to Foot Patrols," *The New York Times*, July 20, 2008, http://www.nytimes.com/2008/07/20/us/20patrol.html (accessed November 30, 2013).

32. U.S. Department of Transportation, National Highway Traffic Safety Administration, "Motorcycle Traffic Enforcement," www.nhtsa.dot.gov/people/injury/pedbimot/motorcycle/motorcycle_traffic03/preface.htm#2 (accessed March 5, 2013).

33. U.S. Department of Justice, Bureau of Justice Statistics, "Local Police Departments, 2007," p. 6, http://bjs.ojp.usdoj.gov/content/pub/pdf/lpd07.pdf (accessed November 8, 2013).

34. Chris Menton, "Bicycle Patrols: An Underutilized Resource," **Policing: an International Journal of Police Strategies & Management 31(1), 2008.** pp. 98–103.

35. See Officer.com, "Vehicles and Equipment," directory.officer.com/list/Vehicles_Equipment (accessed March 5, 2013).

36. Carl B. Klockars and Stephen D. Mastrofski, "Police Discretion: The Case of Selective Enforcement," in *Thinking About Police: Contemporary Readings*, 2nd ed., eds. Carl B. Klockars and Stephen D. Mastrofski (Boston: McGraw-Hill, 1991), p. 330.

37. James Q. Wilson and George L. Kelling, "'Broken Windows': The Police and Neighborhood Safety," *Atlantic Monthly*, March 1982, pp. 28–29.

38. David H. Bayley and Egon Bittner, "Learning the Skills of Policing," in *Critical Issues in Policing: Contemporary Readings*, eds. Roger G. Dunham and Geoffrey P. Alpert (Prospect Heights, IL: Waveland Press, 1989), pp. 87–110.

39. Kenneth Culp Davis, *Police Discretion* (St. Paul, MN: West, 1975), p. 73.

40. Kenneth Culp Davis, *Discretionary Justice* (Urbana: University of Illinois Press, 1969), p. 222.

41. Klockars and Mastrofski, "Police Discretion," p. 331.

42. Ibid.

43. Richard J. Lundman, "Routine Police Arrest Practices: A Commonweal Perspective," *Social Problems* 22 (1974): 127–141; Donald Petersen, "Informal Norms and Police Practices: The Traffic Quota System," *Sociology and Social Research* 55 (1971): 354–361.

44. Lawrence W. Sherman, "Experiments in Police Discretion: Scientific Boon or Dangerous Knowledge?" *Law and Contemporary Problems* 47 (1984): 61–82.

45. For a thorough discussion, see Gregory Howard Williams, "The Politics of Police Discretion," in *Discretion, Justice and Democracy: A Public Policy Perspective*, ed. Carl F. Pinkele and William C. Louthau (Ames: Iowa State University Press, 1985), pp. 19–30.

46. Davis, *Police Discretion*, p. 22.

47. See James F. Doyle, "Police Discretion, Legality, and Morality," in *Police Ethics: Hard Choices in Law Enforcement*, ed. William C. Heffernan and Timothy Stroup (New York: John Jay Press, 1985), pp. 47–68.

48. *Tennessee v. Garner*, 471 U.S. 1 (1985).

49. U.S. Department of Justice, Bureau of Justice Statistics, *Characteristics of Drivers Stopped by Police, 2002* (Washington, D.C.: Author, 2006), pp. 1–2, 5.

50. National Highway Traffic Safety Association, "New NHTSA Analysis Shows 2011 Traffic Fatalities Declined by Nearly Two Percent," December 10, 2012, http://www.nhtsa.gov/About+NHTSA/Press+Releases/2012/New+NHTSA+Analysis+Shows+2011+Traffic+Fatalities+Declined+by+Nearly+Two+Percent (accessed December 11, 2012.).

51. See, for example, Terry C. Cox and Mervin F. White, "Traffic Citations and Student Attitudes Toward the Police: An Examination of Selected Interaction Dynamics," *Journal of Police Science and Administration* 16(2) (fall 1988): 105–121.

52. Adam F. Carr, John F. Schnelle, and John F. Kirchner, "Police Crackdowns and Slowdowns: A Naturalistic Evaluation of Changes in Police Traffic Enforcement," *Behavioral Assessment* 2 (Spring 1980): 33–41; Tom Robinson, "Extinction Rate Measurement of the Mobile Radar Display Trailer" (unpublished manuscript, Department of Political Science, University of Nevada, Reno, 1993).

53. Richard J. Lundman, "Working Traffic Violations," in *Policing Society: An Occupational View*, ed. W. Clinton Terry III (New York: Wiley), pp. 327–333.

54. City of Berkeley City Council, "Agenda: June 27, 2000," www.ci.berkeley.ca.us/citycouncil/2000citycouncil/agenda/062700A.html (accessed March 5, 2013).

55. Paul N. Tinsley and Darryl Plecas, "Studying Public Perceptions of Police Grooming Standards," *The Police Chief*, November 2003, policechiefmagazine.org/magazine/index.cfm?fuseaction=display_arch&article_id=152&issue_id=112003 (accessed November 5, 2013).

56. 425 U.S. 238 (1976).

57. Ibid., pp. 247–248.

58. Richard R. Johnson, "The Psychological Influence of the Police Uniform," *FBI Law Enforcement Bulletin*, March 2001, pp. 27–32; Tinsley and Plecas, "Studying Public Perceptions of Police Grooming Standards," p. 2.

59. Ibid., p. 29.

60. Ibid., p. 3.

61. Ibid., p. 2.

62. Ibid., p. 3.

63. Ibid., p. 3.

64. Adapted from the Minneapolis, Minnesota Police Department Policy and Procedure Manual #3-100, "Personal Appearance and Uniforms," http://www.minneapolismn.gov/police/policy/mpdpolicy_3-100_3-100 (accessed October 8, 2013).

65. "Tattooed State Police Job Applicant Sues Over Policy," http://dailyitem.com/0100_news/x46896383/State-police-job-applicant-sues-over-tattoo-policy (accessed November 5, 2013).

66. Carolyn Feibel, "Ban on Beards at HPD Could Grow Costly," *Houston Chronicle*, May 29, 2008, www.chron.com/disp/story.mpl/metropolitan/5806843.html (accessed November 5, 2013).

67. "Des Moines Police Ban New Tattoos," http://www.foxnews.com/story/0,2933,379203,00.html (accessed November 5, 2013).

68. Park, "HPD Weighs Tattoo Cover-up," p. 1.

69. U.S. Department of Labor, Bureau of Labor Statistics, "Police, Fire, and Ambulance Dispatchers," http://www.bls.gov/ooh/office-and-administrative-support/police-fire-and-ambulance-dispatchers.htm (accessed November 5, 2013).

Practices and Challenges

Part 2 considers contemporary policing practices and challenges and begins with a discussion of community policing community-oriented policing and problem solving (Chapter 4), and includes this strategy's principles, strategies, and various applications. Next, Chapter 5 focuses on criminal investigation, including some discussion of how this field evolved, the roles of detectives, working undercover, DNA and other forms of analysis and technologies, uses of behavioral science, and recent developments in the field. This part's concluding chapter, Chapter 6, examines selected personnel issues: stress, labor relations, higher education, and the private police.

4 Community-Oriented
Policing and Problem Solving

LEARNING OBJECTIVES

As a result of reading this chapter, the student will be able to:

1 *Define community-oriented policing and problem solving (community policing and problem solving) and to describe how this concept differs from traditional policing*

2 *Delineate the four parts of the SARA problem-solving process for police*

3 *Provide an example of how social media can be utilized for community policing*

4 *Describe some important considerations for implementing and evaluating community policing and problem-solving initiatives*

5 *Explain what is meant by the term CompStat, as well as how it functions and why it is now a rapidly growing tool for crime suppression*

Describe some methods, problems, and successes that are involved with evaluating community policing and problem-solving efforts

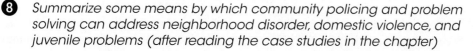 Explain what is meant by crime prevention, and be able to describe how it relates to community policing and problem solving

8 Summarize some means by which community policing and problem solving can address neighborhood disorder, domestic violence, and juvenile problems (after reading the case studies in the chapter)

9 Explain what is meant by a new policing paradigm, "Smart Policing," to include its origins and the outcomes of several test sites

10 Describe what is meant by, and uses of two complementary concepts: intelligence-led policing and predictive policing

Introduction

This is a uniquely challenging time to be entering police work. As mentioned in Chapter 1, a strategy that runs counter to the professional model of policing is spreading across the country: **community-oriented policing and problem solving**. This chapter examines the rationale for and methods of that strategy, which represent a return to the philosophy and practices of policing of the early nineteenth century.

Until the 1980s, the dominant police strategy emphasized motorized patrol, rapid response time, and retrospective investigation of crimes. Those strategies have some merit for police operations, but they were not designed to address root community problems but, rather, to detect crime and apprehend criminals—hence the image of the "crime fighter" cop. Current wisdom holds that the police cannot unilaterally attack the burgeoning crime, drug, and gang problems that beset our society, draining our federal, state, and local resources. Communities must police themselves. We also understand that it is time now for new police methods and measures of effectiveness.

This chapter begins by examining **community-oriented policing (COP)**, and then it reviews a more recent development, which extends COP by using the community to address crime and disorder: **problem-oriented policing (POP)**. Included is an overview of the scanning, analysis, response, assessment (SARA) problem-solving process. Following that, we look at how COP and POP, two inter-related and complementary concepts, work to engage the community in crime fighting through what has been termed community-oriented policing and problem solving (community policing and problem solving). We review how community policing and problem solving should be implemented and evaluated; a new and rapidly growing concept, CompStat; problems and methods involved with evaluating problem-solving efforts; and how this strategy relates to two elements of crime prevention: environmental design and repeat victimization. Next is an instructive case study of problem-solving efforts by police in Tulsa, Oklahoma, as concerned juvenile problems. Following is a review of a new policing paradigm, Smart Policing, that emphasizes the use of data and analytics as well as improved crime analysis, performance measurement, and evaluation research.

Three exhibits in this chapter will provide further insight; the first concerns the use of social networking in community policing; the second provides several examples of crime prevention through environmental design (CPTED); and the third describes a Smart Policing project in Los Angeles. A summary, key terms, review questions, and several scenarios and activities that provide opportunities for you to "learn by doing" conclude the chapter.

Also note that two related topics of discussion, intelligence-led policing (ILP) and predictive policing, are included in Chapter 12 as potential tools for addressing the problem of terrorism.

▶ Basic Principles of Community Policing

Redefined Role

There is a growing awareness that the community can and must play a vital role in problem solving and crime fighting. A fundamental aspect of COP has always been that the public must be engaged in the fight against crime and disorder. As we noted in Chapter 1, Robert Peel emphasized in the 1820s in his principles of policing that the police and community should work together.[1]

In the early 1980s, the notion of community policing emerged as the dominant model for thinking about policing. It was designed to reunite the police with the community.[2] No single program describes community policing. Community policing has been applied in various forms by police agencies in the United States and abroad and differs according to community needs, local politics, and available resources.

COP is much more than a police–community relations program; it attempts to address crime control through a working partnership with the community. Community institutions such as families, schools, and neighborhood and merchants' associations are seen as key partners with the police in creating safer, more secure communities. The views of community members have greater status under community policing than under the traditional policing model.[3]

COP is a long-term process that involves fundamental institutional change. This concept redefines the role of the officer on the street from crime fighter to problem solver and neighborhood ombudsman. It forces a cultural transformation of the entire department, including a decentralized organizational structure and changes in recruiting, training, awards systems, evaluations, and promotions. This philosophy also requires officers to break away from the binds of incident-driven policing and to seek proactive and creative resolution to the problems of crime and disorder.

The major points at which COP departs from traditional policing are shown in Table 4-1 ■.

Community Building: New Station House Design and Amenities

Even traditional monolithic police station houses are being changed in terms of design and amenities in some jurisdictions in order to better engage in community building.

▲ Citizen input is crucial to the police for crime detection and prevention.

(Courtesy © pojoslaw—Fotolia.com.)

TABLE 4-1 Traditional Versus Community Policing: Questions and Answers

Question	Traditional Policing	Community Policing
Who are the police?	A government agency principally responsible for law enforcement	The police are the public, and the public are the police: The police officers are those who are paid to give full-time attention to the duties of every citizen
What is the relationship of the police force to other public-service departments?	Priorities often in conflict	One department among many responsible for improving the quality of life
What is the role of the police?	To focus on solving crimes	To take a broader problem-solving approach
How is police efficiency measured?	By detection and arrest rates	By the absence of crime and disorder
What are the highest priorities?	Crimes that are high value (e.g., bank robberies) and those involving violence	Whatever problems disturb the community most
What, specifically, do police deal with?	Incidents	Citizens' problems and concerns
What determines the effectiveness of police?	Response times	Public cooperation
What view do police take of service calls?	Deal with them only if there is no real police work to do	View them as a vital function and a great opportunity
What is police professionalism?	Responding swiftly and effectively to serious crime	Keeping close to the community
What kind of intelligence is most important?	Crime intelligence (study of particular crimes or series of crimes)	Criminal intelligence (information about the activities of individuals or groups)
What is the essential nature of police accountability?	Highly centralized; governed by rules, regulations, and policy directives; accountable to the law	Emphasis on local accountability to community needs
What is the role of headquarters?	To provide the necessary rules and policy directives	To preach organizational values
What is the role of the press liaison department?	To keep the "heat" off operational officers so they can get on with the job	To coordinate an essential channel of communication with the community
How do the police regard prosecutions?	As an important goal	As one tool among many

Source: Traditional Versus Community Policing: Questions And Answers, Malcolm K. Sparrow, "Implementing Community Policing, (Washington, DC: U.S. Government Printing Office), U.S. Department of Justice, 1988.

Generally, the public areas of most station houses are very stark, cold, and unfriendly places. As is true for trips to the dentist, few people go to their police station voluntarily, but some jurisdictions are hoping to change that.

In the Los Angeles Police Department (LAPD) West Valley Station, in Reseda, California, residents will find ATMs in the light-filled lobby, kitchen-equipped meeting rooms for public use, and even an inviting outdoor courtyard with barbecue facilities. Gone from such "second-generation" station houses are the small windows that were located high off the ground to deter drive-by shootings but made the buildings look like bunkers and armed camps. These newer police stations also typically offer more areas that are open to the public (such as cafeterias where officers and civilians can eat together), bigger lobbies where people can comfortably sit, and community rooms where people can hold meetings and training sessions.[4]

▶ Major Step Forward: Problem-Oriented Policing

Problem solving is not new—police officers have always tried to solve problems. The difference is that officers in the past received little guidance, support, or technology from police administrators for dealing with problems, so the routine application of problem-solving techniques is new. It is premised on two facts: that problem solving can be applied by officers throughout the agency as part of their daily work and that routine problem-solving efforts can be effective in reducing or resolving problems.

Problem-oriented policing was grounded on different principles than COP, but they are complementary. POP is a strategy that puts the COP philosophy into practice because it advocates that police examine the underlying causes of recurring incidents of crime and disorder. The problem-solving process helps officers identify problems, analyze them completely, develop response strategies, and assess the results.

Herman Goldstein is considered by many to be the principal architect of POP. Goldstein coined the term *problem-oriented policing* in 1979 out of frustration with the dominant model for improving police operations: "More attention [was] being focused on how quickly officers responded to a call than on what they did when they got to their destination."[5]

Goldstein argued for a radical change in the direction of efforts to improve policing. The first step in POP is to move beyond just handling incidents and to recognize that incidents are often overt symptoms of problems. It requires that officers take a more in-depth interest in incidents by acquainting themselves with some of the conditions and factors that cause them. (The expanded role of police officers under POP is discussed later.)

The Problem-Solving Process: SARA

39 POP has at its nucleus, a four-stage problem-solving process known as scanning, analysis, response, assessment (SARA).[6]

Scanning: Problem Identification

Scanning involves problem identification. As a first step, officers should identify problems on their beats and look for a pattern or persistent repeat incidents. At this juncture, the question might well be asked "What is a problem?" *Problem* may be defined as a group of two or more incidents that are similar in one or more respects, causing harm and, therefore, being of concern to the police and the public. Incidents may be similar in various ways:

- *Behaviors.* People's behaviors are the most frequent indicator and include activities such as drug sales, robberies, thefts, and graffiti.
- *Locations.* Problems may occur in area hot spots, such as in downtown areas, in housing complexes plagued by burglaries, and in parks in which gangs commit crimes.
- *People.* Both repeat offenders and repeat victims account for a high proportion of crime.
- *Time.* Incidents may be similar in terms of the season, day of the week, or hour of the day; examples include rush hours, bar closing times, and tourist seasons.
- *Events.* Crimes may peak during events such as university spring break, rallies, and gatherings.

There appears to be no inherent limit on the types of problems patrol officers can face because all types of problems are candidates for problem solving.

Numerous resources are available to the police to help them identify problems, including calls for service (CFS) data, especially repeat calls from the same location or a series of similar incidents. Other means include citizen complaints, census data, data from other government agencies, newspaper and media coverage of community issues, officer observations, and community surveys.

The primary purpose of scanning is to conduct a preliminary inquiry to determine whether a problem really exists and whether further analysis is needed. During this stage, priorities should be established if multiple problems exist, and a specific officer or team of officers should be assigned to handle the problem. Scanning initiates the problem-solving process.

Analysis: Heart of Problem Solving

The second stage, analysis, is the heart of the problem-solving process. Crime analysis has been defined as "a set of systematic, analytical processes providing timely and pertinent information to assist operational and administrative personnel."[7]

Effective tailor-made responses cannot be developed unless people know what is causing the problem. Thus, the purpose of analysis is to learn as much as possible about a problem in order to identify its causes. Complete analysis includes identifying the seriousness of the problem, knowing all the individuals or groups involved and affected, listing all the causes of the problem, and assessing current responses and their effectiveness.

Over time, several methods have been developed for analyzing crime and disorder. We examine some of them now: the problem-analysis triangle, mapping and offense reports, CFS analysis, and community surveys.

Problem-Analysis Triangle One tool that may be used for analyzing problems is the problem-analysis triangle, which helps officers visualize the problem and understand the relationship between the three elements of the triangle (see Figure 4-1 ■). In addition, it suggests where more information is needed and helps with crime control and prevention. Generally, three elements must be present before a crime or harmful behavior—a problem—can occur: an offender (someone who is motivated to commit harmful behavior), a victim (a desirable and vulnerable target), and a location (although the victim and offender are not always in the same place at the same time; locations is discussed later). If these three elements show up over and over again in patterns of recurring problems, removing one of these elements can stop the pattern and prevent future harm.[8]

Mapping and Offense Reports Computerized crime mapping (discussed in greater detail in Chapter 14) also assists with crime analysis. Mapping combines geographic information from global positioning satellites with crime statistics gathered by the department's computer-aided dispatching (CAD) system and demographic data provided by private companies or the U.S. Census Bureau.

Police offense reports can also be useful, analyzed for suspect characteristics, modi operandi (MOs), victim characteristics, and many other factors. Offense reports are also a potential source of information about high-crime areas and addresses, since they capture exact descriptions of locations. In a typical department, however, patrol officers may write official reports on only about 25 to 30 percent of all calls to which they respond. Another limitation is that there may be a considerable lag between when the officer files a report and when the analysis is complete.[9]

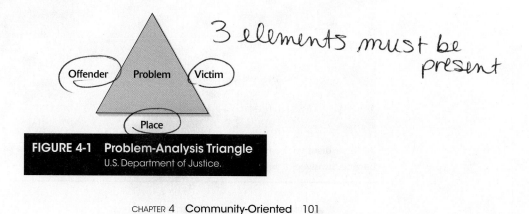

3 elements must be present

FIGURE 4-1   Problem-Analysis Triangle
U.S. Department of Justice.

Computer software can now assist with profiling beats and demographics, finding patterns of problems, helping plan daily officer activities, balancing beat and officer workloads, and identifying current levels of performance. Such software can scan through hundreds of millions of pieces of data for patterns, trends, or clusters in beats and neighborhoods while ranking and reranking problems. In the field, the officer simply highlights the neighborhood, beat, or grid under consideration and then selects the problem or problems to be worked on from a menu on the computer.

CFS Analysis With the advent of CAD systems, a more reliable source of data on CFS has become available. CAD systems, containing information on all types of CFS, add to information provided by offense reports, yielding a more extensive account of what the public reports to the police.[10] The data captured by CAD systems can be sorted to reveal hot spots of crime and disturbances—specific locations from which an unusual number of calls to the police are made.

A study in Minneapolis on hot spots analyzed nearly 324,000 CFS for a one-year period over all 115,000 addresses and intersections. The results showed relatively few hot spots accounting for the majority of calls to the police:[11]

- In all the calls, 50 percent came from 3 percent of the locations.
- All robbery calls came from 2.2 percent of the locations.
- All rape calls came from 1.2 percent of the locations.
- All auto thefts came from 2.7 percent of the locations.

Many police agencies have the capability to use CAD data for repeat-call analysis (which is related to repeat victimization, discussed later). The repeat-call locations identified in this way can become targets of directed patrol efforts, including problem solving.

▲ Once disorder begins to descend on a location, crime soon follows—and the police will become involved. *(Courtesy of City of Reno Police Department.)*

For example, a precinct may receive printouts of the top twenty-five CFS areas to review for problem-solving assignments. In Houston, the police and Hispanic citizens were concerned about violence at cantinas (bars). Through repeat-call analysis, police learned that only 3 percent of the cantinas in the city were responsible for 40 percent of the violence. The data narrowed the scope of the problem and enabled a special liquor-control unit to better target its efforts.[12]

Repeat alarm calls are another example of how CAD data can be used to support patrol officer problem solving. In fact, when an experiment began in Baltimore County, Maryland, some commanders preferred that officers start with alarm projects. Data documenting repeat alarm calls by address were readily available, and commanders anticipated that solving alarm problems would be relatively simple and would bring considerable benefits compared to the investment of time.[13]

Community Surveys Not to be overlooked in crime analysis is the use of community surveys to analyze problems. For example, an officer may canvass all the business proprietors in shopping centers on his or her beat. In Baltimore, an officer telephoned business owners to update the police department's after-hours business contact files. Although the officer did not conduct a formal survey, he used this task to inquire about problems the owners might want to bring to police attention.

On a larger scale, a team of officers may survey residents of a housing complex or neighborhood known to have particular crime problems. The survey could assist in determining residents' priority concerns, acquiring information about hot spots, and learning more about residents' expectations of police.[14] Residents are also more likely to keep the police abreast of future problems when patrol officers leave their business cards and encourage residents to contact them directly. The accompanying Career Profile describes the duties and training of a crime analyst under community policing and problem solving, while Exhibit 4-1 ■ describes how social networking sites can also assist with this function (the use of social media is discussed more in Chapter 14, Technology Review).

EXHIBIT 4-1

SOCIAL NETWORKING AND COMMUNITY POLICING

Because of social media, today's police officers who are engaged in community policing and problem solving are more connected and have access to more information than ever before. If a citizen is following the local police department on, say, Twitter, then the citizen will receive all of the police "tweets" on the user's Twitter home page in their e-mail, or on a smartphone or PDA. If the police are looking for an offender, they can send a message to their community followers. Amber Alerts for missing children, pursuit-in-progress notices, reports of persons apprehended, reminders of neighborhood watch meetings, or other relevant bulletins can also be provided. Citizens can reply to these messages using the same system. Facebook is also used to advantage, by promoting community events, drawing attention to its podcasts, and adding video clips it has produced. Blogs—sort of an online diary—are an excellent means for police to elevate their community profile as well; it can serve as a daily "police blotter"—a log of what officers are doing; they can include photos and YouTube video clips. When a new blog is posted, citizens can be alerted to it on Twitter and Facebook.

Sources: Adapted from Dan Alexander, "Using Technology to Take Community Policing to the Next Level," *The Police Chief*, October 2012, http://www.policechiefmagazine.org/magazine/index.cfm?fuseaction=display&article_id=2425&issue_id=72011; also see Terry Collins, "Police embrace emerging social media tool," *Associated Press*, August 11, 2012, http://news.yahoo.com/police-embrace-emerging-social-media-tool-150141734.html (accessed October 25, 2013).

Career Profile

(Courtesy Lisa Reagan.)

Name: Lisa Reagan

Position: Crime Analyst

City, State: Portland, Maine

College attended: University of Southern Maine (Bachelors) and American Military University (Masters)

Majors: BA, Psychology; master's degree, Homeland Security (currently enrolled)

How long have you occupied this position/assignment?

I've worked as a crime analyst for 8 years.

How would you briefly describe this position/assignment:

In the budget-cut, post 9/11 era, and community policing and problem solving, you must be willing to wear many different hats in order to accomplish your job and any other tasks which may appear. For example, I have to be extremely flexible and frequently switch from a crime analyst to being an intelligence analyst. One minute I'm functioning as a crime analyst by doing a motor vehicle burglary analysis, preparing and reporting the weekly COMPSTAT (computer statistics) report or *Uniform Crime Reports* (UCR) data. At any given time I may have to shift tasks completely, from conducting intelligence analyses (such as assisting detectives' investigations by completing toll call analysis, cell phone tower analysis) to information-gathering in support of tactical operations. I also assist universities, hospitals, the department's community service and patrol divisions, as well as citizens, by preparing crime statistics. I also work collaboratively with agencies (local, state, and federal) by gathering and sharing information as it pertains to their open investigations.

What attracted you to this position/assignment?

With the skills I learned in the military as an intelligence analyst, this was a natural progression.

What qualities/characteristics are most helpful for this position/assignment?

It can be difficult to operate as a civilian crime analyst because you're not a sworn officer and thus don't have firsthand knowledge of the work in the field. Therefore, listening to what officers need and building bridges between yourself and them to meet their needs is a major challenge. Being a good listener and observer, however, and using your inductive reasoning skills and uppermost professionalism in general will assist you in building that bridge. In addition, always ensure your work and recommendations can be backed up with data; there isn't any room for error, and so corroborating your findings will give you more credibility. Be steadfast with your work and others in the agency will eventually support your analytical suggestions as well. Also, if you don't know the answer (or question) concerning something, make sure you get clarification from a supervisor. You must also ensure that you're not violating anyone's rights under the Code of Federal Regulations—specifically, 28 CFR, Part 23, which covers agencies that receive, store, analyze, and exchange or disseminate data regarding criminal activities, and basically governs how criminal intelligence information is to be entered, reviewed, and purged where cases are no longer active (see: http://www.it.ojp.gov/documents/28cfr_part_23.pdf).

How would you describe a typical day for one in this position/assignment?

A typical day consists of reading a lot of e-mails, attending community and department meetings, issuing requests for information, and attending to projects with approaching deadlines. Therefore, you need to have good time management skills. Try to manage your workload based on which mission is most critical at the given point in time.

What advice would you offer someone who is beginning their studies of policing and criminal justice?

If you're interested in being an analyst, get as much training as possible in statistics, Microsoft Excel, and Access. Pay attention in classes when your professors discuss *Uniform Crime Reporting* and the aforementioned 28 CFR, Part 23. Take advantage of training. Education is key, so stay in school for as long as you can. Also, try to either intern or volunteer at a police department so that you can be exposed to the law enforcement environment and its own culture. Most importantly, do not break the law. You might have a Ph.D., but would still have a hard time gaining employment if you've even bought your underage friends alcohol. Polygraph examinations and extensive background checks for applicants for analyst and officers' positions are a common practice.

Response: Formulation of Tailor-Made Strategies

After a problem has been clearly defined and analyzed, the officer confronts the ultimate challenge in POP: the search for the most effective way of dealing with it. The response may be quite simple (such as reprogramming a public telephone at a convenience store where drug dealers conduct their "business" so that it only makes outgoing calls) or quite involved (e.g., screening and evicting some tenants from a housing complex; cleaning up a neighborhood that is overcome with graffiti, debris, and junk cars; taking legal action to create a curfew; or condemning and razing a drug house).[15] (A number of examples of responses are provided in the case study.)

This stage of the SARA process focuses on developing and implementing responses to the problem. Before entering this stage, the police agency must overcome the temptation to implement a response prematurely and be certain that it has thoroughly analyzed the problem; attempts to fix problems quickly are rarely effective in the long term.

Assessment: Evaluation of Overall Effectiveness

In the assessment stage, officers evaluate the effectiveness of their responses. A number of measures have traditionally been used by police agencies and community members to assess effectiveness. These include numbers of arrests; levels of reported crime; response times; clearance rates; citizen complaints; and various workload indicators, such as CFS and the number of field interviews conducted.[16] Several of these measures may be helpful in assessing the impact of a problem-solving effort.

A number of nontraditional measures will also shed light on whether a problem has been reduced or eliminated:[17]

- Reduced instances of repeat victimization
- Decreases in related crimes or incidents
- Neighborhood indicators, including increased profits for businesses in the target area, increased usage of the area, increased property values, less loitering and truancy, and fewer abandoned cars
- Increased citizen satisfaction regarding the handling of the problem, determined through surveys, interviews, focus groups, electronic bulletin boards, and so on
- Reduced citizen fear related to the problem

Assessment is obviously key in the SARA process; knowing that we must assess the effectiveness of our efforts emphasizes the importance of documentation and baseline measurement. Supervisors can help officers assess the effectiveness of their efforts.

▶ Collaborative Approach: Basic Principles

The two concepts of community policing and problem-oriented policing (COP and POP) are separate but complementary notions that can work together. Both share some important characteristics: (1) decentralization (to encourage officer initiative and the effective use of local knowledge), (2) geographically defined rather than functionally defined subordinate units (to encourage the development of local knowledge), and (3) close interactions with local communities (to facilitate responsiveness to, and cooperation with, the community).[18] The following definition accurately captures the essence of this concept:

> Community-Oriented Policing and Problem Solving is a proactive philosophy that promotes solving problems that are criminal, affect our quality of life, or increase our fear of crime, as well as other community issues. Community policing and problem solving involves identifying, analyzing, and addressing community problems at their source.[19]

For this strategy to succeed, the following measures are required:[20]

- Conducting accurate community needs assessments
- Mobilizing all appropriate players to collect data and brainstorm strategies
- Determining appropriate resource allocations and creating new resources where necessary

- Developing and implementing innovative, collaborative, comprehensive programs to address underlying causes and causal factors
- Evaluating programs and modifying approaches as needed

—PEAK, KEN; GLENSOR, RONALD W., COMMUNITY POLICING AND PROBLEM SOLVING, 5th, © 2008. Printed and Electronically reproduced by permission of Pearson Education, Inc., Upper Saddle River, New Jersey.

▶ Implementation

Principle Components

Since community policing and problem solving came into being, most police executives have implemented the strategy throughout the entire agency. Some executives, however, have attempted to introduce the concept in a small unit or an experimental district,[21] often in a specific geographic area of the jurisdiction.

It is strongly argued that a department-wide implementation of this strategy be accomplished. When it is established as a distinct unit within patrol rather than department-wide, the introduction of this "special unit" seems to exacerbate the conflict between community policing's reform agenda and the more traditional outlook and hierarchical structure of the agency. A perception of elitism is created—a perception that is ironic because community policing and problem solving is meant to close the gap between patrol and special units and to empower and value the rank-and-file patrol officer as the most important functionary of police work.

The key lesson from research in implementation, however, is that there is no golden rule or any universal method to ensure the successful adoption of this philosophy. Two general propositions are important, however, for implementing the concept: the role of the rank-and-file officer and the role of the environment (or "social ecology") where community policing and problem solving is to be implemented.[22] Moving an agency from the reactive, incident-driven mode to the community policing and problem-solving approach is a complex endeavor, often requiring a complete change in the culture of the police organization. Four principal components of implementation profoundly affect the way agencies do business: leadership and administration, human resources, field operations, and external relations.[23] These factors are discussed next.

Leadership and Administration It is essential that the chief executive communicate the idea that this approach and philosophy is department-wide in scope. To get the whole agency involved, the chief executive must adopt four practices as part of the implementation plan:[24]

1. Communicate to all department members the vital role of community policing and problem solving in serving the public. They must understand why handling problems is more effective than just handling incidents.

2. Provide incentives to all department members to engage in community policing and problem solving. This includes a new and different personnel evaluation and reward system as well as positive encouragement.

3. Reduce the barriers to community policing and problem solving that can occur. Procedures, time allocation, and policies all need to be closely examined.

4. Show officers how to address problems. Training is a key element of community policing and problem-solving implementation. The executive must also set guidelines for innovation. Officers must know they have the latitude to innovate.

Human Resources With regard to human resources, middle managers (captains and lieutenants) and first-line supervisors (sergeants) also play a crucial role in planning and implementing this philosophy and in encouraging their officers to be innovative, take risks, and be creative.[25] First-line supervisors and senior patrol officers seem to generate the greatest resistance to community policing, largely because they have long-standing working styles cultivated from years of traditional police work and because these officers can feel disenfranchised by a management system that takes the best and brightest out of patrol and (they often believe) leaves them behind.

Field Operations Furthermore, the mechanisms that motivate, challenge, reward, and correct employees' behaviors in the field must be compatible with the community policing principles. These include recruiting, selection, training, performance evaluation, promotion, honors and awards, and discipline, all of which should be reviewed to ensure that they promote and support the tenets of community policing and problem solving. First, recruiting literature should reflect the principles to be applied. A job-task analysis identifying the new knowledge, skills, and abilities should be conducted and become a part of the testing process for entry-level employees. community policing and problem solving should also be integrated into academy training, field-training programs, and in-service training. Performance evaluations and reward systems should reflect new job descriptions and officers' application of their training. Also, promotion systems should be expanded from their usual focus on tactical decision making, should include knowledge of the research on community policing, and should test an officer's ability to apply problem solving to various crime and neighborhood problems.

External Relations Collaborative responses to neighborhood crime and disorder are essential to the success of community policing and problem solving. This requires new relationships and the sharing of information and resources among the police and the community, local government agencies, service providers, and businesses. The media provide an excellent means for police to educate the community about this strategy and its applications to crime and disorder.

Political support is another essential consideration when implementing community policing and problem solving. The political environment varies considerably, say, with the strong mayor and council-manager forms of government. These and other rapidly changing political environments make the implementation of the approach more difficult—especially when we add to the mix the at-will employment of most police executives.

▶ Broader Role for the Street Officer

A major departure of POP from the conventional style lies with POP's view of the line officer, who is given much more discretion and decision-making ability and is trusted with a much broader array of responsibilities.

POP values "thinking" officers, urging that they take the initiative in trying to deal more effectively with problems in the areas they serve. This concept effectively uses the potential of college-educated officers, "who have been smothered in the atmosphere of traditional policing."[26] It also gives officers a new sense of identity and self-respect; they are more challenged and have opportunities to follow through on individual cases—to analyze and solve problems—which will give them greater job satisfaction. Using patrol officers in this manner allows the agency to provide sufficient challenge for both those who are better educated and those who remain patrol officers throughout their entire career.[27]

Under POP, officers continue to handle calls, but they also do much more. They combine the information gathered in their responses to incidents with information obtained from other sources to get a clearer picture of the problem. They then address the underlying conditions. If they are successful in ameliorating these conditions, fewer incidents may occur, and those that do occur may be less serious; the incidents may even cease. At the very least, information about the problem can help police design more effective ways of responding to each incident. Police administrators ought to be recruiting people as police officers who can "serve as mediators, as dispensers of information, and as community organizers."[28]

CompStat: Utilizing Information Technology to Manage Crime

A relatively new crime management tool used in the problem-solving process is known as CompStat (for "comparative or computer statistics"), which is designed for the collection and feedback of information on crime and related quality-of-life issues. This strategy is said to be "revolutionizing law enforcement management and practice,"[29] and some have called it "perhaps the single most important organizational/administrative innovation in policing during the latter half of the 20th century."[30]

Since the CompStat process was introduced by the New York City Police Department in 1994, it has been widely adopted: a national survey found that 58 percent of large agencies (those with hundred or more sworn officers) had either adopted or were planning to implement a CompStat-like program.[31] The key elements of CompStat are as follows:

- Specific objectives
- Accurate and timely intelligence
- Effective tactics
- Rapid deployment of personnel and resources
- Relentless follow-up and assessment[32]

CompStat pushes all precincts to generate weekly or monthly crime activity reports. Crime data are readily available, offering up-to-date information that is then compared at citywide, patrol, and precinct levels.

▲ At CompStat meetings, police officials discuss crime patterns in their assigned area(s) and brainstorm about tactics and resources that might be used to address them. *(Courtesy Washoe County Sheriff's Office.)*

Under CompStat, police begin proactively thinking about ways to deal with crime in terms of suppression, intervention, and prevention. Commanders must explain what tactics they have employed to address crime patterns, what resources they have and need, and with whom they have collaborated. Brainstorming problem-solving sessions ensue about proactively responding to the crime problems, and suggestions for strategies are made at subsequent meetings, with relentless follow-up by top brass to further ensure accountability. Many scholars and practitioners believe that CompStat has played a prominent role in the significant crime reductions seen across the nation.

A Career Profile describes the work of a patrol officer under the community policing and problem-solving philosophy.

▶ Does It Work? Evaluation

People consistently agree about two aspects of community policing and problem solving: first, there is a need for partnerships between the police and the public; second, there must be a focus on solving problems underlying criminal incidents.[33]

(Courtesy of William Cameron.)

Career Profile

Name: Will Cameron

Position: Senior Patrol Officer, Community Action Policing Team (CAP Team)

City, State: Anchorage, Alaska

College Attended: University Of Wyoming

Major: BA—Criminal Justice

How long have you occupied this position/assignment?

I've been with the Anchorage Police Department for 7.5 years, and assigned to the CAP Team for the last four years.

How would you briefly describe the position/assignment?

My role as a CAP Team officer, first and foremost, is to uphold state and local laws, while also addressing what the general community needs and desires and working in conjunction with several community groups/councils/individuals to solve long-term/short-term problems.

What attracted you to this position?

A strong desire to make my community a better place for me as well as my fellow neighbors. I felt that community policing was the best means of getting involved with these issues and topics as well as getting to know local community leaders.

What qualities/characteristics are most helpful for this position?

An officer in a community policing unit needs to be willing to listen to concerns within the community—from both individuals as well as community at-large. The officer needs to think creatively for solving different issues as well as seeing projects through to completion. Proficient communication with community members and leaders is very important. The officer must also be able to use predictive policing as well as problem-oriented policing theories to solve crime and/or a problem before a major problem arises.

How would you describe a typical day for one in this position?

It can include going from working in plainclothes in a project area to walking a beat in a high-crime area to attending a community council meeting and listening to the concerns of residents within our community. My unit also runs surveillance on problem areas/businesses via plainclothes details to determine a true problem exists in a given area, using the SARA [scanning, analysis, response, and assessment] process. During this process we attempt to brainstorm with members of the community for developing proper responses and solutions to the neighborhood problems.

What advice would you offer someone who is beginning their studies of policing and criminal justice?

First and foremost, attain your university degree. Your degree will benefit you within the police recruitment process, as well in your future promotional opportunities. Having a degree also demonstrates that you have the ability begin and complete a problem solving project. During your academic life, try to gain life experience through participating in research studies, internships, travel, and so on. Joining a reserve program or Explorer post can also add to your life experience. Do ride-alongs with your local police or sheriff's department to better understand the job and the culture of the organization. Finally, during the application and testing process, be honest about everything.

Empirical studies of this strategy also suggest that its impact is twofold: first, community policing reduces disorder and increases positive community—police relations; second, community policing initiatives increase the positive attitudes that police officers have both toward their jobs and toward the community.[34]

Beyond these areas of agreement, however, studies have been scant and inconclusive. The first problem has been that, because community policing and problem solving serves to improve on several aspects of policing, its impact on crime has not always been the focus of evaluations; as one academic stated, "There needs to be an evaluation process/system that makes reality out of conjecture."[35] Studies have focused on fear of crime, public disorder, police response, and community support.[36]

Compounding this "scattergun" approach to evaluating this tactic are three additional issues:

1. The definition of community policing today is still ambiguous: What one department implements as a community policing and problem-solving strategy may be very different from other departments, resulting in very little consistency across implementations and evaluations.

2. This model is still implemented in a fractional manner: agencies that do not focus on complete departmental and institutional change will confound evaluations, because without that level of adoption, community policing and problem-solving evaluations are limited to studying only those components that were implemented by the agency.

3. Studies have generally had a restricted focus on large cities: Evaluations have generally overlooked the potential success of a community policing model when instituted in a sector or beat as opposed to the entire department jurisdiction.[37]

A 2008 study by Connell et al. sought to address these three issues by evaluating a clearly defined and comprehensive community policing and problem-solving initiative where the initiative pervaded a single unit; the goal was to examine the effects of community policing and problem solving on violent, drug, and property crimes; and the initiative was situated in a suburban setting. Using a time-series design, the researchers' findings suggested that community policing and problem solving does have the capacity to affect crime rates. Indeed, such efforts resulted in an abrupt and permanent decline in the levels of violent and property crime in the treatment site (although the intervention may not have been as effective with drug crimes). The findings suggest that community policing and problem solving can be successful in reducing serious crimes and need not be limited to larger jurisdictions with greater resources.[38]

Attention must be paid in the future to the aforementioned problems and shortcomings as found in evaluations, which to this point have been very limited both in terms of their conclusions and generalizability. It is essential for this strategy—with emphasis on the fact that policing is now in the community policing *era*—that they, the public, and policy makers know unequivocally "what works."

▶ Crime Prevention

An important corollary of community policing and problem solving—and a critical and rapidly developing concept that all police officers should understand—is crime prevention. It stands to reason that it is preferable as well as much less expensive (in terms of both financial and human resources) to prevent a crime from occurring in the first place than to try to solve the offense and arrest, prosecute, and possibly incarcerate the offender. A focus on crime prevention shifts a police organization's purpose. Once the question becomes "How can we prevent the next crisis?" all kinds of approaches become possible.[39]

Crime prevention once consisted primarily of exhorting people to "lock it or lose it" and giving advice to citizens about door locks and window bars for their homes and businesses. It typically was (and often still is) an add-on program for the police agency, which normally included a few officers who were trained to go to citizens' homes and perform security surveys or to speak publicly on the subject of target hardening. Times are rapidly changing in this regard.

Crime prevention and community policing are close companions, attempting to define the problem, identify the contributing causes, seek out the proper people or agencies to assist in identifying potential solutions, and work as a group to implement the solution. The problem drives the solution.[40] At its heart, community policing and problem solving is about preventing crime.

Next we briefly discuss two important aspects of crime prevention—crime prevention through environmental design and repeat victimization—and briefly mention a drug-prevention program.

Crime Prevention Through Environmental Design

Crime prevention through environmental design (CPTED) is defined as the "proper design and effective use of the environment that can lead to a reduction in the fear and incidence of crime, and an improvement in the quality of life."[41] At its core are three principles that support problem-solving approaches to crime:[42]

1. *Natural access control.* Employ elements such as doors, shrubs, fences, and gates to deny access to a crime target and to create a perception among offenders that the target presents risk.

2. *Natural surveillance.* Place windows, lighting, and landscaping properly to increase the ability to observe intruders as well as regular users, allowing observers to challenge inappropriate behavior or to report it to the police or to the property owner.

3. *Territorial reinforcement.* Use elements such as sidewalks, landscaping, and porches to distinguish between public and private areas and to help users exhibit signs of ownership that send hands-off messages to would-be offenders.
   Five types of information are needed for CPTED planning:[43]

   1. *Crime-analysis information.* Crime mapping, police crime data, incident reports, and victim and offender statistics are all included.
   2. *Demographics.* Statistics about residents, such as age, race, gender, income, and income sources, are used.
   3. *Land use information.* Zoning information (such as residential, commercial, industrial, school, and park zones) and occupancy data for each zone are analyzed.
   4. *Observations.* Information includes observations of parking procedures, maintenance, and residents' reactions to crime.
   5. *Resident information.* Resident crime surveys and interviews with police and security officers are assessed.

Exhibit 4-2 ■ provides several examples of CPTED in action.

EXHIBIT 4-2

CPTED AT WORK: SOME EXAMPLES

Under the CPTED approach to problem solving, the overarching question that is asked is this: "What is it about this location that places people at risk or that results in opportunities for crime?" In other words, *why here*? As few examples will illustrate this point:

Case #1: Custodial workers routinely find evidence of smoking, drinking and vandalism in a high school lavatory.

Why here? The lavatory is in an isolated area of the building, adjacent to a ticket booth and concession stand that are active only during athletic events. The school's open lunch policy allows students to eat anywhere on campus, while monitors are assigned only to the cafeteria.

CPTED response: A lock is installed on the lavatory door, and it remains locked unless there is an athletic event. The open lunch policy has been revised: students are still allowed to leave the cafeteria but must eat in designated areas, and a faculty member is charged with patrolling these areas during lunch periods.

Case #2: The back wall of a building in an office center is repeatedly tagged with graffiti.

Why here? The area is out of the view of passers-by: a rear corner location where two buildings come together at the end of a poorly lit service lane. Visibility is further reduced by hedges at the site's perimeter. Businesses in the office center are open from 9 AM to 5 PM during the week; however the tagged building is next to a roller skating rink where activity peaks at night and on weekends.

CPTED response: Hedges are trimmed and wall-mounted light fixtures installed along the service lane, with motion detection lighting in the problem area. The skating rink agrees to change to a "no re-admission" policy to keep skaters inside the building and away from the office property.

Case #3: ATM patrons at a bank are being robbed after dark.

Why here? The bank is situated along a commercial strip in a neighborhood with vacant properties and abandoned businesses. The ATM is in the front corner of the bank building, and the drive-through teller windows are at the side of the building, around the corner from the ATM. Robbers hide in the darkened drive-through teller area and attack unsuspecting ATM users after they complete a transaction.

CPTED response: The bank installs a fence at the corner of the building, creating a barrier between the ATM and the drive-through teller area.

Repeat Victimization

U.S. society—including the police—gives far greater attention to criminal offenders than to crime victims. Just as at the zoo, where more spectators seem to gather around the lions and tigers than around wildebeests and antelope, more attention is focused on the predators than on their prey. However, an evolving body of research in Great Britain suggests that crime victims should be placed on the national agenda. In the United States—where POP has spread across the country—patterns of repeat victimization (RV) have not been examined or assimilated into problem solving. Police officers in the United States would benefit from this developing body of knowledge, which can play a major role in crime prevention and analysis.

The premise underlying RV is that if the police want to know where a crime will occur next, they should look at where it happened last. RV is not new; police officers have always been aware that the same people and places are victimized again and again. What is new, however, are attempts abroad to incorporate RV knowledge into formal crime-prevention efforts. One in three burglaries reported in the United States is a repeat burglary of a household. Furthermore, a 48 percent RV rate was found for sexual incidents (including

▲ Abandoned cars can affect residents' feelings about safety and overall quality of life. *(Courtesy spirit of america/Shutterstock.)*

grabbing, touching, and assault), 43 percent for assaults and threats, and 23 percent for vehicle vandalism.[44] A study of white-collar crime indicated that the same people are victims of fraud and embezzlement time and time again and that banks that have been robbed also have high rates of RV.[45] These data show that providing crime-prevention assistance to potential victims is not only morally justifiable in most instances but also an efficient and practical way of allocating limited police resources.

Why would a burglar return to burgle the same household again? One could argue that, for several reasons, the burglar would be stupid not to return: Temporary repairs to a burgled home will make a subsequent burglary easier, the burglar is familiar with the physical layout and surroundings of the property, the burglar knows what items of value were left behind at the prior burglary, and the burglar also knows that items that were taken at an earlier burglary are likely to have been replaced through insurance policies.

RV is arguably the best single predictor routinely available to the police in the absence of specific intelligence information. A small number of victims accounts for a disproportionate number of victimizations.[46]

Drug Abuse Resistance and Education

A related attempt to prevent crime should be discussed briefly: the well-known Drug Abuse Resistance and Education (DARE) program. The program, launched in 1983 and now administered by police in 80 percent of schools, has not fared well among researchers. Beginning in the late 1990s, however, studies began establishing that the program did not keep kids from abusing drugs. Indeed, one such study's grim findings were that "20-year-olds who'd had DARE classes were no less likely to have smoked marijuana or cigarettes, drunk alcohol, used 'illicit' drugs like cocaine or heroin, or caved in to peer pressure than kids who'd never been exposed to DARE."[47] One of its key flaws, researchers allege, has been that students are taught that all drugs are equally dangerous; when students find that this is not true, the DARE message is undercut.[48]

Now DARE officials are admitting that the program needs a new direction. Officials are revamping the program, reducing the lecturing role of local officers and involving kids in a more active way. A new curriculum is being developed for use in some schools that will show brain scans after drug use to demonstrate the harm, shift officers into more of a coaching role, and have kids engage in role-playing about peer pressure.[49]

▶ Community Policing and Problem Solving at Work

Ameliorating Juvenile Problems in Tulsa

Following is an excellent case study of community policing and problem-solving efforts using the SARA model in Tulsa, Oklahoma.[50] Note that, instead of merely showing up at a crime scene, taking offense reports, and leaving the scene, the police employed a variety of responses to combat crime and disorder.

Scanning North Tulsa experienced consistently higher crime rates than the rest of the city. Nearly half of the violent crimes that were reported occurred in this section of the city—a depressed low-income area lacking adequate services. The Tulsa Housing Authority was established to support the city's low-income public housing. In an attempt to determine the nature of the crime problem in North Tulsa, a special management team of Tulsa police officials conducted a study and decided to concentrate on five public-housing complexes where high crime rates and blatant street dealing existed.

Analysis A residential survey conducted by patrol officers revealed that 86 percent of the occupants lived in households headed by single females. Officers in the target area noticed large groups of school-age youth in the housing complexes who appeared to be selling drugs during school hours. A comparison of the dropout and suspension rates in North Tulsa schools with those in other areas of the city determined that the city's northernmost high school, serving most of the high school–age youth in the five complexes, had the highest suspension (4.4 percent) and dropout (10 percent) rates of any school in the city. It also reported the highest number of pregnant teenagers in the school system. Few of the juveniles observed in the complexes had legitimate jobs, and most of them appeared to be attracted to drug dealing by the easy money.

Supervisors at Uniform Division North placed volunteers into two-officer foot teams, assigned to the complexes on eight-hour tours. The teams established a rapport with residents and assured them that police were present to ensure their safety. Within a month, officers verified juvenile involvement in drug trafficking. A strategy was needed to provide programs to deter youth from selling or using drugs.

Response Officers S. and N., assigned to foot patrol at one of the complexes, believed that the youth needed programs that would improve their self-esteem, teach them values, and impart decision-making skills. Because 86 percent of the boys came from homes without fathers, the officers started a Boy Scout troop in the complex for boys between eleven and seventeen years of age to provide positive role models for them. Officer N., a qualified Boy Scout leader, and Officer S. began meeting with the boys on Saturdays in a vacant apartment.

Officers J. and E. also organized a Boy Scout troop. In addition, they started a group that worked to raise money for needy residents and police-sponsored youth activities. Officer J. spoke at civic group meetings and local churches throughout the city to solicit donations and increase awareness of the needs of young people on the city's north side. Volunteers came from the churches and the civic groups where Officer J. spoke.

Officers B. and F., foot patrol officers at another complex, developed plans for unemployed young people. Officer B. organized a group called the Young Ladies Awareness Group, which hosted guest speakers who taught different job-related skills each week. Programs instructed young women how to dress for job interviews and employment;

role-playing officers demonstrated proper conduct during interviews. The women were also instructed in résumé writing, makeup, hair care, and personal hygiene. Officer F. worked with a government program that sponsored sessions on setting goals and building self-esteem to prepare young people to enter job-training programs. Officer F. also helped area youth apply for birth certificates and arranged for volunteers from the Oklahoma Highway Patrol and a local school to help teach driver's education. Officers even provided funds for young people who were unable to pay the fees to obtain birth certificates or driver's licenses. Officers F. and B. also tried to explain the value of an education and persuade youth in their complex to return to school. Unfortunately, parents too often appeared unconcerned when their children missed classes.

The foot patrol officers became involved in a day camp project conducted at "the Ranch," a twenty-acre northside property that the police had confiscated from a convicted drug dealer. The project used the property for a day camp for disadvantaged youth recruited from the target projects. Tulsa's mayor and chief of police came to the Ranch to meet with the youth, as did psychologists, teachers, ministers, and celebrities. Guests tried to convey the value of productive and drug-free lives, among other ethical values.

To combat dropout and suspension problems, a program called Adopt a School had police officers patrol the schools during classes, not to make arrests but rather to establish rapport with the students. The program was intended to reduce the likelihood of student involvement in illegal activities.

Assessment The police noted a decline in street sales of illegal drugs in the five target complexes. Youth reacted positively to the officers' efforts to help them, and the programs seemed to deter them from drug involvement. The police department continued to address the problems of poor youth in North Tulsa. Foot patrol officers met with the Task Force for Drug Free Public Housing to inform the different city, county, and statewide officials of the needs of youth in public housing. Other social service agencies began working with the police department, establishing satellite offices on the north side of the city, scheduling programs, and requesting police support in their efforts.

▶ An Emerging Paradigm: Smart Policing

Smart Policing is an emerging paradigm in American policing. It emphasizes the use of data and analytics as well as improved crime analysis, performance measurement, and evaluation research. Next is a brief discussion of this strategy's origin and application in its ten initially selected cities.

Origins

In 2008 and 2009, local police agencies throughout the United States were hard-hit with budget reductions and other problems (hiring stoppages, employee layoffs, deferred technology, and equipment purchases) wrought by the "Great Recession." In addition, many agencies were compelled to cease responding to nonemergency calls, pulled personnel from specialized functions, and even slowed or ceased their community policing and problem-solving activities. Ironically, after years of progress in community policing and problem solving—to include tremendous advances in technologies and thinking in crime analysis and responses, agencies were again forced to focus mainly on reactively responding to calls for service.

As history has shown in policing, however, crises stimulate progress. And so it was against this backdrop of fiscal gloom, "do more with less" situation that the police were again forced to rely on their genius. But first, the federal Bureau of Justice Assistance lived up to its name, however, soliciting the first grant proposals for "Smart Policing" initiatives (SPI) in June 2009, seeking proposals that would identify or confirm effective, crime-reduction techniques that were also efficient (i.e., reasonably affordable) for most agencies to replicate.[51]

A Unique Requirement: Research Partnerships

Perhaps the most important element of SPI is the research partnership. Significantly, the Bureau of Justice Assistance (BJA) emphasized police and criminal justice scholar partnerships for these efforts, working together to test solutions that were informed by crime science theories and assessed with sound evaluation methods. The need for a focus on developing a stronger base of evidence in policing, and for more sophisticated research designs in evaluations of police strategies, was reinforced early in the development of SPI.

How It Works: An Array of Strategies and Tactics

Since BJA made its first ten SPI awards to police agencies in 2009, to date, more than $12.4 million has been awarded to thirty-three local law enforcement agencies conducting thirty-six SPI projects.

Because the initial SPI did not prescribe any particular policing model or approach, but stressed the importance of in-depth problem analysis and definition to guide their later efforts, an impressive array of strategies and tactics were developed and implemented by the local SPI sites. For example, while some sites focused primarily on hot spot and place-based policing strategies, others focused primarily on offender-based approaches (e.g., focused deterrence through identification of prolific offenders and strategic application of suppression and social support strategies). Some first identified hot spots and then pinpointed the prolific offenders within them. Some sites begin with a distinct problem-oriented policing approach (e.g., application of the SARA (scanning, analysis, response, assessment) problem-solving model), and others adopt a distinctly community-oriented policing approach (e.g., strong emphasis on community and victim engagement); again, some sites combine these two approaches. Several sites have implemented initiatives with a strong predictive-analytic approach, others have incorporated elements of intelligence-led policing or have implemented strategies to move their entire agency toward an intelligence-led policing model, others have adopted technological approaches to improving police operations (e.g., strategic use of surveillance cameras, enhanced crime analysis capabilities, enhancements to "real-time crime centers," or enhanced predictive analytic capabilities).

The Philadelphia SPI employed an experimental design in its testing of foot patrol, problem-oriented policing, and offender-focused strategies. The Boston SPI employed a quasi-experimental design using propensity score matching techniques to evaluate the implementation of SPI in thirteen hot spots. The Los Angeles SPI employed an interrupted time-series analysis methodology to evaluate the effectiveness of its SPI in one historically violent police district. The Glendale SPI employed comparative analysis to assess the effectiveness of its problem-oriented policing approach to reducing convenience store theft. The research results from each of these initiatives describe significant crime decreases in the targeted areas and, after accounting for crime levels in the control or comparison areas, for the targeted offenses. In addition to the instrumental (crime reduction) impacts noted earlier, several local SPI sites report positive organizational impacts as a result of their endeavors. In some instances, Smart Policing concepts and materials have been incorporated into police academy training and departmental (e.g., roll call) training. Other sites have reported the incorporation of SPI in police officer performance assessment, and the integration of SPI into CompStat meetings. Initial results indicate that Smart Policing has had a positive impact on these police agencies that have been involved in SPI, which is encouraging and consistent with the original aims of the initiative.

Findings thus far also suggest that: smart policing programs can significantly reduce violent crime (Philadelphia); creative use of crime analytics and crime analysis resources, coupled with targeted problem-solving approaches, can also reduce violent crime in historically violent police districts (Los Angeles); problem-solving teams can prevent violence in stubborn chronic hot spots (Boston); and reduce service calls and property crime at troubled high-traffic convenience stores (Glendale, Arizona). Other SPI projects now underway seek to examine patrol officer body-worn camera testing (Phoenix, Arizona), explore the links between traffic violations/vehicle crashes and other criminal activity (Shawnee, Kansas, and York, Maine) and video camera surveillance of high-density, order-maintenance areas (Pullman, Washington), and test intelligence-led policing (Columbia, South Carolina) and predictive policing (in Cambridge, Massachusetts and Indio, California).

Lessons Learned

Continue the Move Away from Tradition If SPI is to work to its maximum effect, first, police must make a conscious effort to overcome traditional organizational cultures and barriers to collaboration. SPI reinforces the fact that traditional police methods simply do not work in today's society. For example, it has long been held that the best police intervention is enforcement, that is, arrest is the most effective and direct intervention to deal with crime. Several SPI sites challenge this axiom. For example, the Boston SSTs, after advanced training in police problem solving, used the support of analysts to unravel the nature of violence in each micro hot spot. Working with the research team the SSTs developed and implemented 396 distinct problem-oriented strategies. Contrary to traditional police thinking, the data reveal that enforcement accounted for the fewest number of interventions—far outnumbered by the other two response categories.

Furthermore, SPI underscores the futility of merely treating crime and disorder through saturation patrols or massive amounts of overtime. SPI can help to determine the right amount of police effort required to treat a chronic problem, and researcher partners can help with this diagnosis. With a targeted and research-based approach, police can use their resources more effectively.

Technologies and Information Systems for "Deep Analysis" Technologies and information systems are also integral to this strategy: Smart Policing is concerned with using knowledge, evidence, data, and technology to improve the outcomes of police decisions and operations. Technology and human intelligence must be combined in order to inform patrol units as to how to focus their efforts in the right places and on the right people in order to reduce crime. This serves to move the police from merely relying on their personal knowledge, experiences, and connections when implementing the SARA model.

Comprehensive problem analysis is the overarching theme that sets SPI sites apart. The SPI sites placed researchers and police professionals in mutually supportive roles. In addition, under Smart Policing, researchers are engaged early on in the process, so that they can contribute significantly to both scanning and analysis, thereby helping police agencies to refine and strengthen their understanding of the nature and extent of the problem(s) identified.

▼

Certainly technology was an essential piece of these early SPI projects. As shown in Exhibit 4-3 ■, in addition to traditional police resources, LASER involved a criminal intelligence detail (CID) in the Newton Division to develop special criminal bulletins on violent offenders. A Real-Time Crime Center (RACR) involved multiple databases and high-speed analytic capability, so that the police in LASER were equipped with more comprehensive information about violent crime, place and suspects than ever before. Other early SPIs used sophisticated spatial analysis, time-series analysis, and geomapping to plot crime and translate incidents into clusters that led to the identification of priority micro-places; such technologies convey complex information, allowing officers to better visualize problems and develop targeted and efficient solutions.

Where from Here? Future Considerations

The aforementioned SPI efforts provide tremendous wisdom for those agencies that wish to adopt this approach. Hopefully, police executives will realize the essential role research and analysis play in their decision making, and value research and evidence-based approaches. These early studies provide clear and convincing proof that evidence-based policing works. The conditions necessary for a given approach to work vary based on structural, organizational, and environmental factors specific to the location and the agency.

EXHIBIT 4-3

SMART POLICING IN LOS ANGELES: A CASE STUDY

The Los Angeles Police Department Smart Policing Initiative (SPI) sought to reduce gun violence in the Newton Division, one of 21 areas the LAPD serves. The SARA problem-solving process—scanning, analysis, response, and assessment—was first applied. During scanning, the LAPD and its research partner examined gun-related crimes by the Newton Division for 2011, determining it was ranked third in gun violence among the 21 Divisions. Next the Los Angeles SPI team sought to identify specific areas for intervention in the division, employing a geographic analysis of data on gun-related crimes, arrests, and calls for service over a six-year period (2006–2011). The location-based analysis resulted in the identification of five large hot spots. Once the target areas were identified, SPI team developed their intervention strategy, which it termed the Los Angeles Strategic Extraction and Restoration Program (or Operation LASER). Established in September 2011, LASER's overall goal was to target the violent repeat offenders and gang members who committed crimes in the target areas. LASER involved both location- and offender-based strategies, most notably the creation of a Crime Intelligence Detail (CID). CID's primary mission centered on the development of proactive, real-time intelligence briefs called *Chronic Offender Bulletins*. The bulletins assist officers in identifying crime trends and solving current investigations, and gave officers a tool for proactive police work. The SPI team also assessed the impact of LASER using interrupted time-series analysis, looking at monthly crime data for the Newton Division and 18 other divisions from January 2006 to June 2012. Results show that Part I violent crimes, homicide, and robbery all decreased significantly in the Newton Division after Operation LASER began. After the program was implemented, Part I violent crimes in the Newton Division dropped by an average of 5.4 crimes per month, and homicides dropped by 22.6 percent per month. Meanwhile, the crime declines did not occur in the other LAPD divisions, which provided strong evidence that LASER caused the declines in the Newton Division.

Source: A Case Study, California Smart Policing Initiative Reducing Gun-Related Violence through Operation LASER, U.S. Department of Justice, 2012.

Although relatively new, progress against crime fighting under SPI is impressive. Police operations are much better informed when research partners are used in new and innovative ways, and officers engage in problem analysis, intelligence, and comprehensive responses. SPI will help to inform other academics who are engaged in the police research, perhaps also changing the ways in which police research is carried out. Meanwhile, the police can become much more knowledgeable about research methodologies, cause-and-effect, and contribute significantly to future research projects that attempt to attack neighborhood crime and disorder.

The Los Angeles SPI experience described in Exhibit 4-3 offers a number of lessons learned for both police managers and line officers. First, the value of the SARA problem-solving process is underscored, when used as an evidence-based framework for crime control, and it highlights the central role of both crime analysis and technology in data-driven decision making. LASER strongly involved a close working relationship between line officers and crime analysts, and the investment paid off in the target areas.

► Intelligence-Led Policing and Predictive Policing

This section discusses two concepts/policing paradigms—intelligence-led policing (ILP) and predictive policing—that are also useful for crime analysis in the SARA problem-solving process, as well as being complementary to the Smart Policing approach discussed above.

Intelligence-Led Policing: Understanding the "Who" of Crime

Intelligence-led policing (ILP) originated in Great Britain, where police believed that a relatively small number of people were responsible for a comparatively large percentage of crimes; they believed that officers would have the best effect on crime by focusing on the most prevalent offenses occurring in their jurisdiction.[52]

The word *intelligence* is often misused; the most common mistake is to consider intelligence as secretly collected data that were analyzed. Intelligence is information; furthermore, "information plus analysis equals intelligence," and without analysis, there is no intelligence. Intelligence is what is produced after collected data are evaluated and analyzed by a trained intelligence professional.[53]

To better comprehend ILP, let's break it down into its core components. For example, many police agencies have both crime analysts and intelligence analysts. Crime analysts keep their fingers on the pulse of crime in the jurisdiction: which crime trends are up, which ones are down, where the hot spots are, what type of property is being stolen, and so on. Intelligence analysts, on the other hand, are likely to be more aware of the specific *people* responsible for crime in the jurisdiction—who they are, where they live, what they do, whom they associate with, and so on. Integrating these two functions—crime analysis and intelligence analysis—is essential for obtaining a comprehensive grasp of the crime picture. *Crime analysis* allows police to understand the "who, what, when, and where," while *intelligence analysis* provides an understanding of the "who"—the crime networks and individuals.

The National Criminal Intelligence Sharing Plan (NCISP)[54] categorizes the intelligence gathering process into six steps: planning and direction, collection, processing/collation, analysis, dissemination, and reevaluation.

Levels of Intelligence In general, law enforcement agencies can be categorized according to four levels of intelligence operations.[55]

Level 1 intelligence is the highest level, wherein agencies produce tactical and strategic intelligence products that benefit their own department as well as other law enforcement agencies. The law enforcement agency at this level employs an intelligence manager, intelligence officers, and professional intelligence analysts. Examples of level 1 intelligence agencies include the High Intensity Drug Trafficking Area (HIDTA, discussed below), Intelligence Support Centers, and the National Drug Intelligence Center.

Level 2 intelligence includes police agencies that produce tactical and strategic intelligence for internal consumption, generally to support investigations rather than to direct operations. These departments may have intelligence units and intelligence officers, analysts, and an intelligence manager. Some examples are state police agencies, large city police departments, and some investigating commissions, where intelligence supports investigations into complex crimes such as organized crime, insurance fraud, and environmental crime.

Level 3 intelligence is the most common level of intelligence function in the United States. It includes law enforcement agencies with anywhere from dozens to hundreds of sworn employees, and they do not normally employ analysts or intelligence managers; however, they may have named one or more sworn individuals as their "intelligence officers" and may have sent them to intelligence and/or analytic training. These agencies may be capable of developing intelligence products internally, but they are more likely to rely on products developed by partner agencies, such as HIDTAs, federal intelligence centers, and state agencies.

Level 4 intelligence is the category that comprises most agencies in the United States. These agencies, often with a few dozen employees or less, do not employ intelligence personnel. Officers may be involved in a limited information-sharing network made up of county or regional databases. Some departments have received intelligence awareness training and may be able to interpret analytic products.

Intelligence operations have led to the creation of the fusion center (discussed in Chapter 12) and are compatible with the community-oriented policing and problem concepts.[56]

Predictive Policing: Systematic Knowledge of Where Crimes Will Occur

The term predictive policing, according to the U.S. Department of Justice (DOJ), is a relatively new law enforcement concept that "integrates approaches such as cutting-edge crime analysis, crime-fighting technology, intelligence-led policing, and more to inform forward thinking crime prevention strategies and tactics."[57] The DOJ states that, ultimately, predictive policing is intended as a framework to advance strategies like community policing, problem-oriented policing, intelligence-led policing, and hot-spots policing.[58]

The police have always known that robberies surge near check-cashing businesses, that crime spikes on hot days and plummets during the rain, that residential burglaries often occur on Sunday mornings (while people are attending church services), and that Super Bowl Sunday is usually the slowest crime day of the year.[59] But officers' minds can store and remember only so much data. So when the police monitor crime data and query a computer system for historical and real-time patterns, they can predict, more systematically, over a bigger area, and across shifts and time spans, where crimes are likely to occur.

More important, the crime-analysis software does not forget details, get sick, take vacation, or transfer to a different precinct.

So if commercial robberies were high in, say, March 2011, their software will predict another spike in March 2012, and the police can then look at the types of businesses that were hit, their locations, and time of day. The system can even analyze a robber's modus operandi—what was said, type of weapon used, and so on.[60]

Summary

This chapter examined the basic principles and strategies of the current community era—the era in which policing now resides (as noted in Chapter 1). It examined community policing and problem solving (community policing and problem solving), which is the best strategy for addressing neighborhood crime and disorder now and in the future. Blending the two concepts of community policing and problem-oriented policing results in a better, more comprehensive, and long-term approach to providing quality police service, combining the emphasis on forming a police–community partnership to fight crime with the use of the SARA problem-solving process. It was shown that two very important components of this philosophy are the expanded role of the street officer and the focus on crime analysis.

The associated strategy of crime prevention, including crime prevention through environmental design (CPTED) and repeat victimization (RV), is equally important. It is clear that the field of crime prevention has "matured" from its earlier forms, originally involving strategic placement of rocks by early cave dwellers and more recently having to do primarily with target hardening one's home with better locks. This chapter has shown the various elements of CPTED and RV as well as the results of research efforts concerning what good can occur when measures are taken to prevent crimes.

The overarching theme is that the police realize that they alone cannot prevent or address crime and disorder and that a partnership with the community is essential if the physical and social problems that plague communities are to be reduced or eliminated.

Key Terms

community-oriented policing (COP)
community-oriented policing and problem solving
CompStat
crime prevention through environmental design (CPTED)

evaluations
implementation
Intelligence-led policing
Predictive policing
problem-analysis triangle
problem-oriented policing (POP)

repeat victimization (RV)
scanning, analysis, response, assessment (SARA)
Smart Policing

Review Questions

1. How would you define community policing, and what are some of the major ways this concept differs from traditional policing?
2. What are the four parts of the SARA problem-solving process?
3. What are the major elements of implementation and evaluation phases of community policing and problem solving, and why are they so critical?
4. What is CompStat? How does it function, and why is it now sweeping the nation's police agencies as a means toward crime suppression?

5. What are some methods, problems, and successes that are involved in evaluating community policing and problem solving?
6. What is meant by crime prevention, and how does it relate to community policing and problem solving?
7. How can social networking assist community policing and problem solving?
8. What does the Tulsa case study demonstrate in terms of how community policing and problem solving functions and what this strategy accomplished with that city's juvenile problems?
9. What is Smart Policing? How did it originate, and what has been learned from the test sites and where has it been tested?

Learn by Doing

1. Assume that for the past six months a small neighborhood market in the western part of the city has generated dozens of calls for service about drug dealing because of several drug dealers and users frequenting the area. Part I ("Index") crimes are beginning to increase in the area as well. A nearby drug house contributes heavily to the problem, and a T-shaped alley behind the store provides easy ingress and egress for buyers, both on foot and in vehicles. The lighting is poor, and pay telephones in front of the store are constantly in use by traffickers. You are assigned to launch a POP/SARA initiative at the location to effect long-term results. What kinds of information would you collect about the area and the drug problem? What kinds of responses might be considered? What types of assessment would you perform?

2. Using media reports or local crime data (oftentimes available from your local police agency Web site), identify a particularly crime-ridden neighborhood, beat, or area of your jurisdiction. Then, using techniques described in this chapter, including the problem-analysis triangle and SARA, explain what your approach would be to bringing a sense of order to that area through the use of a problem-solving exercise.

3. Your chief executive has assigned you, as head of the agency's research, planning, and analysis unit, the task of developing a comprehensive report containing recommendations for establishing a CompStat program. Explain what your report would contain.

4. Develop a one-hour course on the fundamentals of "Crime Prevention" for your area police academy (to include CPTED and repeat victimization).

Notes

1. W. L. Melville Lee, *A History of Police in England* (London: Methuen, 1901), ch. 12.
2. Robert Trojanowicz and Bonnie Bucqueroux, *Community Policing: A Contemporary Perspective* (Cincinnati, OH: Anderson, 1990), p. 154.
3. Mark H. Moore and Robert C. Trojanowicz, *Corporate Strategies for Policing* (Washington, D.C.: Government Printing Office, 1988), pp. 8–9.
4. Sheila Muto, "Arresting Design: Police Stations Get a Lift," *Wall Street Journal*, January 5, 2005, p. B-1.
5. Herman Goldstein, "Problem-Oriented Policing" (paper presented at the Conference on Policing: State of the Art III, National Institute of Justice, Phoenix, June 12, 1987).
6. Ibid., pp. 43–52.
7. Noah Fritz, *Crime Analysis* (Tempe, AZ: Tempe Police Department, n.d.), p. 9.
8. John Eck, *A Dissertation Prospectus for the Study of Characteristics of Drug Dealing Places* (College Park: University of Maryland, November 1992).
9. Barbara Webster and Edward F. Connors, *Community Policing: Identifying Problems* (Alexandria, VA: Institute for Law and Justice, March 1991), p. 9.
10. See Lawrence W. Sherman, Patrick R. Gartin, and Michael E. Buerger, "Hot Spots of Predatory Crime: Routine Activities and the Criminology of Place," *Criminology* 27 (1989): 27.
11. Ibid., p. 36.
12. William Spelman, *Beyond Bean Counting: New Approaches for Managing Crime Data* (Washington, D.C.: Police Executive Research Forum, January 1988).
13. Webster and Connors, *Community Policing*, p. 11.
14. For an example of this type of survey process, see William H. Lindsey and Bruce Quint, *The Oasis Technique* (Fort Lauderdale: Florida Atlantic University/Florida International University Joint Center for Environmental and Urban Problems, 1986).
15. Rana Sampson, "Problem Solving," in *Neighborhood-Oriented Policing in Rural Communities: A Program Planning Guide* (Washington, D.C.: U.S. Department

of Justice, Office of Justice Programs, Bureau of Justice Assistance, 1994), p. 4.

16. Darrel Stephens, "Community Problem-Oriented Policing: Measuring Impacts," in *Quantifying Quality in Policing*, ed. Larry T. Hoover (Washington, D.C.: Police Executive Research Forum, 1995).

17. U.S. Department of Justice, Office of Community Oriented Policing Services, *Problem-Solving Tips: A Guide to Reducing Crime and Disorder Through Problem-Solving Partnerships* (Washington, D.C.: Author, 2002), p. 20.

18. Moore and Trojanowicz, *Corporate Strategies for Policing*, p. 11.

19. Kenneth J. Peak and Ronald W. Glensor, *Community Policing and Problem Solving: Strategies and Practices*, 5th ed. (Upper Saddle River, NJ: Prentice Hall, 2008), p. 85.

20. Ibid.

21. Herman Goldstein, *Problem-Oriented Policing* (New York: McGraw-Hill, 1990), p. 172.

22. Gregory Saville and D. Kim Rossmo, "Striking a Balance: Lessons from Community-Oriented Policing in British Columbia, Canada" (unpublished manuscript, June 1993), pp. 29–30.

23. Ronald W. Glensor and Kenneth J. Peak, "Implementing Change: Community-Oriented Policing and Problem Solving," *FBI Law Enforcement Bulletin* 7 (July 1996): 14–20.

24. John E. Eck and William Spelman, *Problem-Solving: Problem-Oriented Policing in Newport News* (Washington, D.C.: Police Executive Research Forum, 1987), pp. 100–101.

25. Ibid., p. 9.

26. Herman Goldstein, "Toward Community-Oriented Policing," *Crime and Delinquency* 33 (1987): 6–30.

27. Ibid., p. 21.

28. Ibid.

29. Daniel DeLorenzi, Jon M. Shane, and Karen L. Amendola, "The CompStat Process: Managing Performance on the Pathway to Leadership," *The Police Chief* 73 (September 2006), http://www.policechiefmagazine.org/magazine/index.cfm?fuseaction=display&article_id=998&issue_id=92006 (accessed October 24, 2013).

30. Ibid.

31. Ibid.

32. Heath B. Grant and Karen J. Terry, *Law Enforcement in the 21st Century* (Boston: Allyn & Bacon, 2005), pp. 329–330.

33. David M. Kennedy and Mark Moore, "Underwriting the Risky Investment in Community Policing: What Social Science Should Be Doing to Evaluate Community Policing," *Justice System Journal* 17(1995):271–289; Robert Trojanowicz and Bonnie Bucqueroux, *Community Policing: A Contemporary Perspective* (Cincinnati, OH: Anderson, 1990).

34. A. Lurigio and D. P. Rosenbaum, "The Impact of Community Policing on Police Personnel," in *The Challenge of Community Policing: Testing the Promise*, ed. D. P. Rosenbaum, (Thousand Oaks, CA: Sage, 1994).

35. Donald S. Quire, "Models for Community Policing Evaluation: The St. Petersburg Experience," September 2008, p. 13, www.fdle.state.fl.us/Content/Florida-Criminal-Justice-Executive-Institute/Docs/Quire.aspx (accessed October 25, 2013).

36. Gary W. Cordner, "Community Policing: Elements and Effects," in *Critical Issues in Policing: Contemporary Readings*, 4th ed., eds. Roger G. Dunham and Geoffrey P. Alpert, (Prospect Heights, IL: Waveland, 2001), pp. 493–510.

37. Nadine M. Connell, Kristen Miggans, and Jean Marie McGloin, "Can a Community Policing Initiative Reduce Serious Crime? A Local Evaluation," *Police Quarterly*, 11(2) (2008): 130–132.

38. Ibid., p. 146.

39. Jim Jordan, "Shifting the Mission: Seeing Prevention as the Strategic Goal, Not a Set of Programs," in *Subject to Debate* (Washington, D.C.: Police Executive Research Forum, December 1999), pp. 1–2.

40. Ibid., p. 8.

41. C. R. Jeffrey, *Crime Prevention Through Environmental Design* (Beverly Hills, CA: Sage, 1971).

42. National Crime Prevention Council, *Designing Safer Communities: A Crime Prevention Through Environmental Design Handbook* (Washington, D.C.: Author, 1997), pp. 7–8.

43. Ibid., p. 3.

44. G. Farrell and W. Sousa, "Repeat Victimization in the United States and Ten Other Industrialized Countries" (paper presented at the National Conference on Preventing Crime, Washington, D.C., October 13, 1997).

45. Ibid.

46. G. Farrell, "Preventing Repeat Victimization," in *Building a Safer Society*, eds. M. Tonry and D. P. Farrington (Chicago: University of Chicago Press, 1995), pp. 469–534.

47. Jessica Reaves, "Just Say No to DARE," *Time.com*, February 15, 2001, www.time.com/time/nation/article/0,8599,99564,00.html (accessed October 25, 2013).

48. Rocky Anderson, quoted in Claudia Kalb, "DARE Checks into Rehab," *Newsweek*, February 26, 2001, p. 56.

49. Ibid.

50. U.S. Department of Justice, Bureau of Justice Assistance, *Problem-Oriented Drug Enforcement: A Community-Based Approach for Effective Policing* (Washington, D.C.: Police Executive Research Forum, October 1993), pp. 27–28.

51. Information concerning the origins and initial grant funded test sites for SPI was obtained from the following sources: James R. Coldren Jr., Alissa Huntoon, and Michael Medaris, "Introducing Smart Policing: Foundations, Principles, and Practice," *Police Quarterly* 16(3) (September 2013): 275–286; and Nola M. Joyce, Charles H. Ramsey, and James K. Stewart, "Commentary on Smart Policing," *Police Quarterly* 16(3) (September 2013): 358–368. This special issue of *Police Quarterly* contains a number of other, site-specific articles that discuss SPI.

52. U.S. Department of Justice, Office of Justice Programs, Bureau of Justice Statistics, *Intelligence-Led Policing: The New Intelligence Architecture* (Washington, D.C.: Author, 2005), p. 9.

53. Ibid., p. 3.

54. See U.S. Department of Justice, Office of Justice Programs, *National Criminal Intelligence Sharing Plan*, p. 6, www.fas.org/irp/agency/doj/ncisp.pdf (accessed October 25, 2013).

55. Ibid., pp. 12–13.

56. Ibid., pp. 10–11.

57. U.S. Department of Justice, "Predictive Policing: A National Discussion," blogs.usdoj.gov/blog/archives/385 (accessed October 24, 2013).

58. U.S. Department of Justice, National Institute of Justice, "Predictive Policing Symposium: The Future of Prediction in Criminal Justice," http://www.nij.gov/topics/law-enforcement/strategies/predictive-policing/symposium/future.htm (accessed October 25, 2013).

59. Ellen Perlman, "Policing by the Odds," *Governing*, December 1, 2008, www.governing.com/article/policing-odds (accessed October 25, 2013).

60. Ibid.

(Courtesy mikeledray/Shutterstock.)

5 Criminal Investigation
The Science of Sleuthing

LEARNING OBJECTIVES

As a result of reading this chapter, the student will be able to:

1 *Distinguish between* forensic science *and* criminalistics

2 *Understand the origins of criminalistics as well as the types of information that physical evidence can provide*

3 *Compare anthropometry and dactylography*

4 *Explain how Bertillon, Locard, Vollmer, and others contributed to the development of criminal investigation techniques*

5 *Describe the kinds of qualities that detectives and undercover officers need to possess*

(6) *Delineate the functions of medical examiners and coroners*

(7) *Explain the basic functions of the polygraph and its legal status in the courts*

(8) *Describe how DNA analysis operates (including a new approach, using familial DNA) as well as recent developments and some legal and policy issues concerning its use*

(9) *Explain the contributions of social networking sites to criminal investigations*

(10) *Describe the purpose and operation of a cold case squad*

(11) *Clarify whether or not there is a "CSI effect" relating to criminal cases*

(12) *Relate the contributions of dogs to the investigative process*

Introduction

The challenges involved with investigating crimes may well be characterized by a quote from Ludwig Wittgenstein: "How hard I find it to see what is right in front of my eyes!" Investigating crimes has indeed become a complicated art as well as a science, as will be seen in this chapter.

The art of sleuthing has long fascinated the American public. People appear to be completely enthralled with anything involving forensics and criminal psychoses (e.g., *CSI, Dexter, Criminal Minds*), as well as the exploits of detectives as they pursue serial killers (e.g., *Silence of the Lambs, Se7en*). Nor is this public interest in sleuthing a recent phenomenon: for decades, Americans have feasted on the exploits of dozens of fictional masterminds and detectives in books and movies, such as Arthur Conan Doyle's Sherlock Holmes, Agatha Christie's Hercule Poirot and Miss Marple, and Clint Eastwood's Detective "Dirty Harry" Callahan, to name a few.

In reality, investigative work is largely misunderstood, often boring, and overrated; it results in arrests only a fraction of the time; and it relies strongly on the assistance of witnesses and even some luck. Nonetheless, the related fields of forensic science and criminalistics are the most rapidly developing areas of policing—and probably in all of criminal justice. This is an exciting time to be in the investigative or forensic disciplines.

This chapter begins by defining forensic science and criminalistics and by looking at their origins; included is a brief discussion of crime scenes. Then we review the evolution of criminal investigation, emphasizing the identification of people and firearms. Next we analyze the application of forensic science within the larger context of the criminal justice system, followed by a review of the qualities detectives and undercover officers should have, and the role of the medical examiner. We then briefly touch on the use of polygraph testing.

The status of DNA analysis is covered next; here we consider some new policy and legal developments—whether DNA testing should be employed for property crimes as well as for convicted offenders; also in this connection we consider a new testing approach of what is termed "familial DNA." We then look at the contributions to investigations made by criminal profiling and psycholinguistics, and then we examine several developing areas in the field: using social networking sites, the handling of cold cases, and the use of dogs. Finally, we consider whether or not the ubiquitous use of DNA and other forensic tools in television and movie portrayals has created an unrealistic expectation of such evidence in the eyes of the jury—the so-called CSI Effect. After a discussion of three investigative techniques—use of informants, interviewing, and interrogating—the chapter concludes with a summary, key terms, review questions, and several scenarios and activities that provide opportunities for you to learn by doing.

► Scope of Forensic Science and Criminalistics

Definitions of Terms

The terms *forensic science* and *criminalistics* are often used interchangeably. Forensic science is the broader term and is that part of science used to answer legal questions. It is the examination, evaluation, and explanation of physical evidence in law. Forensic science encompasses pathology, toxicology, physical anthropology, odontology (the study of tooth anatomy and development and diseases of the teeth and related structures), psychiatry, questioned documents, ballistics, tool work comparison, and serology (the study of reactions and properties of serums), among other fields.[1] Criminalistics is one branch of forensic science; it deals with the study of physical evidence related to crime. From such a study, a crime may be reconstructed.

Career Profile

(Courtesy Renee Romero)

Name: Renee Romero

Position: Director, Washoe County Sheriff's Office-Forensic Science Division (FSD)

City, State: Reno, NV

College attended: Michigan State University (MSU) and University of Nevada, Reno

Academic Major: Bachelor degree-MSU-chemistry and forensic science; master's degree-UNR-cell and molecular biology

How long have you occupied this position/assignment?

I have been at the Washoe County Sheriff's Office Forensic Science Division for 23 years. I started as a student intern in 1988 then moved on the becoming a criminalist, supervising criminalist, and now have been the director of the division for the past 5 years.

How would you briefly describe this position/assignment?

As director of the FSD, I manage people, budgets, and human resources issues much like a director of any organization. I also constantly work to meet or exceed international forensic accreditation requirements. A criminalist (forensic scientist) is responsible for performing casework in a specific forensic discipline such as DNA, toxicology, firearms, breath alcohol, or controlled substances. Upon completion of casework, a report is issued to a law enforcement agency. The criminalist may then be called upon to testify to their findings during a legal proceeding.

What attracted you to this post/assignment?

I was initially attracted to forensic science at Michigan State University while I was working on a chemistry degree. While at MSU, I found out about and completed their forensic science program. At the time there were no TV shows such as *CSI*. There was an older TV show, *Quincy*, that portrayed a medical examiner but forensics was not nearly as popular or glamorized as it is today. I liked science and forensics science appeared to me to be a very meaningful way to apply science to criminal investigations.

What qualities/characteristics are most helpful for this position/assignment?

Attention to detail is probably the biggest quality a forensic scientist can have. An aptitude for science, organizational skills, and public speaking abilities are necessary as well. One needs to be able to communicate forensic results effectively to a jury.

How would you describe a typical day for one in this position/assignment?

A forensic scientist's typical day can range from performing laboratory examinations, interpreting data, performing quality assurance or validations, or testifying in court. As a Director, a typical day involves reviewing forensic case reports, emphasizing quality assurance expectations, and meeting with various groups to further the overall forensic science division goals.

What advice would you offer someone who is beginning their studies of policing and criminal justice?

If you are interested in criminalistics, obtain a minimum of a bachelor's degree in a scientific discipline. If you are interested in DNA you should obtain a Master's degree. *CSI* TV shows are pretty far from reality. Talk to somebody who works in the field to find out if this is something you are really interested in. The job of a crime scene investigator is very different from a criminalist. On TV they are one and the same. A crime scene investigator lives a life of being on call at all hours of the day and night to go out to scenes in a variety of conditions. A criminalist spends their days in a laboratory environment. Neither one of them interviews suspects and victims; that is the job of a law enforcement detective or investigator. Be prepared to work on emotionally charged casework with an unbiased approach.

Criminalistics is interdisciplinary, drawing on mathematics, physics, chemistry, biology, anthropology, and many other scientific fields.[2] The Career Profile on the previous page describes the work and preparation for one who works in a forensic laboratory.

Basically, the analysis of physical evidence is concerned with identifying traces of evidence, reconstructing criminal acts, and establishing a common origin of samples of evidence. Peter DeForest and colleagues described the types of information that physical evidence can provide:[3]

- *Information on the* corpus delicti *(body of the crime)*. Physical evidence, such as tool marks, a broken door or window, a ransacked home, missing valuables in a burglary, a victim's blood, a weapon, or clothing torn in an assault, shows that a crime was committed.

- *Information on the* modus operandi *(method of operation)*. Physical evidence points to the means used by the criminal to gain entry, the tools used in the crime, the types of items taken, and other signs, such as urine left at the scene, an accelerant used at an arson scene, and the way crimes are committed. Many well-known criminals have left their "calling card" at their crimes, in terms of either what they did to their victims or the physical condition of the crime scene.

- *Linking of a suspect with a victim.* One of the most important linkages, particularly with violent crimes, is the connection to the suspect. This can include hair, blood, clothing fibers, and cosmetics that may be transferred from the victim to the perpetrator. Items found in a suspect's possession, such as bullets or a bloody knife, can also be linked to a victim.

- *Linking of a person to a crime scene.* Also a common and significant type of linkage, this includes fingerprints, glove prints, blood, semen, hairs, fibers, soil, bullets, cartridge cases, tool marks, footprints or shoe prints, tire tracks, and objects that belonged to the criminal. Stolen property is the most obvious example.

- *Disproving or supporting of a witness's testimony.* Evidence can indicate whether or not a person's version of events is true. An example is a driver whose car matches the description of a hit-and-run vehicle. If blood is found on the underside of the car and the driver claims that he hit a dog, tests on the blood can determine whether the blood is from an animal or from a human.

- *Identification of a suspect.* One of the best forms of evidence for identifying a suspect is fingerprints, which prove "individualization." Without a doubt, that person was at the crime scene.

A Word About Crime Scenes

On the subject of the crime scene, we will not go into detail concerning the roles of patrol officers, crime-scene technicians, and investigators; however, it should be emphasized that the protection of the crime scene and all evidence contained therein is of utmost importance for these personnel if the scene is to be properly preserved and evidence properly collected and analyzed. It is critical that at the moment they arrive, responding personnel are trained to (1) describe vehicles (make, model, color, condition, license plate number) and individuals (height, weight, race, age, clothing, sex, distinguishing features), including their direction of travel from first observation; (2) assess the scene for officer safety (downed power lines, animals, biohazards, chemicals, weapons); (3) watch for violent persons and attend to any emergency medical needs; and (4) prevent any unauthorized persons from entering the scene. A very good resource for crime-scene investigation, published by the National Institute of Justice, is titled *Crime Scene Investigation: A Reference for Law Enforcement Training*.[4]

▲ Technology is rapidly advancing in forensic laboratories. Here (clockwise from upper-left), lab technicians perform drug, toxicology (alcohol or drugs), document, and DNA examinations. *(Courtesy Washoe County Sheriff's Office and FBI.)*

▶ Origins of Criminalistics

The study of criminalistics began in Europe. The first major book describing the application of scientific disciplines to criminal investigations was written in 1893 by Hans Gross, a public prosecutor and later a judge from Graz, Austria.[5] Translated into English in 1906, the book remains a highly respected work in the field. Two prominent aspects of criminalistics, personal identification and firearms analysis, are covered next, followed by a discussion of individual contributions, investigative techniques, and state and federal developments in the field.

Personal Identification: Anthropometry and Dactylography

Anthropometry Historically, two major systems for personal identification of criminals have been used: *anthropometry* and *dactylography*. Dactylography, better known as fingerprint identification, is widely used throughout the world today.

Anthropometry, a system that did not survive long, was developed in 1882 by Alphonse Bertillon (1853–1914). The Bertillon system, the first attempt at criminal identification that was thought to be reliable and accurate, was based on the theory that human beings differ from each other in the exact measurements of their bodies and that the sum of these measurements yields a characteristic formula for each individual.[6]

Bertillon performed menial tasks in 1879 for the Paris Police Department, filing cards that described criminals so vaguely as to have little meaning—"stature: average . . . face: ordinary."[7] He began comparing photographs of criminals and taking measurements of those who had been arrested, and eventually concluded that if eleven physical measurements of a person were taken, the chances of finding another person with the same eleven measurements were 4,191,304 to 1.[8] Bertillon's report of his findings to his superiors was treated as a "joke," however[9]; but in 1883 his "joke" was given worldwide attention when it was implemented on an experimental basis and Bertillon correctly made his first criminal identification.[10]

Around the start of the twentieth century, many countries abandoned anthropometry, or the Bertillon system, adopting the simpler and more reliable system of fingerprint identification.[11] Still, Bertillon's pioneering work in personal identification has earned him a place in history, and today he is considered the "father of criminal investigation."[12]

ABSTRACT OF
THE ANTHROPOMETRICAL SIGNALMENT

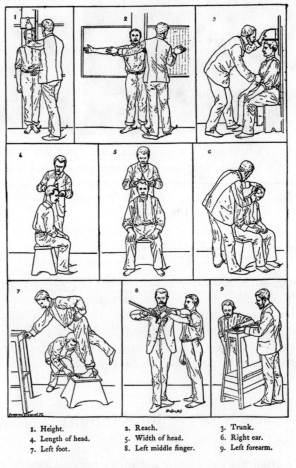

1. Height.	2. Reach.	3. Trunk.
4. Length of head.	5. Width of head.	6. Right ear.
7. Left foot.	8. Left middle finger.	9. Left forearm.

▲ A police officer taking Bertillon measurements. (*Courtesy Science Source.*)

The major breakthrough for fingerprints was made by Edward Henry (1850–1931), who developed a fingerprint-classification system in 1897 that was adopted throughout British India. In 1901, Henry published his *Classification and Use of Finger Prints* and was appointed assistant police commissioner of London, rising to the post of commissioner two years later.[13]

The Jones Case. In 1904, Detective Sergeant Joseph Faurot of New York City was sent to England to study fingerprints. Upon his return to New York, Faurot was told by his superiors to forget such scientific nonsense, and he was transferred to a walking beat. In 1906, Faurot arrested a man who was creeping out of a suite at the Waldorf-Astoria Hotel; the man claimed to be a respected citizen named James Jones, but Faurot sent the man's fingerprints to Scotland Yard and learned that "James Jones" was actually Daniel Nolan, who had twelve prior convictions for hotel thefts. Nolan confessed to several thefts in the Waldorf-Astoria and was sent to prison for seven years. Publicity surrounding this case greatly advanced the credibility of fingerprinting in America.[14]

The West Case. An even more important incident that furthered the use of fingerprints in America occurred in 1903 when Will West arrived at the federal penitentiary in Leavenworth, Kansas. While West was being processed into the institution, a staff member said that a photograph was already on file for him, along with Bertillon measurements. West denied ever having been in Leavenworth. A comparison of fingerprints showed that despite nearly identical physical appearance and Bertillon measurements, the

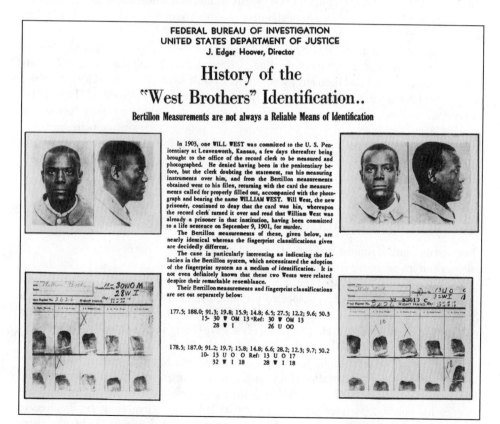

▲ The "West Brothers" case: Two men having close physical resemblance, nearly identical measurements, and the same name (William West) at the same penitentiary caused much confusion about their true identities. The case showed the fallacies of the Bertillon system and the superior nature of fingerprints as a means of identification. *(Courtesy FBI.)*

identification card on file belonged to a William West who had been in Leavenworth since 1901. The incident served to establish the superiority of fingerprints over anthropometry as a system of personal identification.

Locard's Exchange Principle

Due in large part to Bertillon's influence, Dr. Edmond Locard developed, in 1910, what is today widely regarded as the cornerstone of the forensic sciences: Locard's exchange principle (also known as Locard's Theory). Basically this principle or theory asserts that when any person comes into contact with an object or other person, a cross-transfer of evidence—in the form of fingerprints, hairs, fibers, and all manner of residue or other materials—will occur.[15] An example is when a victim is strangled to death (by an assailant who is not wearing gloves), the suspect may well have the victim's skin cells under his nails, the victims hair on his clothing, and other such residual material on his person.

For these reasons, it is obviously of utmost importance that the crime scene be protected against contamination in order that any such trace evidence may be properly collected and preserved.

Firearms Identification

Firearms are involved in nearly 500,000 fatal and nonfatal violent crimes per year in this country; of those incidents, about 11,000 results in murder, while about 52,000 result in nonfatal shooting.[16] The frequency of shootings in this country has obviously made firearms identification very important.

Chicago witnessed the St. Valentine's Day Massacre in 1929. A special grand jury inquiring into the matter noted that there were no facilities for analyzing the numerous bullets and cartridge cases that had been strewn about. As a result, several influential jury members raised funds to establish a permanent crime laboratory. Colonel Calvin Goddard (1858–1946) was appointed director of the lab and is the person most responsible for raising the status of firearms identification to a science and for perfecting the bullet comparison microscope.[17]

Firearms identification goes beyond comparing a bullet found in the victim and a test bullet fired from the defendant's weapon. It also includes identifying types of ammunition, designing firearms, restoring obliterated serial numbers on weapons, and estimating the distance between a gun's muzzle and a victim when the weapon was fired.[18]

Contributions of August Vollmer and Others

The contributions of August Vollmer (discussed in Chapter 1) to the development of criminalistics and investigative techniques should not be overlooked. In 1907, as police chief of Berkeley, California, he enlisted the services of a University of California chemistry professor named Loeb to identify a suspected poison during a murder investigation. Vollmer instituted a formal training program to ensure that his officers properly collected and preserved criminal evidence. He also called on scientists on campus on several other occasions, and his support helped John Larson produce the first workable polygraph in 1921.

Vollmer also established in Los Angeles in 1923 the first full forensic laboratory; the concept soon spread to other cities, including Sacramento (a state laboratory), San Francisco, and San Diego. Because Vollmer's subsequent efforts to establish a relationship between his police department and the university led other scientists to get involved in forensic science, eventually courses in forensics were offered as part of the biochemistry curriculum at the University of California at Berkeley,[19] with many graduates of that program becoming criminalists.

Other early major contributors included Albert Osborn, who in 1910 wrote *Questioned Documents*, a definitive work; Edmond Locard, who maintained a central interest in locating microscopic evidence; and Leone Lattes, who in 1915 developed a blood-typing procedure from dried blood, a key event in serology.[20]

The forerunner of what was to become the Federal Bureau of Investigation (FBI; discussed in Chapter 10) was created in 1908. In 1924, J. Edgar Hoover assumed leadership of the Bureau of Investigation; eleven years later, Congress enacted legislation giving the FBI its present designation. Under Hoover, who understood the importance and uses of information, records, and publicity, the FBI became known for investigative efficiency. In 1932, the FBI established a crime laboratory and made its services free—they remain free of charge today to state and local police. In 1935, it opened its National Academy, providing training courses for state and local police as well as federal officers. And in 1967, the National Crime Information Center (NCIC) was made operational by the FBI, providing data on wanted persons and stolen property in all fifty states. These developments gave the FBI considerable influence over policing in America; Hoover and the FBI vastly improved policing practices in the United States, keeping crime statistics and assisting investigations.[21]

▶ Forensic Science and the Criminal Justice System

Investigative Stages and Activities

The police (more specifically, investigators and criminalists) operate on the age-old theory that there is no such thing as a perfect crime: Criminals either leave a bit of themselves (such as a hair or clothing fiber) at the crime scene or take a piece of the crime scene away with them. Thus it is the job of the police and the crime lab to unify their efforts and to find that incriminating piece of evidence, which they can use in conjunction with other pieces of evidence to determine "whodunit" and to bring the guilty party to justice.

In the apprehension process, when a crime is reported or discovered, police officers respond, conduct a search for the offender (it may be a "hot" crime-scene search where the offender is likely present, a "warm" search in the general vicinity, or a "cold" investigative search), and check out suspects. If the search is successful, evidence for charging the suspect is assembled, and the suspect is apprehended.[22] Cases not solved in the initial phase of the apprehension process are assigned either to an investigative specialist or, in smaller police agencies, to an experienced uniformed officer who functions as a part-time investigator. According to Paul Weston and Kenneth Wells, what follows are the basic investigative stages:[23]

Preliminary investigation. The work of the preliminary investigation is crucial, involving the first police officer at the scene. Duties to be completed include establishing whether a crime has been committed; securing from any witnesses a description of the perpetrator and his or her vehicle; locating and interviewing the victim and all witnesses; protecting the crime scene (and searching for and collecting all items of possible physical evidence); determining how the crime was committed and what the resulting injuries were, as well as the nature of property taken; recording in field notes and sketches all data about the crime; and arranging for photographs of the crime scene.

Continuing investigation. The next stage, which begins when preliminary work is done, includes conducting follow-up interviews; developing a theory of the crime; analyzing the significance of information and evidence; continuing the search for witnesses; beginning to contact crime lab technicians and assessing their analyses of the evidence; conducting surveillances, interrogations, and polygraph tests, as appropriate; and preparing the case for the prosecutor.

Reconstruction of the crime. The investigator seeks a rational theory of the crime. Most often, inductive reasoning is used: The collected information and evidence are carefully analyzed to develop a theory. Often, a rational theory of a crime is developed with some assistance from the careless criminal. *Verbrecherpech,* or "criminal's bad luck," is an unconscious act of self-betrayal. One of the major traits of criminals is vanity; their belief in their own cleverness, not chance, is the key factor in their leaving a vital clue. Investigators look for mistakes.

Focus of the investigation. When the last stage is reached, all investigative efforts are directed toward proving that one suspect (perhaps with accomplices) is guilty of the crime. This decision is based on the investigator's analysis of the connections between the crime, the investigation, and the habits and attitudes of the suspect.

Arrest and Case Preparation

A lawful arrest brings the investigation into even greater focus and provides the police with several investigative opportunities. The person arrested can be searched and booked at the police station, and fingerprints can be taken for positive identification and possible future use. Evidence may be found at these stages. The prisoner may wish to talk to the police. Here, the officer must obviously know and understand the laws of arrest and search and seizure as well as the laws of evidence (especially the "chain of custody"). Any evidence found during the arrest must be collected, marked, transported, and preserved as carefully as that found at a crime scene.

"Case preparation is organization."[24] For an investigation to succeed at trial, all reports, documents, and exhibits must be arrayed in an orderly manner. This package must then be forwarded to the prosecutor. At this point, the investigator never injects personal opinions or conclusions into the case. The identification of the accused leads to an array of witnesses and physical evidence. The corpus delicti of the crime has been established, and the combination of "what happened" and "who did it" has occurred, at least in the mind of the investigator. The investigator must also prepare for the almost inevitable negative evidence that must be countered at trial, where the accused may contend that he or she did not commit the crime. (He or she may try to attack the investigative work, use an alibi, or get the evidence suppressed.) The defendant may offer an affirmative defense, admitting that he or she committed the acts charged but claiming that he or she was coerced, acted in self-defense, was legally insane, and so forth. Or the defendant may attack the corpus delicti, contending that no crime was committed or that there was no intent present.[25]

In the prosecutor's office, the case is reviewed, assigned for further investigation, and (if warranted) prepared for trial. Conferences with the investigator and witnesses are usually held. The prosecutor may waive prosecution if the case appears to be too weak to result in a conviction; if the accused will inform on other (usually more serious) offenders; if a plea bargain is more attractive than a trial; or if there are mitigating circumstances in the case (such as emotional disturbance).

An investigation is successful when the crime being investigated is solved and the case closed. Often a case is considered cleared even if no arrest has been made, as when the offender dies, the case is found to be a murder–suicide, the victim refuses to cooperate with the police or prosecutor, or the offender has left the jurisdiction and the cost of extradition is not justified.[26]

▶ Detectives: Qualities, Myths, and Attributes

The detective function is now well established within the police community. A survey by the RAND Corporation revealed that every city with a population of more than 250,000, along with 90 percent of the smaller cities, has officers specifically assigned to investigative duties.[27]

Several myths surround police detectives, who are often portrayed in movies as rugged, confident (sometimes overbearing), independent, streetwise individualists who bask in glory, are rewarded with big arrests, and are adorned by beautiful women. Detective work carries a strong appeal for many patrol officers, young and veteran alike. In reality, detective work is seldom glamorous or exciting. Investigators, like their bureaucratic cousins, often wade in paperwork and spend many hours on the telephone. Furthermore, studies have not been kind to detectives, showing that their vaunted productivity is overrated. Not all cases have a good or even a 50–50 chance of being cleared by an arrest. Indeed, in a study of over 150 large police departments, a RAND research team learned that only about 20 percent of their crimes could have been solved by detective work.[28] Another study, involving the Kansas City, Missouri, Police Department, found that fewer than 50 percent of all reported crimes received more than a minimal half hour's investigation by detectives. In many of these cases, detectives merely reported the facts discovered by the patrol officers during the preliminary investigations.[29]

Yet the importance and role of detectives should not be understated. Detectives know that a criminal is more than a criminal. As Weston and Wells said:

> John, Jane and Richard are not just burglar, prostitute and killer. John is a hostile burglar and is willing to enter a premises that might be occupied. Jane is a prostitute who wants a little

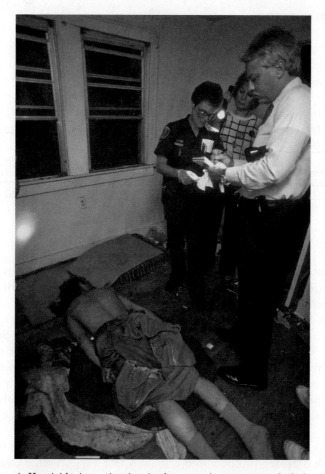

▲ Homicide investigation is the most important and challenging work performed by detectives. *(Courtesy Photo by Shelly Katz//Time Life Pictures/Getty Images.)*

more than pay for services rendered and is suspected of working with a robbery gang and enticing her customers to secluded areas. Richard is an accidental, a person who, in a fit of rage, killed the girl who rejected him.[30]

To be successful, the investigator must possess four personal attributes to enhance the detection of crime: an unusual capability for observation and recall; an extensive knowledge of the law, rules of evidence, scientific aids, and laboratory services; a powerful imagination; and a working knowledge of social psychology.[31] Successful detectives (and even patrol officers) also appear to empathize with the suspect; if a detective can appear to understand why a criminal did what he or she did ("You robbed that store because your kids were hungry, right?"), a rapport is often established that results in the suspect's telling the officer his or her life history—including how and why he or she committed the crime in question. Perhaps first and foremost, however, detectives need logical skills, the ability to exercise deductive reasoning, to assist in their investigative work. (An interesting example of the logical skills needed for police work was provided by Al Seedman, former chief of detectives for the New York Police Department, in Chapter 2.)

▶ Officers Who "Disappear": Working Undercover

Undercover work is a highly sought after and valued type of investigative police work. Undercover work can be defined as the assignment of police officers to investigative roles in which they adopt fictitious civilian identities for a sustained period of time in order to uncover criminal activities that are not usually reported to police.[32]

Undercover police operations have increased greatly since the 1970s, owing largely to expanded drug investigations. The selection process typically is intense and very competitive. Since only a few officers are actually selected for undercover assignments, these officers enjoy a professional mystique, in large measure because of wide discretionary and procedural latitude in their roles, minimal departmental supervision, ability to exercise greater personal initiative, and higher degree of professional autonomy than regular patrol officers.[33]

Problems with the Role

The conditions of undercover work, however, may lessen officer accountability and lower adherence to procedural due process and confidence in the rule of law.[34] One of the most important requirements is the ability to cultivate informants for information on illegal activities and for contacts with active criminals. Deals and bargains must be struck and honored. Therefore close association with criminals—both the informants and the targeted offenders—heightens the challenges of the undercover role considerably. Undercover officers must sustain a deceptive front over extended periods, thereby facing increased risk of stress-induced illness, physical harm, and corruption. One study determined that the greater the number of undercover assignments undertaken, the more drug, alcohol, and disciplinary problems federal officers had during their careers.[35]

Undercover agents can experience profound changes in their value systems, often resulting in an overidentification with criminals and a questioning of certain criminal statutes they are sworn to enforce.[36] These isolated assignments may also involve a separation of self, disrupting or interfering with officers' family relationships and activities and perhaps even leading to a loss of identity and the adoption of a criminal persona as they distance themselves from a conventional lifestyle.[37] Author Gary Marx cites one instance: A good example of this is the case of a Northern California police officer who participated in a "deep cover" operation for eighteen months, riding with the Hell's Angels. He was responsible for a very large number of arrests, including previously almost untouchable higher-level drug dealers. But this was at the cost of heavy drug use, alcoholism, brawling, the break-up of his family, an inability to fit back into routine police work, resignation from the force, several bank robberies, and a prison term.[38]

Return to Patrol Duties

Ending an undercover assignment, and then returning to patrol duty, is an awkward experience for the many officers who have difficulty adjusting to the everyday routine of traditional police work. These officers may suffer from emotional problems such as anxiety, loneliness, and suspiciousness, and they may experience marital problems. Officers will quickly have less autonomy and diminished initiative in job performance; they are no longer working in a tight-knit unit with expanded freedom and control and no longer feel as though they are behind enemy lines in the battle against crime, where their work experiences are intense and inherently dangerous. The return to routine patrol may be analogous to coming down from an emotional high, and officers in this position may feel depressed and lethargic.[39]

▶ Contributions of Medical Examiners and Coroners

"*Hic locus est ubi mors gaudet succurrere vitae.*" This Latin phrase—popular in forensic pathology—means "This is the place where death rejoices to help those who live." Indeed, this is the motto seen at the website of the National Association of Medical Examiners. Death investigations in every jurisdiction are conducted by either a medical examiner or coroner. An important distinction between the two offices typically concerns their training. Medical examiners are usually physicians or pathologists who are appointed for unspecified terms; they may serve a county, a group of counties, or a state. Coroners, conversely, are usually lay individuals who are elected to serve a fixed term of office in their county; depending on the laws of the jurisdiction, the coroner may or may not be trained in the medical sciences. Obviously, in the absence of medical expertise, a nonphysician coroner might have difficulty in examining and determining causes of death. However, coroners are often authorized to employ physicians, pathologists, or forensic pathologists to perform autopsies. Ten states use coroners as their only official death investigation professional.[40]

The individual performing the medical examination will gather the past medical history of the deceased and then perform an autopsy—examining the body externally and internally and taking biopsies of tissues for microscopic examination for disease. Various laboratory tests may also be undertaken, including x-rays, cultures of body fluids, and tests of organs for evidence of infection.

Next, all such information is correlated and conclusions may be drawn as to the cause and manner of death. A report is then prepared summarizing these findings. Finally, the forensic pathologist may later be subpoenaed to testify in court concerning those findings and conclusions; their official reports may also be given to other parties or agencies that have a legitimate interest in the cause and manner of death.[41]

▶ Uses of the Polygraph

Discussed in Chapter 2 in terms of its use in police recruiting and hiring, the polygraph has also been used by the police in the investigation of serious crimes since at least the early 1900s.

With a downturn in police budgets and related resources, leading to increased investigative caseloads, use of the polygraph for identifying the guilty has become highly desirable in order to make more efficient use of the investigator's time.

The diagnostic function of the polygraph seeks to determine truth or deception, and thus requires an examiner with considerable training and education as well as the use of carefully constructed questioning techniques. The psychophysiology of the polygraph instrument lies with its ability to record physical changes related to the autonomic nervous system. These are involuntary reactions, controlled by various centers in the brain, and are related to the emotion of fear (i.e., of being caught in a lie) and conflict between what one knows to be the truth vis-a-vis his physical and verbal attempt to convey the opposite.[42] Corrugated rubber tubes (or electronic sensors) placed over the examinee's chest and abdominal area will record respiratory activity. Two small metal plates or disposable adhesive electrodes, attached to the fingers, will record sweat gland activity, and a blood pressure cuff or similar device will record cardiovascular activity.[43]

The investigator should first provide the polygraph examiner with pertinent case facts to address the issue that the investigator wishes resolved. Other related matters may also need to be addressed: does the subject first need to be read his Miranda rights? Who will be given the examination results, and be allowed to observe the examination (e.g., legal counsel)? Is the subject a juvenile (if so, someone will likely need to accompany him and sign the necessary release forms). Is the examination to be videotaped?[44]

At some point prior to the actual examination, the examiner will conduct a pre-test interview with the subject, to discuss the test questions and familiarize the examinee with the testing procedure and gain an understanding of the subject's knowledge of related case facts and circumstances. The examiner will also attempt to assess whether the subject is in the necessary mental, physical, and emotional state for polygraph testing at that particular point in time.[45] Doing so will assist in avoiding two types errors during the examination: false positive (a truthful examinee is reported as being deceptive) and false negative (a deceptive examinee is reported as truthful). The commonly held belief that polygraph examination results are not admitted into evidence in court is untrue. Some courts admit polygraph evidence even over the objection of counsel; in other jurisdictions, polygraph results are admitted by stipulation. At the federal level, no single standard governs admissibility. It is also common for prosecutors to use polygraph results to decide which charges to file, if any, and defense attorneys rely on polygraph testing to plan their defense and to negotiate pleas. Some judges also use polygraph results in sentencing decisions.[46]

▶ DNA Analysis

Discovery and Types of Analyses

Deoxyribonucleic acid (DNA) is, in essence, a molecule containing the instructions that organisms need to develop, live, and reproduce—instructions that are found inside every cell, and are the same for each cell of an individual's body, including skin, organs, and all body fluids (Figure 5-1 ■).[47] Developed in England in 1984 by Alec Jeffreys,[48] we know that portions of the DNA structure are as unique to each individual as fingerprints

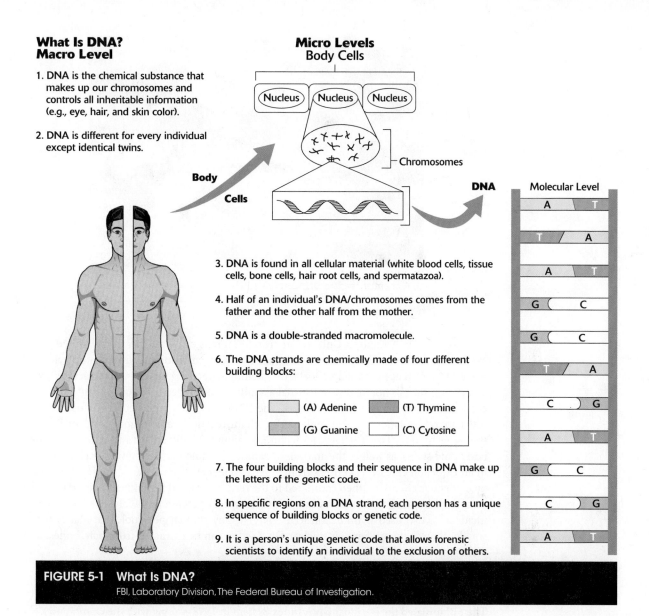

What Is DNA?
Macro Level

1. DNA is the chemical substance that makes up our chromosomes and controls all inheritable information (e.g., eye, hair, and skin color).

2. DNA is different for every individual except identical twins.

Micro Levels
Body Cells

Nucleus Nucleus Nucleus

Chromosomes

Body Cells

DNA

Molecular Level

A — T
T — A
A — T
G — C
G — C
T — A
C — G
A — T
G — C
C — G
A — T

3. DNA is found in all cellular material (white blood cells, tissue cells, bone cells, hair root cells, and spermatazoa).

4. Half of an individual's DNA/chromosomes comes from the father and the other half from the mother.

5. DNA is a double-stranded macromolecule.

6. The DNA strands are chemically made of four different building blocks:

(A) Adenine   (T) Thymine
(G) Guanine   (C) Cytosine

7. The four building blocks and their sequence in DNA make up the letters of the genetic code.

8. In specific regions on a DNA strand, each person has a unique sequence of building blocks or genetic code.

9. It is a person's unique genetic code that allows forensic scientists to identify an individual to the exclusion of others.

FIGURE 5-1   What Is DNA?
FBI, Laboratory Division, The Federal Bureau of Investigation.

and that inside each of the sixty trillion cells in the human body are strands of genetic material—chromosomes. Arranged along the chromosomes, like beads on a thread, are nearly a hundred thousand genes, which are the fundamental units of heredity; they instruct the body cells to make proteins that determine everything from hair color to susceptibility to diseases, and they pass genetic instructions from one generation to the next.[49] DNA profiling, also called genetic fingerprinting or DNA typing, has shown much promise in helping investigators to solve crimes and to ensure that those guilty of crimes are convicted in court by the examination of DNA samples from body fluid, hair, and bones to determine whether they came from a particular subject. For example, semen on a rape victim's jeans can be positively or negatively compared with a suspect's semen. DNA is thus powerful evidence. Indeed, in April 2007 it was reported that the two-hundredth person—a former Army cook who spent nearly twenty-five years in prison for a rape he did not commit—was exonerated by DNA evidence (the tenth exoneration since January 2002).[50]

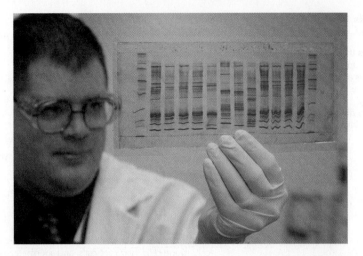

▲ A chemist reads a DNA profile. *(Courtesy U.S. Customs and Border Protection.)*

The FBI's DNA Analysis Unit and many other forensic laboratories in the United States examine items of evidence from a wide variety of alleged crimes including counterterrorism and intelligence gathering efforts, threatening letters (e.g. anthrax threat letters), violent crimes such as homicides and sexual assaults, bank robberies, extortion and organized crime cases, and many other violations. The DNA analysis method currently used by the FBI Laboratory is termed the "polymerase chain reaction-based–Short Tandem Repeat" typing technique. This (PCR–STR) technique allows for the analysis of extremely small body fluid stains, as well as the analysis of samples with no visible staining (e.g., envelopes in an extortion case or a ski mask from a bank robbery). The results of the DNA analyses on evidentiary items are then compared to the results obtained from known blood or saliva samples submitted from the victims and/or suspects potentially involved in the alleged incident.[51] Also used is mitochondrial DNA—a tiny ring-shaped molecule that is much smaller than the more familiar nuclear DNA—that can be extracted from hair, bones, and teeth when little else remains of a body.[52]

CODIS

The FBI initiated the National DNA Index System in 1998—along with the Combined DNA Index System (CODIS) software to manage the program; since that time it has become the world's largest repository of known offender DNA records. Each year, CODIS aids federal, state, and local agencies in more than 25,000 criminal investigations. CODIS contains DNA profiles obtained from subjects convicted of homicide, sexual assault, and other serious felonies. Investigators are able to search and compare evidence from their individual cases against the system's extensive national file of DNA genetic markers. CODIS also provides software and support services to state and local laboratories for establishing their databases of convicted offenders, unsolved crime scenes, and missing persons. Therefore, forensic laboratories can exchange and compare DNA profiles electronically and link serial violent crimes, especially sexual assaults, and identify suspects by matching DNA from crime scenes to convicted offenders.[53]

DNA Policy Nightmare: Solving Property Crimes

A recent study compared burglary investigations in which traditional police practices were used to collect and analyze DNA in the usual manner, as well as through "touch" DNA. The latter process has been available for several years and is so-named because DNA profiles can be obtained from such nontraditional sources of evidence as computer cords, jewelry boxes, and door handles. The study revealed that when DNA was analyzed:[54]

- more than twice as many suspects were identified,
- twice as many suspects were arrested,
- more than twice as many cases were accepted for prosecution, and
- suspects were five times as likely to be identified through DNA evidence as through fingerprints.[55]

The question as to whether DNA should be applied to property crimes should be a no-brainer—right? Unfortunately, the answer is not an emphatic yes, and the whole matter has the potential to turn the criminal justice system on its head.

First, consider that in a given year more than 2.1 million burglaries are reported to the police[56] and that only about one in eight of them will be solved. Lurking in this question of using DNA in property offenses are some huge policy decisions, such as the following:

- How will U.S. crime laboratories process the increase in evidence? And how many new labs would need to be built to accommodate the log of new cases?
- Are we willing to hire more prosecutors and public defenders to handle an increased volume of cases?
- How can we ensure that using DNA to solve burglaries will not pull investigative resources away from other criminal investigations, such as sex crimes, robbery, and domestic violence?
- Even if the preceding issues were addressed, do we need to revisit sentencing guidelines—or are we going to pay the cost to build many more prisons and jails that would be needed to handle these newly arrested property offenders?[57]

Perhaps the major policy implication surrounding this matter would be how to reduce the current backlog of evidence needing to be analyzed in U.S. crime labs. Would Americans be willing to have a large measure of cases outsourced to for-profit DNA labs?[58] Such questions would need to first be answered in determining whether or not to extend the reach of DNA testing. The truth is, DNA works, but it costs a lot of money.[59]

Postconviction DNA Tests: The Supreme Court Speaks

A major issue involving DNA has concerned postconviction testing. Because the speed and accuracy of testing have improved and because there are stories of convicted people who were exonerated because of DNA tests, many inmates want to be tested if there is any evidence from which DNA can be extracted. They have everything to gain and nothing to lose.

In June 2009, the U.S. Supreme Court addressed the question of whether or not convicts enjoyed a constitutional right to such testing in hopes of proving their innocence; in a 5–4 decision, the Court said such persons had *no* such right. (The plaintiff in this case, William Osborne, was an Alaska citizen who had been convicted of a brutal attack on a prostitute sixteen years ago.[60]) The decision, however, was seen as having limited impact because the federal government and forty-seven states already had laws allowing convicts some access to genetic evidence.

A Wider Net: New Law Expands DNA Gathering

In early 2007, the U.S. Department of Justice finalized guidelines for allowing the collection of DNA from most people arrested or detained by federal authorities, a vast expansion that will include hundreds of thousands of illegal immigrants each year. The new forensic DNA sampling was authorized by Congress in the January 2006 renewal of the Violence Against Women Act, and it permits DNA collection from anyone under arrest by federal authorities and from illegal immigrants detained by federal agents.

Familial DNA

Police agencies now have another way to solve cases: searching DNA databases to match crime-scene evidence with the DNA of a suspect's family members. This technique involves using what is termed "familial DNA" and is successful for identifying a lead to a suspect of a crime if a parent, a child, or a sibling of the suspect has previously provided a DNA sample. So-called familial DNA searches involve investigators looking for close-but-not-exact matches between DNA evidence collected at crime scenes and the state's data bank of DNA collected from convicted felons. Although some states allow familial DNA searches only for violent crimes, the apparent success of familial DNA testing in some high-profile cases (such as the 2010 arrest in Los Angeles of Lonnie Franklin Jr., for ten counts of murder) may encourage other states to adopt it. Meanwhile, some civil-liberties groups and legal scholars have concerns about privacy and ethical issues.[61]

▶ Criminal Profiling and Psycholinguistics

The criminal profiling of serial killers has probably captured the public's fancy more than any other investigative technique used by the police. The success of profiling depends on the profiler's ability to draw on investigative experience, training in forensic and behavioral science, and empirically developed information about the characteristics of known offenders. It is more art than science. The focus of the analysis is the behavior of the perpetrator while at the crime scene.[62]

There are various types of investigative profiles. Drug-courier profiles have been developed from collections of observable characteristics that experienced investigators believe indicate a person who is carrying drugs. Other types of profiles include loss-control specialists' profiles of shoplifters as well as threat assessments, such as the Secret Service's profiles of potential presidential assassins. Criminal profiling of violent offenders, however, is the area for which the most descriptive information has been collected and analyzed and the most extensive training programs have been developed.[63] Unfortunately, most people associate criminal profiling with the psychic profiler on television's *The Profiler* or with Agent Starling in the film *The Silence of the Lambs*—both of which are inaccurate portrayals.[64]

Profiling is not a new discovery; indeed, Sir Arthur Conan Doyle's fictional character Sherlock Holmes often engaged in profiling. For example, in "A Study in Scarlet," published in 1887, Holmes congratulated himself on the accuracy of his psychological profile: "It is seldom that any man, unless he is very full-blooded, breaks out in this way through emotion, so I hazarded the opinion that the criminal was probably a robust and ruddy-faced man. Events proved that I had judged correctly."[65] Profiling was used by a psychiatrist to study Adolph Hitler during World War II and to predict how he might react to defeat.[66]

Psychological profiling, while not an exact science, is obviously of assistance to investigators; however, it does not replace sound investigative procedures. Profiling works in harmony with the search for physical evidence. Victims play an important role in the development of a profile, as they can provide the investigator with the offender's exact conversation. Other items needed for a complete profile include photographs of the crime scene and any victims, autopsy information, and complete reports of the incident, including the weapon used. From this body of information, the profiler looks for motive.[67]

Serial murderers—killers who are driven by a compulsion to murder again and again—are also profiled. Many psychologists believe that serial murderers fulfill violent sexual fantasies they have had since childhood. They satisfy their sexual needs by thinking about their killings, but when the satisfaction wears off they kill again. Most serial murderers, the FBI has learned, are solitary males; an alarming number are doctors, dentists, or other health-care professionals. Almost one-third of them are ex-convicts and former mental patients. Many, like Kenneth Bianchi, the Los Angeles Hillside Strangler, are attracted to policing. (Bianchi, who was working as a security guard when he was finally caught in Washington State, often wore a police uniform during his crimes.) Serial killers seem normal, and they principally attack lone women, children, older people, homeless people, hitchhikers, and prostitutes.[68]

Another psychology-related investigative tool is psycholinguistics, which provides an understanding of those who use criminal coercion and strategies for dealing with threats. The 1932 kidnapping case of Charles Lindbergh's infant son (perpetrated by a German-born illegal alien, whose notes revealed his background and ethnicity) marked the beginning of this investigative method. Concentrating on evidence obtained from a message, spoken or written, the psycholinguistic technique microscopically analyzes the threats or messages for clues to the origins, background, and psychology of the maker. Every sentence, syllable, phrase, word, and comma is computer scanned. A "threat dictionary" containing more than 350 categories and 15 million words is consulted; these "signature" words and phrases are then used to identify possible suspects.[69]

Clearly, profiling can be useful in criminal inquiries in several ways: focusing the investigation on more likely types of offenders, suggesting proactive strategies, suggesting trial strategies, and preventing violent crimes. The FBI has trained dozens of state and local investigators in the profiling process. The program required twelve months of intensive training and hands-on profiling experience and consisted of an academic phase and an application phase.[70]

▶ Developing Areas in Forensic Science and Investigation

Technological opportunities—as well as new scientific and investigative problems—are rapidly developing for federal, state, and local police practitioners. In this section, we discuss several of them.

Using Social Networking Sites

Add to the use of wiretaps, undercover operations, cooperative witnesses, and other types of evidence in the investigator's toolbox, the use of Facebook (whose membership reached one billion in late 2012),[71] YouTube, Twitter, and other popular social networking sites that can assist police in their investigations. Indeed, police and prosecutors now obtain search warrants to scour such sites for postings, videos, contact information, photos, private messages, and proof of criminal conspiracies. Defendants are even known to update their social networking sites (to include descriptions of their offenses, their aliases, and "friends") while in jail using contraband cellphones.[72]

One survey found that 92 percent of all police agencies in the United States are using digital tools to fight crime.[73] Investigators are also using social networking sites to research suspects, solicit crime tips, and collect evidence. Citizens are more willing to share information online, and even criminals—such as one gang member in New York—are showing photos, illegal drugs, gang signs, and sinister threats on their web posts. Collaborating with the University of Cincinnati's Institute of Crime Science, police there dismantled a local street gang and arrested seventy-one people using social media to identify key members and create databases of information from social networks, existing police records and phone records.[74]

One controversial aspect of police using such information is their going undercover online by creating fake profiles to "friend" suspects. Facebook, for example, not only does not condone such practices, but doing so also violates its terms of service, even for the police. However, obtaining evidence in this manner still holds up in court—it is widely known that the police pose as young girls to nab people for soliciting a minor for sexual activities, or act as potential drug buyers for enticing traffickers. Furthermore, most social networking sites require a subpoena or a warrant for turning over members' profile information and correspondence; in one Minnesota case where a man used a fake Facebook page to talk to underage girls, detectives used a search warrant to obtain the man's profile and Facebook turned over more than two years of data (which included more than 800 chat conversations, primarily with girls under 18); the defendant's Facebook profile was used as evidence in court, and he was sentenced to 12 years in prison.[75]

No Stone Unturned: Cold Cases

Many jurisdictions plagued by a significant number of unsolved murders, or cold cases, have created a cold case squad. These squads can be especially useful in locating and working with past and potential witnesses and in reviewing physical evidence to identify suspects.

The most important component of cold case squads is personnel—the squads must have the right mix of investigative and supervisory talent. Squads may also use, as needed, the services of federal law enforcement agencies, medical or coroners' offices, retired personnel, criminalists or other specialists, or college or student interns. Cold cases selected for investigation are usually at least a year old and cannot be addressed by the original investigative personnel because of workload, time constraints, or the lack of viable leads. Cases are prioritized on the basis of the likelihood of an eventual solution. The highest-priority cases are those in which there is an identified homicide victim, suspects were previously named or identified through forensic methods, an arrest warrant was previously issued, significant physical evidence can be reprocessed, newly documented leads have arisen, and critical witnesses are available and willing to cooperate.[76]

An Institute for Cold Case Evaluation (ICCE) at West Virginia University provides lawenforcement agencies a diverse array of scientists in fields ranging from anthropology to entomology. The ICCE will provide departments with free or discounted services from at least two dozen scientists. It will launch a website as well, with a free electronic newsletter and a secure chat room for investigators. The public can also browse the site and search through cases.[77]

Use of "Nonhuman Detectives": Dogs

Dogs (and, more particularly, their noses) have proven very useful for public safety agencies; they are used to detect bombs, search for drugs, and find survivors and human remains in the aftermath of natural disasters (in fact, thirty-two dog teams were used in New York and New Jersey to search for survivors following Hurricane Sandy in late 2012).[78]

Police dogs thus play an increasingly vital role in investigative work in addition to their historical use for tracking and catching criminals and controlling crowds. The most popular breed for police work is the German shepherd. Chosen for its intelligence and highly developed senses, this breed tends to be more instinctively suspicious of strangers than

▼

▲ Police dogs occupy vital roles in investigative work, being used to find drugs, explosives, and human remains. *(Courtesy © B Christopher/Alamy.)*

other breeds. However, Springer Spaniels and Labrador retrievers are often used for police work as well because of their natural tracking abilities.

As the threat of terrorism has increased, these specialist police dogs have become even more important to the police. Just as police work is making increasing use of new technology, so is the training police dogs receive. Police dogs are now being trained to work with cameras attached to their heads, enabling them to enter dangerous places and send pictures back to officers.[79]

▶ Is There a "CSI Effect"?

Television programs focusing on criminal investigations and forensic techniques may be creating unrealistic courtroom expectations among jurors that cannot be achieved in real life. This phenomenon has been labeled the "CSI effect." Some court officers believe this "effect" is truly present: prosecutors indicate that jurors want to see all evidence subjected to substantial forensic examination, whether warranted in a specific case or not, while some defense attorneys believe that jurors deem all scientific evidence to be flawless and thus establishing guilt. The *voir dire* jury selection process may also be altered to ensure that those jurors who are unduly influenced by shows like *CSI* are screened from jury service. Such modifications to the usual process could result in longer trials and increased use of expert witnesses to aid the jury in understanding the presence or absence of physical evidence.[80]

A survey of Kentucky circuit court judges found that the impact has been strong—but not in areas where one might expect. First, three-fourths of the judges indicated that jurors have come to expect more forensic evidence; furthermore, 82 percent of the judges believed that "shows like *CSI* have distorted the public's perception of time needed to obtain forensic results." In that same connection, a slight majority (53.4 percent) believed that the popularity of shows like *CSI* has made it harder to convict defendants. The responding judges also perceived that these television programs create unrealistic representations concerning the state of the forensic art in their jurisdiction, as well as the speed of forensic testing.[81]

It may be that the "CSI effect" is, in reality, more of a nuisance for those who engage in the administration of justice, rather than a substantial factor in criminal justice processing. Or it may be that the "CSI effect" is substantial in only certain types of cases involving certain issues.[82]

▶ Investigative Tools: Informants, Interviews, and Interrogations

No discussion of police involvement in criminal investigations would be complete without consideration of police using informants as well as conducting interviews and interrogations—all of which occupy a central role in this arena. Next, we briefly discuss these three investigative tools.

Use of Confidential Informants

Sometimes common citizens act as informants, contacting the police in order to report suspicious or criminal activity, such as when seeing people coming and going at all hours of the day and night and in high volume at a home in their neighborhood. In such cases, if the person contacting the police provides his or her name, then greater weight is normally given to his or her credibility than if the caller prefers to remain anonymous.

The more controversial use of informants, however, is where the person providing information is a criminal himself. The police must often rely heavily on such persons in order to obtain information about crimes, arrest offenders, and obtain probable cause for arrest and search warrants. Prosecutors also must become involved with such persons when, as part of the plea negotiation process, pressure is applied on such informants—particularly in drug cases—to give up information about other criminals in exchange for dropped charges or shorter sentences.

Such informants are rarely upstanding citizens who possess an altruistic desire to assist police and benefit society. Rather, in exchange for providing information, they expect some benefits from the state in return, which can include monetary payments, immunity from prosecution, sentence reductions, dropped charges, and even the freedom to continue criminal activity. This situation becomes problematic when such informants engage in outright lying, exaggeration, and contribute significantly to wrongful convictions—all of which has historically contributed to suspicions toward and challenges of confidential informants.[83]

Thus it is key that police agencies properly manage their confidential informants, through: (1) having policies and procedures and training in techniques for working with informants; (2) maintaining an informant file system that not only maintains personal, descriptive, and criminal information about informants but also clearly establishes informants' credibility and reliability; and (3) requiring that supervisory approval be obtained before confidential informants are used in an investigation. Investigators must receive supervisory approval from the appropriate authority. Furthermore, informants must not entice persons to commit an offense he or she would otherwise not have committed—which is entrapment. Informants who do so can cause defense attorneys to argue that the police and informants' actions were outrageous or shocking to fundamental fairness. Therefore, informants' activities must be documented thoroughly enough to show that their actions did not lead to entrapment.[84]

On the other side of the coin, informant's identities must be protected so as to protect them and to maintain the service they provide. If they are not protected, their lives may be put in jeopardy.

Conducting Interviews and Interrogations

There are countless books, articles, and manuals that attempt to describe complicated, cognitive techniques for conducting interviews and interrogations. Most law enforcement personnel, however, learn such techniques through attendance at advanced training sessions and via practical experience. Here, as with the use of informants above, we will only look at some of the basic techniques involved. It should also be mentioned that not only do detectives conduct interviews and interrogations, patrol officers do so as well.

It is first important to define and distinguish between interviews and interrogations. Interviewing someone is to merely question him or her in order to obtain superficial information; for example, a field interview by a patrol officer would include obtaining one's name, address, place of employment, and so on. These questions might be said to be "inquisitory," and because the questions do not focus on or involve a specific criminal-related event, the person has no reason to withhold information and will normally be cooperative. Interrogations, however, are more purposeful, focusing on a crime and thus involve the formal questioning of a suspect in order to obtain incriminating information and/or a confession. As such, persons being interrogated may well be reluctant, uncooperative, and even hostile toward such questioning.

At the beginning, interrogators are advised to remember certain "articles of faith" in this regard: take your time; keep a written record of information that is gleaned; avoid yes/no questions; and, if appropriate, allow the suspect a "way out" or to save face (e.g., "You robbed that store to get food for your kids, right?"). The interrogation should begin by asking several nondistressing questions. Then, with that baseline of behavior, it now becomes very important to begin observing any changes in the suspect's behavior and any visual cues: nonverbal communication often due to stress. Specifically, the experienced interrogator will pick up on such cues as lack of eye contact, foot or finger tapping, short breaths, tightly clenched or wringing hands, clearing of the throat, and fidgeting in the chair. Such cues can also convey that the interviewee is being defensive or withdrawn. Other axioms among interrogators are that "Liars deny in detail, truthful people deny categorically," and that "Liars give rambling and indirect answers—truthful people answer directly."[85]

Again, this is a very simplistic description, and any serious—and successful—attempt at interrogating suspects must typically involve considerable training and experience.

Summary

This chapter has presented the evolution of criminal investigation, including definitions of key terms, identification of people and firearms, ways investigators work within the larger context of the criminal justice system, qualities needed by detectives, undercover police work, polygraph testing, DNA analysis, profiling, using social networking sites and dogs, investigating cold cases, and whether or not there is a "CSI Effect."

The evolution of forensic evidence, criminalistics, and criminal investigation is the product of a successful symbiosis of science and policing. This chapter has shown the truly interdisciplinary nature of police work; we discussed not only the influence of the so-called hard sciences—computer science, chemistry, biology, and physics—but also the assistance of psychology.

Forensic science is arguably the most rapidly progressing area of criminal justice, and there is little doubt that the future holds even greater advances in this realm. This discipline has traveled a great distance, especially in laboratory processes, in DNA analysis and application, and in ever-expanding uses of the computer. The potential of the computer to assist in solving crimes is limited only by our funds and imagination. Thus policing should continue indefinitely to reap the benefits of applying scientific aids to criminal justice matters.

Certainly this area of policing carries with it a high degree of fascination and mystique for the public, and rightfully so. Although policing certainly has its limitations, such as paperwork, boredom, failures, and other liabilities, there is nothing quite like using "gee whiz" investigative tools and techniques to catch bad guys—at least in the public's mind.

Key Terms

anthropometry
Bertillon system
cold cases
Combined DNA Index Systems
   (CODIS)
corpus delicti
crime scene

criminalistics
criminal profiling
dactylography
detective
forensic science
Interrogation
Interviewing

investigative stages
Locard's exchange principle
medical examiner
modus operandi
polygraph examiner
postconviction testing
psycholinguistics

Review Questions

1. How would you differentiate the terms *forensic science* and *criminalistics*?
2. What are the origins of criminalistics, and what are the differences between anthropometry and dactylography?
3. What types of information can physical evidence provide?
4. What does a "body farm" do?
5. What contributions did Bertillon, Vollmer, and Locard make to the development of criminal investigation techniques?
6. What qualities do detectives and undercover officers need and use?
7. What contributions do medical examiners provide to criminal investigators?
8. What are the basic functions of the polygraph, and what is its legal status in the courts?
9. In lay terms, how does DNA analysis operate?
10. What policy implications are involved with the use of DNA analysis for investigation of property offenses?
11. What was the purpose of the U.S. Supreme Court rule concerning the right of prison inmates to receive a DNA analysis?
12. What is familial DNA, and how does it function?
13. What contributions have behavioral science and dogs made to criminal investigation?
14. What contributions are social networking sites making to criminal investigation?
15. What is the purpose of a cold case squad, and how does it operate?
16. Is there a "CSI effect" in criminal investigation? Provide reasons in support of, and opposition to this question.
17. What are the concerns and controversies involving the use of confidential informants?
18. How do interviewing and interrogating differ, and what techniques are used with the latter?

Learn by Doing

1. Unequivocally, the best means of learning about investigative techniques and forensic methods/equipment is to tour a modern forensics laboratory. A related aspect of investigation that should not be overlooked is that agency's means of safeguarding the chain of evidence and its storage prior to and following trial. If, for security or other reasons, you are unable to personally (or as a class) tour a forensic laboratory, then attempt to interview one or more detectives who work with crimes against persons and/or property concerning their methods, training and education; primary obstacles in successfully bringing a case to trial; greatest challenges in their work; methods employed in interviewing suspects; constitutional and other legal aspects of their role; recent changes in the investigative field; and so on.

2. To fully understand what kinds of investigative efforts are being made by police to address real-world problems, go to www.popcenter.org/Problems/?action =alpha&type=pdf#webguides. There you will find a selection of individual problem-solving guides—now more than fifty in number—published by the federal Center for Problem-Oriented Policing. Select two guides and describe what they say police are using to succeed in their investigative and problem-solving efforts.

Notes

1. Marc H. Caplan and Joe Holt Anderson, *Forensics: When Science Bears Witness* (Washington, D.C.: Government Printing Office, 1984), p. 2.
2. Charles R. Swanson, Neil C. Chamelin, Leonard Territo, and Robert W. Taylor, *Criminal Investigation*, 9th ed. (Boston: McGraw-Hill, 2006), p. 10.
3. Peter R. DeForest, R. E. Gaensslen, and Henry C. Lee, *Forensic Science: An Introduction to Criminalistics* (New York: McGraw-Hill, 1983), p. 29.
4. U.S. Department of Justice, National Institute of Justice, *Crime Scene Investigation: A Reference for Law Enforcement Training* (Washington, D.C.: Author, 2004).
5. Richard Saferstein, *Criminalistics: An Introduction to Forensic Science*, 9th ed. (Upper Saddle River, NJ: Prentice Hall, 2007), p. 8.
6. Jurgen Thorwald, *Crime and Science* (New York: Harcourt, Brace and World, 1967), p. 4.
7. Jurgen Thorwald, *The Century of the Detective* (New York: Harcourt, Brace and World, 1965), p. 7.
8. Ibid., pp. 9–10.
9. Ibid., p. 12.
10. Swanson et al., *Criminal Investigation*, p. 12.
11. Ibid., pp. 12–13.
12. Ibid., p. 12.
13. Thorwald, *The Century of the Detective*, p. 18.
14. Thorwald, *The Marks of Cain* (London: Thames & Hudson, 1965), pp. 78–79.
15. W. Jerry Chisum and Brent E. Turvey, "Evidence Dynamics: Locard's Exchange Principle & Crime Reconstruction," *Journal of Behavioral Profiling* 2(1) (2000): 3.
16. U.S. Department of Justice, Bureau of Justice Statistics, *Firearm Violence, 1993–2011* (May 2013), pp. 2, 11, http://www.bjs.gov/content/pub/pdf/fv9311.pdf (accessed October 18, 2013).
17. Swanson et al., *Criminal Investigation*, p. 17.
18. Saferstein, *Criminalistics*, pp. 460–461.
19. DeForest et al., *Forensic Science*, pp. 13–14.
20. Ibid., p. 19.
21. Swanson et al., *Criminal Investigation*, pp. 8–9.
22. President's Commission on Law Enforcement and the Administration of Justice, *Task Force Report: Science and Technology* (Washington, D.C.: Government Printing Office, 1967), pp. 7–18.
23. Paul B. Weston and Kenneth M. Wells, *Criminal Investigation: Basic Perspectives*, 4th ed. (Englewood Cliffs, NJ: Prentice Hall, 1986), pp. 5–10.
24. Ibid., p. 207.
25. Ibid., pp. 207–209.
26. Ibid., p. 214.
27. Peter W. Greenwood and Joan Petersilia, *The Criminal Investigation Process, vol. 1: Summary and Policy Implications* (Santa Monica, CA: RAND, 1975). The entire report is found in Peter W. Greenwood, Jan M. Chaiken, and Joan Petersilia, *The Criminal Investigation Process* (Lexington, MA: D.C. Heath, 1977).
28. Ibid.
29. Ibid., p. 19.
30. Weston and Wells, *Criminal Investigation*, p. 5.
31. DeForest et al., *Forensic Science*, p. 11.
32. Mark R. Pogrebin and Eric D. Poole, "Vice Isn't Nice: A Look at the Effects of Working Undercover," *Journal of Criminal Justice* 21 (1993): 383–394.
33. Ibid., pp. 383–384.
34. Peter K. Manning, *The Narc's Game: Organizational and Informational Limits on Drug Enforcement* (Cambridge, MA: MIT Press, 1980).
35. M. Girodo, "Drug Corruption in Undercover Agents: Measuring the Risk," *Behavioral Sciences and the Law* 3 (1991): 299–308; also see David L. Carter, "An Overview of Drug-Related Conduct of Police Officers: Drug Abuse and Narcotics Corruption," in *Drugs, Crime, and the Criminal Justice System*, ed. Ralph Weisheit (Cincinnati, OH: Anderson, 1990).
36. Federal Bureau of Investigation, *The Special Agent in Undercover Investigations* (Washington, D.C.: Author, 1978).
37. A. L. Strauss, "Turning Points in Identity," in *Social Interaction*, eds. C. Clark and H. Robboy (New York: St. Martin's, 1988).
38. Gary T. Marx, "Who Really Gets Stung? Some Issues Raised by the New Police Undercover Work," in *Moral Issues in Police Work*, eds. F. Ellison and M. Feldberg (Totowa, NJ: Bowman and Allanheld, 1988), pp. 99–128.
39. G. Farkas, "Stress in Undercover Policing," in *Psychological Services for Law Enforcement*, eds. J. T. Reese and H. A. Goldstein (Washington, DC: Government Printing Office, 1986).
40. National Association of Medical Examiners, "What is a Coroner?" http://thename.org/index.php?option=com_content&task=view&id=36&Itemid=42 (accessed October 25, 2013).
41. Ibid., "What does a forensic pathologist do?" http://thename.org/index.php?option=com_content&task=view&id=39&Itemid=42 (accessed June 23, 2011).

42. Dan Sosnowski, "Investigator's Use of the Polygraph," http://www.patc.com/weeklyarticles/print/polygraph-investigation.pdf (accessed October 29, 2013).

43. American Polygraph Association, "Frequently Asked Questions," http://www.polygraph.org/section/resources/frequently-asked-questions (accessed October 29, 2013).

44. Sosnowski, "Investigator's Use of the Polygraph" (accessed October 29, 2013).

45. Ibid.

46. Frank Horvath, "Polygraph," in *The Encyclopedia of Police Science*, 2nd ed., ed. William G. Bailey (New York: Garland, 1995), p. 642.

47. Livescience, "DNA Definition, Structure, & Discovery," http://www.livescience.com/37247-dna.html (accessed October 25, 2013).

48. Massachusetts Institute of Technology, "Inventor of the Week Archive: Alec Jeffreys—DNA Fingerprinting," June 2005, web.mit.edu/invent/iow/jeffreys.html (accessed October 25, 2013).

49. Saferstein, *Criminalistics*, pp. 382–383.

50. Richard Willing, "DNA to Clear 200th Person," www.usatoday.com/news/nation/2007-04-22-dna-exoneration_N.htm (accessed October 25, 2013).

51. Federal Bureau of Investigation, "DNA—Nuclear," www.fbi.gov/hq/lab/html/dnau1.htm (accessed October 25, 2013).

52. Federal Bureau of Investigation, "DNA—Mitochrondrial," http://www.fbi.gov/about-us/lab/biometric-analysis/mtdna (accessed October 25, 2013).

53. Federal Bureau of Investigation, "The FBI and DNA," http://www.fbi.gov/news/stories/2011/november/dna_112311 (accessed October 25, 2013).

54. U.S. Department of Justice, National Institute of Justice, *DNA Solves Property Crimes (But Are We Ready for That?)* (Washington, D.C.: Author, October 2008), p. 2.

55. Ibid., p. 3.

56. Federal Bureau of Investigation, "Crime in the United States, 2012: Burglary," http://www.fbi.gov/about-us/cjis/ucr/crime-in-the-u.s/2012/crime-in-the-u.s.-2012/property-crime/burglary(accessed October 25, 2013).

57. U.S. Department of Justice, *DNA Solves Property Crimes*, p. 10.

58. Ibid., p. 3.

59. Ibid., p. 10.

60. Adam Liptak, "Justices Reject Inmate Right to DNA Tests," *New York Times*, www.nytimes.com/2009/06/19/us/19scotus.html (accessed October 25, 2013).

61. Matthew Cella, "Familial DNA gives investigators another tool," *The Washington Times*, March 21, 2011, http://www.washingtontimes.com/news/2011/mar/21/familial-dna-gives-investigators-another-tool/ (accessed October 25, 2013).

62. Patrick E. Cook and Dayle L. Hinman, "Criminal Profiling: Science and Art," *Journal of Contemporary Criminal Justice* 15 (August 1999): 230.

63. Ibid., p. 232.

64. Steven A. Egger, "Psychological Profiling," *Journal of Contemporary Criminal Justice* 15 (August 1999): 243.

65. Ibid., p. 242.

66. Walter C. Langer, *The Mind of Adolph Hitler* (New York: World, 1978).

67. Swanson et al., *Criminal Investigation*, 4th ed., pp. 601–602.

68. Brad Darrach and Joel Norris, "An American Tragedy," *Life*, August 1984, p. 58.

69. Swanson et al., *Criminal Investigation*, pp. 606–607.

70. Cook and Hinman, "Criminal Profiling," p. 234.

71. Aaron Smith, Laurie Segall, and Stacy Cowley "Facebook Reaches One Billion Users," *CNNMoney*, October 4, 2012, http://money.cnn.com/2012/10/04/technology/facebook-billion-users/index.html (accessed October 27, 2013).

72. Jim McElhatton, "Feds Use Facebook to Collect Crime Evidence," http://www.washingtontimes.com/news/2011/apr/27/feds-use-facebook-to-collect-crime-evidence/?page=all (accessed October 29, 2013).

73. International Association of Chiefs of Police, IACP Center for Social Media, "2012 Survey Results," http://www.iacpsocialmedia.org/Resources/Publications/2012SurveyResults.aspx (accessed October 29, 2013).

74. Heather Kelly, "Police embrace social media as crime-fighting tool," *CNN Tech*, August 30, 2012, http://www.cnn.com/2012/08/30/tech/social-media/fighting-crime-social-media/index.html (accessed October 29, 2013).

75. Ibid.

76. Ryan Turner and Rachel Kosa, *Cold Case Squads: Leaving No Stone Unturned* (Washington, DC: U.S. Department of Justice, Bureau of Justice Assistance, July 2003), pp. 2–4.

77. "Case Studies," *Law Enforcement News*, November 15/30, 2003, p. 7. John Jay College of Criminal Justice, CUNY, 899 Tenth Avenue, New York, NY 10019.

78. Jesse J. Holland, "Drug-Sniffing Dogs Have Their Day in Court as Justices Hear 2 Arguments," http://www.nytimes.com/2012/11/01/us/justices-hear-arguments-involving-drug-sniffing-dogs.html?_r=0 (accessed November 1, 2012).

79. BBC, "Dog Cameras to Combat Gun Crime," http://news.bbc.co.uk/2/hi/uk_news/england/4497212.stm (accessed March 5, 2013).

80. Thomas Hughes and Megan Magers, "The Perceived Impact of Crime Scene Investigation Shows on the Administration of Justice," *Journal of Criminal Justice and Popular Culture* 14(3) (2007): 262, http://www.albany.edu/scj/jcjpc/vol14is3/HughesMagers.pdf (accessed October 28, 2013).

81. Ibid., p. 265.

82. Ibid., p. 271.

83. Alexandra Natapoff, "Snitching and Use of Criminal Informants," *Oxford Bibliographies*, http://www.oxfordbibliographies.com/view/document/obo-9780195396607/obo-9780195396607-0044.xml (accessed October 7, 2013).

84. Brian Lieberman, "Ethical Issues in the Use of Confidential Informants for Narcotic Operations," *The Police Chief*, June 2007, http://www.policechief magazine.org/magazine/index.cfm?fuseaction=display_arch&article_id=1210&issue_id=62007 (accessed October 7, 2013).

85. See, for example, Clayton Browne, "Police Interview Techniques," *Chron (2013)*, http://work.chron.com/police-interview-techniques-11580.html (accessed October 7, 2013); Ronald P. Fisher and R. Edward Geiselman "The Cognitive Interview Method of Conducting Police Interviews: Eliciting Extensive Information and Promoting Therapeutic Jurisprudence," *International Journal of Law and Psychiatry* 23(5) (November–December 2010): 321–328, http://www.sciencedirect.com/science/article/pii/S0160252710000762 (accessed October 7, 2013); Steve Finney, "Interview & Interrogation," the University of Texas at Dallas (n.d.), http://www.learningace.com/doc/2638370/4822684bc121a8f797316ce9c5fe573a/interview-interrogation (accessed October 7, 2013).

6 Personnel Issues and Practices
Stress, Labor Relations, Higher Education, and Private Police

LEARNING OBJECTIVES

As a result of reading this chapter, the student will be able to:

1. *Describe the causes and effects of stress in policing, to include the primary stressors for officers and ways in which officers may reduce stress levels*

2. *Explain the employment rights of police officers, including the provisions of the Peace Officer Bill of Rights*

3. *Explain the development of police unions and their influence today*

4. *Describe the three models of collective bargaining*

Describe the four kinds of job actions

 Explain the extent of higher (postsecondary) education requirements for police by hiring agencies, and the major arguments for and against officers possessing such education

7 Explain how and why private policing/security evolved, some issues and concerns concerning the field, legislative attempts to improve the field, and rationales for unifying private and public police

Introduction

This chapter addresses a number of important policing matters that could have been included in previous chapters. But because of their common nature—all represent a substantial degree of change, controversy, and/or influence within society and the operations of their agencies—they are consolidated and set apart here for discussion.

First we examine police stress, which can certainly be debilitating to those who are engaged in police service as well as their peers, supervisors, and the public; included in this discussion are its myriad causes and physical and emotional effects. Next we look at the broad area of labor relations, which includes police officers' rights, unionization, and collective bargaining. This is a significant yet often overlooked aspect of policing across the nation, particularly in the East and the West, and it warrants a substantial amount of attention for all who are in, or might enter, policing.

Then we consider the topic of higher education for police, which has been a topic of debate for nearly a century. Finally, we examine the extent and nature of private police/security forces, and attempts to improve such organizations and to align them more closely with public police organizations. A summary, key terms, review questions, and several scenarios and activities that provide opportunities for you to learn by doing conclude the chapter.

▶ The Silent Epidemic: Stress

We would prefer to ignore one side of policing—the stress that is induced by the job—and its supervision and management. Indeed, Sir W. S. Gilbert observed that "When constabulary duty's to be done, the policeman's lot is not a happy one."[1] Furthermore, William A. Westley observed that "The policeman's world is spawned of degradation, corruption and insecurity. He walks alone, a pedestrian in Hell."[2]

Many people with whom the police interact are heavily armed and arrogant. The job of policing has never been easy, but the danger, frustration, and family disruption of the past have been made worse by the drug war and violent criminals who have more contempt for the police than ever before. Furthermore, as will be seen later in this chapter, compounding this situation is that the officer's own organizational policies and practices often generate more stress than the streets.

Nature and Types of Stress

The police work environment itself can and does have adverse effects on police officers. It creates stress, which may be defined as a force that is external in nature that causes both physical and emotional strain upon the body. The late Hans Selye, who is known as "the father of stress research," defined stress as a nonspecific response of a body to demands placed on it. Succinctly, stressors are situations or occurrences outside of ourselves that we allow to turn inward and cause problems.[3]

Stress can be positive or negative. Positive stress is referred to as *eustress,* while negative stress is called *distress*. When people think about stress, they usually focus on negative stress and negative situations; however, positive events in our lives can create stress. For example, an officer's promotion to sergeant is a positive experience, but at the same time it creates stress. The officer has to react and adjust to the new position. The promotion, although positive for the officer's career, is somewhat psychologically disruptive.

Traumatic stress is the result of an extremely stressful event, such as a line-of-duty shooting or a hostage situation. This stress is immediate and has a significant and profound impact on the officer. *Chronic stress,* on the other hand, generally represents the accumulation of the effects of numerous stressful events over time. Each can adversely affect a police officer and result in physical, emotional, and psychological problems. Traumatic stress may subside over time, but chronic stress for many police officers is ever present. If an officer cannot cope with a traumatic stressful event or manage the long-term effects of chronic stress, he or she may suffer from its consequences.

No human being can exist in a continuous state of stress. The body strives to maintain its normal state, homeostasis, and to adapt to the alarm, but it can actually develop disease in the process. Thus, it is extremely important for police agencies to recognize stress and its impact on officers and their productivity.

Sources of Stress

Stress can come from a number of directions, so police officers can experience job stress as the result of a wide range of problems and situations. The four general categories of stress are (1) organizational and administrative practices, (2) the criminal justice system, (3) the public, and (4) stress intrinsic to police work itself.

Organizational and Administrative Practices A primary source of stress is the police organization itself. Police departments typically are bureaucratic and authoritarian

▲ Police work presents a variety of stressors, including felony car stops and critical incidents. *(Courtesy Western Nevada State Peace Officer Academy.)*

in nature, and this type of organization creates stress for individual officers in at least two ways. First, police departments follow strict rules and regulations that are dictated by top management. Line officers and first-line supervisors seldom have direct input into their formulation, resulting in officers feeling powerless and alienated about the decisions that directly affect their jobs. Second, these rules dictate how officers specifically perform many of their duties and responsibilities. They are created to provide officers with guidance and direction. Police officers, however, sometimes view them as mechanisms used by management to restrict their freedom and discretion or to punish them. Officers also view rules as protection for the department when officers make incorrect decisions or errors. In these instances, departments sometimes use rules to avoid liability when officers' actions are challenged in civil actions.

Problems are also faced by female police officers (see Chapter 4). Because policing has traditionally been a male-dominated occupation, in many agencies female officers do not have the same standing as their male counterparts. The primary sources of stress for female officers are sexual harassment and treatment different from that which males receive in the workplace. Some women officers have reported that they were given different assignments, were the object of jokes (often concerning sexual orientation), were propositioned by male officers, and were generally victimized by gender stereotyping in the department.[4]

The Criminal Justice System Each component of the criminal justice system affects the other components. For example, judges have openly displayed hostile attitudes toward the police, or prosecutors have not displayed proper respect to officers, arbitrarily dismissing cases, having them appear in court during regularly scheduled days off, and advocating rulings restricting police procedures.[5] Another example occurs when parole officers and probation officers do an inadequate job of supervising parolees, which results in their being involved in an inordinate amount of crime. The courts have the most direct impact on police officers and probably are the greatest source of stress from the criminal justice system.

The Public When police officers perform community services, they also become involved in conflicts or negative situations. They arrest citizens, write tickets, and give citizens orders when intervening in domestic violence or disorder situations. Often, to resolve problems, they make half of the participants happy, but the other half are unhappy. The problem is that police officers develop unrealistic or inaccurate ideas about citizens as a result of their negative encounters. Officers must keep their relationship with citizens in proper perspective. This is achieved by open, straightforward discussions of public attitudes and encounters with citizens. It also means that managers must emphasize the importance of good police–public relations and of the majority of citizens supporting and respecting the police.

Stressors Intrinsic to Police Work Police work is fraught with situations that pose physical danger to officers. Domestic violence, felonies in progress, and fight calls often require officers to physically confront suspects. It would seem that police work itself, since it includes dealing with dangerous police activities and dangerous people, would be the most stressful part of police work. Certainly traumatic incidents can require long-term follow-up support for law enforcement personnel.

Another major job-related stressor involves undercover work. The glamorous depiction of undercover officers in books, movies, and other media does not adequately portray the stress that is caused by the overall nature of the work—the isolation, danger, relationships with suspects, loss of personal identity, protracted periods of removal from family and friends, and fear of discovery.[6]

EXHIBIT 6-1

DELIVERING DEATH MESSAGES AND TRAGIC NEWS

An often overlooked aspect of police work—and one that certainly can be stressful for officers—is the task of delivering tragic news to citizens concerning the death of a loved one or other catastrophic information. Sometimes this topic is addressed in academy training, sometimes it is not; but in either case, it is a task for which one is never fully prepared, and the manner in which this task is handled may make a major difference in how soon the recipient(s) of the news begins to recover from their loss. A case in point is the state trooper in Florida who told the parents of a girl who had been involved in a head-on auto accident that she had been taken to a trauma unit of a hospital. Later, as the parents were on their way to the hospital, the trooper called to ask the parents where they were; they told him, and he stated "I thought I told you [she] didn't make it."

There are obviously right and wrong methods for making such notifications. First, the officer should confirm the identity of the person who is deceased as well as the identity of the person to receive the notification, and their address. Certainly the officer must be sympathetic and compassionate, and deliver the message in person. Preferably, the officer will be accompanied by someone, such as a police chaplain or a friend or relative of the recipient(s); this person can remain there after the officer leaves and until other relatives or friends arrive. The officer should also be prepared for different reactions on the part of the recipient(s); not everyone responds in the same manner, and may even faint or become hostile.[7]

Source: Kenneth Peak.

Effects of Stress

It has been estimated that 15 percent of a department's officers will be in a burnout phase at any time. These officers account for 70 to 80 percent of all the complaints against their department, including physical abuse, verbal abuse, and misuse of firearms. If officers do not relieve the pressure, they eventually may suffer heart attacks, nervous breakdowns, back problems, headaches, psychosomatic illnesses, and alcoholism. They may also manifest excessive weight gain or loss; combativeness or irritability; excessive perspiration; excessive use of sick leave; excessive use of alcohol, tobacco, or drugs; marital or family disorders; inability to complete an assignment; loss of interest in work, hobbies, and people in general; more than the usual number of "accidents," including vehicular and other types; and shooting incidents.[8] An extreme reaction to stress is suicide. Police are at a higher risk for committing suicide because of their access to firearms, continuous exposure to human misery, shift work, social strain, marital difficulties, physical illness, and alcohol addiction.

It is imperative that officers learn to manage their stress before it causes deep physical and/or emotional harm. One means is to view the mind as a "mental bucket" and strive to keep it full through hobbies or activities that provide relaxation. Exercise, proper nutrition, and positive lifestyle choices (such as not smoking and moderation with alcohol) are also essential for good health.

Employee Assistance Programs

To help officers deal with stress and its effects, a comprehensive wellness program is needed that should include five elements: (1) physical fitness, (2) stress management, (3) psychological and mental health, (4) nutrition and dietary-related behaviors, and (5) alcohol/chemical dependency. Police agencies need a comprehensive wellness program to assist officers in coping with stress, but if that fails or is absent, an employee assistance program (EAP) should be available to help officers to cope with alcohol and substance abuse, psychological problems such as depression, or family management problems.

Excessive drinking and alcoholism remain a problem in policing. When officers' drinking becomes excessive, other officers and frequently supervisors and the department cover up for them. In the end, however, covering up drinking problems postpones officers' seeking or being required to obtain assistance. Drug abuse can also be present among officers, although it is not known if it is a significant problem. What is known, however, is that drug testing reduces the incidence of drug usage among police officers. If officers know they are going to be tested, they are less likely to use drugs. A number of departments require officers in selected assignments such as narcotics or special response teams to submit to drug testing, and some departments require testing of officers being transferred to such units.

If an officer is found to be using illegal drugs, what should be done with the employee? A number of arguments can be made for immediate termination. First, the police officer has committed a crime. Second, the officer has associated with known criminals when obtaining the illegal drugs. And third, the officer's drug use poses a liability problem for the police department. Immediate termination is counter to a humane view of police personnel administration, however. It should be realized that job stress may be the primary contributing factor to the drug usage. Second, the department has a significant investment in each of its officers, and a termination decision should not be taken lightly; problem officers can be salvaged and returned to work. Thus, termination, although an acceptable choice for officers with chronic drug problems, may not be the best solution for officers who had not previously caused the department any problems or had not otherwise been in trouble. Factors considered in making this decision include the severity of the offense (type and amount of drug used and whether or not the officer went beyond mere usage), prior drug and disciplinary problems, and the probability of the officer being rehabilitated.

► Labor Relations: Officers' Rights, Unionization, and Collective Bargaining

A long line of court cases has established that public employees have a property interest in their employment. The U.S. Supreme Court has provided some general guidance on how the question of a constitutionally protected property interest is to be resolved:

> To have a property interest in a benefit, a person . . . must have a legitimate claim of entitlement to it. It is a purpose of the ancient institution of property to protect those claims upon which people rely in their daily lives, reliance that *must not be arbitrarily undermined* [emphasis added].[9]

Labor relations—a broad term that includes officers' employment rights and the related concepts of unionization and collective bargaining—has become an important issue in policing. This section explores these topics.

Police Officers' Rights Chapter 8 will examine several restrictions that are placed on the rights of police officers (such as place of residence, religious practices, freedom of speech, and search and seizure). Given those numerous restrictions, in this section we look at some measures the police have taken to maintain their rights on the job to the extent possible.

In the 1980s and 1990s, police officers began to insist on greater procedural safeguards to protect themselves against what they perceived as arbitrary infringements on their rights. These demands have been reflected in a statute enacted in many states, generally known as the Peace Officer Bill of Rights. This legislation confers on police employees a property interest in their position and mandates due process rights for peace officers who are the subject of internal investigations that could lead to disciplinary action. The legislation identifies the type of information that must be provided to the accused officer, the officer's responsibility to cooperate during the investigation, the officer's rights to representation during the process, and the rules and procedures concerning the collection of certain types of evidence. Following are some provisions of the Peace Officer Bill of Rights:

- *Written notice.* The department must provide the officer with written notice of the nature of the investigation, a summary of the alleged misconduct, and the name of the investigating officer.

- *Right to representation.* Although not a universal right, many, if not most, states allow the officer to have an attorney or a representative of his or her choosing present during any phase of questioning or any hearing.

- *Polygraph examination.* The officer may refuse to take a polygraph examination unless the complainant submits to an examination and is determined to be telling the truth. In this case, the officer may be ordered to take a polygraph examination or may be subject to disciplinary action.

Officers expect to be treated fairly, honestly, and respectfully during the course of an internal investigation. In turn, the public expects that the agency will develop sound disciplinary policies and will conduct thorough inquiries into allegations of misconduct. It is imperative that supervisors be thoroughly familiar with statutes, contract provisions, and existing rules between employer and employee to ensure that procedural due process requirements are met, particularly in disciplinary cases in which an employee's property interest is affected.

Police officers today are also more likely to file a grievance when they believe their rights have been violated. Grievances may cover a broad range of issues, including salaries, overtime, leaves, hours of work, allowances, retirement, opportunities for advancement, performance evaluations, workplace conditions, tenure, disciplinary actions, supervisory methods, and administrative practices. The preferred method for settling an officer's grievance is through informal discussion during which the employee explains his or her grievance to the immediate supervisor, and most complaints can be handled this way. Complaints that cannot be dealt with informally are usually handled through a more formal grievance process, which may involve several different levels of action.

Unionization The first campaign to organize the police started shortly after World War I when the American Federation of Labor (AFL) reversed a long-standing policy and issued charters to police unions in Boston, Washington, D.C., and about thirty other cities.[10] The unions' success was short-lived, however. The Boston police commissioner refused to recognize the union, forbade officers to join it, and filed charges against several union officials. Shortly thereafter, on September 9, 1919, the Boston police initiated a famous strike of three days' duration, causing major riots and a furor against the police all across the nation; nine rioters were killed, and twenty-three were seriously injured. During the strike, Massachusetts Governor Calvin Coolidge uttered his now-famous statement: "There is no right to strike against the public safety by anybody, anywhere, anytime." Then in the early 1950s, many benevolent and fraternal organizations of police were formed in cities such as Chicago, New York, and Washington, D.C.; others were fraternal orders of police (FOPs). Soon a new group of highly vocal rank-and-file association leaders came into power, supporting higher salaries and pensions, free legal aid, low-cost insurance, and other benefits.[11] Since the 1970s, the unionization of the police has continued to flourish. Today the majority of U.S. police officers belong to some form of association;[12] indeed, there are numerous unions and associations that are willing to represent, and do represent police employees at several levels (i.e., nonsupervisory, supervisory, and management). The Fraternal Order of Police claims to hold the largest membership of sworn police officers in the world, with 325,000 members in more than 2,100 lodges.[13]

Collective Bargaining In this section, different models, negotiations, and impasses associated with collective bargaining (the process of negotiations between employer and employees) are covered.

Three Models. Each state is free to decide which public-sector employees (if any) will have collective-bargaining rights and under what terms, so there is considerable variety in collective-bargaining arrangements across the United States. Three basic models are used in the states: (1) binding arbitration, (2) meet and confer, and (3) bargaining not required.[14]

Under the binding-arbitration model, used in twenty-five states, public employees are given the right to bargain with their employers. If the bargaining reaches an impasse, the matter is submitted to a neutral arbiter, who decides what the terms and conditions of the new collective-bargaining agreement will be.[15]

Only three states use the meet-and-confer model, which grants very few rights to public employees. As with the binding-arbitration model, police employees in meet-and-confer states have the right to organize and to select their own bargaining representatives.[16] However, when an impasse is reached, employees are at a distinct disadvantage: Their only legal choices are to accept the employer's best offer, try to influence the offer through political tactics (such as appeals for public support), or take some permissible job action.[17]

The twenty-two states that follow the bargaining-not-required model have statutes that either do not require or do not allow collective bargaining by public employees.[18] In the majority of these states, laws permitting public employees to engage in collective bargaining have not been passed.

Negotiations. Figure 6-1 ■ depicts a typical configuration of the union and management bargaining teams. Positions shown in dashed boxes typically serve in a support role and may or may not actually partake in the bargaining. The management's labor relations manager (lead negotiator) is often an attorney assigned to the human resources department who reports to the city manager or assistant city manager and represents the city in grievances and arbitration matters. The union's chief negotiator will normally not be a member of the bargaining unit; rather, he or she will be a specialist brought in to

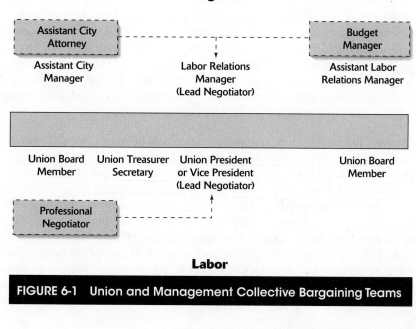

FIGURE 6-1 Union and Management Collective Bargaining Teams

represent the union's position and to provide greater experience, expertise, objectivity, and autonomy. The union's chief negotiator may be accompanied by individuals who have conducted surveys on wages and benefits, trends in the consumer price index, and so on.[19]

Management's chief negotiator may be the director of labor relations or the human resources director for the unit of government involved or a professional labor relations specialist. The agency's chief executive should not appear at the table personally—it is extremely delicate for the chief to represent management one day and then return to work among the employees the next. Management is represented by a key member of the command staff who has the executive's confidence.

Impasses. The purpose of bargaining is to produce a bilateral written agreement to which both parties will bind themselves during the lifetime of the agreement. Even parties bargaining in good faith may not be able to resolve their differences by themselves, and an impasse may result. In such cases, a neutral third party may be appointed to facilitate, suggest, or compel an agreement. Three major forms of impasse resolution are mediation, fact-finding, and arbitration:

1. *Mediation.* Mediation occurs when a third party, called the mediator, comes in to help the adversaries with the negotiations.[20] This person may be a professional mediator or someone in whom both parties have confidence. In most states, mediation may be requested by either labor or management. The mediator's task is to build agreement about the issues involved by reopening communication between the two sides. The mediator has no way to compel an agreement, so an advantage of the process is that it preserves the nature of collective bargaining by maintaining the decision-making power in the hands of the parties involved.[21]

2. *Fact-finding.* Fact-finding primarily involves the interpretation of facts and the determination of what weight to attach to them. Appointed in the same way as mediators, fact-finders also do not have a way to impose a settlement of the dispute. Fact-finders may sit alone or as part of a panel, which normally consists of three people. The fact-finding hearing is quasi-judicial, although less strict rules of evidence are applied. Both labor and management may be represented by legal counsel, and verbatim transcripts are commonly made. In most cases, the fact-finder's recommendations are made public at some point.[22]

3. *Arbitration.* Arbitration parallels fact-finding but differs in that the "end product of arbitration is a final and binding decision that sets the terms of the settlement and with which the parties are legally required to comply."[23] Arbitration may be compulsory or voluntary: It is compulsory when mandated by state law and binding on the parties even if one of them is unwilling to comply; it is voluntary when the parties of their own volition decide to use the procedure. Even when entered into voluntarily, arbitration is binding on the parties who have agreed to it.

Grievances. The establishment of a working agreement between labor and management does not mean that the possibility for conflict no longer exists; the day-to-day administration of the agreement may also be the basis for strife. Questions can arise about the interpretation and application of the document and its various clauses. Grievances— complaints or expressions of dissatisfaction by an employee concerning some aspect of employment—may arise. The grievance procedure is a formal process that involves the seeking of redress of the complaints through progressively higher channels within the organization. The sequence of the grievance process will be spelled out in the collective-bargaining agreement and will typically include the following steps: The employee presents the grievance to his or her immediate supervisor; if the employee does not receive satisfaction, a written grievance is presented to the division commander, then to the chief executive officer, then to the city or county manager, and finally to an arbiter, who is selected according to the rules of the American Arbitration Association.[24]

The burden of proof is on the grieving party except in disciplinary cases, in which it is always on the employer. The parties may be represented by counsel at the hearing, and the format will include opening statements by each side, examination and cross-examination of any witnesses, and closing arguments in the reverse order in which opening arguments were made.[25]

Job Actions. A job action is an activity in which employees engage to express their dissatisfaction with a particular person, event, or condition or to attempt to influence the outcome of some matter pending before decision makers.[26] Job actions are of four types: vote of confidence, work slowdown, work speedup, and work stoppage.

1. *Vote of confidence.* The vote of confidence is used sparingly. A vote of no confidence signals employees' collective displeasure with the chief administrator of the agency. Although such votes have no legal standing, they may have high impact due to the resulting publicity.

2. *Work slowdown.* In work slowdowns, employees continue to work, but they do so at a leisurely pace, causing productivity to fall. As productivity declines, revenues decline (through fewer citations being issued), and the public may pressure government officials to bring about normal operations (e.g., to slow down speeders in school zones, and so forth).[27]

3. *Work speedup.* A work speedup involves accelerated activity in the level of services. For example, a police department may conduct a "ticket blizzard" to pressure public officials into granting pay increases, to make more concessions at the bargaining table, or to abandon some policy change that affects their working conditions. In any case, the idea is to raise public ire by the police doing their jobs—with too much gusto, and with an impact on wallets and purses.

4. *Work stoppage.* Work stoppages constitute the most severe job action. The ultimate work stoppage is the strike, or the withholding of all employee services. This tactic is most often used by labor to force management back to the bargaining table when negotiations have reached an impasse. However, criminal justice employee strikes are now rare. Briefer work stoppages, which do not involve all employees and are known in policing as "blue flu," last only a few days.

Fair Labor Standards Act. An area of policing that is at the heart of management–labor relations is the Fair Labor Standards Act (FLSA). For some police administrators, the FLSA is, as one observer termed it, the criminal justice administrator's "worst nightmare come true."[28] On the other hand, it has been said that the FLSA is one of the most important labor laws ever passed, and forever changed American policing: it meant that police officers could no longer be required to work more than eight hours a day or forty hours a week without compensation, nor did local police unions and associations have to argue at the collective bargaining table for their members to be paid overtime.[29] The act provides minimum pay and overtime provisions covering both public- and private-sector employees and contains special provisions for firefighters and police officers. The FLSA was first enacted in 1938 to protect the rights and working conditions of employees in the *private* sector; in 1985, however, the U.S. Supreme Court brought state and local governmental employees under its coverage as well (in *Garcia* v. *San Antonio Transit Authority*).[30] Police operations, which take place twenty-four hours a day, seven days a week, often require overtime and participation in off-duty activities such as court appearances and training sessions. The FLSA provides that an employer must generally pay employees time and a half for all hours worked over forty per week; overtime must also be paid to personnel for all work in excess of 43 hours in a seven-day cycle or 171 hours in a twenty-eight-day period. Public-safety employees may accrue a maximum of 480 hours of "comp" (compensation) time, which, if not utilized as leave, must be paid off upon separation from employment at each employee's final rate of pay or at the average pay over the last three years, whichever is greater.[31] Furthermore, employers usually cannot require employees to take comp time in lieu of cash. Today, an officer who works the night shift must receive pay for attending training or testifying in court during the day. Furthermore, officers who are ordered to remain at home in anticipation of emergency actions must be compensated. Notably, however, FLSA's overtime provisions do not apply to those who are employed in a bona fide executive, administrative, or professional capacity. In criminal justice, the act has generally been held to apply to detectives and sergeants but not to those of the rank of lieutenant and above.

▶ Higher Education

Lagging Behind

That policing lags well behind our society-at-large in terms of its emphasis on educational attainment is evident: first, according to the latest survey by the U.S. Census Bureau, the percentage of the population aged twenty-five and over with a bachelor's degree or higher now stands at 30 percent.[32] Conversely, although the proportion of local (county and municipal) police officers holding at least a bachelor's degree is unknown, the latest survey of the Bureau of Justice Statistics found that only 1 percent of all local police agencies required at least a bachelor's degree for hiring, and less than one-third—32 percent—offered officers some form of educational incentive pay.[33]

Certainly the shift to community policing and problem-solving era of policing (discussed in Chapters 1 and 4) would seem to make the case that postsecondary education is more critical than ever before. The problem analysis and skills needed to develop tailor-made responses to neighborhood crime and disorder appears to practically cry out for postsecondary preparation. In a similar way, the threat of terrorism—and the relatively recent inception of such concepts as intelligence-led policing, predictive policing, fusion centers, and so on—would seem to make college preparation the degree of necessity. Nonetheless, for nearly a century there has been a debate over whether or not a college education is beneficial for police officers.[34]

An Enduring Controversy

The aforementioned small percentage of agencies requiring a college degree is certainly surprising in light of the reports of numerous studies, courts, and national commissions (some of which are discussed below) that have concluded that higher education is essential for police officers. As will be seen, this remains one of policing's most enduring and controversial issues.

Efforts to involve college-educated personnel in police work were first made by August Vollmer (discussed in Chapter 1) in 1917 when he recruited University of California students as part-time police officers in Berkeley.[35] However, few departments elsewhere in the country took any immediate steps to follow Vollmer's example. Rank-and-file officers strongly resisted the concept of college-level studies for police, and officers with a college education remained very much an exception; they were often referred to disparagingly as "college cops."[36]

However, the movement toward higher education for police continued to spread: By 1975, there were 729 community college and 376 four-year applicable programs.[37] The Law Enforcement Education Program (LEEP) provided tuition assistance for in-service

▲ Whether or not police officers should be compelled to possess college degrees is a source of enduring controversy. *(Courtesy aastock/Shutterstock.)*

police officers and preservice students. In 1973, ninety-five thousand college and university students were receiving LEEP assistance—unquestionably the "glory days" of higher education in criminal justice.[38] Many patrol officers who otherwise could not have afforded it received quality higher education.

Rationales for and Against Higher Education for Police

The issue of higher education for police officers has been addressed by a number of notable entities, going back more than forty years. First, the President's Commission on Law Enforcement and the Administration of Justice made this statement in 1967:

> It is nonsense to state or assume that the enforcement of law is so simple that it can be done by those unencumbered by the study of liberal arts. Officers of any department should certainly be conversant with the structure of government, [and] be well grounded in sociology, criminology, and human relations in order to understand the ramifications of the problems which confront them daily.[39]
>
> —"Statement made by Enforcement and the Administration of Justice" from TASK FORCE REPORT: THE POLICE. Published by U.S. Government Printing Office, © 1973.

In 1973, the National Advisory Commission on Criminal Justice Standards and Goals, concurring that college-educated officers were needed, recommended that all police officers have a four-year college education by 1982,[40] a goal that obviously went unmet. Nevertheless, from 1967 to 1986, every national commission that studied crime, violence, and policing in America came to the conclusion that a college education could help the police do their jobs better.[41] Advocates of higher education for the police maintain that it will improve the quality of policing by making officers more tolerant of people who are different from themselves; in this view, college-educated officers are more professional, communicate better with citizens, are better decision makers, and have better written and verbal skills than less educated officers.

A ringing endorsement for higher education for the police also came in 1985 when a lawsuit challenged the Dallas, Texas, Police Department's requirement that all applicants for police officer positions possess forty-five credit hours and at least a C average at an accredited college or university. The Fifth Circuit Court of Appeals, and eventually the U.S. Supreme Court, upheld the educational requirement. The circuit court said:

> Even a rookie police officer must have the ability to handle tough situations. A significant part of a police officer's function involves his ability to function effectively as a crisis intervenor, in family fights, teen-age rumbles, bar brawls, street corner altercations, racial disturbances, riots and similar situations. Few professionals are so peculiarly charged with individual responsibilities as police officers. Mistakes of judgment could cause irreparable harm to citizens or even to the community. The educational requirement bears a manifest relationship to the position of police officer. We conclude that the district court's findings . . . are not erroneous.[42]
>
> —Statement by The Fifth Circuit Court of Appeals, Davis v. City of Dallas, 777 F.2d 205 (5th Cir. 1985), The Supreme Court of the United States, 1985.

Abundant empirical evidence also indicates that college-educated police officers are better officers. Compared to less educated officers, research indicates they have significantly fewer founded citizen complaints[43]; have better peer relationships[44]; are likelier to take a leadership role in the organization[45]; tend to be more flexible[46]; are less dogmatic and less authoritarian[47]; take fewer leave days, receive fewer injuries, have less injury time, have lower rates of absenteeism, use fewer sick days, and are involved in fewer traffic accidents[48]; and have a more desirable system of personal values.[49] Furthermore, college graduates are significantly less likely to violate their department's internal regulations regarding insubordination, negligent use of a firearm, and absenteeism than officers who lack a college degree.[50]

A major argument by police administrators against requiring a college degree for entry-level officers is that the recruitment of minorities will greatly suffer, which is particularly problematic at a time when agencies seek to diversify their ranks. However, a number of jurisdictions argue just as strongly that this is not a problem and offer evidence (albeit anecdotal) that the reverse is actually true and that maintaining the college requirement has a number of benefits:[51] Some studies, however, have identified some negative effects of higher education. Critics believe that educated officers are more likely to become frustrated with their work and that their limited opportunities for advancement will cause them to leave the force early. Furthermore, they argue that police tasks that require mostly common sense or street sense are not performed better by officers with higher education.[52] These studies found that it had no positive effect on officers' public-service orientation (those with a degree displayed less orientation toward public service than those without a degree)[53] and that college-educated officers attach less value to obedience to supervisors than do officers without a college education.[54]

Given the above benefits and today's challenges to policing, however, and if the field is to ever truly achieve the level of a true profession, it remains a paradox to many that higher educational standards have not yet been established for police officers.

▶ On Guard: The Private Police

Nature and Types

Much has certainly changed in society and the private security industry since 1851, when Allan Pinkerton initiated the Pinkerton National Detective Agency, specializing in railroad security. Pinkerton established the first private security contract operation in the United States. His motto was "We Never Sleep," and his logo, an open eye, was probably the genesis of the term private eye.

▲ William A. Pinkerton, principal of the western branch of Pinkerton's National Detective Agency. *(Reprinted from The Blue and the Brass: American Policing, 1890–1976. Copyright held by the International Association of Chiefs of Police. Further reproduction without express written permission from IACP is strictly prohibited.)*

Today, according to loss-prevention expert Saul Astor, "We are a nation of thieves"[55]—and, it might be added, a nation that needs to be protected against would-be terrorists, rapists, robbers, and other dangerous people. According to the National Crime Victim Survey, there are about 5.8 million violent-crime victimizations and 17.1 million property crime victimizations each year in this nation.[56] As a result, and especially since 9/11, this nation has become highly security minded concerning its computers, lotteries, celebrities, college campuses, casinos, nuclear plants, airports, shopping centers, mass transit systems, hospitals, and railroads. Such businesses, industries, and institutions have recognized the need to conscientiously protect their assets against threats of crime and other disasters—as well as the limited capabilities of the nation's full-time sworn officers and agents to protect them—and have increasingly turned to the "other police"—those of the private sector—for protection.

In-house security services, directly hired and controlled by the company or organization, are called proprietary services; contract services are those outside firms or individuals hired by the individual or company to provide security services for a fee. The most common security services provided include contract guards, alarm services, private investigators, locksmith services, armored-car services, and security consultants.

Although some of the duties of the security officer are similar to those of the public police officer, their overall powers are entirely different. First, because security officers are not police officers, court decisions have stated that the security officer is not bound by the *Miranda* decision concerning suspects' rights. Furthermore, security officers generally possess only the same authority to effect an arrest as does the common citizen (the exact extent of citizen's arrest power varies, however, depending on the type of crime, the jurisdiction, and the status of the citizen). In most states, warrantless arrests by private citizens are allowed when a felony has been committed and reasonable grounds exist for believing that the person arrested committed it. Most states also allow citizen's arrests for misdemeanors committed in the arrester's presence.

The tasks of the private police are very similar to those of their public counterparts: protecting executives and employees, tracking and forecasting security threats, monitoring alarms, preventing and detecting fraud, conducting investigations, providing crisis management and prevention, and responding to substance abuse.[57]

Still, there are concerns about the field: as one author noted, "Of those individuals involved in private security, some are uniformed, some are not; some carry guns, some are unarmed; some guard nuclear energy installations, some guard golf courses; some are trained, some are not; some have college degrees, some are virtually uneducated."[58] Studies have shown that security officer recruits often have minimal education and training; because the pay is usually quite low, the jobs often attract only those people who cannot find other jobs or seek temporary work. Thus much of the work is done by the young and the retired, and the recruitment and training of lower-level private security personnel can present a real concern.[59] Clearly, today's security officer needs to be highly trained and competent.

Another long-standing issue that concerns private police is whether or not they should be armed. In the past, much has been made about security officers who have received little or no prior training or have undergone no checks on their criminal history records but are carrying a weapon. Twenty-three hours of firearms instruction is recommended for all security personnel, as well as another twenty-four hours on general matters and proper legal training.[60]

Attempts to Unify Public–Private Police

In the new millennium there has been a formal movement to attempt to bring the public and private police closer together, due in large measure to the following special strengths that are possessed by the private security industry:

Size of the industry: Employment in private security is nearly three times that of the public police, and its spending is more than double. Furthermore, while public policing has seen spending levels remain steady or even decrease, that of private security has been growing rapidly.

Expertise and resources: The private security industry is advanced in (a) the use of technology to both prevent and detect crime, (b) the investigation of high-tech and economic crime, and (c) crime and loss prevention. Further, security organizations that work in corporations, businesses, and such locations as schools are generally well equipped to address such crimes as school shootings, workplace violence, or computer crimes.[61]

In 2000, a program entitled "Operation Cooperation" was funded by the Bureau of Justice Assistance and the U.S. Department of Justice, and supported by the American Society for Industrial Security (now ASIS International), the International Association of Chiefs of Police, and the National Sheriffs' Association. The purpose of the project was to persuade police, sheriffs, and security professionals to work together, and to establish that the public and private police organizations need each other. The program's underlying theme was that "No city or metropolitan area should be without at least one public–private cooperative program."[62]

In addition, the Federal Law Enforcement Training Center launched "Operation Partnership," a two- to three-day training program for instructing public and private police managers in how to build productive, cooperative relationships between their organizations. This program emphasizes the similarities and differences between the missions of the police and private security, provides examples of effective law enforcement private security partnerships, reviews strategies and processes for developing such partnerships, and identifies the skills needed to plan, implement, and evaluate partnerships.[63]

Attempts to Legislate Advancement

The United States Congress has indicated a willingness to help move private security services in the right direction. In December 2004, the Intelligence Reform and Terrorism Prevention Act of 2004 (Public Law 108–458) was enacted. Section 6402 of that legislation, known as the Private Security Officer Employment Authorization Act of 2004, authorizes a fingerprint-based criminal history check of state and national criminal history records to screen prospective and current private security officers.[64]

More recently, the 112th Congress (2011–2012) saw the introduction of H.R. 4112, the "Private Security Screening Improvement Act," which would "allow screening entities to submit, receive, and screen criminal history record" information and allow searches of private security officers under the above employment authorization act; this bill was referred to committee in February 2012, and no further action has been taken.[65]

An Organization at the Forefront

The private security industry has been advanced significantly by a national, nonprofit organization that has existed for more than a half-century to "increase the effectiveness and productivity of security professionals."[66] Founded in 1955 as the American Society for Industrial Security, in 2002 its official name was changed to ASIS International. The organization develops educational programs and materials that address broad security interests, conducts annual seminars, provides members with a full range of programs and services, and publishes a trade magazine, *Security Management*.[67]

Perhaps as beneficial is that ASIS International publishes and espouses a number of standards and guidelines for the field, such as recommended minimum selection and training qualifications for personnel (e.g., the *Private Security Officer Selection and Training Guideline*)[68] as well as a related code of conduct.[69]

Summary

This chapter has examined several contemporary trends and issues in policing. Despite its 180-year-plus history and many advances, policing still has many issues that have not been resolved.

This chapter first addressed police officer stress, where it was demonstrated that police agencies must recognize and address the needs of their human resources just as they plan for the purchase of capital equipment or for operations. Too often, police departments neglect or take their personnel for granted. People are a department's most important asset.

Certainly the section on labor relations and collective bargaining would be completely foreign to the major figures (Peel, Vollmer, Parker, and so on) who were instrumental in the development of American policing (discussed in Chapter 1). It was shown that the balance of power is certainly different today, as compared with the earlier unilateral, serve-at-the-pleasure-of-the-boss era, when officers had little protection against the whims of their leadership or complaints by the public; furthermore, their employment and ability to negotiate for better working conditions and benefits have greatly increased over time.

Higher education also remains a questionable element of policing for many people—notwithstanding that several major national commissions and court decisions as well as other entities and police executives have been advocating this requirement for nearly three decades. The major argument against having a college education requirement—that it greatly diminishes the minority hiring pool—was also brought into question in this chapter.

Finally, it is evident that the private security services are becoming a much more vital segment of public safety in the United States; many reasons were given for the continuing unification of the public and private police, and it can only be for the better that formal efforts by legislatures and related national organizations continue to strive to improve the industry and reduce or eliminate some of its long-term issues and challenges.

Key Terms

collective bargaining
contract services
employee assistance program
  (EAP)
Fair Labor Standards Act (FLSA)

grievance
higher education
homeostasis
impasse
job action

labor relations
Peace Officer Bill of Rights
private police
proprietary services
stress

Review Questions

1. How would you define stress, and what are the four general areas of police work that contribute to stress?
2. How may police personnel attempt to manage their stress levels?
3. What are the functions of an employee assistance program?
4. What employment rights do today's police officers possess, and what are some of the common provisions of the Peace Officer Bill of Rights?
5. What are the major reasons for the development and expansion of police unions, and what is their impact today?

6. What are the three models of collective bargaining, and what happens under each model when there is an impasse?
7. What are the four kinds of job actions?
8. How would you describe the Fair Labor Standards Act and the way it operates in policing?
9. Why is the possession of higher education by police officers controversial, and what are some rationales given for and against officers having such education?
10. How did private policing evolve, how does it differ from public policing, and what are some issues and concerns it presents to the public?

Learn by Doing

1. Unquestionably, the best way for you to determine the kinds of stressors that exist in policing is to interview a municipal police officer or county deputy sheriff. Encourage your interviewee to identify the degrees of stress that are caused by the stressors described in this chapter; the stressors caused by personnel; the issues that originate both inside and outside the organization; which type of calls for service create the most stress; and how he or she attempts to cope with stress.
2. Your criminal justice professor assigns a project in class wherein you are to debate the pros and cons of police officers and higher education—specifically,

whether or not they should be required to possess a four-year or graduate degree. Taking either a pro or con side, develop your debating points.
3. Recently there has been a movement in your tourism-based community to examine the field of private policing. Today while you are guest lecturing before a local civic group's luncheon, a member of the audience asks you to describe the kinds of duties, rights, and training that should exist under the law for the private police. Also of interest to the audience is the interface between the public and private police—advantages and disadvantages of one as compared with the other. With what specifics do you respond?

Notes

1. Quoted in J. Bartlett, ed., *Familiar Quotations*, 16th ed. (Boston: Little, Brown, 1992).
2. William A. Westley, *Violence and the Police* (Cambridge, MA: The MIT Press, 1970), p. 3.
3. Hans Selye, *Stress Without Distress* (Philadelphia: Lippincott, 1981).
4. Merry Morash and Robin Haarr, "Gender, Workplace Problems, and Stress in Policing" (Paper presented at the annual meeting of the Academy of Criminal Justice Sciences, Nashville, TN, March 12, 1991).
5. L. Brooks and N. Piquero, "Police Stress: Does Department Size Matter?" *Policing: An International Journal of Police Strategies and Management* 21(1) (1998): 600–617.
6. S. R. Band and D. C. Sheehan, "Managing Undercover Stress: The Supervisor's Role," *FBI Law Enforcement Bulletin* (February 1999): 1–6.
7. Adapted from Larry Copeland, "Police trained in delivering tragic news," *USA Today*, October 26, 2011, http://usatoday30.usatoday.com/news/nation/story/2011-10-25/death-notification-mourning/50913338/1 (accessed October 16, 2013)
8. G. L. Fishkin, *Police Burnout: Signs, Symptoms and Solutions* (Gardena, CA: Harcourt Brace Jovanovich, 1988).
9. *Board of Regents v. Roth*, 408 U.S. 564 (1972), at 578.
10. W. Clinton Terry III, *Policing Society: An Occupational View* (New York: Wiley, 1985), p. 168.
11. Ibid., pp. 170–171.
12. Samuel Walker, *The Police in America: An Introduction*, 3rd ed. (Boston: McGraw-Hill, 1999), p. 368.
13. Fraternal Order of Police homepage, http://www.fop.net/ (accessed November 1, 2012).
14. Will Aitchison, *The Rights of Police Officers*, 3rd ed. (Portland, OR: Labor Relations Information System, 1996), p. 7.
15. Ibid.
16. Ibid.
17. Ibid., p. 8.
18. Ibid., p. 9.
19. Charles R. Swanson, Leonard Territo, and Robert W. Taylor, *Police Administration: Structures, Processes, and Behavior*, 6th ed. (Upper Saddle River, NJ: Prentice Hall, 2005), p. 517.
20. Arnold Zack, *Understanding Fact-Finding and Arbitration in the Public Sector* (Washington, U.S. Government Printing Office, 1974), p. 1.
21. Thomas P. Gilroy and Anthony V. Sinicropi, "Impasse Resolution in Public Employment," *Industrial and Labor Relations Review* 25 (July 1971): 499.
22. Robert G. Howlett, "Fact Finding: Its Values and Limitations—Comment," in *Arbitration and the Expanded Role of Neutrals* (Proceedings of the Twenty-Third Annual Meeting of the National Academy of Arbitrators) (Washington, D.C.: Bureau of National Affairs, 1970), p. 156.
23. Zack, *Understanding Fact-Finding and Arbitration in the Public Sector*, p. 1.
24. Charles W. Maddox, *Collective Bargaining in Law Enforcement* (Springfield, IL: Charles C Thomas, 1975), p. 54.
25. Swanson et al., *Police Administration*, p. 530.
26. Ibid., p. 423.
27. Ibid.
28. L. Lund, "The 'Ten Commandments' of Risk Management for Jail Administrators," *Detention Reporter* 4 (June 1991): 4.
29. International Union of Police Associations, "I.U.P.A. History Timeline," http://www.iupa.org/index.php?option=com_content&view=article&id=112&Itemid=164 (accessed October 31, 2013).
30. *Garcia v. San Antonio Transit Authority*, 469 U.S. 528 (1985).
31. Swanson et al., *Police Administration*, p. 392.
32. U.S. Census Bureau, Educational Attainment in the United States: 2009 (February 2012, p. 1), http://www.census.gov/prod/2012pubs/p20-566.pdf (accessed October 31, 2012).
33. U.S. Department of Justice, Bureau of Justice Statistics, *Local Police Departments, 2007* (Washington, D.C.: Author, December 2010), pp. 11–36.
34. Roy Roberg and Scott Bonn, "Higher Education and Policing: Where Are We Now?" *Policing* 27(4) (2004), http://0-search.proquest.com.innopac.library.unr.edu/docview/211270803/13A1CFE821B41F9D7D2/4?accountid=452 (accessed October 31, 2012).
35. Albert Deutsch, *The Trouble with Cops* (New York: Crown, 1955), p. 122.
36. Herman Goldstein, *Policing a Free Society* (Cambridge, MA: Ballinger, 1977), pp. 283–284.
37. Deutsch, *The Trouble with Cops*, p. 213; *Law Enforcement and Criminal Justice Education: Directory, 1975–76* (Gaithersburg, MD: International Association of Chiefs of Police, 1975), p. 3.
38. Law Enforcement Assistance Administration, *Fifth Annual Report, Fiscal Year 1973* (Washington, D.C.: Government Printing Office, 1973), p. 119.
39. President's Commission on Law Enforcement and the Administration of Justice, *The Police* (Task Force

Report) (Washington, D.C.: Government Printing Office, 1973), p. 155.

40. National Advisory Commission on Criminal Justice Standards and Goals, *Police* (Washington, D.C.: Government Printing Office, 1973), p. 369.

41. Gerald W. Lynch, "Why Officers Need a College Education," *Higher Education and National Affairs* (September 20, 1986): 11.

42. *Davis v. City of Dallas,* 777 F.2d 205 (5th Cir. 1985).

43. Victor E. Kappeler, Allen D. Sapp, and David L. Carter, "Police Officer Higher Education, Citizen Complaints and Departmental Rule Violations," *American Journal of Police* 11 (1992): 37–54. Also see Mayo, "College Education and Policing," *The Police Chief* 73 (8) (August 2006), http://www.policechiefmagazine. org/magazine/index.cfm?fuseaction=display_ arch&article_id=955&issue_id=82006 (accessed October 16, 2013).

44. Charles L. Weirman, "Variances of Ability Measurement Scores Obtained by College and Non-College Educated Troopers," *Police Chief* 45 (August 1978): 34–36.

45. Ibid.

46. Robert Trojanowicz and T. Nicholson, "A Comparison of Behavioral Styles of College Graduate Police Officers Versus Non-College Going Police Officers," *Police Chief* 43 (August 1976): 56–59.

47. A. F. Dalley, "University and Non-University Graduated Policemen: A Study of Police Attitudes," *Journal of Police Science and Administration* 3 (1975): 458–468.

48. Wayne F. Cascio, "Formal Education and Police Officer Performance," *Journal of Police Science and Administration* 5 (1977): 89–96; Bernard Cohen and Jan M. Chaiken, *Police Background Characteristics and Performance* (New York: RAND, 1972); B. E. Sanderson, "Police Officers: The Relationship of College Education to Job Performance," *Police Chief* (August 1977): 62–63.

49. James W. Sterling, "The College Level Entry Requirement: A Real or Imagined Cure-All?" *Police Chief* 41 (April 1974): 28–31.

50. Gerald W. Lynch, "Cops and College," *America,* April 4, 1987, pp. 274–275.

51. Mayo, "College Education and Policing."

52. Robert E. Worden, "A Badge and a Baccalaureate: Policies, Hypotheses, and Further Evidence," *Justice Quarterly* 7 (September 1990): 565–592.

53. Jon Miller and Lincoln Fry, "Reexamining Assumptions About Education and Professionalism in Law Enforcement," *Journal of Police Science and Administration* 4 (1976): 187–198.

54. John K. Hudzik, "College Education for Police: Problems in Measuring Component and Extraneous Variables," *Journal of Criminal Justice* 6 (1978): 69–81.

55. Saul D. Astor, "A Nation of Thieves," *Security World* 15 (September 1978).

56. Department of Justice, Bureau of Justice Statistics, *Criminal Victimization, 2011* (October 2012), http://www.ojp.usdoj.gov/newsroom/pressreleases/ 2012/ojppr101712.pdf (accessed October 16, 2013).

57. Ibid., p. 238.

58. Lawrence J. Fennelly, ed., *Handbook of Loss Prevention and Crime Prevention,* 2nd ed. (Boston: Butterworths, 1989), in foreword.

59. George F. Cole and Christopher E. Smith, *The American System of Criminal Justice,* 11th ed. (Belmont, CA: Thomson Wadsworth, 2007), p. 253.

60. National Advisory Commission on Criminal Justice Standards and Goals, Private Security (Washington, D.C.: U.S. Government Printing Office, 1976), p. 99.

61. U.S. Department of Justice, Bureau of Justice Assistance, *Operation Cooperation: Guidelines for Partnerships between Law Enforcement and Private Security Organizations* (2000), http://www.ilj.org/ publications/docs/Operation_Cooperation.pdf (accessed November 2, 2012).

62. Ibid., p. 1.

63. Ibid., p. 11.

64. Federal Register, "Implementation of the Private Security Officer Employment Authorization Act of 2004," https://www.federalregister.gov/regulations/ 1110-AA23/implementation-of-the-private-security- officer-employment-authorization-act-of-2004 (accessed November 1, 2012).

65. See govtrack.us, http://www.govtrack.us/congress/ bills/112/hr4112 (accessed November 1, 2012).

66. ASIS International, "About ASIS," http://www. asisonline.org/about/history/index.xml (accessed November 2, 2012).

67. Ibid., https://www.asisonline.org/ (accessed November 2, 2012).

68. Ibid., http://www.abdi-secure-ecommerce.com/ASIS/ ps-1128-37-2001.aspx (accessed November 2, 2012).

69. ASIS Management System for Quality of Private Security Company Operations—Requirements with Guidance, http://www.abdi-secure-ecommerce.com/ ASIS/ps-1128-37-2001.aspx (accessed November 2, 2012).

Adhering to Law, Ethical Principles, and Public Expectations

7 Rule of Law: Expounding the Constitution

8 Accountability: Ethics, Use of Force, Corruption, and Discipline

9 Civil Liability: Failing the Public Trust

The three chapters composing Part 3 together examine several means by which police authority is constrained. More specifically, Chapter 7 looks at the rule of law: court decisions and constitutional enactments that direct and constrain police actions; the focus here is on the Bill of Rights in the Constitution, particularly the Fourth, Fifth, and Sixth Amendments. Chapter 8 considers police accountability from several perspectives, including the issue of police ethics, use of force, corruption, and discipline. Potential civil liability of the police is then examined in Chapter 9, which includes various areas in which officers may be liable, and the means by which citizens may seek legal redress when they believe their civil rights have been violated.

(Courtesy Francesco Carucci/Shutterstock.)

7 Rule of Law
Expounding the Constitution

LEARNING OBJECTIVES

As a result of reading this chapter, the student will be able to:

1 *Explain what is meant by the rule of law*

2 *Outline the protections afforded citizens by the Fourth, Fifth, and Sixth Amendments*

3 *Define and give examples of probable cause*

4 *Describe the rationale for and ramifications of the exclusionary rule*

5 *Distinguish between arrests and searches and seizures with and without a warrant*

6 *Explain what is permitted and prohibited with respect to searches of automobiles*

7 Describe three recent court decisions concerning warrantless searches of homes by police under exigent circumstances to render emergency aid

8 Describe some significant ways in which the Miranda decision has been modified

9 Explain the law regarding the use of GPS systems for surveilling suspects' vehicles

10 Delineate the major rights of juveniles as well as the major philosophical differences in the law for treatment of juvenile and adult offenders

11 Define "stand your ground" laws and describe its impact on police and prosecutors

Introduction

The Bill of Rights—the first ten amendments to the U.S. Constitution—was passed largely to protect all citizens from excessive governmental power. The police are expected to control crime within the framework of these rights; they must conduct themselves in a manner that conforms to the rule of law as set forth in the U.S. Constitution, state constitutions, statutes passed by state legislatures, and the precedent of prior interpretations by the courts.

What is meant by the **rule of law**? This commonly used phrase was comprehensively defined in 1885 by Albert Venn Dicey in his now-classic *Introduction to the Study of the Law of the Constitution*.[1] Dicey identified three principles that together establish the rule of law:

1. Absolute supremacy or predominance of regular law as opposed to the influence of arbitrary power

2. Equality before the law or the equal subjection of all classes to the ordinary law of the land administered by the ordinary courts

3. Law of the U.S. Constitution as a consequence of the rights of individuals as defined and enforced by the courts

In other words, under the rule of law of the United States, the means are more important than the ends. A nation's democratic form of government would be of little value if the police could arrest, search, and seize its citizens and their property at will.

This chapter examines three constitutional amendments that regulate the police and prevent abuses of power: the Fourth Amendment (probable cause, exclusionary rule, arrest, search and seizure, electronic surveillance, and lineups), the Fifth Amendment (confessions, interrogation, and entrapment), and the Sixth Amendment (right to counsel and interrogation). To avoid overwhelming the reader with case titles, only better-known court cases—such as *Miranda v. Arizona*—are included in the body of the chapter; others are cited in the Notes section. Also discussed is a related, yet in some ways very different, area of law and procedure: the law pertaining to juvenile offenders. Finally, an exhibit includes a review of the new (and highly controversial) "stand your ground" law that has been enacted in several states. A summary, review questions, and several scenarios and activities that provide opportunities to learn by doing conclude the chapter.

It is also important to remember that our nation's laws are dynamic—that is, like our society in general, they are constantly changing. Laws are enacted by courts and legislatures as well as by acts of Congress and treaties and are found in the U.S. and state constitutions and statutes, administrative laws (i.e., those laws involving the powers and duties of government agencies), and city and county ordinances; therefore, the laws are constantly in flux as new ones are created and old ones are repealed or overturned. Therefore, aspiring police officers, students of criminal justice, and of course judges, prosecutors, and defense attorneys must keep abreast of changes in the laws. Although many police agencies will have the benefit of a legal advisor assigned by their city or county attorney's office to render legal advice for persons working in the field, most agencies probably do not have that luxury and thus must make an extra effort to read and understand new court decisions and other enactments. Publications such as the following will help one to keep abreast of such changes: the *FBI Law Enforcement Bulletin*, *The Police Chief* magazine, the *Criminal Law Reporter*, *U.S. Law Week*, and the *Supreme Court Bulletin*.

▶ Fourth Amendment

The right of the people to be secure in their persons, papers, and effects, against unreasonable searches and seizures, shall not be violated, and no Warrants shall issue, but upon probable cause, supported by Oath or affirmation, and particularly describing the place to be searched, and the persons or things to be seized.

—*U.S. Constitution, U.S. Department of Justice.*

The Fourth Amendment is intended to limit overzealous behavior by the police. Its primary protection is the requirement that a neutral detached magistrate, rather than a police officer, issue warrants for arrest and search and seizure. Crime, though a major concern to society, is balanced by the concern that officers might thrust themselves unnecessarily into our homes. The Fourth Amendment requires that the necessity for a person's right of privacy to yield to society's right to search is best decided by a neutral judicial officer, not by an agent of the police.[2]

Probable Cause

The standard for a legal arrest is probable cause. This important concept is elusive at best; it is often quite difficult for professors to explain and even more difficult for students to understand. One way to define probable cause is to say that for an officer to make an arrest, he or she must have more than a mere hunch, yet less than actual knowledge, that the arrestee committed the crime. I often use the following example from my own experience to better explain the concept:

At midnight, a fifty-five-year-old woman, having spent several hours at a city bar, wished to leave the bar and go to a nightclub in a rural part of the county. A man offered her a ride, but rather than driving directly to the nightclub, he drove to a remote place and parked the car. There he raped the woman and forced her to orally sodomize him. She fought him and later told the police she thought she had broken the temples (side pieces) of his black glasses. After the act, he drove her back to town; when she got out of the car, she saw the license plate number and thought that the hood of the car was colored red. Her account of the crime and her physical description of the rapist immediately prompted a photograph lineup; a known rape/sodomy suspect's picture was shown to her, along with photos of several other men with a similar description. She tentatively identified the suspect in the mug shot but could not be certain; the suspect's mug shot had been taken several years earlier.

With this preliminary information, two police officers (one of whom was this author) hurried to the suspect's home to question him. They did not have a warrant. Upon entering the suspect's driveway, the officers observed a beige car—with a red hood. Probable cause was beginning to build. Next the officers noted that the vehicle's license plate number matched the one given by the victim; probable cause was now growing by leaps and bounds. Then the suspect exited the house and walked toward his car; the officers observed that the frame of his eyeglasses was black but that the temples were gold, indicating that the black temples had probably been broken and replaced by spare gold temples. The officers now had, by any standard, adequate probable cause to lead a "reasonable and prudent" person to believe that this suspect was the culprit; the failure to arrest him would have been a gross miscarriage of justice. The suspect was thus arrested and placed in an actual lineup, where the victim identified him. This was one of those rare cases where the evidence was so compelling that the defendant pleaded guilty at his initial appearance and threw himself on the judge's mercy.

Of course, the facts of each case and the probable cause present are different; the court will examine the type and amount of probable cause that the officer had at the time of the arrest. It is important to note that a police officer cannot add to the probable cause used to make the arrest after effecting the arrest; the court will determine whether there existed sufficient probable cause to arrest the individual based on the officer's knowledge of the facts at the time of the arrest.

The Supreme Court has upheld convictions when probable cause was provided by a reliable informant,[3] when it came in an anonymous letter,[4] and when a suspect fit a Drug Enforcement Administration profile of a drug courier.[5] The Court has also held that police officers who "reasonably but mistakenly conclude that probable cause is present" are granted qualified immunity from civil action.[6]

Exclusionary Rule

The Fourth Amendment recognizes the right to privacy, but its application raises some perplexing questions. First of all, not all searches are prohibited—only those that are unreasonable. Another issue has to do with how to handle evidence that is illegally obtained. Should murderers be released, Justice Benjamin Cardozo asked, simply because "the constable blundered"?[7] The Fourth Amendment says nothing about how it is to be enforced, a problem that has stirred a good amount of debate for a number of years. Most of this debate has focused on the wisdom of, and the constitutional necessity for, the so-called exclusionary rule, which requires that all evidence obtained in violation of the Fourth Amendment be excluded from government's use in a criminal trial.

The 1961 Supreme Court decision in *Mapp v. Ohio*[8] helped in explaining the admissibility of illegally seized evidence in the state courts (see Court Closeup: *Mapp v. Ohio*).

▲ Officers have a responsibility to testify in court. (*Courtesy Washoe County Sheriff's Office.*)

In May 1957, three Cleveland police officers went to Dolree Mapp's house to follow up on an informant's tip that a suspect in a recent bombing was hiding there. They also had information that a large amount of materials for operating a numbers game would be found. Upon arrival at the house, officers knocked on the door and demanded entrance, but Mapp, after telephoning her lawyer, refused them entry without a search warrant.

Three hours later, the officers again attempted to enter Mapp's house, and again she refused them entry. They then forcibly entered the house. Mapp confronted the officers, demanding to see a search warrant; an officer waved a piece of paper at her, which she grabbed and placed in her bosom. The officers struggled with Mapp to retrieve the piece of paper, at which time Mapp's attorney arrived at the scene. The attorney was not allowed to enter the house or to see his client. Mapp was forcibly taken upstairs to her bedroom, where her belongings were searched. One officer found a brown paper bag containing books that he deemed to be obscene.

Mapp was charged with possession of obscene, lewd, or lascivious materials. At the trial, the prosecution attempted to prove that the materials belonged to Mapp; the defense contended that the books were the property of a former boarder who had left his belongings behind. The jury convicted Mapp, and she was sentenced to an indefinite term in prison.

In May 1959, Mapp appealed to the Ohio Supreme Court, claiming that the obscene materials were not in her possession and that the evidence was seized illegally. The court disagreed, ruling the evidence admissible. In June 1961, the U.S. Supreme Court overturned the conviction, holding that the Fourth Amendment's prohibition against unreasonable search and seizure had been violated:

> [Because] the right to be secure against rude invasions of privacy by state officers is . . . constitutional in origin, we can no longer permit that right to remain an empty promise. We can no longer permit it to be revocable at the whim of any police officer who, in the name of law enforcement itself, chooses to suspend its enjoyment.

But the Court's decision in *Mapp* did not end the controversy surrounding the exclusionary rule: Opponents of the rule are left with the suspicion that the rule is invoked only by someone—usually a guilty person—who does not want evidence of his or her crimes to be used at trial; furthermore, they believe that the suspect's behavior has been much more reprehensible than that of the police.[9]

The Supreme Court has objected to police behavior when it "shocks the conscience," excluding evidence, for example, that was obtained by forcible extraction (by stomach pump) from a man who had swallowed two morphine capsules in the police's presence.[10]

Modifications of the Exclusionary Rule Three major decisions during the 1983–1984 term of the Supreme Court served to modify the exclusionary rule. Then Associate Justice William Rehnquist (appointed Chief Justice in 1986) established a "public safety exception" to the doctrine. In that case, the defendant was charged with criminal possession of a firearm after a rape victim described him to the police. The officers located him in a supermarket, and upon questioning him about the weapon's whereabouts (without giving him the *Miranda* warning), they found it located behind some cartons. Rehnquist said that the case presented a situation in which concern for public safety outweighed a literal adherence to the rules. The police were justified in questioning the defendant on the grounds of "immediate necessity."[11]

Another 1984 decision announced the "inevitability of discovery exception." A ten-year-old girl was murdered and her body hidden. While transporting the suspect, detectives—who had promised the suspect's attorney that they would not question him while in transit—appealed to his sensitivities by saying it would be proper to find the body so that the girl's parents could give her a Christian burial. (This became known as the "Christian Burial Speech.") The suspect, Robert Williams, directed them to the body while, at the same time, a large search party was two-and-one-half miles away, combing both sides of the highway. Williams was tried and convicted of murder. In 1977, the Supreme Court overturned the conviction, ruling that the detectives had violated the defendant's rights by inducing him to incriminate himself without the presence of counsel (although it was noted that, even though his statements could not be admitted at a second trial, evidence of the body's location and condition might be admissible as the body would have been discovered even if the incriminating statements had not been elicited from respondent). Using this "inevitability of discovery" rationale, at a second trial, evidence concerning the body's location and condition was admitted, Williams was again convicted of first-degree murder. Using this "inevitability of discovery" rationale, at a second trial, evidence concerning the body's location and condition was admitted and Williams was again convicted of first-degree murder; in 1984 the Supreme Court upheld his conviction.[12]

Also in 1984, the Court ruled that evidence can be used even if obtained under a search warrant that is later found to be invalid. The Court held that evidence obtained by police officers acting in good faith on a reasonable reliance on a search warrant issued by a neutral magistrate could be used at trial even if the warrant was later found to be lacking in probable cause. This decision prompted a strong dissenting opinion by three justices, including William Brennan Jr., who said, "It now appears that the Court's victory over the Fourth Amendment is complete."[13]

Another ruling favorable to the police was handed down in 1988. Federal agents, observing suspicious behavior in and around a warehouse, illegally entered the building (with force and without a warrant) and observed marijuana in plain view. They left and obtained a search warrant for the building; then they returned and arrested the defendant for conspiracy to deliver illegal drugs. The Court allowed the evidence to be admitted at trial, saying that it ought not to have been excluded simply because of unrelated illegal conduct by the police. If probable cause could be established apart from their illegal activity, the Court said, evidence obtained from the search should be admitted.[14]

In summary, since the Warren Court expanded the rights of criminal defendants in the 1960s, a surge of cases to the Supreme Court has raised further questions concerning the exclusionary rule. Many observers expected the Court to overturn *Mapp*, yet the Court has not done so, apparently believing that without *Mapp* the flagrant abuses that occurred before it could resurface.

Arrests

A restriction on the right of the police to arrest is the hallmark of a free society. A basic condition of freedom is that one cannot be legally seized in an arbitrary and capricious manner at the discretion or whim of any government official. It is customary to refer to the writ of *habeas corpus*—the "Great Writ"—as the primary guarantee of personal freedom in a democracy. *Habeas corpus* is defined simply as a writ requiring an incarcerated person to be brought before a judge for an investigation of the restraint of that person's liberty. It should be noted that habeas corpus is the means of remedying wrongful arrest or other detention that has already occurred and that may have been illegal. The constitutional or statutory provisions for making an arrest are of crucial importance because they prevent police action that could be very harmful to the individual.[15]

Arrests with a Warrant It is always best for a police officer to effect an arrest with a warrant. In fact, in 1980, the Supreme Court required police officers to obtain warrants when making felony arrests, should there be time to do so—that is, when there are no exigent circumstances.[16] To obtain an arrest warrant, the officer or a citizen swears in an affidavit (as an "affiant") that he or she possesses certain knowledge that a particular person has committed an offense. For example, a private citizen tells police or the district attorney that he or she attended a party at a residence where drugs or stolen articles were present, or (as is often the case) a detective gathers physical evidence or interviews witnesses or victims and determines that probable cause exists to believe that a particular person committed a specific crime. In any case, a neutral magistrate, if he or she agrees that probable cause exists, will issue the arrest warrant. Officers will execute the warrant, taking the suspect into custody to answer the charges.

Warrantless Arrests An arrest without a warrant requires exigent circumstances and that the officer possess probable cause (as explained previously in the sodomy case). Street officers rarely have the time or opportunity to effect an arrest with a warrant in hand. Although the following real-life case involves a search preceding an arrest, it will make the point. One afternoon, a police officer was sent to the residence of several college students. They reported that four men left their party and that soon afterward another guest discovered that a stereo had been taken from a car parked in the yard. A description of the men and their vehicle was given to the officer, who soon observed a vehicle and four men matching the description. The men were stopped in their vehicle, and the officer called for backup.

The law does not require that the officer ask the subjects to stay put while he speeds off to the courthouse to attempt to secure a search warrant. The doctrine of probable cause allows the officer to search the vehicle and arrest the occupants if stolen or contraband items are found (as in this case, where the stolen stereo was found under the driver's seat). Police officers encounter these kinds of situations thousands of times each day. Such searches and arrests without benefit of a warrant are legally permissible, provided the officer had probable cause (which can later be explained to a judge) for his or her actions.

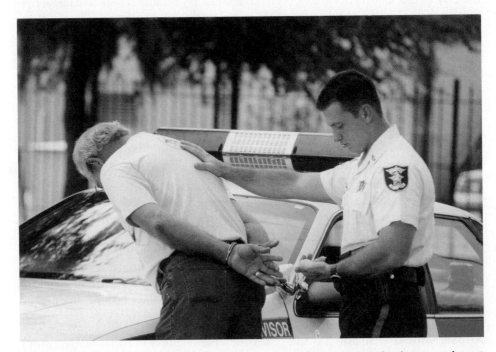

▲ Police officers frequently engage in warrantless arrests, searches, and seizures, and must therefore fully understand related court decisions as well as the concept of probable cause. *(Courtesy FBI.)*

Court Cases In 1979, the Supreme Court rendered two decisions relating to arrests. Police, the Court said, must have probable cause to take a person into custody and to the police station for interrogation.[17] Police may not randomly stop a single vehicle to check the driver's license and registration; there must be probable cause for stopping the driver.[18] However, in 1990 the Court ruled that the stopping of all vehicles passing through sobriety checkpoints—a form of seizure—did not violate the Constitution, although singling out individual vehicles for random stops without probable cause is not authorized.[19] Several days later, it ruled that police were not required to give drunk-driving suspects a *Miranda* warning and could videotape their responses.[20]

In related decisions in the 2003–2004 term, the Supreme Court held that police may arrest *everyone* in a vehicle in which drugs are found. A Baltimore officer, stopping a speeding car and finding cocaine in an armrest in the backseat, was told by the driver and the two passengers that none of them owned the contraband; he arrested all three. Chief Justice Rehnquist wrote that in a small space like a car, officers can reasonably infer "a common enterprise" among a driver and passengers and would have probable cause to suspect that the drugs might belong to any or all of them.[21] A few months later, the Court ruled that police may set up roadblocks to collect information from motorists about crime. Short stops, "a very few minutes at most," are not too intrusive considering the value in crime solving; police may also hand out fliers or ask drivers to volunteer information, the Court noted.[22]

Finally, since 1975, police practice has been to ensure that a person arrested without a warrant receives a "prompt" initial appearance for a probable cause determination to see if the police were justified in arresting and holding the detainee. In its 1990–1991 term, the Supreme Court said that "prompt" does not mean "immediate" and that within forty-eight hours is generally soon enough.[23]

Searches and Seizures

Because of the serious nature of police invasion of private property, the Supreme Court has had to examine several issues, particularly as they relate to searches of suspects' homes. In late 2003, the Court clarified how long police must wait before breaking into a home to serve a warrant, ruling unanimously that it was constitutional for police to wait fifteen to twenty seconds before knocking down the door of a drug suspect because to wait any longer would give the suspect time to flush evidence down the toilet. (The justices refused, however, to state exactly how long is reasonable in serving warrants.)[24] However, in 1995, the Court affirmed without decision an opinion of the Pennsylvania Supreme Court that the police violated the Fourth Amendment when they broke down the door of a residence only one or two seconds after they knocked, announced their presence, and said that they had a warrant. There were no exigent circumstances present.[25] Furthermore, in *Wilson v. Arkansas* (1995),[26] the Court found a search invalid when police in Arkansas, armed with a search warrant after receiving an informant's tip that drugs were being sold at the defendant's home, identified themselves *as they entered* the residence, where they subsequently found drugs and paraphernalia.

Figure 7-1 ■ shows the pertinent parts of a search and seizure warrant form for persons or property that is used by the U.S. District Courts, for execution by agents of the federal government.

Another decision relating to the area of police conduct at a private home during a search was rendered in March 2005. Following a drive-by shooting, police in Simi Valley, California, were searching a suspected gang member's house for *evidence* of a crime—weapons, ammunition, and gang paraphernalia, in the present case—rather than for contraband. Because of the high-risk nature of the case, a special weapons team entered the home, handcuffed the four occupants, and so detained them in a garage for two to three

UNITED STATES DISTRICT COURT
for the

<table>
<tr><td>In the Matter of the Search of
(Briefly describe the property to be searched
or identify the person by name and address)</td><td>)
)
)
)
)
)</td><td>Case No.</td></tr>
</table>

SEARCH AND SEIZURE WARRANT

To: Any authorized law enforcement officer

An application by a federal law enforcement officer or an attorney for the government requests the search of the following person or property located in the _____ District of _____
(identify the person or describe the property to be searched and give its location):

The person or property to be searched, described above, is believed to conceal *(identify the person or describe the property to be seized):*

I find that the affidavit(s), or any recorded testimony, establish probable cause to search and seize the person or property.

YOU ARE COMMANDED to execute this warrant on or before _____
(not to exceed 14 days)

❏ in the daytime 6:00 a.m. to 10 p.m.   ❏ at any time in the day or night as I find reasonable cause has been established.

Unless delayed notice is authorized below, you must give a copy of the warrant and a receipt for the property taken to the person from whom, or from whose premises, the property was taken, or leave the copy and receipt at the place where the property was taken.

The officer executing this warrant, or an officer present during the execution of the warrant, must prepare an inventory as required by law and promptly return this warrant and inventory to United States Magistrate Judge

_____ .
(name)

❏ I find that immediate notification may have an adverse result listed in 18 U.S.C. § 2705 (except for delay of trial), and authorize the officer executing this warrant to delay notice to the person who, or whose property, will be searched or seized *(check the appropriate box)* ❏ for _____ days *(not to exceed 30)*.

❏ until, the facts justifying, the later specific date of _____ .

Date and time issued: _____   _____
Judge's signature

City and state: _____   _____
Printed name and title

FIGURE 7-1 The Form Used by U.S. District Courts for Searches and Seizures of Persons and Property
Federal Court Search & Seizure Warrant Form, U.S. District Courts, Office of the United States Courts, United States Courts, 2013.

hours. The plaintiff alleged a violation of her Fourth Amendment rights. Supreme Court disagreed, finding that her detention was permissible, nor did the Court see a distinction between detention for a search for criminal evidence and detention for a search for contraband, because her detention was based on the existence of a warrant for a residence; furthermore, her being handcuffed was reasonable because of the officers' continuing safety interests.[27]

Furthermore, the Court upheld a search (with a warrant) of a third party's property when police had probable cause to believe it contained fruits or instrumentalities of a crime (e.g., a newspaper office containing photographs of a disturbance),[28] a search of a wrong apartment conducted with a warrant but with a mistaken belief that the address was correct,[29] and a warrantless search and seizure of garbage in bags outside the defendant's home.[30]

The Court has also attempted to define when a person is considered "seized"—an important issue because seizure involves Fourth Amendment protections. Is a person "seized" while police are pursuing him or her? Basically, there is no rule that determines the point of seizure in all situations—the standard is whether a suspect believes his or her liberty is restrained. This is ultimately a question for a judge or jury to decide.[31] In a recent roadblock case, the Court did provide some guidance, however. Where a police roadblock resulted in the death of a speeder, the Court said roadblocks involve a "governmental termination of freedom of movement," that the victim was therefore seized under the Fourth Amendment, and that the police were liable for damages.[32]

Two decisions in the 1990–1991 Supreme Court term expanded police practices. The Court looked at a police drug-fighting technique known as "working the buses." Police board a bus at a regular stopping place, approach seated passengers, and ask permission to search their luggage for drugs. Justice Sandra Day O'Connor, writing for the majority, said that such a situation should be evaluated in terms of whether a person in the passenger's position would have felt free to decline the officer's request or to otherwise terminate the encounter; it was held that such police conduct does not constitute a search.[33] In a companion decision in 2002, the justices held that the police—focusing on possible terrorists as well as drug couriers—may question passengers on buses and trains and may search for evidence without informing passengers that they can refuse. Police in Florida were on a Greyhound bus, asking questions of each passenger, when two men wearing heavy clothing on a warm day consented to a search of their luggage and bodies; police found bricks of cocaine strapped to their legs. The Court said the men were not coerced into consenting and that nothing about the fact that they were seated on a bus forced them to give their consent (searches with consent are discussed more fully below).[34]

The Court also decided that no "seizure" occurs when a police officer seeks to apprehend a person through a show of authority but applies no physical force (such as in a foot pursuit). In this case, a juvenile being chased by an officer threw down an object, later determined to be crack cocaine. The Supreme Court found no seizure or actual restraint in this situation.[35] Also, it should be noted that the Court held that no individualized suspicion of misconduct was required in either of these cases.

Supreme Court decisions have authorized a warrantless seizure of blood from a defendant to obtain evidence. (This was a case of driving under the influence, the drawing of blood was done by medical personnel in a hospital, and there were exigent circumstances—the evidence would have been lost by dissipation in the body.)[36] However, when police compelled a robbery suspect to submit to surgery to remove a bullet, the Court held that such an intrusion to seize evidence was unreasonable; this case said there are limits to what police can do to solve a crime.[37]

Searches and Seizures with and Without a Warrant As is the case with making an arrest, the best means by which the police can search a person or premises is with a search warrant issued by a neutral magistrate. Such a magistrate has determined, after receiving information from a sworn affiant, that probable cause exists to believe that a person possesses the fruits or instrumentalities of a crime or that they are present at a particular location. Again, as with arrest, the "luxury" of searching and seizing with a warrant is usually confined to investigative personnel, who can interview victims and witnesses and gather other available evidence and then request the warrant. Street officers rarely have the opportunity to perform such a search, as the flow of events normally requires quick action to prevent escape and to prevent evidence from being destroyed or hidden.

Court Cases The U.S. Supreme Court recently rendered three important decisions that involved—and clarified—warrantless searches of homes by police under exigent circumstances to render emergency aid. A brief overview of the facts is provided for each case, to assist in understanding why the Court arrived at the three decisions.

First, in _Brigham City v. Stuart_,[38] the Court considered whether police may enter a home without a warrant if they reasonably believe that an occupant is or is about to be seriously injured. At about 3:00 A.M., four officers were dispatched to a loud house party where they observed two juveniles consuming alcohol; officers then entered the backyard and witnessed an altercation occurring inside the house involving four adults and a juvenile. Because of the chaos inside, two of the officers opened the screen door, identified themselves, entered the home, and placed the adults under arrest for contributing to the delinquency of a minor, disorderly conduct, and intoxication. At trial the defendants claimed that the officers' warrantless entry into the home violated the Fourth Amendment; the trial court agreed to suppress, as did both the state court of appeals and the Utah Supreme Court. The U.S. Supreme Court reversed the state courts, holding that the officers' warrantless entry into the home was justified under the emergency aid exception because their entry "was plainly reasonable under the circumstances."

In _Michigan v. Fisher_,[39] police officers responding to a disturbance call were directed to a residence where a man was said to be "going crazy." Upon arrival the officers observed drops of blood in the area and the defendant inside the home, yelling and throwing objects. Fisher refused to answer the door and ignored officers' questions concerning his medical condition. One officer saw Fisher pointing a gun in his direction; eventually, Fisher was subdued and charged with assault with a dangerous weapon and possessing a weapon during the commission of a felony. The lower courts suppressed the gun as evidence, stating it was seized in violation of his Fourth Amendment rights, that the situation did not rise to the level of an emergency and thus did not justify the warrantless entry into Fisher's home; nor did they believe the drops of blood indicated a serious, life-threatening injury. The U.S. Supreme Court reversed in view of its long line of cases involving exigent circumstances, particularly _Brigham City v. Stuart_. Here, in Fisher, the Supreme Court said the relevant consideration is whether the officer has an "objectively reasonable basis for believing that a person is in need of aid." Using that standard, the Court found ample support for application of the emergency aid exception, stating, "Officers do not need ironclad proof of a likely serious, life-threatening injury to invoke the emergency aid exception," and should not be required to "walk away from a situation like the one they encountered here. The role of a peace officer includes preventing violence and restoring order, not simply rendering aid to casualties."

Finally, in mid-2011 the U.S. Supreme Court again made it easier for police to enter a home without a warrant. In _Kentucky v. King_,[40] the Court upheld the warrantless search of an apartment after police smelled marijuana and feared that persons inside were destroying evidence. Police in Lexington, Kentucky, were pursuing a drug suspect and banged on the door of an apartment where they thought they smelled marijuana. After identifying themselves, the officers heard movement inside the apartment and, suspecting that evidence was being destroyed, kicked in the door and found King smoking marijuana (he also possessed cocaine). King was convicted of multiple drug crimes and sentenced to eleven years in prison. Kentucky's highest court ruled that the drugs found in the apartment were inadmissible as evidence, not finding any "emergency circumstances" present, and that instead police should have sought a search warrant. The U.S. Supreme Court disagreed, saying that the police acted reasonably: when police knock on a door and there is no response, and then hear movement inside that suggests evidence is being destroyed, they are justified in breaking in.

Other Types of Warrantless Searches

Five types of searches may be conducted without a warrant: (1) searches incidental to lawful arrest, (2) searches during field interrogation (stop-and-frisk searches), (3) searches of automobiles that are carried out under special conditions, (4) seizures of evidence in "plain view," and (5) searches when consent is given.

Searches Incidental to Lawful Arrest. In *United States v. Robinson* (1973), the defendant was arrested and taken to the police station for driving without a permit—an offense for which a full-scale arrest could be made. Robinson was taken to jail and searched, and heroin was found. He tried to suppress the evidence on the grounds that the full-scale arrest and custodial search were unreasonable for a driver's license infraction. The Supreme Court disagreed, saying that the arrest was legal and that when police assumed custody of Robinson, they needed total control and therefore could perform a detailed inventory of his possessions: "It is the fact of the lawful arrest that establishes the authority to search and we hold that in the case of lawful custodial arrest a full search of the person is not only an exception to the warrant requirement of the Fourth Amendment, but is also a 'reasonable' search under that Amendment."[41]

The rationale for this decision was in part the possibility that the suspect might destroy evidence unless swift action was taken. But in *Chimel v. California* (1969), when officers without a warrant arrested an individual in one room of his house and then proceeded to search the entire three-bedroom house, including the garage, attic, and workshop, the Supreme Court said that searches incidental to lawful arrest are limited to the area within the arrestee's immediate control or that area from which he or she might obtain a weapon. Thus if the police are holding a person in one room of the house, they are not authorized to search and seize property in another part of the house, away from the arrestee's immediate physical presence.[42]

The Court approved the warrantless seizure of a lawfully arrested suspect's clothes even after a substantial time period had elapsed between the arrest and the search.[43] Another advantage given the police was the Court's allowing a warrantless in-home "protective sweep" of the area in which a suspect is arrested to reveal the presence of anyone else who might pose a danger. Such a search, if justified by the circumstances, is not a full search of the premises and may only include a cursory inspection of those spaces where a person could be hiding.[44]

Searches During Field Interrogation (Stop-and-Frisk Searches). In 1968, the U.S. Supreme Court heard a case challenging the constitutionality of on-the-spot searches and questioning by the police. The case, *Terry v. Ohio*, involved a suspect who was stopped and searched while apparently "casing" a store for robbery (see the Court Closeup: *Terry v. Ohio*).

The Court's dilemma in this case was whether to rule that in some circumstances the police do not need probable cause to stop and search people, and thus appear to invalidate *Mapp v. Ohio*, or to insist on such a high standard for action by the police that they could not function on the streets.[45] The Court held that a brief on-the-spot stop for questioning, accompanied by a superficial search (a pat-down search) of external clothing for weapons, was something less than a full-scale search and therefore could be performed with less than the traditional amount of probable cause. This case instantly became—and remains—a major tool for the police.

While *Terry* said the stop and frisk is legal under the Fourth Amendment in cases involving direct police observation, other cases have said that such a stop is legal when based on information provided by an informant[46] and when an individual is the subject of a "wanted" flier from another jurisdiction.[47] In summary, police officers are justified, both to provide for their own safety and to detect past or future crimes, in stopping and questioning people. A person may be frisked for a weapon if an officer fears for his or her life, and the officer may go through the individual's clothing if the frisk indicates the presence of a weapon. Regardless of the rationale for the stop and frisk, there will always be some argument about whether this type of search is being used frivolously or to harass individuals. However, in balancing the public's need for safety against individual rights, the Court was willing to tip the scales in favor of community protection, especially where the safety of the officer was concerned.[48]

An important expansion of the *Terry* doctrine was handed down in 1993 in *Minnesota v. Dickerson*,[49] in which a police officer observed a man leave a notorious crack house and then try to evade the officer. The man was eventually stopped and patted down, during which time the officer felt a small lump in the man's front pocket that was suspected to be drugs. After manipulating and squeezing the lump, the officer removed it from the man's pocket; the object was crack cocaine wrapped in a cellophane container. Although the defendant's arrest and conviction were later thrown out (the Supreme Court reasoned that the search was illegal because it went beyond the limited frisk for weapons, as permitted by *Terry*), the Court also allowed such seizures in the future when officers' probable cause is established by the sense of touch.

Another case extending *Terry*, *Illinois v. Wardlow*,[50] was decided in January 2000. The Court held that a citizen's running away from the police—under certain conditions—supports reasonable suspicion to justify a search. Two Illinois police officers investigating drug transactions in an area of heavy drug activity observed Wardlow holding a bag. Upon

Court Closeup — *Terry v. Ohio*, 319 U.S. 1 (1968)

Cleveland Detective McFadden, a veteran of nineteen years of police service, first noticed Terry and another man at about 2:30 P.M. on the afternoon of the arrest in October 1963. McFadden testified that it appeared the men were "casing" a retail store. He observed the suspects making several trips down the street, stopping at a store window, walking about a half block, turning around, walking back, and pausing to look inside the same store window. At one point they were joined by a third party, who spoke with them and then moved on. McFadden claimed that he followed them because he believed it was his duty as a police officer to investigate the matter further.

Soon the two rejoined the third man; at that point McFadden decided the situation demanded direct action. The officer approached the subjects, identified himself, and then requested that the men identify themselves. When Terry said something inaudible, McFadden "spun him around so that they were facing the other two, with Terry between McFadden and the others, and patted down the outside of his clothing." In a breast pocket of Terry's overcoat, the officer felt a pistol. McFadden found another pistol on one of the other men. The two men were arrested and ultimately convicted of concealing deadly weapons. Terry appealed on the ground that the search was illegal and that the evidence should have been suppressed at trial.

The U.S. Supreme Court disagreed with Terry, holding that the police have the authority to detain a person briefly for questioning even without probable cause if they believe that the person has committed a crime or is about to commit a crime. Such detention does not constitute an arrest. If the officer reasonably suspects that he or she is in danger, the officer may also frisk a person.

Source: The Supreme Court of the United States, 1968.

seeing the two officers, Wardlow fled, but he was soon stopped. The officers conducted a protective pat down and then squeezed the bag; they felt a gun and arrested Wardlow. The Court reasoned that, taken together, several factors (the stop occurred in a high-crime area; the suspect acted in a nervous, evasive manner; and the suspect engaged in unprovoked flight upon noticing the police)[51] were sufficient to establish reasonable suspicion.

Another important Supreme Court decision in February 1997 took officer safety into account. In *Maryland v. Wilson*,[52] the Court held that police may order passengers out of vehicles they stop, regardless of any suspicion of wrongdoing or threat to the officers' safety. Chief Justice Rehnquist cited statistics showing officer assaults and murders during traffic stops and noted that the "weighty interest" in officer safety is present whether a vehicle occupant is a driver or a passenger. (Here, a Maryland state trooper initiated a traffic stop and ordered an apparently nervous passenger, Wilson, to exit the vehicle. While doing so, Wilson dropped a quantity of crack cocaine, for which he was arrested and convicted.)

Searches of Automobiles Carried Out Under Special Conditions. The third general circumstance allowing a warrantless search is when an officer has probable cause to believe that an automobile contains criminal evidence. The Supreme Court has traditionally distinguished searches of automobiles from searches of homes on the grounds that a car involved in a crime can be rapidly moved and its evidence irretrievably lost. The Court first established this doctrine in *Carroll v. United States* (1925). In this case, officers searched the vehicle of a known bootlegger without a warrant but with probable cause, finding sixty-eight bottles of illegal booze. On appeal, the Court ruled that the seizure was justified. However, *Carroll* established two rules: First, to invoke the *Carroll* doctrine, the police must have enough probable cause that if there had been enough time, a search warrant would have been issued; second, urgent circumstances must exist that require immediate action.[53]

Extending the creation of the *Carroll* doctrine, however, two new questions confronted the justices: whether impounded vehicles were subject to warrantless search and whether searches could be made of vehicles stopped in routine traffic inspections. In *Preston v. United States* (1964), the Court ruled that once the police had made a lawful arrest and then towed the suspect's car to a different location, they could not conduct an incidental search of the vehicle. The Court reasoned that because such a search was remote in time and place from the point of arrest, it was not incidental and therefore was unreasonable.[54]

Harris v. United States (1968) upheld the right of police to enter an impounded vehicle following a lawful arrest in order to inventory its contents.[55] Building on this decision, the Court later upheld a warrantless search of a vehicle in custody, saying that because the police had probable cause to believe it contained evidence of a crime and could be easily moved, it made little difference whether a warrant was sought or an immediate search conducted.[56]

In 1974, the expectation of citizens to privacy in their vehicles was further diminished when the Court said an automobile has "little capacity for escaping public scrutiny [as] it travels public thoroughfares where both its occupants and its contents are in plain view."[57] This position was reinforced in 1976 when the Court said that a validly impounded car may be searched without probable cause or warrant as it is reasonable for an inventory of its contents to be made as a protection against theft or charges of theft while the car is in police custody.[58]

An automobile may be searched following the lawful search of its driver or another occupant. Following the rationale of *Chimel*, the Court ruled that the entire interior of the car, including containers, may be examined even if the items are not within the driver's reach.[59] The Court went on to say that a warrantless search of an automobile incidental to a lawful arrest, including its trunk and any packages or luggage, is permissible if there is probable cause to believe that it contains evidence of a crime.[60] The Court also authorized a protective pat down of vehicle passenger compartments for weapons (similar to that of persons in *Terry v. Ohio*) after a valid stop and when officers have a reasonable belief that they may be in danger.[61] Finally, it was decided in 1987 that evidence seized by opening a closed container during a warrantless inventory search of a vehicle incidental to lawful arrest is admissible.[62]

During its 1990–1991 term, the Supreme Court extended the long arm of the law with respect to automobiles. In a May 1991 decision, the Court declared that a person's general consent to a search of the interior of an automobile justifies a search of any closed container found inside the car that might reasonably hold the object of the search; thus, an officer, after obtaining a general consent, does not need to ask permission to look inside each closed container.[63] One week later, the Court ruled that probable cause to believe that a container within a car holds contraband or evidence allows a warrantless search of that item under the automobile exception, even in the absence of probable cause extending to the entire vehicle.[64] This decision clarified the *Carroll* doctrine.

During its 1998–1999 term, the Court held that when an officer has probable cause to search a vehicle, the officer may search objects belonging to a passenger in the vehicle, provided the item the officer is looking for could reasonably be in the passenger's belongings.[65] (Here the officer was searching an automobile for contraband, searched a passenger's purse, and found drug paraphernalia there.)

In early 2013 the Supreme Court ruled on the constitutionality of police using trained drug-sniffing dogs outside of a home to determine the presence of drugs within. The Court held,[66] 5–4, that such use of dogs constitutes a "search" under the Fourth Amendment, and thus required a warrant. Here, officers from the Miami-Dade Police Department approached Jardines' home with a drug dog after receiving a tip that marijuana was being grown in the house. The Labrador retriever alerted officers to the presence of marijuana in the house, and the officers obtained a search warrant and discovered the plants. Justice Antonin Scalia's opinion stated that: "To find a visitor knocking on the door is routine (even if sometimes unwelcome); to spot that same visitor exploring the front path with a metal detector, or marching his bloodhound into the garden before saying hello and asking permission, would inspire most of us to—well, call the police." Scalia said using the dog was no different from using thermal imaging technology from afar to peer inside homes without a warrant. However, just one month earlier the Court unanimously held that an alert by a trained police dog during a traffic stop gave officers probable cause to further search a *vehicle*.[67]

More recently regarding vehicle searches, in April 2009 the Supreme Court overturned nearly three decades of a particular police practice by holding that, where an individual has been arrested and is in police custody away from his or her vehicle, unable to access the vehicle, officers may not then search the vehicle without a warrant. Here, the officers did so, and discovered a handgun and a plastic bag of cocaine; the Court said it is a violation of the Fourth Amendment's protection against unreasonable searches and seizures.[68] In essence, the Court is saying that police may search the passenger compartment of a vehicle incident to a recent occupant's arrest only if it is reasonable to believe that the arrestee might access the vehicle at the time of the search or that the vehicle contains evidence of the offense of arrest.

Finally, in 2012 the U.S. Supreme Court ruled[69] that police violated the Constitution when they attached a Global Positioning System (GPS) device to a suspect's vehicle without a search warrant. Police had followed a drug trafficking suspect for a month and eventually found nearly 100 kilograms of cocaine and $1 million in cash when raiding the suspect's home in Maryland. Justice Scalia noted that the Fourth Amendment's protection of "persons, houses, papers, and effects, against unreasonable searches and seizures" extends to automobiles as well, and that even a small trespass, if committed in "an attempt to find something or to obtain information," constituted a "search" under the Fourth Amendment. This decision is anticipated to primarily affect major narcotics investigations.

Seizures of Evidence in "Plain View." The police do not have to search for items that are in plain view. If such items are believed to be fruits or instrumentalities of a crime and the police are lawfully on the premises, they may seize them. For example, if an officer has been admitted into a home with an arrest or search warrant and sees drugs and paraphernalia on a living room table, he or she may arrest the occupants on drug charges as well as the other charges. If an officer performs a traffic stop for an offense and observes drugs in the backseat of the car, he may arrest for that as well. Provided that the officer was lawfully in a particular place and that the plain-view discovery was inadvertent, the law does not require the officer to ignore contraband or other evidence of a crime that is in plain view.

The Supreme Court has said that officers are not required to immediately recognize an object in plain view as contraband before it may be seized. (For instance, an officer may see a balloon in a glove box with a white powdery substance on its tip and later determine the powder to be heroin.)[70] Furthermore, fences and the posting of "No Trespassing" signs afford no expectation of privacy and do not prevent officers from viewing open fields without a search warrant,[71] nor are police prevented from making a naked-eye aerial observation of a suspect's backyard or other curtilage (the grounds around a house or building).[72]

Two decisions in the late 1980s have further defined the plain-view doctrine. In one case, an officer found a gun under a car seat while looking for the vehicle identification number; the Court upheld the search and the resulting arrest as being a plain-view discovery.[73] However, in another similar situation, the Court disallowed an arrest when an officer, during a legal search for weapons, moved a stereo system to locate its serial number, saying that this constituted an unreasonable search and seizure.[74]

Searches When Consent Is Given. Another permissible warrantless search involves citizens waiving their Fourth Amendment rights and consenting to a search of their persons or effects. It must be established at trial, however, that a defendant's consent was given voluntarily. In some circumstances, as with metal detectors at airports, an agent's right to search is implied.

▲ The U.S. Supreme Court, Washington, D.C. (*Courtesy Kenneth J. Peak.*)

In the leading case on consent searches, *Schneckloth v. Bustamonte* (1973), a police officer stopped a car for a burned-out headlight. Two other backup officers joined him. When asked if his car could be searched, the driver consented. The officers found several stolen checks in the trunk. The driver and passenger were arrested and convicted. On appeal, the defendants argued that the evidence should have been suppressed, as they did not know they had the right to refuse the officers' request to search the car. The Supreme Court upheld their convictions, reasoning that the individuals, although poor, uneducated, and alone with three officers, could reasonably be considered capable of knowing and exercising their right to deny officers permission to search their car.[75]

However, police cannot deceive people into believing they have a search warrant when they in fact do not. For example, the police, looking for a rape suspect, announced falsely to the suspect's grandmother that they had a search warrant for her home; the evidence they found was ruled to be inadmissible.[76] A hotel clerk cannot give a valid consent to a warrantless search of the room of one of the occupants; hotel guests have a reasonable expectation of privacy, and that right cannot be waived by hotel management.[77]

Finally, the right of police to search a home when one occupant consents and the other objects was the subject of a Supreme Court decision in March 2006. There, police responded to the home of a Georgia couple following a domestic disturbance. The wife told the officers that her husband was a drug user and had drugs in their home. An officer asked the husband for permission to search the residence and was denied. The wife granted consent, however, and led the officers to a bedroom where cocaine was kept. The defendant-husband appealed on the grounds that the drugs were the product of an unlawful search, and the Supreme Court agreed on the grounds that the Fourth Amendment should not ignore the privacy rights of an individual who is present and asserting his rights.[78] Note, however, that an occupant may still give police permission to search when the other resident is absent or does not protest.

Electronic Surveillance

It was the original view of the Supreme Court, in *Olmstead v. United States* (1928), that wiretaps were not searches and seizures and did not violate the Fourth Amendment; this represented the old rule on wiretaps.[79] However, that decision was overruled in 1967 in *Katz v. United States*, which held that any form of electronic surveillance, including wiretapping, is a search and violates a reasonable expectation of privacy.[80] The case involved a public telephone booth, deemed by the Court to be a constitutionally protected area where the user has a reasonable expectation of privacy. This decision expressed the view that the Constitution protects people, not places. Thus the Court has required that warrants for electronic surveillance be based on probable cause, describe the conversations to be overheard, be for a limited period of time, name subjects to be overheard, and be terminated when the desired information is obtained.[81]

However, the Supreme Court has held that while electronic eavesdropping (i.e., an informant wearing a "bug," or hidden microphone) did not violate the Fourth Amendment (a person assumes the risk that whatever he or she says may be transmitted to the police),[82] the warrantless monitoring of an electronic beeper in a private residence violated the suspect's right to privacy. A federal drug agent had placed a beeper inside a can of ether, which was being used to extract cocaine from clothing imported into the United States, and had monitored its movements.[83]

Lineups

A police lineup, as well as other face-to-face confrontations after the accused has been arrested, is considered a critical stage of criminal proceedings; therefore, the accused has a right to have an attorney present. If counsel is not present, the evidence obtained is inadmissible.[84] However, the suspect is not entitled to the presence and advice of a lawyer before being formally charged.[85]

Lineups that are so suggestive as to make the result inevitable violate the suspect's right to due process. (In one case, the suspect was much taller than the other two people in the lineup, and he was the only person wearing a leather jacket similar to that worn by the robber. In a second lineup, the suspect was the only person who had participated in the first lineup.[86]) In short, lineups must be fair to suspects; a fair lineup guarantees no bias against the suspect.

The Supreme Court has held that a suspect may be compelled to appear before a grand jury and give voice exemplars for comparison with an actual voice recording. Appearance before a grand jury is not a search, and the giving of a voice sample is not a seizure that is protected by the Fourth Amendment.[87]

▶ Fifth Amendment

No person shall be held to answer for a capital, or otherwise infamous crime, unless on a presentment or indictment of a Grand Jury, except in cases arising in the land or naval forces, or in the Militia, when in actual service in time of war or public danger; nor shall any person be subject for the same offense to be twice put in jeopardy of life or limb; nor shall be compelled in any criminal case to be a witness against himself, nor be deprived of life, liberty, or property, without due process of law; nor shall private property be taken for public use, without just compensation.

—U.S. Constitution, U.S. Department of Justice.

A major tool used in religious persecutions in England during the sixteenth century was the oath. Ministers were called before the Court of Star Chamber (which, during much of the sixteenth and seventeenth centuries, enforced unpopular political policies and meted out severe punishments, including whipping, branding, and mutilation, without a jury trial) and questioned about their beliefs. Being men of God, they were compelled to tell the truth and admitted to their nonconformist views; for this, they were often severely punished or even executed.[88] In the 1630s, the Star Chamber and similar bodies of cruelty were disbanded by Parliament. People had become repulsed by compulsory self-incrimination; the privilege against self-incrimination was recognized in all courts when claimed by defendants or witnesses. Today, the Fifth Amendment applies not only to criminal defendants but also to any witness testifying in a civil or criminal case and anyone testifying before an administrative body, a grand jury, or a congressional committee. However, the privilege does not extend to blood samples, handwriting exemplars, and other such items that are not considered to be testimony.[89]

The right against self-incrimination is one of the most significant provisions in the Bill of Rights. Basically it states that no criminal defendant shall be compelled to take the witness stand and give evidence against himself or herself. No one can be compelled to answer any question if his or her answer can later be used to implicate or convict him or her. Some people view the defendant's "taking the Fifth" as an indication of guilt; others view this as a basic right in a democracy, wherein a defendant does not have to contribute to his or her own conviction. In either case, the impact of this amendment is felt daily by the criminal justice system.

Decisions Supporting *Miranda*: Confessions

Traditionally, the U.S. Supreme Court has excluded physically coerced confessions on the grounds that such confessions might very well be untrustworthy or unreliable in view of the duress surrounding them. As the quality of police work has improved, police use of physical means to obtain confessions has diminished. Some cases that have come before the Supreme Court involved psychological rather than physical pressure on the defendant to confess. One such case involved an accused who was questioned for eight hours by six police officers in relays and was told falsely that the job and welfare of a friend who was a rookie cop depended on his confession. He was also refused contact with his lawyer. The Court reversed his conviction, not so much on the grounds that the confession was unreliable but on the grounds that it was obtained unfairly.[90]

In the 1960s, the Supreme Court ruled in *Escobedo v. Illinois* (1964)[91] (discussed later) and in *Miranda v. Arizona* (1966)[92] (see Court Closeup: *Miranda v. Arizona*) that confessions made by suspects who have not been notified of their constitutional rights cannot be admitted into evidence. In these cases, the Court emphasized the importance of a defendant having the "guiding hand of counsel" present during the interrogation process.

Once a suspect has been placed under arrest, the *Miranda* warning must be given before interrogation for any offense, be it a felony or a misdemeanor. An exception is the brief routine traffic stop; however, a custodial interrogation of a suspect for driving under the influence (DUI) requires the *Miranda* warning.[93] Moreover, after an accused has invoked the right to counsel, the police may not interrogate the same suspect about a different crime.[94] Once a "Mirandized" suspect invokes his or her right to silence, interrogation must cease. The police may not readminister *Miranda* and interrogate the suspect later unless the suspect's attorney is present. If, however, the suspect initiates further conversation, any confession he or she provides is admissible.[95] (This decision involved a suspect who was arrested on a state criminal charge and invoked his right to have counsel present at questioning; then, one day later, the police returned, re-Mirandized him, and during this period of questioning he said that he was willing to talk; he then confessed to child molestation.)

However, in a significant decision in February 2010, the U.S. Supreme Court modified this ruling in *Maryland v. Shatzer*.[96] There, a detective attempted to question a prison inmate concerning allegations of sexually abusing his son; Shatzer invoked his *Miranda* right to have counsel present during interrogation, so the questioning ceased, Shatzer was released back into the general prison population, and the investigation was closed. Three years later, Shatzer had been released from prison, rearrested, and returned to prison; the earlier investigation was reopened and another detective sought to question Shatzer in prison. This time Shatzer waived his *Miranda* rights and confessed. On appeal, the U.S. Supreme Court held that, because Shatzer had experienced a break in *Miranda* custody of *more than two weeks* between the first and second attempts at interrogation, his confession did not have to be suppressed. Justice Antonin Scalia wrote, "The Court concludes that the appropriate period is 14 days, which provides ample time for the suspect to get reacclimated to his normal life, consult with friends and counsel, and shake off any residual coercive effects of prior custody."[97]

Decisions Modifying *Miranda*: Interrogations

Miranda, *Escobedo*, and *Mapp* combined to represent the centerpiece of the "due process revolution" of the Court of Chief Justice Earl Warren in the 1960s. However, several decisions, including many by the Court of Chief Justice Warren Burger, have dealt severe blows to *Miranda*.

It has been held that a second interrogation session held after the suspect had initially refused to make a statement did not violate *Miranda*.[98] If a suspect waives his or her *Miranda* rights and makes voluntary statements while irrational (allegedly "following the advice of God"), those statements too are admissible.[99] The Court also decided that when a suspect waived his or her *Miranda* rights, believing the interrogation would focus on minor crimes, but the police shifted their questioning to a more serious crime, the confession was valid—there was no police deception or misrepresentation.[100] When a suspect invoked his or her right to assistance of counsel and refused to make written statements but then voluntarily gave oral statements to police, the statements were admissible (defendants have

While walking to a Phoenix, Arizona, bus stop on the night of March 2, 1963, eighteen-year-old Barbara Ann Johnson was accosted by a man who shoved her into his car, tied her hands and ankles, and drove her to the edge of the city, where he raped her. He then drove Johnson to a street near her home, letting her out of the car and asking that she pray for him.

The Phoenix police subsequently picked up Ernesto Miranda for investigation of Johnson's rape and included him in a lineup at the police station. Miranda was identified by several women; one identified him as the man who had robbed her at knifepoint a few months earlier, and Johnson thought he was the rapist.

Miranda was a twenty-three-year-old eighth-grade dropout with a police record dating back to age fourteen, and he had also served time in prison for driving a stolen car across a state line. During questioning, the police told Miranda that he had been identified by the women; Miranda then made a statement in writing that described the rape incident. He also noted that he was making the confession voluntarily and with full knowledge of his legal rights. He was soon charged with rape, kidnapping, and robbery.

At trial, Miranda's court-appointed attorney got the officers to admit that during the interrogation the defendant was not informed of his right to have counsel present and that no counsel was present. Nonetheless, Miranda's confession was admitted into evidence. He was convicted and sentenced to serve twenty to thirty years for kidnapping and rape.

On appeal, the U.S. Supreme Court ruled:

> [T]he current practice of incommunicado interrogation is at odds with one of our Nation's most cherished principles—that the individual may not be compelled to incriminate himself. Unless adequate protective devices are employed to dispel the compulsion inherent in custodial surroundings, no statement obtained from the defendant can truly be the product of free choice.

Source: The Supreme Court of the United States, 1966.

"the right to choose between speech and silence").[101] Finally, a suspect need not be given the *Miranda* warning in the exact form that it was outlined in *Miranda v. Arizona*. In one case, the waiver form said the suspect would have an attorney appointed "if and when you go to court." The Court held that as long as the warnings on the form reasonably convey the suspect's rights, they need not be given verbatim.[102]

In 1994, the Supreme Court ruled that after police officers obtain a valid *Miranda* waiver from a suspect, they may continue questioning him or her when he or she makes an ambiguous or equivocal request for counsel during questioning. In this case,[103] the defendant stated during an interview and after waiving his rights, "Maybe I should talk to a lawyer." The officers inquired about this statement, determined that he did not want a lawyer, and continued their questioning. When a suspect unequivocally requests counsel, all questioning must cease. However, here the Court held that when the suspect mentions an attorney, the officers need not interrupt the flow of the questioning to clarify the reference but may continue questioning until there is a clear assertion of the right to counsel, such as "I want a lawyer."

Finally, in June 2010, the Supreme Court held (5–4) that suspects' mere silence—when they do not expressly waive their *Miranda* rights and speak only after remaining silent through a period of interrogation—does not mean they intend to invoke *Miranda*. There, a Michigan murder suspect remained silent during almost three hours of interrogation and finally answered yes to the following question: "Do you pray to God to forgive you for shooting that boy down?" This affirmative response was later used against him at trial, and he was convicted of first-degree murder. The majority held that earlier decisions concerning *Miranda* have put a greater burden on suspects to invoke their rights, while the dissenting opinion argued that the decision created a kind of paradox: "A suspect who wishes to guard his right to remain silent must, counterintuitively, speak." The Criminal Justice Legal Foundation, explaining the decision, stated, "The Supreme Court recognized the practical realities that the police face in dealing with suspects. They don't always answer the waiver question clearly. When they do not, Miranda should not apply, and the statement should be admissible as long as it is not compelled."[104]

Entrapment

The due process clause of the Fifth Amendment requires "fundamental fairness"—government agents may not act in a way that is "shocking to the universal sense of justice." Thus the police may not induce or encourage a person to commit a crime that he or she would otherwise not have attempted, that is, entrapment.[105] This is the current test used by many courts to evaluate police behavior. Some states take a broader view than others as to what constitutes entrapment. For example, a police department in a western state had police officers impersonate homeless people. The decoys pretended to be asleep or passed out from intoxication on a public bench, and paper money visibly protruded from their pockets. Several passersby helped themselves to the money and were arrested on the spot. On appeal, the prosecution argued that a thief is a thief, the people had the intent to commit theft, and the decoy operation simply provided an opportunity for dishonest people to get caught. The state's Supreme Court disagreed, calling the operation entrapment, adding that the situation could cause even honest people to be overcome by temptation.

However, the U.S. Supreme Court approved an undercover drug agent's provision of an essential chemical for the manufacture of illegal drugs. (The defendant, the majority said, was an "unwary criminal" who was already "predisposed" to commit the offense.)[106] Nor is it entrapment when a drug agent sells drugs to a suspect, who then sells it to government agents. Government conduct in this case is shocking to civil libertarians, but the focus here is the conduct of the defendant, not the government. As long as government's conduct is not outrageous and the defendant was predisposed to crime, the arrest is valid.[107]

The Supreme Court has held that police officers "may not originate a criminal design, implant in an innocent person's mind the disposition to commit a criminal act, and then induce commission of the crime."[108]

▶ Sixth Amendment

In all criminal prosecutions the accused shall enjoy the right to a speedy and public trial, by an impartial jury of the State and district wherein the crime shall have been committed, which district shall have been previously ascertained by law, and to be informed of the nature and cause of the accusation; to be confronted with the witnesses against him; to have compulsory process for obtaining witnesses in his favor; and to have the assistance of counsel for his defense.

—U.S. Constitution, U.S. Department of Justice.

Right to Counsel

Many people believe that the Sixth Amendment right of the accused to have the assistance of counsel before and at trial is the greatest right we enjoy in a democracy. Indeed, a close reading of the cases mentioned here would reveal the negative outcomes that are possible when a person—rich or poor, illiterate or educated—has no legal representation.

Over seventy years ago, in *Powell v. Alabama* (1932), it was established that in a capital case, when the accused is poor and illiterate, he or she enjoys the right to assistance of counsel for his or her defense and due process.[109] In *Gideon v. Wainwright* (1963), the Supreme Court mandated that all indigent people charged with felonies in state courts be provided counsel.[110]

Note that *Gideon* applied only to felony defendants. In 1973, *Argersinger v. Hamlin* extended the right to counsel to indigent people charged with misdemeanor crimes if they face the possibility of incarceration (however short the incarceration may be).[111]

Another landmark decision concerning the right to counsel is *Escobedo v. Illinois* (1964).[112] Danny Escobedo's brother-in-law was fatally shot in 1960; Escobedo was arrested without a warrant and questioned, but he made no statement to the police. He was released after fourteen hours of interrogation. Following police questioning of another suspect, Escobedo was again arrested and questioned at police headquarters. Escobedo's request to confer with his lawyer was denied, even after the lawyer arrived and asked to see his client. The questioning of Escobedo lasted several hours, during which time he was handcuffed and forced to remain standing. Eventually, he admitted being an accomplice to murder. Under Illinois law, an accomplice was as guilty as the person firing the fatal bullet. At no point was Escobedo advised of his rights to remain silent or to confer with his attorney.

Escobedo's conviction was ultimately reversed by the Supreme Court, based on a violation of Escobedo's Sixth Amendment right to counsel. However, the real thrust of the decision was his Fifth Amendment right not to incriminate himself; when a defendant is scared, flustered, ignorant, alone, and bewildered, he or she is often unable to effectively make use of protections granted under the Fifth Amendment without the advice of an attorney.[113] The *Miranda* decision set down two years later simply established the guidelines for the police to inform suspects of all of these rights.

What Constitutes an Interrogation?

The Supreme Court has stated that an interrogation takes place not only when police officers ask direct questions of a defendant but also when the police make remarks designed to appeal to a defendant's sympathy, religious interest, and so forth. This has been deemed soliciting information through trickery and deceit. The "Christian Burial Speech" case (discussed previously) and *Escobedo* demonstrated that even before (and certainly after) a suspect has been formally charged, a suspect in police custody should not be interrogated without an attorney present unless he or she has waived the right to counsel.

However, the Supreme Court upheld a conviction when two police officers, in a suspect's presence, discussed the possible whereabouts of the shotgun used in a robbery and expressed concern that nearby schoolchildren might be endangered by it. Hearing this conversation, the suspect led officers to the shotgun, thereby implicating himself. On appeal, the Court said that interrogation includes words and actions intended to elicit an incriminating response from the defendant and that no such interrogation occurred here; this was a mere conversation between officers, and the evidence was admissible.[114]

In another case, the Court ruled that if the police were present at and recorded a conversation between a husband and wife (this tape was later used against the husband at trial, where he claimed insanity in the killing of his son), an interrogation did not occur. The Court believed that the police merely arranged a situation in which it was likely the suspect would make incriminating statements, so anything recorded could be used against him in court.[115]

Two cases on police interrogations were heard during the 1990–1991 Supreme Court term. First, the Court held that a defendant who is in custody and has been given the *Miranda* warning may be questioned later on a separate as-yet-uncharged offense. In this case, the defendant appeared with an attorney at a bail hearing on robbery charges. Later, while he was still in custody, the police, after reading him his rights, questioned him about a murder; the defendant agreed to discuss the murder without counsel and made incriminating statements that were used to convict him.[116] In the second case, representing a victory for the defense, the Court held that once a criminal suspect has asked for and consults with a lawyer, interrogators may not later question him without his lawyer being present.[117]

Two recent decisions have expanded defendants' rights under the Sixth Amendment. First, in mid-2009, the U.S. Supreme Court ruled that criminal defendants have a constitutional right to cross-examine forensic analysts who prepare laboratory reports on illegal drugs and other evidence used at trial. The defendant—convicted for distributing and trafficking cocaine—challenged on appeal the lab analysis that confirmed cocaine was in plastic bags found in the vehicle in which he was riding. He argued, successfully, that the Sixth Amendment allowed him to confront witnesses against him and that he should have been allowed to question the lab analyst about testing methods and how the evidence was preserved.[118] Then, in early 2010, the Supreme Court held that the Sixth Amendment requires that immigrants have a right to be told by their lawyers whether pleading guilty to a crime could lead to their deportation; Justice John Paul Stevens wrote for the majority that "Our long-standing Sixth Amendment precedents, the seriousness of deportation, and the concomitant impact of deportation on families living lawfully in this country demand no less."[119]

▶ Juvenile Rights

The criminal justice system's philosophy toward juveniles is very different from its philosophy toward adults. Consequently, police officers, who are constantly dealing with juvenile offenders, must know and apply a different standard of treatment in these situations. The approach is generally that society, through poor parenting, poverty, and so forth, is primarily responsible for the criminal behavior of juvenile offenders.

The prevailing doctrine that guides our treatment of juveniles is parens patriae, meaning that "the state is the ultimate parent" of the child. In effect, as long as we adequately care for and provide at least the basic amenities for our children as required under the law, they are ours to keep, but when children are physically or emotionally neglected or abused by their parents or guardians, the juvenile court and police may intervene and remove the children from that environment. Then the doctrine of in loco parentis takes hold, meaning that the state will act in place of the parent. The author can state from experience that there is probably no more overwhelming or awe-inspiring duty for a police officer than having to testify in juvenile court that a woman is an unfit mother and that parental ties should be legally severed. However, when a person chooses to be a negligent or abusive parent, it is clearly in everyone's best interest for the state to assume care and custody of the child.

The juvenile justice system, working through and with the police, seeks to protect the child. It seeks to rehabilitate, not punish; its procedure is generally amiable, not adversarial. That is why the term *in re*, meaning "concerning" or "in the matter of," is commonly used in many juvenile case titles—for example, a case would be called *In Re Smith* rather than the adversarial and more formal *State v. Smith*. Juvenile court proceedings are generally shrouded in privacy—that is, heard before a judge only. However, when a juvenile commits an act that is so heinous that the protective and helpful juvenile court philosophy will not work, the child may be remanded to the custody of the adult court to be tried as an adult.

Juvenile delinquency (an ambiguous term that has no widespread agreed-on meaning but has a multitude of definitions under state statutes[120]) became recognized as a national problem in the 1950s. As a result, several important decisions by the Supreme Court between 1960 and 1970 addressed the rights of juveniles. *Kent v. United States* (1966)[121] involved a sixteen-year-old male who was arrested in the District of Columbia for robbery, rape, and burglary. The juvenile court, without holding a formal hearing, waived the matter to a criminal court, and Kent was tried and convicted as an adult. Kent appealed, arguing that the waiver without a hearing violated his right to due process. The Supreme Court agreed.

Another landmark case extending due process to juveniles was *In Re Gault* (1967).[122] Gerald Gault was a fifteen-year-old who resided in Arizona and allegedly made obscene telephone calls. When a neighbor complained to police, Gault was arrested and eventually sent to a youth home (a previous crime, stealing a wallet, was also taken into account), to remain there until he either turned twenty-one or was paroled. Before his hearing, Gault did not receive a timely notice of charges. At his hearing, Gault had no attorney present, nor was his accuser present; no transcript was made of the proceedings, and Gault was not read his rights or told he could remain silent. Gault appealed on the grounds that all of these due process rights should have been provided. The Supreme Court reversed his conviction, declaring that these Fourteenth Amendment protections applied to juveniles as well as adults. This case remains the most significant juvenile rights decision ever rendered.

In 1970, the Supreme Court decided *In Re Winship*, which involved a twelve-year-old boy convicted in New York of larceny.[123] At trial, the court relied on the "preponderance of the evidence" standard of proof against him rather than the more demanding "beyond a reasonable doubt" standard used in adult courts. At that time, juvenile courts could apply any of three standards of proof (the third was "clear and convincing evidence"). The Court reversed Winship's conviction on the grounds that the "beyond a reasonable doubt" standard had not been used.

Other precedent-setting juvenile cases followed. In *McKeiver v. Pennsylvania* (1971), the Supreme Court said juveniles do not have an absolute right to trial by jury; whether or not a juvenile receives a trial by jury is left to the discretion of state and local authorities.[124] In *Breed v. Jones* (1975), the Court concluded that the Fifth Amendment protected juveniles from double jeopardy, or being tried twice for the same offense.[125] (Breed had been tried both in California Juvenile Court and later in Superior Court—the state's trial courts, which exist in each of the state's fifty-eight counties—for the same offenses.)

In March 2005, the U.S. Supreme Court, in *Roper v. Simmons*, ruled that the Eighth and Fourteenth Amendments forbid the execution of offenders who were under the age of eighteen when their crimes were committed.[126]

Finally, in May 2010, the U.S. Supreme Court ruled that the Eighth Amendment's ban on cruel and unusual punishment prohibits juveniles who commit crimes not involving murder from serving life without parole (LWOP) sentences. The justices stated that the sentences at issue had been "rejected the world over" and that only the United States and perhaps Israel had imposed the punishment even for homicides committed for juveniles.[127]

An area of law that recently garnered nationwide attention (and involved the shooting of a juvenile) is the "stand your ground" law, which is discussed in Exhibit 7-1 ∎.

EXHIBIT 7-1

THE SHOOTING OF TRAYVON MARTIN: "STAND YOUR GROUND" LAWS

Although not specifically a federal court decision that constrains police behavior like others discussed in this chapter, the killing in Florida of Trayvon Martin by George Zimmerman in February 2012 caused a major controversy that, by its nature, implicates the entire criminal justice system and binds the police and prosecutors under a controversial "rule of law" in particular. The law essentially expands the common law "castle doctrine" which provided that if a stranger entered one's home without permission, the home owner could use deadly force to protect himself. "Stand your ground" became law in Florida in 2005; since then, at least 21 states have enacted a similar expansion of the castle doctrine. Essentially, "stand your ground" says that the old common law should extend not only to the outside of one's home but to any other place

where he or she has a right to be; under the law, when killers state they acted in self-defense, they cannot be convicted of murder unless it can be proven *beyond a reasonable doubt* (the highest legal standard) that the dead person did not attack the killer. The law, enacted in the aftermath of Florida's Hurricane Ivan after which there occurred a lot of looting of homes and businesses, was intended to give citizens a presumption of innocence when defending themselves. It also does not give police the right to hold someone if they have evidence that the shooter was attacked "in a place he had a right to be." Prosecutors largely despise the law because of the aforementioned burden of proof, while defense attorneys have found it to be a means of arguing for all manner of people who can now claim that they had a right to meet force with force. One irony now under

(Continued)

Florida's "stand your ground" law: while pointing a gun at someone can earn them three years in prison, pointing a gun and shooting at that same person may well allow them to go free.

Zimmerman was found not guilty of either second-degree murder or manslaughter, by a jury of six women, in July 2013; the judge instructed the jury to acquit if it found "he had no duty to retreat and had the right to stand his ground and meet force with force, including deadly force, if he reasonably believed it was necessary." Legal experts do not believe such laws will be repealed in the aftermath of the verdict—which prompted many protests across the nation. In fact, to the contrary, many state legislatures are conservative towards crime and lean heavily in favor of gun owners' rights.

Source: Kenneth J. Peak.

Summary

U.S. society places great importance on individual freedom, and the power of government has traditionally been feared; therefore, the U.S. Constitution, courts, and legislatures have seen fit to restrain the power of government agents through what is commonly referred to as the *rule of law*. This necessary aspect associated with having police in a democracy carries with it a responsibility for police practitioners to understand the law and—more important, perhaps—to keep abreast of the legal changes society is constantly undergoing.

The law is dynamic—that is, it is constantly changed by the Supreme Court and other federal courts and by state courts and legislatures. It is imperative that police agencies have a formal mechanism for imparting these legal changes to their officers.

The number of successful criminal and civil lawsuits against police officers today demonstrates that the police have not always done their homework and simply do not apply the law in the manner in which the federal courts intended. Officers must understand and enforce the law properly. In this grave business of adult cops and robbers, the means are in many respects more important than the ends. The courts and the criminal justice system should expect and allow nothing less.

Key Terms

affidavit

consent

entrapment

exclusionary rule

exigent circumstances

Fifth Amendment

Fourth Amendment

in loco parentis

interrogation

juvenile rights

life without parole

lineup

parens patriae

probable cause

rule of law

search and seizure

Sixth Amendment

"stand your ground" laws

Review Questions

1. What is meant by the rule of law?
2. What protections are afforded to citizens by the Fourth, Fifth, and Sixth Amendments?
3. What is an example of probable cause?
4. From both the police and community perspectives, what are the ramifications of having and not having the exclusionary rule?

5. How would you distinguish between arrests and searches and seizures with and without a warrant, and which form is best? Provide examples of each.
6. Explain when and under what circumstances the police may enter a home without a warrant under exigent circumstances to render emergency aid.
7. In what significant ways has the original *Miranda* decision been modified, and what is its long-term outlook, given the shifting composition of judges on the Supreme Court?
8. What major legal rights exist for juveniles, and what are the major differences in philosophy and treatment between juvenile and adult offenders?

Learn by Doing

1. Your criminal justice professor has assigned a class project wherein class members are to determine which amendment to the Bill of Rights—the Fourth, Fifth, or Sixth—contains the most important rights that are protected by citizens under a democracy. You are to analyze the three and present your findings as to which one is the most important.
2. You are assigned the task of debating which period was the most important—the so-called "due process revolution" of the Warren Court (particularly during the 1960s, when the U.S. Supreme Court granted many rights to the accused through such decisions as *Gideon, Miranda, Escobedo,* and so forth), or the more conservative era that followed under the Rehnquist Court, during which time many of the Warren Court decisions were eroded and more rights were given to the police. Choose a side, and make your defenses.
3. From the time of his confirmation in 1969, Chief Justice Warren Burger viewed the exclusionary rule as an unnecessary and unreasonable intrusion on law enforcement. Prepare a pro/con paper that examines why there should and should not be an exclusionary rule as a part of our system of justice.

Notes

1. Albert Venn Dicey, *Introduction to the Study of the Law of the Constitution*, 10th ed. (London: Macmillan, 1959), p. 187.
2. David W. Neubauer and Henry F. Fradella, *America's Courts and the Criminal Justice System*, 10th ed. (Belmont, CA: Wadsworth, 2011), pp. 294–300.
3. *Draper v. U.S.*, 358 U.S. 307 (1959).
4. *Illinois v. Gates*, 462 U.S. 213 (1983).
5. *U.S. v. Sokolow*, 109 S.Ct. 1581 (1989).
6. *Hunter v. Bryant*, 112 S.Ct. 534 (1991).
7. *People v. Defore*, 242 N.Y. 214, 150 N.E. 585 (1926).
8. *Mapp v. Ohio*, 367 U.S. 643 (1961).
9. John Kaplan, Jerome H. Skolnick, and Malcolm M. Feeley, *Criminal Justice: Introductory Cases and Materials*, 5th ed. (Westbury, NY: Foundation Press, 1991), pp. 258–259, 269.
10. *Rochin v. California*, 342 U.S. 165 (1952).
11. In *New York v. Quarles*, 467 U.S. 649 (1984).
12. *Nix v. Williams*, 52 LW 4732 (1984). This case began as *Brewer v. Williams*, 430 U.S. 387 (1977).
13. *U.S. v. Leon*, 82 L.Ed.2d 677 (1984).
14. *Murray v. U.S.*, 487 U.S. 533 (1988).
15. Alexander B. Smith and Harriet Pollack, *Criminal Justice: An Overview* (New York: Holt, Rinehart and Winston, 1980), pp. 154–155.
16. *Payton v. New York*, 445 U.S. 573 (1980).
17. *Dunaway v. New York*, 442 U.S. 200 (1979).
18. *Delaware v. Prouse*, 440 U.S. 648 (1979).
19. *Michigan Department of State Police v. Sitz*, 110 S.Ct. 2481, 110 L.Ed.2d 412 (1990).
20. *Pennsylvania v. Muniz*, 110 S.Ct. 2638, 110 L.Ed.2d 528 (1990).
21. *Maryland v. Pringle*, 124 S.Ct. 795 (2004).
22. *Illinois v. Lidster*, 124 S.Ct. 885 (2004).
23. *Riverside County, Calif. v. McLaughlin*, 59 LW 4413 (May 13, 1991).
24. *U.S. v. Banks*, 124 S.Ct. 521 (2003).
25. *Pennsylvania v. Bull*, 63 LW 3695 (1995).
26. *Wilson v. Arkansas*, 115 S.Ct. 1914 (1995).
27. *Muehler v. Mena*, 125 S.Ct. 1465 (2005).
28. *Zurcher v. Stanford Daily*, 436 U.S. 547 (1978).
29. *Maryland v. Garrison*, 480 U.S. 79 (1987).
30. *California v. Greenwood*, 486 U.S. 35 (1988).
31. Rolando V. Del Carmen and Jeffrey T. Walker, *Briefs of One Hundred Leading Cases in Law Enforcement* (Cincinnati, OH: Anderson, 1991), p. 49.
32. *Brower v. County of Inyo*, 109 U.S. 1378 (1989).
33. *Florida v. Bostick*, 59 LW 4708 (June 20, 1991).
34. *U.S. v. Drayton*, 536 U.S. 194, 231 F.3d 787 (2002).
35. *California v. Hodari D.*, 59 LW 4335 (April 23, 1991).

36. *Schmerber v. California*, 384 U.S. 757 (1966).
37. *Winston v. Lee*, 470 U.S. 753 (1985).
38. *Brigham City v. Stuart*, 547 U.S. 398 (2006).
39. *Michigan v.* Fisher, 130 S. Ct. 546 (2009).
40. *Kentucky v. King*, 563 U.S. (2011).
41. *U.S. v. Robinson*, 414 U.S. 218 (1973).
42. *Chimel v. California*, 395 U.S. 752 (1969).
43. *U.S. v. Edwards*, 415 U.S. 800 (1974).
44. *Maryland v. Buie*, 58 LW 4281 (1990).
45. Smith and Pollack, *Criminal Justice*, p. 161.
46. *Adams v. Williams*, 407 U.S. 143 (1972).
47. *U.S. v. Hensley*, 469 U.S. 221 (1985).
48. Smith and Pollack, *Criminal Justice*, p. 162.
49. *Minnesota v. Dickerson*, 113 S.Ct. 2130 (1993).
50. *Illinois v. Wardlow*, 120 S.Ct. 673 (2000).
51. Ibid., p. 673.
52. *Maryland v. Wilson*, 117 S.Ct. 882 (1997).
53. *Carroll v. United States*, 267 U.S. 132 (1925).
54. *Preston v. United States*, 376 U.S. 364 (1964).
55. *Harris v. United States*, 390 U.S. 234 (1968).
56. *Chambers v. Maroney*, 399 U.S. 42 (1970).
57. *Cardwell v. Lewis*, 417 U.S. 583 (1974).
58. *South Dakota v. Opperman*, 428 U.S. 364 (1976).
59. *New York v. Belton*, 453 U.S. 454 (1981).
60. *U.S. v. Ross*, 456 U.S. 798 (1982).
61. *Michigan v. Long*, 463 U.S. 1032 (1983).
62. *Colorado v. Bertine*, 479 U.S. 367 (1987).
63. *Florida v. Jimeno*, 59 LW 4471 (May 23, 1991).
64. *California v. Acevedo*, 59 LW 4559 (May 30, 1991).
65. *Wyoming v. Houghton*, 119 S.Ct. 1297 (1999).
66. *Florida v. Jardines*, No. 11-564 (2013); also see Matthew DeLuca, "Supreme Court limits drug-sniffing dog use," NBCNews.com, http://usnews.nbcnews.com/_news/2013/03/26/17473347-supreme-court-limits-drug-sniffing-dog-use?lite (accessed March 27, 2013).
67. *Florida v. Harris*, No. 11-817 (2013).
68. *Arizona v. Gant*, 07-542 (2009).
69. *U.S. v. Jones*, 565 U.S. ___, 132 S.Ct. 945 (2012).
70. *Texas v. Brown*, 460 U.S. 730 (1983).
71. *Oliver v. U.S.*, 466 U.S. 170 (1984).
72. *California v. Ciraolo*, 476 U.S. 207 (1986).
73. *New York v. Class*, 54 LW 4178 (1986).
74. *Arizona v. Hicks*, 55 LW 4258 (1987).
75. *Schneckloth v. Bustamonte*, 412 U.S. 218 (1973).
76. *Bumper v. North Carolina*, 391 U.S. 543 (1968).
77. *Stoner v. California*, 376 U.S. 483 (1964).
78. *Georgia v. Randolph*, 126 S.Ct. 1515 (2006).
79. *Olmstead v. U.S.*, 277 U.S. 438 (1928).
80. *Katz v. U.S.*, 389 U.S. 347 (1967).
81. *Berger v. New York*, 388 U.S. 41 (1967).
82. *Lee v. U.S.*, 343 U.S. 747 (1952).

83. *U.S. v. Karo*, 468 U.S. 705 (1984).
84. *U.S. v. Wade*, 388 U.S. 218 (1967).
85. *Kirby v. Illinois*, 406 U.S. 682 (1972).
86. *Foster v. California*, 394 U.S. 440 (1969).
87. *U.S. v. Dionisio*, 410 U.S. 1 (1973).
88. Kaplan et al., *Criminal Justice*, pp. 219–20.
89. Ibid., pp. 220–21.
90. *Spano v. New York*, 360 U.S. 315 (1959).
91. *Escobedo v. Illinois*, 378 U.S. 478 (1964).
92. *Miranda v. Arizona*, 384 U.S. 436 (1966).
93. *Berkemer v. McCarty*, 468 U.S. 420 (1984).
94. *Arizona v. Roberson*, 486 U.S. 675 (1988).
95. *Edwards v. Arizona*, 451 U.S. 477 (1981).
96. *Maryland v. Shatzer*, No. 08-680 (February 24, 2010).
97. Ibid., p. 13.
98. *Michigan v. Mosley*, 423 U.S. 93 (1975).
99. *Colorado v. Connelly*, 479 U.S. 157 (1986).
100. *Colorado v. Spring*, 479 U.S. 564 (1987).
101. *Connecticut v. Barrett*, 479 U.S. 523 (1987).
102. *Duckworth v. Eagan*, 109 S.Ct. 2875 (1989).
103. *Davis v. U.S.*, 114 S.Ct. 2350 (1994).
104. *Berghuis v. Thompkins*, No 08-1470 (June 2010); also see Adam Liptak, "Mere Silence Doesn't Invoke *Miranda*, Justices Say," *New York Times*, http://www.nytimes.com/2010/06/02/us/02scotus.html (accessed March 5, 2013).
105. *Sherman v. U.S.*, 356 U.S. 369 (1958).
106. *U.S. v. Russell*, 411 U.S. 423 (1973).
107. *Hampton v. U.S.*, 425 U.S. 484 (1976).
108. Ibid., p. 1540.
109. *Powell v. Alabama*, 287 U.S. 45 (1932).
110. *Gideon v. Wainwright*, 372 U.S. 335 (1963).
111. *Argersinger v. Hamlin*, 407 U.S. 25 (1973).
112. *Escobedo v. Illinois*, 378 U.S. 478 (1964).
113. Smith and Pollack, *Criminal Justice*, p. 177.
114. *Rhode Island v. Innis*, 446 U.S. 291 (1980).
115. *Arizona v. Mauro*, 481 U.S. 520 (1987).
116. *McNeil v. Wisconsin*, 59 LW 4636 (June 13, 1991).
117. *Minnick v. Mississippi*, 59 LW 4037 (1990).
118. *Melendez-Diaz v. Mass.*, No. 07-591 (June 2009).
119. *Padilla v. Kentucky* (No. 08-651), 253 S. W. 3d 482 (March 2010).
120. Arnold Binder, Gilbert Geis, and Dickson Bruce, *Juvenile Delinquency: Historical, Cultural, Legal Perspectives* (New York: Macmillan, 1988), pp. 6–9.
121. *Kent v. U.S.*, 383 U.S. 541 (1966).
122. *In Re Gault*, 387 U.S. 9 (1967).
123. *In Re Winship*, 397 U.S. 358 (1970).
124. *McKeiver v. Pennsylvania*, 403 U.S. 528 (1971).
125. *Breed v. Jones*, 421 U.S. 519 (1975).
126. *Roper v. Simmons*, 543 U.S. 551 (2005).
127. *Graham v. Florida*, 560 U. S. ____ (2010).

(Courtesy Africa Studio/Shutterstock.)

8 Accountability
Ethics, Use of Force, Corruption, and Discipline

LEARNING OBJECTIVES

As a result of reading this chapter, the student will be able to:

1 *Explain what is meant by police accountability*

2 *Describe what is meant by ethics, to include the principles of double effect, noble cause corruption, the "Dirty Harry problem"*

3 *Review some potential ethical problems posed by community policing*

4 *Describe how Packer's crime-control model and due process model are implicated in the matter of ethics*

5 Explain the uses and limits of police force, and how a force continuum can help officers to gauge the appropriate use of force for different situations

6 Define the types of police brutality

7 Describe some factors that contribute to police violence

8 Explain what constitutes inappropriate use of force by the police

9 Define bias-based policing, and know how it can be addressed

10 Explain how and why police corruption began and what factors within both the community and policing seem to foster and maintain it

11 Discuss the constitutional limitations that federal courts have placed on officers' rights and behaviors

12 Explain how Brady v. Maryland *has affected policing, and can affect one's career*

13 Describe how social networking sites have affected policing and how agency policies might prevent problems

14 Describe the general process that police agencies use to deal with citizen complaints

15 Explain some of the factors used for determining sanctions for officers who are to be disciplined

Introduction

"Character," it might be said, "is who we are when no one is watching." Unfortunately, character cannot be trained at the police academy nor given to someone in a pill or intravenously. Character and ethical conduct, for police officers, means they would never betray their oath of office, their public trust, or their badge. Character and ethics are *sine qua non* for the police—without those attributes, nothing else matters. These qualities constitute the foundation of their occupation and will certainly affect the officers' philosophy concerning when to use force and whether or not to engage in corruption or report other officers who do. Therefore, perhaps no general area of policing carries more controversy, concerns, problems, and questions than the aspects of policing that are discussed in this chapter concerning police accountability: ethics, use of force, corruption, and discipline.

First the subject of police ethics—its definitions, types, and problems—is examined. Incorporated in this discussion are ethical ideals, including differing views of how much latitude the police should be permitted in doing their work, as well as some ethical issues that are posed in this era of community policing and problem solving. Next, we consider the equally controversial area of police use of force, including use-of-force continuum, police shootings and brutality, vehicle pursuits, bias-based policing, and domestic violence. We then consider police corruption: types and causes, problems posed by the police code of silence, and some possible solutions for dealing with it. Next is an overview of areas in which the federal courts have placed limitations on behaviors of the police by virtue of their unique role (e.g., speech, search and seizure, self-incrimination, freedom of religion, sexual misconduct) and then turn to the very important matter of the use of so-called "*Brady* material"—the ramifications of an officer's lying, and its effects on one's career. Then we discuss recent problems caused by officers' personal use of social networking sites. The chapter concludes with an examination of disciplinary policies and practices, including handling citizens' complaints and doling out sanctions. A summary, key terms, review questions, and several scenarios and activities that provide opportunities to learn by doing conclude the chapter.

▶ Police Ethics

In a broad sense, for the police, being ethical should include holding themselves and others accountable for their actions. Accountability, like character and ethics, is also a significant watchword for today's police, and certainly all citizens expect their public servants to be accountable. What does *accountability* mean for the police? Beyond the obvious, such as having character and ethics and being good stewards of the public's trust, the term can also include the following: Police officers will treat all persons with dignity and respect and in a lawful manner; they will not use more force than necessary; they will not demonstrate bias for or against any particular group of persons; they will make every effort to ensure that all officers are well trained to meet the highest standards of professionalism; and they will maintain adequate policies, procedures, rules, regulations, general orders, and so forth for ensuring the public's trust, which includes procedures for investigating alleged incidents of bias and unprofessional behavior. Consider the following scenario.

A Scenario

Assume that the police have strong suspicions that Jones is a serial rapist, but they have not secured enough probable cause to obtain a search warrant for Jones's car and home, where evidence might be found. Officer Brown feels frustrated and, early one morning, uses a razor blade to remove the current registration decal from the license plate on Jones's

▲ The police have long been criticized for a variety of reasons, as shown in this 1874 caricature of the police as pigs. *(Courtesy Library of Congress Prints and Photographs Division Washington, D.C. 20540 USA http://hdl.loc.gov/loc. pnp/pp.print.)*

car. The next day he stops Jones for operating his vehicle with an expired registration; he impounds and inventories the vehicle and finds evidence of several sexual assaults, which ultimately leads to Jones's conviction on ten counts of forcible rape and possession of burglary tools and stolen property. Brown receives accolades for the apprehension. Was Officer Brown's removal of the registration decal legal? Should Brown's actions, even if improper or illegal, be condoned for "serving the greater public good"? Did Brown use the law properly?

This hypothetical sequence of events and the accompanying questions should be kept in mind as we consider the definitions and problems of police ethics. Exhibit 8-1 ■ describes some means by which a police agency's culture of integrity can be measured.

Definitions and Types of Problems

Proper ethical behavior has always been the cornerstone of policing (based on the Law Enforcement Code of Ethics, discussed in Exhibit 8-2 ■) and is what the public expects of its public servants. Ethics usually involves standards of moral conduct and what we call "conscience"—the ability to recognize right from wrong and to act in ways that are good and proper; it concerns choices of good and bad actions as well as moral duties and obligations.

There are both absolute and relative ethics. Absolute ethics is a concept wherein an issue only has two sides: Something is either good or bad, black or white. The original interest in police ethics focused on such unethical behaviors as bribery, extortion, excessive force, and perjury. Few communities can tolerate the absolute unethical behavior of rogue officers; for instance, anyone would have a hard time trying to rationally defend a police officer's stealing.

Relative ethics, as demonstrated in the preceding scenario, can be much more complicated and can have varying shades of gray. The problem here is this: What is considered ethical behavior by one person may be deemed highly unethical by someone else. Not

---

MEASURING A POLICE DEPARTMENT'S "CULTURE OF INTEGRITY"

Researchers believe they have found a quantitative method that allows police executives to assess their agency's level of resistance to corruption. A national survey of 3,235 officers in thirty police departments asked them to examine eleven common scenarios of police misconduct. The study was based on the premise that organizational and occupational culture can create an atmosphere in which corruption is not tolerated. Survey questions were designed to indicate whether officers knew the rules governing misconduct and how strongly they supported those guidelines, whether they knew the disciplinary penalties for breaking those rules and believed them to be fair, and whether they were willing to report misconduct. Respondents found some types of transgressions to be significantly less serious than others. The more serious the transgression was perceived to be, the more willing officers were to report a colleague and to believe that severe discipline was appropriate. Four scenarios that were not considered major transgressions by officers included operating a private security business while off duty, receiving free meals, accepting free holiday gifts, and covering up a police drunk-driving accident. Indeed, a majority of respondents said they would not report a fellow officer for accepting free gifts, meals, or discounts or for having a minor traffic accident while under the influence of alcohol.

The intermediate levels of misconduct included using excessive force on a car thief following a foot pursuit, a supervisor's offering time off during holidays in exchange for a tune-up on his personal vehicle, and accepting free drinks in return for ignoring a late bar closing. Very serious forms of misconduct, as perceived by the respondents, included accepting a cash bribe, stealing money from a found wallet, and stealing a watch from a crime scene.

Source: "Measuring a Police Department's 'Culture of Integrity'" from HOW DO YOU RATE? THE SECRET TO MEASURING A DEPARTMENT'S "CULTURE OF INTEGRITY". LAW ENFORCEMENT NEWS. Published by Belcher, Ellen, © 2000.

LAW ENFORCEMENT CODE OF ETHICS AND LAW ENFORCEMENT OATH OF HONOR

The Law Enforcement Code of Ethics (LECE) was first adopted by the International Association of Chiefs of Police in 1957 and has been revised several times since then. It is a powerful proclamation, and tens of thousands of police officers across the United States have sworn to uphold this code upon graduating their academies. Unfortunately, however, the LECE is also quite lengthy, covering rather broadly the following topics as they relate to police officers: primary responsibilities, performance of one's duties, discretion, use of force, confidentiality, integrity, cooperation with other officers and agencies, personal/professional capabilities, and private life.

Recently the IACP adopted a separate, shorter code that would be mutually supportive of the LECE—but also easier for officers to remember and call to mind when they come face-to-face with an ethical dilemma. It is the Law Enforcement Oath of Honor, and the IACP is hoping this oath will be implemented in all police agencies and by all individual officers. It may be used at swearing-in ceremonies, graduation ceremonies, promotion ceremonies, beginnings of training sessions, police meetings and conferences, and so forth.

The Law Enforcement Oath of Honor is as follows:

> On my honor,
> I will never betray my badge[1],

my integrity, my character,
or the public trust.
I will always have
the courage to hold myself
and others accountable for our actions.
I will always uphold the constitution[2],
my community[3] and the agency I serve.

The Law Enforcement Oath of Honor is also flexible, and can be adjusted as appropriate for nations, countries, or governments by inserting the appropriate terms. For example:

At the[1], insert the appropriate term, such as badge; profession; country.

At the[2], insert the appropriate term, such as constitution; laws; monarch.

At the[3], insert the appropriate term, such as community; country; land; nation.

all police ethical issues are clear-cut. For example, communities seem willing at times to tolerate extralegal behavior by the police if there is a greater public good, especially in dealing with such problems as gangs and the homeless or with offenders like the serial rapist in our scenario.

A community's acceptance of relative ethics may send the wrong message: that there are few boundaries placed on police behaviors and that, at times, "anything goes" in the fight against crime. Giving false testimony to ensure that a public menace is "put away" or using illegal wiretapping to get evidence from an organized crime figure's telephone conversations might sometimes be viewed as "necessary" and "justified," though illegal. This viewpoint—the principle of double effect—holds that if one commits an act to achieve a good end, even though an inevitable but intended effect is negative, then the act might be justified. Other related catchwords for this phenomenon are noble cause corruption and the "Dirty Harry problem.[1]" (The latter is based on the 1971 Warner Brothers film of the same title in which Detective Harry Callahan [Clint Eastwood] uses extralegal methods to accomplish legitimate police goals. For example, Callahan tortures a vicious kidnapper until he learns where he has hidden the victim. Such treatment might be condoned by many people because the heinous treatment of the offender is viewed as less shocking than what the offender did to his victim.)

The discussion of noble cause corruption and double effect is closely entwined with Herbert Packer's two classic models of law enforcement: crime control and due process.[2]

The crime-control model holds that repression of criminal conduct is the most important function of the police; police efficiency, with an emphasis on speed and finality, is a top priority; the due process model, conversely, operates under the principle that efficiency is less important than eliminating errors and that the protection of the process of law is more important than any end result of conviction (both models were introduced in Chapter 9). Under the due process model, there is a recognition that the coercive power of the state (including all the tools and resources at the disposal of the police and prosecutors) is sometimes subject to abuse and must be guarded against by due process.

Noble cause corruption is a type of wrongdoing that stems from a crime-control orientation. It is a type of means-end thinking in that the end of crime control justifies the means, even if the means are otherwise unethical or illegal. Therefore, in this view, police officers may feel compelled to lie ("testilying") under oath, use physical coercion during an interrogation, ignore exculpatory evidence if they feel they have the right offender in custody, overlook criminal acts of an informant, plan or manufacture evidence, and so on. What sets apart these acts from other ethical issues is that they are done for arguably good motives.[3]

The accompanying Career Profile provides some insight from one who has worked in an internal affairs unit—and therefore dealt with citizens' complaints and investigated officers' actions that were called into question.

Ethics and Community Policing

With the shift to community-oriented policing and problem solving (COPPS, discussed in Chapter 6), some concerns have been raised about the increased number of ethical dilemmas that COPPS officers confront because they have greater discretion and more

(Courtesy Dan Olivas, Lieutenant, City of Madison Police Department.)

Career Profile

Name: Dan Olivas

Position: Lieutenant, Professional Standards & Internal Affairs

City, State: Madison, Wisconsin

College attended: Luther College, Decorah, IA

Academic Major: B.A. Music

How long have you occupied this position/assignment?

Two years

How would you briefly describe this position/assignment:

This position involves managing and oversight of internal investigations for the Department. The position also involves active investigative work on more serious cases.

What attracted you to this position/assignment?

Personnel investigations are quite different from criminal investigations and involve employment law. The work is always interesting, and quite important. How a department responds to citizen complaints and misconduct is integral to the community perception of the agency and the level of trust the community has with the department.

What qualities/characteristics are most helpful for this position/assignment?

It is absolutely critical that the person working in this position display honesty, integrity, and fairness. Organization and investigative competence are also important.

How would you describe a typical day for one in this position/assignment?

A typical day involves accepting citizen complaints, reviewing dispositions, active investigative work, and meeting with Command Staff. I also regularly update the Chief of Police on investigations.

What advice would you offer someone who is beginning their studies of policing and criminal justice?

This profession is constantly changing and evolving—you are at the beginning of a lifelong learning process. It is important to educate yourself in current research, trends, technologies, and best practices throughout your career, regardless of rank or assignment. Something that will never change, however, is the need for professionals with the highest levels of honesty and integrity in this field. The responsibilities that come with this career are significant, and the communities we serve, fellow professionals, and the agencies we work for place a great deal of trust in each of us. Live your life with integrity.

public interaction than other officers. Gratuities—free gifts that are supposedly given to the police without obligation—are an example of an ethical problem that can arise with more frequency under COPPS. Whether the police should receive such minor gratuities as free coffee and meals is a long-standing and controversial issue, one for which there will probably never be widespread consensus. Proponents argue that police deserve such perks and that minor gratuities are the building blocks of positive social relationships. Harmless gratuities, it is maintained, may create good feelings in the community toward police officers, and vice versa. Opponents believe, however, that the receipt of gratuities can lead to future deviance. This is the slippery slope perspective, which holds that the acceptance of minor gratuities begins a process wherein the recipient's integrity is gradually subverted, which eventually leads to more serious unethical conduct.[4] Given that judges, educators, and other professionals neither expect nor receive such gifts, some people (and police agencies) conclude that gratuities are unethical. As an example, after firing an officer for stealing cigars, sandwiches, magazines, and other goods from merchants, the Bradenton, Florida, Police Department established a policy prohibiting sworn personnel from accepting discounted meals from restaurant owners.[5]

The following scenario involves COPPS and gratuities:

> The sheriff's department has a long-standing policy concerning the solicitation and acceptance of gifts. A deputy has been working a problem-solving project in a strip mall area that has experienced juvenile loitering, drug use, prostitution, and vandalism after hours in the parking lot. The mall manager, Mr. Chang, believes it is his moral duty to show his appreciation to the deputy and has made arrangements for the deputy and his family to receive a 15 percent discount at every store in the mall. Knowing that the department policy requires that such offers be declined, the deputy is also aware that Chang will feel very hurt if the proffered gift is refused.[6]

A particularly strong consideration in this scenario is that the mall manager is Asian American and might be extremely hurt if his gift were rejected. Some policy issues are also presented in this scenario. For example, in developing rapport with a mall restaurant manager, is an officer who was formerly prohibited from accepting a free meal now free to do so? Assume that other deputies learn of Chang's new discount arrangement and go to the mall expecting to be treated similarly, resulting in complaints to the sheriff by several business owners. Certainly some people would hold this action to be unethical, given the officers' motivation (personal gain) and their exploitation of the situation.

In sum, the subject of police ethics is not simplistic in nature. We all know that officers should do right, not wrong, but the existence and use of relative ethics make this a complicated issue at best. What can be said is that police officers must be recruited and trained with ethics in mind because they will be given much freedom to become more involved in their community and given wider discretion to make important decisions when addressing neighborhood disorder.

Exhibit 8-2 shows the very important Law Enforcement Code of Ethics, which police officers are sworn to uphold; the code not only contributes to the professional image of law enforcement, but it also brings about self-respect among officers and affords feelings of mutual respect among police personnel.

▶ Use of Force

A Tradition of Problems

Throughout U.S. history, police agencies have faced allegations of brutality and corruption. In the late nineteenth century, New York Police (NYPD) Sergeant Alexander "Clubber" Williams epitomized police brutality; he spoke openly of using his nightstick to knock a man unconscious, batter him to pieces, or even kill him. Williams supposedly coined the term *tenderloin* when he commented, "I've had nothing but chuck steaks for a long time, and now I'm going to have me a little tenderloin."[7] Williams was referring to opportunities for graft in an area in New York City that was the heart of vice and nightlife, often termed Satan's Circus. This was Williams's beat, where his reputation for brutality and corruption became legendary.[8]

Although police brutality and corruption are no longer openly tolerated, a number of events have demonstrated that the problem still exists and requires the attention of police officials. Several of these events, such as the so-called police riot in 1968 during the Democratic National Convention, were discussed in Chapter 1.

Legitimate Uses of Force

American society recognizes three legitimate and responsive forms of force: the right of self-defense, including the valid taking of another person's life in order to protect oneself from harm; the power to control those for whom one is responsible (such as a prisoner or a patient in a mental hospital); and the relatively unrestricted authority of police to use force as required. Police work is dangerous—a routine arrest may result in a violent confrontation, sometimes triggered by drugs, alcohol, or mental illness. To cope, police officers are given the unique right to use force, even deadly force, against others. There are, of course, limitations on when an officer may exercise deadly force (they will be discussed later in this chapter).

Egon Bittner defined police use of force as the "distribution of non-negotiably coercive remedies."[9] He asserted that the duty of police intervention in matters of societal disorder "means above all making use of the authority to overpower resistance. This feature of police work is uppermost in the minds of people who solicit police aid. Every conceivable police intervention projects the message that force may . . . have to be used to achieve a desired objective."[10] The exercise of force by police can take several forms, ranging from a simple verbal command to the use of lethal force. These forms of force are discussed next as continuums.

Use-of-Force Continuums

Use-of-force continuums have been evolving for over three decades and have been explained and depicted in very simple (e.g., as a staircase, wheel, or ladder) to more elaborate illustrations. A basic-force continuum (and one that existed for a long while) instructed officers to move up the "ladder" or "staircase" and employ increasing levels or types of force as an aggressor became more physical or violent; it typically contained the following five escalating steps: officer presence/verbal direction, touch control, empty-hand tactics and chemical agents, hand-held impact weapons, and lethal force.[11]

Today, however, more and more police executives and force experts believe this simplistic, sequential depiction of the force continuum is ill-suited for today's police and that police use of force cannot always be employed in such a sequential, stair-step fashion. Even with policies and procedures accompanying such a continuum, confusion remained among many officers: "Where am I now on the ladder?" or "Is it now time to climb up to the next rung of the ladder?" Such a simple continuum also fails to properly represent the dynamic encounter between the officer and a resistant suspect and to take into account the wide array of tools that are available to today's officers. How can a department dictate definitively with a continuum in what situations, say, a baton or pepper spray, and electronic control device, or other less-lethal weapons should be used?

As a result of this confusion, many agencies now have policies requiring their officers to be "objectively reasonable" in their use of force; in essence, "objectively reasonable" means that in determining the necessity for force and the appropriate level of force, officers shall evaluate each situation in light of the known circumstances; such an assessment includes the seriousness of the crime, the level of threat or resistance presented by the subject, and the danger to the community.

A new approach to determining proper use of force has recently been developed by two special agents of the Federal Bureau of Investigation and attempts to "more accurately reflect the intent of the law and the changing expectations of society" and provide officers with "simple, clear, unambiguous, and consistent guidelines in the use of force."[12] Known as the dynamic resistance response model (DRRM), this approach combines a use of force continuum with an application of four broad categories of suspects. *Dynamic* indicates that the model is fluid, and *resistance* demonstrates that the suspect controls the interaction. In this view, a major failing of past continuums has been that the emphasis is on the officer and the amount of force used. DRRM instead emphasizes that the suspect's level of resistance determines the officer's response. The model also delineates suspects into one of four categories (see Figure 8-1 ■).

As shown in Figure 8-1, if a passively resistant suspect fails to follow commands and perhaps attempts to move away from the officer or escape, appropriate responses include using a firm grip, control holds, and pressure points to gain compliance. On the other hand, an aggressively resistant suspect—one who is taking offensive action by attempting to push, throw, strike, tackle, or physically harm the officer—would call for such responses as the use of personal weapons (hands, fists, feet), batons, pepper spray, and a stun gun. Finally, because a deadly resistant suspect can seriously injure or kill the officer or another person, the officer is justified in using force, including deadly force, as is *objectively reasonable* to overcome the offender.

In the DRRM, a suspect's lack of resistance (compliance) is in the center of the triangle, which is emphasized as the goal of every encounter. If a suspect's resistance level places him or her on one of the three corners of the triangle, the officer's response is intended to move the suspect's behavior to the center of the triangle and compliance. The sole purpose of the application of force is to gain compliance.

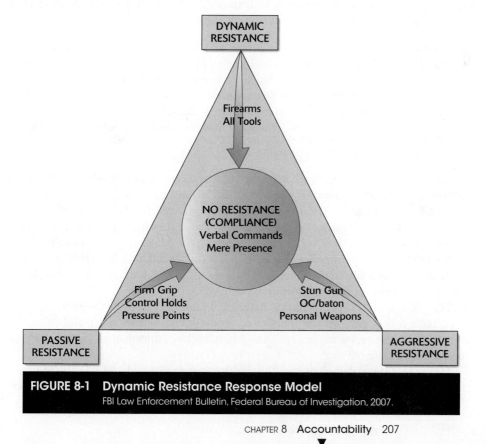

FIGURE 8-1   Dynamic Resistance Response Model
FBI Law Enforcement Bulletin, Federal Bureau of Investigation, 2007.

Police Shootings: Conundrum and Controversy

Clearly, nothing can inflame a community and raise tensions like police shootings, and there has been no dearth of high-profile police shooting incidents during the early part of this millennium:

- In early 2012, a police officer in Phoenix, Arizona, came under scrutiny following his sixth involvement in a fatal shooting (and one shooting in which a person was wounded) in a decade.[13]

- In late 2012, a trio of incidents where Los Angeles officers allegedly used excessive force (i.e., a woman died after struggling with officers trying to arrest her for child endangerment; a registered nurse slammed to the ground twice by two male officers who exited her car when pulled over and did not comply with their demand that she re-enter her vehicle; a college student stopped for skateboarding on the wrong side of the street appearing to be punched in the face while on the ground) threatened to erode the goodwill gained by the agency over the past several years.[14]

- Five current or former New Orleans police officers were convicted (of twenty who were charged) in mid-2011 of civil rights violations for shooting and killing two people and wounding four others in the aftermath of Hurricane Katrina.[15]

The U.S. Justice Department issued a report in late-2011 saying inadequate supervision and training have led Seattle, Washington, officers to be too quick to grab weapons and engage in excessive force; the probe began after the fatal shooting of a homeless native American.[16] These incidents that also involve minority group members will often heighten the tension and lead to charges of racism against the entire police agency. One *Washington Post* columnist offered that "it is the police culture, more than race, that is at the crux of the problem . . . a mentality of brutality."[17] Such kinds of police uses of force even caused one organization, Human Rights Watch, to state the following in a report titled *Shielded from Justice: Police Brutality and Accountability in the United States*:

> Police abuse remains one of the most serious and divisive human rights violations in the United States. The excessive use of force by police officers, including unjustified shootings, severe beatings, fatal chokings, and rough treatment, persists because overwhelming barriers to accountability make it possible for officers who commit human rights violations to escape due punishment and often to repeat their offenses.[18]
>
> —Excerpt from "Shielded from Justice: Police Brutality and Accountability in the United States" from SHIELDED FROM JUSTICE: POLICE BRUTALITY AND ACCOUNTABILITY IN THE UNITED STATES. Published by Human Rights Watch, © 1998.

Human Rights Watch also noted in the report that officers who repeatedly commit human rights violations tend to be a small minority but that "they are protected, routinely, by the silence of their fellow officers and by flawed systems of reporting, oversight, and accountability; by the scarcity of meaningful information about trends in abuse; data lacking regarding the police departments' response to those incidents; and their plans or actions to prevent brutality."[19]

Even though killings by police are a very serious matter and have damaged law enforcement's standing in some communities, no one knows the actual number of such deaths or exactly how many of them were deemed unjustified.

The FBI and the Bureau of Justice Statistics, the statistical arm of the Justice Department, both collect data on the number of people killed by the police and other law enforcement agencies, but no one is required to submit this information, and many police departments choose not to.[20]

Moreover, federal data does not distinguish between justified and unjustified homicides, in which the victim was not a threat. The FBI says it tracks "justifiable homicides" and then defines these as "the killing of a felon by a law enforcement officer in the line of duty." In some cases, however, such killings have been ruled unjustified. The FBI data also does not provide details on where or under what circumstances deadly force was used.[21]

News media reports reveal a dramatically higher number of police shootings than federal statistics. Tracking media reports for 2011, Jim Fisher, a law professor and former FBI agent, identified 607 fatal shootings, compared with 393 homicides listed by the FBI for that year.[22]

Notwithstanding this lack of data collection for such incidents, the U.S. Department of Justice has relatively new legal means to investigate allegations of racial bias in police departments. The law authorizing such investigations, passed in 1994 after the Rodney King beating in Los Angeles, compels police agencies to initiate safeguards against excessive force and racial bias (for instance, computer systems to track complaints and disciplinary actions) to determine whether the police engaged in "a pattern and practice" of racial discrimination or brutality.[23]

Legal Restrictions

When the colonists came to this country from England, they brought with them a principle of common law that authorized the use of deadly force to apprehend any and all fleeing felony suspects. As American laws and society evolved, however, it became possible for police to use deadly force against people who were at great distances from them, including people suspected of nonviolent property crimes. The justification and necessity for the fleeing-felon rule came into question.[24] Then the U.S. Supreme Court's 1985 decision in *Tennessee v. Garner*[25] greatly curtailed the use of deadly force. The Court held that the use of deadly force to prevent the escape of all felony suspects was constitutionally unreasonable. It is not better, the Court reasoned, that all felony suspects die than that they escape. Where the suspect poses no immediate threat to the officer or to others, the harm resulting from failing to apprehend him or her does not justify the use of deadly force to do so. (The misuse of firearms will be discussed in detail later in this chapter.)

Police Brutality

Many people contend that there are actually three means by which the police can be "brutal." There is the literal sense of the term, which involves the physical abuse of others. There is the verbal abuse of citizens, exemplified by slurs or epithets. And, for many who feel downtrodden, the police symbolize brutality because the officers represent the Establishment's law, which serves to keep minority groups in their place. It is perhaps the last form of police brutality that is of greatest concern for anyone who is interested in improving community relations. Because it is a philosophy or frame of mind, it is probably the most difficult to overcome.

Citizens' use of the term *police brutality* encompasses a wide range of practices, from profane and abusive language to actual physical force or violence.[26] Some would claim that there is little (if any) police brutality in today's enlightened police agencies. Others acknowledge that police brutality exists today but add that "*brutality is the prerogative of the police state. To tolerate any of it is to differ from the police state only in degree*" (emphasis in original).[27]

While no one can deny that some police officers use brutal practices, it is impossible to know with any degree of accuracy how often and to what extent these incidents occur. They are low-visibility acts, and many victims decline to report them. Although it is widely believed that brutality is a racial matter primarily involving white police and black victims, Albert Reiss found that lower-class white men were as likely to be brutalized by the police as lower-class black men.[28] What is most disturbing is that 37 percent of the instances of excessive force occurred in settings controlled by the police—station houses and patrol cars. In half the situations, a police officer did not participate but did not restrain his or her colleague, indicating that the informal police culture did not disapprove of the behavior.[29]

It is doubtful that police brutality will ever disappear forever. There are always going to be, in the words of A. C. Germann, Frank Day, and Robert Gallati, "Neanderthals" who enjoy their absolute control over others and become tyrannical in their arbitrary application of power.[30] Therefore, many people support the use of formal citizen complaint review procedures for investigating allegations of brutality and excessive use of force.

Vehicle Pursuits

In 2007, the U.S. Supreme Court issued a major decision concerning the proper amount of force the police may use during high-speed vehicle pursuits (which are also discussed in Chapter 9, concerning their related civil liability). The fundamental question was whether or not the serious danger created by the fleeing motorist justifies the use of deadly force to eliminate the threat. In other words, was the level of force used proportionate to the threat of reckless and dangerous driving? The incident involved Harris, a nineteen-year-old Georgia youth, driving at speeds up to ninety miles per hour and covering nine miles in six minutes, with a deputy sheriff in pursuit; the chase ended in a violent crash that left Harris a quadriplegic. His lawyers argued that the Fourth Amendment protects against the use of excessive force, such as high-speed drivers having their cars rammed by police (by intentionally stopping a fleeing vehicle in such a manner, a "seizure" occurs for Fourth Amendment purposes). Conversely, the deputy's lawyers argued that such drivers pose an escalating danger to the public and must be stopped to defuse the danger (the deputy's supervisor had authorized the use of the precision immobilization technique, or PIT, where the officer uses his patrol vehicle to cause the speeder's to spin out; PIT was not used in the Harris chase, however). The Court's 8–1 opinion, authored by Justice Antonin Scalia, stated, "A police officer's attempt to terminate a dangerous high-speed car chase that threatens the lives of innocent bystanders does not violate the Fourth Amendment, even when it places the fleeing motorist at risk of serious injury or death."[31]

Bias-Based Policing and Other Field Tactics

Bias-based policing—also known as "driving while black or brown" (DWBB)—involves unequal treatment of any person on the basis of race, ethnicity, religion, gender, sexual orientation, or socioeconomic status. A 2007 study released by the Bureau of Justice Statistics found that while black, Hispanic, and white drivers are equally likely to be pulled over by the police, blacks and Hispanics are much more likely to be searched and arrested, and police are much more likely to threaten or use force against blacks and Hispanics than against whites in any encounter, whether at a traffic stop or elsewhere. The report warned that the findings do not prove that police treat people differently along racial lines and that the differences could be explained by driver conduct or other circumstances.[32] Nonetheless, traffic stops are a politically volatile issue, and such studies underscore minority groups' complaints that many stops and searches are based on race rather than on legitimate suspicions. This dynamic was certainly at the root of the controversy over a law enacted in Arizona in mid-2010, authorizing police to stop and determine someone's immigration status if they suspected that he or she was an illegal immigrant (a federal judge quickly issued a preliminary injunction against that and other highly controversial provisions of the law).

Some police executives defend officers' selective stopping of citizens as effective crime fighting, based not on prejudice but on probabilities: the statistical reality that certain people are disproportionately likely to commit crimes. Bernard Parks, former African-American police chief of Los Angeles, explained:

> We have an issue of violent crime against jewelry salespeople. The predominant suspects are Colombians. We don't find Mexican-Americans, or blacks, or other immigrants. It's a

▲ Scenes from the Walker Report of the 1968 Chicago Democratic National Convention. *(Courtesy National Commission on the Causes and Prevention of Violence.)*

collection of several hundred Colombians who commit this crime. If you see six in a car in front of the Jewelry Mart, and they're waiting and watching people with briefcases, should we play the percentages and follow them? It's common sense.[33]

—*Excerpt from "Suspect Policy" by Randall Kennedy, NEW REPUBLIC. Copyright © 1999 by The New Republic. Used by permission.*

Still, bias-based policing has become a despised police practice in the new millennium. Profiling on the basis of race is given no public support. The best defense for the police may be summarized in two words: *collect data.* Collecting traffic-stop data helps chiefs and commanders to determine whether officers are stopping or searching a disproportionate number of minorities and enables them to act on this information right away. Technology—including mobile data computers and wireless handheld devices—can be used for this purpose.

Other police field practices, such as the following, also can be sources of tension between minorities and police:

- **Delay in responding to calls for service.** Studies of police work have found that patrol officers sometimes delay responding to calls for service, especially in cases of family disturbances.[34] Although this delay may be justified on grounds of officer safety (i.e., an officer must await backup), and while these studies did not demonstrate any pattern of racial bias, delays do not improve public perceptions of the police.

- **Verbal abuse, epithets, and other forms of disrespect.** Offensive labels for people are a regular aspect of the working language of some police officers. One study found that 75 percent of all officers used some racially offensive words, most of which were not uttered in the presence of citizens; however, police openly ridicule and belittle citizens in 5 percent of all encounters.[35] In some situations, the police use the terms as a control technique in an attempt to establish their authority.[36] Nonetheless, verbal abuse should be avoided at all times.

- **Excessive questioning and frisking of minority citizens.** Allegations of harassment by police are often raised by racial minorities who believe they have been unnecessarily subjected to field interrogations. Many officers, because they are trained to be suspicious and must often confront individuals in questionable circumstances, regard such activities as legitimate and effective crime-fighting tactics.

- **Discriminatory patterns of arrest and traffic citations.** African Americans are arrested more often than whites relative to their numbers in the population.[37] African-American complainants request arrests more often than whites. Since most incidents are intraracial, this can result in more arrests of African Americans.[38] Police have been found more likely to arrest both white and African-American suspects in low-income areas. Insofar as African Americans are disproportionately represented among the poor, however, this factor is likely to result in a disproportionately high arrest rate for African Americans.[39]

- **Excessive use of physical force.** Police have been found to use force in about 5 percent of all encounters involving offenders. In about two-thirds of the incidents involving force, its application was judged to be reasonable. White and African-American officers used excessive force at nearly the same rate. It is known that "a sizable minority of citizens experience police misconduct at one time or another."[40] The result, of course, is that many racial minorities perceive that their race is being unduly brutalized. And, to them, perception is reality.

A Related Issue: Domestic Violence

A 1996 federal law, titled the Domestic Violence Offender Gun Ban (popularly known as the Lautenberg Amendment), bars anyone—including police and military personnel—from carrying firearms if they have a conviction for domestic violence. Although no figures are available regarding loss of jobs, that has been the case for hundreds of police officers across the United States. In many cases, officers found to have past misdemeanor convictions have lost their jobs.[41]

No one denies that a police officer who beats a spouse or child should be fired. The ban's supporters maintain that the police must also be held accountable when they commit any type of domestic violence and that their easy access to firearms can cause a domestic argument to escalate to homicide.[42] However, critics of the law, including many politicians, police associations, and unions, argue that the law is too broad.

Assume, for example, that a police officer tells her fifteen-year-old son that he cannot leave the house and hang out with some kids she knows to be using drugs. He attempts to leave and calls her some names, so she grabs him by the arm and sits him down. Except for a bruise on his arm, he is not injured, but he calls the police, a report is filed, and she is convicted of misdemeanor assault in a trial by judge with no right to trial by jury. Because of the domestic-violence law, she loses her right to carry a gun and, thus, her career is ended.[43] Because police agencies typically have no unarmed positions, the law in effect ends the careers of officers who are affected by it.

The issue is not whether abusive police officers should be fired but whether the law as it is written is effective and legal. Several state lawsuits, including lawsuits by the National Association of Police Officers (which argues that officers are being "sacrificed on the altar of political correctness"[44]), have challenged the constitutionality of the law. In August 1998, the U.S. Court of Appeals for the District of Columbia Circuit exempted police and federal law enforcement agents within its jurisdiction from the law.

▶ Police Corruption

History: A Long-Standing "Plague"

"For as long as there have been police, there has been police corruption," observed Lawrence Sherman concerning the oldest and most persistent problem in American policing.[45] To make the point, corruption has long plagued the NYPD, as determined by the Knapp Commission, which investigated police corruption there in the early 1970s.[46] Knapp's 1973 report stated that there are two primary types of corrupt police officers: the "meat-eaters" and the "grass-eaters." Meat-eaters, who probably constitute a small percentage of police officers, spend a good deal of their working hours aggressively seeking out situations that they can exploit for financial gain, including gambling, narcotics, and other lucrative enterprises. No change in attitude is likely to affect meat-eaters; their income is so large that the only way to deal with them is to get them off the force and prosecute them. Grass-eaters constitute the overwhelming majority of those officers who accept payoffs; they are not aggressive but will accept gratuities from contractors, tow-truck operators, gamblers, and the like.

The Knapp Commission also identified several factors that influence how much graft police officers receive, the most important of these being the character of the individual officer. The branch of the department and the type of assignment also affect opportunities for corruption. Typically, plainclothes officers have more varied opportunities than uniformed patrol officers, and uniformed officers located in beats with, say, several vice dens will have more opportunities for payoffs. Another factor is rank: the amount of the payoff received generally ascends proportionally with rank.

Police corruption can be defined broadly, from major forms of police wrongdoing to the pettiest forms of improper behavior. Another definition is "the misuse of authority by a police officer in a manner designed to produce personal gain for the officer or for others."[47] Police corruption is not limited to monetary gain, however. Gains may be made through the acceptance of services received, status, influence, prestige, or future support for the officer or someone else.[48]

Events like those described in Los Angeles and other cities have focused attention on the broader issue of rogue cops in police departments across the country, especially in minority neighborhoods.[49] The brazenness and viciousness of today's corrupt police officers trouble even their staunchest defenders.

Types and Causes

Several factors contribute to police corruption, among them the rapid hiring of personnel, civil service, and union protections that make it difficult to fire officers,[50] and temptations from money and sex.

Two theories—the "rotten apple" theory and the "environmental" theory—have been suggested to explain police corruption. The rotten apple theory holds that corruption is the result of having a few bad apples in the barrel that probably had character defects prior to employment. The environmental theory suggests that corruption is more the result of a widespread politically corrupt environment; politically corrupt cities create an environment in which police misconduct flourishes.[51]

Police corruption takes two basic forms: external and internal. External corruption includes those activities (such as gratuities and payoffs) that occur from and through police contacts with the public. Internal corruption involves the relationships among police officers within the workings of the police department; this includes payments to join the police force, to get better shifts or assignments, to receive promotions, and the like.[52]

Ellwyn Stoddard, who coined the term *blue-coat crime*, described several different forms of deviant practices among both police and citizens. In the following list, those coming first would probably elicit the least fear of prosecution, and those at the end would probably invoke major legal ramifications:[53]

- **Mooching.** Receiving free coffee, meals, liquor, groceries, laundry services, and so forth.
- **Chiseling.** Demanding free admission to entertainment or price discounts on goods and services.
- **Favoritism.** Using license tabs, window stickers, or courtesy cards to gain immunity from traffic arrest.
- **Prejudice.** Behaving less than impartially toward minority group members or others who are less likely to have influence in city hall.
- **Bribery.** Receiving payments of cash or gifts for past or future assistance in avoiding prosecution, including political payoffs for favoritism in promotions. Police officers who accept payoffs or protection money are said to be "on the pad."
- **Shakedown.** Stealing expensive items for personal use and attributing the loss to criminal activity when investigating a burglary or unlocked door.
- **Perjury.** Following the "code" that demands that officers lie to provide an alibi for fellow officers apprehended in unlawful activity.
- **Premeditated theft.** Being involved in planned burglaries that involve the use of tools or keys to gain entry; also any prearranged act of unlawful acquisition of property that cannot be explained as a spur-of-the-moment theft.

The most common and extensive form of corruption involves the receipt by police officers of small gratuities or tips. Officers may regard discounts and free services as relatively unimportant, while the payment of cash—bribery—is a very different matter.[54] Former New York City Police Commissioner Patrick V. Murphy was one of those who "drew the short line," telling his officers that "except for your paycheck, there is no such thing as a clean buck."[55] Such police officials would argue that even the smallest gratuities can create an expectation of some patronage or favor in return. Retail establishments do not offer gratuities to other persons in professional positions (doctors, lawyers, educators) for performing their duties, and the argument can certainly be made that the police should be similarly viewed and treated.

Withrow and Dailey offered a uniquely different viewpoint toward gratuities.[56] They propose a "model of circumstantial corruptibility," stating that the exchange of a gift is influenced by two elements: the role of the giver and the role of the receiver. The role of the *giver* determines the level of corruptibility, in this model; the giver is either taking a position as a:

- *presenter,* who offers a gift voluntarily without any expectation of a return from the receiver;

- *contributor,* who furnishes something toward a result and expects something in return; or a
- *capitulator,* who involuntarily responds to the demands of the receiver.

The role of the receiver of the gift is obviously very important as well; the receiver can act as an:

- *acceptor,* who receives the gift humbly and without any residual feelings of reciprocity;
- *expector,* who looks forward to the gift and regards it as likely to happen, and will be annoyed by the absence of the gift; or
- *conqueror,* who assumes total control over the exchange and influence over the giver.

The function of the model is centered on the intersection of the giver and the receiver. For example, when the giver assumes the role of the presenter and the receiver is the acceptor, the result is a giving exchange, and corruption does not occur. However, if giver and receiver occupy other roles, corruptibility can progress to higher levels of social harm, which Withrow and Dailey termed a "hierarchy of wickedness." Bribery results when something of value is given and the giver expects something in return, while the receiver agrees to conform his or her behavior to the desires of the giver. It is therefore of great importance that the police consider the role of the giver as well as their own intentions when deciding whether or not to accept a gratuity. In certain circumstances, the exchange of *any* gratuity is ethical or unethical regardless of its value.

Another serious form of police corruption is related to drugs. Until the 1960s, most police corruption was associated with the protection of gambling operations, illegal liquor establishments, prostitution, and similar "victimless" activities. More recently, however, drug-related police corruption has probably surpassed those earlier forms of deviance. A typology of drug-related corruption has been developed by David Carter, who believes that the numbers of such cases "have notably increased":[57]

> *Type I drug corruption* occurs when an officer seeks to use his or her position simply for personal gain. This type of drug corruption includes giving information to drug dealers about investigations, names of informants, planned raids, and so forth; accepting bribes from drug dealers in exchange for nonarrest, evidence tampering, or perjury; stealing drugs from the police property room for personal consumption; "seizing" drugs for personal use without arresting the person possessing the drugs; taking either the profits of drug dealers' sales or the drugs themselves for resale; and extorting money or property from drug traffickers in exchange for nonarrest or nonseizure of drugs.
>
> *Type II drug corruption* involves the officer's search for legitimate goals and may not even be universally perceived as being corrupt. Officer gain may involve organizational benefit, perhaps a form of "winning" or "revenge." Included are such actions as giving false statements to obtain arrest or search warrants against suspected or known drug dealers, committing perjury during hearings and trials of drug dealers, planting or creating evidence against known drug dealers, using entrapment, and falsely spreading rumors that a dealer is a police informant in order to endanger that person.

—Excerpt from "A Typology of Drug-Related Corruption" by David L. Carter from POLICING PERSPECTIVES: AN ANTHOLOGY, edited by Larry K. Gaines and Gary W. Cordner. Published by Roxbury Publishing Company, © 1999.

Code of Silence

Patrick V. Murphy wrote that "the most difficult element to overcome in the fight against corruption in the department was the code of silence."[58] This keeping quiet in the face of misconduct by other officers has been well documented. Evidence of the fraternal bond that exists in policing was first reported by William Westley as early as 1970, when more than 75 percent of the officers surveyed said that they would not report another officer for taking money from a prisoner, nor would they testify against an officer accused by a prisoner.[59] (In a related vein, see Exhibit 8-1.)

For example, Officer Jack Smith finds himself in a moral dilemma. He knows of another officer's misconduct; he witnessed the officer putting expensive ink pens in his pocket while securing an unlocked office supply store on the graveyard shift. If reported, the misconduct will ruin the officer, but if not reported, the behavior could eventually cause enormous harm. To outsiders, this is not a dilemma at all; the only proper path is for Smith to report the misconduct. To philosophers, the doctrines of utilitarianism (the ethic of good consequences) and deontology (the ethic of rights and duties) require that Officer Smith work to eliminate corruption. But the outsiders and the philosophers are not members of the close fraternity of police, nor do they have to depend on other officers for their own safety.

There are several arguments for and against Officer Smith's informing on his partner. Reasons for informing include the fact that the harm caused by a scandal would be outweighed by the public's knowledge that the police department is free of corruption; also, individual episodes of corruption would be brought to a halt. The officer, moreover, has a sworn duty to uphold the law. Any employee has a right to be allowed to do his or her duty, including blowing the whistle on employers or colleagues. Reasons against Officer Smith's informing include the fact that a skilled police officer is a valuable asset whose social value far outweighs the damage done by moderate corruption. Also, discretion and secrecy are obligations assumed by joining and remaining within the police fraternity; dissenters should resign rather than inform. Furthermore, it would be unjust to inflict punishment of dismissal and disgrace on an otherwise decent officer.[60]

How does one reconcile these two varying points of view? Probably the first thing to do is to realize that each view is morally defensible. A person who is in charge of investigating police corruption would no doubt be warmer toward the punitive view, while at the other extreme would be the person who would overlook such behaviors at all times. The ideal position might be in the middle—to maintain a commitment to professionalism and ethics without overreacting (e.g., without insisting that officers report on their fellows every time they see someone napping or conducting personal business while on duty).

The good news is that a recent survey by the National Institute of Justice found that about 83 percent of all officers in the United States do not accept the code of silence as an essential part of the mutual trust necessary to good policing.[61]

Investigation and Prosecution

Federal powers and jurisdiction for investigating and prosecuting police corruption were significantly expanded through the Hobbs Act in 1970.[62] Two important elements of this federal statute that allow the investigation of police corruption are extortion and commerce. Whenever a police officer solicits a payoff from a legitimate business owner to overlook law violations (e.g., a tavern owner who was selling alcohol to minors), extortion (involving fear) occurs, and that extortion affects legitimate commerce. The Hobbs Act may be employed by the prosecutor when these two elements are present. The meaning of extortion has been expanded so that it now covers most payoff arrangements that involve public officials.[63] The only areas of police corruption that may be beyond the reach of the Hobbs Act are internal corruption and the acceptance of isolated gratuities.

The federal perjury statute (18 U.S.C. 1621) and the federal false sworn declaration statute (18 U.S.C. 1623), both enacted in 1970, have also become powerful weapons for prosecutors in investigating public corruption. Both statutes deal with false testimony under oath, and in an investigation of corruption they are pertinent at the grand jury stage.[64]

Possible Solutions

Several other measures are possible for overcoming the pernicious effects of police corruption. In addition to the obvious need for an honest and effective police administration, it is also necessary to train recruits on the need for a corruption-free department. The creation and maintenance of an internal affairs unit and the vigorous prosecution of law-breaking police officers are also critical to maintaining the integrity of officers. In addition, there should be some mechanism for rewarding the honest police officers that should minimally include protection from retaliation when they inform on crooked cops. All police officers should be given formal written guidelines on the departmental policy on soliciting and accepting gifts and gratuities. This apprises officers of the administration's view of such behavior and assists the chief executive in maintaining integrity and disciplining wayward officers. Figure 8-2 ■ is an example of a good policy concerning gratuities.

Also, computers can assist with investigations of police corruption. Indeed, information that was uncovered about corruption within the Chicago Police Department was obtained through an $850 software program known as Brainmaker, an early-warning program intended to flag at-risk officers before they commit acts that could get them arrested or fired. With this type of approach, at-risk officers can be provided with counseling before serious problems occur.[65]

Exhibit 8-3 ■ shows what one city has done, and the kind of software that it used, to create an early-warning system.

1. Without the express permission of the Sheriff, members shall not solicit or accept any gift, gratuity, loan, present, or fee where there is any direct or indirect connection between this solicitation or acceptance of such gift and their employment by this office.

2. Members shall not accept, either directly or indirectly, any gift, gratuity, loan, fee, or thing of value, the acceptance of which might tend to improperly influence their actions, or that of any other member, in any matter of police business, or which might tend to cast an adverse reflection on the Sheriff's Office.

3. Any unauthorized gift, gratuity, loan, fee, reward, or other thing falling into any of these categories coming into the possession of any member shall be forwarded to the member's commander, together with a written report explaining the circumstances connected therewith. The commander will decide the disposition of the gift.

FIGURE 8-2   A Sample Gratuity Policy
Kenneth Peak.

EXHIBIT 8-3

A MEANS OF POLICING THE POLICE

A lawsuit filed recently by dozens of plaintiffs, alleging that they were roughed up by a band of Oakland, California, officers calling themselves "the Riders," was settled for $11 million and resulted in a new Personnel Information Management System (PIMS) being implemented in 2005. PIMS will document use-of-force incidents, citizen complaints, attendance, shootings, and accidents, as well as commendations, awards, and letters of appreciation. Its main purpose is to help supervisors identify trends that might indicate [when] an officer needs an intervention. Based on a Phoenix, Arizona, model, the system holds the supervisor all the way up the chain accountable for doing something and is a tremendous risk management tool; it emphasizes guiding employees, not merely disciplining them.

At the extreme, it allows for getting to people before they "crash and burn, and kill somebody in a police pursuit, traffic accident, or whatever." The system refreshes itself nightly by collecting new information added that day. An Oakland police captain emphasized that a lot of use-of-force problems, incidents, or attendance issues do not make one a bad officer; an officer working in a busy area abundant with shootings will be involved in more car chases and fights and have more use-of-force incidents than one working in a less active downtown area.

Source: "A Means of Policing the Police" by Jim Mckay from POLICING THE POLICE: OAKLAND, CALIF., TACKLES POLICE MISCONDUCT ISSUES WITH DATABASE. Copyright © 2004 by Government Technology. Used by permission.

▶ Limitations on Officers' Constitutional Rights

Police officers are generally afforded the same rights, privileges, and immunities outlined in the U.S. Constitution for all citizens. However, by virtue of their position, they may be compelled to give up certain rights in connection with an investigation of on-duty misbehavior or illegal acts. These rights are the basis for legislation such as the Peace Officers' Bill of Rights (discussed at length in Chapter 8), labor agreements, and civil service and departmental rules and regulations that guide an agency's disciplinary process.

Following is a brief overview of some areas in which the federal courts have placed limitations on officers' constitutional rights and have held sworn officers more accountable by virtue of the higher standard required by their occupation.

Free Speech Although the right of freedom of speech is one of the most fundamental and cherished of all American rights, the Supreme Court has indicated that "the State has interests as an employer in regulating the speech of its employees that differ significantly from those it possesses in connection with regulation of the speech of the citizenry in general."[66] Thus the state may impose restrictions on its police employees that it would not be able to impose on civilians; however, these restrictions must be reasonable. For example, a department may not prohibit "any activity, conversation, deliberation, or discussion which is derogatory to the Department," as such a rule obviously prohibits all criticism of the agency by its officers, even in private conversation.[67]

Another First Amendment–related area is that of personal appearance. The Supreme Court has upheld several grooming standards for officers (regarding length of hair, sideburns, and mustaches) to make officers readily recognizable to the public and to maintain the esprit de corps within the department.[68]

Searches and Seizures The Fourth Amendment to the U.S. Constitution protects "the right of the people to be secure in their persons, houses, papers, and effects, against unreasonable searches and seizures." The Fourth Amendment usually applies to police officers when they are at home or off duty in the same manner as it applies to all citizens. However, because of the nature of their work, police officers can be compelled to cooperate with investigations of their behavior when ordinary citizens would not. For example, regarding equipment and lockers provided by the department to the officers, the officers have no expectation of privacy that affords or merits protection.[69]

However, lower courts have established limitations on searches of employees themselves. The question of whether prison authorities have the right to search their employees arose in a 1985 Iowa case in which employees were forced to sign a consent form as a condition of hire. The court disagreed with such a broad policy, ruling that the consent form did not constitute a blanket waiver of all Fourth Amendment rights.[70] Police officers may also be forced to appear in a lineup, a clear "seizure" of their person.

Self-Incrimination The Supreme Court has addressed questions concerning the Fifth Amendment as it applies to police officers who are under investigation. In *Garrity v. New Jersey*,[71] a police officer was ordered by the attorney general to answer questions or be discharged. The officer testified that information obtained as a result of his answers was later used to convict him of criminal charges. The Supreme Court held that the information obtained from the officer could not be used against him at his criminal trial because the Fifth Amendment forbids the use of coerced confessions. However, it is proper to fire a police officer who refuses to answer questions that are related directly to the performance of his or her duties, provided that the officer has been informed that any answers may not be used later in a criminal proceeding.[72]

Religious Practices Police work requires that personnel be available and on duty twenty-four hours a day, seven days a week. Although it is not always convenient or pleasant, shift configurations require that many officers work weekends, nights, and holidays. It is generally assumed that an officer who takes such a position agrees to work such hours and abide by other such conditions; it is usually the personnel with the least seniority on the job who must work the most undesirable shifts. However, there are occasions when the requirements of the job interfere with an officer's ability to attend religious services or observe religious holidays. The carrying of firearms may even conflict with an officer's beliefs. In these situations, the employee may be forced to choose between his or her job and religion.

Title VII of the Civil Rights Act of 1964 prohibits religious discrimination in employment. It requires reasonable accommodation of religious beliefs but not to the extent that the employee has complete freedom of religious expression.[73]

Sexual Misconduct To be blunt, there is ample opportunity for police officers to become involved in adulterous or extramarital affairs. Few other occupations or professions offer the opportunities for sexual misconduct that police work does. Police officers frequently work alone, usually without direct supervision, in activities that involve frequent contact with citizens, usually in relative isolation. The problem seems to be pervasive in police departments of all sizes. Unfortunately, it is also an area of police behavior that is not easily quantified or understood.[74]

Allen D. Sapp suggested several possible categories of sexually motivated behaviors by police officers (again, the extent to which each occurs is unknown):[75]

- **Sexually motivated nonsexual contacts.** Officers initiate contacts with female citizens, without probable cause or any legal basis, for the purpose of obtaining names and addresses for possible later contact.
- **Voyeuristic contacts.** Officers seek opportunities to view unsuspecting women partially clad or nude, such as in parked cars on "lovers' lanes."
- **Contacts with crime victims.** A wide variety of behavior can occur, including unnecessary callbacks to homes of female victims, bodily contact with accident victims, and sexual harassment by officers.
- **Contacts with offenders.** Officers may also harass female offenders by conducting body searches and pat downs or frisks.
- **Sexual shakedowns.** Officers may demand sexual services from prostitutes or other citizens.
- **Citizen-initiated sexual contacts.** "Police groupies"—often young women who are sexually attracted to the uniform, weapons, or power of the police officer—may seek to participate in sexual activities with officers. This category may also include offers of sexual favors in return for preferential treatment or calls to officers from lonely or mentally disturbed women seeking officers' attention.
- **Sex crimes by officers.** Officers may sexually assault jail inmates and citizens.

  —*Several possible Categories of Sexually Motivated Behaviors by Police Officers by Allen D. Sapp from CRIME AND JUSTICE IN AMERICA: PRESENT REALITIES AND FUTURE PROSPECTS, edited by Paul F. Cromwell and Roger G. Dunham. Published by Pearson Education, © 1997.*

In a related vein, several federal courts have recently considered whether police agencies have a legitimate interest in the sexual activities of their officers when such activities affect job performance. In one such case, the court held that the dismissal of a married police officer for living with another man's wife was a violation of the officer's privacy and associational rights.[76]

Other courts, however, have found that off-duty sexual activity can affect job performance. When a married city police officer was found to be having consensual sexual relations with unmarried women other than his wife, the department contended that the officer's conduct—which became public—severely damaged public confidence in the department. A Utah court held that adultery was not a fundamental right and refused to strike down a statute criminalizing adultery.[77] In a Texas case, when a male officer's extramarital affair led to his being passed over for promotion, the city civil service commission, the Texas Supreme Court, and the U.S. Supreme Court upheld the denial; they concurred with the city police chief's argument that such a promotion would adversely affect the efficiency and morale of the department and would be disruptive.[78]

Residency Requirements Many government agencies specify that all or certain members in their employ must live within the geographic limits of their jurisdiction— that is, employees must reside within the county or city of employment. Such residency requirements have been justified on the grounds that officers should become familiar with and be visible in the jurisdiction of employment or that they should reside where they are paid by the taxpayers to work.[79] Perhaps the strongest rationale given by employing agencies is that criminal justice employees must live near their work so they can respond quickly in the event of an emergency.

Moonlighting The term *moonlight* means to hold a second job in addition to one's normal full-time occupation. The courts have traditionally supported the limitations police agencies have placed on the amount and kind of outside work their employees can perform.[80] For example, police restrictions on moonlighting range from a complete ban on outside employment to permission to engage in certain forms of work, such as investigations, private security, and criminal justice education. The rationale for agency limitations is that "outside employment seriously interferes with keeping the [police and fire] departments fit and ready for action at all times."[81]

Misuse of Firearms As noted above, the use of firearms by police, whether justified or not, can have drastic consequences on both the officer(s) involved and the community. Police agencies typically attempt to restrain the use of firearms through written policies and frequent training of a "shoot/don't shoot" nature. Still, a broad range of potential and actual problems remains with respect to the use and possible misuse of firearms. Police agencies generally have policies regulating the use of handguns and other firearms by their officers, both on and off duty. The courts have held that such regulations need only be reasonable and that the burden rests with the disciplined police officer to show that the regulation was arbitrary and unreasonable.[82]

Police firearms regulations may address several basic topics: shooting in defense of life, shooting to stop fleeing felons, identifying juveniles, shooting at or from vehicles, firing warning shots, shooting animals, carrying secondary weapons, carrying weapons off duty, and registering weapons.[83] Next we briefly discuss each of these topics.

Following the 1985 *Tennessee v. Garner* decision (discussed previously), firearms policies are likely to be written from the "defense of life" perspective, which permits shooting only to defeat an imminent threat to an officer's life or to another person's life (as opposed to previous policies, which included and allowed for the killing of fleeing felons).[84] Regarding juveniles, agencies generally do not instruct their officers to make a distinction between adults and juveniles when using deadly force, based on the pragmatic view that an armed juvenile can kill as well as an adult and that it is often impossible to tell if an offender is a juvenile or an adult.[85]

Shooting at or from moving vehicles has been severely limited in recent years. Some of the reasons include difficulty in hitting the target, ricochets striking innocent bystanders, difficulty in penetrating the automobile body and tires, and injuries and damages that might result should the vehicle go out of control.[86] A general consensus among police administrators is that warning shots should be prohibited as they might strike an innocent person. From a safety standpoint, "what goes up must come down," so firing a warning shot into the ground or into a tree, if allowed at all, is restricted to only a few kinds of situations.

Police agencies generally allow their officers to kill animals in self-defense, either for prevention of substantial harm to others or for relief from suffering when the animal is injured so badly that humaneness requires its killing.[87] Secondary, or backup, weapons are generally permitted so that officers who are disarmed during a confrontation have a second weapon and so that they can less conspicuously be prepared to protect themselves during routine citizen stops. A concern is that backup weapons may be used as "throwaways" in the event that an officer shoots an unarmed suspect, but the practice is generally accepted as long as the weapons are registered.[88] Similarly, carrying weapons off duty has also been controversial; however, given that while in their jurisdictions they are viewed as being on duty twenty-four hours a day, officers are generally allowed to carry such weapons, provided the weapons are registered and officers qualify on the pistol range regularly with them.[89]

Most agencies require their officers to use only department-approved weapons on and off duty and may require that the weapons be inspected, fired, and certified by the department's armorer. In addition, some agencies require that the firearms be registered by make, model, serial number, and even ballistics sample.[90]

Courts and juries are increasingly becoming harsher in dealing with police officers who misuse their firearms. The current tendency is to investigate police shootings to determine whether the officer acted negligently or whether the employing agency was negligent in training and supervising the officer.

Alcohol and Drug Abuse

Alcoholism and drug abuse problems are much more acute when they involve police employees. It is obvious, given the law of most jurisdictions and the nature of their work, that police officers must not be walking time bombs; they must be able to perform their work with a clear head that is unbefuddled by alcohol or drugs.[91] Police departments typically specify in their policy manual that no alcoholic beverages may be consumed within a specified period prior to reporting for duty. Such regulations have uniformly been upheld as rational because of the hazards of police work.

Enforcing such regulations occasionally means that police employees are ordered to submit to drug or alcohol tests. In 1989, the U.S. Supreme Court issued a major decision on drug testing: *National Treasury Employees Union v. Von Raab*,[92] which dealt with drug-testing plans for U.S. customs workers. This decision addressed all three of the most controversial drug-testing issues: whether testing should be permitted when there is no indication of a drug problem in the workplace, whether the testing methods are reliable, and whether a positive test proves there was on-the-job impairment.[93]

The Supreme Court held that although only a few customs employees tested positive, drug use is such a serious problem that the program was warranted. Second, the Court found nothing wrong with the testing protocol. In addition, while tests may punish and stigmatize a worker for extracurricular drug usage that may have no effect on his or her on-the-job performance, the Court indicated that this dilemma is still no impediment to testing.

▶ "*Brady*" Material

Consider the following scenario: At the end of his duty shift, Officer Jones acknowledges a dispatch to assist an animal control unit that is struggling to pick up a large, vicious dog. Because he has social plans after work and believes the incident to be minor in nature, Jones opts instead to drive to the police station and leave for home. The animal control officer, thus acting alone, incurs a number of severe dog bites, $10,000 in medical costs (she has medical insurance), the loss of two week's work, and potential long-term injuries. As a result, Jones is contacted by his supervisor to justify his lack of response; he explains that he was enroute to the call, but was diverted by seeing what he felt was a robbery in progress that needed "checking out" (no robberies being reported). Largely owing to the animal control officer's injuries, the matter is referred to the department's Internal Affairs (IA) office for investigation. Upon being questioned, Jones initially lied to IA investigators, but when presented with evidence that he never reported a potential robbery, Jones finally admits to IA that he thought the dog call was a minor problem and opted to ignore it. He is given two weeks' leave without pay, and placed on a performance review for six months.

To Jones, this matter may appear to be over with, a lesson learned for the future. However, it is doubtful that Jones could have ever conceived of its ramifications or what lie ahead for his career. Jones lied to his supervisor and the IA investigators. Police officers, by virtue of their position, are—first and foremost—required to tell the truth; to do any less can be career-ending. An officer with credibility issues is unable to make cases because he or she can no longer testify effectively in court from that point forward. His or her department is required to advise the prosecutor's office of this issue—and the prosecutor is required to disclose it to the defense—in every criminal case in which Jones will testify during the remainder of his career. Furthermore, Jones may well have to endure the following type of cross examination and/or closing argument by the defense attorney:

> Ladies and gentlemen of the jury, as you consider the testimony of Officer Jones, whom the prosecution has called as its witness, it is my duty to inform you that you are being asked to believe the testimony of an officer who will lie in his reports.

To further sully Jones' reputation, the prosecutor's office may also inform the chief of police or sheriff that they will not take any future cases in which Jones was a witness.[94]

Questions for you to consider:

1. What *internal* (department-level, per agency policies and procedures) punishment, if any, would you deem appropriate for Jones in this incident?

2. (Looking ahead at information presented in Chapter 9, on civil liability) Assume the animal control officer files a civil suit against the city and Jones for his negligence, seeking (1) compensatory damages (medical costs, pain and suffering, loss of wages, etc.) and (2) punitive damages (money due to Jones' acting in a wanton, malicious, vindictive, or oppressive manner). How much is the animal control officer due?

Such is the current status of policing, a result of *Brady v. Maryland* (1963),[95] with one large Western police agency recently discovering more than 135 of its officers having potential Brady problems in a disciplinary case.[96] Brady was convicted of first-degree murder and sentenced to death. He testified at trial about his participation in the crime, but also stated that his companion, Boblit, was the actual murderer. Before trial, Brady's attorney had requested to see Boblit's statements. The government provided some of his statements, but did not turn over those in which Boblit actually admitted to the murder. Brady was convicted, and later his attorney, then knowing of Boblit's statement admitting guilt, filed an appeal. The U.S. Supreme Court stated that Brady was entitled to obtain and use Boblit's statement, and that the government's failure to provide the statement amounted to a denial of his right to due process.

Brady thus established that in a criminal case the accused has a right to any exculpatory evidence (sometimes termed "Brady material"—that is, any evidence in the government's possession that is favorable to the accused and is material to either guilt or punishment). Prosecutors must therefore disclose to the defense all exculpatory evidence.[97]

Today many police agencies take the "Brady officer" matter quite seriously, training officers about its existence, sanctions, and ramifications. They are generating policies and procedures that address this issue, explaining that the agency may be placed in a position where the officer's termination is the only appropriate outcome.

Finally, agencies are encouraged to review all officers' personnel files to determine if any of them has a disciplinary history that would seriously impeach his or her credibility as a witness. Any such information should also be made available to the prosecutor before such officers are allowed to testify in a criminal prosecution.[98]

▶ Social Networking: Issues and Policy Guidance

With Facebook membership reaching one billion in late 2012,[99] it is probably no surprise to anyone that there have been related issues and problems in policing. As examples:

- A deputy in Georgia was fired hours after he posted an entry on Facebook supporting a candidate for sheriff who was running against his boss, the current sheriff.[100]

- An Indiana state trooper faced an internal investigation for posting what were termed "compromising" photographs and statements on the Internet and bragging about his lewd activities and heavy drinking, and activities at work (which included threatening people who resisted arrest).[101]

- A female officer in Massachusetts was investigated for uploading a crime scene photograph of a deceased male on her Facebook page.[102]

Social networking sites are providing benefits to police who are engaged in community policing, problem solving, and investigative activities (see Chapters 4 and 5). But the above examples show unequivocally that the sites can pose serious problems and challenges as well. Police officers today must assume that, in our connected world, anything they put in a report, letter, memo, email, blog, online post, or any other medium will be open for the whole world to see. Not only do such online postings make headlines, reflect poorly on the agency, and cost people their jobs, but they also affect agency morale and credibility but even court cases (such postings can be subpoenaed and used to discredit and impeach an officers' testimony).[103]

These kinds of problems are thus compelling police administrators to consider such questions as the following: what conduct should be allowed—and prohibited—by our agency? How can we ensure our officers are not posting sensitive, disturbing, and confidential information and photographs? How do we prevent their engaging in posting materials during on-duty time?

Several police organizations have addressed these questions and proactively provided clear guidance to their officers by developing a policy that leaves no doubt as to what is expected of them, both on and off duty, while also being cognizant of their First Amendment rights. Such policies typically prohibit employees from posting any digital material that:

- expresses the opinions of the police organization.

- refers to the person posting the material as being a member of the police organization.

- is unprofessional, unbecoming, or illegal, such as lewd sexual conduct, or refers to excessive alcohol consumption, or similar behaviors.

- could have an adverse effect on agency morale, discipline, operation of the agency, safety of staff, or perception of the public.

- contains any recording or image obtained during the course of one's official duties (i.e., enforcement activities, tactical situations).[104]

Such policies do not bar their employees from using social networking sites; nor do they require officers to provide their agencies with department access to their personal sites. The policies do, however, remind employees that their online behavior directly bears on their organization's integrity and function as well as its successfully ensuring public safety.

The International Association of Chiefs of Police (IACP) has developed a model policy on social networking (see http://www.theiacp.org/portals/0/pdfs/socialmediapolicy.pdf), and the IACP's Center for Social Media offers police executives a tremendous resource with fact sheets, and case studies.[105] These are extremely valuable resources for police leadership to use as they attempt to understand and confront the new and powerful instruments of communication that now exist.

▶ Disciplinary Policies and Practices

Maintenance of Public Trust

Clearly, the public's trust and respect are precious commodities, quickly lost through improper behavior by police employees and the improper handling of an allegation of misconduct. Serving communities with professionalism and integrity should be the goal of every police agency and its employees in order to ensure that trust and respect are maintained. The public expects that police agencies will make every effort to identify and correct problems and respond to citizens' complaints in a judicious, consistent, fair, and equitable manner.

Employee misconduct and violations of departmental policy are the two principal areas in which discipline is applied.[106] Employee misconduct includes acts that harm the public, such as corruption, harassment, brutality, and violations of civil rights. Violations of policy may involve a broad range of issues, from substance abuse and insubordination to tardiness or minor violations of dress.

Due Process Requirements

There are well-established minimum due process requirements for discharging public employees:

- They must be afforded a public hearing.

They must be present during the presentation of evidence against them and have an opportunity to cross-examine their superiors.

They must have an opportunity to present their own witnesses and other evidence concerning their side of the controversy.

- They may be represented by counsel if they so choose.

- They must have an impartial referee or hearing officer presiding.

There must be an eventual decision for or against them based on the weight of the evidence introduced during the hearing.

Such protections apply to any disciplinary action that can significantly affect a police employee's reputation or future chances for special assignment or promotion.[107]

At times, police administrators determine that an employee must be disciplined or terminated. Grounds for discipline or discharge can vary widely from agency to agency, and the agency's formal policies and procedures should specify what constitutes proper and improper behavior.

Complaints

Origins A personnel complaint is an allegation of misconduct or illegal behavior against an employee by anyone inside or outside the organization. Internal complaints—those made from within the organization—may involve supervisors who observe officer misconduct, officers who complain about supervisors, civilian personnel who complain about officers, and so on. External complaints originate from outside the organization and usually involve the public.

Every complaint, regardless of the source, must be accepted and investigated in accordance with established policies and procedures. Anonymous complaints are the most difficult to investigate because there is no opportunity to obtain further information or to question the complainant about the allegation. Such complaints can have a negative impact on employee morale, as officers may view them as unjust and frivolous.

Types and Causes Complaints may be handled informally or formally, depending on the seriousness of the allegation and the preference of the complainant. A formal complaint occurs when a written and signed or tape-recorded statement of the allegation is made and the complainant asks to be informed of the investigation's disposition. Figure 8-3 ■ provides an example of a complaint form used to initiate a personnel investigation.

****

Control Number _____

Date & Time Reported   Location of Interview   Interview

_____   _____   _____ Verbal _____ Written _____ Taped

Type of complaint: _____ Force _____ Procedural _____ Conduct
      _____ Other (Specify)

Source of complaint: _____ In Person _____ Mail _____ Telephone
      _____ Other (Specify)

Complaint originally   _____ Supervisor _____ On Duty Watch Commander _____ Chief
received by: _____ IAU _____ Other (Specify)

Notifications made: _____ Division Commander _____ Chief of Police
received by: _____ On-Call Command Personnel
      _____ Watch Commander _____ Other (Sepcify)

Copy of formal personnel complaint given to complainant? _____ Yes _____ No

****

Complainant's Name: Address:

_____   _____ Zip _____

Residence Phone: Business Phone:

DOB: Race: Sex: Occupation:

****

Location of Occurrence: Date & Time of Occurrence:

Member(s) Involved: Member(s) Involved:
(1)_____   (2) _____
(3)_____   (4) _____

Witness(es) Involved: Witness(es) Involved:
(1)_____   (2) _____
(3)_____   (4) _____

****

(1) _____ Complainant wishes to make a formal statement and has requested an investigation into the matter with a report back to him/her on the findings and actions.
(2) _____ Complainant wishes to advise the Police Department of a problem, understands that some type of action will be taken, but does not request a report back to him/her on the findings and actions.

****

CITIZEN ADVISEMENTS

(1)   If you have not yet provided the department with a signed written statement or a tape-recorded statement, one may be required in order to pursue the investigation of this matter.
(2)   The complainant(s) and/or witness(es) may be required to take a polygraph examination in order to determine the credibility concerning the allegations made.
(3)   Should the allegations prove to be false, the complainant(s) and/or witness(es) may be liable for criminal and/or civil prosecution.

_____   _____
Signature of Complainant   Date & Time

_____
Signature of Member Receiving Complaint

FIGURE 8-3   **Formal Complaint Form**
Kenneth Peak.

An informal complaint is an allegation of minor misconduct, made for informational purposes, that can usually be resolved without the need for more formal processes. The supervisor may simply discuss the incident with the employee and resolve it through informal counseling as long as more serious problems are not discovered and there is no history of similar complaints.

The majority of complaints against officers fall under the general categories of verbal abuse, discourtesy, harassment, improper attitude, and ethnic slurs.[108] It is clear that the verbal behavior of officers generates a significant number of complaints.

In addition, minority citizens and those with less power and fewer resources are more likely to file complaints of misconduct and to allege more serious forms of misconduct than citizens with greater power and more resources.

Receipt and Referral Administrators must have a process for receiving complaints that is clearly delineated by departmental policy and procedures. Generally, a complaint is made at a police facility and is referred to a senior officer in charge to determine what its seriousness is and whether immediate intervention is needed.

In most cases, the senior officer will determine the nature of the complaint and will identify the employee involved; he or she then refers the matter to the employee's supervisor to conduct an initial investigation. The supervisor completes the investigation, recommends any discipline, and sends the matter to the internal affairs unit (IAU) and the agency head to finalize the disciplinary process. This method of review ensures that consistent and fair standards of discipline are applied.

Investigative Process Generally, the employee's supervisor will conduct a preliminary inquiry of the complaint, commonly known as fact-finding. If it is determined that further investigation is necessary, the supervisor may question employees and witnesses, obtain written statements from those who were involved in the incident, and gather any necessary evidence, including photographs. Care must be exercised that the accused employee's rights are not violated. The initial investigation is sent to the appropriate division commander and forwarded to the IAU for review.

Determination and Disposition Once an investigation has been completed, the supervisor or IAU officer must make a determination about the culpability of the accused employee and report that determination to the administrator. The following categories of dispositions are commonly used:

- **Unfounded.** The alleged act did not occur.
- **Exonerated.** The act occurred but was lawful, proper, justified, or in accordance with departmental policies, procedures, rules, and regulations.
- **Not sustained.** There was insufficient evidence to prove or disprove the allegation made.
- **Misconduct not based on the complaint.** Sustainable misconduct was determined but was not a part of the original complaint. For example, a supervisor investigating an allegation of excessive force may find that the force used was within departmental policy but that the officer made an unlawful arrest.
- **Closed.** An investigation may be halted if the complainant fails to cooperate or if it is determined that the action does not fall within the administrative jurisdiction of the police agency.
- **Sustained.** The act did occur and was a violation of departmental rules and procedures. Sustained allegations include misconduct that falls within the broad outlines of the original allegation.

Once a determination of culpability has been made, the complainant should be notified of the department's findings. Details of the investigation or recommended punishment should not be included in the correspondence. As shown in Figure 8-4 ■, the complainant will normally receive only information concerning the outcome of the complaint.

Appeal of Disciplinary Measures If an officer disagrees with a supervisor's recommendation for discipline, the first step of an appeal may involve a hearing before the division commander, who usually holds the rank of captain or deputy chief. The accused employee may be allowed labor representation or an attorney to assist in asking questions of the investigating supervisor, clarifying issues, and presenting new or mitigating evidence. If the employee is still not satisfied, an appeal hearing before the chief executive, which is usually the final step in appeals within the agency, is granted. The chief or sheriff communicates a decision to the employee in writing. Depending on labor agreements and civil service rules and regulations, some agencies extend their appeals of discipline beyond the department. For example, employees may bring their issue before the civil service commission or city or county manager for a final review. Employees may also have the right to an independent arbiter's review.

Level of Discipline and Type of Sanction

When an investigation against an employee is sustained, the level of discipline and type of sanction must be decided. Management must be very careful when recommending and

---

POLICE DEPARTMENT
3300 Main Street
Downtown Plaza
Anywhere, U.S.A. 99999

June 20, 2007

Mr. John Doe
2200 Main Avenue
Anywhere, U.S.A.

Re: Internal Affairs #000666-98
       Case Closure

Dear Mr. Doe,

Our investigation into your allegations against Officer Smith has been completed. It has been determined that your complaint is SUSTAINED, and the appropriate disciplinary action has been taken.

Our department appreciates your bringing this matter to our attention. It is our position that when a problem is identified, it should be corrected as soon as possible. It is our goal to be responsive to the concerns expressed by citizens so as to provide more efficient and effective services.

Your information regarding this incident was helpful and of value in our efforts to attain that goal. Should you have any further questions about this matter, please contact Sergeant Jane Alexander, Internal Affairs, at 555-9999.

Sincerely,

I.M. Boss
Lieutenant
Internal Affairs Unit

FIGURE 8-4   Citizen's Notification of Discipline Letter
Kenneth Peak.

imposing discipline because of its impact on the overall morale of the agency's employees. If employees view the recommended discipline as too lenient, it may send the wrong message that the misconduct was insignificant; on the other hand, discipline that is viewed as too harsh may have a demoralizing effect on the officer involved and on other agency employees and may result in allegations that the leadership is unfair.

Listed here, in order of severity from least to most, are the seven types of sanctions that police agencies commonly use:[109]

1. **Counseling.** This counseling is usually a conversation between the supervisor and the employee about a specific aspect of the employee's performance or conduct. It is warranted when an employee has committed a relatively minor infraction or when the nature of the offense is such that oral counseling is all that is required. No documentation or report is placed in the employee's personnel file.

2. **Documented oral counseling.** Usually the first step in a progressive disciplinary process, documented oral counseling is intended to address relatively minor infractions. It takes place when the employee has had no previous reprimands or more severe disciplinary action of the same or similar nature.

3. **Letters of reprimand.** These letters are formal written notices regarding significant misconduct, more serious performance violations, or repeated offenses. It is usually the second step in the disciplinary process and is intended to provide the employee and the agency with a written record of the violation of behavior. It identifies what specific corrective action must be taken to avoid subsequent and more serious disciplinary action.

4. **Suspension.** The step of suspension is a severe disciplinary action that results in an employee being relieved of duty, often without pay. It is usually administered when an employee commits a serious violation of established rules or after written reprimands have been given and no change in behavior or performance has resulted.

5. **Demotion.** In a demotion, an employee is placed in a position of lower responsibility and pay. It is normally used when an otherwise good employee is unable to meet the standards required for the higher position or when the employee has committed a serious act requiring that he or she be removed from a position of management or supervision.

6. **Termination.** The most severe disciplinary action that can be taken is termination. It usually occurs when previous serious discipline has been imposed and there has been inadequate or no improvement in behavior or performance, but it may also occur when an employee commits an offense so serious that continued employment would be inappropriate.

7. **Transfer.** Many agencies use the disciplinary transfer to deal with problem officers. Officers can be transferred to a different location or assignment, and this action is often seen as an effective disciplinary tool.

—From POLICE SUPERVISION AND MANAGEMENT: In an Era of Community Policing, 3rd ed. by Kenneth J. Peak, Larry K. Gaines, Ronald W. Glensor, 2010. Printed and Electronically reproduced by permission of Pearson Education, Inc. Upper Saddle River, NJ.

Summary

This chapter has examined ethics as well as several topics that might well be termed the *underbelly* of the field: police use of force, police brutality, bias-based policing, police corruption, and the code of silence. We also considered a number of areas in which federal courts have placed limitations on police behaviors by virtue of the unique role of the police and the necessary higher standard of behavior: freedom of speech, search and seizure, self-incrimination, freedom of religion, sexual misconduct, residency requirements, moonlighting, misuse of firearms, and alcohol and drug abuse. The chapter also examined disciplinary policies and practices.

Clearly, it would be a much better profession—and society—if these unsavory topics could be omitted, but ours is not a perfect world, nor are the police perfect. This chapter underscored the serious nature of police misbehavior and society's attempts to hold officers accountable. Police behavior is being closely scrutinized today, and the police are held to a much higher standard of behavior than ever before, especially since incidents involving violations of public trust often harm innocent or undeserving people and receive national attention.

The next chapter, on civil liability, examines the high legal cost of the kinds of failures in policing that were discussed in this chapter. Although liability is a form of accountability, it stands alone because it is a reflection of the standard of accountability owed to the public and a means of measuring public dissatisfaction with improper police performance.

Key Terms

absolute ethics
accountability
bias-based policing
Brady material
code of silence
complaint
"Dirty Harry problem"
Domestic Violence Offender
    Gun Ban
double effect

dynamic resistance response
    model (DRRM)
ethics
Garrity v. New Jersey
Lautenberg Amendment
limitations on officers'
    constitutional rights
model of circumstantial
    corruptibility
noble cause corruption

police brutality
police corruption
police firearms regulations
police shootings
police use of force
relative ethics
slippery slope perspective
social networking
Tennessee v. Garner
use-of-force continuums

Review Questions

1. What is meant by police ethics, and what are some of the unique ethical problems that community policing can pose?

2. What is meant by noble cause corruption and the "Dirty Harry problem," and how do they each relate to Packer's crime-control and due process models of law enforcement?

3. What is meant by use of force continuum, how can it be problematic, and what is the general structure and function of the dynamic resistance response model (DRRM)?

4. What are the types of police brutality and use-of-force incidents?

5. What did the Supreme Court relatively recently decide with regard to police use of deadly force in stopping speeding vehicles in high-speed pursuits?

6. What are some organizations recommending be done in terms of tracking and dealing with incidents of police use of force?

7. What is meant by bias-based policing, what do recent studies say about police stops and searches of

minorities, and what is the result in relations between minorities and police?

8. What are the purposes of the Lautenberg Amendment and the Domestic Violence Offender Gun Ban, and how can they affect the police?

9. How and why does police corruption occur, and what factors within both the community and policing seem to foster and maintain it?

10. Which constitutional limitations have federal courts placed on officers' rights and personal behavior?

11. How did *Brady v. Maryland* affect policing in general and, potentially, individual officers' careers?

12. What are some examples of actual and potential misuse of social networking sites by police officers, and how are such problems being addressed by agency policies?

13. What is the general process that police agencies use to deal with citizen complaints?

14. What are some factors used to determine the level of discipline and type of sanction for officers who are to be disciplined?

Learn by Doing

1. As the head of your professional standards unit in your sheriff's office, you are assigned to address the following letter, received by your sheriff. What will be your actions in response to the matter?

   Last night my seventeen-year-old daughter, Jamie, was stopped by one of your deputies for speeding. I do not know the deputy's name, but his badge number is 336. I don't know what kind of people you have in your agency, but this one got very sarcastic with my daughter and said some things that weren't very nice. He even told her that if she would go out with him on a date, he wouldn't give her a ticket. When she told him that she would not go out with him, he gave her a ticket.

   I know a dispatcher there, and if I don't hear that this deputy is disciplined for his behavior, I will send a letter to the County Commission as well.

   Signed: A Concerned, Irate Taxpayer

2. Officer King has been a member of your agency for six years and one of your subordinates for two years. Her productivity, both in terms of quality and quantity, as well as her interactions with the public, have generally been at or above standard, and her performance evaluations have been satisfactory or above. In recent weeks, however, all aspects of her work have shown a significant decline; furthermore, there have been complaints from other officers about her not responding to calls for service in a timely manner (resulting in their having to cover for her) as well as inadequate investigations of traffic collisions and other matters. In addition, King's reports are often late or submitted only after you have sent her several reminders. Today a citizen contacts you to complain about her rudeness while taking a burglary report yesterday. You decide it is time to call her into your office to discuss these matters. How will you address this situation?

3. Your police agency has a policy concerning the solicitation and acceptance of gifts; essentially, it states that no personnel shall accept any gift, gratuity, loan, fee, or thing of value which might tend to improperly influence their actions in any manner. Your subordinate, Officer Fisher, recently addressed a problem at a municipal country club that involved a lot of after-hours juvenile loitering and vandalism problems in the club's parking lot. The club manager, Mr. Chang, wishes to show appreciation to the officer and has made arrangements for the officer and family to receive a 15 percent discount when eating or golfing there. Fisher approaches you for guidance: accept the offer or not? What would be your response and accompanying explanation?

Notes

1. See Carl Klockars, "The Dirty Harry Problem," in *Police and Society: Touchstone Readings*, 2nd ed., ed. Victor E. Kappeler (Prospect Heights, IL: Waveland Press, 1999), pp. 329–346.

2. Herbert Packer, *The Limits of the Criminal Sanction* (Stanford, CA: Stanford University Press, 1968).

3. Jocelyn M. Pollack, "Ethics and Law Enforcement," in *Critical Issues in Policing: Contemporary Readings*, 5th ed., eds. Roger G. Dunham and Geoffrey P. Alpert (Long Grove, IL: Waveland Press, 2005), pp. 280–303.

4. Brian Withrow and Jeffrey D. Dailey, "When Strings Are Attached: Understanding the Role of Gratuities in Police Corruptibility," in *Contemporary Policing Controversies, Challenges, and Solutions: An Anthology*, eds. Quint Thurman and Jihong Zhao (Los Angeles: Roxbury, 2004), pp. 319–326.

5. "No Free (or Discounted) Lunch for Bradenton Cops," *Law Enforcement News*, October 15, 2000, p. 6.

6. Kenneth J. Peak, B. Grant Stitt, and Ronald W. Glensor, "Ethics in Community Policing and Problem Solving," *Police Quarterly* 1 (1998): 30–31.

7. L. Morris, *Incredible New York* (New York: Bonanza, 1951).

8. James A. Inciardi, *Criminal Justice*, 5th ed. (Orlando, FL: Harcourt Brace, 1996).

9. Egon Bittner, "The Functions of the Police in Modern Society," in *Policing: A View from the Street*, eds. Peter K. Manning and John Van Maanen (Santa Monica, CA: Goodyear, 1978), pp. 32–50.

10. Ibid., p. 36.

11. Adapted from Lorie A. Fridell, "Improving Use-of-Force Policy: Policy Enforcement and Training," in *Chief Concerns: Exploring the Challenges of Police Use of Force*, eds. Joshua A. Ederheimer and Lorie A. Fridell (Washington, DC: Police Executive Research Form, April 2005), p. 48.

12. Charles Joyner and Chad Basile, "The Dynamic Resistance Response Model," *FBI Law Enforcement Bulletin*, September 2007, p. 17.

13. Bob Christi, "Police Officer in Ariz. Shooting has Shot 6 Others," *Associated Press*, February 16, 2012, http://www.standard.net/stories/2012/02/16/police-officer-ariz-shooting-has-shot-6-others (accessed October 26, 2012).

14. Christine Hoag, "Forceful Arrests Could Harm LAPD Goodwill Efforts," *Associated Press*, September 2, 2012, http://news.yahoo.com/forceful-arrests-could-harm-lapd-goodwill-efforts-035215501.html (accessed October 26, 2012).

15. Cain Burdeau, "5 Ex-Cops Sentenced in Katrina Killings Case," *Associated Press*, April 4, 2012, http://usatoday30.usatoday.com/news/nation/story/2012-04-04/katrina-case-ex-cops-sentenced/54002168/1 (accessed October 16, 2013).

16. "Justice Dept.: Seattle Police Used Excessive Force," *Associated Press*, http://www.cbsnews.com/8301-501363_162-57344323/justice-dept.-seattle-police-used-excessive-force/ (accessed October 26, 2012).

17. "L.A. Police Corruption Case Continues to Grow," *Washington Post*, February 13, 2000, p. 1A.

18. Human Rights Watch, *Shielded from Justice: Police Brutality and Accountability in the United States* (New York: Author, 1998).

19. Ibid.

20. The Cap Times (Madison, Wis.), Feb. 19, 2013, http://host.madison.com/news/local/writers/pat_schneider/no-comprehensive-reliable-database-of-police-shootings-exists/article_9a0e40a2-7ac5-11e2-9f0d-001a4bcf887a.html

21. Las Vegas Review-Journal, Nov. 28, 2011, http://www.reviewjournal.com/news/deadly-force/142-dead-and-rising/national-data-shootings-police-not-collected

22. Jim Fisher, True Crime, Dec. 25, 2013, http://jimfishertruecrime.blogspot.com/2012/01/police-involved-shootings-2011-annual.html

23. Kit R. Roane, "Policing the Police Is a Dicey Business: But the Feds Have a Plan to Root Out Racial Bias," *U.S. News and World Report*, April 30, 2001, p. 28.

24. James J. Fyfe, Jack R. Greene, William F. Walsh, et al., *Police Administration*, 5th ed. (New York: McGraw-Hill, 1997), pp. 197–198.

25. *Tennessee v. Garner*, 471 U.S. 1, 105 S.Ct. 1694, 85 L.Ed.2d 1 (1985).

26. George F. Cole and Christopher E. Smith, *The American System of Criminal Justice*, 12th ed. (Florence, KY: Cengage, 2010), p. 228.

27. A. C. Germann, Frank D. Day, and Robert R. J. Gallati, *Introduction to Law Enforcement and Criminal Justice* (Springfield, IL: Charles C Thomas, 1976), p. 225.

28. Albert J. Reiss Jr., "Police Brutality: Answers to Key Questions," *Transaction* (July–August 1968): 10–19.

29. Ibid.

30. Germann, Day, and Gallati, *Introduction to Law Enforcement and Criminal Justice*, p. 225.

31. *Scott v. Harris*, 550 U.S. 372 (2007), at p. 13.

32. Office of Justice Programs, Department of Justice, "Police Stop White, Black, and Hispanic Drivers at Similar Rates According to Department of Justice Report," www.ojp.usdoj.gov/newsroom/pressreleases/2007/BJS07020.htm (accessed March 5, 2013).

33. Quoted in Randall Kennedy, "Suspect Policy," *New Republic*, September 13, 1999, pp. 30–35.

34. Donald Black, *Manners and Customs of the Police* (New York: Academic Press, 1980), p. 117; Richard J. Lundman, "Domestic Police-Citizen Encounters," *Journal of Police Science and Administration* 2 (March 1974): 25.

35. Jerome Skolnick, *The Police and the Urban Ghetto* (Chicago: American Bar Foundation, 1968).

36. Samuel Walker, *The Police in America: An Introduction* (New York: McGraw-Hill, 1983), p. 234.

37. Ibid., p. 235.

38. Robert Friedrich, "Racial Prejudice and Police Treatment of Blacks," in *Evaluating Alternative Law Enforcement Policies*, ed. Ralph Baker and Fred A. Meyers (Lexington, MA: Lexington Books, 1979), pp. 160–161.

39. Douglas A. Smith and Christy A. Visher, "Street-Level Justice: Situational Determinants of Police Arrest Decisions," *Social Problems* 29 (December 1981): 167–187.

40. Albert J. Reiss, *The Police and the Public* (New Haven, CT: Yale University Press, 1971), p. 151.

41. "Beat Your Spouse, Lose Your Job," *Law Enforcement News*, December 31, 1997, p. 9.

42. Ibid.

43. Adapted from Jerry Hoover, "Brady Bill Unfair in Broad Approach to Police Officers," *Reno Gazette Journal*, September 25, 1998, p. 11A.

44. "Denver Cop's Case Galvanizes Opponents of Lautenberg Gun Ban," *Law Enforcement News*, February 14, 1999, p. 1.

45. Lawrence W. Sherman, ed., *Police Corruption: A Sociological Perspective* (Garden City, NY: Anchor, 1974), p. 1.

46. See Peter Maas, *Serpico* (New York: Viking, 1973); *The Knapp Commission Report on Police Corruption* (New York: George Braziller, 1973).

47. Herman Goldstein, *Policing a Free Society* (Cambridge, MA: Ballinger, 1977), p. 188.
48. Ibid.
49. Gordon Witkin, "When the Bad Guys Are Cops," *Newsweek*, September 11, 1995, p. 20.
50. Ibid., p. 22.
51. Lawrence W. Sherman, "Becoming Bent," in *Moral Issues in Police Work*, eds. F. A. Elliston and M. Feldberg (Totowa, NJ: Rowan and Allanheld, 1985), pp. 253–265.
52. Christian P. Potholm and Richard E. Morgan, eds., *Focus on Police: Police in American Society* (New York: Schenkman, 1976), p. 140.
53. Ellwyn R. Stoddard, "Blue Coat Crime," in *Thinking about Police: Contemporary Readings*, ed. Carl B. Klockars (New York: McGraw-Hill, 1983), pp. 338–350.
54. Walker, *The Police in America*, p. 175.
55. David Burnham, "Police Aides Told to Rid Commands of All Dishonesty," *New York Times*, October 29, 1970, p. 1.
56. Withrow and Dailey, "When Strings Are Attached," pp. 319–326.
57. David L. Carter, "Drug Use and Drug-Related Corruption of Police Officers," in *Policing Perspectives: An Anthology*, ed. Larry K. Gaines and Gary W. Cordner (Los Angeles: Roxbury, 1999), pp. 311–323.
58. Patrick V. Murphy and Thomas Plate, *Commissioner: A View from the Top of American Law Enforcement* (New York: Simon and Schuster, 1977), p. 226.
59. William A. Westley, *Violence and the Police* (Cambridge, MA: MIT Press, 1970), pp. 113–114.
60. Thomas E. Wren, "Whistle-Blowing and Loyalty to One's Friends," in *Police Ethics: Hard Choices in Law Enforcement*, ed. William C. Heffernan (New York: John Jay Press, 1985), pp. 25–43.
61. David Weisburd and Rosanne Greenspan, *Police Attitudes Toward Abuse of Authority: Findings from a National Study* (Washington, DC: U.S. Department of Justice, National Institute of Justice, Research in Brief, May 2000), p. 5.
62. See 18 U.S.C., Section 1955.
63. See, for example, *United States v. Hyde*, 448 F.2d 815 (5th Cir. 1971), cert. den., 404 U.S. 1058 (1972); *United States v. Addonizia*, 451 F.2d 49 (3d Cir.), cert. den., 405 U.S. 936 (1972); and *United States v. Kenney*, 462 F.2d 1205 (3d Cir.), as amended, 462 F.2d 1230 (3d Cir.), cert. den., 409 U.S. 914 (1972).
64. Herbert Beigel, "The Investigation and Prosecution of Police Corruption," in *Focus on Police: Police in American Society*, eds. Christian P. Potholm and Richard E. Morgan (New York: Schenkman, 1976), pp. 139–166.
65. "Artificial Intelligence Tackles a Very Real Problem—Police Misconduct Control," *Law Enforcement News*, September 30, 1994, p. 1.
66. *Pickering v. Board of Education*, 391 U.S. 563 (1968), p. 568.
67. *Muller v. Conlisk*, 429 F.2d 901 (7th Cir. 1970).
68. *Kelley v. Johnston*, 425 U.S. 238 (1976).
69. See *People v. Tidwell*, 266 N.E.2d 787 (Ill. 1971).
70. *McDonell v. Hunter*, 611 F. Supp. 1122 (SD Iowa 1985), aff'd. as mod., 809 F.2d 1302 (8th Cir. 1987).
71. *Garrity v. New Jersey*, 385 U.S. 483 (1967).
72. See *Gabrilowitz v. Newman*, 582 F.2d 100 (1st Cir. 1978).
73. *United States v. City of Albuquerque*, 12 EPD 11, 244 (10th Cir.); also see *Trans World Airlines v. Hardison*, 97 S.Ct. 2264 (1977).
74. Allen D. Sapp, "Police Officer Sexual Misconduct: A Field Research Study," in *Crime and Justice in America: Present Realities and Future Prospects*, eds. Paul F. Cromwell and Roger G. Dunham (Upper Saddle River, NJ: Prentice Hall, 1997), pp. 139–151.
75. Ibid.
76. See *Briggs v. North Muskegon Police Department*, 563 F. Supp. 585 (W.D. Mich. 1983), aff'd. 746 F.2d 1475 (6th Cir. 1984).
77. *Oliverson v. West Valley City*, 875 F. Supp. 1465 (D. Utah 1995).
78. *Henery v. City of Sherman*, 928 S.W.2d 464 (Sup. Ct. Texas), cert. den., 17 S.Ct. 1098 (1997).
79. See, for example, *Cox v. McNamara*, 493 P.2d 54 (Ore. 1972); *Brenckle v. Township of Shaler*, 281 A.2d 920 (Pa. 1972); *Flood v. Kennedy*, 239 N.Y.S.2d 665 (1963); and *Hopwood v. City of Paducah*, 424 S.W.2d 134 (Ky. 1968).
80. Richard N. Williams, *Legal Aspects of Discipline by Police Administrators*, Traffic Institute Publication 2705 (Evanston, IL: Northwestern University, 1975), p. 4.
81. See *Lally v. Department of Police*, 306 So.2d 65 (La. 1974).
82. Charles R. Swanson, Leonard Territo, and Robert W. Taylor, *Police Administration*, 5th ed. (Upper Saddle River, NJ: Prentice Hall, 2005), p. 586.
83. Ibid.
84. Ibid.
85. Kenneth James Matulia, *A Balance of Forces: Model Deadly Force Policy and Procedure* (Alexandria, VA: International Association of Chiefs of Police, 1985), pp. 23–24.
86. Catherine H. Milton, Jeanne Wahl Halleck, James Larndew, et al., *Police Use of Deadly Force* (Washington, DC: Police Foundation, 1977), p. 52.

87. Matulia, *A Balance of Forces*, p. 52.
88. Ibid., p. 177.
89. Ibid.
90. Ibid., p. 78.
91. See *Krolick v. Lowery*, 302 N.Y.S.2d 109 (1969), p. 115; and *Hester v. Milledgeville*, 598 F. Supp. 1456, 1457 (M.D. Ga. 1984).
92. *National Treasury Employees Union v. Von Raab*, 489 U.S. 656 (1989).
93. Robert J. Alberts and Harvey W. Rubin, "Court's Rulings on Testing Crack Down on Drug Abuse," *Risk Management* 38 (March 1991): 36–41.
94. Jaxon Van Derbeken, "Police with Problems are a Problem for the D.A.," *San Francisco Chronicle*, May 16, 2010, http://www.sfgate.com/cgi-bin/article.cgi?f=/c/a/2010/05/15/MNKC1DB57E.DTL (accessed November 14, 2013).
95. *Brady v. Maryland*, 373 U.S. 83 (1963).
96. See Richard Lisko, "Agency Policies Imperative to Disclose *Brady v. Maryland* Material to Prosecutors," *The Police Chief* 77(3) (March 2011), http://www.policechiefmagazine.org/magazine/index.cfm?fuseaction=display_arch&article_id=2329&issue_id=32011 (accessed November 14, 2013).
97. Lisko, "Agency Policies Imperative to Disclose *Brady v. Maryland* Material to Prosecutors;" also see Val Van Brocklin, "*Brady v. Md* Can Get You Fired," Officer.com (August 16, 2010), http://www.officer.com/article/10232477/brady-v-md-can-get-you-fired (accessed November 14, 2013).
98. Jack Ryan, "Police Officers may be Liable for Failure to Disclose Exculpatory Information under the Brady Rule Managing Risks," Policelink (n.d.), http://policelink.monster.com/training/articles/2123-police-officers-may-be-liable-for-failure-todisclose-exculpatory-information-under-the-brady-rule-managing-risks- (accessed November 14, 2013).
99. Aaron Smith, Laurie Segall and Stacy Cowley "Facebook Reaches One Billion Users," *CNNMoney*, October 4, 2012, http://money.cnn.com/2012/10/04/technology/facebook-billion-users/index.html (accessed October 27, 2012).
100. Policeone.com, "Deputy Fired After Facebook Post Supporting Candidate Running Against Sheriff," July 18, 2012, http://www.policeone.com/chiefs-sheriffs/articles/5839590-Deputy-fired-after-Facebook-post-supporting-candidate-running-against-sheriff/ (accessed October 27, 2012).
101. Eric P. Daigle, "Social Networking Policies: Just Another Policy?" *The Police Chief*, May 2010, http://www.policechiefmagazine.org/magazine/index.cfm?fuseaction=display_arch&article_id=2091&issue_id=52010 (accessed October 27, 2012).
102. Ibid., p. 2.
103. Michael Masterson and William Bones, "Protecting Officers Online, Off Duty: How Police Chiefs Can Safeguard Officers with Policy Guidance on Social Networking," *The Police Chief*, October 2012, http://www.policechiefmagazine.org/magazine/index.cfm?fuseaction=display&article_id=2426&issue_id=72011 (accessed October 27, 2012).
104. Ibid.
105. See Center for Social Media, http://www.iacpsocialmedia.org/.
106. V. McLaughlin and R. Bing, "Law Enforcement Personnel Selection," *Journal of Police Science and Administration* 15 (1987): 271–276.
107. Ibid.
108. Allen E. Wagner and Scott H. Decker, "Evaluating Citizen Complaints Against the Police," in *Critical Issues in Policing: Contemporary Readings*, 3rd ed., eds. Roger G. Dunham and Geoffrey P. Alpert (Prospect Heights, IL: Waveland Press, 1989), pp. 302–318.
109. Kenneth J. Peak, Larry K. Gaines, and Ronald W. Glensor, *Police Supervision and Management: In an Era of Community Policing*, 3rd ed. (Upper Saddle River, NJ: Prentice Hall, 2010), p. 260.

9 Civil Liability
Failing the Public Trust

LEARNING OBJECTIVES

As a result of reading this chapter, the student will be able to:

1. *Explain the incidence, expense, and benefits of lawsuits against the police*

2. *Describe the legal definition of a frivolous lawsuit*

3. *Discuss several fundamental terms and concepts relating to liability*

4. *Explain the meaning and uses of U.S. Code Title 42, Section 1983*

5. *Describe types of actual and potential (e.g., use of less-lethal weapons, special relationships) police actions that can lead to Section 1983 claims*

6. *Explain how police officers might be held criminally liable for their misconduct*

7 *Describe how police facilities may bring about police liability*

8 *Discuss the areas of police liability in vehicle pursuits, and what kinds of related elements are contained in a pursuit policy*

9 *Describe how police supervisors may be held liable for their inaction or their officers' misconduct*

10 *Delineate some of the liability issues related to computer evidence*

11 *Explain the doctrine of qualified immunity as it relates to police officers*

• •

Introduction

No one knows for certain how much money is paid by local police agencies each year to settle lawsuits, although one source estimates the total tab is $2 billion.[1] What is known, however, is that some cities have seen lawsuits against their city's police force soar: New York's price tag is $150 million a year and growing, due to a record 2,004 cases in 2011 to 2012—a 28 percent increase over the previous fiscal year.[2] Put another way, from 2002 to 2011 the Los Angeles Police Department paid nearly 1,000 settlements and judgments to resolve lawsuits (for as much as $12,860,000 in one case), the majority of which were for civil rights cases, but about 400 of them—involving about $24 million in settlements—stemmed from traffic crashes involving police officers.[3]

A police sergeant once commented to the author, "The decision-making process is not directed by the question 'Is it right or wrong?' but rather 'How much will it cost us if we're sued?'" While that may be a bit overstated or in jest, the specter of lawsuits certainly looms large over police officers, their supervisors, and their unit of government; however, we will see that civil liability has arguably provided a number of benefits to policing. This chapter focuses on this omnipresent facet of contemporary police work, discussing civil liability from a number of perspectives, and it cannot be overstated how important it is for students of criminal justice and in-service police personnel to know and understand this indispensable aspect of policing. To assist in this endeavor, dozens of examples and actual court cases are provided.

Policing is a challenging occupation. The police must enforce the laws, perform welfare tasks, protect the innocent, and attempt to prevent crime. They see people at their worst and participate each year in tens of thousands of arrests, searches, seizures, major incidents (such as hostage situations), and high-speed pursuits. They make split-second decisions, and they function as custodians of offenders in local jails. Perhaps no other occupation, with the exception of medicine, is as vulnerable to legal attack for the actions of its practitioners. Some observers even believe that community-oriented policing and problem solving (COPPS, discussed in Chapter 6) could lead to an increase in civil liability filings because of the greater degree of involvement of police in the lives of citizens.[4]

The chapter begins by discussing the incidence, expense, benefits, and sometimes frivolous nature of lawsuits against the police. Next, with an eye toward helping readers develop a better comprehension of liability, is an overview of a number of basic terms and concepts. We then analyze the legal history of the major tool that is used against the police by citizens who believe the police have violated their constitutional rights: U.S. Code Title 42, Section 1983; included here is a comprehensive discussion, with many examples, of the kinds of police actions that foster liability suits. The liability of supervisors who fail to control their personnel is then reviewed. Finally, other areas of potential liability are examined: duty of care, failure to protect, vehicle pursuits (including a sample agency policy addressing them), and computer evidence. The chapter concludes with a summary, key terms, review questions, and several scenarios and activities that provide opportunities to learn by doing.

• •

▶ Incidence, Expense, Benefits, and Nature of Lawsuits

The police are not irrationally paranoid when it comes to their being sued—to some officers, it probably seems to be a contemporary rite of passage or a fact of life that one "isn't really a cop" unless he or she has been sued. There is some basis in fact for this belief: Between 1980 and 2005, federal court decisions involving lawsuits against the police nearly tripled, and according to one study, the police are currently faced with more than thirty thousand civil actions annually.[5] Yet this number might seem small given that the police have millions of interactions with citizens each day.

One contemporary indication of police concern about liability is that many police officers are now purchasing their own miniature video cameras that can be concealed in writing pens. They believe the devices, which cost as little as $50 each, can help to guard against false allegations of misconduct or abuse. Agency administrators, however, are thus scrambling to develop policies for the use of such recording devices, in order to address potential privacy concerns.[6]

The cost of civil suits against police can be quite high. For example, according to one study, from 1990 to 1999 Los Angeles paid in excess of $67.8 million in judgments and settlements in eighty lawsuits targeting police use of excessive force as well as police officers involved in sexual assault, sexual abuse, molestation, and domestic violence. This amount does not include the millions of dollars the city spent defending itself against any civil suits or lawsuits stemming from the Rampart Division scandal of the late 1990s,[7] during which a former Los Angeles Police Department (LAPD) officer testified that he and other officers routinely lied in court, stole and resold drugs, beat handcuffed suspects in the police station, and killed unarmed people and then planted guns and drugs on them; dozens of lawsuits were filed.[8]

Facing potential judgments amounting to millions of dollars, municipalities are forced to secure liability insurance to protect against civil litigation—insurance that is very expensive. But such expenditures are necessary: The cost of an average jury award of liability against a municipality is reported to be about $2 million.[9] In an attempt to prevent such large judgments, many cities and their insurers have made it a routine practice to settle many claims of police misconduct out of court as opposed to having a jury give the plaintiff(s) a large award. A U.S. Justice Department study of Los Angeles County (not including the LAPD) found that county officials, in settling sixty-one police misconduct cases, paid plaintiffs between $20,000 and $1.75 million per case.[10]

Such litigation, although costly in terms of both money and police morale, does have beneficial effects. Proponents of civil liabilities argue that these lawsuits keep the police accountable, give real meaning to citizens' rights, foster better police training, and can force police agencies to correct any deficiencies and review all policies, practices, and customs.[11]

It would be understandable if some officers felt that most (if not all) such lawsuits are frivolous in nature, merely an attempt to gain revenue from the officer(s) or jurisdiction defending against the suit; however, their perception of what constitutes a frivolous lawsuit may be very different from the legal definition: that it lacks an arguable basis in law or fact.[12] In fact, frivolous lawsuits against the police are quite rare. A study of published cases by the federal district courts indicates that less than 0.5 percent of those cases resulted in a judicial sanction against plaintiffs for cases that clearly lacked merit.[13]

▶ Basic Terms and Concepts

Laws are enacted in three ways: by legislation, by regulation, and by court decision. Statutes and ordinances are laws passed by legislative bodies, such as the U.S. Congress, state legislatures, county commissions, and city councils. These bodies sometimes create a general outline of the laws they enact, leaving to a particular governmental agency the authority to fill in the details of the law through rules and regulations. During the past two decades, administrative rules and regulations constituted one of the fastest-growing bodies of new law.

When the solution to a legal dispute cannot be found in the existing body of law—statutes, rules, or regulations—judges must rely on prior decisions that their own or other courts have made on similar issues. These judicial decisions are known as stare decisis (meaning "let the decision stand"), and the judges who follow them are said to be relying on precedent. Of course, prior court decisions can be overruled or modified by a higher court or by the passage of new legislation. Furthermore, judges sometimes create their own tests to fairly resolve an issue. Statutes, judicial decisions, and tests may differ greatly from state to state; therefore, it is important for lawyers and criminal justice practitioners to read and understand the laws as they apply in their own jurisdictions.

It is also important to have a basic understanding of tort liability, a tort being an injury inflicted on one person by another. Three categories of torts generally cover most of the lawsuits filed against criminal justice practitioners: negligence, intentional torts, and constitutional torts.

Negligence arises when a police officer's conduct creates a danger to others; in other words, the officer did not conduct his or her affairs in a manner so as to avoid subjecting others to a risk of harm. The officer will be held liable for the injuries caused to others through his or her negligent acts. The law recognizes various levels or degrees of negligence: simple, gross, and willful or criminal negligence. Simple negligence involves a reasonable act performed by a reasonable officer in the scope of employment but performed without due care; the result is usually a charge of mental pain and anguish, for which an employer or an insurance company will pay damages. Gross negligence involves an unreasonable act for which damages for mental pain and anguish will be paid by either the employer (if the officer's acts were within the scope of employment) or the officer. Willful or criminal negligence involves an intentional act rather than negligence; the plaintiff will receive actual damages, mental pain and anguish damages, and punitive damages. These damages will be paid by the officer involved; neither the employer nor the insurance company will be compelled to pay.[14]

Intentional torts occur when an officer engages in a voluntary act that had a substantial likelihood of resulting in injury to another; examples are assault and battery, false arrest and imprisonment, malicious prosecution, and abuse of process. Constitutional torts involve police officers' duty to recognize and uphold the constitutional rights, privileges, and immunities of others, and violations of these guarantees may subject officers to civil suits, most frequently brought in federal court under 42 U.S. Code Section 1983[15] (discussed later).

Allegations of false arrest, false imprisonment, criminal behavior (such as assault and battery), and police misconduct (invasion of privacy, negligence, defamation, and malicious prosecution) are examples of torts that are commonly brought against police officers.[16] False arrest is the arrest of a person without probable cause—an arrest that is made even though an ordinarily prudent person would not have concluded that a crime had been committed or that the person arrested had committed it. False imprisonment is the intentional illegal detention and confinement of a person in a specified area, including but not limited to jail. Most false arrest suits result in a false imprisonment charge as well, but a false imprisonment charge sometimes can follow a valid arrest. For example, the police might fail to release an arrested person after a proper bail or bond has been posted, they might delay the arraignment of an arrested person unreasonably, or they might fail to release a prisoner after they no longer have authority to hold him or her. "Brutality" is not a legal tort action per se; rather, charges must be made as a civil assault and/or battery.

A single act may also be a crime as well as a tort. For example, if Officer Smith, in an unprovoked attack, injures Citizen Jones, the state will attempt to punish Smith in a criminal action by sending him to prison or fining him or both. The state would have the burden of proof at a criminal trial, having to prove Smith guilty "beyond a reasonable doubt." Furthermore, Jones may sue Smith for money damages in a civil action for the personal injury he suffered. Jones would argue that Smith failed to carry out his duty to act reasonably and prudently and that this failure resulted in Jones's injury. This legal wrong, of course, is a tort; Jones would have the burden of proving Smith's acts were tortious by a "preponderance of the evidence"—a lower standard and thus easier to satisfy in civil court.

The U.S. system of government has both federal and state courts. Federal courts are intended to have somewhat limited jurisdiction and tend not to hear cases involving private (as opposed to public) controversies unless federal law is involved or both parties agree to have their dispute settled there. Thus most tort suits are filed in state courts. There are two means by which a federal court may acquire jurisdiction of police misconduct suits. The first is the predominant source of our later discussions, referred to as a "1983 suit," a name that is derived from the fact that the suits are brought under the provisions of Title 42, Section 1983, of the U.S. Code. The significant part of this statute and its legislative history follow.

The second means by which a federal court may assume jurisdiction over a police misconduct suit is to allege what some legal commentators call a *Bivens* tort, a name that derives from a 1971 case, *Bivens v. Six Unknown Named Agents of the Federal Bureau of Narcotics*.[17] The U.S. Supreme Court held that a civil suit based directly on the Fourth Amendment could be filed. In *Bivens*, federal narcotics agents conducted an illegal search, arrest, and interrogation, but a suit by the plaintiffs could not be filed under Section 1983 because that section covers only police agents acting under state law. Civil suits to recover damages for violations of constitutional rights by federal officers have thus become known as *Bivens* suits.

A suit may also be filed against an employer under the doctrine of respondeat superior, an old legal maxim meaning "let the master answer"; this doctrine is also termed vicarious liability. In sum, an employer is liable in certain instances for the wrongful acts of its employee. It is generally inapplicable if a jury determines that the employee's negligent or malicious acts were outside the legitimate scope of the employer's authority. Although U.S. courts have expanded the extent to which employers can be sued for the torts of their employees, the courts are still reluctant to extend this doctrine to police supervisors (sergeants and lieutenants) and administrators. The courts realize that, first of all, police supervisors have little discretion in hiring decisions. Second, the duties of police officers are largely established by the governmental authority that hired them rather than by their supervisors. However, if a supervisor has abused his or her authority, was present when the misconduct occurred and did nothing to stop it, or otherwise participated in the misconduct, he or she can be held liable for the tortious behavior of his or her officers.[18] (This issue is discussed at greater length later in this chapter.)

Another issue that involves the question of who may be sued involves immunity and whether police departments and the employing governmental unit can be sued for damages caused by police misconduct. Under common law, the government could not be sued because the king could do no wrong. This doctrine, known as sovereign immunity, was also adopted in 1795 in the Eleventh Amendment to the U.S. Constitution, which states, "The judicial power of the United States shall not be construed to extend to any suit in law or equity, commenced or prosecuted against one of the United States by citizens of another state, or by citizens or subjects of any foreign state." This amendment therefore bars suits against states, state agencies, and instrumentalities in federal courts; the Supreme Court has also said it bars suits by citizens of the same state.[19]

Municipal governments, however, do not enjoy the same protection since they are creations of state laws and, as such, are not truly "sovereigns." Thus, they do not enjoy blanket immunity and are only cloaked with immunity to the extent that the state sees fit to do so.[20]

▶ Section 1983 Litigation

History and Escalation

Prior to discussing specific kinds and examples of civil litigation against the police and their supervisors, it is prudent to first gain an understanding of a major legal instrument that is used by citizens against the police when they feel the police have acted in such a manner as to violate their individual rights: U.S. Code Title 42, Section 1983.

In the years following the Civil War, Congress, in reaction to the states' inability to control the Ku Klux Klan's lawlessness, enacted the Ku Klux Klan Act of 1871. This was later codified as Title 42, Section 1983, of the U.S. Code. Its statutory language is as follows:

> Every person who, under color of any statute, ordinance, regulation, custom, or usage of any State or Territory, subjects, or causes to be subjected, any citizen of the United States or any other person within the jurisdiction thereof to the deprivation of any rights, privileges, or immunities secured by the Constitution and laws, shall be liable to the party injured in an action at law, suit in equity, or other proper proceeding for redress.
> —Statute, Title 42, Section 1983 of the U.S. Code., U.S Department of Justice.

This legislation was intended to provide civil rights protection to all persons protected under the act when a defendant acted "under color of any statute" (misused power of office). It was also meant to provide an avenue to the federal courts for relief of alleged civil rights violations.

The original intent of the law did not include police misconduct litigation. In fact, the law was virtually ignored for ninety years until the U.S. Supreme Court's 1961 decision in *Monroe v. Pape*,[21] where thirteen members of the Chicago Police Department broke into a home without a warrant, forced the family out of bed at gunpoint, made them stand naked while the officers ransacked the house, and subjected the family to verbal and physical abuse. The plaintiffs (Monroe and his family) claimed that the officers acted "under color of law" as set forth in Section 1983, thus violating their constitutional rights. The U.S. Supreme Court agreed, holding the officers liable.

There was a virtual boom of Section 1983 suits from 1967 through 1976.[22] Several factors contributed to this surge in Section 1983 actions. First, some lawyers believe that clients receive more competent judges and juries in the federal forum than in state courts because federal judges, who are appointed for life, may be less concerned about the political ramifications of their decisions than locally elected judges often are. Also, federal prosecutors may be more aggressive in arguing to jurors from a multicounty area, whereas local prosecutors must argue to jurors who elected them and who may know the defendant-officer. Furthermore, federal rules of pleading and evidence are uniform, federal procedures of discovery are more liberal, and lawyers have easier access to published case law in assisting them to prepare a federal suit.[23] Just as important, Congress passed Section 1988 of the Civil Rights Act in 1976, which allows attorney's fees to the prevailing party over and above the award for compensatory and punitive damages, meaning that a plaintiff's verdict in a police shooting case can be quite profitable.

Also, in 1978, in *Monell v. Department of Social Services*,[24] the Supreme Court held that Congress, in the 1871 act, *did* intend that municipalities and other local governments be included as "persons" to whom Section 1983 applies. Local governing bodies and corporate "persons," therefore, can be sued for damages under Section 1983 if such deprivation was the direct result of an official policy or custom of a local unit of government.

Defenses and immunities against Section 1983 suits exist, however. The states themselves, for example, are granted absolute immunity from Section 1983 suits,[25] as are judges, prosecutors, legislators, and federal officials. Federal officials usually act under color of federal law, as opposed to state law, as specified in the act.

Police Actions Leading to Section 1983 Liability

Following are some cases based on Section 1983 liability:

- In 1991, Los Angeles motorist Rodney King was beaten following a pursuit by police officers, an incident that was captured on an eighty-one-second videotape that captured the nation's attention. He was awarded $3.8 million.[26]

- In 1995, federal law enforcement officers at Ruby Ridge, Idaho, used deadly force to seize two citizens, resulting in the federal government's agreement to pay survivors almost $4 million because of unconstitutional use of deadly force. That same year, a federal jury awarded Ramona Africa, the sole survivor of a bombing of her residence by Philadelphia police, $1.5 million (the police had dropped explosives into the home of a radical group trying to make members leave their home). The bombing destroyed sixty-one other homes and killed eleven people, and the total cost to the city exceeded $59 million.[27]

- A jury acquitted four New York police officers of criminal charges in the shooting death of Amadou Diallo. The officers had mistaken Diallo's wallet for a gun and opened fire, discharging forty-one rounds and striking him nineteen times. His parents were awarded $3 million in a settlement with the city.[28]

The common thread in all these highly publicized cases (other than the fact that all involved an unconstitutional use of force by the police) was that they used U.S. Code Title 42, Section 1983. Exhibit 9-1 ▪ provides an example of a recent Section 1983 lawsuit—an outgrowth of the 2011 pepper spraying of Occupy protestors by campus police officers at the University of California at Davis.

As suggested, Section 1983 is an appropriate legal tool for citizens who believe they have been victims of police brutality. In *Jennings v. City of Detroit*,[29] a twenty-two-year-old single African-American man was permanently paralyzed following a beating at a police station; the jury award was $8 million (settled for $3.5 million). In *Gilliam v. Falbo*,[30] the U.S. District

---

EXHIBIT 9-1

AN EXAMPLE OF U.S. CODE TITLE 42, SECTION 1983

In November 2011, students non-violently demonstrating against a tuition hike were pepper-sprayed by a campus police officer, handcuffed and arrested. Some students were hospitalized due to the highly potent chemical, sprayed at close range. Defending his actions, the officer said the students had refused to leave and surrounded him.

However, a university task force report found the use of force was "unreasonable" and dismissed the officer's claim he was trapped. The students filed a lawsuit against the university alleging use of excessive force, and the university paid about $1 million to settle the suit. Each student involved was awarded $30,000. Later,

the officer was given more than $38,000 in workers' compensation for the psychological suffering he experienced in being blamed for the incident.

Sources: University of California to pay nearly $1 million in deal with 21 pepper-sprayed UC-Davis Occupy protesters NBC News, Sept. 26, 2012 http://usnews.nbcnews.com/_news/2012/09/26/14112860-university-of-california-to-pay-nearly-1-million-in-deal-with-21-pepper-sprayed-uc-davis-occupy-protesters?lite; UC Davis pepper-spray officer awarded $38,000 Joe Garofoli San Francisco Gate, Oct. 23, 2013 http://www.sfgate.com/politics/joegarofoli/article/UC-Davis-pepper-spray-officer-awarded-38-000-4920773.php; The Reynoso Task Force Report University of California at Davis, April 11, 2012 http://reynosoreport.ucdavis.edu/reynoso-report.pdf

Court for Ohio awarded $72,000 to a young man beaten by two officers, and in *Haygood v. City of Detroit*,[31] a thirty-five-year-old plaintiff was awarded $2.5 million in punitive damages and $500,000 in compensatory damages after being subjected to racial slurs, beaten, and chained to a bed for twelve hours (charges against the officers were never filed).

Even off-duty activities may get police officers into serious difficulty for acting "under color of law." Part-time work as security guards often opens the door to legal problems. In *Carmelo v. Miller*,[32] two off-duty officers were working security at a baseball game. They received information that someone was displaying a gun and stopped a man who fit the description. The officers searched, arrested, beat, and kicked the suspect and his companion. No gun was found in the area, and one of the beaten men required medical treatment. The officers were found liable. In *Stengel v. Belcher*,[33] an off-duty officer entered a bar carrying a .32-caliber handgun (which he was required to carry off duty at all times) and a can of Mace. An altercation broke out, and without identifying himself the officer got involved, killing two men and seriously wounding another. The plaintiffs recovered $800,000 in compensatory damages.

Clearly, the use of off-duty weapons and policies requiring that they be carried pose a risk of liability. In *Bonsignore v. New York*,[34] a mentally unstable twenty-three-year veteran police officer shot his wife five times and then killed himself, using a .32-caliber pistol that departmental policy required him to carry when off duty. Evidence produced at trial demonstrated that Officer Bonsignore's unsuitability for police duties was well known by the department—it had even provided him a limited-duty assignment as station house janitor—yet the police code of silence protected him. The jury awarded Mrs. Bonsignore nearly a half million dollars.

Suits involving wrongful death are also becoming more frequent, and the following cases illustrate how the law applies in this regard. In *Prior v. Woods*,[35] a twenty-four-year-old man was killed outside his home by police officers who mistook him for a burglar; the jury awarded his estate $5.75 million. In *Burkholder v. City of Los Angeles*,[36] a Los Angeles police officer killed a man in his early twenties who, while naked and under the influence of drugs, was climbing a light pole (the man had seized the officer's club but had not struck the officer). The jury awarded $450,000 in damages and $150,000 in attorney's fees to his survivors.

Generally, police officers are not liable for damages under Section 1983 for merely arresting someone, but that protective shroud vanishes if the plaintiff proves the officer was negligent or violated an established law or right (as in cases of false arrest). As an illustration, in *Murray v. City of Chicago*,[37] Murray's purse and checkbook were stolen; she reported the theft to the police. Later, some of the stolen checks were cashed (by another party) and Murray was arrested; she appeared in court and cleared up the matter, explaining that she had been the victim, and all charges were dropped. Several months later, she was arrested again at her home by Chicago officers who used an invalid arrest warrant that was related to the earlier mix-up. Murray was taken to the police station, strip-searched by male officers, and detained for six hours before being released. The federal court ruled that the officers acted in good faith but that if the policy or custom of the city was shown to have encouraged such unwarranted arrests, the city could be held liable.

Search and seizure, an especially complicated area of criminal procedure, is ripe for Section 1983 suits, primarily because of the ambiguous nature of the probable cause doctrine. In *Duncan v. Barnes*,[38] police officers obtained a warrant to search a suspect's home for heroin and executed the warrant in early morning hours. With guns drawn, officers entered two bedrooms, forcing the two females and one male inside to stand nude, spread-eagled against a wall, while their rooms were searched. Soon the officers realized that they had entered the wrong apartment, and they left the apartment in total disarray. The occupants, students at a court-reporting school, were so upset that they missed classes for two weeks; as a result, their certification and employment as court reporters were delayed. The court had little difficulty finding that the officers had acted in an unreasonable manner.

Negligence by police officers is another cause of action under Section 1983. Negligence can be found in the supervision and training of personnel, among other things. In *Sager v. City of Woodland Park*,[39] an officer accidentally killed a person when the shotgun he was pointing at the head of the prisoner discharged while the officer was attempting to handcuff the prisoner with his other hand. At trial, the officer stated that he had seen the technique in a police training film. The training officer, however, testified that the film was intended to show how *not* to handcuff a prisoner; unfortunately, none of the trainers had made that important distinction to the class, so the court ruled that improper training resulted in the prisoner's death. In *Popow v. City of Margate*,[40] an innocent bystander was killed on his front porch at night by a police officer engaged in foot pursuit, and the court held the city negligent because the officer had had no training on night firing, shooting at moving targets, or using firearms in a residential area.

The accompanying Career Profile addresses the very weighty matter of police civil liability.

(Courtesy Samuel G. Chapman.)

Career Profile

Name: Samuel G. Chapman

Degrees: Bachelor's and master's, criminology, University of California, Berkeley

What CJ-related jobs have you held?

Consultant on police functions and use of police dogs; professor emeritus, University of Oklahoma; Assistant Director, President's Commission on Law Enforcement and the Administration of Justice, Washington, D.C.; Chief, Multnomah County Sheriff's Office, Portland, Oregon; police officer, Berkeley, California

As a long-time police practitioner, university professor, and expert witness, what advice do you have concerning police liability?

Police departments must take civil rights litigation seriously. Actually, civil rights lawsuits are seen by many as an occupational hazard in policing.

When a lawsuit has been filed, the allegations should be evaluated by the government's attorneys. Fact-finding may disclose that the allegations appear to have little merit. It could be that the lawsuit is of dubious substance, really seeking what is called a "convenience settlement"—a defendant's paying the plaintiff a dollar amount less than what the defendant's costs would be to prepare for trial. But if after fact-finding it appears that the department and its officers are culpable, the defense team should start settlement negotiations early. The defense should make a meaningful offer, keeping it in the range of settlements for cases of a similar sort elsewhere.

At the same time, the defense (both the government and the officer) must commence their discovery, with the goal of minimizing loss should the case eventually go to trial. Settlements that occur just before trial are invariably costly. The defense team should also evaluate the courtroom record of the plaintiff's law firm and opposing attorneys, since some firms are more competent than others.

Fact-finding will often indicate that a case is realistically defensible. If so, the defense team may decide to reject a convenience settlement and prepare for trial. This will cause the plaintiffs to evaluate whether to expend resources and time in pursuing a case that they are not likely to win. When the defense decides to stand up and fight, it establishes the jurisdiction as a "hard target" and sends a message that lawsuits with little merit are going to be forcefully defended.

Whoever is named to defend officers and police agencies must be skilled in handling civil rights cases. It is a grave mistake for the government to take a "bargain basement" approach by assigning staff attorneys who have little or no experience working with these highly technical types of litigation.

The police can fight back by suing those who sue them, but this means hiring counsel, which is expensive. And even if the lawsuit is successful and brings a dollar judgment against the defendant, such a defendant is usually poor and thus unable to meet any financial judgment levied against him or her.

The government's best defense against an adverse judgment in a civil rights lawsuit is to thoroughly train and regularly retrain its police personnel, and to supervise them well. Also, the police department's rules, regulations, policies, and procedures must be kept current. Then, if officers perform as trained and properly under departmental guidelines, a persuasive defense can be mounted against any allegations of misconduct.

Criminal Prosecutions for Police Misconduct

Whereas Section 1983 is a civil statute, Title 18, Section 242, of the U.S. Code makes it a *criminal* offense for any person acting willfully "under color of law," statute, regulation, or custom to deprive any person of the rights and privileges guaranteed under the Constitution and laws of the United States. This law, like Section 1983, dates from the post–Civil War era and applies to all people regardless of race, color, or national origin. Section 242 applies not only to police officers but also to other public officials; prosecutions of judges, bail-bond agents, public defenders, and even prosecutors are possible under the statute.

An example of the use of Section 242 is the murder of a drug courier by two U.S. customs agents while the agents were assigned to the San Juan International Airport. The courier flew to Puerto Rico to deposit approximately $700,000 in cash and checks into his employer's account. He was last seen being interviewed by the two customs agents in the airport; ten days later, his body was discovered in a Puerto Rico rain forest. An investigation revealed that the agents had lured the victim away from the airport and had murdered him for his money, later disposing of the body. They were convicted under Section 242 and related federal statutes, and each agent was sentenced to a prison term of 120 years.[41]

▶ Liability of Police Supervisors

Negligent supervision and direction of officers involve a breach of a duty to provide effective systems for the evaluation, control, and monitoring of police employees' performance. This breach of duty may come in the form of failure to provide written and verbal directives, to develop adequate policies and guidelines, or to articulate clearly to employees how duties are to be performed. It may also involve a supervisor's direction to an employee to engage in an illegal activity or the supervisor's approval of an illegal activity.[42] In such cases, Section 1983 allows for a finding of personal liability on the part of police supervisory personnel.

McClelland v. Facteau,[43] a Section 1983 suit against a state police agency chief as well as a local police chief, was such a case. McClelland was stopped by Officer Facteau (a state employee) for speeding. He was taken to the city jail; there he was not allowed to make any phone calls, he was questioned but not advised of his rights, and he was beaten and injured by Facteau in the presence of two city police officers. McClelland sued, claiming that the two police chiefs were directly responsible for his treatment and injuries due to their failure to properly train and supervise their subordinates. Evidence was produced of prior misbehavior by Facteau. The court ruled that the chiefs could be held liable if they knew of prior misbehavior yet did nothing about it.

Another related case was that of *Brandon v. Allen*.[44] In this case, two teenagers who were parked in a "lovers' lane" were approached by an off-duty police officer, Allen, who showed his police identification and demanded that the boy exit the car. Allen struck the boy with his fist and stabbed him with a knife; then he attempted to break into the car where the girl was seated. The boy was able to reenter the car and manage an escape. As the two teenagers sped off, Allen fired a shot at them with his revolver, and the shattered windshield glass severely injured the youths to the point that they required plastic surgery. Allen was convicted of criminal charges, and the police chief was also sued under Section 1983. The plaintiffs charged that the chief and others knew of Allen's reputation for being mentally unstable (none of the other police officers wanted to ride in a patrol car with him). At least two formal charges of misconduct had been filed previously, yet the chief had failed to take any remedial action or even to review the disciplinary records of officers. The court called this behavior "unjustified inaction," held the police department liable, and allowed the plaintiffs' damages. The U.S. Supreme Court upheld this judgment.[45]

Police supervisors have also been found liable for injuries arising out of an official policy or custom of their department. Injuries resulting from a chief's verbal or written support of heavy-handed behavior resulting in excessive force by officers have resulted in such liability.[46]

Today's police supervisors are definitely in a "need to know" position where the law is concerned. They are caught in the middle: Not only can they be sued for improper hiring, training, and supervision of their officers, but other civil rights laws can be used by officers who believe they were improperly disciplined or terminated. Indeed, Section 1983 can also be used by unsuccessful job applicants if they can show that the administrator's tests were not job related, included inherent bias, or were not properly administered or graded. The same holds true if it can be shown that proper testing methods were not used in the promotion or the discipline or firing of personnel. Police supervisors have lost in suits in which they disciplined male and female officers who were having a private relationship,[47] in which they disciplined African-American officers who removed the U.S. flag from their uniforms to protest perceived discriminatory acts by the city,[48] and in which they disciplined officers for "improper" political party membership.[49]

▶ Other Areas of Potential Liability

Next we look at several interrelated areas in which liability on the part of the police may be found if they fail to perform their duties properly, perform them in a negligent manner, make poor decisions, or abuse their authority.

Less-Lethal Tools and Technologies

Chapter 14 discusses many of the technologies or "tools for the tasks" that are now employed in policing, and certainly many if not most such tools—from batons to chemicals to dogs—can result in injury and possibly even death if employed improperly. Therefore, the specter of liability is cast over all such tools, and the public is constantly vigilant concerning their use. As an example, in early 2012 Amnesty International—which estimates at least 500 people in the United States have died since 2001 after being shocked with electronic control devices (ECDs) either during their arrest or while in jail—called for national standards and tighter limits on police use of the weapons. Such standards, Amnesty argued, would effectively replace thousands of individual policies now followed by state and local agencies that currently permit a wide use of the weapons, often in situations that are believed to not warrant such a high level of force.[50] Thus far there have been lawsuits involving officer use of ECDs where: they were deployed accidentally (e.g., the officers believed they were deploying their ECDs but instead discharged their firearm), subjects were standing in an elevated position and fell, being seriously injured; and a subject was fleeing on foot and sustained serious injuries as a result of an uncontrolled fall on a hard surface. Questions have also been raised concerning whether or not the use of ECDs in certain situations was excessive.[51]

Duty of Care

While citizens often speak of the broad police duty to serve and protect their community, their lives, and their property, a legal duty is very specific and more limited. This doctrine of duty of care is derived from common law and holds that police have no duty to protect the general public from harm, absent a special kind of relationship (discussed later). The Supreme Court addressed this doctrine in 1856 in *South v. Maryland*,[52] a case in which a sheriff was sued for refusing to protect a citizen from injuries inflicted from a violent crowd. The court said that peace officers protect the general public, not specific individuals. Since *South*, the doctrine of duty of care has been adopted at the state and federal levels, with most courts ruling that the state is not required to provide police services.[53] This may come as a surprise to many people, but the legal view is that police can only act once a crime is or has already been committed and that they cannot be held liable for failure to arrive in time to save any particular individual from harm unless the victim has a special relationship with the police, such as a protected witness. There are neither sufficient resources nor enough police to act as personal bodyguards for every citizen, twenty-four hours a day. No duty of care exists unless it is established that the agency owed a special duty to the injured party.

Police legal duties can arise from many sources, including laws, customs, court decisions, and agency policies. As examples, a state statute prohibiting drunk driving might also order the police to arrest any persons operating motor vehicles while under the influence of intoxicants, and a police department policy in the same state may require officers who stop such suspected motor vehicle operators to perform field sobriety tests at the scene of the traffic stop.[54]

Special Relationships   Special relationships are those where the officer knows or has reason to know the likelihood of harm to someone if he or she fails to do his or her duty; they are thus defined by the circumstances surrounding an injury or damage. A special relationship can be based on the following three areas:

1. Whether the officer could have foreseen that he or she was expected to take action in a given situation to prevent injury is one consideration.[55] (e.g., a police officer failed to remove an intoxicated operator of a motor vehicle from a highway.)

2. Departmental policies or guidelines that prohibit a certain course of action are also examined.[56] (e.g., when a drunk driver killed another driver, the court noted that the police department had a standard operating procedure manual that mandated that an intoxicated individual who would likely do physical injury to himself or others "*will* be taken into protective custody.")

3. Spatial and temporal proximity of the defendant-officer's behavior to the injury damage is another factor.[57] (e.g., an individual was arrested for drunk driving, taken into custody, found to have a 0.166 blood alcohol level, and released three hours later, then had a fatal car accident.)

Proximate Cause   Related to the duty of care and liabilities of the police is the matter of proximate cause. Once a plaintiff has demonstrated the existence of a police duty of care and has shown the officer breached that duty, he or she must still prove that the officer's conduct was the proximate cause of the injury or damage. Proximate cause is established by asking "But for the officer's conduct, would the plaintiff have sustained the injury or damage?" If the answer to this question is no, then proximate cause is established, and the officer can be held liable for the damage or injury. This requirement of negligence limits liabilities, however, in situations where damage would have occurred regardless of the officer's behavior.[58] For example, an officer is involved in a high-speed chase, and the offending driver strikes an innocent third party. Generally, if the officer did not act in a negligent fashion and did not cause the injury, there would be no liability on the officer's part.[59]

Proximate cause may be found in such cases as when an officer leaves the scene of an accident aware of dangerous conditions (spilled oil, smoke, vehicle debris, stray animals) without proper warning to motorists.[60] In such a case, Louisiana state troopers responded to a one-car accident caused by an oil spill on a dangerous portion of the roadway. Initially, the troopers asked the state's department of transportation to cover the spill with sand and then ignited flares to warn oncoming motorists of the danger; the troopers then returned to other patrol duties. Soon the oil had absorbed the sand and the flares went out; then an unsuspecting motorcyclist slid on the oil, struck a tree, and died. The court held that the troopers breached their duty to provide warning to drivers of the danger and that this breach was the proximate cause of the motorcyclist's death.[61]

Persons in Custody Courts generally recognize that police officers have a duty of care to persons in their custody.[62] This means that police officers have a legal responsibility to take reasonable precautions to ensure the health and safety of persons in their custody, keeping detainees free from harm, rendering medical assistance when necessary, and treating detainees humanely.[63] Custody is not restricted to those persons who are incarcerated, however; a duty of care is owed by the police, for example, to persons in their physical custody outside a jail setting, such as when arresting or transporting prisoners and mental patients or when holding persons in booking or interrogation areas regardless of whether they have been formally charged with a crime.[64]

This general duty of care to persons in police custody seldom results in liability for self-inflicted injury or suicide because these acts are normally considered to result from the detainee's own intentional conduct rather than from some form of police negligence.[65] There are exceptions to this rule, however.[66] Most courts, for example, have held that if a prisoner's suicide is "reasonably foreseeable," the jailer owes the prisoner a duty of care to help prevent that suicide. As the court stated in *Joseph v. State of Alaska* (where an intoxicated jail inmate hanged himself with a nylon cord not taken from his sweatpants at booking, and the jail's video camera lens had been obscured):

> While a prisoner's mental illness, intoxication, or other impairment may be the reasons why the jailer knows or should know that the prisoner is suicidal, other signs—such as declared intent to commit suicide—are also sufficient.[67]

If the suicidal tendencies of an inmate are known, the duty of care required of the custodian is elevated.[68] In such special cases, officers must ensure that measures are taken to prevent self-inflicted harm; included here are detainees who suffer from a disturbed state of mind and those who are impaired by drugs or alcohol. Duty of care to an impaired individual may include removing shoes, belts, clothing, and other articles from the detainee.[69]

Safe Facilities Another area of police liability, one that involves both persons in custody and proximate cause, is the need to provide safe facilities. Courts have even considered the design of detention facilities as a source of negligence, such as in a Detroit case where the construction of a jail's holding cell did not allow officers to observe detainees' movements: The construction of the cell doors hampered detainee supervision, there were no electronic monitoring devices for observing detainees, and there was an absence of detoxification cells required under state department of corrections rules. Therefore, following a suicide in this facility, the court concluded that these conditions constituted building defects and were the proximate cause of the decedent's death.[70]

The need to provide a secure environment for detainees extends beyond the confines of the detention center. In a Delaware case, a constable used his private vehicle to transport mental patients and did not handcuff patients while in transport. One patient, who had declared his intention to kill himself, unfastened his seat belt, jumped out of the vehicle while it was in motion, and died. The court found that because the constable knew his vehicle was inadequate for such transports and did not restrain the patient or heed his intention to commit suicide, his misconduct constituted wantonness.[71]

Failure to Protect

A failure to protect may occur if a police officer neglects to protect a person from a known and foreseeable danger, a claim that most often involves battered women. However, other circumstances can create a duty to protect people from crime. Informants, witnesses, and other people dependent on the police can be a source of police liability if the police fail to take reasonable action to prevent victimization—officers' conduct cannot place a person in peril or demonstrate deliberate indifference for his or her safety.

For example, one morning Juan Penilla was on the porch of his home and became seriously ill. His neighbors called 911, and two police officers arrived first. They found him to be in grave need of medical care, cancelled the request for paramedics, broke the lock and door jamb on the front door of Penilla's residence, moved him inside the house, locked the door, and left. The next day, family members found Penilla dead inside the house as a result of respiratory failure. His mother sued under Section 1983, and the court found that the officers' conduct clearly placed Penilla in a more dangerous position than the one in which they found him.[72] Another example is when the Green Bay, Wisconsin, Police Department released the tape of a phone call from an informant, which led to the informant's death.[73]

Vehicle Pursuits

In Chapter 10 we discussed a 2007 decision by the U.S. Supreme Court regarding the proper level of deadly force that may be used by officers during vehicle pursuits. Still, the police must act reasonably in such instances or they may be found civilly liable. In this section, we discuss vehicle pursuits in more detail, including the kinds of actions by officers that may lead to their being civilly liable.

First, police officers are afforded no special privileges or immunities in the routine operation of their patrol vehicles.[74] Police officers driving in nonemergency situations do not have immunity for their negligence or recklessness and are held to the same standard of conduct as private citizens. When responding to emergency situations, however, officers are governed by statutes covering emergency vehicles.[75] In such circumstances, most jurisdictions afford the police limited immunity for violations of traffic laws; in other words, they are accorded some protections and privileges not given to private citizens and are permitted to take greater risks that would amount to negligence if undertaken by citizens.[76]

Few operational patrol issues are of greater concern to police leadership than police pursuits because of the tremendous potential for injury, property damage, and liability that accompanies them. As one police procedure manual describes it, "The decision by a police officer to pursue a citizen in a motor vehicle is among the most critical that can be made."[77] Civil litigation arising out of collisions involving police pursuits reveals such pursuits to be high-stakes undertakings with serious and sometimes tragic results.[78] Indeed, several hundred people are killed each year during police pursuits,[79] and many of them are innocent third parties.

Pursuits place the police in a delicate balancing act. On one hand is the need for police to show criminals that flight from the law is no way to freedom. If a police agency completely bans high-speed pursuits, its credibility with both law-abiding citizens and law violators may suffer; public knowledge that the agency has a no-pursuit policy may encourage people to flee, decreasing the probability of apprehension.[80] Still, according to one observer, because of safety and liability concerns, "a growing number of agencies have the position that if the bad guy puts the pedal to the metal, it's a 'freebie.' They will not pursue him."[81]

On the other hand, there is indeed the high-speed threat to everyone within range of the pursuit, including suspects, their passengers, other drivers, and bystanders. One police trainer asks a simple question to help officers determine whether to continue a pursuit: "Is this person a threat to the public safety other than the fact the police are chasing him?" If the officers cannot objectively answer yes, the pursuit should be terminated.[82]

In May 1990, two Sacramento County, California, deputies responded to a call about a fight. At the scene, they observed a motorcycle with two riders approaching their vehicle at high speed. Turning on their red lights, the deputies ordered the driver to stop. The motorcycle operator began to elude the officers, who initiated a pursuit that reached speeds of more than a hundred miles per hour over about 1.3 miles. The pursuit ended when the motorcycle crashed; the deputies' vehicle could not stop in time and struck the bike's passenger, killing him. The passenger's family brought suit, claiming that the pursuit violated the crash victim's due process rights under the Fourteenth Amendment.

In *County of Sacramento v. Lewis*,[83] decided in May 1998, the U.S. Supreme Court held that the proper standard to be employed in these cases is whether the officer's conduct during the pursuit "shocks the conscience." (Was the conduct offensive to a reasonable person's sense of moral goodness?) The Court further determined that high-speed chases with no intent to harm suspects do not give rise to liability under the Fourteenth Amendment and therefore closed the door on liability for officers involved in pursuits that do not "shock the conscience." But the Court left unanswered many important questions, such as whether it will allow an innocent third party to file a claim against the police for damages and whether a municipality can be held liable for its failure to train officers in pursuit issues.

In sum, a pursuit is justified only when the necessity of apprehension outweighs the degree of danger created by the pursuit. Agencies generally require field supervisors (sergeants) to discontinue the pursuit when it is unjustified or becomes too dangerous.[84]

Exhibit 9-2 ■ shows an example of a police agency's vehicle pursuit policy.

Computer Evidence

It is almost impossible to investigate a fraud, embezzlement, or child pornography case today without dealing with some sort of computer evidence. Even evidence in a homicide or narcotics case may be buried deep within a computer's hard drive. As a result, many police agencies have recruited self-taught "experts" to fill the role of computer evidence specialists. These specialists are usually highly motivated and have some knowledge of the rules of evidence and some experience in testifying in court. Other police agencies have enlisted the support of personnel at local universities or computer repair shops to help them with computer evidence.[85]

The increased exposure to computer evidence by people both inside and outside policing brings an increase in potential legal liabilities. For example, if a police agency seizes the computerized records of an ongoing business, there may be negative financial consequences for the business. If it can be shown that the police accidentally destroyed business records through negligence, a criminal investigation might well become the civil suit of the decade. Furthermore, if a seized computer contains a newsletter, a draft of a book, or any computer bulletin board system, there may be liability under the Privacy Protection Act.[86]

The risk of liability in such cases may be reduced substantially if police investigators follow generally accepted forensic computer evidence procedures. Guidelines approved by the Department of Justice's Computer Crime and Intellectual Property Section dictate how the police are to search, seize, and analyze computers. It is crucial that the police be trained in the proper procedures for handling computers as well as in the rules of evidence. The federal government has made computer evidence training a priority for federal, state, and local law enforcement officers.[87]

▶ Qualified Immunity for Police

Police officers can and are sued for actions they perform in the course of their duties because someone believes their constitutional rights were violated. However, the Supreme Court has indicated a desire to "give (police) breathing room to make reasonable but mistaken judgments."[88] And, in certain circumstances, these lawsuits may be dismissed at an early stage of the litigation.

EXHIBIT 9-2

SAMPLE POLICE VEHICLE PURSUIT POLICY

[Author's Note: Such policies, because of their nature and the need to address many circumstances, are quite lengthy; therefore, the sample below has been greatly abridged and modified, with only the more pertinent aspects included.]

Vehicle Pursuits

A. Justification

   A. Justification for engaging in a vehicle pursuit must be based on facts known by the police member when the decision is made to engage in a pursuit. In all instances of vehicle pursuits, the initiating officer must be able to clearly articulate the reason(s) why a pursuit was initiated.

   B. Vehicle pursuits are justified only when the police member knows or has probable cause reasonable grounds to believe:

   > The suspect presents a clear and immediate threat to the safety of others; or the occupant(s) suspect has committed, or is attempting to commit a violent felony (i.e. armed robbery, recklessly endangering safety, and other crimes against a person in which violence is an element to the felony offense); or the occupant(s) presents a clear and immediate threat to the safety of others and therefore the necessity of immediate apprehension outweighs the level of danger created by the vehicle pursuit, as in the case of a serious traffic violation such as OWI, reckless driving, etc.

B. Decision to Initiate Vehicle Pursuits

The decision to initiate a vehicle pursuit, which is limited by this policy, rests in the sole discretion of the individual police member.

C. Pursuit Procedures

   1. The police member initiating a pursuit shall notify the Communications Division as soon as reasonably possible that a pursuit is underway and provide the following information:

      a. Police unit identification
      b. Location, speed, and direction of travel
      c. Reason for the pursuit
      d. Pursued vehicle description, including license number, if known
      e. Number of occupants
      f. Road conditions
      g. Traffic density

   2. A field supervisor or higher authority must acknowledge that he/she is aware of and monitoring the pursuit as soon as practicable.

D. Decision to Continue Pursuit

   1. The authority of the primary unit to continue the pursuit is, at all times, under the command of:

      a. The watch commander field deputy inspector, if on duty.
      b. His/her immediate district/division commander.
      c. His/her immediate shift commander.
      d. His/her immediate field supervisor.
      e. The field supervisor assigned by Technical Communications Division in the event there is no district field supervisor available from the primary unit's district or division.

E. Decision to Terminate the Pursuit

Officers and field supervisors must continually evaluate the risk assessment criteria and assess whether the seriousness of the incident justifies continuing the pursuit. When a decision is made to terminate a pursuit, police members shall:

   a. Immediately pull over, turn off their emergency lights and siren, radio their position to the dispatcher, and verbally acknowledge the order to terminate the pursuit.
   b. No longer follow the suspect vehicle, nor may they violate any traffic laws in an effort to catch up to, or parallel the suspect vehicle.
   c. Remain at the termination point for the responding field supervisor so that a debrief may occur and the field supervisor can collect the necessary information in order to complete a pursuit report.

Twice the U.S. Supreme Court has addressed the question of when police officers are granted qualified immunity. In the first case, *Saucier v. Katz*,[89] in 2001, the Court established a two-pronged test to determine whether a public employee could claim qualified immunity. The test required the courts to determine: (1) whether the police actions constituted a violation of someone's constitutional rights; and, if such a violation was found, (2) whether that right was "clearly established" at the time of the employee's misconduct (i.e., the right was obvious to a reasonable person). This test, although rather cumbersome and confusing, was applied for eight years until the decision in *Pearson v. Callahan*,[90] in 2009. The facts in this case are important toward understanding the doctrine of qualified immunity.

Police searched Afton Callahan's home without a warrant, and he sued the officers for violating his civil rights. A narcotics task force had first sent a confidential informant into Callahan's house to purchase drugs; then, after the transaction, the informant gave a signal and police officers entered the home and searched without a warrant. The police defended their warrantless search under the "consent once removed" doctrine. (Several federal circuits have approved this doctrine, which provides that if a suspect in a home consents to the entry of an *undercover* police operative (such as a narcotics agent), he or she is also granting permission to the police to enter as well.) This doctrine had *not* been officially adopted in Utah where Callahan lived, however, and thus the officers argued it was not a "clearly established" right and believed they held qualified immunity. Here, in *Pearson*, the Supreme Court broke from *Saucier*, believing its mandatory two-step test was too rigid and that trial courts had to waste too much time and resources analyzing the constitutional question at the outset of the lawsuit. In sum, *Pearson* allowed lower courts discretion in qualified immunity cases over which prong of the qualified immunity analysis to address first—(1) whether there was a constitutional violation or (2) whether the constitutional right at issue was clearly established at the time of the alleged violation. If there is no violation of a clearly established right—one that is so obvious that the employee should have been aware of it—then the employee is immune from suit. Here, in *Pearson*, the police were entitled to qualified immunity in *Pearson* because it was not "clearly established" at the time of the search that their conduct was unconstitutional.

Summary

This chapter examined the incidence, expense, benefits, and sometimes frivolous nature of lawsuits against the police; a number of basic terms and concepts that are ingrained in the area of civil liability; Section 1983, a major litigation tool that is used against the police by citizens who believe the police have violated their constitutional rights; the liability of supervisors who fail to control their personnel; and other areas of potential liability such as duty of care, failure to protect, vehicle pursuits, and computer evidence. Included were many examples of the kinds of police actions that foster liability lawsuits, police actions leading to liability, and new areas of potential police liability such as vehicle pursuits and computer evidence.

The weight and breadth of the chapter's litigated cases and decisions against police officers—and their organizations and cities or counties—speak for themselves. Perhaps what has been shown most unequivocally is that the consequences of failing to properly hire, train, and supervise police personnel can be quite costly, in both human and financial terms. The need is clear and present for officers to know and understand the law regarding liability, to always project themselves in the best possible light, and to conduct themselves in a manner that demonstrates that their behavior was a good-faith effort to do their job properly.

Americans know the police have a difficult job to do and are likely willing to accept less than perfect behavior from them, but the kinds of improper and illegal actions shown in this chapter simply cannot and will not be tolerated.

Key Terms

Bivens tort
"consent once removed" doctrine
constitutional torts
duty of care
failure to protect
frivolous lawsuit
intentional torts

negligence
negligent supervision
proximate cause
qualified immunity
respondeat superior
Section 242
Section 1983

sovereign immunity
special relationship
stare decisis
tort liability
vicarious liability
wrongful death

Review Questions

1. What are the incidence and benefits of lawsuits against the police?
2. What is the legal definition of a frivolous lawsuit?
3. What is meant by Title 42, Section 1983, of the U.S. Code?
4. What would be an example of police behavior that would result in a plaintiff winning a Section 1983 suit?
5. What are some types of police actions that are vulnerable to Section 1983 actions?
6. On what grounds are lawsuits challenging police use of ECDs?
7. What is meant by duty of care and failure to protect?
8. How might police facilities and vehicles be involved in police liability?
9. What are the areas of civil liability in the area of police vehicle pursuits?
10. What are some of the elements of a policy concerning vehicle pursuits?
11. What are some examples of how police supervisors may be held criminally liable for their officers' misconduct?
12. What are some of the liability issues related to computer evidence?
13. How does the doctrine of qualified immunity apply to police officers?

Learn by Doing

1. Sergeant Tom Gresham is newly promoted and assigned to patrol on the graveyard shift; he knows each officer on his shift, and several of them are his close friends; you are his patrol lieutenant. Gresham was an excellent patrol officer and prides himself on his reputation and ability to get along with his peers. He believes that doing so will result in greater productivity from his officers, and he makes efforts to socialize with them after work. Gresham also believes that a supervisor should not "get in the way of good police work," and his officers say he is "a cop's cop." In his view, his duty shift officers perform very well, generating the highest number of arrests and citations in the entire department. Unfortunately, his shift is also generating the highest number of citizen complaints for abusive language and improper use of force. Gresham believes that such complaints are "the price of doing business." One Monday morning, Gresham is surprised at being summoned to your office. You show Gresham a substantial number of use-of-force complaints lodged against his officers during the past two weeks while he was away on vacation. Despite your efforts to explain the gravity of the situation, Gresham fails to grasp the seriousness of the complaints and how his supervisory style may have contributed to them.

   a. What do you believe are some of Sergeant Gresham's problems as a new supervisor? Could anything have been done *before* he assumed his new position to help him understand his role better?

   b. As Gresham's superior officer, what advice would you give to him? Are there any other supervisory or command officers who you should ask to be involved in dealing with the situation?

   c. What corrective action must Sergeant Gresham take immediately with his team of officers?

2. Independently employ a number of methods in order to get a good understanding of police liability, such as the following:

   - Interview a district attorney, judge, or private attorney who is experienced in matters involving police misconduct, or research the literature and news articles to determine the nature of civil suits and amounts of awards against the police, as well as what the police and citizens can do to avoid civil litigation.

- Interview some police executives to determine what they are doing in terms of training and policies to minimize the chances of successful lawsuits against their officers.
- Discuss with police practitioners the technical areas of their work in which they must be constantly be retrained and certified because of possible litigation and to avoid causing unnecessary harm to citizens (focusing on the weapons and tools they use).
- Determine how local police attempt to protect themselves against lawsuits, such as with false arrest insurance, keeping abreast of court decisions involving police negligence, and so on.

Notes

1. TASER, "AXON FLEX On-Officer Camera," http://www.taser.com/flex (accessed October 24, 2013).
2. *The New York World*, "A Tort Time Bomb," October 3, 2012, http://www.thenewyorkworld.com/2012/10/03/nypd-lawsuits-surge/(accessed October 24, 2013).
3. *The Los Angeles Times*, "Legal payouts in LAPD lawsuits," http://spreadsheets.latimes.com/lapd-settlements/ (accessed October 24, 2013).
4. See, for example, John L. Worrall and Otwin Marenin, "Emerging Liability Issues in the Implementation and Adoption of Community Oriented Policing," *Policing: An International Journal of Police Strategies and Management* 22 (1998): 121–136.
5. Isidore Silver, *Police Civil Liability* (New York: Matthew Bender, 2005), p. 4.
6. Kevin Johnson, "Police tap technology to compensate for fewer officers," *USA Today*, April 25, 2012, http://usatoday30.usatoday.com/news/nation/2011-04-24-police-crime-technology-facebook.htm (accessed October 23, 2013).
7. The Feminist Majority Foundation and the National Center for Women & Policing, "Gender Differences in the Cost of Police Brutality and Misconduct: A Content Analysis of LAPD Civil Liability Cases: 1990–1999," http://www.womenandpolicing.org/ExcessiveForce.asp?id=4516 (accessed October 25, 2013).
8. "LAPD Officers Take Stand in Rampart Scandal Trial," archives.cnn.com/2000/LAW/10/16/lapd.corruption.tria (accessed October 25, 2013).
9. Victor E. Kappeler, *Critical Issues in Police Civil Liability*, 4th ed. (Long Grove, IL: Waveland Press, 2005), p. 4.
10. Ibid., p. 11.
11. G. P. Alpert, R. G. Dunham, and M. S. Stroshine, *Policing: Continuity and Change* (Long Grove, IL: Waveland Press, 2006).
12. *Harper v. Showers*, 174 F.3d 716, 718 (5th Cir. 1999).
13. S. F. Kappeler and V. E. Kappeler, "A Research Note on Section 1983 Claims Against the Police: Cases Before the Federal District Courts in 1990," *American Journal of Police* 11 (1): 65–73.
14. H. E. Barrineau III, *Civil Liability in Criminal Justice* (Cincinnati, OH: Pilgrimage, 1987), p. 58.
15. Ibid., p. 5.
16. Charles R. Swanson, Leonard Territo, and Robert W. Taylor, *Police Administration: Structures, Processes, and Behavior*, 6th ed. (Upper Saddle River, NJ: Prentice Hall, 2005), p. 549.
17. *Bivens v. Six Unknown Named Agents of the Federal Bureau of Narcotics*, 403 U.S. 388, 29 L.Ed.2d 619, 91 S.Ct. 1999 (1971).
18. Swanson, Territo, and Taylor, *Police Administration*, pp. 438–439.
19. *Hans v. Louisiana*, 134 U.S. 1 (1890); also see "Sovereign Immunity," www.lectlaw.com/def2/s103.htm (accessed March 5, 2013).
20. Ibid.
21. *Monroe v. Pape*, 365 U.S. 167, 81 S.Ct. 473 (1961).
22. Wayne W. Schmidt, "Section 1983 and the Changing Face of Police Management," in *Police Leadership in America*, ed. William A. Geller (Chicago: American Bar Foundation, 1985), p. 228.
23. Ibid., p. 227.
24. *Monell v. Department of Social Services*, 436 U.S. 6587 (1978).
25. *Alabama v. Pugh*, 438 U.S. 781 (1978).
26. Kappeler, *Critical Issues in Police Civil Liability*, p. 2.
27. J. R. Daughen, "Potential Cost of Philadelphia House-Bombing Incident Up to $59 Million," *Philadelphia Daily News*, April 14, 2005, p. B8.
28. Ibid.
29. *Jennings v. City of Detroit*, Wayne County Circuit Court, Michigan (August 1979).
30. *Gilliam v. Falbo*, U.S. District Court, Southern District of Ohio (April 1982).
31. *Haygood v. City of Detroit*, Wayne County Circuit Court, Michigan, No. 77-728013 (December 29, 1980).
32. *Carmelo v. Miller*, 569 S.W. 365 (1978).

33. *Stengel v. Belcher*, 522 F.2d 438 (6th Cir. 1975).

34. *Bonsignore v. New York*, 521 F. Supp. 394, aff'd., 683 F.2d 635 (2d Cir. 1982).

35. *Prior v. Woods*, U.S. District Court, (E.D. Michigan) (October 1981).

36. *Burkholder v. City of Los Angeles*, L.A. County Superior Court, California (October 1982).

37. *Murray v. City of Chicago*, 634 F.2d 365 (1980).

38. *Duncan v. Barnes*, 592 F.2d 1336 (1979).

39. *Sager v. City of Woodland Park*, 543 F. Supp. 282 (D. Colo. 1982).

40. *Popow v. City of Margate*, 476 F. Supp. 1237 (1979).

41. On appeal, the Section 242 convictions were vacated, as the victim was not an inhabitant of Puerto Rico; therefore, he enjoyed no protection under the U.S. Constitution. On resentencing in January 1991, the agents each received fifty years in prison for convictions of several other federal crimes under Title 18.

42. Kappeler, *Critical Issues in Police Civil Liability*, p. 29.

43. *McClelland v. Facteau*, 610 F.2d 693 (10th Cir. 1979).

44. *Brandon v. Allen*, 516 F. Supp. 1355 (W.D. Tenn. 1981).

45. *Brandon v. Holt*, 469 U.S. 464, 105 S.Ct. 873 (1985).

46. See, for example, *Black v. Stephens*, 662 F.2d 181 (1991).

47. See, for example, *Swope v. Bratton*, 541 F. Supp. 99 (W.D. Ark. 1982).

48. See, for example, *Leonard v. City of Columbus*, 705 F.2d 1299 (11th Cir. 1983).

49. See, for example, *Elrod v. Burns*, 427 U.S. 347 (1975).

50. "Amnesty International Urges Stricter Limits on Police Taser Use as U.S. Death Toll Reaches 500," February 15, 2012, http://www.amnestyusa.org/news/press-releases/amnesty-international-urges-stricter-limits-on-police-taser-use-as-us-death-toll-reaches-500 (accessed October 26, 2013).

51. See, for example, Legal and Liability Risk Management Institute, "ECW/TASER® LEGAL Issues & Litigation," http://www.llrmi.com/training/defending_taser_litigation.shtml (accessed October 26, 2013).

52. *South v. Maryland*, 59 U.S. (18 How.) 396 (1856).

53. *Reiff v. City of Philadelphia*, 477 F. Supp. 1262 (E.D. Pa. 1979).

54. Kappeler, *Critical Issues in Police Civil Liability*, pp. 25–26.

55. *Irwin v. Ware*, 467 N.E.2d 1292 (1984).

56. *Fudge v. City of Kansas City*, 239 Kan. 369, 720 P.2d 1093 (1986), at 373.

57. *Kendrick v. City of Lake Charles*, 500 So.2d 866 (La. App. 1 Cir.1986).

58. Kappeler, *Critical Issues in Police Civil Liability*, p. 27.

59. *Fielder v. Jenkins*, 833 A.2d 906 (N.J. Super. A.D. 1993).

60. Silver, *Police Civil Liability*, p. 4; also see *Coco v. State*, 474 N.Y.S.2d 397 (Ct.Cl. 1984); and *Duvernay v. State*, 433 So.2d 254 (La. App. 1983).

61. *Naylor v. Louisiana Dept. of Public Highways*, 423 So.2d 674 (La. App. 1982).

62. *Joseph v. State of Alaska*, 26 P.3d 459 (2001).

63. *Thomas v. Williams*, 124 S.E.2d 409 (Ga. App. 1962).

64. *Morris v. Blake*, 552 A.2d 844 (Del. Super. 1988).

65. *Guice v. Enfinger*, 389 So.2d 270 (Fla. App. 1980).

66. *Manuel v. City of Jeanerette*, 702 So.2d 709 (La. App. 3 Cir. 1997).

67. *Joseph v. State of Alaska*, 26 P.3d 459 (2001), at 474.

68. *Saunders v. County of Steuben*, 693 N.E.2d 16 (Ind. 1998).

69. *Manuel v. City of Jeanerette*, 702 So.2d 709 (La. App. 3 Cir. 1997).

70. *Davis v. City of Detroit*, 386 N.W.2d 169 (Mich. App. 1986).

71. *Morris v. Blake*, 552 A.2d 844 (De. Super. 1988).

72. *Penilla v. City of Huntington Park*, 115 F.3d 707 (9th Cir., 1997).

73. *Monfils v. Taylor*, 165 F.3d 511 (7th Cir. 1998), cert. den., 528 U.S. 810 (1999).

74. *Seide v. State of Rhode Island*, 875 A.2d 1259 (2005).

75. Silver, *Police Civil Liability*, p. 8.

76. *Seide v. State of Rhode Island*, 875 A.2d 1259 (2005).

77. Tulsa, Oklahoma, "Police Department," *Procedure Manual* (Ronald Palmer, chief of police), June 10, 1998, p. 1.

78. John Hill, "High-Speed Police Pursuits: Dangers, Dynamics, and Risk Reduction," *FBI Law Enforcement Bulletin* 71 (July 2002): 14–18.

79. Voices Insisting on Pursuit Safety, "Facts and Statistics," www.pursuitsafety.org/mediakit/statistics.html (accessed March 5, 2013).

80. C. B. Eisenberg, "Pursuit Management," *Law and Order* 47 (March 1999): 73–77.

81. A. Belotto, "Supervisors Govern Pursuits," *Law and Order* 47 (January 1999): 86.

82. G. T. Williams, "When Do We Keep Pursuing? Justifying High-Speed Pursuits," *Police Chief* 64 (March 1997): 24–27.

83. *County of Sacramento v. Lewis*, 118 S.Ct. 1708 (1998).

84. Oklahoma County Sheriff John Whetsel, quoted in Nicole Marshall, "Hot Pursuit," *Tulsa World* 93 (June 15, 1998), p. A11.

85. Michael R. Anderson, "Reducing Computer Evidence Liability," *Government Technology* (February 1997): 24, 36.

86. Ibid.

87. Ibid.

88. *Ashcroft v. al-Kidd*, 131 S.Ct. 2074 (2011).

89. *Saucier v. Katz* 533 U.S. 194 (2001).

90. *Pearson v. Callahan*, 555 U.S. 223 (2009).

PART **4**

Agency Organization and Administration

10 Federal and State Agencies: Protecting Our Borders and Freedoms

11 Municipal and County Agencies: Organization, Administration, and Roles

Part 4 has as its unifying theme the fact that federal and state law enforcement as well as local (municipal and county) policing in the United States doesn't just "happen" or occur in random, unplanned fashion. Such organizations are in fact organized and administered by virtue of their sovereignty, jurisdiction, and type of assignment so as to be more effective and efficient. Chapter 10 examines the organization and administration of U.S. federal and state law enforcement agencies, and Chapter 11 discusses the organization and administration of local agencies (i.e., municipal police departments and county sheriff's offices); included are profiles of both and comparisons with each other. Also discussed are definitions of organizations; organizational communication; functions of police executive officers, middle managers, and supervisors; influence of politics; media relations; contract and consolidated policing; and agency accreditation.

(Courtesy 1000 Words/Shutterstock.)

10 Federal and State Agencies
Protecting Our Borders and Freedoms

LEARNING OBJECTIVES

As a result of reading this chapter, the student will be able to:

1 List the major organizations that compose the Department of Homeland Security and their primary functions

2 Explain the functions of the primary law enforcement agencies within the Department of Justice as well as other major organizations

3 Describe where and how federal agents are trained

4 Explain the purposes of the Uniform Crime Reports and the National Crime Information Center

5 Describe the types of state-level police and law enforcement agencies, as well as their various functions

Introduction

In large measure, this chapter reflects the impact of the events of September 11, 2001, when foreign terrorists attacked the United States on its own soil. No segment of the U.S. society was altered more than the nation's police organizations, particularly the federal law enforcement agencies (local police agencies will be discussed in Chapter 11). Therefore, this chapter examines how our federal and state law enforcement agencies are now structured and function, particularly during this time when our nation's very existence depends on the ability to be proactive to prevent more terrorist attacks.

This chapter begins with a broad view of federal law enforcement agencies that possess arrest and firearms authority, and then it focuses on the major agencies and offices that comprise the Department of Homeland Security (DHS). Next is a discussion of the U.S. Department of Justice and its four primary law enforcement organizations: the Federal Bureau of Investigation (FBI); the Bureau of Alcohol, Tobacco, Firearms, and Explosives (ATF); the Drug Enforcement Administration (DEA); and the U.S. Marshals Service (USMS); included in this chapter section is an exhibit describing the role and functions of the International Criminal Police Organization, or INTERPOL. Then the chapter reviews the functions of three related organizations: the Central Intelligence Agency (CIA); the Criminal Investigation Division of the Internal Revenue Service (IRS); and the Federal Law Enforcement Training Center (FLETC). Next is an overview of state agencies, to include types and duties. Included at the chapter's end are a discussion of some career requirements and considerations, a summary, key terms, review questions, and several scenarios and activities providing opportunities for you to learn by doing. Also note that terrorism will be discussed more fully in Chapter 12, including legislation that gives the aforementioned federal agencies greater authority for preventing and combating such acts.

▶ Federal Law Enforcement Agencies with Arrest and Firearms Authority

This section describes the major law enforcement arms of the federal government, most of which are found within DHS and the Department of Justice. (Note: As can be seen in Figure 10-1 ■, bear in mind that a number of other federal agencies—such as the U.S. Postal Service, the Veterans Administration, National Park Service, U.S. Capitol Police, Bureau of Indian Affairs, U.S. Fish and Wildlife Service, and U.S. Forest Service—also employ full-time officers with authority to carry firearms and make arrests.)

▲ In the midst of the WTC destruction, agents and professional staff started collecting evidence, conducting interviews, and analyzing data. *(Courtesy FBI.)*

Agency	Number of Officers
Federal Bureau of Prisons	16,835
Federal Bureau of Investigation	12,760
U.S. Immigration and Customs Enforcement	12,446
U.S. Secret Service	5,213
Administrative Office of the U.S. Courts*	4,696
Drug Enforcement Administration	4,308
U.S. Marshals Service	3,313
Veterans Health Administration	3,128
Internal Revenue Service, Criminal Investigation	2,636
Bureau of Alcohol, Tobacco, Firearms, and Explosives	2,541
U.S. Postal Inspection Service	2,288
U.S. Capitol Police	1,637
National Park Service—Rangers	1,404
Bureau of Diplomatic Security	1,049
Pentagon Force Protection Agency	725
U.S. Forest Service	644
U.S. Fish and Wildlife Service	598
National Park Service—U.S. Park Police	547
National Nuclear Security Administration	363
U.S. Mint Police	316
Amtrak Police	305
Bureau of Indian Affairs	277
Bureau of Land Management	255
TOTAL	36,863

Source: Brian Reaves, *Federal Law Enforcement Officers, 2008.* U.S. Department of Justice, Bureau of Justice Statistics, June 2012, p. 2, http://bjs.ojp.usdoj.gov/content/pub/pdf/fleo08.pdf (accessed October 25, 2013).

FIGURE 10-1   Federal Agencies Employing 250 or More Sworn Law Enforcement Personnel

▶ Department of Homeland Security

Within one month of the attack on U.S. soil on September 11, 2001, President George W. Bush issued a proposal to create a new Department of Homeland Security—which would be activated in January 2003 and become the most significant transformation of the U.S. government in over a half-century. All or part of 22 different federal departments and agencies were combined, and 80,000 new federal employees were immediately put to work.[1] Congress committed $32 billion toward safeguarding the nation, developing vaccines to protect against biological or chemical threats, training and equipping first responders (local police, firefighters, and medical personnel), and funding science and technology projects to counter the use of biological weapons and assess vulnerabilities. Since 2003, more than $635 billion has been appropriated by the federal government to support homeland security.[2]

Figure 10-2 ■ shows the current organizational structure of DHS.

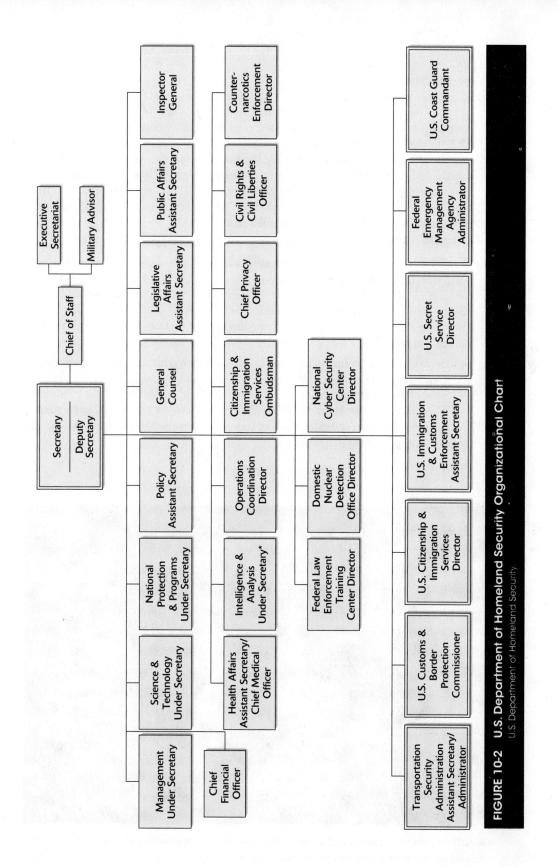

FIGURE 10-2 U.S. Department of Homeland Security Organizational Chart

U.S. Department of Homeland Security.

Following are brief descriptions of the major law enforcement agencies that are organizationally located within the DHS:

- U.S. Customs and Border Protection (CBP) is one of the largest federal law enforcement agencies, with more than 60,000 agents who work as CBP officers (21,000), border patrol agents (21,000), as air, and marine agents (1,200), and agriculture specialists (2,300). CBP is responsible for preventing terrorists and terrorist weapons from entering the United States while facilitating the flow of legitimate trade and travel. On a typical day, the CBP will process nearly a million passengers and pedestrians, execute more than 60 arrests at ports of entry, and seize nearly 11,000 pounds of narcotics in 70 seizures at more than 300 ports of entry. The CBP protects nearly 7,000 miles of border with Canada and Mexico and 95,000 miles of shoreline.[3]

A Career Profile briefly describes the work of a Border Patrol agent.

- Immigration and Customs Enforcement (ICE): This is the largest *investigative* arm of DHS with more than 20,000 employees in more than offices worldwide. ICE is responsible for identifying and shutting down vulnerabilities both in the nation's borders and in economic, transportation, and infrastructure security.[4] Because of its key role in providing national security, a further breakdown of its three main branches (or "directorates") is provided below:

  - Homeland Security Investigations (HSI): This branch is responsible for investigating a wide range of domestic and international activities arising from the illegal movement of people and goods into, within and out of the United States. HSI investigates immigration crime, human rights violations and human smuggling, smuggling of narcotics, weapons and other types of contraband, financial crimes, cybercrime and export enforcement issues.[5]

▲ A CBP agent uses a fiber optic scope to look inside a vehicle gas tank, where traffickers often conceal packages of drugs. *(Courtesy U.S. Customs and Border Protection.)*

▲ ICE works with U.S. Border Patrol and a Florida county sheriff's department to arrest members of a large Mexican-American human smuggling operation. *(Courtesy U.S. Customs and Border Protection.)*

- Enforcement and Removal Operations: This unit identifies, apprehends, and removes undocumented immigrants from the United States. It prioritizes the apprehension, arrest and removal of convicted criminals, those who pose a threat to national security, fugitives and recent border entrants.
- Management and Administration: This directorate oversees ICE's budget, expenditures, accounting and finance, procurement, human resources and personnel, workforce recruitment, equal employment opportunity, information technology systems, facilities, property and equipment needs.[6]

- The *Transportation Security Administration (TSA)* protects the nation's transportation systems. TSA employs 48,000 personnel at 457 airports who screen approximately two million people per day to ensure travel safety. Agents also inspect air carrier operations to the United States, assess security of airports overseas, fly air marshal missions, and train overseas security personnel.[7]

- The *Citizenship and Immigration Services* is responsible for the administration of immigration and naturalization adjudication functions and the establishment of immigration services policies and priorities.

- The *Coast Guard* protects the public, the environment, and U.S. economic interests in the nation's ports, on its waterways, along the coast, on international waters, or in any maritime region as required to support national security.

- The *Secret Service* protects the president and other high-level officials and investigates counterfeiting and other financial crimes, including financial institution fraud, identity theft, computer fraud, and computer-based attacks on our nation's financial, banking, and telecommunications infrastructure. The Secret Service's Uniformed Division protects the White House complex and the vice president's residence as well as foreign embassies and missions in the Washington, D.C., area. The Secret Service has agents assigned to approximately 125 offices located in cities throughout the United States and in select foreign cities.[8]

EXHIBIT 10-1

INTERPOL

INTERPOL is the oldest, the best-known, and probably the only truly international crime-fighting organization for crimes committed on an international scale, such as drug trafficking, bank fraud, money laundering, and counterfeiting. INTERPOL agents do not patrol the globe, nor do they make arrests or engage in shootouts. They are basically intelligence gatherers who have helped many nations work together in attacking international crime since 1923.[1]

Lyon, France, serves as the headquarters for INTERPOL's crime-fighting tasks and its 190 member countries.[2] Today INTERPOL has six priority crime areas: corruption, drugs and organized crime, financial and high-tech crime, fugitives, public safety and terrorism, and trafficking in human beings. It also manages a range of databases with information on names and photographs of known criminals, wanted persons, fingerprints, DNA profiles, stolen or lost travel documents, stolen motor vehicles, child sex abuse images, and stolen works of art. INTERPOL also disseminates critical crime-related data through its system of international notices. There are seven kinds of notices, of which the most well known is the Red Notice, an international request for an individual's arrest.[3]

INTERPOL has one cardinal rule: It deals only with common criminals; it does not become involved with political, racial, or religious matters. It has a basic three-step formula for offenses that all nations must follow for success: pass laws specifying the offense is a crime; prosecute offenders and cooperate in other countries' prosecutions; and furnish INTERPOL with and exchange information about crime and its perpetrators. This formula could reverse the trend that is forecast for the world at present: an increasing capability by criminals for violence and destruction. The following crimes, because they are recognized as crimes by other countries, are covered by almost all U.S. treaties of extradition: murder, rape, bigamy, arson, robbery, burglary, forgery, counterfeiting, embezzlement, larceny, fraud, perjury, and kidnapping.[4]

INTERPOL's annual report may be viewed at: https://www.interpol.int/Public/ICPO/InterpolAtWork/iaw2011.pdf

[1] "INTERPOL: Global crackdown on illicit online pharmacies," October 4, 2012, http://www.interpol.int/News-and-media/News-media-releases/2012/PR077 (accessed October 27, 2013); also see INTERPOL, "Overview," http://www.interpol.int/About-INTERPOL/Overview (accessed October 25, 2013).
[2] Ibid.
[3] Ibid.
[4] Michael Fooner, INTERPOL: Issues in World Crime and International Criminal Justice (New York: Plenum Press, 1989), p. 179.

- The *Federal Law Enforcement Training Center (FLETC)* provides training for more than hundred federal, state, and local agencies, and is discussed more fully later.

Because its roles and purpose are closely related to the protection of the United States against terrorism and other crimes, a discussion of INTERPOL is provided in Exhibit 10-1 ■.

▶ Department of Justice

The Department of Justice is headed by the attorney general, who is appointed by the U.S. president and approved by the Senate. The president also appoints the attorney general's assistants and the U.S. attorneys for each of the judicial districts. The U.S. attorneys in each judicial district control and supervise all federal criminal prosecutions and represent the government in legal suits in which it is a party. These attorneys may appoint committees to investigate other governmental agencies or offices when questions of wrongdoing are raised or when possible violations of federal law are suspected or detected.

▲ Secret Service agents are highly visible wherever U.S. presidents appear, such as at inaugural parades. *(Courtesy U.S. Secret Service.)*

The Department of Justice is the official legal arm of the government of the United States. Within the Justice Department are several law enforcement organizations that investigate violations of federal laws; we will discuss the Federal Bureau of Investigation; Bureau of Alcohol, Tobacco, Firearms, and Explosives; Drug Enforcement Administration; and U.S. Marshals Service. (The Office of Community Oriented Policing Services have already been discussed in Chapter 4.)

Figure 10-3 ■ shows the organizational chart for the Department of Justice.

Federal Bureau of Investigation (FBI)

Beginnings The Federal Bureau of Investigation was created and funded through the Department of Justice Appropriation Act of 1908. The FBI was first known as the Bureau of Investigation. With thirty-five agents, it originally had no specific duties other than the "prosecution of crimes," focusing on bankruptcy fraud, antitrust crimes, neutrality violations, and crimes on Native American reservations. Espionage and sabotage incidents during World War I, coupled with charges of political corruption reaching into the Department of Justice and the bureau itself, prompted angry demands for drastic changes.[9]

A new era was begun for the FBI in 1924 with the appointment of J. Edgar Hoover as director; he served in that capacity until his death in 1972. Hoover was determined that the organization would become a career service in which appointments would be made strictly on personal qualifications and abilities, and promotions would be based on merit. Special agents were college graduates, preferably with degrees in law or accounting. A rigorous course of training had to be completed, and agents had to be available for assignment wherever their services might be needed. Hoover coordinated the development of the Uniform Crime Reporting system, and during his tenure in office many notorious

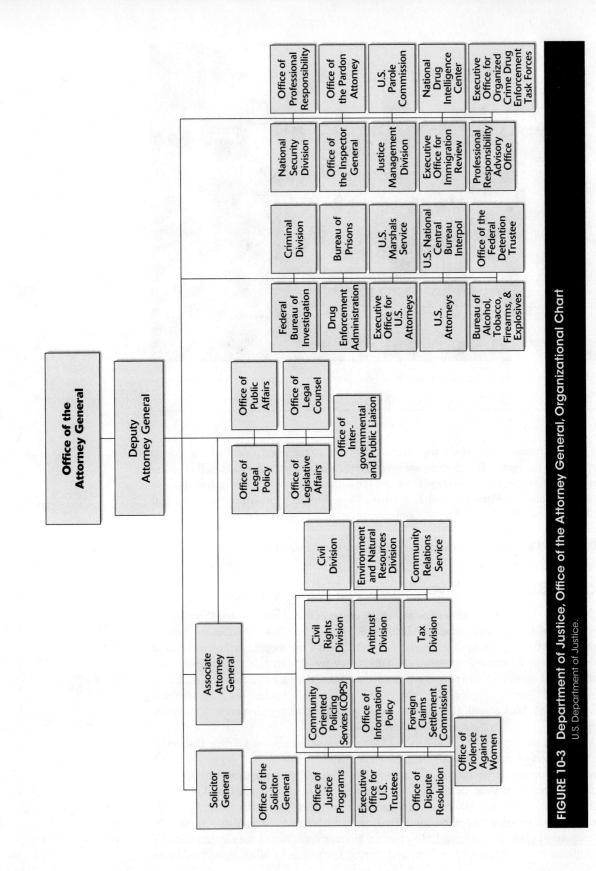

FIGURE 10-3 Department of Justice, Office of the Attorney General, Organizational Chart
U.S. Department of Justice.

▲ J. Edgar Hoover. *(Courtesy The White House.)*

criminals, such as Bonnie Parker, Clyde Barrow, and John Dillinger, were tracked and captured or killed. The building housing the FBI Headquarters in Washington, D.C., bears his name.[10]

The bureau's Identification Division was created on July 1, 1924, and its laboratory opened in 1932. Then, in 1933, all of the bureau's functions were consolidated and transferred to a Division of Investigation, which became the Federal Bureau of Investigation on March 22, 1935.

Contemporary Priorities and Roles Today the FBI has fifty-six field offices, approximately four hundred resident agencies, and more than fifty foreign liaison posts called legal attachés. About 22,000 nonsworn support employees perform professional, administrative, technical, or other functions in support of the FBI's nearly 14,000 sworn special agents.[11]

The national priorities of the FBI have been modified in major fashion since September 11, 2001; today the following are its top three priority areas:[12]

1. Protect the United States from terrorist attack.
2. Protect the United States against foreign intelligence operations and espionage.
3. Protect the United States against cyber-based attacks and high-technology crimes.

Other priorities include combating public corruption, civil rights violations (e.g., hate crimes, human trafficking), organized crime, white-collar crime, and major thefts/violent crimes. Figure 10-4 ■ depicts the organizational chart that is designed to facilitate the accomplishment of these priorities and goals.

Recently, the FBI was given new powers to aid its reform efforts to battle terrorism. The bureau can now monitor Internet sites, libraries, churches, and political organizations. In addition, under revamped guidelines, agents can attend public meetings for the purpose of preventing terrorism.[13] The bureau also participates with local police in dozens of task forces that target fugitives and violent gangs nationwide.

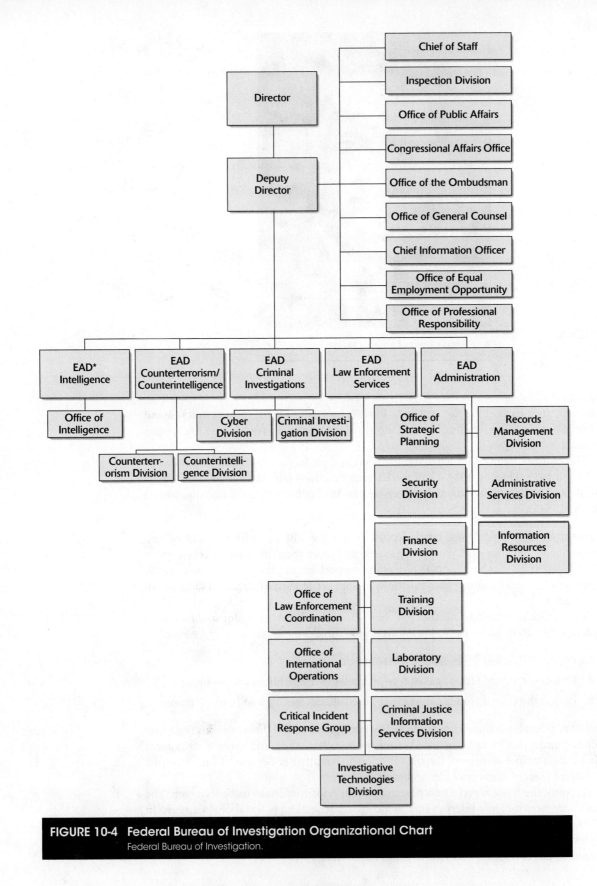

FIGURE 10-4 **Federal Bureau of Investigation Organizational Chart**
Federal Bureau of Investigation.

But counterterrorism still constitutes only a fraction of the bureau's workload; the FBI also continues to investigate bank robberies, white-collar crimes, and organized crime and drug syndicates—staples of the agency's workload for a long time—while it combats radical Islamic fundamentalism and global terrorism with a workforce in which just 1 percent of the FBI's 12,200 agents have any familiarity with the Arabic language.[14]

Ancillary Investigative, Training, and Reporting Services Today the FBI's laboratory examines blood, hair, firearms, paint, handwriting, typewriters, and other types of evidence. Highly specialized techniques are now utilized—at no charge to state police and local police agencies—for analysis of DNA, explosives, hairs and fibers, tool marks, drugs, plastics, and bloodstains.

Another feature of the bureau is its National Academy, which graduated its first class in 1935. Today thousands of local police managers from across the country have received training at the National Academy in Quantico, Virginia, which has twenty-one buildings on 385 acres. The FBI also provides extensive professional training to national supervisory-level police officers at the National Academy. (More information on local police training is provided in Chapter 11.)

A very successful function of the FBI, inaugurated in 1950, is its "Ten Most Wanted Fugitives" list, which over the years has contained many notable fugitives. As of 2000, the bureau had caught about 460 top ten fugitives; the Internet has helped to invigorate the program, with the "Ten Most Wanted" Web page receiving about 25 million hits per month.[15]

The FBI also operates the National Crime Information Center (NCIC), through which millions of records relating to stolen property and missing persons and fugitives are instantaneously available to local, state, and federal authorities across the United States and Canada. Following are some of the categories of individuals and items that are included in the NCIC files.[16]

1. Categories of individuals covered by the system:
   - Wanted persons (for whom warrants are outstanding, who have committed or have been identified with a felony or serious misdemeanor offense); an escaped or wanted juvenile; missing persons (e.g., those with proven physical/mental disability or who are senile, or who are possibly kidnapped, are missing after a catastrophe, are members of violent criminal gangs or terrorist organizations), and unidentified deceased persons.

2. Categories of records in the system:
   - Stolen vehicles, vehicle parts or plates, boats, guns, articles, securities, and vehicles wanted in conjunction with felonies or serious misdemeanors.

In a related vein, one of the FBI's several annual publications is the Uniform Crime Reports (UCR), which includes crime data reported from more than 15,000 state and local police agencies concerning twenty-nine types of offenses: eight Part I (or index) offenses (criminal homicide, forcible rape, robbery, aggravated assault, burglary, larceny–theft, motor vehicle theft, and arson) and twenty-one Part II offenses. The UCR also includes a so-called crime clock, shown in Figure 10-5 ■.

Several shortcomings characterize the UCR data, however. First, the data are dependent on crimes being reported to, and by, the police; many crime victims do not report their victimization to the police, so there is the so-called shadow of crime—those crimes that are hidden and unknown. Furthermore, the reporting system is not uniform, so crimes may be reported incorrectly or inaccurately. In addition, the UCR operates under the hierarchy rule, which means that when a number of separate crimes are committed as

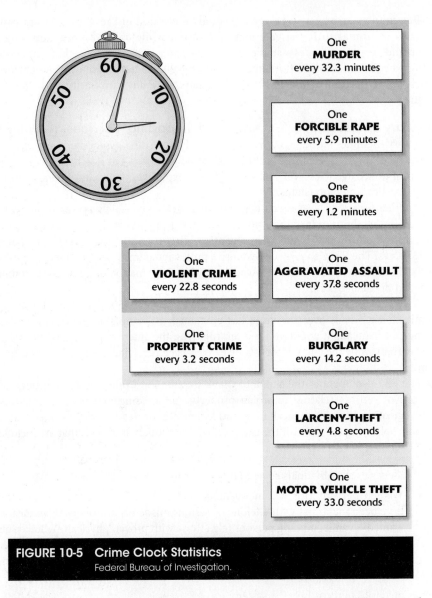

FIGURE 10-5 Crime Clock Statistics
Federal Bureau of Investigation.

part of a single act (e.g., a burglar enters a home and then, at gunpoint, robs the residents living there, and then murders one of them when a struggle ensues), only the most serious crime—the murder—will be reported to the FBI. At best, UCR has several limitations and must be used cautiously.

A large amount of information concerning the FBI's application and hiring process—including its minimum requirements and the kinds of knowledge, skills, and abilities it is now seeking for special agents and professional staff—is available on the agency's Web site at www.fbijobs.gov/1.asp.

Bureau of Alcohol, Tobacco, Firearms, and Explosives (ATF)

- The ATF originated as a unit within the IRS in 1862, when certain alcohol and tobacco tax statutes were created. The next year, Congress authorized the hiring of three "detectives" to aid in the prevention, detection, and punishment of tax evaders. Originally called the Alcohol, Tobacco, Tax Unit, it eventually became the Alcohol, Tobacco, and

Firearms Division within the IRS. In 1972, it became the Bureau of Alcohol, Tobacco, and Firearms, under the direct control of the Treasury Department; in January 2003, it was moved to the Justice Department and renamed the Bureau of Alcohol, Tobacco, Firearms, and Explosives.[17] Like the FBI and several other federal agencies, the ATF has a rich and colorful history, much of which has involved capturing bootleggers and disposing of illegal whiskey stills during Prohibition.[18] From 1920 to 1933, congressional Prohibition legislation (the Volstead Act) made it illegal to manufacture, possess, or sell intoxicating liquors in the United States (with a few exceptions). Still, the country was awash with liquor. History is replete with accounts of violations of Prohibition laws; much has been written and portrayed in movies of that era, when the moonshiners tried to outsmart and outrun the law. Speakeasies (secret bars) proliferated across America to satisfy the American yearning for liquor. This era bolstered the popularity of such G-men (short for "government man," meaning a federal agent) as Eliot Ness; the 1960s television program and later film *The Untouchables* were inspired by his career.

The ATF administers the U.S. Criminal Code provisions concerning alcohol and tobacco smuggling and diversion. The 2,500 agents are responsible for:

- Investigating criminal violations of federal laws within the enforcement jurisdiction of the U.S. Department of Justice.
- Conducting investigations of violations relating to explosives, firearms, arson, and alcohol and tobacco diversion.
- Gathering and analyzing evidence through investigative leads, seizures, arrests, execution of search warrants, and a variety of other means.[19]

ATF also maintains a U.S. Bomb Data Center (to collect information on arson and explosives related incidents) and a Bomb and Arson Tracking System, which allows local, state, and other federal agencies to share information about bomb and arson cases; a National Response Team of highly trained agents that can be deployed to major explosion and fire scenes in the United States; an International Response Team that provides assistance in other countries; accelerant and explosives detection canine teams; and three national laboratory facilities.

Drug Enforcement Administration (DEA)

The Drug Enforcement Administration began with the passage of the Harrison Narcotic Act, signed into law on December 17, 1914, by President Woodrow Wilson. The act made it unlawful for any "nonregistered" person to possess heroin, cocaine, opium, morphine, or any of their by-products. Drug enforcement began in 1915, and during that first year, agents seized forty-four pounds of heroin and achieved 106 convictions (mostly the result of illicit activities of physicians). In 1920, Prohibition was enacted; the Narcotics Division of the Prohibition Unit of the Revenue Bureau consisted of 170 agents working out of seventeen offices around the country. New authority was granted to agents by the Narcotic Drugs Import and Export Act of 1922.[20]

Today's DEA is also an outgrowth of the former Bureau of Narcotics, which was established in 1930 under the direct control of the Treasury Department. In 1968, the Bureau of Narcotics was transferred from the Treasury to the Department of Justice and was renamed the Bureau of Narcotics and Dangerous Drugs. In 1973, the DEA was established, and in 1982, the organization was given primary responsibility for drug and narcotics enforcement, sharing this jurisdiction with the FBI. Succinctly, major responsibilities of the DEA's 5,200 agents, under the U.S. Code, include the following[21]:

- Investigation of, and coordination with major violators of controlled substance laws in domestic and international venues.
- Management of a national drug intelligence program in cooperation with federal, state, local, and foreign officials.

- Seizure and forfeiture of assets derived from, traceable to, or intended to be used for illicit drug trafficking.
- Liaison with the United Nations, INTERPOL, and other organizations on matters relating to international drug control programs.

Figure 10-6 ■ depicts DEA's various programs and operations.

U.S. Marshals Service (USMS)

The U.S. Marshals Service is one of the oldest federal law enforcement agencies, established under the Judiciary Act of 1789; George Washington appointed thirteen marshals, one for

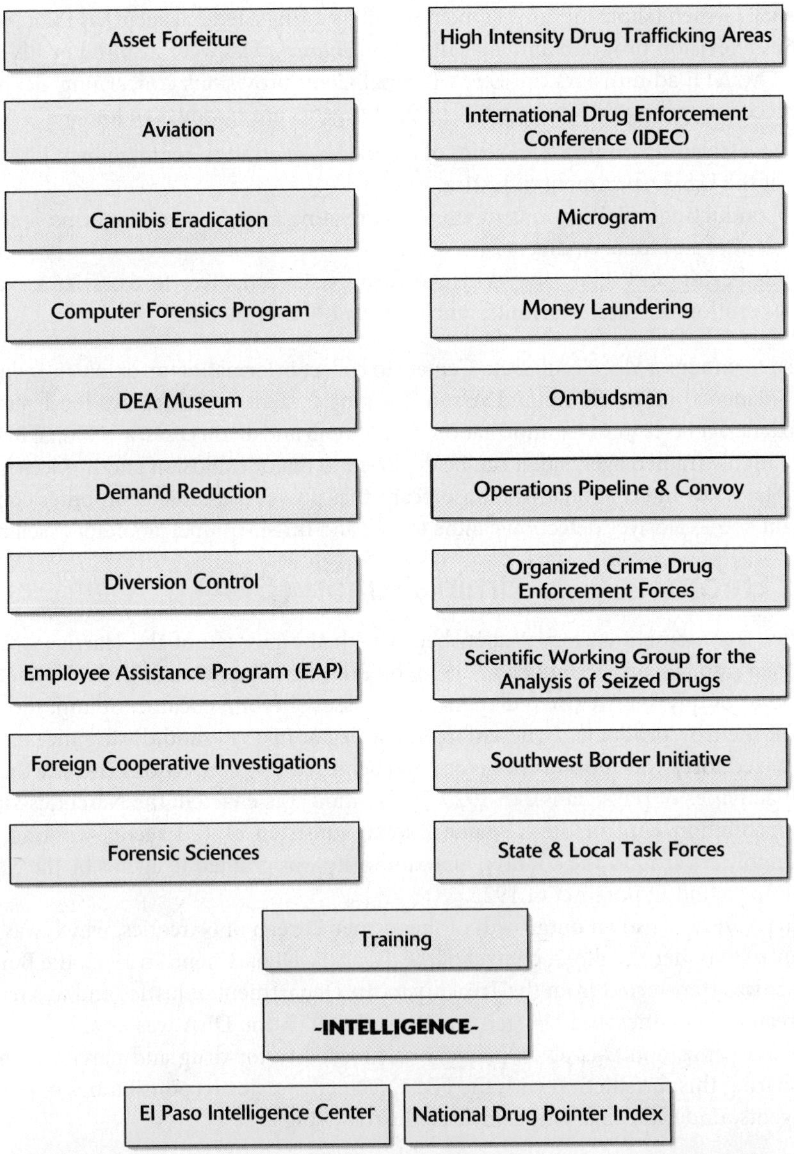

Asset Forfeiture	High Intensity Drug Trafficking Areas
Aviation	International Drug Enforcement Conference (IDEC)
Cannibis Eradication	Microgram
Computer Forensics Program	Money Laundering
DEA Museum	Ombudsman
Demand Reduction	Operations Pipeline & Convoy
Diversion Control	Organized Crime Drug Enforcement Forces
Employee Assistance Program (EAP)	Scientific Working Group for the Analysis of Seized Drugs
Foreign Cooperative Investigations	Southwest Border Initiative
Forensic Sciences	State & Local Task Forces

Training

-INTELLIGENCE-

El Paso Intelligence Center   National Drug Pointer Index

FIGURE 10-6 U.S. Drug Enforcement Administration Programs and Operations
U.S. Drug Enforcement Administration.

▲ U.S. Marshals plan an arrest. *(Courtesy U.S. Marshals Service.)*

each of the original thirteen states. The USMS formally assumed the responsibility for the apprehension of federal fugitives in 1979.[22]

Today the USMS has ninety-four U.S. marshals, one for each federal court district. Each district headquarters office is managed by a politically appointed U.S. marshal and a chief deputy U.S. marshal, who direct a staff of supervisors, investigators, deputy marshals, and administrative personnel. As in the so-called Wild West, the backbone of the USMS today is the deputy U.S. marshals—numbering nearly 4,000 deputy U.S. marshals and criminal investigators today—who pursue and arrest fugitives (about 36,000 per year) wanted for federal violations; pursue escaped federal prisoners; transport federal prisoners (about 360,000 per year); and provide a secure environment for judges, attorneys, witnesses, and others in the federal courts.[23]

In 1971, the USMS created the Special Operations Group (SOG), consisting of a well-trained elite group of deputy marshals. The group provides support in priority or dangerous situations, such as the movement of a large group of high-risk prisoners, and at trials involving alleged drug traffickers or members of subversive groups. Another important function of the USMS is the operation of the Witness Protection Program. Federal witnesses are sometimes threatened by defendants or their associates (e.g., they sometimes testify against organized crime figures). If certain criteria are met, the USMS will provide a complete change of identity for witnesses and their families, including new Social Security numbers, residences, and employment. About 8,300 witnesses and 9,800 of their family members have been protected, relocated, and given new identities since the program began in 1971.[24]

▶ Other Federal Agencies

Central Intelligence Agency (CIA)

Although not a law enforcement agency, the Central Intelligence Agency (CIA is of significance at the federal level to the nation's security and warrants a brief discussion. The National Security Act of 1947 established the National Security Council, which in 1949 created a subordinate organization, the CIA. Considered the most clandestine government service, the CIA participates in undercover and covert operations around the world for the purposes of managing crises and providing intelligence during the conduct of war.[25] In sum, the CIA carries out what is termed "the intelligence cycle," which is defined as the process of collecting, analyzing, and disseminating intelligence information to top U.S. government officials.[26]

The CIA is an independent agency responsible through its director to the U.S. president. The agency Web site states that it offers "exciting career opportunities and a dynamic environment," and that it is "on the forefront of world-altering events—as they happen."[27] The agency offers careers in at least twenty-five different areas, an interest in international affairs and national security, impeccable integrity, strong interpersonal skills, and excellent written and oral skills.[28]

Internal Revenue Service (IRS)

The Internal Revenue Service has as its main function the monitoring and collection of federal income taxes from American individuals and businesses. Since 1919, the IRS has had a Criminal Investigation (CI) Division employing "accountants with a badge."

The CI branch of the IRS is composed of approximately 4,400 employees worldwide, approximately 2,800 of whom are special agents whose investigative jurisdiction includes tax, money laundering, and Bank Secrecy Act laws. While other federal agencies also have investigative jurisdiction for money laundering and some bank secrecy act violations, IRS is the only federal agency that can investigate potential criminal violations of the Internal Revenue Code.[29]

The first chief of the Special Intelligence Unit, Inspector Elmer I. Irey, gained notoriety by participating in investigations that included income tax evasion charges against organized crime kingpin Alphonse ("Al") Capone and the kidnapping of Charles Lindbergh's baby in 1932.[30] Since then, the list of celebrated, prosecuted CI "clients" has been impressive and includes federal judges, prominent politicians, and athletes. Indeed, today there is a much greater appreciation for what a financial investigator can do for almost any type of criminal investigation.[31]

IRS agents are armed; the U.S. Code authorizes them to execute search warrants, make arrests without warrants for tax-related offenses, and seize property related to violations of the tax laws. Agents engage in money-laundering investigations under Title 18 of the U.S. Code and investigate for tax and currency violations any individuals who organize, direct, and finance high-level criminal enterprises.[32]

The CI Division enforces nearly all of the provisions of the Bank Secrecy Act, requiring financial institutions or individuals to report certain domestic and foreign currency transactions to the federal government. The CI Division also enforces the wagering tax laws and conducts investigations related to the pornography industry. Another important area of the division is the Questionable Refund Program, which attempts to detect and stop fictitious claims for tax refunds.

Federal Law Enforcement Training Center (FLETC)

The Federal Law Enforcement Training Center (FLETC) states as its mission: "We train those who protect our homeland." To carry out this mission, the FLETC serves as an interagency law enforcement training organization for ninety-one federal agencies. The FLETC also provides training to state, local, rural, tribal, territorial, and international law enforcement agencies. During a recent year almost 70,000 students received FLETC training, and it was established in 1970 approximately one million law enforcement officers and agents have been trained at FLETC. Although the FLETC trains officers and agents from all federal departments and all three branches of government, it is a component of the Department of Homeland Security. The center is headquartered in Glynco, Georgia, where it occupies a

▲ FLETC training using a scenario simulator. *(Courtesy Federal Law Enforcement Training Center, Department of Homeland Security.)*

1,500-acre campus with state-of-the-art classrooms Other domestic campuses are located in Artesia, New Mexico; Charleston, South Carolina; and Cheltenham, Maryland.

FLETC offers more than 150 basic and advanced training programs, including specialized courses such as: cyberterrorism (such as internet forensics and investigations), financial forensics, international banking and money laundering, critical infrastructure protection, land transportation antiterrorism, weapons of mass destruction, seaport security, and antiterrorism intelligence awareness training for state and local agencies. FLETC increasingly uses technology-based, distance learning when the programs being taught do not require specialized facilities; furthermore, FLETC often uses alternative training technologies, especially simulation and modeling to augment existing training delivery systems and methodologies.[33]

▶ State Agencies

State Police and Law Enforcement Agencies: General Types

As with federal law enforcement organizations, there is a variety of organizations, duties, and specialization found in the fifty states—although, generally, state troopers and highway patrol officers actually perform a lot of the same functions that are found with their county and municipal counterparts: enforcing state statutes, investigating criminal and traffic offenses (and, by virtue of those roles, knowing and applying laws of arrest, search, and seizure), making arrests, testifying in court, communicating effectively in both oral and written contexts, using firearms and self-defense tactics proficiently, and effectively performing pursuit driving, self-defense, and lifesaving techniques until a patient can be transported to a hospital. Such agencies also maintain a wide array of special functions, including special weapons and tactics (SWAT) teams, drug units and task forces, marine and horse patrol, and so on.[34]

▲ State police officers include bureau of investigation agents, highway patrol troopers, and other professionals. Here, state law enforcement agents conduct training on an active-shooter scenario.
(Courtesy bibiphoto/Shutterstock.)

A first distinction to be made between state agencies concerns their name or designation, which will also indicate their primary functions: 24 (48 percent) of the states identify their organizations as "State Police"; 16 (32 percent) are designated in some form of "patrol"—e.g., "Highway Patrol" or "State Highway Patrol"; and nine (18 percent) of the states identify their organizations as a "Department of Public Safety" (one, Alaska's, is termed "State Troopers").[35] *State police* organizations are typically tasked, under state statute, to perform more general law enforcement functions than are highway patrol troopers, to include criminal investigations as well as highway patrol, traffic control, crash investigations, and related functions. The latter, public safety organizations, are often more complex and may encompass several agencies or divisions. For example, the Hawaii Department of Public Safety, by statute, includes a Law Enforcement Division (with general arrest duties, narcotics division, sheriff division, and executive protection unit), a Corrections Division (inmate intake, incarceration, paroling authority, and industries), and a victim compensation commission.[36]

State bureaus of investigation (SBIs), as their name implies, are investigative in nature and might be considered a state's equivalent to the FBI; they investigate all manner of cases assigned to them by their state's laws and usually report to the state's attorney general. SBI investigators are plainclothes agents who usually investigate both criminal and civil cases involving the state and/or multiple jurisdictions. They also provide technical support to local agencies in the form of laboratory or record services and may be asked by the city and county agencies to assist in investigating more serious crimes (e.g., homicide).

Other Special-Purpose State Agencies

In addition to the traffic, investigative, and other units mentioned above, several other special-purpose state agencies, including police and other law enforcement organizations, have developed over time to meet particular needs. For example, many state attorney general's offices have units and investigators that investigate white-collar crimes; fraud against or by consumers, Medicare providers, and food stamp recipients; and crimes against children and seniors.[37]

As shown in Figure 10-7 ■, states may also have limited-purpose units devoted to enforcing the following:

- Alcoholic beverage laws (regarding the distribution and sale of such beverages, monitor bars and liquor stores, and so on).
- Fish and game laws (relating to hunting and fishing, to ensure that such persons have proper licenses, and do not poach, hunt, or fish out of season, exceed their limit, and so on).
- State statutes and local ordinances on college and university campuses.
- Agricultural laws, to include cattle brand inspection and enforcement.
- Commercial vehicle laws, such as those federal and state laws pertaining to interstate carriers' (i.e., tractor-trailer rigs) weights and permits, and ordinances applying to taxicabs.

Most of these organizations have their own training academies, but some—campus police officers and fish and game agents, for example—may attend the regular police academies that train county deputies and local police officers.

Career Considerations

Key elements—known as KSAs (for knowledge, skills, and abilities)—of employment in many federal as well as state law enforcement positions are as follows:

- U.S. citizenship.
- Age requirement—applicants must be under thirty-seven years of age.
- Written test.
- Structured oral interview—typically consisting of situational questions posed by an oral board that do not require technical questions.
- Writing sample assessment—applicants might, for example, be provided with a photograph and then asked to prepare a narrative report describing the overall scene and details shown in the photograph.
- Medical exam—to test for any chronic disease or condition affecting the respiratory, cardiovascular, gastrointestinal, musculoskeletal, digestive, nervous, endocrine, or genitourinary systems that would impair full performance of the job duties; it might also include vision and hearing examinations.
- Drug testing—satisfactory completion of a drug test is a condition of placement
- Background investigation[38]

Furthermore, the following minimum qualifications may also be in effect prior to an offer of employment, depending on the agency:

- Successful hires will attend and successfully complete a mandatory basic training program of about six months' duration.
- Any person convicted of a crime of domestic violence cannot lawfully possess a firearm or ammunition (see 18 U.S.C. Section 1001).
- Persons required to carry a firearm while performing their duties must satisfactorily complete the firearms component.
- Positions may require mobility, not only as concerns some travel related to the duties of the job, but also in terms of assignment to a duty station; applicants must sign a mobility agreement.[39]

Type of special jurisdiction	Agencies	Full-time sworn personnel
Total	1,733	56,968
Public buildings/facilities	1,126	21,418
4-year university/college	508	10,916
Public school district	250	4,764
2-year college	253	2,648
State government buildings	29	1,138
Medical school/campus	18	747
Public hospital/health facility	48	715
Public housing	13	250
Other state-owned facilities	7	240
Natural resources	246	14,571
Fish and wildlife conservation laws	56	5,515
Parks and recreational areas	124	4,989
Multi-function natural resources	16	2,926
Boating laws	10	461
Environmental laws	7	368
Water resources	18	185
Forest resources	9	65
Levee district	6	62
Transportation systems/facilities	167	11,508
Airports	103	3,555
Mass transit system/railroad	18	3,214
Transportation—multiple types	5	2,000
Commercial vehicles	12	1,320
Harbor/port facilities	25	876
Bridges/tunnels	4	543
Criminal Investigations	140	7,310
State bureau of investigation	22	3,527
County/city investigations	66	2,006
Fraud investigations	13	636
Fire marshal/arson investigations	21	478
Tax/revenue enforcement	6	177
Other/multiple types	12	486
Special enforcement	54	2,161
Alcohol/tobacco laws	22	1,280
Agricultural laws	12	387
Narcotics laws	5	233
Gaming laws	10	231
Racing laws	5	30

Note: excludes agencies employing less than one full-time officer or the equivalent in part-time officers.

FIGURE 10-7 **Special Jurisdiction State Law Enforcement Agencies, by Type of Jurisdiction**
Bureau of Justice Statistics, Census of State and Local Law Enforcement Agencies, U.S. Department of Justice, 2008.

Several government and nongovernment Web sites offer information concerning federal state and local law enforcement careers, including the following:

- USAJOBS, jobsearch.usajobs.gov (search for "Corrections Officer")
- Federal Jobs Net, "Law Enforcement Jobs," federaljobs.net/law.htm
- Dennis V. Damp, *The Book of U.S. Government Jobs: Where They Are, What's Available, and How to Get One*, federaljobs.net/us7.htm
- Police Employment, The Police Job Board, "Federal Police Jobs," jobs.policeemployment.com/federal-police
- Copcareer.com, www.copcareer.com/federal/federalpage.htm

More general information concerning federal employment may be obtained from the U.S. Office of Personnel Management, www.opm.gov. The federal hiring process normally takes eighteen to thirty months.

One's academic performance can enhance his or her pay scale in the federal system. For example, in the past, federal agencies have paid higher entry-level salaries to people having higher academic degrees as well as grade-point averages that were higher than 3.0 (or "B" level).

Summary

Although modern policing in the United States is still based on the nineteenth-century British model of the Metropolitan Police of London, a tremendous amount of specialization has evolved in today's sphere of policing, especially among federal, state, and (discussed in Chapter 3) local agencies. Policing has developed into a highly organized discipline with many branches and narrow fields of jurisdiction and responsibility. This has happened not so much because of needs being demonstrated by formal research but because of the necessity of keeping abreast of activities of sophisticated criminals and would-be terrorists who would violate the peace and dignity of people in many different ways.

Specifically, this chapter described the major federal law enforcement agencies of the new Department of Homeland Security, the Department of Justice, and other federal agencies and provided an overview of state police agencies. Perhaps what was most evident is how the law enforcement agencies of the federal government have retooled to meet today's challenge of terrorism.

It is clear that now, more than any other time in the history of the United States, "business as usual" cannot be the order of the day. Federal and state law enforcement agencies must take a more farsighted approach to their work while learning new methods for preventing and responding to potential terrorist attacks. This chapter has demonstrated that law enforcement agencies must be—and are being—flexible as the need arises.

Key Terms

Bureau of Alcohol, Tobacco, Fire-arms, and Explosives (ATF)
Central Intelligence Agency (CIA)
Department of Homeland Security (DHS)
Department of Justice

Drug Enforcement Administration (DEA)
Federal Bureau of Investigation (FBI)
Federal Law Enforcement Training Center (FLETC)

Internal Revenue Service (IRS)
National Crime Information Center (NCIC)
state bureaus of investigation (SBI)
Uniform Crime Reports (UCR)
U.S. Marshals Service (USMS)

Review Questions

1. What are the major component agencies of DHS and their primary functions?
2. What are the major functions of the four agencies of the Department of Justice that are described in this chapter?
3. Where and how are federal agents trained?
4. What functions do the CIA and the IRS perform?
5. What are the primary differences between federal and state law enforcement agencies?

Learn by Doing

1. Your criminal justice professor requires you to prepare a research paper on the measures that have been adopted by federal law enforcement and state and local police for homeland security, to include the training that has been provided in the event of a terrorist attack or other critical incident, cooperative agreements with other agencies that are in place for such situations, and so on.
2. You have been requested to provide a two-hour block of instruction concerning federal and state law enforcement agencies for your police department's Citizens' Police Academy; prepare a lecture covering the major agencies—and their functions—that comprise both the Department of Justice and the Department of Homeland Security; include such ancillary functions as the FBI's Uniform Crime Reports and NCIC, as well as the complementary roles of INTERPOL.
3. As your department's public information officer, you have been invited by a local civic organization to appear at a noon luncheon to discuss your agency's roles and functions. During your presentation, someone in the audience raises her hand and asks how the duties of the local police department and sheriff's offices generally differ from those of your state-level police organization. How would you respond?
4. Assume that you and a fellow student of criminal justice are engaged in a conversation about law enforcement careers. Your friend is undecided about whether to seek employment in a federal, state, or local agency upon graduating; furthermore, he wonders about the possible pros and cons of working at each level, as well as working within a large-, medium-, or small-size agency. How would you respond?

Notes

1. U.S. Department of Homeland Security, "Creation of the Department of Homeland Security," http://www.dhs.gov/creation-department-homeland-security (accessed October 29, 2013).
2. National Priorities Project, "U.S. Security Spending Since 9/11," May 26, 2011, http://nationalpriorities.org/analysis/2011/us-security-spending-since-911/ (accessed October 29, 2013).
3. U.S. Customs and Border Protection, "On a Typical Day," http://www.cbp.gov/linkhandler/cgov/about/accomplish/typical_day_fy12.ctt/typical_day_fy12.pdf (accessed October 24, 2013).
4. Department of Homeland Security, "ICE: Enforcement and Removal Operations," http://www.ice.gov/about/offices/enforcement-removal-operations/ (accessed October 26, 2013).
5. Department of Homeland Security, "Homeland Security Investigations," http://www.ice.gov/about/ offices/homeland-security-investigations/ (accessed October 29, 2013).
6. Department of Homeland Security, Transportation Security Administration, "TSA Workforce," http://www.tsa.gov/about-tsa (accessed October 27, 2013).
7. Department of Homeland Security, Transportation Security Administration, "TSA Workforce," http://www.tsa.gov/about-tsa (accessed October 27, 2013).
8. United States Secret Service, "Frequently Asked Questions About the United States Secret Service," www.secretservice.gov/faq.shtml#employees (accessed March 5, 2013).
9. David R. Johnson, *American Law Enforcement History* (St. Louis: Forum Press, 1981), pp. 166–170.
10. Ibid.
11. U.S. Department of Justice, Federal Bureau of Investigation, "About Us—Quick Facts," http://www.

fbi.gov/about-us/quick-facts/quickfacts (accessed October 29, 2013).

12. U.S. Department of Justice, Federal Bureau of Investigation, "What We Investigate," http://www.fbi.gov/about-us/investigate/what_we_investigate (accessed October 29, 2013).

13. "FBI Seeks Sweeping New Powers," *The Nation*, August 22, 2008, www.thenation.com/article/fbi-seeks-sweeping-new-powers (accessed October 25, 2013).

14. "FBI Agents Still Lacking Arabic Skills," www.washingtonpost.com/wp-yn/content/article/2006/10/10/AR2006101001388.html (accessed October 25, 2013).

15. Jeff Glasser, "In Demand for Fifty Years: The FBI's 'Most Wanted' List—Good Publicity, and a History of Success," *U.S. News and World Report*, March 20, 2000, p. 60.

16. U.S. Department of Justice, Federal Bureau of Investigation, "National Crime Information Center (NCIC)," www.fas.org/irp/agency/doj/fbi/is/ncic.htm (accessed October 25, 2013).

17. Bureau of Alcohol, Tobacco, Firearms, and Explosives, "Changes in ATF Resulting from the Signing of the Homeland Security Bill: Two Separate Bureaus Created" (press release), www.atf.gov/press/releases/2002/11/112702-atf-changes-from-homeland-security-bill.html (accessed October 25, 2013).

18. Bureau of Alcohol, Tobacco, Firearms and Explosives, "ATF's History," http://www.atf.gov/about/history/ (accessed October 27, 2013).

19. Ibid.; see http://www.atf.gov/content/Careers/careers-at-ATF (accessed October 25, 2013).

20. U.S. Department of Justice, Drug Enforcement Administration, "DEA History," http://www.justice.gov/dea/about/history.shtml (accessed October 6, 2013).

21. Ibid., "DEA Mission Statement," http://www.justice.gov/dea/about/mission.shtml (accessed October 29, 2013).

22. U.S. Department of Justice, U.S. Marshals Service, *The FY 1993 Report to the U.S. Marshals* (Washington, DC: Author, 1994), pp. 188–189.

23. Ibid., "Fact Sheets: Facts and s," http://www.usmarshals.gov/duties/factsheets/facts-2011.html (accessed October 7, 2013).

24. U.S. Department of Justice, U.S. Marshals Service, "Witness Security Program," http://www.justice.gov/

marshals/forms/pub3.pdf (accessed October 26, 2013).

25. Central Intelligence Agency, "CIA Vision, Mission, & Values," https://www.cia.gov/about-cia/cia-vision-mission-values/index.html (accessed October 27, 2013).

26. Central Intelligence Agency, "About CIA," https://www.cia.gov/about-cia/index.html (accessed October 27, 2013).

27. Central Intelligence Agency, "Life at CIA," "Clandestine Service," https://www.cia.gov/careers/life-at-cia/our-culture.html (accessed October 25, 2013).

28. Ibid.

29. Internal Revenue Service, "Financial Investigations: Criminal Investigation (CI)," http://www.irs.gov/uac/Financial-Investigations—Criminal-Investigation-(CI) (accessed October 29, 2013).

30. Ludovic Kennedy, "The Airman and the Carpenter: The Lindbergh Kidnapping and the Framing of Richard Hauptmann," *Seton Hall Law Review* 14, 574–598.

31. Don Vogel, quoted in Department of the Treasury, Internal Revenue Service, *CI Digest* 1827, June 1994, p. 12.

32. U.S. Department of Treasury, Internal Revenue Service, "Criminal Enforcement," www.irs.gov/compliance/enforcement/index.html (accessed October 29, 2013).

33. U.S. Department of Homeland Security, Federal Law Enforcement Training Center, "Welcome to FLETC," http://www.fletc.gov/ (accessed October 19, 2013).

34. U. S. Department of Justice, Bureau of Justice Statistics, *Census of State and Local Law Enforcement Agencies, 2008*, July 2011, pp. 1–6, http://www.bjs.gov/content/pub/pdf/csllea08.pdf (accessed October 19, 2013).

35. Ibid.

36. Ibid.

37. See, for example, State of California, Department of Consumer Affairs, http://www.dca.ca.gov/ (accessed October 25, 2013).

38. Gregory M. White, Resident Agent in Charge, U.S. Department of Homeland Security, U.S. Immigration and Customs Enforcement, personal communication, October 29, 2009.

39. Ibid.

(Courtesy Vladru/Shutterstock.)

11 Municipal and County Agencies

Organization, Administration, and Roles

LEARNING OBJECTIVES

As a result of reading this chapter, the student will be able to:

 1 *Explain the elements of a bureaucracy, per Weber*

 2 *Describe the basic organizational structure of a police agency*

 3 *Describe the basic elements of the communications process, including that which occurs in police organizations*

 4 *Explain what is meant by span of control and unity of command*

5 *Explain the definition and uses of policies and procedures*

6 *Distinguish between municipal police departments and county sheriff's offices in terms of hiring, training, and use of selected equipment*

7 *Describe the major roles of police executives, using the Mintzberg model of chief executive officers*

8 *Delineate the roles and functions of contemporary chiefs of police and county sheriffs*

9 *Discuss the roles and functions of mid-level managers and first-line supervisors*

10 *Describe politics in the context of policing*

11 *Describe some of the unique aspects and challenges of policing in small and rural areas*

12 *Explain how police services may stretch resources though contract, consolidated, and civilianized operations*

13 *Explain the process for and benefits of accreditation of police agencies*

Introduction

The public has long held a fascination with all things involving the police, as noted in Chapter 5 concerning the many television programs and movies aired during past decades. While there are not nearly as many police programs on television today as in the past—for example, in the 1970s, forty-two such programs premiered[1]—certainly the manner in which the police are depicted today in film and on television has a strong influence on how the police are viewed by society.

Chapter 10 examined the roles and functions of selected federal law enforcement agencies, including how they have changed their mission and priorities since 9/11; the general nature and duties of state-level law enforcement organizations were also examined. This chapter examines policing at the local (municipal and county) levels, specifically in terms of their organization, administration, and roles. First is a definition of organizations, to include the principles of bureaucracies and organizational communications; then we examine police agencies as organizations, including their structure, command principles, use of policies and procedures, and communications processes. Next we compare local agencies (municipal police departments and county sheriff's offices) in terms of their operations, policies and procedures, equipment, screening and testing of new recruits, and technologies; included is a review of the functions of the municipal police chief and the county sheriff, using a management model developed by Mintzberg to better understand those roles. We then briefly consider the roles and functions of middle managers, and examine more thoroughly the complex role of first-line supervisors.

We then address the relationships between police administrators and politicians as well as the police and media. Following that are descriptions of how agencies may contract, consolidate, and civilianize their services, and then we consider how police agencies may become accredited. At the end of the chapter are a summary, key terms, review questions, and several scenarios and activities that provide opportunities for you to learn by doing.

It should be noted that other important and related topics that concern local police officers—women and minorities, higher education, stress, and collective bargaining—were discussed in Chapter 6.

► Organizations, Generally

What Are Organizations?

It is no surprise that one of the most widely read and long-running cartoon strips is that of "Dilbert," Scott Adams's mouthless engineer who is surrounded by downtrodden workers, inconsiderate bosses, and a dysfunctional organization. Unfortunately, many people in the U.S. society identify with Dilbert: One survey found that more than 70 percent of U.S. workers experience stress at work because of red tape, unnecessary rules, poor communication with management, and other causes.[2] But it does not have to be so, as we will see in this chapter.

Organizations are entities of two or more people who cooperate to accomplish an objective. In that sense, undoubtedly the first organizations were primitive hunting parties. Organization and a high degree of cooperation were required to bring down large animals. Organizations were also used to build pyramids and other monuments.[3] Thus, *organization* may be defined as arranging and utilizing resources of personnel and materiel in such a way as to attain specified objectives.

Every organization is unique. Gaines, Southerland, and Angell provide an excellent analogy that helps us understand organizations:

> Organization corresponds to the bones which structure or give form to the body. Imagine that the fingers were a single mass of bone rather than four separate fingers and a thumb made up of bones. The mass of bones could not, because of its structure, play musical instruments, hold a pencil, or grip a baseball bat. A police department's organization is analogous. It must be structured properly if it is to be effective in fulfilling its many diverse goals. Organization may not be important in a police department consisting of three officers, but it is extremely important in [larger] cities.[4]
>
> —*Excerpt from "Organization" by Larry K. Gaines, Mittie D. Southerland and John E. Angell from POLICE ADMINISTRATION. Published by McGraw-Hill Companies, © 1991.*

As Gaines et al. also note, the development of an organization should be done with careful evaluation or the agency may become unable to respond efficiently to community needs. For example, the implementation of too many specialized units in a police agency (such as community relations, crime analysis, or media relations units) may leave too few people to do the general grassroots work of the organization. (As a rule of thumb, at least 55 percent of all sworn police personnel should be assigned to patrol.[5])

Organizations as Bureaucracies: In Principle and Perception

Prior to looking at the bureaucratic organization of police agencies in America, we need to understand what constitutes a bureaucracy. First, a *bureau* (derived from the French language) is a desk or, by extension, an office. *Bureaucracy* is rule conducted from a desk or office (i.e., by the preparation and dispatch of written documents—or, these days, their electronic equivalent). In the office are kept records of communications sent, received, filed, and archived.[6]

Any discussion of bureaucracies must also include the seminal work of Max Weber, a German sociologist who wrote that bureaucracies generally adhere to the following principles:[7]

1. **Specialization:** The principle of fixed jurisdictional areas. Stated simply, every bureaucracy has its own specialized area; thus, physicians do not arrest criminals, police officers do not teach elementary school, firefighters do not make dentures. Duties are assigned, and everyone has a role (a jurisdiction).

2. **Hierarchy of offices:** A bureaucracy creates a clear system of authority, with superiors and subordinates. The authority to give commands is distributed in a formal way and regulated; certain people have the right to control others, and this is spelled out clearly (as in police department organizational structures, described below). This means that any position has only one immediate supervisor, allowing for clear lines of authority (see the discussions concerning police unity of command and span of control, below).

3. **Rules and regulations:** Every bureaucracy has written rules and files that serve as the organizational memory of the bureaucracy (a police sergeant's threat to a subordinate: "Don't do that, or it will go in your personnel file"). These guide the actions of personnel (see the discussion of policies and procedures) who are in a given position.

4. **Technical competence:** People are appointed to offices based on explicit qualifications. Only qualified persons are employed; therefore, individuals may come and go, but the position is defined by the workflow and the rules guiding behavior of occupants in that position (police training and promotional exams were discussed in Chapter 4).

5. **Official activity demands the full working capacity of the official:** An office holder is responsible for completing the tasks of the office, regardless of the number of hours it might take (thus, many people working in a police organization work until the job is done, not until the clock tells them they can drop their work and go home).

6. **Office management follows exhaustive, stable, written rules, which can be learned:** Weber believed that in a bureaucracy, knowledge of the organization's rules and responsibilities is key to job performance (this is why police chiefs and sheriffs are typically hired based on experience and education, not on-the-job training—unlike, say, politically appointed foreign ambassadors who might do poorly because they do not understand the culture and "rules" of the country to which they are assigned).

Today many people view bureaucracies in negative terms, as too often "going by the book"—relying heavily on rules and regulations and on policies and procedures ("red tape") and not being flexible enough to respond to individual needs and problems. Weber's ideal bureaucracy, however, as described above, was designed to eliminate inefficiency and waste in organizations. As shown for each of the preceding six principles, many of the characteristics that Weber proposed many years ago—well-trained personnel, precision, speed, unambiguity (clear division of labor), knowledge of the files and forms, continuity (when one employee leaves and another replaces), unity, and clear lines of authority (supervisors overseeing subordinates) are found in today's police agencies as well as in other bureaucracies (e.g., political parties, churches, educational institutions, and private businesses).

Organizational Communication

Communication is one of the most important dynamics of an organization. Indeed, a major role of today's administrators and other leaders is communication. Managers of all types of organizations spend an overwhelming amount of time engaged in the process of—and coping with problems in—communication.

Today we communicate via electronic mail, Web sites, facsimile machines, video camcorders, cellular telephones, satellite dishes, and other high-tech means. We converse orally, in written letters and memos, through our body language, via television and radio programs, and through newspapers and meetings. Even private thoughts—which take place four times faster than the spoken word—are part of communication. Every waking hour our minds are full of ideas and thoughts; psychologists say that nearly one hundred thousand thoughts pass through our minds every day, conveyed by a multitude of media.[8]

Studies have long shown that communication is the primary problem in administration, however, and lack of communication is the primary complaint of employees about their immediate supervisors.[9] Managers are in the communications business. Consider the following:

> Of all skills needed to be an effective manager/leader/supervisor, skill in communicating is the most vital. In fact, more than 50 percent of a manager's time is spent communicating. First-line supervisors usually spend about 15 percent of their time with superiors, 50 percent of their time with subordinates, and 35 percent with other managers and duties. These estimates emphasize the importance of communications in everyday . . . operations.[10]

Several elements constitute the communications process: encoding, transmission, medium, reception, decoding, and feedback.[11] Following are brief descriptions of these elements:

Encoding. To convey an experience or idea to someone, we translate, or encode, that experience into symbols. We use words or other verbal behaviors and gestures or other nonverbal behaviors to convey the experience or idea.

Transmission. This element involves the translation of the encoded symbols into some behavior that another person can observe. The actual articulation (moving our lips, tongue, and so on) of the symbol into verbal or nonverbal observable behavior is transmission.

Medium. Communication must be conveyed through some channel, or medium. Media for communication may include our sight, hearing, taste, touch, or smell. Some other media are the television, radio, telephone, and paper and pencil. The choice of the medium is very important; for example, a message that is transmitted via a formal letter from the chief executive officer will carry more weight than if the same message is conveyed via a secretary's memo.

Reception. The stimuli, the verbal and nonverbal symbols, reach the senses of the receiver and are conveyed to the brain for interpretation.

Decoding. The individual who receives the stimuli develops some meaning for the verbal and nonverbal symbols and decodes the stimuli. These symbols are translated into some concept or experience of the receiver.

Feedback. When the receiver decodes the transmitted symbols, he or she usually provides some response, or feedback, to the sender. If someone appears puzzled, we repeat the message or we encode the concept differently and transmit some different symbols to express the same concept. Feedback acts as a guide or steering device and lets us know whether the receiver has interpreted our symbols as we intended.

Communication as it occurs within police organizations is discussed later in this chapter.

▶ Police Agencies as Organizations

Chain of Command

The administration of most police organizations is based on a traditional pyramidal, quasi-military organizational structure that contains the elements of an organization and a bureaucracy. First, these agencies are organized into a number of specialized units. Figure 11-1 ■ shows the hierarchy of managers within the typical police organization and the inverse

FIGURE 11-1 The Hierarchy of Managers Within the Typical Police Organization

relationship between rank and numbers of personnel; in other words, as rank increases, the number of people who occupy that rank decreases. Some larger agencies have additional ranks, such as corporal and major, but this can lead to concerns about becoming too top-heavy. The rank hierarchy allows an organization to designate authority and responsibility at each level and to maintain a chain of command.

Administrators (chiefs and assistant chiefs), mid-level managers (captains and lieutenants), and first-line supervisors (sergeants) ensure that these units work together toward a common goal. If each unit worked independently, fragmentation, conflict, and competition would result, subverting the goals and purposes of the entire organization. Police agencies consist of people who interact within the organization and with external groups, and they exist to serve the public.

Police departments are different from most other kinds of organizations for the simple reason that policing is significantly different from most other kinds of work. A special organizational structure has evolved to help carry out the complex responsibilities of policing. The highly decentralized nature and the varying size of American police departments, however, compel police agencies to vary in organization.

Organizational Structure

Every police agency, no matter what its size, has an organizational structure, which is often prominently displayed for all to see in the agency's facility. Even a community with only a town marshal has an organizational structure, although the structure will be very horizontal, with the marshal performing all of the functions displayed in Figure 11-2 ■, the basic organizational chart for a small agency.[12]

Operations, or line, personnel are engaged in active police functions in the field. They may be subdivided into primary and secondary operations elements. The patrol function—often called the backbone of policing—is the primary operational element because of its major responsibility for policing. (The patrol function was examined in Chapter 3.) In most small police agencies, patrol forces are responsible for all operational activities: providing routine patrols, conducting traffic and criminal investigations, making arrests, and functioning as generalists.[13] The investigative and youth functions are the secondary operations elements. (We discussed the investigative function thoroughly in Chapter 5 and juvenile rights in Chapter 7; youth crimes will be discussed in Chapter 13.)

The support (or nonline) functions and activities can become quite numerous, especially in a large agency. These functions fall into two broad categories: staff (or

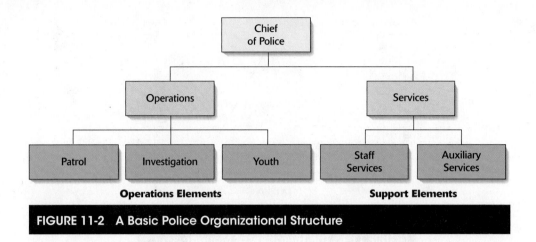

FIGURE 11-2 A Basic Police Organizational Structure

administrative) services and auxiliary (or technical) services. The staff services usually involve personnel and include such matters as recruitment, training, promotion, planning and research, community relations, and public information services. Auxiliary services are the kinds of functions that civilians rarely see. They include jail management, property and evidence, crime laboratory services, communications processes, and records and identification. Many career opportunities exist for those who are interested in police-related work but who cannot or do not want to be a field officer.

Obviously, the larger the agency, the greater the need for specialization and the more vertical the organizational chart will become. With greater specialization come the need and opportunity for officers to be assigned to different tasks, often rotating from one assignment to another after a fixed interval. For example, in a medium-size department serving a community of one hundred thousand or more, it would be possible for a police officer with ten years of police experience to have been a dog handler, a motorcycle officer, a detective, and a traffic officer while simultaneously holding a slot on the special weapons or hostage negotiations team.

The organizational structure of the Metropolitan Police Department (MPD) of St. Louis, Missouri (separate from the St. Louis County Police Department), shown in Figure 11-3 ■, displays the various types of units that might exist in a large agency. Although the city of St. Louis has a population of about 318,000, the Greater St. Louis area totals about 2.8 million;[14] the MPD has nearly 1,900 employees.[15]

This organizational structure provides an excellent illustration of the various components of police organizations while also functionally providing several major functions: (1) it apportions the workload among members and units according to a logical plan; (2) it ensures that lines of authority and responsibility are as definite and direct as possible; (3) it specifies a unity of command throughout, so there is no question about which orders should be followed; (4) it assigns responsibility and authority, and if responsibility is delegated, the delegator is held responsible; and (5) it coordinates the efforts of members so that all will work harmoniously to accomplish the mission.[16] In sum, this structure establishes the chain of command and determines lines of communication and responsibility.

In addition to these generally well-known and visible areas of specialization, other areas of policing are lesser known, such as community crime prevention, child abuse, drug education, and missing children units.[17]

Unity of Command and Span of Control

A related principle is unity of command, an organizational principle dictating that every officer should report to one and only one superior (following the chain of

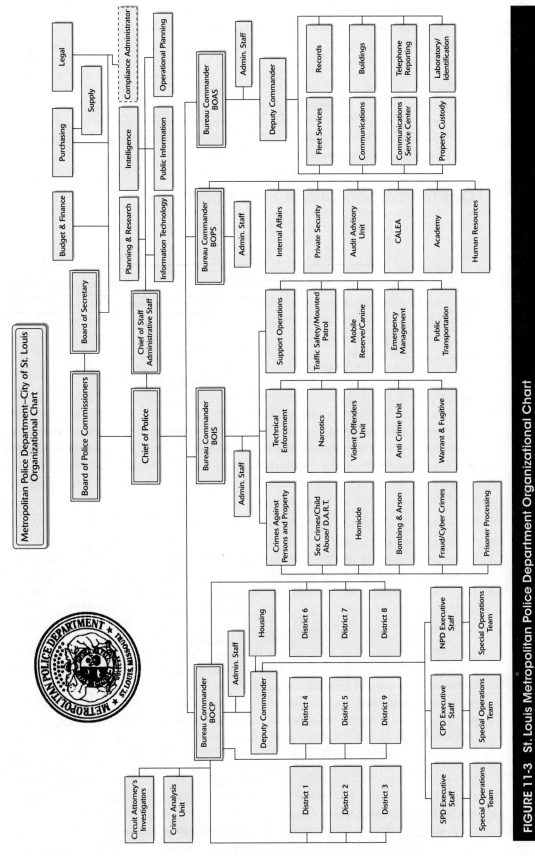

FIGURE 11-3 St. Louis Metropolitan Police Department Organizational Chart

command) until that superior officer is relieved. Ambiguity about authority can and does occur in police organizations—who should handle calls, who is in charge at a crime scene, and so on. Nevertheless, the unity-of-command principle ensures that multiple and/or conflicting orders are not issued to the same officer by several supervisors. It is important that all officers know and follow the chain of command at critical incidents.

The term span of control refers to the number of subordinates one individual can effectively supervise. The limit is small; it is normally three to five at the top level of the organization and is often broader at the lower levels.[18] The tendency in modern police operations is to have supervisors spread too thinly.

Organizational Policies and Procedures

It has been said that a well-written policy and procedure manual serves as the foundation of a professional law enforcement agency.[19] In policing, policies and procedures and rules and regulations are also important for defining role expectations for officers. Police leaders rely on these directives to guide officers' behavior and performance. Because police agencies are intended to be service oriented in nature, they must work within specific and well-defined guidelines designed to ensure that all officers conform consistently to behavior that will enhance public protection.[20]

This tendency for organizations to promulgate policies and procedures as well as rules and regulations has been caused by three contemporary developments. First is the requirement for administrative due process in employee disciplinary matters, encouraged by federal court rulings, police officer bill of rights legislation, and labor contracts. The second development is the threat of civil litigation. Lawsuits against local governments and their criminal justice agencies and administrators have become commonplace; written guidelines by law enforcement agencies prohibiting certain acts provide a hedge against successful civil litigation.[21] The third stimulus is the trend toward the accreditation of police agencies (discussed below). Agencies that either are pursuing accreditation or have become accredited must follow policies and practice procedures.[22]

Policies are quite general and serve basically as guides to thinking rather than action. Policies reflect the purpose and philosophy of the organization and help interpret them for the officers. An example of a policy might be that everyone found to be driving while under the influence of drugs or alcohol must be arrested or that all juveniles who are to be detained must be taken to a Procedures are more detailed than policies and provide the preferred methods for handling matters pertaining to investigation, patrol, booking, radio transmissions, filing of reports, roll call, use of force, arrest, sick leave, evidence handling, promotion, and many other elements of the job. Most police agencies are awash in procedures. Methods for accomplishing certain tasks are also found in myriad city or county administrative regulations and police agency general orders (such as when a new federal court decision relating to search and seizure is announced or a new state or local law regarding the use of force takes effect).

Rules and regulations are specific guidelines that leave little or no latitude for individual discretion. Some examples are requirements that police officers not smoke in public, that they check the operation of their vehicle and equipment before going on patrol, that they not consume alcoholic beverages within a specified number of hours before going on duty, or that they arrive in court or at roll call early. Rules and regulations are not always popular, especially if they are perceived as unfair or unrelated to the job. Nonetheless, it is the supervisor's responsibility to ensure that officers perform these tasks with the same degree of professionalism as they do other job duties.

A sample policy on vehicle pursuits has been provided in Chapter 9.

Communication Within Police Organizations

Communication becomes exceedingly important and sensitive in nature in a police organization because of the nature of the information that is processed by officers—who often see people when they are at their worst and when they are in their most embarrassing and compromising situations. To "communicate" what is known about these kinds of behaviors could be devastating to the parties concerned.

Types of Communication Communication within police organizations may be downward, upward, or horizontal. There are five types of downward communication within such an organization:[23]

1. **Job instruction.** Communication relating to the performance of a certain task.
2. **Job rationale.** Communication relating a certain task to organizational tasks.
3. **Procedures and practice.** Communication about organizational policies, procedures, rules, and regulations.
4. **Feedback.** Communication about how an individual performs an assigned task.
5. **Indoctrination.** Communication designed to motivate the employee.

Upward communication in a police organization may encounter several obstacles. First, the physical distance between superior and subordinate impedes upward communication. Communication is often difficult and infrequent when superiors are isolated. In large police organizations, the administration may be located in headquarters that are removed from the operations personnel. The complexity of the organization may also cause prolonged delays in communication. For example, if a patrol officer observes a problem that needs to be taken to the highest level, normally this information must first be taken to the sergeant and then to the lieutenant, the captain, the deputy chief or the chief, and so on. At each level, the superiors reflect on the problem, putting their own interpretation on it (possibly including how the problem might affect them professionally or even personally) and perhaps diluting or distorting the problem. Thus, delays in communication are inherent in a bureaucracy.

Horizontal communication thrives in an organization when formal communication channels are not open.[24] The disadvantage of horizontal communication is that it is much easier and more natural to achieve than vertical communication; therefore, it often replaces vertical channels. Horizontal channels are usually of an informal nature, including the grapevine (which is discussed next). The advantage is that horizontal communication is essential if the subsystems within a police organization are to function in an effective and coordinated manner. Horizontal communication among peers may also provide emotional and social bonds that build morale and feelings of teamwork among employees.

The Grapevine Something "heard through the grapevine" is a rumor from an anonymous source. The expression "grapevine telegraph" is also sometimes used, referring to the speed with which rumors spread. Rumors are another type of communication, and police agencies certainly have their share of scuttlebutt. Departments even establish rumor control centers during major riots. Compounding the usual barriers to communication is the fact that policing is a twenty-four-hour, seven-day occupation, so rumors are easily carried from one shift to the next.

The grapevine's most effective characteristics are that it is fast, it operates mostly at the place of work, and it supplements regular formal communication. On the positive side, it can be a tool that management can use to get a feel for employees' attitudes, to spread useful information, and to help employees vent their frustrations. The grapevine, however, can also carry untruths and be malicious. Without a doubt, the grapevine is a force for administrators to reckon with every day.

Written Communication Within complex organizations, confidence is generally placed in the written word. It establishes a permanent record, but transmitting information in this way does not necessarily ensure that the message will be clear to the receiver, despite the writer's best efforts. This may be due in large measure to shortcomings in the writer's skills. Nonetheless, police organizations rely heavily on written communication, as evidenced by the proliferation of written directives and reports found in most of these agencies.

In the same vein, written communication is also preferred as a medium for dealing with citizens or groups outside the police agency. This means of communication provides the greatest protection against the growing number of legal actions taken against agencies by activists, citizens, and interest groups. In recent years, e-mail has also proliferated as a communications medium in criminal justice organizations. E-mail can provide an easy-to-use and almost instantaneous communication through a computer—in upward, downward, or horizontal directions. For all its advantages, however, e-mail messages can lack security and be ambiguous not only with respect to the meaning of the contents but also with regard to what they represent. Are such messages, in fact, mail that should be given the full weight of an office letter or memo, or should they be treated more as offhand comments?[25]

Barriers to Effective Communication

In addition to the inaccurate nature of the grapevine and the preponderance of poor writing skills, several other potential barriers to effective communication exist. Some people, for example, are not good listeners. Unfortunately, listening is one of the most neglected and least understood of the communication arts.[26] We allow other things to obstruct our communication, including time, too little or too much information, the tendency to say what we think others want to hear, the failure to select the best word, prejudices, and strained sender–receiver relationships.[27] Also, subordinates do not always have the same "big picture" viewpoint that superiors possess and may not communicate well with more fluent and persuasive superiors.

► Local Agencies

Police Departments and Sheriff's Offices: A Comparison

Today Sir Robert Peel (discussed in Chapter 1) would be amazed because there are about 17,000 general-purpose municipal police departments and county sheriff's departments in the United States.[28] The 12,501 municipal agencies are composed of about 463,000 sworn full-time police officers,[29] and 3,063 sheriff's offices employ about 183,000 sworn full-time deputies.[30] Following is a brief overview of their employee composition, hiring practices, and some authorized equipment. Municipal police departments employ an average of 2.3 officers per 1,000 population; about one in eight of these sworn employees is a woman, and one in four is a member of a racial or ethnic minority. For recruiting qualified personnel, 86 percent of these agencies use physical agility tests, 82 percent use written aptitude tests, and two-thirds employ personality inventories. On average, these officers receive 1,370 hours of recruit training in their academy. Significantly, about half of local police agencies employ fewer than ten sworn personnel. Two-thirds of these agencies require their officers to wear protective body armor at all times while on duty; 61 percent use video cameras in patrol cars, three-fourths authorize the use of electronic control devices (such as a Taser), and more than 90 percent of agencies serving 25,000 or more residents use in-car computers.

More information concerning municipal police agencies may be obtained at: http://bjs.ojp.usdoj.gov/index.cfm?ty=pbdetail&iid=2216).[31] In county sheriff's departments, about one in eight sworn employees is a woman, and 19 percent are members of a racial or ethnic minority. For recruiting qualified personnel, 74 percent of these agencies use physical agility tests, 68 percent use written aptitude tests, and 52 percent employ personality inventories. On average, new deputy recruits receive about 1,500 hours of recruit training in their academy. About three-fifths of sheriff's departments employ fewer than twenty-five sworn personnel. Fifty-seven percent of these agencies require their officers to wear protective body armor at all times while on duty; two-thirds use video cameras in patrol cars, 79 percent authorize the use of electronic control devices (such as a Taser), and about 80 percent of agencies use in-car computers. More information concerning county sheriff's departments may be obtained at: http://bjs.ojp.usdoj.gov/index.cfm?ty=tp&tid=72.[32]

Executive Officers: Police Chief and County Sheriffs

Having analyzed police organizations, we now look at the two primary chief executive officers: the police chief (also known as the police superintendent, commissioner, or director) and the county sheriff. After looking at the qualifications for and functions of these positions, we consider their roles in more detail with the Mintzberg model of chief executive officers.

The chief or sheriff of a ten-person agency faces many of the same problems and expectations as his or her big-city counterpart. The difference between managing large and small departments is a matter of scale. Executives of large departments face a larger volume of many of the same problems that executives of small departments face. The leader of a small department must not only deal with all these managerial concerns but in many cases must also perform the duties of a working officer.

Furthermore, the police manager's style must be flexible. Management style is always contingent on the situation and the people being managed.[33] The police manager would behave one way at the scene of a hostage situation and another way at the scene of a shoplifting. A less experienced employee will require a more authoritarian style of management than a more experienced employee.

Chiefs of Police Qualifications, Selection, and Tenure The required qualifications for the position of chief of police vary widely, depending on the size of the agency and the region of the country. Smaller agencies, especially those in rural areas, may not have any minimum educational requirement for the job. Large agencies, on the other hand, may require college education plus several years of progressively responsible police management experience.[34]

Although it is certainly cheaper to select a police chief from within the organization than to recruit an outsider, the value of doing so is open to debate. There are obvious advantages and disadvantages to both practices. One study of police chiefs promoted from within and hired from outside in the West found significant differences in only one area: educational attainment. The outsiders were more highly educated, but the two groups did not differ in other areas, including background, attitudes, salary, tenure in current position or in policing, and size of agency, community, or current budget.[35] Some states have made it nearly impossible for nonresidents to be hired as police chiefs. For example, California has mandated that the chief be a graduate of its full Peace Officers Standards and Training (POST) academy; New Jersey and New York also encourage "homegrown" chiefs.[36]

A survey of 358 police chiefs in larger jurisdictions (50,000 or more residents) conducted by the Police Executive Research Forum (PERF) found that these chiefs were more educated than ever before (87 percent held a bachelor's degree and 47 percent had a master's degree) and were more likely to have been chosen from outside the agencies they head. Even so, most chiefs spent less than five years in the position.[37]

To obtain the most capable people for executive positions in policing—and to avoid personnel, liability, and other kinds of problems that can arise from poor personnel choices—many agencies have adopted the assessment center method (discussed in Chapter 4), an elaborate yet efficacious means of hiring and promoting personnel. Although more costly and time consuming than conventional testing methods (e.g., candidates' resumes are examined and oral interviews are held), the assessment center method is well worth the extra investment. Money invested at the early stages of hiring or promotion can save untold dollars and problems for many years to come. The process may include interviews; psychological tests; management tasks; group discussions; simulations of interviews with subordinates, the public, and the news media; fact-finding exercises; oral presentation exercises; and written communications exercises.[38]

Job security for police chiefs ranges from full civil service protection in a small percentage of agencies to appointment and removal at the discretion of the mayor or city manager. There is a growing trend for a fixed term of office, such as a four- or five-year contract. Traditionally, however, the tenure of police chiefs has been short. A federal study in the mid-1970s found that the average term in office by chiefs of police was 5.4 years.[39] Another study by PERF a decade later found the average to be practically unchanged: 5.5 years. That figure has not changed in more recent times.[40] Those who are appointed from within the agency tend to have longer tenure than those appointed from outside. This lack of job tenure has several negative consequences, including the difficulty of long-range planning, the possible negative effect of frequently having new policies and administrative styles, the inability of the short-term chief to develop a political power base and local influence, and the time and expense involved in hiring a new chief.

A Career Profile describes the work of the police chief.

Sheriffs Nature of Position As discussed in Chapter 1, the position of sheriff has a long tradition. Sheriffs today tend to be elected; thus most candidates are aligned with a political party, and it is possible that the only qualification a person brings to the office is the ability to get votes.

In some areas of the country, the sheriff's term of office is limited to two years, and the sheriff is prohibited from serving successive terms. In most counties, however, the sheriff has a four-year term and can be reelected. Sheriffs enjoy no guarantee of tenure in office, although a federal study found that sheriffs (who average 6.7 years in office) had longer tenure in office than police chiefs.[41] The politicization of the office of sheriff can obviously result in both high turnover rates of personnel who do not have civil service protection and a lack of long-range (strategic) planning.

Also, largely due to the political nature of the office, sheriffs tend to be older, are less likely to have been promoted through the ranks of the agency, have less specialized training, and are less likely to be college graduates compared to police chiefs. Research has also found that sheriffs in small agencies have more difficulty with organizational problems (e.g., field activities and budget management), whereas sheriffs in large agencies find dealing with local officials and using planning and evaluation to be more troublesome.

Functions. Because of the diversity of sheriffs' offices throughout the country, it is difficult to describe a "typical" sheriff's department; the offices run the gamut from the traditional, highly political, limited-service office to the modern, fairly nonpolitical, full-service police organization.[42] It is possible, however, to list functions commonly associated with the sheriff's office:

- Maintaining and operating the county correctional institutions
- Serving civil processes (protective orders, liens, evictions, garnishments, and attachments) and performing other civil duties, such as extradition and transportation of prisoners
- Collecting certain taxes and conducting real estate sales (usually for nonpayment of taxes) for the county

Career Profile

Name: Theron L. Bowman, Ph.D.

Position: Police Chief

City, State: Arlington, Texas

College attended: University of Texas at Arlington

Academic Majors: Ph.D., urban and public administration; master's, public administration; bachelor's, biology

(Courtesy Theron L. Bowman, Ph.D.)

How long have you occupied this position/assignment?

I served as Arlington, Texas (APD) Police Chief for 13.5 years. I began my career in law enforcement there in 1983 and served in narcotics, patrol, personnel/recruiting, and community affairs before promoting to sergeant, lieutenant, deputy chief and assistant chief. I became police chief in 1999.

How would you briefly describe this position/assignment:

As Chief of Police, I serve as the chief administrator of a department consisting of about 640 sworn officers. I am responsible for policy development, supervision and implementation of programs administered by the APD, and work to ensure that established goals, long-range plans, objectives and policies are being administered across the organization. I am responsible for budgetary oversight of the APD and work closely with law enforcement officials from other jurisdictions. An inordinate amount of time is spent looking at the future, so the position requires being visionary, forward-leaning, and to some extent prophetic. The APD upholds the highest standards in policing and accountability, as evidenced by its accreditation by the Commission on Accreditation for Law Enforcement Agencies.

What attracted you to this position/assignment?

My passion for law enforcement and public safety began as a young boy growing up in Fort Worth, where a police officer in my neighborhood made a lasting and positive impact on my life. Upon graduation from college I applied to the APD because I wanted a rewarding career in law enforcement. I was attracted to the Police Chief's position because I wanted to make a bigger impact on quality in life in our city, specifically in our neighborhoods and with our youth. I wanted to work closer with the city's executive team and our City Council to preserve the quality of life in our neighborhoods. This was an opportunity for me to leverage partnerships and encourage more community investment in making Arlington a safer city. Arlington is also a tourist destination (more than six million visitors travel here annually), so the safety of our guests is also very important to me.

What qualities/characteristics are most helpful for this position/assignment?

It is important to have a proven history as an innovative leader. One must be knowledgeable of the principles and practices of modern police administration; have extensive knowledge of state statutes, codes, federal guidelines, protocols and all local ordinances relating to law enforcement; have a true passion for public service and law enforcement; and have demonstrated success in the areas of communications and planning. He or she must also be able to grow community and regional partnerships and have a good combination of experience and education. The "icing on the cake" would be a healthy dose of political savvy: be capable in political arenas, be politically astute, and drive appropriate legislative agendas without being political.

How would you describe a typical day for one in this position/assignment?

Attending meetings with command staff to discuss and understand the day-to-day issues and challenges occurring in the department and city. We consistently work to identify ways to maintain high-quality, cost-effective services that improve safety for our citizens and visitors. My day may also include meetings with neighborhood groups, youth groups, school officials, business/economic partners, the city manager, mayor and city council members. The day could also include coordination of regional projects that might impact public safety in North Texas.

What advice would you offer someone who is beginning their studies of policing and criminal justice?

Study and learn about policing methods. Learn everything you can about the history and culture of policing because they impact current operational and management philosophies. Seek exposure to disciplines outside of policing as well to assist in developing well-rounded approaches policing communities. Maintain high morals and values and always make good choices. Take advantage of internship opportunities where available. Pursue graduate studies. Seek out opportunities to enhance leadership skills. Understand that with the call into policing comes an obligation to yourself, your agency and the field to make it better than it would have been without your influence.

- Performing routine order-maintenance duties by enforcing state statutes and county ordinances, arresting offenders, and performing traffic and criminal investigations
- Serving as bailiff of the courts

Other general duties vary from one region to another.

Next we continue to discuss the roles of police chiefs and sheriffs but in a different manner, using the Mintzberg model of chief executive officers.

▲ About three-fourths of all sheriff's offices operate a jail. *(Courtesy Washoe County Sheriff's Office.)*

▶ Mintzberg Model of Chief Executive Officers

What do contemporary police executives really do? Ronald Lynch described in simple terms their primary tasks:

> They listen, talk, write, confer, think, decide—about men, money, materials, methods, facilities—in order to plan, organize, direct, coordinate, and control their research service,

production, public relations, employee relations, and all other activities so that they may more effectively serve the citizens to whom they are responsible.[43]

A police executive actually has many roles. Some chief executive officers (CEOs) openly endorse and subscribe to the philosophy of Henry Mintzberg, who described a set of behaviors and tasks of CEOs in any organization.[44] Following is an overview of the roles of the police agency CEO—that is, the chief of police or sheriff—using the Mintzberg model and its interpersonal, informational, and decision-maker roles as an analytic framework.

Interpersonal Role

First we will consider the interpersonal role, which includes figurehead, leadership, and liaison duties. As a figurehead, the CEO performs various ceremonial functions. Examples include riding in parades and attending other civic events; speaking before school and university classes and civic organizations; meeting with visiting officials and dignitaries; attending academy graduations and swearing-in ceremonies and some weddings and funerals; and visiting injured officers in the hospital. Like the mayor who cuts ribbons and kisses babies, the CEO performs these duties simply because of his or her position within the organization; the duties come with being a figurehead. Although police chiefs and sheriffs cannot realistically be expected to commit to every committee meeting, speaking engagement, and other event to which they are invited, they are obligated from a professional standpoint to attend as many as they can.

The leadership function requires the CEO to motivate and coordinate workers while resolving different goals and needs within the department and the community. A chief or sheriff may have to urge the governing board to enact a code or ordinance that, whether popular or not, is in the best interest of the jurisdiction. For example, a police chief recently led a drive to pass an ordinance that prohibited university students parking in residential neighborhoods surrounding the campus, which was a highly unpopular undertaking, but the chief pursued it because of the hardships suffered by the area residents. CEOs also provide leadership in such matters as bond issues (to raise money for more officers or new buildings) and should advise the governing body on the effects of proposed ordinances.

The role as liaison is performed when the CEO of a police organization interacts with other organizations and coordinates workflows. It is not uncommon for police executives from one geographic area—the police chief, the sheriff, the ranking officer of the local highway patrol office, the district attorney, the campus police chief—to meet informally each month to discuss common problems and strategies. Also, the chief executives serve as liaisons between their agencies and others in forming regional police councils, narcotics units, crime labs, dispatching centers, and so forth. They also meet with representatives of the courts, the juvenile system, and other criminal justice agencies.

Informational Role

The second major role of a CEO under the Mintzberg model is the informational role, which involves the CEO in monitoring/inspecting and disseminating information and acting as spokesperson. In the monitoring/inspecting function, the CEO constantly looks at the workings of the department to ensure that things are operating smoothly (or as smoothly as a police agency can be expected to run). This function is often referred to as "roaming the ship," and many CEOs who have isolated themselves from their personnel and from the daily operations of the agency can speak from sad experience of the need to be alert and to create a presence. Many police executives use daily staff meetings to discuss any information about the past twenty-four hours that might affect the department.

The disseminating tasks involve both getting information to members of the department and to the public. The former may include memorandums, special orders, general orders, and policies. For the latter, it must be remembered that news organizations, especially the television and print media, are highly competitive businesses that seek to obtain the most complete news in the shortest amount of time—which often translates to wider viewership and therefore greater advertising revenues for them. From one perspective, the media must appreciate that a criminal investigation can be seriously compromised by premature or excessive coverage. From another perspective, the public has a legitimate right to know what is occurring in the community, especially matters relating to crime. Therefore, the prudent police executive attempts to have an open and professional relationship with the media in which each side knows and understands its responsibilities. Many chief executives employ a public information officer (PIO) who is trained in public speaking as well as what kinds of and how much information should be divulged to media outlets. Unfortunately, however, there is no lack of police executives who failed to develop and maintain an appropriate relationship with the media. Such chief executives must recognize the power of the pen or, as one person put it, "Don't argue with someone who buys his ink by the barrel!"

Decision-Maker Role

As a decision maker, the CEO of a police organization serves as an entrepreneur, a disturbance handler, a resource allocator, and a negotiator. As entrepreneur, the CEO must sell ideas to the governing board or the department. Ideas might include new computers or a new communications system, a policing strategy (such as COPPS), or different work methods, all of which are intended to improve the organization. Sometimes there is a blending of roles, as when several police executives band together (functioning as liaisons) and go to the state attorney general and the legislature to lobby (in an entrepreneurial capacity) for new crime-fighting laws.

As a disturbance handler, the executive's tasks range from the minor (perhaps resolving trivial disputes between staff members) to the major (such as handling riots or muggings in a local park or cleaning up the city's downtown). Sometimes the intradepartmental disputes can reach major proportions; for example, if the patrol commander tells the street officers to arrest more public drunks, it might create a severe strain on the jail division commander's resources, causing enmity between the two commanders and forcing the chief executive to intervene.

As a resource allocator, the CEO must be able to say no to subordinates. However, subordinates should not be faulted for trying to obtain more resources or for trying to improve their unit as best they can. The CEO must have a clear idea of the budget and what the priorities are and must listen to citizen complaints and act accordingly. For example, ongoing complaints of motorists speeding in a specific area will result in a shifting of patrol resources to that area or neighborhood.

As a negotiator, the police manager resolves employee grievances and sits as a member of the negotiating team for labor relations. A survey by PERF found that seven out of ten municipal police departments with more than seventy-five employees have some form of union representation.[45]

Collective bargaining puts the CEO in a difficult position. As a member of management, the CEO is often compelled to argue against salaries and benefits that would benefit the rank and file. As mentioned earlier, however, as long as a limited supply of funds is available to the jurisdiction, managers will have to draw the line at some point and say no to subordinates. Again, the collective-bargaining unit and individual officers cannot be faulted for trying to improve salaries, benefits, and working conditions, but sometimes these associations go outside the boundary of reasonableness and reach an impasse or deadlock in contract negotiations with management. These situations can become uncomfortable and even disastrous, leading to work stoppages, work speedups, work slowdowns, or other such tactics (discussed in detail in Chapter 8).

► Middle Managers: Captains and Lieutenants

Note: A Career Profile in Chapter 12 describes the work of a captain who also commands a department's special operations unit; another Career Profile, in Chapter 8 (concerning police accountability) describes a lieutenant's duties.

Few police administration books discuss the middle managers of a police department: captains and lieutenants. This is unfortunate because they are too numerous and too powerful within police organizations to ignore. Opinions vary about these mid-management personnel, however. Normally, captains and lieutenants are commissioned officers, with the position of captain second in rank to the executive managers. Captains have authority over all officers of the agency below the chief or sheriff, to whom they are solely responsible. Lieutenants are in charge of sergeants and all officers and report to captains. Captains and lieutenants may perform the following functions:[46]

- Inspecting assigned operations.
- Reviewing and making recommendations on reports.
- Helping to develop plans.
- Preparing work schedules.
- Overseeing records and equipment.
- Overseeing recovered or confiscated property.
- Enforcing all laws and orders.

Too often middle managers become glorified paper pushers, especially in the present climate of myriad reports, budgets, grants, and so on. Police agencies should take a hard look at what managerial services are essential and whether lieutenants are needed to perform such services. Recently some communities, such as Kansas City, Missouri, eliminated the rank of lieutenant, finding that this move had no negative consequences and some positive effects.[47]

Obviously, when a multilayered bureaucracy is created, a feudal kingdom and several fiefdoms will occupy the building. As Richard Holden observed, however, "If feudalism was so practical, it would not have died out in the Middle Ages."[48] It is important to remember that the two crucial elements to organizational effectiveness are top administrators and operational personnel. Middle management can pose a threat to the agency by acting as a barrier between these two primary elements. Research has shown an inverse relationship between the size of the hierarchy in an organization and its effectiveness.[49] Normally, the closer the administrator is to the operations, the more effective the agency.

► First-Line Supervisors

At some point during the career of a patrol officer who has acquired the minimum years of experience, he or she has the opportunity to test for promotion to first-line supervisor, or sergeant. Competition for this position is quite keen in most departments. To compete well, officers are often advised to rotate into different agency assignments to gain exposure to a variety of both police functions and supervisors before testing for the sergeant's position. The promotional system, then, favors not only those officers who are skilled at test taking but also those who have experience outside the patrol division.[50]

The supervisor's role, put simply, is to get his or her subordinates to do their very best. This task involves a host of activities, including communicating, motivating, mediating, mentoring, leading, team building, training, developing, appraising, counseling, and

▲ A newly promoted sergeant. The rank of sergeant is one of the most difficult and challenging positions in a police organization. *(Courtesy Kenneth J. Peak.)*

disciplining. As a result, no other rank in the police hierarchy exerts more direct influence over the working environment, morale, and performance of employees.

Adding to the complexity of the supervisor's role is the fact that the supervisor is generally in his or her first leadership position. A new supervisor must learn how to exercise command and be responsible for the behavior of several other employees. Long-standing relationships are put under stress when one party suddenly has official authority over former equals. Expectations of leniency or preferential treatment may have to be dealt with.

The supervisor is caught in the middle, working with rank-and-file employees—labor—on the one hand and middle or upper management on the other. While it is management's job to squeeze as much productivity out of workers as possible, labor's motivation often seems to be to avoid work as much as possible. Supervisors find themselves right in the middle of this contest.

Ten Tasks

For all these reasons, the first-line supervisor has one of the most complex roles in the organization. If the supervisor fails to make sure that employees perform correctly, the unit will not be very successful, causing difficulties for mid-level managers and administrators. The following ten tasks are most important for sergeants and are listed in order of their importance:[51]

1. Supervising subordinate officers in the performance of their duties (including such tasks as maintaining inventory of equipment, training subordinates, preparing monthly activity reports, scheduling vacation leave).
2. Disseminating information to subordinates.
3. Ensuring that general and special orders are followed.
4. Observing subordinates in handling calls and other duties (including securing major crime scenes).
5. Reviewing and approving various departmental reports.
6. Listening to problems voiced by officers.

7. Answering backup calls.

8. Keeping superiors apprised of ongoing situations.

9. Providing direct supervision for potential high-risk calls or situations.

10. Interpreting policies and informing subordinates.

▶ Police and Politics

Good Politics, Bad Politics

As we saw in Chapter 1, the history of policing is so replete with politics that it even experienced a political "era." Still, this is an aspect of policing that is often overlooked, and it has had both good and bad elements. Political influence can range from major beneficial policy, personnel, and budgetary decisions to the overzealous city manager or city council member who wants to micromanage the police department and even appears unexpectedly at night at a crime scene (overheard on his or her police scanner) to "help" the officers.

Norm Stamper, former chief of police in Seattle, Washington, described the relationship between politics and policing very well:

> *Everything* about policing is ultimately political. Who gets which office: political. Which services are cut when there's a budget freeze: political. Who gets hired, fired, promoted: political, political, political. The challenge . . . is to make sure the politics of picking and promoting people is as fair as possible. And as mindful of the *greater good* of the organization and of the community as possible. I hire my brother-in-law's cousin, a certifiable doofus, because he's got a bass boat I wouldn't mind borrowing—bad politics. I promote a drinking buddy—bad politics. I pick an individual because he or she will add value to the organization and will serve the community honorably—good politics.[52]
>
> —*Excerpt from "Relationship between Politics and Policing" by Norm Stamper from BREAKING RANK: A TOP COP'S EXPOSE OF THE DARK SIDE OF AMERICAN POLICING. Published by Nations Book, © 2005.*

Policing can be said to be very similar to politics, which is defined as: "The activities associated with the governance of a country or other area, especially the debate or conflict among individuals or parties having or hoping to achieve power."[53] Both words derive from the Greek terms for "citizen" and "citizenship," and *police* also comes from the Greek word for "city": *polis*; furthermore, both politics and policing certainly involve debate or conflict.

Historically, police departments in the United States have been political bodies, extensions of the municipal political authority.[54] Because of the close relationship between police departments and the political leadership of the community, political power has often been abused (see Exhibit 11-1 ■). From the beginning of the twentieth century, when the journalist Lincoln Steffens exposed corruption in American cities, to more recent times, when police scandals have rocked departments in New York City, Chicago, and Miami, politics has been shown to be entwined in the relationships that often bind criminals and police officers. Partisan politics has often been the cause of police corruption.[55]

Police Executive Relations and Expectations

The chief of police is generally considered to be one of the most influential and prestigious people in local government. However, much of the power of the office has eroded because of the high attrition rate, the increased power of local personnel departments, and the strong influence of police unions. Furthermore, mayors, city managers and administrators, members of the agency, citizens, special-interest groups, and the media all have differing, often conflicting, expectations of the role of chief of police.

The mayor or city manager is likely to believe that the chief of police should be an enlightened administrator whose responsibility is to promote departmental efficiency,

EXHIBIT 11-1

REDUCING OR ELIMINATING POLITICS: THE KANSAS CITY, MISSOURI, BOARD OF POLICE COMMISSIONERS

In the 1920s and 1930s, Thomas Pendergast's political "machine" ran Kansas City, Missouri: workers were provided jobs, handpicked politicians ran the government, and Pendergast profited handsomely. In 1932, the City Council, under Pendergast's influence, approved a home-rule ordinance bringing the police department (KCPD) under city governance for the first time since its inception in 1874. Thus the department was another cog in the Pendergast machine, and officers ignored illegal gambling, prostitution and saloons in order to stay in the boss's favor. In 1939, however, the state attorney general began a campaign against the machine, and the governor had the police department returned to state control. Thus was reinstated the governor-appointed Board of Police Commissioners, the system in use today.

Today, the KCPD Board of Police Commissioners is statutorily mandated to provide police service to the citizens of Kansas City. The state's governor, with the consent of the senate, appoints four citizens to serve on the Board for four-year terms. The fifth member of the Board is the city's mayor, with the Board's secretary appointed by the Commissioners and acting as legal consultant. The KCPD is one of only two police departments in the nation (in addition to St. Louis) that is so governed, as opposed to being overseen by a city council/commission.

It is believed that this concept is excellent for keeping politics and corruption out of policing, given that the Board, except for the mayor, is composed of people who are not elected politicians, not running for office, and not raising campaign funds. Indeed, those four police commissioners *must take an oath not to engage in political activity*.

The city government does, however, provide (and control) the department with funding, and police commanders and others regularly attend city meetings and work on consolidated projects in such areas as radio maintenance, parking control, dispatching, and information technology.

Source: Reducing or Eliminating Politics: The Kansas City, Missouri, Board of Police Commissioners, Kansas City Board of Police Commissioners, KANSAS CITY MISSOURI POLICE DEPARTMENT, 2012.

reduce crime, improve service, and so on. Other mayors and managers will appreciate the chief who simply "keeps the lid on" and manages to keep the morale high and the number of citizen complaints low.[56] However, the mayor or city manager may also properly expect the chief to be part of the city management team, communicate city management's policies to police personnel, establish agency goals and objectives, select and effectively manage people, and be a responsible steward of the budget.[57]

The relationship between the police chief and the mayor is difficult to articulate. However, several points are indispensable in the relationship. First, the mayor is boss; indeed, the mayor possesses the legal or political power to fire or force the police chief out of office almost at whim. Second, the mayor has the responsibility for assuring the public that the police are doing the best they can with available resources. Third, the police executive, if chosen on merit, has considerable knowledge about the problems of the community and a wide array of possible solutions—expertise that will serve city hall well—and the mayor should come to rely on the chief's pragmatism and take-charge approach as well. Finally, the mayor must give the chief the authority to run his or her department day to day; without this autonomy, perhaps guided by the mayor's input, the chief's authority will be eroded.[58]

Members of the police agency may have different expectations of the chief executive. They may be less concerned with cost-effectiveness and more concerned with good salaries, benefits, and equipment. The officers expect the chief to be their advocate, backing them up when necessary and representing the agency well in dealings with judges and prosecutors who may be indifferent or hostile to their interests. Citizens, for their part, expect the chief of police to provide efficient and cost-effective police services while keeping crime and tax rates down and eliminating corruption and illegal use of force.

Special-interest groups expect the chief to advocate desirable policy positions; for example, Mothers Against Drunk Driving (MADD) insists on strong police measures combating driving under the influence. Finally, the media expect the chief to cooperate fully with their efforts to obtain fast and complete crime information.

▶ Policing in Small and Rural Jurisdictions

Fewer People, Greater Needs

Although (and perhaps because) rural America is disappearing according to the latest U.S. census—now accounting for only 16 percent of the nation's population[59]—as indicated above, about half of municipal police agencies employ fewer than ten employees, and about three-fifths of sheriff's offices having fewer than twenty-five employees. Therefore, special mention is warranted of policing in rural and small-town venues.

In 2007, the U.S. Congress formally recognized the important roles and needs of rural police agencies, creating the Rural Policing Institute (RPI) within the Federal Law Enforcement Training Center (FLETC, discussed in Chapter 10) and requiring the RPI to: evaluate the needs of law enforcement agencies and other emergency responders in rural areas; develop expert training programs based on identified needs; deliver training programs to rural law enforcement officers and other emergency response providers; and conduct outreach efforts to ensure rural agencies are aware of the training.[60]

Unique Duties

Police officers and deputy sheriffs in small and rural venues often have vastly different duties than their urban counterparts. First, although the annual reports published by the Federal Bureau of Investigation (FBI) do not indicate a proportionately high number of officers in small towns and rural areas being killed either by felonious or accidental means,[61] the work is more solitary in nature and thus danger is omnipresent, with a county deputy's nearest backup unit—if there is one—possibly being dozens of miles away.

Where actual police work is concerned, because of their much more flattened organizational structure, these officers typically must be generalists rather than having specialized assignments, working all manner of criminal cases from beginning to end (with the possible exception of serious, violent crimes, which might require that the state's bureau of investigation, or SBI, discussed in Chapter 10, be called for assistance). And the work varies considerably; for example, a deputy sheriff may be working a burglary today and a livestock theft tomorrow; protecting a crime scene involving a murder this morning and patrolling the most remote areas in a four-wheel drive truck or on a horse later in the day. Rural and small-town officers may be assigned more mundane chores than their larger counterparts, such as: locking and unlocking municipal parking lots, emptying parking meters, delivering meeting agendas to the homes of governing officials, picking up the daily receipts at the local swimming pool or golf course, and so on. Finally, they work more in the public eye—the "fishbowl effect," which can certainly cause a higher level of stress.

A Career Profile describes some of the challenges of providing police services in a small/rural jurisdiction.

Criminal Activity

According to the FBI's *Uniform Crime Reports*, larceny-theft is the only Part I offense reported by police as committed in rural areas at a higher rate than the national average (in jurisdictions of less than 10,000 population).[62] More problematical, however, is rural

Career Profile

(Courtesy Pat Soukup.)

Name: Pat Soukup

Position: Captain, Administrative Services, Lyon County (Nevada) Sheriff's Office (currently managing the Jail Division and Dispatch Center)

City, State: Yerington, Nevada

College attended: University of Nevada, Reno

Academic Major: Criminal Justice

How long have you occupied this position/assignment?

Employed by the sheriff's office for 23.5 years, serving in the Field and Administrative Services Divisions; have served in this current position for the past 4.5 years.

How would you briefly describe this position/assignment:

My primary roles are: managing the jail and dispatch supervisors and assist with administrative processes; overseeing entry level and promotional testing; securing advanced training for personnel; assisting the sheriff with budgets and policies; completing progress reports on grant funding; and monitoring/enforcing professional standards throughout the agency (via the internal/citizen complaint process.

What attracted you to this position/assignment?

After serving for several years as the Patrol Services Captain, I was attracted to this position because it was new and challenging to me. The Jail Division has more liability than any other division of this agency, and both the jail and dispatch have a mixture of sworn and non-sworn employees, which makes supervision more diverse.

What qualities/characteristics are most helpful for this position/assignment?

Education, confidence, trustworthiness, and most importantly, the ability to trust your subordinate supervisors to do the job they were trained for, with minimal input.

How would you describe a typical day for one in this position/assignment?

Communicating with my lieutenant who is in charge of the jail and also with the dispatch manager, to remain current on any issues facing either division; completing grant reports; reviewing/writing employee evaluations; and researching training and reviewing any administrative situations assigned to me by my superiors. I also might attend meetings involving a multi-agency advisory board and others covering such topics as budgets, training, policies, etc.

What advice would you offer someone who is beginning their studies of policing and criminal justice?

Truly understand the education you are receiving at the college level. It isn't designed to train you how to immediately do a job in law enforcement, but it will give you a well-rounded background to draw from as you deal with diverse groups in our society. Plan your career as well as you can from the beginning, and obtain training that is conducive to attaining those goals.

Challenges of policing in small and rural jurisdictions:

The effects on the smaller agencies caused by budgets and legislation are significant. My county contains several townships that are serviced by the Sheriff's Office, which increases costs for our office space, patrol cars, fuels, manpower, supplies, and support staff. Each patrol area must be supplied with a similar infrastructure. In addition, the jail is located in the county seat requiring each area to transport prisoners. Also, rural areas have the same types of crimes as large urban areas, just not in the same frequency. When serious crimes occur, there can be a major impact on the county budget. Furthermore, rural agencies generally don't have the budgets to maintain seldom-used equipment or personnel (e.g., DNA laboratories, psychiatrists, coroners, and so on), so we must normally contract for such services through larger agencies. In addition, major crimes such as homicides can be very expensive in the investigative phase, trial preparation, and the actual trial. If several homicides occur within a calendar year, the District Attorney and Sheriff's Office budgets could be almost entirely consumed, resulting in contingency requests. Finally, as science and technology increasingly enter crime and the criminal justice system, police training must keep pace. Many agencies conduct their own in-house training for basic (e.g., firearms, defensive tactics) but must pay for and travel to larger jurisdictions to receive advanced training. Unfortunately, when budgets decrease, two of the first items to be cut are usually training and travel; thus the quality of investigations can decrease and threats of lawsuits can increase from investigative shortcomings.

narcotics enforcement; in fact, some authorities argue it cannot be done. One source states that agencies serving less than 7,000 citizens are unable to dedicate sworn officers to full-time narcotics enforcement, so planning and executing investigations is not feasible.[63]

If there does appear to be a drug problem in the area (based perhaps on surveys, arrest statistics, and discussions with local citizens and area police agencies), local agencies are urged to determine the most effective investigative approach, such as use of undercover agents, confidential informants, reverse stings (also known as "buy and bust," where an officer pretends to be a drug dealer and sells to an unsuspecting customer), and so on;

then—depending on their level of resources—the agency can either contact an outside, state bureau of investigation or attempt to perform the investigation itself.

▶ Ways to Stretch Resources

The United States has many small police agencies; in fact, of the estimated seventeen thousand local police departments, nearly half (45.5 percent) employ fewer than ten sworn personnel; three-fourths employ twenty-five or fewer sworn personnel.[64] Many communities that are small in size find it extremely difficult (if not impossible) to maintain a 24/7 police or sheriff's department—particularly one that is trained and staffed well enough to provide a full range of policing services. Therefore, several approaches have been developed by agencies facing staffing and funding shortages for reducing and/or sharing the costs of full enforcement operations: contracting, consolidating, and civilianizing services. Next, we discuss the means by which this can be—and is being—done.

Consolidated Policing

A means of unifying agencies and possibly achieving cost savings is through consolidated policing, which is the merging of two or more city and/or county governments into a single policing entity. There are variations of consolidation that occur to a lesser degree, however, including: *functional* (two or more agencies combine certain functional units, such as jail, communications/dispatch, or records), *cross deputization/overlapping jurisdictions* (such as a county agency permitting a city's police officers to make arrests in the county, or a city allowing a sheriff's department's deputies to make arrests in the city), *public safety* (city or county governments may unite all police, fire, and emergency medical services agencies), *local merger* (two separate police agencies form a single new entity), regional (a number of agencies combine to police a geographic area rather than a jurisdictional one), metropolitan (two or more agencies serving overlapping jurisdictions join forces to become one agency serving an entire metropolitan area), and government (a city and adjoining county consolidate their entire governments, creating a "metro" form of government for all citizens[65]).

Separate jurisdictions that combine into a single agency can have their sworn personnel enforcing a single set of statutes or ordinances, wearing the same uniform, driving the same type of patrol vehicle, and so on. Again, the advantage is in avoiding duplication of services (e.g., by having the ability to purchase equipment in larger volume), which leads to economy of scale. As a caveat, however, the initial cost of implementing consolidation can be high. In some states, the enabling legislation requires that when two or more agencies combine their operations, the best salary and benefits packages that already existed be brought into the newly consolidated organization. This so-called cherry picking can obviously be quite expensive, especially in the initial stages of consolidation when the new consolidated agency may also be top-heavy with administrative personnel. Cost savings to be realized through consolidation, therefore, may not be realized for many years (if ever), depending on how the agency is structured, how the enabling legislation is written, and so on.

Civilianization

Most citizen calls for police service do not involve a crime or require a sworn officer to enforce the laws. For that reason, many agencies are increasingly using civilianization for a lot of functions performed traditionally by sworn personnel. This has worked particularly well for such aspects of policing as dispatching, crime analysis (forensics), crime-scene investigation, report taking, and even supplemental patrol duties. And as with contract and consolidated police services, doing so can be much more cost-effective by using nonsworn personnel, thus freeing sworn officers for critical police work. This is especially important when many agencies today are being tasked to do more with less.

In fact, the use of civilians has become so widespread that an area of controversy has arisen surrounding their use: How civilianized should the department become? Police unions are becoming increasingly wary of management's outsourcing of traditional police tasks to civilians, viewing the latter as potential threats to their livelihood. Therefore, as civilianization becomes more widespread, police chief executives must be mindful of the potential for friction and poor officer morale because no one—citizens, sworn officers, or civilian personnel—will benefit by losing a healthy and productive work environment. Where they exist, the unions should be included in any planning and discussion of civilianization and should help to fashion a plan that benefits the agency in ways that will be received well by the rank and file.[66]

▶ Agency Accreditation

In 1979, the accreditation of police agencies began with the creation of the Commission on Accreditation for Law Enforcement Agencies (CALEA), located in Gainesville, Virginia. Since then, several states have created accrediting bodies for their police and corrections organizations.[67]

CALEA is a nonprofit organization that has developed and administers 464 voluntary standards in nine subject areas for law enforcement agencies to meet. Although its primary program is for police agencies as a whole, there are also separate, stand-alone accreditations available for communications (dispatch) centers, training academies, and campus policing organizations. Prior to being accredited, the agency first completes a self-evaluation questionnaire to determine its current status. Then, when the agency is ready to attempt accreditation, an on-site team appointed by CALEA conducts an assessment and writes a report on its findings.[68] Today nearly 750 agencies are accredited or recognized in one of CALEA's various programs, with several hundred others working toward their first award.[69] Given the resources of time, effort, and funds involved to become accredited, what are the perceived benefits? According to one state-level accrediting body, the benefits of being accredited include:

- enhancing community understanding of the agency and its role in the community, as well as its goals and objectives.

- providing an in-depth review of the agency's organization, management, operations, and administration—and correcting of deficiencies before they become problems.

- evaluation of whether resources are being used in accord with agency goals, objectives, and mission.

- evaluation of agency policies and procedures.

- the opportunity to re-organize without the appearance of personal attacks on any personnel.

- providing objective measures to justify budget and personnel decisions and policies.

- increased employee morale and confidence in the effectiveness and efficiency of their agency[70].

In 2011, CALEA adopted a tiered accreditation model that allows police agencies to choose between levels of accreditation based on budget situations and staff reductions. One level is comprised of 177 standards specifically linked to life, health, and safety issues as well as those standards that are essential to the effective delivery of services for contemporary law enforcement agencies. The second level represents the full complement of CALEA's *Standards for Law Enforcement Agencies*, currently 464 standards.[71]

Summary

This chapter has presented local (municipal and county) police agencies as organizations and bureaucracies and has explored organizational communication and the roles and functions of police executives, middle managers, and first-line supervisors. A management model (per Mintzberg) was employed to clarify the general roles and functions of police administrators, and the relationship between the police and politics and how it permeates the field were also addressed. Consolidated policing and civilianization, policing in small and rural areas, as well as agency accreditation were also examined.

In the past, particularly during the political era of policing, many administrators, managers and supervisors, and officers were hired and attained their level of leadership responsibility through political favoritism. This hiring and promoting of unqualified personnel contributed heavily to the massive growth of employee labor unions. This chapter has demonstrated that today's challenges are too complex and dangerous to leave personnel administration and hiring to chance. Today, to be an effective administrator, the individual must not only know about policing but must also learn all he or she can about the most valuable asset—people. Upon acquiring these human skills, the technical, conceptual, and other necessary skills of the job must follow, lest the new leader walk off the gangplank and then sink in an ocean of "alligators." Poor administration and management skills can and do lead to serious problems of ethics, civil liability, and accountability, as was seen in earlier chapters.

Key Terms

accreditation
bureaucracy
chain of command
chief of police
civilianization
Commission on Accreditation for
    Law Enforcement Agencies
    (CALEA)

communication
consolidated policing
county sheriff's departments
first-line supervisor
middle managers
Mintzberg model
municipal police departments
organizational structure

organizations
policies and procedures
rules and regulations
Rural Policing Institute
sheriff
span of control
unity of command

Review Questions

1. What is an organization, and what elements of an organization, per Weber, are said to constitute a bureaucracy?
2. What are the elements—and purposes—of the basic organizational structure of a police agency? Diagram these basic elements.
3. What is meant by the terms *chain of command, unity of command*, and *span of control*?
4. What are the differences between policies and procedures and between rules and regulations (and what are some examples of each)?
5. What processes of, and barriers to effective communication can exist within a police organization?
6. What are the primary differences between municipal police departments and sheriff's offices?

7. What are the roles of the police executive under the Mintzberg model of chief executive officers?
8. How do the roles and functions differ for contemporary chiefs of police and county sheriffs?
9. What are the roles and functions of mid-level managers and first-line supervisors?
10. How do political influences affect policing, and how is a Board of Police Commissioners reputed to diminish or eliminate them?
11. How do consolidated and civilianized police services operate, and what are their advantages?
12. How does a police organization become accredited, and what are advantages to doing so?

Learn by Doing

1. Your commander comes to you, having heard and personally observed a number of problems concerning the manner in which communication is occurring from one duty shift to another; these problems primarily involve inaccurate information being disseminated as well as a grapevine that seems bent on carrying incorrect, malicious information. You are assigned to look at the problem as well as recommend means by which communications could be improved. How would you proceed, and what kinds of ideas might you put forth?

2. Your county sheriff has recently come out publicly in favor of consolidating all police agencies in your county. Having caught your new police chief off-guard, your police chief asks you—the agency's director of research, planning, and analysis—to explain in a memorandum all that would be involved in creating and maintaining a single county-wide police agency, to include advantages and disadvantages of doing so. How do you respond?

3. While you are working on the assignment in #1 (i.e., preparing a report on creating and maintaining a consolidated police agency in your county), you are asked by a local civic organization to appear at one of its functions and describe and compare the roles and functions of police chiefs and sheriffs. You decide to use the Mintzberg model for chief executive officers to meet this address. Prepare a presentation that does so.

Notes

1. The Museum of Broadcast Communications, "Police Programs," www.museum.tv/archives/etv/P/htmlP/policeprogra/policeprogra.htm (accessed March 5, 2013).
2. Steven Levy, "Working in Dilbert's World," *Newsweek*, August 12, 1996, pp. 52–57.
3. David A. Tansik and James F. Elliott, *Managing Police Organizations* (Monterey, CA: Duxbury, 1981), p. 1.
4. Larry K. Gaines, Mittie D. Southerland, and John E. Angell, *Police Administration* (New York: McGraw-Hill, 1991), p. 9.
5. Ibid.
6. John Kilcullen, "Max Weber: On Bureaucracy," Lecture; Pol., 246, Modern Political Theory, Macquarie University Sydney, Australia, 1996.
7. Adapted from Max Weber, *Essays in Sociology*, ed. and trans., H. H. Gerth and C. Wright Mills (New York: Oxford University Press, 1946), pp. 196–204.
8. Samuel Walker, *The Police in America: An Introduction*, 2nd ed. (New York: McGraw-Hill, 1992), p. 86.
9. *Interpersonal Communication: A Guide for Staff Development* (Athens: University of Georgia, Institute of Government, August 1974), p. 15.
10. Wayne W. Bennett and Karen Hess, *Management and Supervision in Law Enforcement*, 2nd ed. (St. Paul, MN: West, 1996), p. 85.
11. See R. C. Huseman, quoted in Bennett and Hess, *Management and Supervision in Law Enforcement*, pp. 21–27. Material for this section was also drawn from Charles R. Swanson, Leonard Territo, and Robert W. Taylor, *Police Administration: Structures, Processes, and Behavior*, 6th ed. (Upper Saddle River, NJ: Prentice Hall, 2005), pp. 309–311.
12. See George D. Eastman and Esther M. Eastman, eds., *Municipal Police Administration*, 7th ed. (Washington, DC: International City Management Association, 1971), p. 17.
13. Ibid., p. 18.
14. St. Louis Regional & Growth Association, "Greater St. Louis Area," http://www.stlrcga.org/x1044.xml (accessed October 26, 2013).
15. Metropolitan Police Department, St. Louis, Missouri, "Welcome from Chief Dan Isom," http://www.slmpd.org/ (accessed October 25, 2013).
16. President's Commission on Law Enforcement and Administration of Justice, *Task Force Report: The Police* (Washington, DC: Government Printing Office, 1967), p. 46.
17. U.S. Department of Justice, Bureau of Justice Statistics, *Police Departments in Large Cities, 1987* (Washington, DC: Author, 1989), p. 5, Table 10 (Special Report NCJ-119220).
18. M. D. Iannone and Nathan F. Iannone, *Supervision of Police Personnel*, 6th ed. (Upper Saddle River, NJ: Prentice Hall, 2000).
19. Michael Carpenter, "Put It in Writing: The Police Policy Manual," *FBI Law Enforcement Bulletin* 69 (October 2000): 1.
20. Robert Sheehan and Gary W. Cordner, *Introduction to Police Administration*, 2nd ed. (Cincinnati, OH: Anderson, 1989), pp. 446–447.

21. Charles R. Swanson, Leonard Territo, and Robert W. Taylor, *Police Administration: Structures, Processes, and Behavior*, 5th ed. (Upper Saddle River, NJ: Prentice Hall, 2001), p. 248.

22. Stephen W. Mastrofski, "Police Agency Accreditation: The Prospects of Reform," *American Journal of Police* 5(3) (1986): 45–81.

23. D. Katz and R. L. Kahn, *The Social Psychology of Organizations* (New York: John Wiley and Sons, 1966), p. 239; as cited in P. V. Lewis, *Organizational Communication: The Essence of Effective Management* (Columbus, OH: Grid, 1975), p. 36.

24. See R. K. Allen, *Organizational Management Through Communication* (New York: Harper and Row, 1977), pp. 77–79.

25. Alex Markels, "Managers Aren't Always Able to Get the Right Message Across with E-mail," *Wall Street Journal*, August 6, 1996, p. 2.

26. See, for example, Michael P. Nichols, *The Lost Art of Listening: How Learning to Listen Can Improve Relationships*, 2nd ed. (New York: The Guilford Press, 2009).

27. Bennett and Hess, Management and Supervision in Law Enforcement, p. 101.

28. U.S. Department of Justice, Bureau of Justice Statistics, "Census of State and Local Law Enforcement Agencies, 2008" (July 2011), p. 1, http://bjs.ojp.usdoj.gov/content/pub/pdf/csllea08.pdf (accessed October 25, 2013).

29. U.S. Department of Justice, Bureau of Justice Statistics, *Local Police Departments, 2007*, December 2010, p. 6, http://bjs.ojp.usdoj.gov/content/pub/pdf/lpd07.pdf (accessed October 25, 2013).

30. U.S. Department of Justice, Bureau of Justice Statistics, *Sheriff's Offices, 2003*, http://bjs.ojp.usdoj.gov/index.cfm?ty=tp&tid=72 (accessed October 24, 2013).

31. U.S. Department of Justice, Bureau of Justice Statistics, "Local Police," p. 6, http://bjs.ojp.usdoj.gov/index.cfm?ty=tp&tid=71 (accessed October 24, 2013).

32. U.S. Department of Justice, Bureau of Justice Statistics, "Sheriff's Offices," p. 2.

33. Gaines et al., *Police Administration*, pp. 10–11.

34. Ibid., p. 42.

35. Janice Penegor and Ken Peak, "Polices Chief Acquisitions: A Comparison of Internal and External Selections," *American Journal of Police* 11(1) (1992): 17–32.

36. Richard B. Weinblatt, "The Shifting Landscape of Chiefs' Jobs," *Law and Order*, October 1999, p. 50.

37. "Survey Says Big-City Chiefs Are Better-Educated Outsiders," *Law Enforcement News*, April 30, 1998, p. 7.

38. R. J. Filer, "Assessment Centers in Police Selection," in *Proceedings of the National Working Conference on the Selection of Law Enforcement Officers*, ed. C. D. Spielberger and H. C. Spaulding (Tampa: University of South Florida, March 1977), p. 103.

39. National Advisory Commission on Criminal Justice Standards and Goals, *Police Chief Executive* (Washington, DC: Government Printing Office, 1976), p. 7.

40. Weinblatt, "The Shifting Landscape of Chiefs' Jobs," p. 51.

41. National Advisory Commission on Criminal Justice Standards and Goals, *Police Chief Executive*, p. 7.

42. Clemens Bartollas, Stuart J. Miller, and Paul B. Wice, *Participants in American Criminal Justice: The Promise and the Performance* (Englewood Cliffs, NJ: Prentice Hall, 1983), pp. 51–52.

43. Ronald G. Lynch, *The Police Manager: Professional Leadership Skills*, 3rd ed. (New York: Random House, 1986), p. 1.

44. Henry Mintzberg, "The Manager's Job: Folklore and Fact," *Harvard Business Review* 53 (July–August 1975): 49–61.

45. Donald C. Witham, *The American Law Enforcement Chief Executive: A Management Profile* (Washington, DC: Police Executive Research Forum, 1985), p. xii.

46. Bennett and Hess, Management and Supervision in Law Enforcement, pp. 44–45.

47. Richard N. Holden, *Modern Police Management* (Englewood Cliffs, NJ: Prentice Hall, 1986), pp. 294–295.

48. Ibid., p. 295.

49. Thomas J. Peters and Robert H. Waterman Jr., *In Search of Excellence* (New York: Warner, 1982), pp. 306–317.

50. John Van Maanen, "Making Rank: Becoming an American Police Sergeant," in *Critical Issues in Policing: Contemporary Readings*, ed. Roger G. Dunham and Geoffrey P. Alpert (Prospect Heights, IL: Waveland Press, 1989), pp. 146–161.

51. Kenneth J. Peak, Larry K. Gaines, and Ronald W. Glensor, *Police Supervision and Management: In an Era of Community Policing*, 2nd ed. (Upper Saddle River, NJ: Prentice Hall, 2004), pp. 33–34.

52. Norm Stamper, Breaking Rank: A Top Cop's Exposé of the Dark Side of American Policing (New York: Nation Books, 2005), p. 185.

53. Oxford Dictionaries Online, oxforddictionaries.com/view/entry/m_en_us1279217#m_en_us1279217 (accessed October 25, 2013).

54. Richard Brzeczek, "Chief-Mayor Relations: The View from the Chief's Chair," in *Police Leadership in America: Crisis and Opportunity*, ed. William A. Geller (New York: Praeger, 1985), pp. 48–55.

55. George F. Cole and Christopher Smith, *The American System of Criminal Justice*, 9th ed. (Belmont, CA: West/Wadsworth, 2001), p. 237.

56. Bartollas, Miller, and Wice, *Participants in American Criminal Justice*, p. 35.

57. Ibid., pp. 39–40.

58. Ibid., pp. 49–50.

59. Hope Yen, "Rural US disappearing? Population share hits low," Yahoo News, http://news.yahoo.com/rural-us-disappearing-population-share-hits-low-205818711.html (accessed October 25, 2013).

60. See LETN, "Rural Policing Institute," http://www.rpi.letn.com/ (accessed October 25, 2013).

61. See, for example, U.S. Department of Justice, Federal Bureau of Investigation, *Law Enforcement Officers Killed & Assaulted 2012*, (http://www.fbi.gov/about-us/cjis/ucr/leoka/leoka-2010/about-leoka accessed October 25, 2013),

62. Federal Bureau of Investigation, *Crime in the United States: Uniform Crime Reports, 2012*, Table 16, http://www.fbi.gov/about-us/cjis/ucr/crime-in-the-u.s/2011/crime-in-the-u.s.-2011/tables/table_16_rate_number_of_crimes_per_100000_inhabitants_by_population_group_2011.xls (accessed October 26, 2013).

63. Jerry Carlton, "Setting Up Rural Narc Teams," *Law Enforcement Technology* 36(8) (August 2009): 52, 54–57.

64. U.S. Department of Justice, Bureau of Justice Statistics, *Law Enforcement Management and Administrative Statistics: Local Police Departments, 2003* (Washington, DC: Author, May 2006), p. 2.

65. International Association of Chiefs of Police, "Consolidating Police Services," May 2003, pp. 1–2, http://www.theiacp.org/LinkClick.aspx?fileticket=fU9dovj4EGs%3D&tabid=87 (accessed October 25, 2013).

66. Jerome H. Skolnick and James J. Fyfe, *Above the Law: Police and the Excessive Use of Force* (New York: Free Press, 1993).

67. See, for example, New York State Law Enforcement Accreditation, http://www.troopers.ny.gov/Introduction/Accreditation/; the Office of Florida Accreditation, http://www.fdle.state.fl.us/Content/Accreditation/Accreditation.aspx (accessed November 6, 2012).

68. Steven M. Cox, *Police: Practices, Perspectives, Problems* (Boston, MA: Allyn & Bacon, 1996, p. 90.

69. Personal communication, CALEA, October 25, 2006; also see the CALEA Web site, www.calea.org.

70. Adapted from Florida Law Enforcement Accreditation Commission, "Benefits of Accreditation," http://www.flaccreditation.org/Benefits.html (accessed October 26, 2013).

71. Commission on Accreditation for Law Enforcement Agencies, "CALEA Announces Tiered Law Enforcement Accreditation Program,"http://www.calea.org/calea-update-magazine/issue-105/calea-announces-tiered-law-enforcement-accreditation-program (accessed October 25, 2013).

Best Practices: Addressing Special Populations, Using Specialized Equipment

Part 5, like the four previous ones, is intended at having a grouping effect in terms of common attributes, with the emphasis here being on the problems caused by special populations of criminals, the challenges they pose for the police, and some of the methods and tools being used to deal with those problems. Chapter 12 examines several criminal *syndicates* that plague our society, including terrorists, the mob (also known as La Cosa Nostra or the mafia), gangs, and drug traffickers. Methods, relevant legislation, and other tools for coping with these crime collectives is included. Chapter 13 largely moves away from the "collective" grouping of offenders in Chapter 12, looking instead at selected *individual* offenders as well as other "people problems." Included in this chapter are crimes involving illegal immigrants (and the protection of our nation's borders), youth crimes, hate crimes, and dealing with the homeless population. As in Chapter 12, emphases here are placed on the methods, relevant legislation, and other tools that are available to the police for coping with these crimes. Finally, Chapter 14 examines a wide array of exciting police technologies that exist today or are on the horizon for detecting crime, analyzing evidence, and doing everyday work.

(Courtesy Prince James/Getty Images.)

12 Pursuing Criminal Syndicates
Terrorists, Gangs, Drug Traffickers, and the Mob

LEARNING OBJECTIVES

As a result of reading this chapter, the student will be able to:

 Define terrorism as well as its categories and types

2 Explain why cyberterrorism and bioterrorism are particularly ominous

 Review the extent, nature, and police responses to incidents involving active shooters/mass killings

 Delineate some of the basic law enforcement responses to terrorism, including the basic functions of the national incident management system

⑤ Discuss what legislative enactments are in place to help combat terrorism

⑥ Explain fusion centers and other new approaches to investigating terrorism

⑦ Discuss the definition, types, and national extent of street gangs and some successful law enforcement strategies being employed against them

⑧ Describe the nature and extent of illicit drug use and trafficking in this nation, as well as problems and strategies relating to methamphetamine, open-air drug markets, raves, bath salts and synthetic drugs

⑨ Explain the origins of organized crime, its several forms, and some means by which law enforcement agencies have been able to imprison significant numbers of mobsters

· ·

Introduction

This chapter focuses on four areas of criminality that are particularly troublesome and challenging for today's police and consume a tremendous proportion of their resources: terrorism (the structure and function of the federal Department of Homeland Security [DHS] and other federal agencies that deal with terrorism were examined in Chapter 2), the Mob (or La Cosa Nostra—generally referred to as the Mafia or organized crime), gangs, and illicit use of drugs.

Indeed, it is almost painful to dwell on the extent to which our lives would be forever changed if the police failed in their efforts in these areas: if terrorists could radically change our form of government, our freedom of speech and religion, and other protections to be like those of Middle Eastern countries; if the Mob controlled most of our everyday commerce, profited greatly from promoting vice and contraband, and threatened and killed people at will from their underground lair; if large numbers of people could "earn" their living through wide-open, rampant gang-related activities; or if citizens could engage in unfettered drug use and trafficking. We will look at how the police are attempting to ensure that such scenarios never come to pass.

First, regarding terrorism, we will examine terrorism and its different types (to include examples of both foreign and domestic terrorism—the latter including "active shooter" incidents); discuss the National Incident Management System that has evolved to deal with it; examine two pieces of legislation that were enacted for addressing it; review the uniquely formidable and terrifying aspects of bioterrorism; and review some new intelligence- and investigative-based means of confronting it. Then we will essentially use the same approach with both gangs and drugs, looking at their widespread nature, problems posed, and successful initiatives adopted by federal law enforcement and local police agencies for addressing them.

Finally we consider organized crime, specifically La Cosa Nostra, also known as the Mafia or the Mob, to include its definition, origins, and traditional criminal enterprises; included in this chapter section is a look at three major tools that have assisted law enforcement in confronting La Cosa Nostra and imprisoning a large number of its members. A summary, key terms, review questions, and several scenarios and activities that provide opportunities to learn by doing conclude the chapter.

· ·

▶ Terrorism

Osama bin Laden is dead (killed by a team of U.S. Navy SEALs at a compound in Abbottabad, Pakistan, in April 2011), but the fight against terrorism continues. Since September 11, 2001, there has been no cessation of attempts by would-be terrorists to attack people, significant buildings, and military objects in the United States; as examples, in recent years:

- A would-be suicide bomber was intercepted on his way to the nation's Capital.

- A plot to bomb synagogues and shoot Stinger missiles at military aircraft was uncovered in New York.

- A scheme was uncovered that involved flying explosive-laden model planes into the Pentagon and the Capitol.[1]

- An attempted terrorist attack on the New York Federal Reserve Bank building was uncovered by the FBI's Joint Terrorism Task Force.[2]

- The Central Intelligence Agency thwarted a plot by Al Qaeda to have a suicide bomber smuggle an experimental bomb aboard an airliner bound for the United States (the bomb contained no metal parts and was designed to escape detection at airport security).[3]

- A man is sentenced to life in prison after being convicted with two friends of plotting to carry out a coordinated suicide attack on New York City subways.[4]

- A Somali-born teenager who thought he was detonating a car bomb at a packed Christmas tree-lighting ceremony in downtown Portland was arrested by FBI agents who spent nearly six months setting up a sting operation.[5]

Often these planned attacks were foiled by law enforcement agencies using undercover agents and informers who posed as terrorists; in some cases they offered the terrorists a dummy missile, fake C-4 explosives, a disarmed suicide vest. The stings initially also begin oftentimes by identifying would-be attackers through their comments to an informer or angry postings on website.[6]

It is no secret that New York City remains a prime target of terrorists; in fact, more than a decade after the 9/11 attacks, nearly twenty plots against the city have been uncovered by federal and local authorities; plots have been uncovered against the Brooklyn Bridge, Times Square, the city's subway system, Citicorp Center, the New York Stock Exchange, and (as mentioned above) the Federal Reserve Bank—which is viewed as a means of destroying the U.S. economy and thus also destroying America.[7]

As indicated above, notwithstanding that the police have won these "battles" against terrorism, the war on terrorism continues—from 2001 to 2013 costing the lives of more than 6,600 service members[8] and costing nearly $1.5 trillion[9]—and will likely continue into the foreseeable future.

Definition and Types

The Federal Bureau of Investigation (FBI) defines terrorism as the "unlawful use of force against persons or property to intimidate or coerce a government, the civilian population, or any segment thereof, in furtherance of political or social objectives."[10] Terrorism can take many forms, however, and does not always involve bombs and guns. For example, the Earth Liberation Front (ELF) and a sister organization, the Animal Liberation Front, have been responsible for the majority of terrorist acts committed in the United States for several years. These ecoterrorists have burned greenhouses, tree farms, logging sites, ski resorts, and new housing developments.[11] The FBI divides the current international terrorist threat into three categories.[12]

1. *Foreign sponsors of international terrorism.* Seven countries—Cuba, Iran, Iraq, Libya, North Korea, Sudan, and Syria—are designated as such sponsors and view terrorism as a tool of foreign policy. They fund, organize, network, and provide other support to formal terrorist groups and extremists.

▼

WANTED
BY THE FBI

Conspiracy to Commit Arson of United States Government Property and of Property Used in Interstate Commerce; Conspiracy to Commit Arson and Destruction of an Energy Facility; Arson of a Building

JOSEPH MAHMOUD DIBEE

Photo taken in early 1990s

Aliases:
Joe Dibee, "Seattle", "Steve", "God"

DESCRIPTION

Date(s) of Birth Used:	November 10, 1967	Hair:	Black
Place of Birth:	Seattle, Washington	Eyes:	Brown
Height:	6'3"	Sex:	Male
Weight:	150 pounds	Race:	White
NCIC:	W108732930	Nationality:	American
Occupation:	Computer Software Tester		

Scars and Marks:	None known
Remarks:	Dibee may have fled to Syria.

CAUTION

On January 19, 2006, a federal grand jury in Eugene, Oregon, indicted Joseph Mahmoud Dibee on multiple charges related to his alleged role in a domestic terrorism cell. Dibee was charged with two conspiracy violations related to seventeen incidents and one count of arson. These crimes occurred in Oregon, Washington, California, Colorado, and Wyoming, and date back to 1996. Many of the crimes he is accused of participating in were claimed to be committed by the Earth Liberation Front (ELF) or the Animal Liberation Front (ALF).

REWARD

The FBI is offering a reward of up to $50,000 for information leading to the arrest of Joseph Mahmoud Dibee.

SHOULD BE CONSIDERED ARMED AND DANGEROUS

If you have any information concerning this person, please contact your local FBI office or the nearest American Embassy or Consulate.

▲ The FBI frequently posts information concerning individuals being sought for domestic terrorism. *(Courtesy Department of Justice, FBI.)*

---

2. *Formalized terrorist groups.* Autonomous organizations (such as bin Laden's al-Qaeda, Afghanistan's Taliban, Iranian-backed Hezbollah, Egyptian Al-Gama'a al-Islamiyya, and Palestinian HAMAS) have their own infrastructures, personnel, finances, and training facilities. Examples of this type are the al-Qaeda terrorists who attacked the World Trade Center towers and the Pentagon in 2001.

3. *Loosely affiliated international radical extremists.* Examples are the persons who bombed the World Trade Center in 1993. They do not represent a particular nation but may pose the most urgent threat to the United States because they remain relatively unknown to law enforcement agencies.

Terrorist attacks in the United States are caused by both foreign and domestic terrorists. Examples of the former are the attacks in September 2001 with hijacked jetliners on the World Trade Center complex in New York City and the Pentagon in Virginia, with more than 3,000 people killed or missing, and the bombing of the World Trade Center in New York City in February 1993, killing 6 and injuring 1,000 people. An example of the latter is the April 1995 bombing of the Alfred P. Murrah Building in Oklahoma City by Timothy McVeigh, which killed 168 people and injured more than 500.[13] (McVeigh was executed in June 2001.)

Another form of domestic terrorism which requires police training and response is the active shooter situation that often results in mass killings in schools and population centers. This form of terrorism is discussed below.

Companion Threats: Cyberterrorism and Bioterrorism

Certainly the vulnerability of the United States to cybercrime keeps the country's preparedness experts awake at night. The specter of electricity going out for days and perhaps weeks, the gates of a major dam opening suddenly and flooding complete cities, or pipes in a chemical plant rupturing and releasing deadly gas are nightmare scenarios that could be wrought by hackers and/or terrorist groups who have the technical knowledge. Cyberterrorism also greatly challenges the police through such activities as data manipulation, software piracy, industrial espionage, bank card counterfeiting, and embezzlement. Hackers of all ages are breaking into computer systems of major corporations and obtaining credit card, telephone, and account information; some entice children for sexual purposes.

This is the domain of the serious and determined cyberterrorist, and the future of terrorism involves much more than planting a relatively harmless virus in a computer system or hacking into a major corporation's voicemail system. These types of crimes require the development of new investigative techniques, specialized training for police investigators, and employment of individuals with specialized, highly technological backgrounds. If the police are not prepared, these crimes could become the Achilles' heel of our society. Cyberterrorism and unmanned aerial vehicles (UAVs, or drones) are discussed more in Chapter 14, concerning technologies.

Regarding bioterrorism, the use of anthrax in the United States in late 2001 left no doubt about people's vulnerability to biological weapons and the intention of some people to develop and use them for the purpose of bioterrorism. Smallpox, botulism, and plague also constitute major biological threats, and many experts feel that it is only a matter of time before biological weapons get into the wrong hands and are used like explosives were in the past.[14]

Today, the person who controls this type of toxin could then sell it to terrorists (one has to wonder why international terrorists have not already done so). This form of terrorism can wipe out an entire civilization. All that is required is a toxin that can be cultured and put into a spray form that can be weaponized and disseminated into the population. Fortunately, such substances are extremely difficult for all but specially trained individuals to make in large quantities and in the correct dosage; they are tricky to transport because live organisms are delicate; and they must be dispersed in a proper molecule size to infect the lungs of the target. Like chemical weapons, they are also dependent on the wind and the weather and are difficult to control.[15]

Some cities have developed a planned response to such a catastrophic attack, with drills and training exercises that attempt to prepare officers for their roles in getting emergency

▼

antibiotics to every resident, enforcing a quarantine, and using personal radiation detectors to check vehicles.[16]

Responding to Active Shooter/Mass Killing Situations

A sordid form of domestic terrorism—now all too common—that befalls local police is responding to mass killing incidents involving active shooters. We will briefly discuss its extent, nature, and relatively new police procedures that have evolved for such critical incidents.

The horrific killings in December 2012 of twenty-six children and teachers at Sandy Hook Elementary School in Newtown, Connecticut, brought swift calls for greater controls on assault rifles as well as a review of such killings in the United States and calls for better treatment of mental illness. Although one study found that **mass killings**—defined as incidents in which four or more people are killed by the attacker—only account for about 1 percent of all murders, they occur on average about every two weeks. In fact, one review of such killings from 2006 through 2010—thus excluding such high-profile shootings as that in Newtown; a rampage in early 2012 in a movie theater in Aurora, Colorado (which left twelve dead and fifty-seven injured); and an attack on a Sikh temple in Wisconsin that killed six)—found that about one-fourth of mass murders involve two or more killers; one- third of such killings do not involve guns (i.e., they can involve fire, a knife, or a blunt instrument), and that children (ages twelve and under) are frequently victims, representing about one-fifth of all victims.[17]

Much has changed since the April, 1999 mass murders by two shooters at Columbine High School in Littleton, Colorado, where fifteen people were killed (including the two shooters) while on-scene officers waited forty-five minutes for an elite SWAT team to arrive. As was seen in the Newtown active-shooter situation, police have greatly modified their protocols for dealing with such incidents. The most immediate change calls for police to react swiftly to such situations, with responding officers being trained to rush toward gunfire and—if necessary—even step over bodies and bleeding victims in order to stop the active shooter before more lives are lost. Such training is grounded on the assumption that a gunman in a mass shooting kills a person every fifteen seconds. [The approach prior to Columbine was for police to take a contain-and-wait strategy, intended to prevent officers and bystanders from getting killed; first responders would establish a perimeter to contain the situation, protect themselves, and then wait for the special-weapons team to go in and neutralize the shooters(s). This approach came under fire again in April 2009, when officers waited nearly forty-five minutes for a SWAT team to arrive as thirteen people were killed at an immigrant center in Binghamton, New York.[18]]

Since Columbine, police also typically employ what are termed contact teams, where officers from any jurisdiction quickly band together to enter a building in formation and confront the shooter(s), thus shifting the shooters' focus to the officers and away from the indiscriminate killing of innocent persons in the area. Then, special-weapons teams enter to search for any remaining shooters and to rescue any hostages. Another change wrought by Columbine is that special-weapons teams now typically have armed medics and rescue teams trained to remove wounded persons under fire.[19]

An often overlooked aspect of mass killings is the psychological impact on the first responders to the scene—police, firefighters, medics, and so on—who witness firsthand the terrible aftermath of such shootings. Many of them struggle not only with the carnage they witnessed, including being haunted by seeing the faces of victims' family members, but also from guilt caused by the fact that they were not able to do more. They should receive—and are often mandated to receive—treatment and counseling following such traumatic events.[20]

National Incident Management System In DHS Presidential Directive 5, *Management of Domestic Incidents*, President George W. Bush directed the DHS secretary to develop and administer a National Incident Management System (NIMS). This system is structured to provide a consistent nationwide approach for federal, state, and local governments to work together effectively to prepare for, prevent, respond to, and recover from domestic incidents. This directive requires all federal departments and agencies to adopt the NIMS and to use it—and to make its adoption and use by state and local agencies a condition for federal preparedness assistance beginning in fiscal year 2005.[21] The NIMS is a lengthy document that cannot be duplicated here in its entirety, so the following discussion is limited to some of its primary components.

Incident Command System

The **Incident Command System (ICS)** was created to coordinate response personnel from more than one agency or teams from more than one jurisdiction and has been adopted to help local police agencies respond to terrorist incidents. A key strength of ICS is its unified command component, which is composed of four sections: operations, planning, logistics, and finance. Under ICS, all agencies go to the same location and establish a unified command post.[22] The most critical time for controlling a crisis is those initial moments when first responders arrive at the scene. They must quickly contain the situation, analyze the extent of the crisis, request additional resources and special teams if needed, and communicate available information and intelligence to higher headquarters. Their initial actions provide a vital link to the total police response and will often determine its outcome.

The five major functions of ICS are command, operations, planning, logistics, and finance/administration:

1. *Command.* The command staff is responsible for overall management of the incident. When an incident occurs within a single jurisdiction without any overlap, a single incident commander should be designated with overall incident management responsibility to develop the objectives on which an actual action plan will be based. The unified command (UC) concept is used in multijurisdictional or multiagency incidents to provide guidelines for agencies with different legal, geographic, and functional responsibilities to coordinate, plan, and interact effectively. The composition of the UC will depend on the location(s) and type of incident.

2. *Operations.* The operations section is responsible for all activities focused on reducing immediate hazards, saving lives and property, establishing control of the situation, and restoring normal operations. Resources for this section might include specially trained single-agency personnel and equipment, and even special task forces and strike teams.

3. *Planning.* The planning section collects, evaluates, and disseminates incident situation information and intelligence to the incident commander or UC, prepares status reports, displays situation information, and maintains status of resources assigned to the incident.

4. *Logistics.* The logistics section is responsible for all support requirements needed to facilitate effective incident management: facilities, transportation, supplies, equipment maintenance and fuel, food services, communications and technology support, and emergency medical services.

5. *Finance/administration.* The finance/administration section is not required at all incidents but will be involved where incident management activities require finance and other administrative support services such as compensation/claims, determination of costs, and procurement. Law enforcement executives should also create budget line-item codes and emergency purchase orders before such an event so that they will be readily available and accessible.

Legislative Measures

Usa Patriot Act A number of new investigative measures were provided to federal law enforcement agencies through the enactment of the Uniting and Strengthening America by Providing Appropriate Tools Required to Intercept and Obstruct Terrorism Act (commonly termed the USA PATRIOT Act) shortly after the 9/11 attacks. The act dramatically expanded the federal government's ability to investigate Americans without establishing probable cause for "intelligence purposes" and to conduct searches if there are "reasonable grounds to believe" there may be national security threats. Federal agencies, including the FBI and others, are given access to financial, mental health, medical, library, and other records.[23] The act was reauthorized in March 2006, providing additional tools for protecting mass transportation systems and seaports from attack, taking steps to combat the methamphetamine (meth) epidemic, closing loopholes in the ability to prevent terrorist financing, and creating a National Security Division at the Department of Justice. Among the new version's more controversial provisions are the "roving wiretap" portion and the "sneak and peek" section. The first allows the government to get a wiretap on every phone a suspect uses, while the second allows federal investigators to get access to library, business, and medical records without a court order.[24]

The USA PATRIOT Act has not been without its critics. Because of the broad language the act contains and because of what it permits federal agents to do, many fear that these new governmental powers will be abused or that the act will become a "permanent fixture" in the U.S. legal system.[25] Critics also bemoan the fact that federal agents are using the act in cases that "have nothing to do with terrorism"; an example cited is the act's money-laundering language, which allows the government to search every financial institution in the country for the records of suspected terrorists.[26] Furthermore, the treatment of Arab Americans since 9/11 has been termed a form of "persecution," as many of those under scrutiny have been fingerprinted, photographed, detained, and deported under the act's mandatory registration program. Tensions also have been raised among Arab Americans and Muslims because hate crimes against them have increased dramatically after 9/11.[27] Still, Americans seem more willing to sacrifice civil liberties in the interest of homeland security and to allow the government to use "every legal means" at its disposal to prevent further terrorist activity.[28]

Electronic Communications Protection Act of 1986 (as amended) The USA PATRIOT Act of 2001 also amended the Electronic Communications Protection Act of 1986 (ECPA, at P. L. 99–508, 100 Stat.1848), in order to make it more effective in the fight against terrorism. It extends federal wiretap laws to new forms of communication, adds terrorist activities to the list of crimes that justify a wiretap, allows law enforcement to seize voice-mail messages when they have a warrant, and have electronic communications providers record the email addresses from messages coming in to or going out from tapped email accounts. Law enforcement can also intercept and use any information or communications left by a trespasser on someone else's computer, if the computer owner agrees. Under the Act, federal authorities need only a subpoena approved by a federal prosecutor, rather than a judge, to obtain electronic messages that are six months old or older; to get more recent communications, a warrant from a judge is required. Use of the ECPA was demonstrated in late-2012 with the downfall of CIA Director (and former four-star Army General) David Petraeus, who confessed to an extramarital affair with his biographer. Federal investigators can quickly gain access to, and examine e-mail accounts and computer records maintained by Internet providers if they believe a crime was committed.[29] [Also see the Stored Communications Act, discussed in Chapter 14.]

Military Commissions Act of 2006 The fight against terrorism was also aided and expanded in October 2006 when President George W. Bush signed Public Law 109–366, the

Military Commissions Act (MCA) of 2006, which he hailed as "one of the most important pieces of legislation in the War on Terror."[30] Under the MCA, the president is authorized to establish military commissions to try unlawful enemy combatants, the commissions are authorized to sentence defendants to death, and defendants are prevented from invoking the Geneva Conventions as a source of rights during commission proceedings. The law contains a provision stripping detainees of the right to file habeas corpus petitions in federal court and also allows hearsay evidence to be admitted during proceedings, so long as the presiding officer determines it to be reliable. This law allows the Central Intelligence Agency (CIA) to continue its program for questioning key terrorist leaders and operatives—a program felt by many to be one of the most successful intelligence efforts in American history. The MCA excludes all statements obtained by use of torture, makes U.S. interrogators subject to only a limited range of "grave breaches," and clarifies what actions would subject interrogators to liability under the existing federal War Crimes Act.[31]

Fusion Centers

Note that two of the following three topics of discussion that are used for combating terrorism—intelligence-led policing (ILP) and predictive policing—are described in Chapter 4, Community-Oriented Policing and Problem Solving, as they are essentially a part—and an extension—of the *analysis* phase of the problem-solving process. They are therefore an essential tool that, when used as a tool of and in conjunction with fusion centers, can be applied to the problem of terrorism.

A number of cities and counties have partnered with the Federal Bureau of Investigation to form terrorism early warning groups or fusion centers.[32] The fusion center provides overarching coordination of all response and counterterrorism elements within a community or metropolitan area. As information or intelligence is gathered by local and federal agencies, it is fed into the fusion center, where it is analyzed (see Figure 12-1 ■). The fusion center is a comprehensive approach in that it allows for the analysis of information from a variety of sources. It is the most comprehensive manner by which to collect and analyze data for a particular

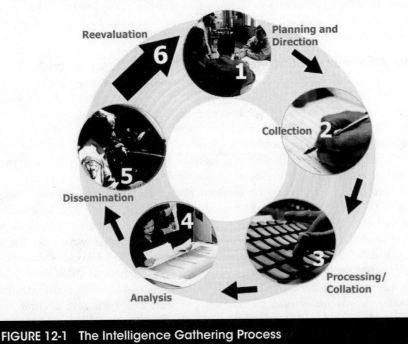

FIGURE 12-1 The Intelligence Gathering Process
U.S. Department of Justice, Office of Justice Programs, The National Criminal Intelligence Sharing Plan, U.S. Department of Justice.

▲ At fusion centers, information or intelligence is gathered and analyzed by local and federal agencies for a particular geographical area. *(Courtesy Washoe County, Nevada, Sheriff's Office.)*

geographical area. Once analyzed, terrorist threat or activity information is generated and supplied to affected constituents. The fusion centers include medical personnel and fire department personnel as well as law enforcement personnel. The medical personnel can provide the fusion center with information about suspicious diseases or illnesses—and early warning system for a biological attack—and the firefighter personnel can provide information about suspicious fires or chemical problems. The fusion center also allows for more comprehensive planning and a better coordinated response should a terrorist event occur.

▶ Street Gangs

Definition and Membership

A definition of "criminal street gangs" is provided in Title 18, Sec. 521 of the *United States Code*, where, for they are "ongoing groups, clubs, organizations, or associations of five or more individuals that have as one of their primary purposes the commission of one or more criminal offenses."

Street gang activities may be traced back to the early 1900s in southern California, where most gangs were small (six to twenty members) and generally formed in socially disorganized neighborhoods. Gangs were generally agreed to be the result of disintegration of the family life, low-wage occupations, unemployment, a lack of wholesome recreational opportunities, and other socio-economic factors.

Since the 1980s gangs have exploded in membership, with estimates of approximately 1.4 million active street, prison, and motorcycle gang members comprising more than 33,000 gangs in the United States. Ethnic-based and nontraditional (i.e., hybrid) gangs have also expanded and now include African, Asian, Eurasian, Caribbean, and Middle Eastern gangs. The Northeast and Southeast regions of the United States have seen the greatest increases in gang memberships since the 1980s, but the West and Great Lakes regions now hold the greatest numbers of gang members.[33]

Irrespective of city size, where they exist, street gangs can significantly damage a community, inciting fear in citizens, dictating where they will and will not travel, and also playing a role in homicides, graffiti, intimidation, firearms transactions and violence, drug sales and use, burglaries, car thefts, vandalism, and a number of other crime problems.[34] Of course, gang members can be of any age, but "gang-banging" tends to be a young person's enterprise: about 70 percent of gang members are between the ages of fifteen and twenty-four, while only about 13 percent are older than age twenty-four. As a result, many jurisdictions report a growing problem involving juvenile gangs and violence. This problem is often attributed to the increased incarceration of older gang members as well as aggressive recruiting of juveniles in schools; young prospects have historically been highly sought after due to a belief that there is less likelihood that they will receive a harsh sentence if arrested, as well as their willingness to perform acts of violence. Recruiters often exploit the social media as well as the gangsta rap culture to facilitate their efforts.[35]

In contrast to popular belief, gangs do not tend to migrate across the country to set up satellite operations; in reality, most, if migrating at all, typically form other gang operations within 100 miles of their city of origin. Possibly for this reason, gangs are basically loose-knit in nature and there tends to be little homogeneity among them; thus there is so single "model" of gangs—rather, there is a wide variety of forms. However, as a general rule, the more structured the gang, the more dangerous the gang tends to be.[36]

Certainly two of the more violent and fear-inducing gangs in the United States at present are the Mexico-based La Familia and El Salvador's MS-13. La Familia is a violent, heavily armed organization that is heavily engaged in drug smuggling, money laundering, and weapons trafficking across the border into the United States. In late 2009, more than 3,000 U.S. federal agents and local police in nineteen states unleashed a massive coast-to-coast sweep against La Familia, arresting 305 reputed gang members and confiscating more than ten tons of narcotics in the United States.[37] And, according to the 2009 National Gang Threat Assessment, there could be as many as 50,000 MS-13 (or Mara Salvatrucha) members worldwide, with 10,000 members in the United States; the MS-13 gang is known for its highly violent ways, and its members are involved in all kinds of illegal activities, including drugs, robbery, extortion, weapons trafficking, and murder.[38]

Both the North Carolina Gang Investigators Association (NCGIA) and the New Jersey State Police provide excellent online guides and resources on their websites for learning much more about common gangs' "identifiers": colors; clothing, graffiti, hand signs, writing, and symbols; and tattoos.[39]

Criminal Activities Gang membership fosters criminal behavior. Studies show that youths living in high-crime areas and who belong to gangs are responsible for far more criminal acts than their non-crime counterparts; more specifically, gang members are responsible for four times as many offenses as their total population share would suggest, while gang members' violent offense rates are about seven times higher than those of youths who are not members of gangs.[40]

Research has also shown that gang members who belong to older (or early-onset) gangs are far more likely to be involved in violent crimes (e.g., homicide, aggravated assault, robbery) and property crimes than those gangs in localities that were late-onset (i.e., forming in the last decade); the same holds true with drug distribution, where trafficking activities were far less likely to be significant problems in jurisdictions with late-onset gangs.[41]

Considering gang members of all ages and in all locations, even considering that gangs' criminal activities are often overstated and wax and wane, it is clear that gangs represent a significant crime problem. According to a federal report:

- Criminal gangs commit nearly half of all violent crimes in many communities, and typical gang-related crimes include alien smuggling, armed robbery, assault, auto theft, drug trafficking, extortion, fraud, home invasions, identity theft, murder, and weapons trafficking.[42]

- Gang members are the primary retail-level distributors of most illicit drugs. U.S. gangs also are banding with Central American and Mexican gangs to establish far-reaching drug networks as well as for smuggling of gun and illegal immigrants. Of particular concern with the drug trade is their tendency to move into suburban and rural communities to recruit new members, form new alliances, and even collaborate with rival gangs.[43]

What Works? Police Responses

Prevention As with any type of crime, proactively preventing a criminal act from taking place is better than having it occur and law enforcement having to reactively devote time, effort, and resources to investigate, prosecute, and incarcerate the offender. With regard to gangs, the goal of prevention is to stop youths from joining gangs, so prevention responses should target the largest segment of the problem: youths at risk for gang membership. Prevention programs, therefore, include a broad potential audience and are typically aimed at groups that pose some risk. For example, a prevention program may focus on preschool children who reside in gang neighborhoods before they show any symptoms of having joined the gang life.

A well-known police response to gangs is the Gang Resistance Education and Training (GREAT) program, which originated in 1991 in Phoenix, Arizona. GREAT emphasizes the acquisition of information and skills needed by students to resist peer pressure and gang influences; the curriculum contains a nine-hour curriculum offered to middle-school students, mostly seventh-graders.[44]

SARA Problem-Solving Process When prevention fails, as with any attempt to engage in problem solving, after scanning the problem to determine that a problem does in fact exist (using the SARA problem-solving process discussed in Chapter 4), the next task for the police is problem analysis. This step is a crucial one, and should begin by considering how specific gang problems are being dealt with locally and the successes and shortcomings of each approach. It is also helpful to try to identify and understand the events and conditions that precede and accompany the problem. Then, a working hypothesis can be developed concerning why the problem is occurring.

The problem analysis triangle (also discussed in Chapter 4) can be useful as well—a consideration of the characteristics of *offenders*, *places*, and *victims* or targets as they relate to the gang problem. During the analysis, it is also helpful to identify the data to be used. Possible sources of information and data can include, but are not be limited to, the following sources:

- Police computer-aided dispatch system, especially for determining hot spots, calls for service relating to gang activities, shots fired, and so on
- School personnel—teachers, administrators—and students, who can provide information about gang-related incidents in schools
- Hospital records, for evidence of gang-related gunshot and other wounds and the presence of gang tattoos
- Juvenile court records of gang membership
- Jails and prisons (especially the gang status of returning offenders).
- Findings of the annual National Youth Gang Survey of police agencies concerning the extent of youth gang problems
- Interviews with gang members and associates[45]

After the gang problem has been clearly defined and analyzed, the police next seek to develop effective responses for dealing with it. Regardless of the scope of responses, in general, responses should include prevention, intervention, and suppression, which are discussed next.

Responses: Intervention and Suppression Responses to the local gang problem must be tailored to the analysis and typically involve some form(s) of intervention and suppression.

▶ Intervention

Intervention involves a broad approach, targeting youths who are at risk of becoming a gang member, in the early stages of membership, or at some stage of membership where they can be pushed out of the gang. The primary aim is to persuade these youths to abandon the gang lifestyle or to reduce their gang-related crime.

The National Crime Prevention Council provides an overview of gang intervention: it is a coordinated effort that involves both the community and the police for reducing the likelihood that high-risk youth with become involved in gangs. This coordinated effort can also involve educators, job-training resources, parents, and community groups, and can combine efforts by those agencies with other community efforts such as neighborhood mobilization and job training for youth. For such a coordinated intervention approach to be successful, it is important that the type of gang be identified (no two gangs being alike) as well as the level of the individual's involvement in the gang. Then, police, probation personnel, and prosecutors share information about gang activity, diffuse crises that arise from gang conflict, and refer the individual to community-based services. Street outreach through community organizations and parents can also be used to supplement partnerships among agencies to make well-integrated services available to at-risk youth. Intervention is most effective when it paired with the aforementioned prevention strategies.[46]

▶ Suppression: Use of Focused Deterrence

Although most police agencies understand that suppression alone is not effective as a long-term gang prevention and intervention strategy, suppression tactics have a part to play in addressing gang problems. Suppression programs revolve around the goal of reducing or eliminating gang activities, typically relying on the criminal law and the collaboration of several criminal justice agencies for their success.

One approach to reducing high rates of gang and youth gun violence that has demonstrated success and rapidly spread across the country is modeled on one that began in Boston in May 1996, known as Operation Ceasefire, which entailed a problem-oriented approach and focused on specific places that were crime hot spots. This approach—involving local, state, and federal criminal justice agencies as well as community leaders, gang outreach workers, and public/private social service agencies—has been implemented in Chicago, Cincinnati, Indianapolis, and, recently, in five California cities.[47] Exhibit 12-1 ■ briefly describes one such project in Newport News, Virginia.

After performing an in-depth analysis of the problem—e.g., geographic location of violent incidents, demographic information on individuals involved in gun violence, and patterns of gang violence—a working group is then organized for designing and implementing the local strategy. This process of implementation typically includes such activities as: communicating directly with gang members a violence prevention message, linking these gang members and youth to training and employment opportunities, and coordinating law enforcement efforts. Law enforcement efforts include a strategy of focused deterrence that embraces a tactic termed "pulling levers"; in other words, if a youth or gang member is engaged in violent behavior and is caught with a gun during their time on

EXHIBIT 12-1

NEW PROGRAM FOCUSES ON DETERRENCE

A new deterrence program implemented in several U.S. cities has been shown to keep drug dealers off the streets, build confidence in the police and restore high-crime neighborhoods. Usually, when drug dealers are arrested, soon they're back on the streets or are quickly replaced, and the neighborhood continues to decline. But under the drug-market intervention program, low-level dealers are not arrested but are invited to rehabilitate themselves.

The dealers are brought into a meeting where they are confronted by police, social workers and neighborhood leaders, as well as neighbors and family members. The dealers are told they will get a second chance if they agree to stop dealing and work with social services to rehabilitate themselves.

The dealers are warned that if they do not cooperate, authorities have enough evidence to prosecute them. Police follow up by maintaining a strong presence in the neighborhood. A key objective is to create a peaceful, cohesive community.

The program was developed by New York-based criminologist David Kennedy. When it was deployed in several high-crime neighborhoods in High Point, N.C., in 2003, crime in those areas fell by as much as 40–50 percent. It is now being deployed in other cities, including Newport News, Va., where outcomes are not yet available.

Sources: **Policing Drug Sales: Cleaning up the 'hood'** The Economist, March 3, 2012 http://www.economist.com/node/21548989; **Newport News, Virginia: Using New Tools to Reduce Crime** Lauren Monsen, American News and Views (U.S. Embassy), Aug. 6, 2012 http://iipdigital.usembassy.gov/st/english/article/2012/08/20120806134195.html#axzz2oblwGZCb; **The High Point Drug Market Intervention Strategy** Kennedy & Wong, National Network for Safe Communities http://www.cops.usdoj.gov/Publications/e08097226-HighPoint.pdf

probation or parole, every available resource would be brought to bear, such as more stringent bail, swift prosecution, and enhanced penalties). Meanwhile, as indicated above, social services are made available to gang members to support an alternative to life in the gang.[48]

This comprehensive, focused approach to deterrence has resulted in declines in youth homicides, firearm assaults, and shots-fired calls for service. In addition, typical outcomes include the gangs' drug markets being disrupted, arrests being made for outstanding warrants, and strict enforcement of probation and federal sanctions.[49]

Gang Units and Civil Injunctions

Across the country, many cities have responded to their gang problems by forming some type of specialized gang unit (GIU) as an initial response to major episodes of gang violence.[50] Today nearly 400 of the nation's large (more than hundred officers) police agencies have such dedicated unit for addressing gang-related activities.[51] Regarding their duties and functions, these units spend the greatest percentage of time on either intelligence gathering (33 percent) or investigative functions (32 percent). About nine in ten gang units monitor gang graffiti (94 percent), track individual gang members (93 percent), monitor internet sites for communication among gang members (93 percent), engage in directed patrols (91 percent), and performed undercover surveillance operations (87 percent).[52]

Some gang units also employ civil gang injunctions in their efforts. A civil gang injunction is a court-ordered instrument used for such things as barring gang members from congregating in specified public areas, engaging in specified criminal and nuisance-type behaviors (such as selling drugs), driving through certain neighborhoods, loitering, cursing, making certain hand gestures, listening to loud music, and even talking on cell phones. This strategy has legal implications and often requires a considerable standard of proof, with law enforcement and prosecutors bearing the legal burden of developing probable cause, collecting evidence and documenting gang membership and activity. Once such information has been presented to a judge, the injunction may be granted forbidding the above types of acts.[53]

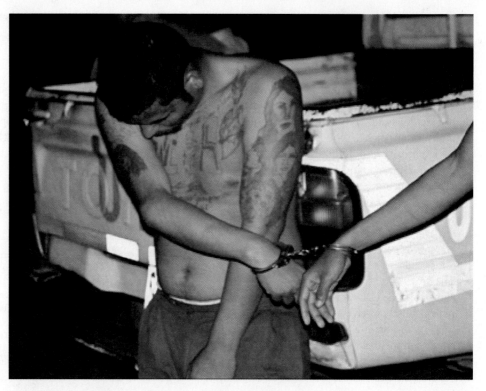

▲ An MS-13 suspect is handcuffed. In 2004, the FBI created the MS-13 National Gang Task Force. A year later, the FBI helped create the National Gang Intelligence Center. *(Courtesy FBI.)*

Did the Responses Work?

Finally, in the assessment phase of the SARA problem-solving process, the police evaluate the effectiveness of their responses. In addition to looking at such indicators as numbers of arrests, levels of reported crime and citizen complaints, clearance rates, and calls for service (CFS), and depending on the nature of problems that were present, some types of questions that might be posed for determining whether or not the responses were effective are as follows (some questions require citizen surveys):

- Were reduced calls for police service concerning gang activities realized?
- Was the amount of gang-related graffiti reduced?
- Were fears and perceptions reduced concerning gangs and related graffiti?
- Was open–air drug-related activity by gang members visibly reduced?
- Did youth gun homicides involving gang members decrease?[54]

▶ Our National Nightmare: Drug Abuse

Although the nation's drug scene recently witnessed a sea change with the legalization of marijuana (i.e., possession up to one ounce, to include a system of state-licensed grows, processors, and retail stores) for recreational use in the states of Oregon and Washington to take effect in December 2012 and January 2013, respectively,[55] advocates of legalizing "pot" should not expect such laws to sweep the country soon. In fact, changing U.S. drug-law culture may well be more like "bending granite" than "curving wood" in the foreseeable future. Polls show only about half (48 percent) of all Americans favoring legalization of marijuana, and legalizing marijuana still puts state laws in direct opposition with federal drug laws[56]—even though by the end of 2012, eighteen states and the District of Columbia had medical marijuana laws.[57] Furthermore, the federal Drug Enforcement Administration has taken a strong position against such legalization and a dim view of its medical value.[58]

Types of Usage and Social Costs: A Snapshot

The following data concerning types of drug usage, arrests, crimes, and costs of drug paint a grim picture and demonstrate that the United States remains in the throes of a severe drug abuse problem.

A study by the federal Substance Abuse and Mental Health Services Administration found that an estimated 22.5 million Americans aged twelve or older are current (during the previous month) illicit drug users (illicit drugs include marijuana/hashish; cocaine, including crack; heroin; hallucinogens; inhalants; or prescription-type psychotherapeutics used nonmedically). Following is a breakdown of that illicit drug use:

- Marijuana is the most commonly used illicit drug (18.1 million past-month users).

- There are about 2.1 million current cocaine users aged twelve or older.

- Hallucinogens were used in the past month by 972,000 million persons aged twelve or older, including 922,000 who had used Ecstasy.

- Of the 6.1 million persons aged twelve or older who used prescription-type drugs non-medically in the past month, 5.2 million used pain relievers (such opioids act on the nervous system to relieve pain and are particularly dangerous; long-term use and abuse can lead to physical dependence and withdrawal symptoms).

- There are an estimated 439,000 current users of methamphetamine aged twelve or older.

- About the same proportion of illicit drug users aged eighteen or older were unem-ployed(17.2 percent) as were employed (either part- or full-time) (19.6 percent).[59]

The abuse of alcohol in America should not be overlooked:

- 28.6 million persons age twelve or older reported driving under the influence of alcohol during the past year; the rate was highest among young adults aged eighteen to twenty-five (21.9 percent); heavy drinking was reported by 15.5 million people.[60]

The direct impact of this drug and alcohol abuse on the U.S. criminal justice system is substantial when looking at apprehensions: about 1.5 million arrests by state and local agencies for drug abuse violations per year (about 82 percent of these arrests are for posses-sion, and the remainder are for trafficking).[61] These arrest figures probably reflect only the tip of the iceberg in comparison to the actual levels of manufacturing, use, and trafficking.

Furthermore, drug use fuels crime; the percentage of booked arrestees testing posi-tive for at least one illicit drug ranged from 49 percent in Washington, D.C., to 87 percent in Chicago. The most common substances present during tests, in descending order, are marijuana, cocaine, opiates, and methamphetamine.[62]

Certainly the economic toll on the United States due to this illicit drug abuse is astro-nomical. As an example, for fiscal year 2013, the federal Office of National Drug Control Policy was appropriated $25.6 billion (its previous year allocation: $25.2 billion) to reduce drug use and availability in four major policy areas: (1) substance abuse prevention, (2) substance abuse treatment, (3) domestic law enforcement, and (4) interdiction and international counterdrug support.[63]

Fighting Methamphetamine The police have long been involved with meth abusers. Meth is cheap and addictive and causes a variety of physical and emotional

▲ Federal agents work abroad to stem the flow of illegal drugs into the United States. Above, DEA agents and Ecuadorian drug authorities seize a submarine carrying multi-ton quantities of cocaine near the border with Colombia; below, DEA, ATF, and Puerto Rican agents execute 70 arrest warrants in targeting a violent trafficking organization. *(Courtesy Drug Enforcement Administration, Department of Justice.)*

problems. It is a serious health hazard to anyone who comes in contact with the precursor drugs used to produce it, including police, medical, and fire personnel. Although meth use is a serious problem across the nation, it has been particularly prevalent in the United States in the West and Midwest.

Indeed, training police officers in lab identification and removal is an important first step in any meth initiative. Training public works and hotel/motel staff is another successful strategy for helping to identify meth lab operations. Drug courts are an additional beneficial option for the criminal justice system because they immediately expose meth-addicted individuals to treatment and provide them with a rigid structure with little tolerance for infractions. Another major part of meth initiatives involves establishing the partnerships that are essential for addressing the problem, such as those developed with prosecutors' offices, environmental protection agencies, agencies involved in cleaning up hazardous materials, child welfare and family services agencies, treatment centers, and federal drug enforcement agencies.[64]

The police battle against meth has been lengthy, focused, and intense; in fact, since 1994 the federal Office of Community Oriented Policing Services has funded nearly $160 million in meth related projects,[65] Federal legislation has also helped by limiting sales of the nasal decongestant pseudoephedrine, and appears to have greatly reduced the number of small, clandestine methamphetamine laboratories in the United States (most states limit individuals to a daily purchase of no more than 3.2 grams, and no more than 9 grams per month, of pseudoephedrine HCl.[66] However, such legislation has also created a vast market for the cold medicine, with pill buyers recruiting homeless people and even college students to purchase the pills for them (a process known as "smurfing"),[67] and driving the underground market for a box of Sudafed that costs about $8 to be sold to meth cooks for $100.[68] Meanwhile, Mexican drug cartels have quietly filled the void in the nation's drug market created by the U.S. crackdown against meth, flooding U.S. cities with exceptionally cheap, extraordinarily potent meth from "superlabs."[69] Given these kinds of persistent efforts, the police and other agencies of criminal justice—prosecutors' offices in particular—have had to develop several new methods and tactics in their ongoing fight against meth, such as the following:

- Educating community organizations and schoolchildren about meth dangers and helping them to form local coalitions against meth

- Participating in joint state-federal efforts to investigate and prosecute meth crimes

- Using their state's attorney general's office to assist county attorneys in prosecuting drug crimes that cross county borders and develop expertise in the investigation and prosecution of meth crimes

- Forming multi-county antidrug task forces and "meth response teams" to help understaffed sheriffs' offices and local police departments in investigating and dismantle multiple meth labs

- Calling on the U.S. Attorneys' Offices and DEA to prosecute federal drug crimes, particularly those that are larger or more sophisticated meth crimes[70]

Open-Air Drug Markets

Open-air drug markets represent the lowest level of the drug distribution network. We address these low-level markets, however, because of the risks posed to market participants and the harm that drug use can inflict on the entire community.

Open markets have several advantages for both buyers and sellers: Buyers know where to go in order to find the drugs they want and can weigh quality against price, and sellers are able to maximize customer access. Open-air markets also generate or contribute to a wide range of problems and disorder in the community, including traffic congestion, noise, disorderly conduct, loitering, prostitution, robberies, burglaries, thefts from motor vehicles, fencing of stolen goods, weapons offenses, assaults, and clandestine drug labs.[71]

Dealing with open-air markets presents a considerable challenge for the police. Simply arresting market participants will have little impact on reducing the size of the market or the amount of drugs consumed. However, the nature of open markets means that market participants are vulnerable both to police enforcement and to the dangers of buying from strangers, which may include rip-offs and robberies.

Following are some open-air drug activities that the police have undertaken—with a caveat by two researchers, Harocopos and Hough, that no matter which approach is taken, it is unlikely that they will be able to eradicate the open-air drug market completely;[72] furthermore, a police crackdown or sweep will only be a deterrent if appropriate criminal sentences are used:

- *Policing the area in a highly visible fashion.* A police presence (including foot patrol) may disrupt the drug market and make it inconvenient for sellers and buyers to engage in drug transactions.

- *Enforcing the law intensively.* The effect of a crackdown is dependent on the drug market that is targeted and the amount of resources available, such as street surveillance and intelligence gathering, a hotline for area residents, and increases in drug-treatment services.

- *Using intelligence-led investigative work.* Information from drug hotlines and local residents can help to identify and analyze a problem. In addition, any arrest may produce information if officers debrief the offender, and drug buyers may lead undercover officers to drug locations.

- *Arresting drug buyers in "reverse stings."* The reverse sting (the sale or purported sale of drugs by a government agent to the target of an investigation) serves to impact the demand side of the market and is most successful against new or occasional drug users. Miami, Florida, police found that the process of being arrested, charged, forced to appear in court, and have a vehicle impounded acted as a deterrent.

Raves

A serious problem that can involve serious drug abuse is raves—dance parties that feature fast-paced, repetitive electronic music and light shows. Drug use is intended to enhance ravers' sensations and boost their energy so they can dance for long periods, usually starting late at night and going into the morning hours. Rave party problems are unique: They create a blend of attitudes, drugs, and behaviors not found in other forms of youth culture. Dealing with raves is difficult for police. On the one hand, police often face pressure from society to put an end to raves; on the other hand, raves are enormously popular (a June 2010 rave in Los Angeles, with 16,000 attendees, resulted in one death).[73] In addition, raves pose a number of concerns for police, including drug overdoses, drug trafficking, noise, persons driving under the influence, and traffic control. Of particular concern is evidence that suggests Ecstasy (also known as MDMA or "Eve")—the drug most closely associated with rave parties—can cause permanent brain damage when used habitually.

To understand the extent of the local rave problem, police should conduct an analysis that answers a number of questions concerning rave incidents, locations, and management. Some police responses that have met with success include regulating rave venues to ensure basic health and safety measures are in use, encouraging property owners to exercise control over raves, prohibiting juveniles and adults from being admitted to the same raves, applying nuisance abatement laws where appropriate, prosecuting rave operators and property owners for drug-related offenses, and educating ravers about the risks of drug use and overexertion.[74]

New Ways to Get "High"—and Die: Bath Salts and "Fake Pot"

Bath salts—named for their fine, crystalline appearance—are the latest designer drug in use and are synthetically made central nervous stimulants. Bath salts imitate the effects of methamphetamine, ecstasy, cocaine, and LSD, and can cause euphoria and hallucinations, and result in violence and psychotic episodes.[75] They are easier to obtain—online or at head shops and convenience stores—and cheaper than cocaine or ecstasy, and they are lethal; by the end of 2012 more than twenty people had died in Florida alone from ingesting bath salts.[76] The use of bath salts has also been implicated in many people committing shocking acts; as reported by users themselves: A California man attacked an elderly woman with a shovel; a Pennsylvania man kicked a trooper and bit a paramedic; a Georgia man went wild at a golf course and threatened to eat people; and it is suspected that a Miami, Florida, man used bath salts when he chewed off most of a homeless man's face.[77]

The number of people calling police and poison control centers about such reactions to the drug began to decline in July 2012, however, when President Obama signed into law a ban on thirty-one compounds and substances found in bath salts as well as synthetic marijuana (see below) and hallucinogens.[78] Although that decline does not mean the bath-salt fad has ended, it may suggest that the countrywide binge is subsiding.[79]

A late-2012 report by the Substance Abuse and Mental Health Services Administration (SAMHSA) stated that more than 11,000 drug-related emergency department visits in 2010 were due to synthetic cannabinoids (SC). Commonly known on the street as "K2" or "Spice," these substances are not actually derived from the marijuana plant, but are reported to have the same effect as the drug. SAMHSA reported that symptoms from SC

▲ Bath salts cause some to die horrible deaths as temperatures skyrocket, causing the muscles to break down and release toxins. *(Courtesy Drug Enforcement Administration, Department of Justice.)*

include: agitation, nausea, vomiting, tachycardia (rapid heartbeat), elevated blood pressure, tremor, seizures, hallucinations, paranoid behavior and non-responsiveness. Youths aged two to twenty-nine represented 75 percent of all emergency hospital visits.[80]

Legislation signed by President Obama in July 2012, mentioned above, also banned SC. Dozens of states and local governments had already enacted such laws against these synthetic cannabinoids, which have been blamed for hundreds of emergency room visits and a handful of fatalities.[81]

High-Intensity Drug Trafficking Area Program

An initiative that provides additional federal resources to areas most in need of help to reduce or eliminate drug trafficking is the High-Intensity Drug Trafficking Area (HIDTA) program. In considering whether to designate an area as a HIDTA, the federal Office of

Career Profile

(Courtesy Daniel W. Gerard.)

Name: Daniel W. Gerard

Position: Police Captain/ Special Operations Commander

City, State: Cincinnati, Ohio

College attended: University of Cincinnati

Academic Major: Criminal Justice

How long have you occupied this position/assignment?
Seven years

How would you briefly describe this position/assignment:
Special Operations consists of all citywide patrol based units that are highly specialized and do not fit neatly into a geographic patrol district. The various units that make up Special Operations include: Traffic; K9 (patrol, narcotics detection and explosive detection); Safe Streets (violent crime/gang enforcement squad); and the Violent Crime Enforcement Team (federal firearms trafficking task force in partnership with the Bureau of Alcohol, Tobacco, Firearms and Explosives) and total over 100 officers.

What attracted you to this position/assignment?
The wide variety of activities the position encompasses. No two days are ever the same. One day I could be coordinating the traffic route for a Presidential motorcade and the next day serving multiple SWAT search warrants while dismantling a violent street gang after a lengthy investigation. Having so many different functions in one command allows me to combine their resources in nontraditional ways such as having traffic officers conduct an operating a vehicle while impaired traffic checkpoint in an area in which a violent street gang operates a drive through drug market. By using nontraditional approaches, we can disrupt illegal activities in unexpected ways and have a longer lasting positive impact than by using only traditional policing tactics.

What qualities/characteristics are most helpful for this position/assignment?
The ability to multitask and the ability to delegate less essential tasks to others. Being involved in so many different areas over the course of a day, the ability to effectively manage many diverse situations at once is crucial. This is not possible if you are unable to delegate. Without both of these abilities, a command officer could easily become so bogged down with the minor peripheral details of an operation that a critical assignment could be overlooked and result in an unfortunate consequence.

How would you describe a typical day for one in this position/assignment?
Special Operations is not a Monday to Friday 8 A.M to 4 P.M. job. I have officers who work in high risk situations, both in uniform and also in a covert capacity. The majority of the units assigned to me operate 24 hours a day, 7 days a week. A typical work day includes: current and future operational planning meetings and case status updates with my various units; meetings with prosecutors about pending cases; responding as needed to manage any critical incidents that either involve my personnel or that require them to assist in the resolution of an incident; and also performing the myriad of daily administrative functions that come with a command assignment including processing a seemingly endless volume of paperwork. After work hours, I am on call and spend large amounts of time on the telephone being briefed about current operations and providing operational guidance and direction as needed to my officers.

What advice would you offer someone who is beginning their studies of policing and criminal justice?
Even if you plan to focus on one area of study, such as policing or corrections, take as many courses as you can in the criminal justice areas you do not plan to specialize in. Although I am in policing, I regularly interact with the court system, the correctional system, probation and parole. By acquiring at least a basic knowledge of the other criminal justice functions, a student will be much better equipped to both make the right career choice and to ultimately operate successfully within the system as a whole upon graduation.

▼

National Drug Control Policy considers the extent to which the area is a center for illegal drug production, manufacturing, importation, or distribution. The priorities of HIDTA are to assess regional drug threats, design strategies to combat those threats, and develop and fund initiatives to implement strategies. The program receives about $240 million per year to fund its efforts. There are now twenty-eight HIDTAs, which include approximately 16 percent of all counties in the United States and 60 percent of the U.S. population.[82]

The accompanying Career Profile is provided by a commander of a Special Operations unit that works to address gang, drugs, and other problems that involve violent criminals.

▶ Policing The Mob

In April 2010, Manhattan, New York, U.S. Attorney Preet Bharara announced the arrest of fourteen members and associates of the Gambino organized crime family on charges including racketeering, murder, sex trafficking, jury tampering, extortion, assault, narcotics trafficking, wire fraud, loansharking, and illegal gambling; Bharara added:

> The mafia is not dead. It is alive and kicking. Modern mobsters may be less colorful, less flamboyant, and less glamorous than some of their predecessors, but they are still terrorizing businesses, using baseball bats, and putting people in the hospital.[83]
>
> —Bharara's statement, Manhattan U.S. Attorney Charges Fourteen Gambino Crime Family Members and Associates with Racketeering, Murder, Sex Trafficking, and Other Crimes, U.S. Department of Justice.

Mr. Bharara's statement put to rest any notion that the Mafia (also known as the Mob, or La Cosa Nostra) has faded into oblivion or lost its appetite for sordid activities.

Imagine devoting your entire police career making few or even no arrests but, rather, devoting those years to the collection and analysis of intelligence information. Visualize yourself investigating crime by watching newspaper obituaries and appearing at funerals to log license plates and take photographs from a safe distance away from the mourners, then tracing names to the fifth cousins. Consider spending years to investigate a single case, combing through records and files that go back twenty years. Picture yourself going undercover for several years to investigate a crime organization, never knowing if or when your cover will be blown and you will be targeted for death. Enter the world of organized crime. These are only some of the unusual methods and schemes that are employed by police agents who are assigned to the underworld.

Definition, Origin, and Enterprises

Herein we define organized crimes as the management and coordination of illegal enterprises connected with vice (gambling, prostitution, high-interest personal loans, pornography, and drug trafficking) and racketeering (labor and business extortion).[84] Under this definition, several organized-crime syndicates or organizations exist in America, such as street youth gangs, prison gangs, gangs from several Asian countries (such as the Chinese Triads, some Vietnamese and Tong immigrants, and the Japanese Boryokudan), bikers, and Gypsies. Probably the oldest, most profitable, and most dangerous form of organized crime in the United States is La Cosa Nostra (LCN; Italian for "this thing of ours").[85] It is also commonly termed the Mafia.

Nor is there any scarcity of theories surrounding the origin of LCN, which is clearly shrouded in mystery and confusion. One of the earliest (and most romanticized) concerns the origin of the term *Mafia* in 1282, with the killing of an Italian maiden by a soldier of the French occupation; this led to a rallying cry among the Sicilians—"Morte alle Francia Italia anela" or M.A.F.I.A. (meaning "Death to the French is Italy's cry")—and an underground, guerrilla-type criminal lifestyle against the French army.[86]

LCN has represented a blight on the American way of life for more than a century. Indeed, following a half century of widespread mob activity and a virtual heyday during

Prohibition (1920–1933), in the early 1950s the U.S. Senate's Kefauver Committee,[87] the American Bar Association, and the President's Commission on Law Enforcement and Administration of Justice,[88] among other groups and commissions, concluded that LCN was a threat to America's economy and security. All of this scrutiny culminated with Congress enacting the Organized Crime Control Act of 1970, which prohibited the creation or management of a gambling organization involving five or more people, gave grand juries new powers, permitted detention of unmanageable witnesses, and authorized the U.S. attorney general to protect witnesses, both state and federal, and their families.[89]

Even with all this public scrutiny, however, inquiries into traditional organized crime[90] have often failed the public due to the Mob's underlying goals of maintaining secrecy and avoiding the limelight at all costs. Indeed, the Mob's primary objective—aside from gleaning illicit profits—has been to remain invisible; this is the organization's law of *omerta*, which prohibits publicly speaking or divulging information about certain activities, especially the activities of the criminal organization.[91]

Many Sicilian and Italian LCN immigrated to the United States in the late 1800s and early 1900s, maintaining their criminal lifestyle of intimidation and force. It has been argued that organized crime existed even in the Wild West, focusing on the crimes of gambling, prostitution, robbery, and cattle rustling.[92]

The Mob in Popular Culture

Today, and for at least a half century, LCN is an immensely popular topic for book authors as well as the print and electronic media. The recent and very successful television programs such as "Mob Wives"[93] and *The Sopranos*, and such movies as *The Untouchables*, *Blood Ties*, *Scarface*, *The Godfather* trilogy, *Goodfellas*, *Donnie Brasco*, *Gotti*, and *Casino* are but a sample of the genre; many of these portrayals of organized criminals have romanticized the Mob and made it difficult to discern fact from fiction, valid from invalid. (Today one can even "be the mobster" with an action/adventure video game entitled "Mafia Wars," where violence is a central theme and every completed mission of death and mayhem leads to a rise up the family tree.[94])

LCN families have a formally organized nature (see Figure 12-2 ■) consisting of the El Capo (or "godfather"), Sotto Capo ("underboss"), the consigliere ("counselor"), caporegimas ("lieutenants" or enforcers), and the soldatos (or "soldiers"). The major obstacle to investigating and apprehending these criminals is that they shun the public spotlight. In fact, their primary, centuries-old code of honor is that of omerta—silence.

Members Of LCN Loathe Unwelcome Attention For The Most Part; It Has Been Said that it is almost as if the Mafiosi are products of parthenogenesis—as if they just arose out of the dust, like the mythical phoenix bird. When confronted by a police officer and asked questions about himself (LCN is an all-male organization), he seems to have no roots, parentage, or any other background that the police can maintain as intelligence information.

Successful Police Initiatives

For forty years, FBI Director J. Edgar Hoover denied that LCN even existed (it has long been believed—although never proven—that Hoover was compromised by LCN figures who possessed photographs and other documentation of his alleged homosexuality). As a result, until very recently the LCN had a virtual chokehold on America, being involved in killing for hire, extortion, loan sharking, money laundering, narcotics, prostitution, smuggling, bookmaking, bribery, business infiltration, embezzlement, hijacking, horserace fixing, racketeering, pornography, bank fraud, and fencing. By the 1960s the LCN's influence extended from America's largest labor unions into trucking, construction, longshoring, waste disposal, gambling, and garment making; it had grown into a multi-billion-dollar syndicate of criminal enterprises run by twenty-six "families" nationwide.[95]

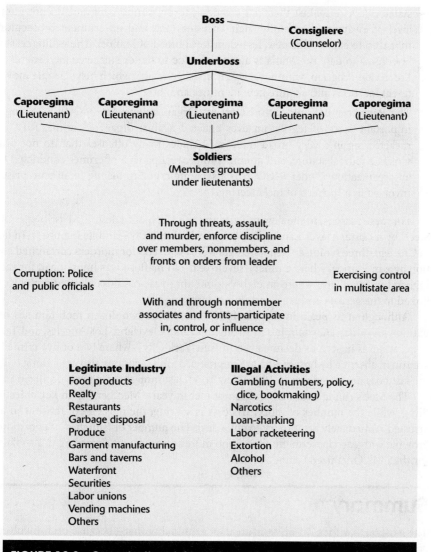

FIGURE 12-2 Organizational Chart for a Mafia Family

Beginning in the mid-1980s, however, the FBI spearheaded an unprecedented assault on LCN, putting away two generations of godfathers on racketeering charges. That initiative continues today and has met with tremendous success toward dealing with this very elusive group.

How has this success been obtained? Through tenacity, hard work, and some luck—and for three very practical reasons:

- *The expanded use of electronic eavesdropping ("wiretapping").* With federal agents listening in on more conversations each year, mobsters are forced to operate in a climate of constant suspicion. Cooperation between federal and state law enforcement authorities also speeds up convictions. Furthermore, the Internal Revenue Service can legally share information, enabling it to assist in complicated tax cases in almost two-thirds of all organized crime prosecutions.

- *The use of informants.* A significant tool in the toppling of Mob kingpins has been the use of former gangsters who have proved willing to violate the code of omerta, turning state's evidence against their old cronies. More youthful gangsters do not possess the level of loyalty to the family their ancestors did, and government prosecutors have managed to exploit this new, less-than-loyal breed of Mafiosi. The willingness of some hoodlums to defy the Mafia is also partly due to the existence of the Federal Witness Protection Program, within the U.S. Marshals Service, which helps people move to different locations and acquire new identities and jobs.

- The Racketeer Influenced and Corrupt Organizations Act (RICO). The single most important piece of legislation ever enacted against organized crime, RICO defines racketeering in a very broad manner, includes many offenses that do not ordinarily violate a federal statute, and attempts to prove a pattern of crimes conducted through an organization. Under RICO, it is a separate crime to belong to an enterprise that is involved in a "pattern of racketeering."

For these reasons, in the new millennium the LCN, once described as "bigger than U.S. Steel" by mobster Meyer Lansky, has lost much of its sway—and its members. In late 2007 in Chicago, three senior-citizen mobsters were locked up for murders committed a generation ago; in Florida, where a ninety-seven-year-old mafioso was imprisoned for racketeering; and in New York, where an eighty-something-year-old boss pleaded guilty to charges linked to the garbage industry and union corruption.[96]

Although at its peak, in the late 1950s, more than two dozen mob families operated nationwide, today LCN families in strongholds like Cleveland, Los Angeles, and Tampa are gone, and it is in serious decline even in New York City—where two of five crime families are run in absentia by bosses who are in prison. Mob executions also are a thing of the past; the last boss murdered was in 1985, New York's last mob shooting war occurred in 1992.[97]

The Mob's ruling commission has not met in years. Membership in key cities is dwindling, while the number of mob turncoats is soaring; the majority of those who are now arrested immediately want to try to cut a deal. The number of "snitches" is enormous—and growing with each indictment; there is no more secret society, according to a spokesperson for the FBI's Organized Crime Section.[98]

Summary

This chapter has focused on four areas of criminality that—because each involves group criminal behavior in the form of a syndicate—are particularly troublesome and challenging for today's police and that consume a tremendous proportion of their resources: terrorism, street gangs, illicit drugs, and La Cosa Nostra. Emphasis for each of these areas was placed on describing the nature of each problem, the extent of its effects on society, and several police responses for coping with each of them.

Perhaps a point that needs to be underscored is that these three problems are not found to the same degree or depth from state to state, city to city. Although police work generally tends to be very much the same from region to region and jurisdiction to jurisdiction, the threat of terrorism, gang activities, and drug problems will differ and will require unique approaches in venues that are dissimilar. The potential dangers of terrorist attacks, gangs, and drugs that are posed to a tourist mecca such as Las Vegas will be quite different in kind and scope than those posed for a hub of business and industry such as Chicago. The police, to borrow a phrase, must "put on different faces for different people."

Related to that reality is another fact: The police will be compelled to adapt their training and operations so as to cope with these problems. As society becomes more diverse, the police will continue to face new challenges that rise to the level of the four posed in this chapter (and in the following chapter, which deals with crimes involving youth, illegal immigrants, homeless, and hate; although perhaps not carrying the potential for societal disasters of a magnitude such as those discussed in this chapter, these problems still command a great deal of attention, resources, and training).

It is of utmost importance that police officers begin receiving adequate training and education to allow them to be prepared for these sorts of crimes, as each can also involve cybercrimes, on the Internet.

Key Terms

active shooter
bioterrorism
cyberterrorism
domestic terrorism
Electronic Communications
    Protection Act of 1986
focused deterrence
fusion center
gang intelligence unit
    (GIU)

High-Intensity Drug Trafficking
    Area (HIDTA) program
Incident Command System (ICS)
La Cosa Nostra
Mafia
methamphetamine (meth)
Military Commissions Act
    (MCA)
National Incident Management
    System (NIMS)

organized crime
predictive policing
The Racketeer Influenced and
    Corrupt Organizations Act
    (RICO)
raves
street gang
terrorism
USA PATRIOT Act

Review Questions

1. What are the three types of terrorism?
2. What are the USA PATRIOT Act, the Electronic Communications Protection Act, and the Military Commissions Act, and how do these pieces of legislation benefit police authorities in their efforts to thwart terrorism?
3. What are the major portions of the National Incident Management System?
4. How do cyberterrorism and bioterrorism present a particularly ominous terroristic threat to U.S. communities, and what would be the police role and functions in the case of such attacks?
5. How are police trained to respond to critical incidents involving active shooters at scenes of mass killings, and why?
6. What are the FBI's new investigative methods for fighting terrorism?
7. How can fusion centers help to fight terrorism?
8. What are some forms of organized crime besides the Mafia?
9. How did La Cosa Nostra originate, and what have traditionally been its preferred forms of criminal behavior?
10. How would you describe the three very successful police methods that have been developed to investigate and prosecute mobsters?
11. What is the nature, cause, and extent of the nation's gang problems, and what are some options used by the police to deal with gang members?
12. How would you describe this nation's drug problem and the part that methamphetamine plays in it?
13. How does HIDTA work to assist a community to combat drug crimes?
14. What is meant by open-air drug markets and raves, and what are the police doing to control these problems?
15. What are "bath salts," and how have they proven to be a serious problem in the U.S.?

Learn by Doing

1. Terrorists would prefer to attack critical targets—several of which exist in nearly any city or county. You, as a lieutenant in your local police agency, have been assigned to your countywide fusion center. The captain who oversees the unit informs you that your first task is to identify all critical targets; then, once identified, the center must consider responses for the time when a terrorist attack or other significant event occurs.

a. What types or categories of critical infrastructure should concern you?

b. What structures in your county do you feel should be listed as critical targets?

c. Might local politics come into play when developing this list, especially if someone's business is (or is not) included? If so, how will you deal with it?

d. What should your fusion center do once this list is compiled?

2. You are a small-town police chief. Early one morning—although you don't yet know it—a man rows his small fishing boat, containing a duffel bag and two fishing rods, down the remote side of a river that runs through your city. After a slow, thirty-minute ride, the fisherman approaches the dam's spillway. He then removes four interconnected backpacks from the duffel bag and lowers them into the water along the sloping spillway. A button on a control device is depressed, and a large explosion is heard for miles. The underwater explosion blows a massive hole in the earthen wall, leading to a huge avalanche of water carving a wide chasm in the dam. Within minutes, the first call of the dam break reaches you; a frantic scramble ensues as media and emergency rescue teams begin to alert everyone living downstream. Reports are also quickly coming in about people drowning near the dam. People are in a state of panic and trying frantically to escape. Several miles of roads have been wiped out.

Your task: Consider the kinds of advance planning that should have been done to prepare for such a situation. Also, what would be the initial duties and responsibilities of law enforcement and other first-response personnel? The types of technologies and equipment needed? Public information responsibilities? What multiagency coordination must be accomplished?

3. Your criminal justice professor is planning a class debate on the USA PATRIOT Act. Pick a side, and develop your arguments.

4. To better grasp the methods of, and problems confronted by, the police in this chapter's subject matter, you could do no better than to seek out and interview those individuals who work in these arenas on a daily basis (e.g., for terrorism: federal, state, or local officers assigned to homeland security or a regional fusion center; for organized crime, gang, or drug investigations: federal or state investigators assigned to those areas). Better yet, if your interests are keen in any one of these areas, you could attempt to accomplish a university-sponsored internship with one of those agencies or, perhaps, offer to volunteer your time at the agency (be forewarned, however: either of these latter objectives would likely involve a thorough and lengthy background check prior to your being accepted).

Notes

1. David Shipler, "Terrorist Plots, Hatched by the F.B.I.," April 28, 2012, http://www.nytimes.com/2012/04/29/opinion/sunday/terrorist-plots-helped-along-by-the-fbi.html?pagewanted=all (accessed November 2, 2013).

2. Chris Barth, "FBI Thwarts Terrorist Plot To Bomb NY Federal Reserve," October 17, 2012, http://www.forbes.com/sites/chrisbarth/2012/10/17/fbi-disables-1000-pound-bomb-thwarts-terrorist-plot-against-ny-federal-reserve/ (accessed November 2, 2013).

3. Scott Shane and Eric Schmitt, "Qaeda Plot to Attack Plane Foiled, U.S. Officials Say," The New York Times, May 7, 2012, http://www.nytimes.com/2012/05/08/world/middleeast/us-says-terrorist-plot-to-attack-plane-foiled.html (accessed November 2, 2013).

4. Mosi Secret, "Man Convicted of a Terrorist Plot to Bomb Subways Is Sent to Prison for Life," The New York Times, November 16, 2012, http://www.nytimes.com/2012/11/17/nyregion/adis-medunjanin-convicted-of-subway-bomb-plot-gets-life-sentence.html?_r=0 (accessed November 3, 2013).

5. Colin Miner, Liz Robbins, and Eric Eckholm, "F.B.I. Says Oregon Suspect Planned 'Grand' Attack," The New York Times, November 27, 2010, http://www.nytimes.com/2010/11/28/us/28portland.html?pagewanted=all&_r=1& (accessed November 2, 2013).

6. Shipler, "Terrorist Plots, Hatched by the F.B.I."

7. Kevin Johnson, USA Today, "Terror Arrest Highlights New York's Spot on Target," October 18, 2012, http://www.usatoday.com/story/news/nation/2012/10/18/terror-arrest-new-york-city/1641109/ (accessed November 2, 2013).

8. The Washington Post, "Faces of the Fallen," http://apps.washingtonpost.com/national/fallen/ (accessed November 2, 2013).

9. Kimberley Amadeo, "What Are the Facts About the War on Terror Costs?" About.com US Economy, http://

useconomy.about.com/od/usfederalbudget/f/War_on_ Terror_Facts.htm (accessed November 3, 2013).

10. Quoted in M. K. Rehm and W. R. Rehm, "Terrorism Preparedness Calls for Proactive Approach," *Police Chief* 67 (December 2000): 38–43.

11. D. Westneat, "Terrorists Go Green," *U.S. News and World Report*, June 4, 2001, p. 28.

12. J. F. Lewis, Jr., "Fighting Terrorism in the 21st Century," *FBI Law Enforcement Bulletin* 68 (March 1999): 3.

13. Ibid., p. 3.

14. K. Strandberg, "Bioterrorism: A Real or Imagined Threat?" *Law Enforcement Technology* (June 2001): 88–97.

15. D. Rogers, "A Nation Tested: What Is the Terrorist Threat We Face and How Can We Train for It?" *Law Enforcement Technology* (November 2001): 16–21.

16. "With Biochem Terror No Longer 'Unthinkable,' NYPD Gets Ready," *Law Enforcement News* (Spring 2004): 1, 13.

17. Meghan Hoyer and Brad Heath, "Mass Killings Occur in USA Once Every Two Weeks," *USA TODAY*, December 19, 2012, http://www.usatoday.com/story/news/nation/2012/12/18/mass-killings-common/1778303/(accessed November 21, 2013).

18. "Shoot First: Columbine Tragedy Transformed Police Tactics," USA TODAY, April 19, 2009, http://usatoday30.usatoday.com/news/nation/2009-04-19-columbine-police-tactics_N.htm (accessed November 2, 2013).

19. Ibid.

20. Michael Melia, "Newtown First Responders Carry Heavy Burdens," *Associated Press*, December 20, 2012, http://news.yahoo.com/newtown-first-responders-carry-heavy-burdens-205638335.html (accessed November 2, 2013)

21. U.S. Department of Homeland Security, *National Incident Management System* (Washington, DC: Author, March 2004), pp. viii, ix.

22. J. Buntin, "Disaster Master," *Governing* (December 2001): 34–38.

23. Gary Peck and Laura Mijanovich, "Give Us Security While Retaining Freedoms," *Reno Gazette Journal*, August 28, 2003, p. 9A.

24. "House Approves Patriot Act Renewal," www.cnn.com/2006/POLITICS/03/07/patriot.act (accessed November 5, 2013).

25. Peck and Mijanovich, "Give Us Security While Retaining Freedoms," p. 9A.

26. Michael Isikoff, "Show Me the Money," *Newsweek*, December 1, 2003, p. 36.

27. Lorraine Ali, "We Love This Country," *Newsweek*, April 7, 2003.

28. John Ashcroft, quoted in Sharon Begley, "What Price Security?" *Newsweek*, October 1, 2001, p. 58.

29. See Charles Doyle, "Privacy: An Overview of the Electronic Communications Privacy Act," March 30, 2011, http://www.fas.org/sgp/crs/misc/R41733.pdf (accessed November 3, 2013); Richard Lardner, "Not That Hard for Authorities to Get to Your Email," *Associated Press*, November 13, 2012, http://bigstory.ap.org/article/not-hard-authorities-get-your-email (accessed November 13, 2013).

30. Jeannie Shawl, "Bush Signs Military Commissions Act," *Jurist: Legal News and Research*, http://jurist.org/paperchase/2006/10/bush-signs-military-commissions-act.php (accessed November 5, 2013).

31. Ibid.

32. J. Sullivan, "Terrorism Early Warning Groups: Regional Intelligence to Combat Terrorism," in *Homeland Security and Terrorism*, ed. R. Howard, J. Forest, and J. Moore (New York: McGraw-Hill, 2006), pp. 235–245.

33. U.S. Department of Justice, Federal Bureau of Investigation, *National Gang Threat Assessment 2011: Emerging Trends* (Washington, DC: National Gang Intelligence Center, 2011), p. 9, http://www.fbi.gov/stats-services/publications/2011-national-gang-threat-assessment/2011-national-gang-threat-assessment-emerging-trends (accessed November 5, 2013).

34. U.S. Department of Justice, Federal Bureau of Investigation, *National Gang Threat Assessment 2011: Emerging Trends*, p. 11.

35. Ibid., pp. 9–10.

36. James C. Howell and Arlen Egley, Jr., (2005, June). *Gangs in Small Towns and Rural Counties* (Washington, DC: Office of Juvenile Justice and Delinquency Prevention, 2005), http://www.nationalgangcenter.gov/Content/Documents/Gangs-in-Small-Towns-and-Rural-Counties.pdf (accessed November 5, 2013); also see: U.S. Department of Justice, Bureau of Justice Assistance, *History of Street Gangs in the United States* (Washington, DC: Author), http://www.nationalgangcenter.gov/Content/Documents/History-of-Street-Gangs.pdf (accessed November 5, 2013).

37. James McKinley, Jr., "U.S. Arrests Hundreds in Raids on Drug Cartel," *New York Times*, www.nytimes.com/2009/10/23/us/23bust.html (accessed November 5, 2013).

38. U.S. Department of Justice, Federal Bureau of Investigation, "A Courageous Victim: Taking a Stand Against MS-13," www.fbi.gov/page2/may09/ms13_050109.html (accessed November 5, 2013).

39. For the NCGIA site, see http://www.ashevillenc.gov/Portals/0/city-documents/police/policeservices/

NCGangAwareness.pdf; for the NJSP site, see: http://www.senatenj.com/uploads/district9/know-the-signs2.pdf (accessed November 5, 2013)..

40. U.S. Department of Justice, Office of Juvenile Justice Programs, *Gang Prevention*, http://www.ojjdp.gov/mpg/progTypesGangPrevention.aspx (accessed November 6, 2013).

41. National Gang Center, *Review of Risk Factors for Juvenile Delinquency and Youth Gang Involvement*, http://www.nationalgangcenter.gov/SPT/Risk-Factors/Research-Review-Criteria (accessed November 6, 2013).

42. Federal Bureau of Investigation, *National Gang Threat Assessment 2011: Emerging Trends*, p. 15.

43. Ibid., p. 11.

44. U.S. Department of Justice, Office of Justice Programs, National Institute of Justice, *Evaluating G.R.E.A.T.: A School-Based Gang Prevention Program*, pp. 1–7, www.ncjrs.gov/pdffiles1/198604.pdf (accessed November 5, 2013).

45. Scott H. Decker, *Strategies to Address Gang Crime: A Guidebook for Local Law Enforcement* (Washington, DC: U.S Department of Justice, Office of Community Oriented Policing Services (April 2008), pp. 21–23, http://www.cops.usdoj.gov/Publications/e060810142Gang-book-web.pdf (accessed November 4, 2013).

46. National Crime Prevention Council, *Strategy: Gang Prevention through Community Intervention with High-risk Youth*, http://74.205.83.203:8181/NCPC/training/topics/violent-crime-and-personal-safety/strategies/strategy-gang-prevention-through-community-intervention-with-high-risk-youth (accessed November 14, 2013).

47. David M. Kennedy, Anthony A. Braga, and Anne M. Piehl, *Reducing Gun Violence: The Boston Gun Project's Operation Ceasefire* (Washington, D.C.: National Institute of Justice, 2001), https://www.ncjrs.gov/pdffiles1/nij/188741.pdf (accessed November 4, 2013); also see State of California, Governor's Office of Gang and Youth Violence Policy, "Safe Community Partnerships," http://www.sgc.ca.gov/hiap/docs/publications/issue_briefs/Health_and_Public_Safety.pdf (accessed November 4, 2013).

48. Ibid.

49. Ibid.

50. D. L. Weisel and E. Painter, *The Police Response to Gangs: Case Studies of Five Cities* (Washington, D.C.: Police Executive Research Forum, 1997).

51. Lynn Langton, *Gang Units in Large Local Law Enforcement Agencies, 2007* (Washington, D.C.: U.S. Department of Justice, Bureau of Justice Statistics, October 2010), p. 1, http://bjs.ojp.usdoj.gov/content/pub/pdf/gulllea07.pdf (accessed November 4, 2013).

52. Ibid.

53. Ibid., p . 10.

54. Decker, *Strategies to Address Gang Crime: A Guidebook for Local Law Enforcement*, p. 37.

55. Gene Johnson, "Strategy, Timing Key to States' Pot Legalization," *Associated Press*, ABC News.com, December 2, 2012, http://bigstory.ap.org/article/strategy-timing-key-states-pot-legalization (accessed December 3, 2013).

56. Susan Page, "Public to feds: Back off state pot laws," *USA Today*, December 7, 2012, http://usatoday30.usatoday.com/NEWS/usaedition/2012-12-07-Poll-Feds-should-back-off-when-states-legalize-pot_ST_U.htm (accessed November 1, 2013).

57. ProCon.org, "18 Legal Medical Marijuana States and DC," http://medicalmarijuana.procon.org/view.resource.php?resourceID=000881 (accessed November 3, 2013).

58. See *The DEA Position on Marijuana* (January 2011), http://www.justice.gov/dea/docs/marijuana_position_2011.pdf (accessed November 2, 2013).

59. U.S. Department of Health and Human Services, Substance Abuse and Mental Health Services Administration, "Results from the 2011 National Survey on Drug Use and Health: Summary of National Findings," pp. 1–4, http://www.samhsa.gov/data/NSDUH/2k11Results/NSDUHresults2011.pdf (accessed November 1, 2013).

60. Ibid., pp. 30–31.

61. U.S. Department of Justice, Federal Bureau of Investigation, Uniform Crime Reports, *Crime in the United States 2012:* "Persons Arrested," http://www.fbi.gov/about-us/cjis/ucr/crime-in-the-u.s/2012/crime-in-the-u.s.-2012/persons-arrested/persons-arrested (accessed November 1, 2013).

62. Office of National Drug Control Policy, "New Study Reveals Scope of Drug and Crime Connection; As Many as 87 Percent of People Arrested for Any Crime Test Positive for Drug Use," May 28, 2009, www.whitehousedrugpolicy.gov/news/press09/052809.html (accessed November 5, 2013).

63. Office of National Drug Control Policy, National Drug Control Strategy, "The National Drug Control Budget: FY 2013 Funding Highlights," http://www.whitehouse.gov/ondcp/the-national-drug-control-budget-fy-2013-funding-highlights (accessed November 1, 2013).

64. Ibid.

65. Office of Community Oriented Policing Services, "COPS History," http://www.cops.usdoj.gov/default.asp?item=44 (accessed November 3, 2013).

66. David Kroll, "Do Pseudoephedrine Sales Predict the Number of Meth Labs in Your Community?" *Forbes*, October 16, 2012, http://www.forbes.com/sites/davidkroll/2012/10/16/do-pseudoephedrine-sales-predict-the-number-of-meth-labs-in-your-community/ (accessed November 3, 2013).

67. Jim Salter, "Meth Flourishes Despite Tracking Laws," CNSNews.com, http://cnsnews.com/news/article/meth-flourishes-despite-tracking-laws (accessed November 3, 2013).

68. Judy Keen, "Missouri grapples with one of the USA's worst meth problems," *USA Today*, December 21, 2011, http://usatoday30.usatoday.com/news/nation/story/2011-12-20/meth-lab-missouri/52132328/1 (accessed November 3, 2013).

69. Jim Salter, "Mexican Cartels Using 'Superlabs' to Flood U.S. with Cheap Meth," *Associated Press*, October 11, 2012, http://www.standard.net/stories/2012/10/11/mexican-cartels-using-superlabs-flood-us-cheap-meth (accessed November 23, 2013).

70. Adapted from Illinois Attorney General, "Strategies for Fighting Meth," http://illinoisattorneygeneral.gov/methnet/fightmeth/law.html (accessed November 3, 2013).

71. Alex Harocopos and Mike Hough, *Drug Dealing in Open-Air Markets* (Washington, DC: U.S. Department of Justice, Office of Community Oriented Policing Services, January 2005), p. 1.

72. Ibid., pp. 21–22.

73. Michael S. Scott, *Rave Parties* (Washington, D.C.: U.S. Department of Justice, Office of Community Oriented Policing Services, 2002), p. 1.

74. Ibid., pp. 1–2, 13–14.

75. Jaclyn O'Malley, "The New High: 'Bath Salts,'" *Reno Gazette Journal*, March 21, 2012, pp. 1, 4A.

76. Jessica Vander Velde, "As Florida Bath Salts Deaths Rise, Drug Enforcers Stymied," *Tampa Bay Times*, October 14, 2012, http://www.tampabay.com/news/publicsafety/as-florida-bath-salts-deaths-rise-drug-enforcers-stymied/1256057 (accessed November 3, 2013).

77. Ibid.

78. Senator Charles E. Schumer, "Schumer Legislation Banning Bath Salts and 29 Other Deadly Synthetic Substances Signed into Law Today by President Obama," *Press Release*, July 9, 2012, http://www.schumer.senate.gov/record.cfm?id=337207 (accessed November 3, 2013).

79. Michael McLaughlin, "Bath Salts Incidents Down Since DEA Banned Synthetic Drug," *Huffington Post*, September 4, 2012, http://www.huffingtonpost.com/2012/09/04/bath-salts-ban_n_1843420.html (accessed November 2, 2013); also see Lee Ferran, "DEA Announces Emergency Ban on 'Bath Salts,'" September 7, 2011, http://abcnews.go.com/Blotter/bath-salts-dea-announces-emergency-ban/story?id=14467134#.UEEgWaN62So (accessed November 3, 2013).

80. Substance Abuse and Mental Health Services Administration, "First-of-its-kind Report Finds that Street Forms of 'Synthetic Marijuana' Products Linked to Thousands of Hospital Emergency Departments Visits Each Year," December 4, 2012, http://www.samhsa.gov/newsroom/advisories/1212040915.aspx (accessed November 5, 2013).

81. Joel Rose, "Fake Pot Is a Real Problem For Regulators," *NPR*, July 12, 2012, http://www.npr.org/2012/07/12/156615024/fake-pot-is-a-real-problem-for-regulators (accessed November 5, 2013).

82. Office of National Drug Control Policy, *National Drug Control Strategy—FY 2012 Budget Summary*, p. 2., http://www.hsdl.org/?view&did=6522 (accessed November 23, 2013); see also Office of National Drug Control Policy, "High Intensity Drug Trafficking Areas (HIDTA) Program," http://www.whitehouse.gov/ondcp/high-intensity-drug-trafficking-areas-program(accessed November 3, 2013).

83. *United States Attorney, Southern District of New York*, Press Release, "Manhattan U.S. Attorney Charges Fourteen Gambino Crime Family Members and Associates with Racketeering, Murder, Sex Trafficking, and Other Crimes," http://msnbcmedia.msn.com/i/MSNBC/Sections/NEWS/gambinoarrestspr.pdf (accessed November 3, 2013).

84. Gary W. Potter, *Criminal Organizations: Vice, Racketeering, and Politics in an American City* (Prospect Heights, IL: Waveland Press, 1994), p. 116.

85. This term for the Mob was used often from January 1957 to March 1960 by the United States Senate's "Select Committee on Improper Activities in the Labor or Management Field," popularly known as the McClellan Committee, which examined the extent to which criminal or other improper practices were engaged in the field of labor management. See *Final Report of the Select Committee on Improper Activities in the Labor or Management Field, United States Senate, pursuant to S. Res. 44 and 249, 86th Congress* (Washington, D.C.: U.S. Government Printing Office, 1960).

86. *New York Times Archives*, "Origin of the Term Mafia," query.nytimes.com/gst/abstract.html?res=9D05E1D61239E033A25750C0A9639C94609ED7CF

(accessed March 5, 2013); also see Henner Hess, *Mafia and Mafiosi: Origin, Power, and Myth* (New York: New York University Press, 1998); Claire Sterling, *Octopus: The Long Reach of the Sicilian Mafia* (New York: Touchstone Books, 1991); and Gaia Servadio, *Mafioso: A History of the Mafia from Its Origins to the Present Day* (New York: Stein and Day, 1976).

87. United States Senate, "Kefauver Crime Committee Launched," www.senate.gov/artandhistory/history/minute/Kefauver_Crime_Committee_Launched.htm (accessed November 5, 2013); the official name of the committee was the "Special Committee to Investigate Organized Crime in Interstate Commerce."

88. President's Commission on Law Enforcement and Administration of Justice, *Task Force Report: Organized Crime* (Washington, D.C.: U.S. Government Printing Office, 1967).

89. Organized Crime Control Act of 1970, Pub.L. 91-452, 84 Stat. 922 (October 15, 1970).

90. This article focuses on "traditional" organized crime, which is associated with Italian-American and Sicilian crime families, as opposed to "nontraditional" organized crime, which is associated with the newer emerging groups, such as outlaw motorcycle gangs, Chinese triads, and youth gangs.

91. Umberto Santino, "Mafia and Mafia-Type Organizations in Italy," www.centroimpastato.it/otherlang/mafia-in-italy.php3 (accessed November 5, 2013).

92. James N. Gilbert, "Organized Crime on the Western Frontier" (paper presented at an annual conference of the Western Social Science Association, Oakland, CA, April 27, 1995), p. 1.

93. See Mary Billard, "Silent Partners No Longer," *The New York Times*, March 28, 2012, http://www.nytimes.com/2012/03/29/fashion/with-mob-wives-silent-partners-no-longer.html?pagewanted=all (accessed November 4, 2013).

94. IGN.com, "Mafia Wars," http://www.ign.com/wikis/mafia-wars (accessed November 5, 2013).

95. See, for example, J. R. de Szigethy, "Blackmail in America: A Dark History," www.americanmafia.com/feature_articles_274.html (accessed November 5, 2013); Christian Lehmann-Haupt, "Books of The Times; Catalogue of Accusations Against J. Edgar Hoover," http://www.nytimes.com/1993/02/15/books/books-of-the-times-catalogue-of-accusations-against-j-edgar-hoover.html (accessed March 5, 2013); David E. Kaplan, "Getting It Right: The FBI and the Mob," *U.S. News and World Report*, June 18, 2001, p. 20.

96. Larry McShane, "Crime's Fraying Families," *Seattle Times*, http://seattletimes.com/html/nationworld/2003977818_mafia27.html (accessed March 5, 2013).

97. Ibid.

98. Ibid.

(Courtesy Lisa F. Young/Shutterstock.)

13 Addressing "People Problems"
Immigrants, Youth Crimes, Hate Crimes, the Mentally Ill, and Homeless

LEARNING OBJECTIVES

As a result of reading this chapter, the student will be able to:

 Explain several issues—political, economic, and social—that underlie immigration and border security

2 Explain what measures some state and local units of government are adopting to attempt to reduce the number of undocumented immigrants residing in their jurisdictions

3 Delineate some new police methods for controlling illegal border crossings

4 Explain the nature and extent of youth crime and violence

Describe how the police are addressing selected problems involving youth, such as school violence, and gun violence

6 Discuss the problems with determining the actual numbers of hate crimes, how such crimes differ from other crimes, and some potential responses to the problem

7 Describe the social factors that contribute to mental illness and homelessness, and what police are doing to assist those who live on the streets

Introduction

This chapter continues with our "extraordinary problems" theme established in Chapter 12 with selected problematical types of offender groups. Whereas Chapter 12 looked at organized, syndicated crime groups, this chapter concerns more individualized offenders who confront the police (although the argument could be made that some of these individuals are in fact organized in their criminal activities; in fact, some problems discussed in this chapter, such as illegal immigration and youth violence, can and do evolve into problems that are gang- or drug-oriented in nature).

Put another way, a common thread running through the types of offenders who are discussed in this chapter—undocumented immigrants who wish to live in the United States or to maintain cross-international criminal activities, violent and disorderly youth, persons who perpetrate crimes because of their hatred for others, and those who are homeless—is that each poses unique challenges for the police, who are often compelled to utilize some unique practices in order to deal with them.

This chapter begins with an examination of what might be viewed as the dual problem of illegal immigration and border security. Included is a review of several rationales that underlie the immigration problem; also included is a discussion of several federal and state laws, methods (e.g., the Southwestern fence), and technologies that attempt to address the problem.

Next we examine crime from the perspective of youth; it has long been said by people working in criminal justice that "Crime is a young person's game," and certainly that holds true; we examine youth crime and violence from several vantage points, including guns, disorderly conduct, and the problem of underage drinking. Following that we look at another increasingly serious matter: crimes committed by individuals who are motivated out of hate; we also consider some police hate-crime initiatives involving enforcement and prevention. Then we review the problems of mental illness and homelessness, including the nature and extent of the problems; as with the preceding topics, we also look at some police "best practices" for helping these individuals.

The chapter concludes with a summary, key terms, review questions, and several scenarios and activities that provide opportunities for you to learn by doing.

▶ Policing U.S. Borders

Extent and Rationales

There are an estimated 11.5 million illegal immigrants residing in the United States.[1] The annual influx of unauthorized immigrants into the United States began to decline in 2007 and even stabilized during 2012, given tougher state immigration laws, fewer available domestic jobs, greater levels of border enforcement, and improved social conditions as well as changing demographics (i.e., lower fertility rates) in Mexico.[2]

▼

The status and numbers of persons now living in the United States illegally could change dramatically if pending legislation is fully implemented, however. A bill, originally called the Development, Relief and Education for Alien Minors Act (the "DREAM Act") was first introduced in Congress in 2001, but has failed to pass since; however, it is expected to be re-introduced by both Houses of Congress in 2013.[3] An estimated 1.8 million immigrants could be affected in the United States who are, or could become eligible for citizenship. Current versions of the legislation would offer a two-year, renewable reprieve from deportation to unauthorized immigrants who: are below the age of thirty-one; entered the United States prior to age sixteen and have lived here continuously for at least five years; have not been con-victed of a felony or "significant" misdemeanor, or three other misdemeanors; and are either now in school, have graduated from high school, earned a GED, or served in the military.[4]

The reasons for persons wishing to immigrate to the United States are varied. Historically, however, income and lifestyle stand at the root of the matter: Many people, like those persons attempting to cross the Southwest border from Mexico, want to relocate here primarily in order to live a productive and more comfortable life. The difference in per capita income between the United States and Mexico is staggering, and until the Mexican economy can become even moderately robust, people will attempt to breach borders and barriers in order to enter the United States. As David Von Drehle stated, "Given the historic ties, family ties, and economic ties connecting the two countries, the long-term solution to border security is a robust Mexican economy."[5] Other motivations for immigrating to the United States include: to escape persecution and corrupt governments, to join their fami-lies, and to provide better education for their children. Unfortunately, however, history has shown there are also those persons who would cross U.S. borders in order to plan, facilitate, and commit terrorist acts on U.S. soil.

Issues, Crime—and a Fence

A number of long-standing social and economic questions remain in the minds of many American citizens concerning immigration and border security: Do illegal immigrants

▲ Illegal immigrants are placed in holding facilities by Customs and Border Protection agents before they are returned to Mexico. *(Courtesy U.S. Customs and Border Protection.)*

commit a disproportionately high number of crimes? Do they take jobs and money away from American citizens and reduce wages? Are U.S. local school districts overtaxed by the needs of immigrant children? Do undocumented immigrants in emergency rooms who are uninsured drive up the costs of premiums for the insured?[6]

The latter three questions—if answerable at all—can be addressed by economists or related federal agencies and are beyond the reach of this chapter section. However, the first question was recently considered by the Congressional Research Service, which looked at arrests of illegal and criminal immigrants for a three-year period and determined that criminality by immigrants is not insignificant: These arrests involved 159,286 individuals and 205,101 arrests. About 26,412 (17 percent) of the database's illegal and criminal immigrants had been detained for some crime and were then released from custody—and later accounted for a total of 42,827 arrests and 57,763 alleged violations. Of these arrests, about 8,500 (14.6 percent) were for driving under the influence, 6,000 (10.9 percent) were for drug violations, 4,000 (7.1 percent) involved major crimes (i.e., murder, assault, battery, rape, and kidnapping), and about 1,000 (2.1 percent) were for other violent offenses (including carjacking, child cruelty, child molestation, domestic abuse, lynching, stalking, and torture). Also included were 59 murders, 21 attempted murders, and 542 sex crimes.[7]

Protecting the nation's 7,000 miles of borders is also a highly-charged—and expensive—political issue. President George W. Bush signed into law the Secure Fence Act of 2006, which allocated $1.2 billion for a "double-layer," nearly 650-mile system of physical barriers between the United States and Mexico, including 299 miles of vehicle barriers, 350 miles of pedestrian fencing, checkpoints, lighting, cameras, satellites, and unmanned aerial vehicles along the southwestern border in areas of California, Arizona, New Mexico, and Texas, where more than 95 percent of all border crossings occur.[8] Then, in June 2013, an immigration reform bill was passed by the U.S. Senate and sent to the House that would deploy 20,000 additional border agents and complete the 700-mile border fence, while also addressing other related issues.[9]

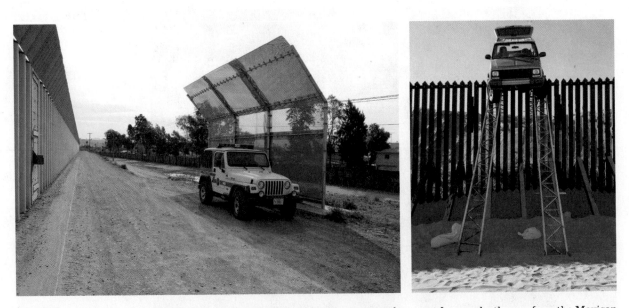

▲ Vehicles at the border. One is parked under an improvised fence to protect the agent from rocks thrown from the Mexican side of the border; the other got stuck while its driver attempted to drive over a 14´1 fence. *(Courtesy U.S. Customs and Border Protection (left); AP Photo/U.S. Customs and Border Protection (right)).*

State Immigration Legislation—and a Supreme Court Decision

Several state and local lawmakers, frustrated with this influx of illegal immigrants and the federal government's lack of success in dealing with it, have sought to check the problem by limiting their opportunities to get work, housing, and driver's licenses. In 2008, more than 200 state laws were enacted relating to immigration, the majority of which clamped down on illegal immigrants and their employers,[10] and during the first quarter of 2011, more than 1,500 immigration-related bills were introduced in the states, most of which dealt with employment, identification/driver's licenses and law enforcement.[11]

Then in April 2010, the Arizona legislature enacted Senate Bill 1070 (Support Our Law Enforcement and Safe Neighborhoods Act)—the toughest immigration enforcement law ever—which:

- Made it a violation of state law to be in the country illegally, and requiring immigrants to have proof of their immigration status; violations are punishable by up to six months in jail and a $2,500 fine; repeat offenses become a felony.

- Required police officers to "make a reasonable attempt" to determine the immigration status of a person if "reasonable suspicion" exists that he or she is an illegal immigrant (race, color, or national origin cannot be the only elements to be considered in initiating such a determination).

- Allowed local or state government agencies to be sued if having policies that hinder enforcement of immigration laws.

- Made it a crime to stop one's vehicle on a road to offer employment to illegal immigrants as day laborers.[12]

In June 2012, however, the U.S. Supreme Court[13] voted 5–3 to strike down most of the law and essentially upheld the federal government's authority to set immigration policy and laws. One provision of the law that was allowed to stand by the Court's decision—and its most controversial—is one that allows police to check a person's immigration status while enforcing other laws if "reasonable suspicion" exists that the person is in the United States illegally. This provision—dubbed by opponents as the "show me your papers" or "papers please" law—has long been condemned by critics of the law that it opens the door to racial profiling.

Arizona's police chiefs and county sheriffs were quick to find problems with the administration of the Court's ruling—particularly the "show me your papers" clause. They wonder how long must officers wait for federal authorities to respond when they encounter someone illegal—especially given President Obama's new policy to only deport dangerous criminals and repeat offenders. (If federal agents decline to pick up immigrants, the state has no means of forcing federal authorities to pick them up, and will likely have to release them unless they're suspected of committing a crime that would require them to be put in jail.) If they release a person too soon, are they exposing themselves to a lawsuit from residents who accuse them of failing to enforce the law? How do they avoid being sued for racial profiling? What justifies reasonable suspicion that someone is in the country illegally? Until such questions are answered, the Court's decision will certainly make enforcement of the law challenging.[14]

States' Reactions in the Aftermath

The Supreme Court's 2012 decision in the Arizona case end this trend: Frustrated with the federal government's failure to secure the southern border, in early 2013 dozens of state lawmakers throughout the nation had begun drafting measures designed to address illegal immigration, including at least six states that planned to introduce bills similar to Arizona's, and others that intended to limit access to public benefits for undocumented immigrants and to punish employers who hire them. Oklahoma initiated a plan to enact a law allowing authorities to seize and keep the vehicle of anyone who harbors an illegal immigrant and Missouri, Mississippi, and Nebraska are among the states where legislators will offer bills similar to Arizona. In several other states, lawmakers plan to push for laws that require employers to verify the immigration status of their workers. Newly elected governors in Georgia, South Carolina, and Florida vowed to enact tough immigration control laws during their high-profile campaigns, and Georgia's governor-elect (Nathan Deal) also wants to revoke birthright U.S. citizenship for children born to illegal immigrants. Commonly known as anchor babies, the number of children born to undocumented immigrants has nearly doubled to 4 million in the last few years and U.S. taxpayers spend tens of billions of dollars annually just to educate them.[15]

Police Responses

Training As illegal immigration has increased over the past thirty years, so have state, local, and tribal law enforcement officer encounters with illegal immigrants during routine police duties. Furthermore, the Supreme Court's decision concerning the aforementioned Arizona law made immigration enforcement an even more challenging legal arena for the police and triggered the need for formal training to ensure fair and just enforcement of immigration laws. One response to these demands was the federal Office of Community Oriented Policing Services (COPS) providing funding in 2007 for a private corporation and a public university to develop and implement a pilot web-based Basic Immigration Enforcement Training (BIET) program, which is offered at a nominal charge through a private web-based provider. The BIET program was designed to respond to that need by addressing topics such as the following:[16]

- **Identifying false identification. Federal law prohibits the production "without lawful authority an identification document or a false identification document." Technologies now allow counterfeiters to make false documents look absolutely legitimate—to include the state hologram, watermarks, even bar codes. The police dilemma is daunting:** How can they keep citizens safe if they do not know the true identity of the people they arrest? Some federal, state, and local authorities have developed a plan whereby each person who is arrested is fingerprinted, and within thirty minutes the local police receive a reply on their fingerprint apparatus giving them the identity of the person arrested (if they have been charged before). If that person is an illegal immigrant, the ICE agents will give them a call, interview the immigrant, detain them as necessary and, ultimately, if warranted, the immigrant will be deported. Fortunately, local law enforcement officers also have technology to authenticate passports, driver's licenses, and ID cards, and validate employee and visitor identification.

- **Consular notification:** If foreign nationals in the United States are arrested or detained, officers must inform them that they can notify their country's embassy or consulate, and embassy or consulate officials must be allowed access upon request. In some cases, officers must notify the foreign embassy regardless of the individual's wishes. Notification is also required when a foreign national dies or is involved in an airplane crash or shipwreck, or a guardian is appointed for a foreign national who is a minor or an incompetent adult.

- **Nonimmigrant visas:** International visitors wishing to visit the United States temporarily for purposes of business, work, tourism, or study have to obtain nonimmigrant visas. These visas are effective for a limited time—from six months to several years—and can be extended. Most nonimmigrants can be accompanied or joined by spouses and unmarried minor (or dependent) children.

- Differences between immigrant and nonimmigrant status. An *immigrant alien* (also known as a Lawful Permanent Resident [LPR]) is one who has been granted the right by the U.S. Customs and Immigration Service to reside permanently in the United States and to work without restrictions. Such immigrants are issued a "green card" (USCIS Form I-551), which is evidence of their LPR status. A *nonimmigrant* is an alien who has the right to reside temporarily in the United States. Such persons (e.g., a foreign student) may enter the country on an F-1 visa. Nonimmigrant aliens may or may not be allowed to work in the United States, and some may or may not have rigid time limits for their stay. Specific rules apply to each nonimmigrant alien and if they violate even one of these rules for at least 180 days, they can be deported and cannot re-enter the United States for three years. One who violates their conditions for more than one year is deportable and unable to re-enter the United States for ten years.

Programs and Aerial Vehicles   In addition to efforts of, and the beefed-up enforcement by agencies of the Department of Homeland Security (discussed in Chapter 10), and the aforementioned attempts to control illegal immigration, a number of other measures have been undertaken to secure U.S. borders.

In March 2013 the federal Office of Biometric Identity Management (OBIM) was created, to support the Department of Homeland Security by providing biometric identification for accurately identifying people and determining whether they pose a risk. OBIM supplies the technology for collecting and storing biometric data, provides analysis, updates its watchlist, and ensures the integrity of the data.[17,18]

Regarding unmanned aerial vehicles (UAVs, or drones), their deployment has increased tremendously since they were introduced by U.S. Customs and Border Protection (CBP) in 2004: As of mid-2012, CBP had purchased ten drones, costing approximately $18 million each, and had spent an additional $55.3 million for their maintenance and operations. A May 2012 report, however, outlined problems with this drone program. According to the Office of Inspector General, CBP "needs to improve planning of its unmanned

▲ U.S. Customs and Border Protection's Air and Marine office recently obtained several Predator B drones, which can fly for over twenty-seven hours, carry a payload of nearly two tons, and have twice the speed and nine times the power of the original Predator. *(Courtesy U.S. National Guard.)*

aircraft systems program to address its level of operation, program funding, and resource requirements, along with stakeholder needs."[19] Also, despite the CBP's limited mission to safeguard the borders, the report noted that CBP often flies missions for many other federal and local agencies.

There is no question that the technology exists to use UAVs to patrol the borders and perform many other key law enforcement functions. As is often the case with technologies, however, as their abilities increase, so do public concerns about privacy safeguards. There have already been a number of reports and hearings held concerning these issues.[20]

Back to Basics: Horses Sometimes the simplest approaches work the best when guarding the nation's borders. As an example, the U.S. Border Patrol's latest weapon is the return of the use of horses in Texas. Horses have been used for border protection since 1924—with agents being required to provide their own horses, and being paid $1,680 per year to look for bootleggers and illegal Chinese immigrants. Today's equines are trained differently, however: If there is an illegal immigrant squatting in the bushes near the Rio Grande, the border guard's horse will stop immediately, prick up its ears, and give a snort. If the illegal person attempts to run away, the horse will take pursuit through brush and branches. They are accustomed to loud noises (such as gunshots) and people, patrol in pairs, and are able to go into areas where all-terrain vehicles and other vehicles cannot penetrate. Inmates at the Hutchinson Correctional Facility in Kansas trained eleven horses for such use along the southwestern border.[21]

▶ Policing Youth Crimes

Extent of the Problem

In Chapter 12 we discussed gangs and what the police are doing to try to suppress them. Of course, youth crimes are certainly a core feature or outcome of gang activity. But here we take a more expansive view of crimes that are committed by and against youth. Such crimes are as old as crime itself.

"Crime is a young person's enterprise," as any police officer, criminologist, or anyone else employed in the criminal justice system can attest. Arrest data bear that out about one in ten persons arrested for committing a violent crime are under age eighteen, while 40 percent are committed by persons under age twenty-five.[22] In fact, a recent study projects that nearly one in three people will be arrested by the age of twenty-three (excluding minor traffic offenses)—a sharp increase from a previous study that stunned the nation when it was published in 1967, finding that 22 percent of youth would be arrested by age twenty-three. This increase is due to tougher crime policies of today, when youth may be arrested for drugs and domestic violence, which were unlikely offenses in 1967; the high rate of arrest rate of youth is particularly troubling today because it can hinder or prevent their obtaining student loans, jobs, and housing.[23]

News accounts of serious crimes committed by children and adolescents have encouraged a general belief that young people are increasingly violent and uncontrollable and that the response of the juvenile justice system has been inadequate. Most states have enacted laws that make the juvenile system more punitive and that allow younger children and adolescents to be transferred to the adult system for a greater variety of offenses and in a greater variety of ways. Indeed, at 645 per 100,000, the U.S. incarceration rate of juveniles is second only to that of Russia, at 685 per 100,000 population.[24]

Next we briefly consider several significant problems involving young offenders: school violence and bullying, gun violence, disorderly youth in public places, and underage drinking.

Gun Violence

Although overall U.S. homicide rates declined in the 1980s and 1990s, youth violence, particularly gun homicide, began increasing dramatically. In urban areas, gun violence takes a particularly heavy toll, as large numbers of young minority males are injured and killed. Research has also linked urban youth gun violence to the gang conflicts over drug markets as well as gun availability.[25]

The numbers speak loudly about the violent nature of American youth, with persons ages eighteen to twenty-four historically having the highest homicide offending rates, and their rates nearly doubling from 1985 to 1993. After increasing dramatically in the late 1980s—while rates for older age groups declined—offending rates of fourteen- to seventeen-year-olds and young adults (eighteen to twenty-four years old) have now stabilized. Homicide offending rates for twenty-five- to thirty-four-year-olds, however, declining from 1980 through 1999, have been increasing since then.[26] Youth gun violence is related to several other problems, including those of disorderly conduct of youth in public and underage alcohol use (both of which will be discussed in the pages that follow).

A very promising approach to addressing the problem of guns and youth is the use of focused deterrence, discussed in Chapter 12, modeled Boston's Operation Ceasefire and entailing a problem-oriented approach that focuses crime hot spots.

Disorderly Conduct in Public Places

The disorderly conduct of youth in public places constitutes one of the most common problems many police agencies must handle, particularly in suburban and rural communities. Disorderly youth are a common source of complaints from urban residents, merchants, and shoppers. Among the kinds of behaviors (some legal and some not) associated with youth disorderly conduct are playing loud music; cursing; blocking pedestrians and traffic; using alcohol, tobacco, and drugs; fighting; littering; vandalizing; and spreading graffiti.[27]

Police responses to this problem might include the following:[28]

- Creating alternative legitimate places and activities for youth (such as youth clubs, drop-in centers, and recreation centers) and employing youth at businesses negatively affected by disorderly behavior.
- Encouraging youth to gather where they will not disturb others.
- Reducing the comfort level, convenience, or attraction of popular gathering places (such as eliminating places to sit or lean, changing the background music).
- Installing and monitoring closed-circuit television cameras.
- Establishing and enforcing rules of conduct.
- Denying youth anonymity by getting to know the names and faces of young people (without being antagonistic or accusatory).

Underage Drinking

As with the statistics provided for other problems discussed in this chapter, unfortunately the numbers concerning underage drinking are not any better: The average age when youth first try alcohol is eleven years for boys and thirteen years for girls. The average age at which Americans begin drinking regularly is 15.9 years old, and adolescents who begin drinking before age fifteen are four times more likely to develop alcohol dependence than those who begin drinking at age twenty-one. It has been estimated that over 3 million teenagers are out-and-out alcoholics; several million more have a serious drinking problem that they cannot manage on their own. Finally, of the three leading causes of death for fifteen- to twenty-four-year-olds—automobile crashes, homicides, and suicides—alcohol is a leading factor in all three.[29]

▲ Youths who are involved with alcohol, drugs, and gangs will soon be involved with the police as well. *(Courtesy Monkey Business Images/Shutterstock.)*

Although underage drinking (alcohol consumption while under the age of twenty-one) is prohibited throughout the nation, young people use alcohol more than any other drug, including tobacco. Many of the harms associated with underage drinking, such as traffic fatalities, driving under the influence, assaults, cruising, street racing, raves, disorderly conduct, acquaintance rape, vandalism, and noise complaints, arise from the overconfidence, recklessness, lack of awareness, aggression, and loss of control that often accompany alcohol abuse.[30] The pressure to drink—whether to experience a rite of passage, to become part of a group, to reduce tension, or to forget worries—also contributes heavily to this problem.[31]

Police have responded in various ways to the problem of underage drinking:[32]

- *Target reduction of the community's overall alcohol consumption.* This may sound impossible to do, but some available means for doing so are discouraging price discounts on alcohol, restricting the hours or days when retailers can sell alcohol, and limiting the number of alcohol outlets.

- *Use of a comprehensive approach.* The police can use a combination of examining motivations for drinking, addressing drunk driving, targeting fake IDs, providing counseling or treatment about drinking patterns, enforcing minimum-age purchase laws, conducting undercover "shoulder tap" operations (police have an underage undercover operative ask adult strangers outside a store to purchase alcohol), checking IDs at bars and nightclubs, applying graduated sanctions to retailers who break the law, requiring keg registration (primarily to identify adults who provide alcohol to minors at large house parties or keg parties on college campuses; several states use keg registration to link information about those who purchase a keg to the keg itself), developing house party guidelines and walk-through procedures, and imposing fines for each underage person drinking at a party.

▶ Policing Hate Crimes

Types of Hate Crimes and Hate Groups

Hate crimes are major issues for the police because of their unique impact on victims and the community. Federal and state laws have given the police considerable ammunition, however, for attempting to suppress hate crimes and prosecute those who commit such crimes. In 1990, Congress passed the Hate Crimes Statistics Act, which forced the police to collect statistics on hate crimes, and several states have since enacted statutes that place higher penalties on crimes that have a hate motive. Then, nearly two decades later, Congress enacted the Matthew Shepard and James Byrd, Jr., Hate Crimes Prevention Act of 2009,[33] to help investigate and prosecute hate crimes. The Act makes it a federal crime to willfully cause bodily injury (or attempting to do so) with fire, firearm, or other dangerous weapon when: the crime was committed because of the actual or perceived race, color, religion, national origin of gender, sexual orientation, gender identity, or disability of any person. Such laws have not completely eliminated such crimes. Exhibit 13-1 ■ describes the recent resurgence of hate crime groups in the United States.

A Conundrum: Determining the Number of Hate Crimes Committed

Certainly preventing and responding to hate crimes can be a daunting task. However, this problem is exacerbated by the fact that it is nearly impossible to determine the statistical extent of the problem because the two different data sets reporting hate crimes provide two very different pictures. Specifically, the Federal Bureau of Investigation's *Hate Crimes Statistics 2011* reported a total of 6,222 hate crimes (with 7,713 victims)—46.9 percent of which were racially motivated, 20.8 percent involved sexual orientation bias, 19.8 percent motivated by religious

---

EXHIBIT 13-1

SURGE IN EXTREMIST GROUPS LINKED TO DEMOGRAPHIC SHIFT

A rise in the number of right-wing extremist groups since 2000 has been linked to alarm over the nation's weak economy and the growth of non-whites, symbolized by the 2008 election of Barack Obama, the nation's first African-American president.

The Southern Poverty Law Center reported that the number of right-wing hate groups—including neo-Nazis, Klansmen, white nationalists, neo-Confederates and racist skinheads—rose from 602 in 2000 to more than 1,000 in 2010, and then leveled off. Also, each group is smaller than before, making it more difficult for FBI informants to penetrate it.

Meanwhile, the Associated Press reported that explicit prejudice against blacks and Hispanics continued to rise by several percentage points during Obama's first term. And "Patriot" groups—those responsible for domestic terrorist plots in the 1990s like the Oklahoma City bombing—enjoyed a comeback, reaching an all-time high of 1,360 in 2012, the center said.

Right-wing extremists experienced major setbacks in 2012, including Obama's re-election and a report by the Census Department that non-Hispanic whites would become a minority by 2050. But the news only strengthened membership. White News Now, a website run by white supremacist Jamie Kelso, reported "an incredible year," reaching more people than ever before, and the secessionist Texas National Movement said membership rose four-fold after Obama was re-elected.

Sources: **Hate Groups Grow as Racial Tipping Point Changes Demographics** Colleen Curry, ABC News, May 18, 2012 http://abcnews.go.com/US/militias-hate-groups-grow-response-minority-population-boom/story?id=16370136; **The Year in Hate and Extremism** SPLC Intelligence Report, Spring 2013 http://www.splcenter.org/home/2013/spring/the-year-in-hate-and-extremism; **'Swimming upstream,' white supremacist groups still strong** CNN, Aug. 7, 2012 http://www.cnn.com/2012/08/07/us/white-supremacist-groups/

▼

bias, and 12 percent stemming from ethnicity/national origin bias.[34] However, the National Crime Victim Survey (NCVS) reports an annual average of *169,000* violent hate crime victimizations. This large discrepancy is largely due to the fact that about 54 percent of victims in the NCVS did not report their crimes to the police. Furthermore, in the NCVS, hate-related victimizations are based on victims' suspicion of the offenders' motivation, rather than that of the police.[35] The UCR statistics, as noted in Chapter 10, are based on crimes reported to, and by, the police, while the NCVS reports on what is reported by people surveyed through its survey and includes crimes that are not reported to the police. The limitations and advantages of both data sets are well known, for example, the UCR cannot report unreported crimes, uses a "hierarchy rule" (reporting only the most serious crime committed in a single incident), and are subject to police reporting error, while the NCVS is more prone to error as a result of respondent mistakes or falsifications, since no one investigates the respondents' claims. Furthermore, for an act to be classified as a hate crime by the NCVS, respondents need report only one of three types of activity: "the offender used hate language, left behind hate symbols, or the police investigators confirmed that the incident was a hate crime."[36]

Initiatives for Enforcement and Prevention

According to the Congressional Research Service, at least forty-five states and the District of Columbia have hate-crime statutes that cover bias-motivated crimes and provide specific penalty enhancements to deter such crimes.[37] At the federal level, investigating hate crime is a high priority of the Civil Rights Program of the FBI.[38] Furthermore, the federal Bureau of Justice Assistance (BJA) has provided funding for the Center for the Prevention of Hate Violence at the University of Southern Maine to produce a series of reports on successful projects. As a result of such funding, many recommendations and "best practices" have emerged over the past decade.[39] At the local level, responses to hate crime include: changes in legislation; enhancing law enforcement training for responding to such crimes; investigation, prosecution,

▲ Purveyors of hate and discrimination may, at some point, require action by the police. *(Courtesy Timothy R. Nichols/Shutterstock.)*

and prevention of hate crimes; and diversity and tolerance education programs. Most states and larger cities also have some form of government-sponsored hate-crime initiative involving criminal justice agencies, while municipal police departments in many large urban areas also have dedicated hate-crime units within their organizations. Furthermore, police departments are often involved as members of state or regional hate-crime task forces.[40]

A final note: One unique problem that exists with hate crimes is that they can be difficult to prosecute. Hate-crime charges are the only type where proving motive becomes as important as proving method. Juries often find it too difficult to conclude with any certainty what was going on in a suspect's mind during the crime. Defending a hate crime can also be a daunting task. Defense attorneys argue that a defendant may, for example, dress and talk like a skinhead but not identify with being one, while juries can be prejudiced toward guilt by the mere allegation of affiliation with such a cruel group. Furthermore, attorneys maintain that defending against such allegations can take on the appearance of defending a hate group and that jurors may force a defendant to pay for the sins of a group.[41]

▶ Coping with Mental Illness and Homelessness: Crucially Needed Programs

A National Model: Memphis's CIT Program

In 1988, police in Memphis, Tennessee, shot and killed a twenty-seven-year-old emotionally disturbed man who was wielding a knife. To its credit, the police department then set about partnering with a local mental illness alliance toward creating a program specifically designed to develop a more intelligent and safe approach to handling mental crisis events.[42] The result was the Crisis Intervention Team, or CIT, which offers specialized training for officers in dealing with the emotionally disturbed and linking police with mental health professionals. Today more than 2,700 police agencies have adopted the program.[43]

The program could not be more needed and timely than it is today, when it is estimated that up to 20 percent of police calls for service involve people whose behavior ranges from dysfunctional to serious mental illness.[44] Indeed, the National Alliance on Mental Illness (NAMI) estimates that there now one in four adults—approximately 61.5 million Americans—experience mental illness in a given year; furthermore, one in seventeen, about 13.6 million, live with a serious mental illness such as schizophrenia, major depression, or bipolar disorder.[45]

Mental illness is defined as "a medical condition that disrupts a person's thinking, feeling, mood, ability to relate to others, and daily functioning."[46] Mental illnesses are medical conditions that often result in reducing one's ability to cope with the ordinary demands of life. CIT uses volunteer officers from each patrol district who, although performing regular patrol functions, are trained to respond to crisis calls that present officers face-to-face with people suffering from these effects.[47]

Memphis has approximately 225 such officers—about 8 percent of the total force—who work with mental health providers, family advocates, and mental health consumer groups. CIT training consists of a four-stage, forty-hour comprehensive program that includes the following and emphasizes mental health-related topics, crisis resolution skills, de-escalation training, and access to community-based services:

- First is a lecture program in which participants learn about such related issues as medications and side effects, alcohol and drug assessment, developmental disabilities, suicide prevention, commitment, post-traumatic stress disorders (PTSD), legal aspects and officer liability, and community resources.

- Second, officers visit mental health centers and participate in discussions with mental health providers.

- Next, officers participate in realistic practical scenarios that emphasize crisis de-escalation, basic verbal skills.
- Finally, there is a broad discussion of the appropriate handling of various situations involving the mentally ill.[48]

After twenty-five years of existence, the results of CIT have been impressive. National advocates for the mentally ill, such as the NAMI and the American Association of Suicidology have recognized the CIT program for distinguished service to the mentally ill. CIT is also credited with saving lives and preventing injuries, both for consumers and officers. Officer injury data have decreased substantially since the program began, and studies have shown that the CIT program has resulted in a decrease in arrests rates for the mentally ill, greatly increased diversion into the health care system, and a resulting low rate of mental illness in our jails. Perhaps most important is that CIT officers give those persons suffering from mental illness a sense of dignity.[49]

Addressing Homelessness

Homelessness is a condition of people who lack regular legal access to adequate housing. Specific reasons for homelessness vary, but research indicates that most people are homeless because they cannot find affordable housing—a situation that has been exacerbated by the recession of the mid- and late-2000s. Families or individuals who pay more than 30 percent of their income for housing are considered "cost-burdened" and can have difficulty affording necessities such as food, clothing, transportation, and medical care. The lack of affordable housing is a significant hardship for low-income households and can prevent them from meeting their other basic needs, such as nutrition and health care, or saving for their future.[50]

According to the National Alliance to End Homelessness, approximately 643,000 people experiencing homelessness on any given night in the United States; of that number, 238,110 are people in families, and 404,957 are individuals. There are also about 26,500 homeless military veterans of the Iraq and Afghanistan wars, due largely to the economic crisis and post-traumatic stress disorder.[51] The new or temporarily homeless—people still hanging on to the remnants of their housed life, within the first six months of homelessness—often end up living in their vehicles.[52] In addition, at any given time 45 percent of homeless people have indicators of mental health problems—25 percent of whom have some form of serious mental illness (e.g., chronic depression, bipolar disorder, and schizophrenia). People experiencing homelessness also have a high rate of substance use: 46 percent of homeless respondents reported having an alcohol use problem, and 38 percent reported a problem with drug use in the past year.[53]

Certainly the police—from both humanitarian as well as financial perspectives—have an interest in working to resolve or at least minimize the extent of, and problems involving their homeless populations. First, assume, conservatively, costs of $80 to $175 for one to spend a night in jail, $300 per day for substance abuse detoxification, $3,700 per night in an emergency room, $4,500 for a typical three-day hospital stay, and $215 per ambulance ride, and the costs become staggering.[54] Homeless individuals, particularly the chronically homeless, are generally heavy users of municipal services such as police, fire, emergency response, and health care. Therefore, as with the mentally ill, discussed above, the solutions to homelessness involve police working with service providers and mental health experts in order to break the cycle of homelessness. Some communities have also implemented the following innovative approaches:

- Trained clinicians accompany police on calls involving chronically homeless individuals who are involved in "public nuisance" or other inappropriate behavior; the police and the trained mental health workers then determine the optimal strategy to address the particular situation.
- A chronic substance abuser program that uses the same basic principles as a drug court. A collaborative team consisting of law enforcement, court officials, prosecutors, and

▲ Homelessness can contribute to crime, fear, and neighborhood disorder. *(Courtesy Pojoslaw/Shutterstock.)*

substance abuse treatment agencies follows up on arrests for public drunkenness or nuisance. The offenders are offered the option of treatment in lieu of custody, followed by ongoing continuum of care and wrap around services.

- Increased use of civil commitments for chronic substance abusers: some jurisdictions allow their district courts to involuntarily commit an alcoholic or substance abuser for up to thirty days to an inpatient facility.[55]

In sum, as with any other problems involving crime and disorder, a well-planned analysis and response to homeless populations, following the standard community-policing and problem-solving approach can allow police departments to implement long-term solutions.

Summary

As noted in the introduction, this chapter has continued the "extraordinary problems" theme established in Chapter 12, focusing more on certain types of individuals in the United States—immigrants, youth crimes, crimes committed by people where the motive is hate, and persons who are homeless—than on criminogenic groups or syndicates. These individuals pose unique challenges for the police through their actions or status. A number of strategies being employed by the police to address these problems were presented as well.

A common theme running through the types of offenders who are discussed in this chapter is that the police are often compelled to engage in clandestine operations in order to arrest or deal with them. Another connecting link for all these problems is that the police must constantly develop *new* methods, technologies, and practices for dealing with these individuals as well as understand and apply the specific laws that are involved. As different crimes and situational problems have arisen, police have also been compelled to adapt their training and operations in order to cope. Still, the unusual policing problems and circumstances discussed in this chapter are not exhaustive. Certainly other circumstances require even further adaptation as the police attempt to guard U.S. borders, keep youthful offenders at bay, address hate groups, and deal with problems involving the homeless.

Key Terms

disorderly conduct

drones

hate crimes

Hate Crimes Statistics Act

homelessness

Office of Biometric Identity

  Management

Secure Fence Act of 2006

underage drinking

unmanned aerial vehicles (UAVs)

youth crimes

Review Questions

1. How would you explain the several issues—including the political, economic, and social—that revolve around the subject of immigration and border security?

2. What are some of the reasons why illegal immigration is currently declining in the United States? What approaches are some state and local units of government taking to attempt to further reduce the number of undocumented immigrants who are living and working in their jurisdictions?

3. What methods have some federal and local law enforcement agencies adopted for controlling illegal border crossings?

4. What is OBIM, and how does it function to help secure U.S. borders?

5. How would you explain the nature and extent of youth crime and violence?

6. What means are being used by the police for addressing gun violence, disorderly conduct in public places, and underage drinking?

7. How would you define a hate crime, and how does it differ from other crimes? What are some police responses to the problem?

8. What factors contribute to mental illness and homelessness, and what are some police agencies doing to assist those who live on the streets?

Learn by Doing

1. You are temporarily assigned to your regional fusion center to collect border information. Assuming that funding and technology acquisition is not restricted, determine what you would do with the following, real-life situation: The border with Canada to the north has quietly developed into a source of concern. If, for example, someone headed north on the gravel road into Noyan, Quebec, to a point just a few miles from Alburgh, Vermont, they would find there is nothing to mark the international divide. There are cameras and sensors to alert the Border Patrol when southbound people enter the United States—but nothing to stop them physically from making the two- or three-mile dash onto Route 2 and disappearing. Smugglers know the road is unguarded. Even more astonishingly, a dozen similarly unmarked back roads are found between Vermont and Quebec, constituting a major, direct threat to national security.

   Source: Adapted from Wilson Ring, "Unguarded Paths Challenge Border Patrol," *Associated Press*, October 28, 2007, www.usatoday.com/news/nation/2007-10-04-border_N.htm (accessed November 5, 2013).

2. Recently a number of local businesses along a city river have been suffering from a rash of problems involving burglaries, panhandling, thefts, and vandalism. Many homeless individuals have been identified as living at nearby campsites in cardboard, plywood, and tarpaulin huts. Many of the transients booby-trap their campsites to ward off intruders. A large number of them also suffer from sexual and skin diseases and mental illness. Garbage, human waste, and litter in the campsites is a serious health concern, and there has been an alarming increase in transient aggression toward river users.

   You are assigned to develop a strategy to "reclaim" the river, to address the crime and disorder, and to discourage illegal camping and other activities. What will you do? Include how other stakeholders might assist in this project and any new ordinances that might be sought.

   Note: A number of communities have programs to assist the homeless; see, for example, the Los Angeles program at www.bringlahome.org/links.htm and the Chicago Coalition for the Homeless at www.chicagohomeless.org.

3. To better grasp the methods of, and problems confronted by, the police in this chapter's subject matter, you should seek out and interview individuals who work in these arenas on a daily basis (e.g.,

federal agents with Customs and Border Protection or Immigration and Customs Enforcement (immigration); police detectives or juvenile probation officers who work with youthful offenders; federal agents and prosecutors who have experience with hate crimes; and a police agency that has a homeless program.

Notes

1. U.S. Department of Homeland Security, *Estimates of the Unauthorized Immigrant Population Residing in the United States: January 2011*, http://www.dhs.gov/xlibrary/assets/statistics/publications/ois_ill_pe_2011.pdf (accessed November 9, 2013).
2. Haya El Nasser, "More Mexicans Returning Home, Fewer Immigrating to U.S.," http://usatoday30.usatoday.com/news/nation/story/2012-04-23/mexican-immigration-united-states/54487564/1 (accessed November 18, 2013).
3. Dream Act 2013, "Overview of the Dream Act," http://www.dreamact2009.org/ (accessed February 18, 2013).
4. Immigration Policy Center, "The Dream Act," http://www.immigrationpolicy.org/issues/DREAM-Act (accessed November 8, 2013).
5. David Von Drehle, "A New Line in the Sand," *Time*, June 20, 2008, p. 31.
6. Ibid.
7. United States House of Representatives, Judiciary Committee, "CRS Report Highlights," http://judiciary.house.gov/news/pdfs/Criminal%20Aliens%20Report.pdf (accessed November 7, 2013).
8. Von Drehle, "A New Line in the Sand," p. 35.
9. Elise Foley, "Senate Immigration Reform Bill Passes With Strong Majority," *Huffington Post*, July 22, 2013, http://www.huffingtonpost.com/2013/06/27/senate-immigration-reform-bill_n_3511664.html (accessed November 5, 2013).
10. National Conference of State Legislatures, "2009 State Laws Related to Immigrants and Immigration," http://www.ncsl.org/issues-research/immig/2009-state-immigration-laws.aspx (accessed November 19, 2013).
11. Ibid.; "2011 Immigration-Related Laws, Bills and Resolutions in the States: Jan. 1–March 31, 2011," http://www.ncsl.org/issues-research/immig/immigration-laws-and-bills-spring-2011.aspx#8 (accessed November 8, 2013).
12. Tom Cohen and Bill Mears, "Supreme Court mostly rejects Arizona immigration law; gov says 'heart' remains," CNN Politics, June 26, 2012, http://articles.cnn.com/2012-06-25/politics/politics_scotus-arizona-law_1_arizona-immigration-law-immigration-status-arizona-association?_s=PM:POLITICS (accessed January 7, 2014); Paul Davenport and Jonathan J. Cooper, "Gov. Jan Brewer Signs Controversial Arizona Immigration Bill: Decision Not 'Made Lightly'," Huffington Post, http://www.huffingtonpost.com/2010/04/23/jan-brewer-arizona-govern_n_549290.html (accessed November 3, 2013).
13. See *Arizona v. U.S.*, No. 11-182 (2012).
14. Elliot Spagat, "Arizona Police Face Questions After Court Ruling," *Associated Press*, June 17, 2012, http://news.yahoo.com/arizona-police-face-questions-court-ruling-081001363.html (accessed January 18, 2013); see also Davenport and Cooper, "Gov. Jan Brewer Signs Controversial Arizona Immigration Bill: Decision Not 'Made Lightly'," p. 1.
15. Judicial Watch, "States Will Push Tough Immigration Laws in 2011," http://www.judicialwatch.org/blog/2011/01/states-push-tough-immigration-laws-2011/ (accessed November 19, 2013).
16. U.S. Department of Justice, Office of Community Oriented Policing Services, "Basic Immigration Enforcement Training," http://www.cops.usdoj.gov/default.asp?Item=2044 (accessed November 9, 2013).
17. U.S. Department of Homeland Security, Office of Biometric Identity Management, "Overview," http://www.dhs.gov/obim (accessed November 5, 2013).
18. U.S Department of Homeland Security, Office of Inspector General, "CBP's Use of Unmanned Aircraft Systems in the Nation's Border Security," May 2012, p. 4, http://www.oig.dhs.gov/assets/Mgmt/2012/OIG_12-85_May12.pdf (accessed November 9, 2013).
19. "U.S. Airports Boost Security," *Reno Gazette-Journal*, January 6, 2004, p. 2A.
20. See, for example, Electronic Privacy Information Center, "Unmanned Aerial Vehicles (UAVs) and Drones," http://epic.org/privacy/drones/ (accessed November 9, 2013).
21. Rick Jervis, "Mounted Patrols Beefed Up At the Border," *USA Today*, http://usatoday30.usatoday.com/news/nation/story/2011-11-27/mounted-patrols-horses-Mexico-border/51425978/1 (accessed November 4, 2013).
22. Federal Bureau of Investigation, *Crime in the United States 2012*, Tables 32 and 38, http://www.fbi.gov/about-us/cjis/ucr/crime-in-the-u.s/2012/crime-in-the-u.s.-2012/tables/32tabledatadecoverviewpdf (accessed November 5, 2013).

23. Donna Leinwand Leger, "Study: Nearly 1 in 3 Will be Arrested by Age 23," *USA Today*, December 19, 2011, http://usatoday30.usatoday.com/news/nation/story/2011-12-19/youth-arrests-increase/52055700/1 (accessed November 3, 2013).

24. Joan McCord, Cathy Spatz Widom, and Nancy A Crowell, eds., *Juvenile Crime, Juvenile Justice: Panel on Juvenile Crime, Prevention, Treatment, and Control* (Washington, DC: National Academy Press, 2001), p. 25.

25. Anthony A. Braga, *Gun Violence Among Serious Young Offenders* (Washington, DC: U.S. Department of Justice, Office of Community Oriented Policing Services, June 2003), pp. 1–2.

26. U.S. Department of Justice, Bureau of Justice Statistics, "Homicide Trends in the U.S.: Age Trends," http://www.bjs.gov/content/pub/pdf/htus8008.pdf (accessed November 5, 2013).

27. Michael S. Scott, *Disorderly Youth in Public Places* (Washington, DC: U.S. Department of Justice, Office of Community Oriented Policing Services, June 2002), pp. 2–5.

28. Ibid., pp. 14–21.

29. Focus Adolescent Services, "Alcohol and Teen Drinking," www.focusas.com/Alcohol.html (accessed November 5, 2013).

30. Kelly Dedel Johnson, *Underage Drinking* (Washington, DC: U.S. Department of Justice, Office of Community Oriented Policing Services, September 2004), pp. 1, 4.

31. Ibid., p. 5.

32. Ibid., pp. 23–39.

33. Codified at 18 U.S.C. § 249.

34. Federal Bureau of Investigation, "Hate Crimes Accounting," http://www.fbi.gov/news/stories/2012/december/annual-hate-crimes-report-released/annual-hate-crimes-report-released (accessed February 18, 2013).

35. Lynn Langton and Michael Planty, *Hate Crime, 2003–2009* (Washington, D.C.: U.S. Department of Justice, Bureau of Justice Statistics, June 2011), p. 2, http://bjs.ojp.usdoj.gov/content/pub/pdf/hc0309.pdf (accessed November 17, 2013).

36. Ibid., p. 4.

37. Congressional Research Service, *State Statutes Governing Hate Crimes*, p. 1, http://www.fas.org/sgp/crs/misc/RL33099.pdf (accessed February 18, 2013).

38. Human Rights Campaign, "State Hate Crimes Laws," http://www.hrc.org/resources/entry/hate-crimes-law (accessed November 5, 2013).

39. U.S. Department of Justice, National Institute of Justice, *Response to Hate Crimes*, http://www.nij.gov/topics/crime/hate-crime/research-findings.htm (accessed November 8, 2013).

40. Ibid.

41. Sean Webby, "Hate-Crime Prosecutions Have Proved to Be Difficult," *Reno Gazette-Journal*, October 25, 2002, p. 8C.

42. Memphis Police Department, "Crisis Intervention Team: The Memphis Model," http://www.memphispolice.org/crisis%20intervention.htm (accessed October 7, 2013).

43. Kevin Johnson, "Memphis Program Offers Example for Police and Mentally Ill," *USA Today*, October 2, 2013, http://www.usatoday.com/story/news/nation/2013/10/02/police-navy-yard-mental-illness-alexis-shooting/2910763/ (accessed October 6, 2013).

44. Ibid.

45. National Alliance on Mental Illness, "Fact Sheet," http://www.nami.org/factsheets/mentalillness_factsheet.pdf (accessed October 7, 2013).

46. Ibid.; "What Is Mental Illness," http://www.nami.org/Template.cfm?Section=By_Illness (accessed October 7, 2013).

47. Memphis Police Department, "Crisis Intervention Team: The Memphis Model," http://www.memphispolice.org/crisis%20intervention.htm (accessed October 7, 2013).

48. The University of Memphis, *Crisis Intervention Team Core Elements*, http://www.cit.memphis.edu/information_files/CoreElements.pdf (accessed October 7, 2013).

49. Memphis Police Department, "Crisis Intervention Team: The Memphis Model," http://www.memphispolice.org/crisis%20intervention.htm (accessed October 7, 2013).

50. National Alliance to End Homelessness, "Snapshot of Homelessness: The Big Picture," http://www.endhomelessness.org/pages/snapshot_of_homelessness (accessed November 9, 2013).

51. Gregg Zeroya, "Number of Homeless Iraq, Afghan Vets Doubles," *USA Today* (December 26, 2012). http://www.armytimes.com/news/2012/12/gannett-homeless-iraq-afghanistan-veterans-122612/ (accessed November 8, 2013).

52. Judy Keen, "Winter Problem: More Homeless are Living in Cars," *USA Today*, http://www.usatoday.com/story/news/nation/2012/12/01/homeless-living-in-cars-winter/1738363/ (accessed November 3, 2013).

53. Ibid. "Mental/Physical Health," http://www.endhomelessness.org/pages/mental_physical_health (accessed November 9, 2013).

54. Jaclyn O'Malley, "Assembly Tackles Homeless Problem," *Reno Gazette-Journal*, February 20, 2007, p. 5A.

55. See, for example, "A Strategy to End Chronic Homelessness in Lynn, Massachusetts: Ten Year Action Plan, Lynn, Massachusetts," September 2006, pp. 6–8, http://www.endhomelessness.org/page/-/files/3070_file_Lynn_TYP.doc (accessed November 8, 2013).

Courtesy © Kim Karpeles/Alamy.)

14 Technology Review
Uses (The Good), Concerns (The Bad), and Legislation

LEARNING OBJECTIVES

As a result of reading this chapter, the student will be able to:

1 *Describe how new technologies are assisting police in dealing with some old problems*

2 *Describe the uses of, outlook for, and concerns about unmanned aerial vehicles (UAVs, or "drones")*

3 *Review how smartphones and social media are assisting the police, as well as some problems and concerns involving their use*

4 *Explain the problem of cybercrime, and what can be done with cybercrooks*

5 Review new developments with electronic control devices

6 Delineate the purposes for which robots are being used in policing

7 Discuss how wireless technology is assisting the police in terms of access to information, crime mapping, and locating serial offenders

8 Explain how electronics are helping to address traffic-related functions

9 Discuss what fingerprint and mug shot databases are contributing to crime-control efforts

10 Explain some of the recent developments in firearms training functions

11 Explain how augmented reality and nanotechnology might benefit law enforcement in the future

Introduction

Previous chapters included discussions of several types of technologies, such as several used for criminal investigation in Chapter 5 and crime analysis tools in Chapter 6. This chapter continues those discussions, focusing on technologies that are having a tremendous impact in policing, rapidly expanding, and changing the work of patrol officers, criminal investigators, forensics, and other specialized assignments (e.g., bomb). Many more technologies are now in research and development. Indeed, one might say that our only limitations are our imagination and the amount of money that we are willing and able to devote to this field.

This chapter begins by showcasing several new uses of technologies for addressing old crime and security problems. Then we consider the current and potential uses of, and concerns with drones (or unmanned aerial vehicles). Following that are discussions of the growing areas of smartphones and social media (including their good and bad aspects). Next is a discussion of the problem of cybercrimes, and what the police are doing to combat them. Then we consider developments that have occurred with electronic control devices, and then we examine the expanding development and uses of robots in policing. A review follows of wireless technology for use in databases, in crime mapping, and in analyses of serial offenders. Then we examine how electronic capabilities are being applied to several traffic functions. Following a review of developments with fingerprints and mug shots, we then consider how computers are assisting with regard to firearms, particularly in training officers and in solving cases involving guns. Next is a brief examination of police use of intelligence systems to address gang activity and, and then we review two exciting technologies that loom on the horizon in terms of research and development: nanotechnology and augmented reality. The five exhibits in the chapter explain some new uses for technologies. The chapter concludes with a summary, key terms, review questions, and several scenarios and activities that provide opportunities for you to learn by doing.

▶ Selected Examples: New Technologies for Old Problems

Following are examples of new technologies and techniques in use by police help address problems of crime, disorder, and related problems:

- An expanding method for police and corrections agencies to check arrestees' identity when they are booked into jail is by taking a high-resolution photograph of one's iris—the colored part of the eye which contains 240 unique points for reference for identification. Arrestees are known to claim to be another individual while awaiting arraignment, so the iris recognition information is entered into a database for later use, to reduce the possibility that the wrong person will be released from jail. More than 2,100 police agencies in twenty-seven states use this form of recognition.[1]

- Sending the police a crime tip via text message might seem "old hat" at this point, but in reality it is a relatively new practice now spreading across the United States Residents in several states now have the ability to anonymously report a crime through an online system that accepts text messages. For example, more than fifty Utah law enforcement agencies utilize TipSoft—a national, privately operated program that allows the public to submit anonymous crime tips via texting through a **smartphone** app or online at the program's website. Some smartphone users may download a free app to submit tips; the app also can take tips via videos or photos. One out of fourteen tips sent through TipSoft results in an arrest. Dallas, Texas, police launched a similar program to allow citizens to report crimes or suspicious behavior that could possibly be linked to terrorism.[2] (Exhibit 14-1 ■ discusses a similar program launched by Kentucky's Office of Homeland Security.)

EXHIBIT 14-1

KENTUCKY'S HOMELAND SECURITY EFFORTS

Kentucky probably is not the first place one would expect to see terrorist-related behavior, but instances of domestic terrorism such as the Oklahoma City bombing are a reminder that criminal activities are not exclusive to highly populated cities or states. With vigilance in mind, the Kentucky Office of Homeland Security (KOHS) recently released a smartphone app that mirrors the "Eyes and Ears on Kentucky" Web site (see accompanying photograph) for reporting "suspicious activity." The free app is designed to allow citizens to send tips to the KOHS—anonymously if they wish—on any activity that may be linked to a terrorist act. Customers can quickly bring up the app on their [smartphone] and basically enter any suspicious information while they're observing the activity.

Examples of such activity that could be reported to either the portal or the app include seeing someone showing an unusual interest in a building's security system—asking several questions about how security's accomplished and how many people are involved in the facility's security. Suspicious activity may also include someone sketching the location, using GPS to get a facility's coordinates, or having "just more than the casual curiosity that tourists or sightseers would take in," Lawson said. Citizens can also report the presence of suspicious items or objects.

Source: Adapted from Kentucky Office of Homeland Security, "Eye on Kentucky," http://homelandsecurity.ky.gov/eyeonky.htm (accessed November 28, 2012).

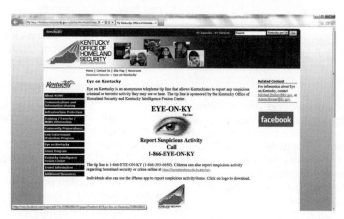

▲ Prior to 9/11, none of the states had a robust intelligence capability. Most now have created offices that connect their state homeland security efforts with law enforcement, intelligence organizations, federal agencies, and even foreign intelligence services.

(Courtesy Kentucky Office of Homeland Security.)

- Standard strip searches conducted at jails for drugs and other contraband require about fifteen minutes' time for arrestees to remove their clothing and officers of the same sex to conduct the search; furthermore, some states require a court order before a body-cavity search can be performed. The "21st century strip search," however, using full-body scanning technology, requires only that arrestees remove their shoes, and requires about seven seconds' time to identify any metallic or organic materials. As the beam passes through the inmate's body, the system measures how much density is left in the beam; that information is processed and related to the officer who is informed if anything looks out of place.[3]

- An immersive simulation training suite uses video and audio feeds to monitor real-time decision making during critical incident drills. Termed "Hydra," the system is used in sixty cities and provides training for high-level, command staff officers in everything from crimes and terrorist attacks to natural disasters, press briefings, meeting with victims' families, and community forums. Trainees are divided into Incident Management teams and housed in different rooms; they are given a stream of information, which can consist of newscasts, intelligence briefings, and police and fire radio traffic. Once the exercise is ended, everyone is brought in for debriefing and the team's decisions are discussed.[4]

Career Profile

Name: Grant Humerickhouse
Position: Police officer
City, State: Madison, Wisconsin
College attended: Michigan State University
Major: Criminal justice
Year hired: 2006

(Courtesy Grant Humerickhouse, City of Madison Police Department.)

Please give a brief description of your job.

My department is very progressive in its diversity and with problem-oriented policing. Therefore, I must be comfortable with technology: I am expected to master computer-aided dispatching, mobile data computers, and mobile audio and video recordings, to name a few applications. During my second year in patrol, I had an opportunity to be part of a community policing team, working with property managers and owners who wanted their property to be safe—and with college students who wanted to have parties and stay out late. Finding the balance was not only good for me as a young officer but challenging and exciting from a problem-oriented policing standpoint.

What appealed to you most about the occupation?

While I was in college, an Introduction to Criminal Justice course instructor told many tales about high-speed pursuits, gory homicide scenes, and arrests during his career. This fueled my dreams of driving fast, catching bad guys, and experiencing something new each day. I wanted to talk to all types of people, learn their problems and help them, assist victims, be the voice for the oppressed, and work for justice.

How would you describe the interview process?

The application process was grueling. I was asked to admit things very few people in my life knew about and to discuss every person I had ever lived with, every place I had worked, every boss, every co-worker, every phone number, and the list was endless.

What is a typical day like?

There is nothing predictable and nothing ordinary about policing. Although rewarding, fulfilling, and challenging, it is extremely difficult on a person emotionally, mentally, and physically. I have learned that I am not omniscient, omnipotent, or able to solve every problem. I remember my first suicide investigation, my first child abuse case, my first car crash, the first time a bad guy got away—including the colors, sounds, and feelings.

What qualities and characteristics are most helpful for this position?

Policing should not be a choice but a calling. The unpredictable hours, missed holidays, graveyard shifts, and tears are offset by the rewards. Know your limitations, and always tell the truth; integrity is your professional life.

What career advice would you give someone in college beginning their criminal justice studies?

Talk to people about the job, go on a ride-along, explore the myriad different paths that law enforcement has to offer. Talk to your family about your career choice; you are going to have to lean on them after a bad day. Be honest and forthright about your drug use, traffic tickets, and every other dirty little secret the department asks you to admit.

- The Locard theory, discussed in Chapter 5, basically asserts that criminals leave something of themselves—fingerprints, hairs, fibers, and so on—at the crime scene.[5] Certainly most crime scenes involve the perpetrator's leaving behind shoe prints. However, even if located, lifted, and preserved, searching through images and catalogs to find a match and identify a footprint can take several days if not weeks or months. Now, however, software exists that contains about 24,000 types of shoes in its database and can reduce that time frame to twenty minutes.[6]

- QR (for "Quick Response") codes are gaining in use and utility round the world. Similar to the barcodes used by retailers to track inventory and price products (which are linear and one-dimensional), QR codes are two-dimensional and can hold thousands of alphanumeric characters of information. When a QR code is scanned with a camera-enabled smartphone, the user can link to digital content on the Web and activate a number of other functions. As examples of their spreading use, police in Vancouver, Canada, are using QR codes to obtain crime clues, tips, and leads. Some cities in Texas seeking to reduce drunk driving, display posters with QR codes that can be scanned by a smartphone and then directs the user to a mobile site called "Choose Your Ride." The mobile site also allows users to enter a ZIP code or location, and then they are shown a list of nearby taxi services and their phone numbers, information on limo services, bus routes, and walking paths.[07]

- "Kelsey's Law," originally enacted in Kansas in 2009 and now in at least eight other states, required cell phone carriers to provide police with a customer's location in certain emergency circumstances (the Kansas case involved an eighteen-year-old girl being abducted).[08]

One potentially helpful use of technology by the police has been curtailed, however (as noted in Chapter 7), was the U.S. Supreme Court's holding[09] in 2012 that police attaching a Global Positioning System (GPS) device to a suspect's vehicle without a search warrant violates the Fourth Amendment. This decision will likely have its greatest effect on major narcotics investigations. The accompanying Career Profile includes the views of an officer who has had to develop—and use, particularly in his community policing and problem-solving endeavors—considerable knowledge about as well as the proper applications of police technologies.

▶ Drones: Uses, Related Concerns, and Legislation

Here Today—and More Tomorrow

Drones, also termed unmanned aerial vehicle (UAV), or as the military prefers to call them, "remotely piloted aircraft" or RPA, were discussed briefly in Chapter 10 in relation to border security. They are powered aerial vehicles that do not carry human operators and are designed to carry nonlethal payloads for missions such as reconnaissance, command and control, and deception. UAVs, which are directed by a ground or airborne controller, come in a variety of designs, from one that fits into a backpack to one with a longer wingspan than a Boeing 747. More than two dozen companies in the United States are currently involved in production of prototype UAV products.[10]

Both commercial and civilian unmanned drones are in the air, although the Federal Aviation Administration (FAA) forbids the operation of such aircraft in national air space. That will likely change soon, however: In February 2012 the U.S. Senate sent President Obama legislation that would require the FAA to devise ways to allow drones to share airspace with passenger planes within three years. Therefore, more drones will likely be aloft in 2015; in fact, the FAA predicts that 15,000 flying robots will be in the skies by 2020, and that number will double by 2030. Certainly as their costs continue to decline (some agencies now purchasing one for about $36,000), more police will be adopting drones. State and local officials will have to draft ordinances and statutes for the use of these devices, so that their use will be secure and avoid trampling on privacy rights.[11] One interim approach by the Mesa County, Colorado, Sheriff's Office, was to negotiate an agreement with the FAA to fly a two-pound drone up to 400 feet altitude so its camera could snap photographs of crime scenes or accidents and its infrared camera can assist with searching for missing persons.[12]

Potential Uses

While UAV research and development are almost totally focused on military applications at present, the potential uses for law enforcement should not be ignored. For example, a low-flying UAV could patrol a given stretch of road, on vigil for speeders; images could be piped to a monitor in a patrol car along with rate of speed, direction of travel, and Global Positioning System (GPS) coordinates, which can be overlaid on a map for the officer on the ground.[13] UAVs could also provide real-time reconnaissance, surveillance, and target spotting in a variety of situations.[14] Following are some uses of drones in a number of states and municipalities for police functions:

- In what was said to be the first known arrests of U.S. citizens with help from a drone, in December 2011, the sheriff of Nelson County, North Dakota, had to search for three possibly armed men and were suspected of stealing six cows. The men could have been anywhere in a 3,000-acre area, so the sheriff called in help from the state patrol, a nearby SWAT team, and deputies from three other counties. They also brought in a military drone, which circled two miles overhead. Using sophisticated sensors, the three suspects were located, and police made the arrest.[15]

- In Seattle, police have received approval to employ drones, and police say they are training officers in how to fly them.

- The Fairfax County, Virginia, police have announced that soon drones will be patrolling the Washington Beltway (which is noted for its traffic congestion).

- Police in Shelby County (Memphis), Tennessee, estimate they can fly UAVs for $3.80 an hour, compared to $600 per hour to fly a large helicopter; the county wants to buy two small drones that could be used to find missing persons, investigate traffic accidents, and locate illegal marijuana crops.

- Miami-Dade police have permission to fly two drones acquired from a military contractor, Honeywell. The device is intended for use with situations where a suspect with a gun has hidden where it would be dangerous for a manned helicopter to fly.[16]

Concerns with Use and Privacy

The above police uses of drones demonstrate their potential utility given they can fly anywhere that is too dangerous or remote for an officer to go. However, as with any high-tech device that can monitor people and their doings, there are privacy concerns. Civil liberties advocates have expressed concerns about the potential for UAV use to violate citizens' rights, and it was expected that during 2013, bills would be introduced in Congress and at least ten states to limit the use of the camera-equipped aircraft.[17] Advocates, however, argue that people have become accustomed to such monitoring, given the widespread use of cell phone cameras, parking lot videos, convenience store taping devices, and cameras mounted on street lights.[18]

In late 2012, the largest association of police executives—the International Association of Chiefs of Police (IACP)—issued a national advisory for the use of drones and recommended that drones not be armed for purposes relating to domestic law enforcement.

Some drones have the capacity to use stun-gun projectiles, tear gas, and rubber balls from as high up as 300 feet, and the IACP believes it is very important for the public to understand that if drones are to be used, the police "will not be up there with armed predator drones firing away" at people. The IACP also recommends that police secure a search warrant prior to launching them for investigative purposes.[19]

Finally, commercial pilots have raised concerns. They note that, while there are strict trainings and tests before pilots can fly airplanes, there are no such requirements for controllers of drones; they are thus concerned about controllers losing contact with drones as well as drones and jets crashing—as was the case in August 2012 when a drone collided with a C-130 cargo plane in Afghanistan.[20]

▶ Smartphones: The Good and The Bad

Smartphones have changed the way people young and old conduct their lives. By the end of 2012 there were more than 1 billion smartphones in use worldwide, and analysts believe it will only take three years for the next billion smartphones to be put into use.[21]

Unquestionably, smartphones are changing the way police operate as well. As discussed at the beginning of this chapter —as well as in Chapter 4, concerning community policing and problem solving—the benefits are numerous. In addition, one smartphone app now allows officers responding to calls for service to determine instantly if previously reported incidents and convicted criminals are associated with a particular address. Officers can point their phone at a particular location and, using the phone's GPS, check the arrest history or officer safety hazard information of the address in question. When looking for a missing child, an icon appears if any sex offenders are living nearby. The app can also track the location of police units, allowing the officer to determine distances of backup units.[22]

Certainly problems have paralleled the growth of the industry: Teens send an average of 100 text messages per day, and texting drivers are 23 times more likely to be involved in a crash than nontexting drivers. By mid-2012, thirty-nine states and Washington, D.C., had made texting-while-driving illegal. In enforcing the laws, police look for the same telltale signs as they would for an intoxicated driver: drivers going faster or slower than the speed limit, weaving, and not paying attention.[23]

Investigations, Smartphones, and the Stored Communications Act In February 2001, a businessman was gunned down in Fort Lauderdale, Florida. The ensuing police investigation had practically nothing to use in the way of witnesses or physical evidence, but four years later the prosecutor charged three men with the murder. The three suspects awaited trial for over five years, and the evidence to be used focused on the admissibility of two of the suspects' cell phone records—specifically, an analysis of the location data contained in them (which placed two of the men within 500 feet of the murder as it occurred). The defense argued that the use of such evidence violated the defendants' constitutional rights, but the judge refused to suppress the cell phone records, citing federal precedent that indicates cell phone users have no reasonable expectation of privacy in location information gathered by the police.[24]

Such cases are common. Indeed, one survey found that during 2011 there were 1.3 million such requests for cell phone tracking data. The above case points out the legal dilemmas and debates that are now posed by new technologies—in this instance, cell site location information (CSLI). The potential for assisting police investigations is undeniable: In recent years the U.S. Marshals Service has been locating its fugitives in about two days—and it used to average about forty-two days. At issue, however, as shown in the above case, is whether or not—as smartphones have become more sophisticated—law enforcement, phone manufacturers, cell carriers, and software makers are exploiting users' personal privacy data without their knowledge.[25] At present, the Stored Communications Act,[26] enacted in 1986 as part (Title II) of the Electronic Communications Privacy Act of 1986 (discussed in Chapter 12) allows law enforcement access to electronic messages greater than 180 days old without a warrant (or, with a court order or subpoena, such access may be obtained for messages more than 180 days old). The government does not need to establish probable cause, but must only offer facts showing that the information sought is material to an ongoing criminal investigation.[27]

▶ Social Media: The Good and The Bad

Many general uses of social media for community policing and problem solving were discussed in Chapter 4. Here we elaborate on those uses as well as some of the problems.

The power and usefulness of social networking sites was evident during the recent devastation by Hurricane Sandy on the northeastern coast in October 2012, as police and other emergency services relied on such sites to warn citizens and constantly update citizens on evacuations, street closures, flooding, and storm conditions almost as they occur regarding what became known as the "Superstorm." The same social-media value became evident after a mid-2012 shooting near the Oakland airport; using Nixle—a public notification service deployed for crimes in progress, traffic problems, and missing children—police quickly sent text alerts to thousands of nearby residents informing them to stay out of the area.[28]

Some critics question the use of social media, saying it releases too much information without adequate filtering. Furthermore, some authors caution police about their own personal use of social media. First, with social media, officers' community exposure is increased and the usual methods used in the past to protect their identity—post office boxes, license plate confidentiality, and so on—are ineffective. Social media sites offer easy access to an unlimited pool of potential "friends," and constraints do not exist for social media; anyone can post anything online with little fear of repercussions. Through social media, people can easily attack a police officer's character (and, if an officers' integrity is compromised, so is their courtroom testimony and investigations). Cases have arisen where comments posted online have led to disciplinary actions, and people can post questionable videos of police officers on such sites in hopes of their profiting financially from them by filing claims or lawsuits. Finally, some people even engage in "cop-baiting"—intentionally creating confrontational situations with officers to exploit them for personal or political motives.[29] However, such potential drawbacks have not stopped the police from employing social media sites. In fact, by mid-2012 more than forty police agencies were already posting surveillance videos on YouTube to communicate with the public and catch criminals.[30] During times of natural disaster such as hurricanes, social media are a valuable link between the police and the public.[31] Furthermore, as indicated in Chapter 4, the police have benefitted greatly by using such social media sites as Twitter, Facebook, MySpace, Nixle (a text messaging service that can be linked to a press release, photos, or a map), and CrimeDex (described as a "Facebook for cops" or "high-tech Neighborhood Watch," which connects investigators in all agencies to share data and videos in real-time).

As an example, Philadelphia's police officers recently began using Twitter for crime-fighting. With a tight budget, the department plans for officers at all levels to make more use of tweeting and other technologies. Furthermore, the department believes this is a good way to respond to people's questions; provide information about agency programs; and have officers tweet information to the public that is timely and relevant, such as public safety alerts, crimes in the area. One detective, who's been tweeting for two years, has gotten a lot of crime tips, and citizens email him every day.[32]

One officer can reach out to a limited number of people, and a large segment of the community may not read the newspapers or watch television news. The social networking community, on the other hand, is a "force multiplier," allowing the police to share data, photos, and videos as they solicit help in catching crooks.[33] Using such nontraditional, public means to share real-time criminal and investigative information, locate violent crime suspects, track fugitives, and stop theft rings not only helps to make up for the police personnel lost from budget cuts, but also, as Camden, New Jersey, Police Chief Scott Thomson put it, makes police "appear bigger than we are."[34]

▶ Combating Cybercrooks

Extent of the Problem

The online world has no shortage of what is termed "hacktivism"—cyberhacking committed with political and social objectives in mind—and it is on the rise. In 2011, reportedly 855 data breaches occurred around the globe. While only 3 percent of such attacks were traced to hacktivist groups, they tend to compromise huge volumes of data. In fact, the work of hacktivists was traced to more than 100,000 million compromised records during that year. Data breaches were traced to thirty-six different countries, up from twenty-two countries, and about two-thirds of such breaches originate in Eastern Europe.[35]

Cybercrime is particularly costly for U.S. businesses and government agencies: A survey of fifty-six such organizations found that they were attacked twice per week on average, that costs associated with cyberattacks averaged $8.9 million, and each organization's cleanup operation cost an average $592,000.[36]

What the Police Can Do

Accordingly, it is essential to stop attacks as early as possible in what EMC, a Massachusetts-based worldwide information technology firm, has termed the "kill chain."[37] The kill chain consists of six stages of attack, which are:

- **Reconnaissance:** This normally consists of reading company Web sites for information on key initiatives and personnel; reading industry whitepapers to identify projects; searching Google for e-mail addresses, contact points, and other bits of information; and identifying social network participation of likely targets

- **Weaponization and delivery:** Here the attacker establishes a target or collection of targets and weaponizes an attack payload and delivers it to the target

- **Exploitation:** Next, the host machine is compromised by the attacker and the delivery mechanism will install malware that will allow the attacker to command execution.

- **Command and control:** Having taken control of a workstation, the attacker will usually install malware that has a command and control mechanism that allows continued access

- **Exfiltration:** Finally, the attacker has successfully entered the target network, taken control of a host, and can now download tools, move laterally onto other hosts

Obviously, the earlier such an attack can be stopped, the less the cost to repair. In fact, the biggest cybercrime costs come from lost information (comprising 44 percent of total cybercrime costs) and disruption in business (30 percent), lost revenue (19 percent), and equipment damages (5 percent). The best preventive measure is to have a good information security monitoring system; indeed, businesses that use such systems cut their cybercrime costs by an average of $1.6 million per year, in part by being able to spot and respond to breaches more quickly.[38]

Battling Cybercrooks: Two National Resources

Detectives were investigating what appeared to be a relatively minor case of financial fraud—$30,000 stolen from a local college; what soon became clear, however, was that the cybercrooks were linked to a worldwide crime ring that was obtaining personal data from infected computers and then were sending it to a foreign venue. Police contacted the nonprofit Center for Internet Security (CIS) in New York, which examines cyberthreat information and coalesces security best practices among state and local governments. CIS analysts confirmed that the servers were infected by a computer code that allowed cybercrooks to steal confidential information, and that seventeen states were victims of the same crime ring; their tracking of information eventually took them to an IP address in Russia that was downloading the stolen information. CIS quickly contacted states that were impacted, warned them of danger, and told them how to block it.[39]

This case study may seem like something out of an INTERPOL training manual, but it is real life—and explains why the CIS may now be the most potent weapon that state and local governments can employ against increasingly complicated cybercrimes and sophisticated cybercriminals. Every state in the union now shares cyberthreat information through CIS, and more local governments are expected to join the effort. CIS also works with the Department of Homeland Security and others in the federal system. The services and memberships are typically free of charge, as is access to its storehouse of best-practice, "what works" information. Information is also provided concerning how agencies can secure their computers.

In CIS's Security Operations Center (SOC), teams of analysts scan the Internet for emerging threats twenty-four hours a day. The Center is full of high-powered computer hardware as well as agents from local police; the FBI; Secret Service; Customs; and Alcohol, Tobacco, Firearms, and Explosives.

Furthermore, since 2010, CIS analysts have worked in the National Cybersecurity and Communications Integration Center (NCCIC), the federal government's cyber-operations center. The NCCIC fuses and coordinates information from:

- DHS operational elements, including:
  - Federal partners, such as the Department of Defense, Department of Justice, Federal Bureau of Investigation, U.S. Secret Service, and the National Security Agency
- State and local representation; and
- Private sector and nongovernment partners.

During a cyberattack, the NCCIC serves as the national response center, coordinating with state, local, and private sector partners. By integrating information from all partners—public and private, state and federal, in both the cyber and communications arenas—the NCCIC creates and shares a common knowledge, coordinates response activities, and protects our nation's critical networks.[40]

▶ Developments with Electronic Control Devices

A federal survey found that about 60 percent of local police departments, employing 75 percent of all officers, and 30 percent of sheriffs' offices authorized their officers to use handheld electronic control devices (ECDs, also known as conducted energy devices, or CEDs), such as a TASER or stun gun.[41] These ECDs have become smaller and easier for police to carry (now as small as six inches by three inches in size and seven ounces in weight) and more effective to use (including a range of up to thirty-five feet; data port storage of date, time, and duration of deployment; a red-dot laser light; and enhanced accountability). Units can be upgraded to include audio and video recordings of usage.

Although the TASER X26 is the standard less-lethal TASER ECD device that is so popular and typically carried by patrol officers, research and development are ongoing at TASER International, Inc., and several new developments have been announced recently. First, the new TASER CAM was introduced, which offers increased protection for officers because the suspect's behavior prior to the TASER ECD's deployment can be recorded with full audio and video, even in zero light conditions. Also new is the TASER X3, a multi-shot ECD that can engage multiple targets and display Warning Arcs while loaded.

TASER International, Inc., claims on its Web site to have saved nearly 100,000 lives.[42] Although some researchers and groups have long claimed that electronic control devices can cause injuries, medical issues, and even death,[43] a study announced in late 2007 by the Wake Forest University School of Medicine—touted as "the first large, independent study to review every TASER deployment and to reliably assess the overall risk and severity of injuries in real world conditions"—reported that 99.7 percent of nearly a thousand cases of TASER use resulted in only mild injuries, such as scrapes and bruises, or no injuries at all; only three subjects (0.3 percent) suffered injuries severe enough to need hospitalization.[44]

In October 2009, TASER International, Inc., issued a training bulletin advising law enforcement officers to aim the TASER at the abdomen, back, and leg areas, rather than the chest area. Although the TASER poses an "extremely rare" risk of inducing a heart attack, TASER observed that "arrest scenarios often involve individuals who are in crisis and are at a heightened risk of serious injury or death, regardless of actions taken by law enforcement"; also, sudden cardiac arrest is "a leading cause of death in the United States, and often occurs in an arrest scenario," and aiming the TASER away from the chest "lessens the risk of shot placement into areas that are undesirable such as the head, face, neck, and female breast."[45]

▶ Robotics

Recent advances in robotics ("bots" in tech-speak) have allowed policing (and soldiering) to become safer. Robots are now fitted with odor sensors, video capability, including night vision; a camera (also useful for photographing crime scenes); a TASER ECD; and even the ability to engage in two-way communications.[46] Robots with seven-foot arms (that scan the inside and undercarriage of vehicles for bombs), lights, video cameras (that zoom and swivel), obstacle-hurling flippers, and jointed arms (that have handlike grippers to disable or destroy bombs) are even relatively commonplace.

A recent application of such a robot for policing—which, it will be seen, could have saved a number of lives—is discussed in Exhibit 14-2 ■.

▶ Use of Wireless Technology

Instant Access to Information

Mobile data systems have been available since the 1970s, but the first-generation systems were based on large proprietary computers that were very costly and were often beyond the reach of many small- and medium-size police agencies. The first digital data were not transmitted from police headquarters to a cruiser until the mid-1980s. Today, armed with a notebook computer and a radio modem, police officers can have almost instant access to information in numerous federal, state, and local databases. Even small agencies can now afford a network and mobile data terminals (MDTs).[47]

Many U.S. police departments, including small agencies, are using laptop computers with wireless connections to crime and motor vehicle databases. These systems are believed to

POLICE USES OF ROBOTS

James Eagan Holmes stands accused of one of the worst mass shootings in American history for killing twelve people and wounding fifty-eight at an Aurora, Colorado, movie theater on July 20, 2012 (during a late-night screening of a Batman movie). Holmes faces 141 felony charges.

After being arrested for the shootings, Holmes informed police that his apartment was booby-trapped, so local, state and federal police officers, firefighters, and bomb-squad experts converged on Holmes's apartment to evacuate neighbors and search for additional evidence.

The officers' first action was to send in a bomb-removal robot to disarm a tripwire guarding the apartment's front door. The robot then neutralized potential explosive devices, incendiary devices and fuel found near the door. Next, the robot's camera—which revealed numerous containers with accelerants and trigger mechanisms—searched for computers or any other evidence to be removed before attempting to disarm additional explosives. Eventually, thirty aerial shells filled with gunpowder, two containers filled with liquid accelerants and numerous bullets left to explode in the resulting fire were found in the apartment, which was obviously designed to kill whoever entered it. Evidence was collected and sent to the FBI laboratory's Terrorist Explosive Device Analytical Center in Quantico, Virginia. Later, another bomb-disposal robot was sent to a potentially related threat on the University of Colorado-Denver's medical campus in Aurora, where Holmes could have shipped some of the items used in the attack.

Sources: John Ingold, "James Holmes Faces 142 Counts, Including 24 of First-Degree Murder," The Denver Post, July 30, 2012, http://www.denverpost.com/breakingnews/ci_21191265/hearing-under-way-man-suspected-killing-12-aurora-theater; Larry Greenmeier, "Bomb-Disarming Robot Was First to Enter Alleged Aurora Shooter's Apartment," July 25, 2012, http://blogs.scientificamerican.com/observations/2012/07/25/bomb-disarming-robot-was-first-to-enter-alleged-aurora-shooters-apartment/; Miranda Leitsinger and Miguel Llanos, U.S. News, "Colorado Shooting Suspect's Apartment was 'Designed to Kill,' Police Say," http://usnews.nbcnews.com/_news/2012/07/21/12875178-colorado-shooting-suspects-apartment-was-designed-to-kill-police-say?lite (accessed December 4, 2012).

pay for themselves in increased fines and officer safety. Officers can access court documents, in-house police department records, and a system of computer-aided dispatch (CAD) and can enter license numbers into their computers. Through a national network of motor vehicle and criminal history databases, they can locate drivers with outstanding warrants, expired or suspended licenses, and so on. Furthermore, rather than using open radio communications, police officers use their computers to communicate with one another via e-mail.[48]

Crime Mapping

Conclusive evidence from clay tablets found in Iraq proves that maps have been around for several thousand years—perhaps tens of millennia.[49] A relatively recent development in policing is computerized crime mapping, which has become increasingly popular among law enforcement agencies.[50] In fact, a federal study found that departments with hundred or more officers used computer crime mapping 35 percent of the time.[51] Computerized crime mapping combines geographic information from global positioning satellites with crime statistics gathered by a department's CAD system and demographic data provided by private companies or the U.S. Census Bureau. (Some agencies acquire information from the Census Bureau's Internet site.) The result is a picture that combines disparate sets of data for a whole new perspective on crime. For example, maps of crimes can be overlaid with maps or layers of causative data: unemployment rates in the areas of high crime, locations of abandoned houses, population density, reports of drug activity, or geographic features (such as alleys, canals, or open fields) that might be the contributing factors.[52] Furthermore, the hardware and software are now available to nearly all police agencies for a few thousand dollars.

The importance of crime mapping is evidenced by the fact that in 1997 the National Institute of Justice (NIJ) established the Crime Mapping Research Center (CMRC) to promote research, evaluation, development, and dissemination of geographic information systems technology for criminal justice research and practice. The CMRC holds annual conferences on crime mapping to give researchers and practitioners an opportunity to gain both practical and state-of-the-art information on the use and utility of computerized crime mapping.[53]

Exhibit 14-3 ■ describes what has become a powerful Web-based crime-fighting tool that provides mountains of information to the police and the public: the Automated Regional Justice Information System, or ARJIS, based in San Diego County, California. The system affords tactical, investigative, statistical, and crime analysis information to police and a wealth of information to the public, including crime mapping.

Locating Serial Offenders

Most offenders operate close to home and tend to operate in target-rich environments to "hunt" for their prey. Geographic profiling—a relatively new development in the field of environmental criminology—analyzes the geography of such locations and the sites of the victim encounter, the attack, the murder, and the body dump and maps the most probable location of the suspect's home.[54]

Geographic profiling is most effective when used in conjunction with linkage analysis. For example, the Washington State Attorney General's office uses a homicide investigation and tracking system (HITS) that includes crime-related databases and links to vice and gang files, sex offender registries, corrections and parole records, and department of motor vehicle databases. HITS can scan these databases simultaneously. When an agency in the state has a major crime in its jurisdiction, the case is loaded into a central system, which scans every database and linking file for connections by comparing eyewitness descriptions of a suspect and vehicle. It then builds a data set containing profiles of the offender, the victims, and the incidents. The data set then goes into a geographic information system (GIS), where the program selects and maps the names and addresses of those suspects whose method of operation fits the crimes being investigated.[55]

EXHIBIT 14-3

ARJIS POWER OF THE WEB

The Automated Regional Justice Information System (ARJIS) was the first multiagency, interactive, publicly accessible crime-mapping Web site in the nation, serving only San Diego County. ARJIS has now evolved into a complex criminal justice enterprise network used by seventy-one local, state, and federal agencies in the two California counties that border Mexico; it integrates more than 6,000 workstations, with more than 11,000 authorized users generating more than 35,000 transactions daily.

ARJIS is used for much more than crime mapping, including tactical analysis, investigations, statistical information, and crime analysis. ARJIS is responsible for major public safety initiatives, including wireless access to photos, warrants, and other critical data in the field, crime and sex offender mapping, crime analysis tools evaluation, and an enterprise system of applications that help users solve crimes and identify offenders. ARJIS also serves as the region's information hub for officer notification, information sharing, and the exchange, validation, and real-time uploading of many types of public safety data.

Source: "ARJIS: Power of the Web" from WHAT IS ARJIS? Copyright © 2013 by ARJIS (Automated Regional Justice Information System). Used by permission of ARJIS.

▶ Electronics in Traffic Functions

Collision Investigations

A multicar traffic collision (also termed a traffic crash) can turn a street or highway into a parking lot for many hours, sometimes even days. The police must collect evidence relating to the collision including measurements and sketches of the scene, vehicle and body positions, skid marks, street or highway elevations, intersections, and curves. These tasks typically involve a measuring wheel, steel tape, pad, and pencil. The cost of traffic delays—especially for commercial truck operators—is substantial.

Some police agencies have begun using GPS to determine such details as vehicle location and damage, elevation, grade, radii of curves, and critical speed. A transmitter takes a series of "shots" to find the exact locations and measurements of collision details like skid marks, area of impact, and debris. That information is then downloaded into the system, and the coordinates are plotted on an aerial shot of the intersection or roadway. Using computer technology, the details are then superimposed on the aerial shot, thus re-creating the collision scene to scale. Digital photos of the collision are incorporated into the final product, resulting in a highly accurate depiction of the collision. Furthermore, with a fatal collision or one with major injuries, what once required up to eighteen hours for several officers is reduced to mere minutes.[56]

Similarly, other agencies use a version of a surveyor's "total station," electronically measuring and recording distances, angles, and elevations as well as the names and features of objects. Data from the system can be downloaded into a computer for display or printed out on a plotter. The system consists of four components: a base station, a data collector, a tripod, and a prism (which reflects an infrared laser beam back to the tripod-mounted base station). With this device, officers can get measurements in an hour or so at major traffic collision scenes, push a button, and have lines drawn for them to scale; this process enables officers to get 40 percent more measurements in about 40 percent less time, allowing the traffic flow to resume much more quickly. This system is also being used at major crime scenes, such as murders.[57]

Arrests of Impaired Drivers

During a vehicle stop for driving under the influence (DUI), officers might spend a long time questioning the driver and conducting a barrage of screening tests. Then, if an arrest is made, the officer necessarily devotes a lot of time transporting and processing the arrestee at the jail before beginning formal testing of urine or blood. This delay in formal testing can skew test results because the alcohol has had time to metabolize.

New instruments now help automate the DUI arrest process. One tool used routinely during a drunk-driving stop is a breath-screening device—a small portable machine that resembles a video game cartridge. The DUI suspect blows into the device, and the officer gets a reading of the amount of alcohol in the suspect's system. It is hoped that this device can be adapted in such a way that the test can be used in court. Fewer hours would then be spent transporting DUI suspects and testing them, only to find that they were below the legal limit and thus cannot be prosecuted for DUI.

The revamped instrument would be attached to a notebook or a laptop computer that officers would use to help speed them through the process; an officer would simply run a magnetic-strip driver's license through a reader on the computer to bring up all of the driver's information. The computer would prompt the officer to start the test and would supply a readout of the results on the screen. The officer would then transmit the test results over telecommunications lines to a central location for recording.[58]

EXHIBIT 14-4

THE "PEACEMAKER" VEHICLE

The City of Fort Lauderdale, Florida, Police Department (FLPD) has 165,000 residents, but an estimated 10 million visitors pass through the jurisdiction every year, making the provision of police services a true challenge. To assist them with addressing crime and neighborhood disorder, city officials decided to mount a few cameras on an armored vehicle and deploy it in crime-prone areas throughout the city. The strategy resulted in a dramatic drop in the city's crime rate during the first few months of the vehicle's (nicknamed "The Peacemaker") deployment. It appears that positioning the vehicle in problem areas achieved remarkable results—deterring crimes and curbing some crime trends. As with any such device that can "see" citizens, there have been complaints from those who believe it is a violation of privacy. In addition, a resident complained she was victimized when The Peacemaker was parked in front of her motel (the FLPD did so because the motel was believed to be used for prostitution). Undeterred, the FLPD later obtained another such vehicle to be parked at the site of city trouble spots.

Source: Adapted from Ihosvani Rodriguez, "Police Roll Out Video Surveillance Truck Called the Peacemaker," Sun Sentinel, January 27, 2012, http://articles.sun-sentinel.com/2012-01-27/news/fl-neighborhood-crime-surveillance-20120126_1_armored-truck-police-roll-brinks (accessed December 3, 2013).

Prevention of High-Speed Pursuits

Chapter 9 examined the current controversy over the tremendous potential for injury, property damage, and liability that accompanies high-speed pursuits by police—this is such a concern that some agency policies completely prohibit such pursuits by officers. Such techniques as bumping, crowding, employing the three-cruiser rolling roadblock, and using tire spikes can all result in personal injuries and significant damage to vehicles.

Tire spikes can be deployed when a fleeing vehicle is approaching and then retracted so that other vehicles and police cars can pass safely. However, tire spikes often do not work effectively, or they result in the suspect losing control of the vehicle (although some spike devices are designed to prevent loss of control by breaking off in the tires and thus deflating them slowly).[59] Furthermore, use of the spikes is limited to times and places where other traffic can be diverted.

One device can stop a stolen vehicle with a short pulse of electric current that disrupts the vehicle's ignition system. When a subscriber reports his or her vehicle stolen to authorities and requests stolen vehicle assistance, the police then provide confirmation to the automotive company that the vehicle is in fact stolen; the company's employees then pinpoint the vehicle's exact GPS location and send a remote signal to prevent the stolen vehicle from starting the next time someone attempts to start it. This capability not only can help authorities recover stolen vehicles but also can prevent dangerous high-speed pursuits from starting.[60] Other similar devices are being refined, miniaturized, and demonstrated for federal, state, and local law enforcement agencies and transportation officials across the United States.

Another traffic-related crime-prevention technique is discussed in Exhibit 14-4 ■.

▶ Databases for Fingerprints and Mug Shots

Though perhaps not as exotic as DNA identification, fingerprints are still a reliable means of positively identifying someone, and advances continue to be made in the field (see Exhibit 14-5 ■). Throughout the country, filing cabinets are filled with ink-smeared cards that hold the keys to countless unsolved crimes if only the data could be located. An automated fingerprint identification system (AFIS) allows this legacy of data to be rapidly

EXHIBIT 14-5

RECENT DEVELOPMENTS WITH FINGERPRINTS

The following are two new developments reported in late 2009 with respect to fingerprinting:

- The Sarasota County, Florida, Sheriff's Office has deployed handheld devices that scan fingerprints to aid officers working in the field. The sheriff's office purchased fourteen of the handheld scanners that connect to federal, state, and local databases to identify individuals. The devices allow police officers to positively identify people in the field, instead of returning to the jail to process the information; they have also allowed officers to identify numerous individuals who gave false names and who entered the U.S. illegally.[1]

- Technology developed by Britain's University of Warwick can identify partial, distorted, scratched, smudged, or otherwise warped fingerprints in just a few seconds. Many other fingerprint techniques have tried to identify a few key features on a fingerprint and match them against a database of templates, but University of Warwick researchers consider the entire detailed pattern of each print and transform the topological pattern into a standard coordinate system, allowing them to "unwarp" any fingerprint that has been distorted by smudging, uneven pressure, or other distortion, that can then be mapped onto an "image space" of all other fingerprints in a database. This unwarping is so effective that it also, for the first time, allows comparison of the position of individual sweat pores on fingerprints.[2]

[1]"Recent Developments with Fingerprints" by Elaine Rundle from HANDHELD FINGERPRINT SCANNERS LET FLORIDA POLICE IDENTIFY INDIVIDUALS IN THE FIELD, GOVERNMENT TECHNOLOGY. Published by e.Republic, © 2009.
[2]"Recent Developments with Fingerprints" by Peter Dunn from NEW TECHNOLOGY REVOLUTIONIZES FINGERPRINT IDENTIFICATION, GOVERNMENT TECHNOLOGY. Published by e.Republic, © 2009.

shared. One such system is the Western Identification Network (www.winid.org), established by nine states as a way to share their 17 million fingerprint records. These states were later joined by local agencies and the Federal Bureau of Investigation, the Internal Revenue Service, the Secret Service, and the Drug Enforcement Administration. The system can generally provide a match within a few hours and has helped solve more than 5,000 crimes. A digital photo exchange facility known as WINPHO is now being added to supplement fingerprint data.[61]

The Boston Police Department, like most others in the United States, was devoting tremendous resources to identifying prisoners with mug shots and fingerprints. Then the department replaced all of its mug shots and inked fingerprints with a citywide integrated electronic imaging identification system—the first system of its kind in North America. The Boston Police Department is also the first city to receive the FBI's certification for electronic fingerprint submission.

Instead of transporting prisoners to a central booking facility in downtown Boston—a task that took forty thousand hours of officers' time per year—officers at the eleven district police stations can electronically scan a prisoner's fingerprints, take digital photographs, and then route the images to a central server for easy storage and access. This network gives investigators timely access to information and mug shot lineups and is saving the police department $1 million per year in labor and transportation costs while freeing officers from prisoner transportation duties.[62]

Technology involving mug shots and imaging systems can be useful in a variety of situations. For example, as a police officer responds to a domestic violence call, the CAD system searches the address and finds a restraining order against the ex-husband or boyfriend; moments later, a street map and digital mug shot of the suspect appear on the officer's laptop computer monitor. The officer is thus aided with an image of the suspect and his or her criminal history before arriving at the scene.[63]

▶ Recent Developments With Firearms

Handguns are, and nearly always have been, the weapon of choice for violent criminals, especially murderers. Handguns are also used with greatest frequency—in about seven of every ten incidents—when police officers are murdered.[64] It is therefore important that everything that is technologically possible be done to train the police to use lethal force against citizens, to identify those who would use lethal force against others, and to keep out of harm's way.

Computer-Assisted Training

A device known as FATS (for firearms training system) is said to be "as close to real life as you can get."[65] Recruits and in-service officers alike use the system. They are given a high-tech lesson in firearms and can be shown a wide variety of computer-generated scenarios on a movie screen, with an instructor at a console controlling the scene. Using laser-firing replicas of their actual weapons, they learn not only sharpshooting but also judgment—when to shoot and when not to shoot. The system, consisting of a container about the size of a large baby buggy with a computer, a laser disc player, a projector, and a hit-detect camera, can be transported to sites throughout the state. Some sites combine FATS with a driving simulator and have recruits drive to the scene of a bank robbery and then bail out of their car into a FATS scenario.[66]

Recent developments have made firearms simulators even more realistic than the basic FATS system just described. One new version has a synchronized "shootback cannon." If an individual on a projection screen pulls a gun and fires toward the trainee, a cannon, which hangs above the screen, pelts the trainee with pain-inducing .68-caliber nylon balls. This newest generation of FATS—which are getting more realistic and better at breaking down how the trainee reacted under stress—now cost between $25,000 for a small system and $200,000 for a trailer that police departments can haul from station to station.[67]

Using Gun "Fingerprints" to Solve Cases

Every gun leaves a unique pattern of minute markings on ammunition. If gun makers test-fire their weapons before the guns leave their factories, the police can use spent ammunition recovered from crime scenes to trace a gun, even when the gun itself is not recovered. This technology could even be taken to the next level: creating an automated database of the fingerprints of new guns. A $45-million multiyear contract was recently awarded to a Montreal, Canada, firm by the U.S. Bureau of Alcohol, Tobacco, Firearms, and Explosives to help fund the development of such technology.[68]

Several problems need to be resolved, however: (1) Criminals can easily use a nail file to scratch a new gun's firing pin; (2) even if the system worked and turned up a serial number, the number could be used to trace the gun to its initial owner and not necessarily to the criminal; (3) the database would not include the estimated 200 million weapons already in circulation; and (4) gun lobbies would undoubtedly oppose the system as being "suspiciously like a national gun registry."[69]

▶ Gang Intelligence Systems

Often a witness to gang violence has only a brief view of the incident—a glimpse of the offenders and their distinguishing characteristics and their vehicles and license plate numbers. Police are now armed with laptop computers and cellular phones to assist in solving gang-related crimes. Recently, for example, the California Department of Justice began installing CALGANG (known as GangNet outside California), an intranet software package linked to nine other sites throughout the state. It is essentially a clearinghouse for information about individual gang members, the places they frequent or live, and the cars they drive. Within a few minutes, a police officer in the field can link to CALGANG through a laptop and cellular phone, type in information, and wait for matches. Other officers can be moving to make the arrest even before the crime laboratory technicians have dusted the scene for fingerprints.[70]

▶ More Technologies for Tomorrow: Augmented Reality and Nanotechnology

The following technologies are still far removed from day-to-day use but promise to greatly alter police methods in the future.

One of the most powerful emerging technologies, augmented reality (AR), uses wearable components to overlay virtual (computer-generated) information onto a real-world view in a way that improves and enhances the ability to accomplish a variety of missions and tasks. Still in the early stages of research and development, AR combines the real and the virtual, displaying information in real time.[71] AR is already here: If you watch televised sports, you may have noticed the yellow first-down lines superimposed on a football field or the driver and speed information tagged to race cars speeding around a track. At a more advanced level, today's military fighter pilots can observe critical information superimposed on the cockpit canopy.[72]

Fundamentally, an AR system consists of a wearable computer, a head-mounted display, and tracking and sensing devices along with advanced software and virtual three-dimensional (3-D) applications. It is a mobile technology designed to improve situational awareness and to speed human decision making. Among the many possible uses in the future of policing are the following (some of which have already been developed but need to be refined for street use and, oftentimes, made more affordable for purchase)[73]:

- Real-time language translation, along with data on cultural customs and traditions
- Real-time intelligence about crimes and criminals in the patrol area
- Facial, voiceprint, and other biometric recognition data of known criminals
- Integration of chemical, biological, and explosives sensors that denote local contamination
- Accessibility of scalable 3-D maps (with building floor plans, utilities systems, and so forth)

Similarly, special weapons and tactics (SWAT) officers could be provided with advanced optics that provide zoom, thermal, and infrared imaging for locating fleeing criminals, as well as a friend-or-foe indicator that could reduce or eliminate friendly-fire casualties. Investigative personnel could use speaker-recognition technology for accurately matching voices against known criminals and for lip reading from a distance; thermal imaging might improve interrogations by indicating the truthfulness of suspects' statements. Supervisors could use video feed from their personnel on the street to determine what their officers are seeing in real time and to monitor their physical status during critical incidents.[74] Certainly a number of issues would accompany the planned adoption of AR. Acceptance by officers themselves may prove problematic, given the bulk and mobility issues associated with additional equipment, and the public (including the courts) may be uncomfortable with the constitutional issues and legal ramifications that AR abilities might raise.

Would AR bring us dangerously close to a real-life "Robo-Cop" scenario? The answer to that question is in the eye of the beholder. It cannot be questioned, however, that AR technology and the uses described above will soon be available and could provide the police with a new degree of efficiency and effectiveness never seen before. The question is whether or not the public—and the police—will be willing to accept this "virtual intrusion" in their daily lives.

In a similar vein, technology will also be available soon to allow realistic simulated humans to be used as a tool for training in decision making. Law enforcement personnel need experience making decisions in which other people—whether suspects, bystanders, or team members—are involved. A 3-D computer graphic would represent a variety of settings; the trainee would have the ability to move about, look around, and direct actions toward a variety of computer representations of human figures that move naturally, display appropriate gestures and expressions, and exhibit realistic patterns of speech. Such simulation technology, which should be available and affordable within the next five to ten years, will have a very positive impact on police training.[75]

The term nanotechnology is based on the root *nanos*, meaning "one billionth." It is the engineering of components that have at least one physical dimension the size of one hundred nanometers or less. (For perspective, a human hair is gigantic in the realm of nanotechnology.) This technology allows for "getting small," which means making objects smarter, more powerful, and more economical (e.g., the computers of the 1940s were the size of a room, compared to those of today). Nanotechnology allows for revolutionary new products using new materials and substances that are not accessible with other technologies. Such products, ranging from knives that never need sharpening to better spaceships and computers, will be stronger, lighter, and even interactive—and may possibly mean the end of disease as we know it.[76]

With regard to policing, a Dutch company has already developed a handheld device that uses nanotechnology to detect marijuana, cocaine, and other drugs in saliva within two minutes.[77] Surely many more nanotechnology applications for the police cannot be too far off—in fact, it is already being tested for the next generation of body armor.[78]

Summary

This chapter examined the exciting high-technology developments in policing (and some with applications in corrections as well), including those in the areas of unmanned aerial vehicles, smartphones, social media, electronic control devices, wireless technology, electronics, firearms, and fingerprint and gang databases.. This is an exciting time for the police—more new technologies than ever are being made available to aid them in their efforts to analyze and address crimes. This chapter has shown the breadth of research and development that is underway.

The rapid expansion in computer technology, while certainly a strong advantage for society overall, bodes ill as well. The first problem lies in adapting the computer technologies to the needs of policing. While the U.S. Air Force can drop a smart bomb down a smokestack and the U.S. Army is rapidly moving toward the electronic battlefield, modern-day crooks and hackers engage in a variety of cybercrimes and (even though the technology exists) the police are still unable to halt all high-speed chases that threaten the lives of officers and citizens.[79]

Obviously, many challenges remain. For example, we must continue to seek a weapon with less-lethal stopping power that can effectively and safely be employed. We must also strive to enhance police effectiveness and efficiency through electronic means. As has been noted, "It is not enough to shovel faster. Criminal justice must enter the Information Age by incorporating technology as a tool to make the system run efficiently and effectively."[80]

Key Terms

ARJIS
augmented reality (AR)
automated fingerprint
    identification system (AFIS)
computer-aided dispatching
    (CAD)
computerized crime mapping

drone
electronic control device (ECD)
FATS
geographic profiling
homicide investigation and
    tracking system (HITS)
Kelsey's Law

mobile data systems
nanotechnology
robotics
social media
smartphones
Stored Communications Act
unmanned aerial vehicle (UAV)

Review Questions

1. What are some of the major developments regarding unmanned aerial vehicles (UAVs)? Concerns with their uses?
2. What are some new applications of smartphone technologies, as well as some problems with their application?
3. How are police using social media, and what are some of the concerns with their application?
4. What is being done about the problem of cybercrime?
5. How are robot technologies being put to use by the police (provide an example)?
6. How has the development of wireless technology benefited the police, specifically with crime mapping and profiling systems?
7. How does technology assist the police traffic function? How has it affected gang intelligence?
8. What are some recent developments in the area of police training?
9. What are augmented reality and nanotechnology, and how might these technologies benefit law enforcement in the future?

Learn by Doing

1. Assume you are in the research, planning, and development unit of your police organization. Your chief executive officer has tasked you to "bring the agency into the new decade" by making recommendations concerning technologies that the department should acquire. Using information and descriptions of the technologies presented in this chapter, select and prioritize ten new technologies (either extant or in development) that you believe your agency should obtain, and write a justification for each in terms of its crime-fighting capabilities.
2. You are preparing a guest lecture at the regional police academy on the subject of police technologies now in use. One of the academy instructors calls you and says the class seems to be very interested in the applications for both unmanned aerial vehicles and robots. Prepare a response.
3. You are a federal law enforcement agent guest lecturing in an area criminal justice class. Eventually the topic of discussion concerns terrorism, and a student poses the following question: "If funding—and peoples' imaginations—were not a limitation, which technologies do you believe should be developed and put into use to thwart any and all terrorist attacks, including those that are chemical or biological in nature?" What is your response?

Notes

1. Elaine Pittman, "Eyeing Offenders," *Government Technology*, April 2011, pp. 40–41.
2. Sara Rich, "Utah Police Taking Anonymous Crime Tips Online," August 2, 2011, http://www.govtech.com/public-safety/Utah-Police-Anonymous-Crime-Tips-Online.html?elq=7128333f79404469b86b4ad6716f0ddd (accessed November 2, 2013).
3. Elaine Pittman, "Inside Out," *Government Technology*, May 2011, pp. 36–37.
4. Elaine Pittman, "Incident Immersion," *Government Technology*, October 2010, pp. 30–31.
5. W. Jerry Chisumn and Brent E. Turvey, "Evidence Dynamics: Locard's Exchange Principle & Crime Reconstruction," *Journal of Behavioral Profiling* 2(1) (2000): 3.
6. Elaine Pittman, "Sole Searcher," *Government Technology*, July 2011, http://www.govtech.com/public-safety/Shoe-Print-Databases-Catch-Up-to-CSI-Fiction.html (accessed November 2, 2013).
7. Hilton Collins, "QR Codes Aim to Curb Drunken Driving in Texas," *Government Technology*, June 6, 2011, http://www.govtech.com/health/QR-Codes-Curb-Drunken-Driving-Texas.html (accessed November 2, 2013); also see BeQRious, "QR Codes Against Drunk Driving," http://beqrious.com/qr-codes-against-drunk-driving/ (accessed November 2, 2013).
8. Jess Rollins, "Missouri to be Eighth State to Enact Kelsey's Law," *USA Today*, August 27, 2012, http://usatoday30.usatoday.com/news/nation/story/2012-08-26/kelseys-law-cellphone-location/57335906/1 (accessed November 3, 2013).
9. *U.S. v. Jones*, 565 US ___, 132 S.Ct. 945 (2012).
10. Brian P. Tice, "Unmanned Aerial Vehicles: The Force Multiplier of the 1990s," www.airpower.maxwell.af.mil/airchronicles/apj/apj91/spr91/4spr91.htm (accessed November 5, 2013).
11. Christina Hernandez Sherwood, "Are You Ready for Civilian Drones?" *Government Technology*, August 2, 2012, http://www.govtech.com/public-safety/Are-You-Ready-for-Civilian-Drones.html?elq=117d5398aecb45709a0c398ae05092d8&elqCampaignId=1626 (accessed November 2, 2013).
12. Bart Jansen, "FAA Told to Make Room for Drones in U.S. Skies," *USA Today*, February 7, 2012, http://usatoday30.usatoday.com/news/nation/story/2012-02-06/unmanned-drones-share-faa-airspace/52994752/1 (accessed November 2, 2013).
13. Anna Broache, "Police Agencies Push for Drone Sky Patrols," *CNET News*, August 9, 2007, news.cnet.com/Police-agencies-push-for-drone-sky-patrols/2100-11397_3-6201789.html (accessed March 5, 2013).
14. Tice, "Unmanned Aerial Vehicles."
15. Brian Bennett, "Police Employ Predator Drone Spy Planes on Home Front," *Los Angeles Times*, December 10, 2011, http://articles.latimes.com/2011/dec/10/nation/la-na-drone-arrest-20111211 (accessed November 8, 2013).
16. Elaine Povich, "More States Testing Drones," *Governing*, May 15, 2012, http://www.governing.com/topics/technology/col-more-states-cities-look-to-test-drones.html (accessed October 9, 2013).
17. Judy Keen, "Citing Privacy, Critics Target Drones Buzzing Over USA," *USA TODAY* (January 10, 2013), http://www.usatoday.com/story/news/politics/2013/01/10/domestic-drones-backlash/1566212/ (accessed November 11, 2013).
18. Sherwood, "Are You Ready for Civilian Drones?"
19. Kevin Johnson, "Police Chiefs Urge Limits on Use of Drones," *USA Today*, September 7, 2012, http://usatoday30.usatoday.com/news/nation/story/2012-09-06/cop-drones/57639048/1 (accessed November 2, 2013).
20. Jansen, "FAA Told to Make Room for Drones in U.S. Skies."
21. Ingrid Lunden, "Mobile Milestone: The Number of Smartphones In Use Passed 1 Billion in Q3, Says Strategy Analytics," *TechCrunch*, October 16, 2012, http://techcrunch.com/2012/10/16/mobile-milestone-the-number-of-smartphones-in-use-passed-1-billion-in-q3-says-strategy-analytics/ (accessed November 2, 2013).
22. Lauren Katims, "Crime Scan," *Government Technology*, April 2011, p. 38.
23. Larry Copeland, "Driver Guide: Steer Clear of Texting Scofflaws or Call 911?" *USA Today*, July 26, 2012, http://content.usatoday.com/dist/custom/gci/InsidePage.aspx?cId=dailyworld&sParam=56511088 story (accessed November 3, 2013).
24. Kyle Malone, "The Fourth Amendment and the Stored Communications Act: Why the Warrantless Gathering of Historical Cell Site Location Information Poses No Threat to Privacy," *Pepperdine Law Review* 39(3) (September 8, 2012), http://digitalcommons.pepperdine.edu/cgi/viewcontent.cgi?article=1368&context=plr&sei-redir=1&referer=http%3A%2F%2Fwww.google.com%2Furl%3Fsa%3Dt%26rct%3Dj%26q%3D1986%2520stored%2520communications%2520a

ct%2520warrantless%2520searches%26source%
3Dweb%26cd%3D7%26ved%3D0CFgQFjAG%2
6url%3Dhttp%253A%252F%252Fdigitalcommo
ns.pepperdine.edu%252Fcgi%252Fviewcontent.
cgi%253Farticle%253D1368%2526context%253
Dplr%26ei%3D3jO9UNDsOMbmiwLDsoC4A
w%26usg%3DAFQjCNEsKOZHRJZkkCfue0F_
QKYroFrfxQ#search=%221986%20stored%20com-
munications%20act%20warrantless%20searches%22
(accessed November 3, 2013).

25. Massimo Calabresi, "The Phone Knows All," *Time*
(August 27, 2012), http://www.time.com/time/
magazine/article/0,9171,2122241,00.html (accessed
November 3, 2013).

26. See 18 U.S.C. Chapter 121 §§ 2701–2712.

27. 18 U.S.C. § 2703(b) (2006).

28. Facebook, "Delaware State Police Prepare for Hurricane Sandy," http://www.facebook.com/notes/del-
aware-state-police-news-room/delaware-state-po-
lice-prepare-for-hurricane-sandy/461858043855465
(accessed November 5, 2013); also see Terry Collins,
"Police Embrace Emerging Social Media Tool," Associated Press, August 11, 2012 (accessed December
3, 2012).

29. Gwendolyn Waters, "Social Media and Law
Enforcement: Potential Risks," *FBI Law Enforcement
Bulletin* 81(11) (November 2012), http://www.fbi.
gov/stats-services/publications/law-enforcement-
bulletin/november-2012/social-media-and-law-
enforcement (accessed November 3, 2013).

30. Natalie DiBlasio, "YouTube: The Latest Crime Solver,"
USA Today, July 5, 2012, http://usatoday30.usatoday.
com/NEWS/usaedition/2012-07-05-youtube-cops_
ST_U.htm (accessed November 3, 2013).

31. Ibid.

32. Jessica Mulholland, "Philadelphia Police Officers to
Start Tweeting at Work," *Government Technology*,25
April 17, 2012 http://www.govtech.com/public-safe-
ty/Philadelphia-Police-to-Start-Tweeting-at-Work.
html?page=2 (accessed November 2, 2013).

33. Jim McKay, "Cops on the Tweet to Solve Crimes and
Educate the Public," *Government Technology* (August
31, 2009), http://www.govtech.com/pcio/Cops-on-the-
Tweet-to-Solve.html (accessed November 3, 2013).

34. Kevin Johnson, "Police Tap Technology to
Compensate for Fewer Officers," *USA Today*, April
25, 2012, http://usatoday30.usatoday.com/news/
nation/2011-04-24-police-crime-technology-face-
book.htm (accessed November 3, 2013).

35. Noelle Knell, "Hacktivism Linked to 100 Million
Compromised Records in 2011," March 23, 2012,
http://www.govtech.com/security/Hacktivism-
Linked-to-100-Million-Compromised-Records-
in-2011.html?elq=752c11796ba24a76abb519eb4842
c9e6&elqCampaignId=207 (accessed November 26,
2012).

36. Ellen Messmer, "Cyberattacks in U.S. Cost an Average $8.9 Million Annually to Clean Up, Study Says,"
http://www.networkworld.com/news/2012/100812-
ponemon-cyberattacks-263113.html (accessed October 8, 2013).

37. EMC, "Stalking the Kill Chain: The Attacker's Chain,"
https://blogs.rsa.com/rsa-first-watch-team/stalking-
the-kill-chain-the-attackers-chain-2/ (accessed November 2, 2013).

38. Adapted from Mathew J. Schwartz, "Cybercrime
Attacks, Costs Escalating," *InformationWeek*, October
08, 2012 (accessed October 8, 2013).

39. Steve Towns, "The Center for Internet Security
Boosts Government Cybersecurity," *Government
Technology*, October 2012, http://www.govtech.com/
security/The-Center-for-Internet-Security-Boosts-
Government-Cybersecurity-VIDEO.html?page=2
(accessed November 2, 2013).

40. Department of Homeland Security, "About the
National Cybersecurity and Communications Integration Center (NCCIC)," http://www.dhs.gov/
about-national-cybersecurity-communications-inte-
gration-center-nccic (accessed November 2, 2013).

41. U.S. Department of Justice, Bureau of Justice Statistics,
Local Police Departments, 2007 (Washington,
DC: Author, 2010), p. 17; U.S. Department of Jus-
tice, Bureau of Justice Statistics, *Sheriff's Offices, 2003*
(Washington, DC: Author, 2006), p. 26.

42. See Taser International, Inc., http://www.taser.com/
(accessed December 4, 2012).

43. See, for example, Total Injury, "Taser Injuries and
Deaths," http://www.totalinjury.com/personal-in-
jury-a-z/police-brutality/taser-injury-and-death.
aspx (accessed November 5, 2013 2013); Barry
E. Mangus, Luke Y. Shen, Stephen D. Helmer, Janae
Maher, and R. Stephen Smith, "Taser and Taser Associated Injuries: A Case Series," *American Surgeon*
74(9): 862-865.,

44. Medical News Today, "Study Suggests TASER
Use by U.S. Police Is Safe," October 9, 2007, www.
medicalnewstoday.com/articles/84955.php
(accessed November 5, 2013).

45. TASER Protect Life, "TASER Training Bulletin
15.0 Regarding Medical Research Update and
Revised Warnings," http://www.ecdlaw.info/out-
lines/10-15-09%20TASER%20ECD%20Trng%20
Memo%20w%20Trng%20Bulletin%20and%20
Warnings.pdf (accessed November 5, 2013).

46. Brian Huber, "Wis. Police Get Robo-Cop's Help," PoliceOne.com, November 14, 2006, www.policeone.com/police-technology/robots/articles/1190983 (accessed November 5, 2013).

47. Blake Harris, "Goin' Mobile," *Government Technology* 10 (August 1997): 1.

48. Kaveh Ghaemian, "Small-Town Cops Wield Big-City Data," *Government Technology* 9 (September 1996): 38.

49. U.S. Department of Justice, National Institute of Justice, *Crime Mapping and Analysis by Community Organizations in Hartford, Connecticut* (Washington, DC: Author, March 2001), p. 1.

50. Donna Rogers, "Getting Crime Analysis on the Map," *Law Enforcement Technology* 26(11) (November 1999): 76–79.

51. U.S. Department of Justice, National Institute of Justice, *Crime Mapping Research Center* (Washington, DC: Author, 2000), pp. 1–3.

52. Lois Pilant, "Computerized Crime Mapping," *Police Chief* 64 (December 1997): 58.

53. U.S. Department of Justice, *Crime Mapping Research Center*, pp. 1–3; the CMRC Web site address is: www.ojp.usdoj.gov/nij/maps/welcome.htm (accessed November 5, 2013).

54. Bill McGarigle, "Crime Profilers Gain New Weapons," *Government Technology* 10 (December 1997): 28–29.

55. Ibid.

56. Alison Bath, "Accident Scene Investigation Is High Tech," *Reno Gazette-Journal* (Sparks Today section), November 18, 2003, p. 4.

57. Bill McGarigle, "Electronic Mapping Speeds Crime and Traffic Investigations," *Government Technology* 9 (February 1996): 20–21.

58. Justine Kavanaugh, "Drunk Drivers Get a Shot of Technology," *Government Technology* 9 (March 1996): 26.

59. Ibid.

60. Christen da Costa, "GM Adds Remote Kill Switch to OnStar Vehicles," *Gadget Review*, July 22, 2009, www.gadgetreview.com/2009/07/gm-adds-remote-kill-switch-to-onstar-vehicles.html#ixzz0vyaGMzgy (accessed November 5, 2013).

61. Ibid., p. 46.

62. Tod Newcombe, "Imaged Prints Go Online, Cops Return to Streets," *Government Technology* 9 (April 1996): 1, 31.

63. Corey Grice, "Technologies, Agencies Converge," *Government Technology* 11 (April 1998): 24, 61.

64. Samuel G. Chapman, *Murdered on Duty: The Killing of Police Officers in America*, 2nd ed. (Springfield, IL: Charles C Thomas, 1998), p. 33.

65. Patrick Joyce, "Firearms Training: As Close to Real as It Gets," *Government Technology* 8 (July 1995): 14–15.

66. Ibid.

67. John McCormick, "On a High-Tech Firing Line," *Newsweek*, December 6, 1999, p. 64.

68. Vanessa O'Connell, "The Next Big Idea: Using 'Fingerprints' of Guns to Solve Cases," *Wall Street Journal* February 10, 2000 http://online.wsj.com/article/SB950142117481201779.html (accessed November 5, 2013).

69. Ibid.

70. Ray Dussault, "GangNet: A New Tool in the War on Gangs," *Government Technology* (January 1998): 34–35.

71. Thomas Cowper, "Improving the View of the World: Law Enforcement and Augmented Reality Technology," *FBI Law Enforcement Bulletin* 73 (January 2004): 13.

72. Ibid.

73. Ibid., p. 15.

74. Ibid., p. 16.

75. Chris Forsythe, "The Future of Simulation Technology for Law Enforcement: Diverse Experience with Realistic Simulated Humans," *FBI Law Enforcement Bulletin* 73 (January 2004): 19–21.

76. National Nanotechnology Initiative, "FAQs: Nanotechnology," http://www.nano.gov/nanotech-101/nanotechnology-facts (accessed March 5, 2013).

77. Nanowerk, "Handheld Nanotechnology Device Detects Cocaine, Marijuana in Saliva," www.nanowerk.com/news/newsid=8328.php (accessed March 5, 2013).

78. Doug Wyllies, "Nanotechnology Being Tested for Next-Gen Body Armor," Policeone.com, www.policeone.com/police-products/body-armor/articles/1888039-Nanotechnology-being-tested-for-next-gen-body-armor (accessed March 5, 2013).

79. George Nicholson and Jeffrey Hogge, "Retooling Criminal Justice: Interbranch Cooperation Needed," *Government Technology* 9 (February 1996): 32.

80. James Q. Wilson, "Six Things Police Leaders Can Do About Juvenile Crime," *Subject to Debate* (Newsletter of the Police Executive Research Forum), September/October 1997, p. 1.

INDEX